INSIDE GOMERY

INSIDE

FRANÇOIS PERREAULT

translated by **CARL ANGERS**

GOMERY

Douglas & McIntyre

TORONTO/VANCOUVER

Douglas & McIntyre Ltd.
2323 Quebec Street, Suite 201
Vancouver, British Columbia
Canada V5T 4S7
www.douglas-mcintyre.com

Éditions de l'Homme
955, rue Amherst
Montreal, Quebec
Canada H2L 3K4

Library and Archives Canada Cataloguing in Publication
Perreault, François, 1950–
Inside Gomery / François Perreault ; translated by Carl Angers.

Translation of: Dans les coulisses de la Commission Gomery.
ISBN-13: 978-1-55365-214-4 · ISBN-10: 1-55365-214-2

1. Canada. Commission of Inquiry into the Sponsorship Program
and Advertising Activities. 2. Sponsorship Scandal, Canada, 1997–.
3. Political corruption—Canada. 4. Patronage, Political—Canada.
5. Government advertising—Canada. I. Angers, Carl, 1964– II. Title.
JL86.P8P4713 2006   352.7'48'0971   C2006-900949-X

Copyediting by Mary Schendlinger
Cover design by Peter Cocking
Text design and typesetting by Ingrid Paulson
Cover photograph by Peter Sibbal
Printed and bound in Canada by Friesens

We gratefully acknowledge the financial support of the Canada Council
for the Arts, the British Columbia Arts Council, and the Government
of Canada through the Book Publishing Industry Development Program
(BPIDP) for our publishing activities.

To my children, Magali and François-Xavier

CONTENTS

FOREWORD

MOST OF THE TIME, judges enjoy the privilege of anonymity. Their work is usually done without attracting public attention or coverage by the media. From time to time, if it happens that a judge is assigned to hear a high-profile case or a trial involving sensational facts, the reports that appear in the press or on television or radio concentrate on the personalities of the parties and lawyers involved, on what they said and the usual facts of the matter. The name and the conduct of the judge presiding over the trial are rarely mentioned.

Fortunately or unfortunately, depending upon your point of view, a commission of inquiry is quite another matter. Often such commissions are called upon to investigate politically sensitive situations that have become matters of public controversy, and, like it or not, the person appointed to head the inquiry, who is invariably recruited from the judiciary, becomes part of the story. Until then, he or she was probably blissfully unaware of the dangers involved in media and public relations, their complexity and the consequences that follow when they are mishandled.

I

Almost immediately after the creation of the Commission of Inquiry into the Sponsorship Program and Advertising Activities, in February 2004, as commissioner I became aware of the enormous public interest in its activities. This interest was shown by what seemed to be an endless number of media requests for interviews, photographs and background information about the personnel of the commission, and particularly about myself, usually described in newspaper articles as an "obscure" Québec judge. Since everyone who had had experience with commissions of inquiry advised me to be very careful about media relations, I realized that we needed the counsel and assistance of an experienced expert in media relations. We were fortunate in being able to find and engage the ideal candidate, François Perreault, as our media spokesman.

For the next eighteen months or so, and especially during the hectic phases of public hearings from September 2004 until June 2005, I leaned on and learned from François. He became not only a trusted advisor and reliable spokesman for the commission, but also a personal friend. We met and talked almost every day. I looked forward to our conversations about the reaction of the media to the latest revelations, and how best we could present ourselves to the public. François asked me questions in the most courteous manner about legal concepts that required long and complicated explanations, and never misunderstood what I told him. In fact, his statements to the media usually simplified what I had told him, making me realize that he had grasped perfectly what I had been trying to explain. Invariably, when difficulties arose that threatened to disturb our generally good relations with those who were closely following the hearings, François found a way to soothe any ruffled feathers. And when I said or did something that exposed me and the commission to unfavourable comment or to the danger of bad press, François usually found a way to minimize the damage and deflect the criticism.

So although I have attempted throughout to conduct the work of the commission in an impartial and objective manner, I confess that I became biased in favour of François Perreault. I like him, I value his friendship, I admire his skills, and I know how fundamentally fair he is, and how sharp are his perceptions. When he told me of his intention to write a book about his experiences in connection with the commission, I encouraged him to go ahead with the project, because I was sure that he would give an honest account of his observations and experiences from the perspective of an insider. I am not sure that I would trust anyone else to give readers a balanced look at the inner workings of a commission, and especially *this* commission, which was the object of particularly intense media attention and comment.

My confidence has proved to be well founded. In this book François has produced a chronicle of the inner workings of the commission that is as fascinating as it is accurate. Of course he writes from the point of view of someone who worked tirelessly and successfully to paint the commission and its personnel in the most favourable light possible. The book certainly cannot be described as a critical look at us, but it is, I believe, a good read for anyone who found the brief life of this dramatic and sometimes sensational commission of inquiry to be an interesting illustration of how a democracy examines its own processes through a quasi-judicial procedure.

—John H. Gomery

PREFACE

Ｎews stories rarely seem fresh or original—all of the scandals of the last few years have had a familiar ring to them. Yet some events still astonish us today—in the way that news of them breaks and in the underlying motives that they reveal. Much has been said and written about the lack of rigour and the questionable behaviour associated with the federal Sponsorship Program. Hearings of the Commission of Inquiry into the Sponsorship Program and Advertising Activities went on from September 2004 to June 2005, and thousands of documents were scrutinized. The revelations have shocked Canadians, who as a result have developed a strong desire to know the truth. Many have placed their trust in Judge John H. Gomery, who set out to uncover it and who quickly became a symbol of justice and integrity—the impartial man who would find out what really happened. For this reason alone, it is important to write about John Gomery, the challenges he has faced and the obstacles he has overcome.

One has to go back to the Pacific Railway scandal of 1873 to find a public inquiry that unveiled as intricate a tangle of political intrigue, influence peddling, breach of trust and misappropriation of public funds. But even compared to that case, the scope and repercussions of the sponsorship scandal are unprecedented.

Although the events examined so closely by John Gomery unfolded over a ten-year period—from 1994 to 2004—it took only a few weeks for the watchful eyes of government auditors and an all-out war between Jean Chrétien and Paul Martin to shake the foundations of the Liberal government. Many months' worth of headlines and revelations, taken from some 172 testimonies, have been enough to turn the Liberal scandal into a national crisis.

Several months before the creation of the Gomery Commission, Jean Chrétien had made decisions whose consequences became a trap for Paul Martin. Gomery was to discover that as early as October 2003, Prime Minister Chrétien, already under attack by his own troops, had been warned by the clerk of the Privy Council of unfavourable findings contained in the auditor general's report. At the time, Chrétien chose to put off its publication, leaving his successor to deal with the crisis that ensued. That may be one of the reasons why Chrétien left office before the scheduled date, December 12. Parliamentary proceedings were put on hold to allow the Martin team to take over, thus delaying the tabling of the auditor general's report in the House of Commons. Chrétien left the Liberal Party and its new leader with a legacy that severely damaged the party and helped to eject the Martin government from office within a very short time. In fact, a long history of animosity between these two powerful men and their factions thrust John Gomery into a pivotal position—he was the man who would get to the bottom of things and reveal a scandal that shook the very foundations of the government.

No stone has been left unturned in reporting the details of the sponsorship affair: the political motivations, the cronyism, the public servants who failed to perform their duties. Over months of public hearings, the commission managed to uncover the facts, which are now crystal clear.

This book is an account of the relentless efforts of the Gomery Commission to find the truth. It does not recap the abuse of authority and misappropriation of funds that came to light and that are patently clear in Gomery's first report. Rather, it tells the story of the commission team itself and its confrontations with the petty behaviour of political giants, the grudges of well-placed senior public servants and the ambushes by reputable lawyers.

There could be no better place from which to observe the day-to-day proceedings than the narrow interface between public and private— an inquiry whose work went on behind closed doors, and a hive of national media people intent on making that work public. My role was a privileged one. I was the spokesperson for a judge beyond suspicion, whose candour and openness rapidly won the trust of all involved— swindled taxpayers and betrayed politicians alike. I stood at the leading edge of a team of experts who grappled with a mandate that was exceptional, and who faced challenges that were just as exceptional.

ACKNOWLEDGEMENTS

THIS BOOK WOULD NOT have been possible without the consent and friendship of John Gomery. While I played out my role at his side and in the preparation of this book, his candour and open mind helped me portray the work done behind the scenes by the members of this commission of inquiry. The same is true of Sheila-Marie Cook, whom I thank for her great kindness and support.

Others have given their time, energy and advice to help me write this book. The assistance of Gaétan Deschênes, a close associate from my years in journalism, was invaluable and essential throughout the writing of this, my first book. Carole Kljajo's friendship and wise advice, and the skill and sustenance of David Giorgi, who helped me evolve from pen and ink to computers and G5s, have been just as supportive in the task. Finally, my mother, Rolande, a devoted reader and critic from the early stages of the writing, knew when to share her reactions during the course of my work.

For the simultaneous publication of this book in both languages, I would especially like to thank Pierre Bourdon from Éditions de l'Homme, and Scott McIntyre from Douglas & McIntyre, my two publishers, as well as the members of their staff, for their commitment in taking up this challenge.

ONE

FIND ME A JUDGE!

LEANING AGAINST THE windowsill, taking in the greys of the paved streets, the St. Lawrence River and the February sky, the man tried to suppress a sudden burst of emotion. Twenty times over he replayed in his memory the conversation of a few minutes ago. His routine of newspaper, coffee and toast had been disrupted suddenly by a telephone call, from someone with an unfamiliar and official voice. It was 8:15 am.

"Mr. Gomery? Judge Gomery, I'm Morris Rosenberg, deputy minister of justice, in Ottawa. Can I have a few minutes? We met once, a long time ago—almost twenty years ago; you were presiding over the Javelin Company case. What a case..."

"What can I do for you? Make it short; I'm expected in court at 9:30."

"I'm calling on behalf of the Privy Council. There's an emergency, sir. The speaker of the House of Commons is in possession of a report from the auditor general, which she will make public in a few hours. Some serious problems are in store for the government. Are you aware of the situation?"

"Yes, somewhat, at least from what I've read in the papers. I gather some department paid for a study coming out of a public relations agency, as many times, I believe, as there were copies made of it."

"It's much more serious. The prime minister, who has been informed of Ms. Fraser's findings, would like to respond to this report by creating a commission of inquiry, which will need to go straight to the heart of the matter. I have been asked to offer you the chair of this commission. If you were to agree to act as commissioner, you would be relieved of your current tasks immediately, given the urgency of the situation."

"Why me?"

"Let me go back to the Javelin case, a seemingly endless affair with years and years of accumulated evidence, motions of all sorts— we need a judge who can take in and process an enormous amount of information within a limited time frame. We see you as the right man for the job!"

What an incredible offer! It was every judge's dream, especially four years away from retirement. A commission of inquiry, no less— just like that, at the start of the day, when he had barely finished shaving. The subject had been well covered during the past several months by the *Globe and Mail* and had already stirred up public opinion. The anxiety in the upper echelons of government was palpable in the caller's voice. Clearly the political will was coming from the highest level. It was a unique opportunity. A commission of inquiry! Gomery had long ago given up hope that he might preside over such an inquiry. To decline the offer was out of the question, although he had two primary conditions.

"I accept, only if you can live with the fact that I will be away for three weeks in Southeast Asia. I made this commitment to my wife some time ago. We leave in ten days."

The silence that ensued seemed endless to Gomery, as his longing to undertake the project grew.

"Not easy, but I think it will be OK. We already have all the information we need about you. The prime minister will make the announcement and answer the questions that will surely come up. In the meantime, we will notify the chief justice of the Québec Superior Court of your appointment. Any questions?"

"A request. I want a free rein and my say with respect to the terms of reference of the inquiry."

"Of course. We will contact you again this morning. I believe ten days will be enough for us to put this together. By the way, congratulations, Mr. Justice!"

.

GOMERY HAD TOO practical a mind to wonder who else had been approached, or what political squabbling had gone into the creation of this commission of inquiry. He was more concerned about the reaction of his wife, who was about to join him for breakfast.

"What? You said yes already, without asking questions or checking how much work is involved or what the time frame of the commission is?"

Her reaction arose from her personal concerns. Two years earlier, the diagnosis had come as a shock: John Gomery had a form of leukemia, and it had been detected just in time. There was a chance of remission, but she had been terrified that she would lose her husband.

Then came the difficult chemotherapy treatments. A balance had to be reached between his immune system, which was at low ebb, and his blood pressure, which was far too high. In the end, the treatment had succeeded in bringing about a remission.

Gomery's reply to his wife came without delay. "You always said that you aspired to be appointed to a commission someday, so I knew there was no way you would oppose my decision." His mischievous smile deflected any further protest.

Montreal's Old Port slowly came to life that winter morning, as if passersby were trying to disperse the icy mist by keeping up a brisk pace. Despite the wind, John Gomery took the rue de la Commune and walked alongside the docks. His mind raced so much faster than his feet that he hardly noticed the frosty paving stones. His thoughts ran from the future to the past, from the immediate implications of his decision to joyful memories that were close to his heart and still fresh in his mind.

In 1969, a young recruit had applied for a job with the Martineau Walker law firm, where Gomery was a partner. The hiring of a female lawyer at the firm would present a few internal management challenges, he knew. But her academic record was compelling, so she joined the firm, specializing in litigation and family law. Very early on, the law student admired the intellect and talent of her boss. He became her mentor and taught her how to listen to clients, to prepare for trial and, in the end, to plead a case.

The year 1972 marked the beginning of their love story. They united their lives and their careers discreetly, and they kept the secret for months to prevent office gossip. Later on, Pierrette Rayle was sworn in as a Québec Superior Court judge, and on May 9, 1995, they became the first couple in Québec to serve as Superior Court judges. At that point their student–mentor relationship ended. From then on, their disagreements were limited to the accuracy of the French wording or the subtleties of the English language in each other's rulings.

Without a doubt, husband and wife shared all they had, the honours as well as the more trivial aspects of their work. This time, however, Gomery had acted impulsively, out of ambition, and by doing so had drafted Pierrette Rayle into the venture without stopping to assess the magnitude of the task. Over the entire course of his work for the commission, she would do at home what she did so well in the Court of Appeal: review and reconsider the rulings of other judges.

Gomery emerged from his thoughts and entered the courthouse. He had never imagined that one day he would have to transfer all of his cases to his colleagues. As eager as he was to work on the commission of inquiry, it was hard to let go of cases he had prepared carefully to preside over.

In the meantime, in Ottawa, the prime minister was getting ready to address a critical issue—a dangerous situation that was developing just before an election. In his parliamentary office he revised his notes for an announcement that he would make to the media in the foyer of the Commons: a mixture of moral indignation, calls for justice and pledges to seek the truth.

Martin knew nothing about the newly appointed commissioner. Gomery, he must have wondered, with only one *M*? From Montreal... bilingual... of Irish descent, I suppose? No? Welsh... well, well. And he's retiring soon? He won't be dragging his feet.

Those in power know full well that a judge appointed as commissioner does not take recommendations or orders. That's why a commission of inquiry grows and changes and eventually eludes the grasp of those who established it. Paul Martin knew this unfailing rule. He would have liked to think, though, that he hadn't given his life to politics just to go down in history as the prime minister with the shortest term in office.

Facing the media, he professed a desire to learn the truth, in the interest of all Canadians. His strategy was based on John Gomery separating the good Liberals from the bad ones, a task that Martin could have taken up, had the Liberal caucus not been so divided and had his leadership enjoyed stronger support.

In the minutes preceding the announcement of the creation of the commission, Gomery received two phone calls. Both were appropriately courteous and encouraging. The first one came from Francis Fox, the prime minister's chief of staff and an ex-cabinet minister who would later be appointed to the Senate. As a lawyer, he was well aware of the scope of the powers conferred on Gomery. He wanted to assure the judge that the whole undertaking stemmed from the will of a head of government who had nothing to hide and who therefore intended to co-operate fully with the inquiry.

The second call, much more formal, came from the justice minister, Irwin Cotler. He had just left a Cabinet meeting and was keen to confirm that the Order-in-Council creating the commission would be signed very shortly.

The two calls—one from a political level and the other from the executive level—complemented each other nicely, making it clear to John Gomery just how politically sensitive his task was, and just how closely the work of the commission would be scrutinized, from many angles.

Whatever the situation, he had just ten days to take care of essential matters: define the framework of his mandate, put together a team and draft a work plan and schedule. First and foremost, he needed to identify and recruit the best lead counsel for the commission.

Paul Martin, on the other hand, had at most ten weeks before he would call an election. When he left the House of Commons, he could have headed for the marble stairs leading to his office in a tactical retreat, but instead, he made his way toward the crowd of eager reporters.

"We will get to the bottom of this," he said. "I will not let a few individuals tarnish the reputation and integrity of the government and its public servants, nor that of the party I lead."

Despite his authoritative tone, the head of government must have been profoundly worried. In order to remain presentable to voters and to maintain an image of integrity, he had just entrusted part of his political destiny to a man before whom he would be appearing as a witness in an explosive affair.

TWO

THE COMMISSIONER'S FIRST STEPS

THE EVENING'S EVENTS made for a restless night for John Gomery. A political storm was brewing, fed by statements, partisan attacks and awkward displays—on television, in the papers, everywhere. The shocking findings of Auditor General Sheila Fraser—the person who knew the most about the situation—had been revealed, the word *scandal* had been uttered by an outraged Opposition, and finally the government had replied by announcing the commission of inquiry.

The long night dragged on for Gomery. At around two in the morning—as was too often the case—he delved into a book. Thus, while a new political chapter was being written in Ottawa, the commissioner was turning the first pages of *The Arctic Grail* by Pierre Berton. At issue in both cases was a question of integrity.

The next day, media pundits and other critics were ruthless in attacking the newly minted prime minister. They charged that he was trying to call an election as quickly as possible and therefore had chosen to delay owning up to a serious offence while shifting the burden of proof to someone else.

The reactions, analyses, reviews and editorials that followed made it clear that John Gomery's name was unknown in Ottawa political circles and missing from newsroom staff memories. Like most judges he was discreet and anonymous, except for the legal decisions he had rendered. For the time being, a few biographical notes contained in a brief press release from the Prime Minister's Office were enough to give him what he later called "the best seat for the best show in town."

When presiding over a case, a judge must keep a tight rein on events. In this instance, the courtroom was taken over by the media, and public opinion became the jury. Gomery knew that at some point he would have to remind everyone that the commissioner was in charge. That is what occupied his thoughts while he waited for his first visitors from Ottawa on February 11, 2004. If everyone was now aware of the task that had been assigned to him, no one except Gomery knew what scope he wished to give to his mandate.

The delegation was impressive, at least for a preliminary meeting. The visitors arrived together at a conference room on the sixteenth floor of the Montreal courthouse. It was John Gomery's first contact with senior members of an administration whose moral standards and management methods he was determined to get to know. For the time being, they came as collaborators: Michel Bouchard, assistant deputy minister of Justice; Yves Côté and Lois Pierce, both from the Privy Council Office, and Elizabeth Nadeau from Public Works—acting as the advance team for the mandarins whom he was soon to meet.

Framework, scope and length of mandate were at the heart of discussions, according to an agenda established in accordance with the independence and authority of the new commissioner, *intuitu personae*. On these issues, Gomery already had a few well-established ideas. Any compromise based on a sense of urgency or on political sensibilities would be too costly in terms of credibility and integrity. The type of legal–political clash that resulted from the commission of inquiry into Canadian military operations in Somalia would have to be avoided at all costs; i.e., the political pressures, the suspension and premature termination of the proceedings of the commission and, above all, the blow to Commissioner Gilles Létourneau's credibility, even though it was re-established afterwards.

John Gomery would not be taken in. He wanted a free hand as to the choice of legal counsel and the time needed to conduct the inquiry. Unrestricted access to all relevant documents—including Cabinet documents—would become the standard. This last crucial point was nevertheless deferred to a future meeting; Gomery's visitors were no doubt aware that opinions on this matter differed in higher circles. The summit meeting with the civil servants was planned for Friday the 13th, forty-eight hours later.

In the meantime, legal counsel had to be identified and recruited. Although the law permits the appointment of more than one judge to preside over a commission of inquiry, John Gomery was on his own. Why had this political decision been made? No one will ever know the real reasons. Some suspected that the motive had been to weaken the credibility or impartiality of an inquiry whose activities were feared by so many. Indeed, placing two or three judges at the head of the commission might have led to a very different outcome. Two commissioners would likely have shared the workload and collaborated closely all along, making it difficult to direct criticism toward one or the other. Decisions on motions presented would also have been the result of a shared position, making them practically impervious to attack. For their part, the proponents of nominating a single commissioner—an anglophone from Québec—could not have imagined that so many Canadians would identify with him, or that Quebecers would be among the first to give him their complete trust. But above all, never could these senior political advisors have imagined that a single commissioner would pursue this task in so little time and take it so far.

Deep down, John Gomery was happy to be alone at the helm. He had no one with whom he had to share his decisions or responsibilities. The same went for the findings of *his* inquiry—he would be the sole author of the Gomery Report. "Too much humility can be detrimental to a judge who dwells on his own weaknesses or is influenced by the perception he has of his weaknesses; he puts his own judgment in jeopardy," he said. And with a smile, he went on to say: "You need confidence to render justice. And then, thank God, there's the Court of Appeal!"

In this situation, however, there was no Court of Appeal where the rulings of a commissioner could be reviewed. Gomery had never thought that the people whose reputation was at stake would attack his judgment and integrity before the federal court. The prime minister's plan to link the publication of the commissioner's final report to a majority win in the next election only added to the pressure on Gomery. It was widely speculated in the news media that by promising to call an election one month after the publication of the commission's final report, Paul Martin was trying to hang on to power for nine more months, during which time, he thought, the scandal would subside.

Despite this pressure, Gomery was unflappable. He never considered that his role was to bail out a beleaguered government. He wanted to defend the institutions and, where appropriate, identify those who misused them. For this reason, he told anyone willing to listen: "At this point in my career, I have nothing to lose. I don't owe anything to anyone. In like manner, I cannot put anyone on trial. I will lead an inquiry and assemble the evidence needed to establish the facts and find those responsible. Those who think they can control me are making a mistake."

And yet, after spending months trying to keep his work at a safe remove from partisan debate, John Gomery would now have to deal with a besieged minority Liberal government that was buying time and placing its fate in his hands. The government's only hope was a favourable outcome. Indeed, on the evening of April 21, 2005, Paul Martin reserved television airtime and promised to call an election thirty days after the publication of Gomery's final recommendations. The commissioner would have to rely on the trust of the media and the general public and ignore the hype and publicity surrounding his work, with its flamboyant witnesses and catchy headlines.

Nothing in the days that followed the prime minister's announcement seemed to alter the public's confidence in Gomery's integrity. In his mind, Martin's promise amounted to a minor news item and had no effect either in the courtroom or in the press room. Gomery's performance from the beginning of his appointment forestalled any suspicion of partiality or leniency. Paul Martin would be alone in dealing with the risk he had just taken.

In John Gomery's eyes, none of the prime minister's statements— including those addressed to all Canadians—would ever outweigh the substance of his testimony before the commission. On that evening in April, as Martin prepared to make his speech, the commissioner reserved a table for dinner with his sisters Barbara and Carol. Reservations are a must at the Bonaparte Restaurant on Saint François-Xavier Street. Diners at neighbouring tables were surprised to see Gomery there at the same time as the prime minister was addressing the nation. Gomery preferred to wait for the next day's newspapers to learn Martin's intentions. After all, Martin's television appearance certainly would not add anything to his testimony in Ottawa a few months earlier.

In spite of his cool confidence, Gomery found himself caught in an unfamiliar process. After many discussions with colleagues, however, he came to the conclusion that this was his opportunity to demonstrate the fairness of the judicial system, and the skills and maturity of its judges. Politicians beware!

Let's go back one year. On Wednesday, February 11, 2004, the newly designated commissioner got a call from his friend Lawrence Poitras, a steadfast supporter. Gomery was not surprised to hear from him.

"John," said Poitras, "I've been following your case—congratulations! But you must be careful. What does Pierrette think of this? We must get together. Have you thought about your legal counsel? You will be on your own; you need the best."

Poitras, a well-known and respected judge since presiding over the commission of the same name, had devoted long hours to examining the investigative methods of the Sûreté du Québec, the provincial police force. "Don't let them suggest candidates," he stressed.

The answer came back loud and clear. "I have no intention of doing that. I just don't know where to look. First I need a lead counsel."

The two men enjoyed a pleasant lunch. Their lively discussion centred on the political stakes of the new commission and the inherent risks of such a thorough inquiry into the federal public administration.

"Let me tell you, they won't back down easily," Poitras told Gomery. "You need an experienced lead counsel who is used to behind-the-scenes politics. For my commission I very much appreciated Bernard Roy's professionalism and determination. He has the right experience."

"Are you kidding? Brian Mulroney's ex-chief of staff interrogating Liberal government witnesses? Come to think of it, why not ask him to lead the examination of his successor in the Prime Minister's Office?"

The two men parted after drawing up a list of suitable candidates. The list included the names of some highly qualified people but was on the short side, considering the tight time frame. Some prospects were interested but already swamped with work. Others were willing but feared political disgrace. Still others wondered whether the inquiry would reach a conclusion before being swept away by the tide of the next election campaign.

Recruiting legal counsel turned out to be a stressful exercise for John Gomery. Those he considered equal to the challenge were not available in large numbers. And once he did find all the qualifications in one individual, he would have to be sure of that person's unfailing loyalty—an essential attribute, in his opinion.

And yet, the impetus that guided Gomery's choices of counsel for the Commission of Inquiry into the Sponsorship Program and Advertising Activities was unusual.

In the hours that followed the announcement of his appointment, Gomery was surprised to hear the voice of an old client, who had since become a close friend. Many years ago Lawrence Finkelstein had asked for his help in a tough battle for the custody of Finkelstein's children. One of them was now an accomplished lawyer, recognized by his peers and eager to be recommended to the bench one day. Finkelstein suggested that his son Neil, of whose talents Gomery was well aware, might be a good candidate for his legal team. The fact that Neil was practising in Toronto, Gomery thought, would add a national dimension to his commission, in an affair that had unfolded essentially in Québec. The next day, Neil Finkelstein showed up before the commissioner in Montreal and was hired.

And although Bernard Roy's past and political alliances worried him, Gomery also decided to hire Roy after an unexpected attack by a Conservative. Still lacking a good feel for handling the media, the recently named commissioner was ambushed by the member of Parliament for Edmonton–St. Albert, John Williams, president of the House Public Accounts Committee, who denounced the creation of a useless and partisan commission headed by a "Liberal hack."

That was quite enough for Gomery—Bernard Roy was offered the job of lead counsel the same day. "I will not let the person presiding over this embarrassing procedural vaudeville tarnish the integrity of my commission, and even less my reputation!"

By asserting his independence in this way, John Gomery was exposing himself to heavier fire, this time from Liberals worried about having to pay the price of revenge. Nevertheless, he preferred honest criticism to cheap shots.

Roy made no secret of the fact that he was pleased to have been named lead counsel. He insisted on engaging a criminal lawyer, Guy Cournoyer, who had assisted him during the Poitras Commission. Roy admitted readily that he hated managing day-to-day details. The only authority he claimed was his experience as a practising lawyer. In all, the commission's legal staff numbered fourteen, with varying experience. Eight days after being appointed commissioner, Gomery had recruited all of the key players he needed.

However, professional disagreements and power struggles would taint the work environment between legal staff who came from Toronto and those who came from Montreal. In the crew's eyes, any hint of discord on board makes a vessel seem much smaller.

THREE

THE MANDARINS ACQUIESCE

J OHN GOMERY LIKES TO TRAVEL by train. In his view, it's the mode of transportation that most enhances his sense of well-being. Just five minutes from his home and offering a comfortable ride for someone of his height (1.8 metres), the train can take one anywhere, from Alaska to Tierra del Fuego. Above all, it is usually on time. This, on John Gomery's scale of values, is fundamental.

In February 2004, on those late-winter evenings when darkness comes early, he rode to Ottawa, deep into government territory. It was a world that he knew nothing about, uncharted territory for a man who had been so busy rendering justice. And yet this was where a good number of the laws that formed the basis of his decisions had been passed.

Gomery was not comfortable with the unknown. He needed an interpreter to fully understand the federal realm and to learn survival tactics. He arranged to meet with Sheila-Marie Cook, who came highly recommended, as she had already been involved in several commissions of inquiry. "I've taken a look at your c.v.," Gomery said.

"I was impressed. You're hired as executive director and secretary of the commission. This will therefore be your fourteenth commission of inquiry, not counting the one I am told you declined to work on. As for your authority, I intend to delegate to you all administrative powers according to Section 34 of the Public Administration Act. We will be meeting on Monday. Now, if you could just tell me how to get to the Treasury Board—I'm expected there in fifteen minutes."

Sheila-Marie Cook was in a spin. "I am flattered," she said. "You know, a commissioner cannot entirely back away from all administrative duties. We have to divide them up..."

"Listen," he said, "a long time ago, I had to choose between law and administration. I opted for law at the time, and I therefore intend to assume this task once again for the commission."

Cook knew all the internal workings of the federal government administration. Even better, she knew the people who made it work. In four decades, she had seen them rise in rank, mingle with the powerful elite and sometimes drop out or be dropped. Sheila-Marie Cook had made her first inroads as a legislative assistant, working for Pierre Elliott Trudeau. That was in 1968. The years that followed marked the beginning of profound changes in our society and, by extension, in the organization of government.

"If I may, what meeting are you going to now?" she asked Gomery.

"Some deputy ministers are going to give me the terms of reference of my mandate."

"Allow me to give you a first bit of advice. Don't sign anything! Take the document they hand to you and leave, then read over all the fine print. Believe me, this isn't their first commission of inquiry."

Never again, she thought, will he go to this type of meeting alone.

That day, though, he was in fact alone as he faced a panel of five men who were intent on observing a judge they had not personally recruited, for a commission whose existence they did not necessarily want. Gomery felt they were annoyed by his take-charge attitude. They must have realized quickly that the agenda of the meeting would soon be in the commissioner's hands. Gomery was tall and calm, and his voice had an assurance that was typical of a high-court judge. He spoke smoothly, but his remarks were so precise and authoritative that they precluded any misunderstanding.

In fact, after the bureaucrats had met Gomery, it was clear that they might eventually have to testify before him. Until that meeting, the question of having one day to account for what they actually knew, what they saw or what they pretended not to have seen, had not been raised. Imagine—senior public servants dragged into this humiliating process!

Judd, Marshall, Rozenberg, Rawling... and the others. They were the highest ranking non-elected personnel, the field marshals of the federal administration. They derived their immense power from the duties and functions delegated to them by their respective ministers or the prime minister himself. Before Gomery, they appeared busy but courteous.

"It's a pleasure to meet you, Mr. Justice," said one.

"We're glad you accepted our offer," said another, more cheekily.

It was no doubt at this meeting that Gomery noticed for the first time how senior public servants from Ottawa use the "we" when referring to their departments.

That private observation later became an irritation that he voiced publicly on many occasions, as government officials, in their testimonies, instinctively tried to recount conversations or written exchanges without revealing the identity of anyone involved. They would admit having met with, e-mailed, obtained authorization from or given instructions to the Treasury Board, Public Works, the Privy Council or the Prime Minister's Office, rather than to Jacques, Paul, Irene or John. Each time, the commissioner would reply, "But with whom, exactly? I'm conducting an inquiry here. Give me some names, please!"

After the deputy ministers had made their presentations, Gomery immersed himself in reading the terms of reference of his mandate, as if he were alone in the room. One of the senior civil servants attempted to break the silence: "As you can see, it's all there, in keeping with the prime minister's announcement. The powers conferred on you are unprecedented for a commission of inquiry."

Absorbed in his reading, Gomery deliberately avoided all the required clauses establishing the legal framework, those endless and unavoidable paragraphs. He went quickly to the heart of his concerns— briefly, the authority given him by the urgency of the situation, independence in his choice of staff and freedom to establish a work schedule. It was all there, except for one essential prerogative. This can't be an oversight, he thought; it's impossible. Did they really think I wouldn't notice?

The silence lay heavy in the room. The bureaucrats must have wondered what he was thinking about. If he wanted more, how far would he go?

This time, Gomery's commanding voice had a clear target. "Gentlemen," he said, "correct me if I'm wrong, but it seems to me that the prime minister insisted that this inquiry would get to the bottom of things, without omitting any fact, any document pertaining to the circumstances of this sponsorship affair. Am I not right?"

"That is true, Mr. Commissioner. You have, as we say, carte blanche."

"Not quite," replied Gomery. "I see no reference in this text to documents coming out of the Prime Minister's Office, nor to minutes of Cabinet meetings, nor to internal memos prepared by the Privy Council. Did Mr. Martin not insist that we uncover the political interference in this scandal? You absolutely must lift this classified status."

An awkward silence ensued. "I'm afraid that will be impossible," answered the boldest deputy sitting at the table. "By their very nature, these documents must remain out of the public eye. The management of state affairs is at stake. To open that door would be reckless."

Gomery lost his composure, throwing his audience off track for a moment. "Well, as far as I'm concerned, the danger is elsewhere. I don't see myself accepting a mandate that I can only half fulfill. In my mind, *that* is what is impossible. Incidentally, the prime minister did not appear to me to have made only a halfway commitment when he announced the creation of my commission."

Whether it is the tone of his voice, the look in his eyes or the expression on his face, Gomery's annoyance always makes an impression on those he confronts. Or maybe it's the combination of all three signals that causes immediate, deep-seated discomfort. Whatever the case, reaction from the bureaucrats was immediate. Nobody in the room dared to consider returning to the prime minister to report that his commissioner, whose nomination had already made the headlines, had been forced to decline the offer on the spot because he lacked the authority he needed to conduct the inquiry.

And yet, one of the senior civil servants excused himself from the room, claiming that he needed authorization from his superiors before he could accept the judge's terms. When he returned, his colleagues reluctantly swallowed the pill: the confidentiality requirement on all documents whose contents might be useful to the inquiry had been lifted.

After the meeting, the bureaucrats must have wondered whether anything at all would remain absolute in their world, much less their own power.

From that point forward, all documents requested by the commission were examined with a fine-tooth comb before being submitted. In certain cases, excessive censoring led to fierce debates and battles as legal staff demanded more complete versions. One such episode concerned the minutes of a special Cabinet meeting held on February 1 and 2, 1996. It was at this meeting that the decision was made to improve federal visibility in Québec, by the government and, by extension, according to the participants, the Liberal Party. In these minutes it was apparent that the two entities had not always been differentiated during Cabinet discussions. The commission had to spend a great deal of time and produce many arguments before finally getting responses to its requests. For example, in a letter to Gomery, Alex Himelfarb, clerk of the Privy Council, stated that in his opinion some of the information contained in the documents requested by the commission was irrelevant, and therefore he had censored certain passages. By wielding his authority in this way, Himelfarb, the highest-ranking public servant in the country, must have thought he had finished with John Gomery. If so, he underestimated the commissioner, who became more and more frustrated and certainly was not deceived by the bluff. Moreover, through his actions, the clerk had exposed the government to the possibility of a court order to hand over the documents. For some items, the negotiations resulted in three different versions of documents being submitted to the counsel, each one with slightly fewer amputations than the last.

The Opposition parties jumped on the bandwagon at this point. The Conservative leader, Stephen Harper, decried Liberal secrecy; Bloc leader Gilles Duceppe compared the blocked-out texts to a game of Mystery Word.

At the meeting with the senior bureaucrats, Gomery was satisfied that he had gained access to restricted documents. He probably did not foresee what a high price he would have to pay for demanding access from people who rarely make such concessions when their personal power is at stake.

After he left the meeting that night, his thoughts were miles away. He imagined himself already in Vietnam or Cambodia, happily far from home. And, as was his custom, he reassured his wife by leaving his work files at home until the two of them returned from their vacation.

FOUR

BACK TO BUSINESS

Since leaving hong kong, John Gomery must have perused the in-flight magazine map of long-haul routes at least ten times. Aside from a dreary film, his only distraction on the aircraft was a selection of bland music—certainly nothing to suit this connoisseur of classical music. Prompted by his wife, who rested on his shoulder, he had tried to sleep several times—to no avail. Fourteen hours later they arrived in Vancouver with aching bodies. After a routine welcome from Customs, baggage transfers and a slight, somewhat predictable delay, they were finally en route for Montreal.

Gomery tried hard to quell his excitement, an emotion he felt more often when he was leaving on a trip than when he was coming home. In fact, the destination he was soon to discover was the sponsorship affair. His impatience was also provoked by the fact that, as he had wished, he had not been informed of what had happened during his three-week absence. Who would be on the legal staff supporting Neil Finkelstein and Bernard Roy in their tasks? Who was being considered to handle communications? John Gomery turned over these and many other questions in his mind.

Unconsciously, he started leafing through a brochure given to all passengers entering Canada. The title was *What You Need to Know about the West Nile Virus*. West Nile was not one of his top priorities at this point, but as he read the document, something dawned on him: the virus was transmitted by mosquitoes, which in turn spread it to other species—including humans, though there had been relatively few such cases. Depending on the region, environment and climate conditions, an epidemic could spread quickly...

He began to wonder what he would eventually find—a few isolated cases of dishonest individuals working for themselves, or a more extensive plague jeopardizing the government's entire immune system. Sooner or later, he would find an answer to this question.

He then found himself thinking about his farm—one of his passions. Havelock! No West Nile virus there—at least, not yet. He wondered what the maple syrup production would be like that year. The *Farmers' Bulletin* was predicting a record season.

There was one last jostle as the flight attendant brought his backrest upright. Then—home at last.

The very next day, he started working on a list of priorities prepared by Sheila-Marie Cook. She had spared him all the tedious details, but nevertheless left him with a good deal of work.

Everything had been carefully worked out—the offices in Ottawa and Montreal, the choice of a venue for the hearings, the administrative support staff, translation and security services and so on. His first concern was his legal team's work plan. The inquiry must get underway. Therefore, he immediately approved the staff and division of workload as Cook had suggested. His only qualm concerned the proposed schedule. In accordance with the scope of his mandate, he established a two-year plan. Neil Finkelstein, who would handle the management and the political roots of the Sponsorship Program, was put in charge of the hearings in Ottawa. Bernard Roy, supported by Guy Cournoyer, was to track the flow of money among the friends of power, those who had benefited from generous government handouts. Finally, another counsel, Marie Cossette, would work with both teams, as necessary.

John Gomery was satisfied with the combination of skills and experience possessed by his legal team. A judge's success rests in large part on the work of those presenting evidence before him: he knew that much but could not guess what would happen next.

Now his lawyers needed an essential tool: investigators. Their recruitment turned out to be a difficult process. All conflicts of interest had to be avoided, and the chosen firm must have no links with the government related to any of the outstanding issues. Gomery, who disliked having to deal with several players at once, asked that all of the services he needed—document management, inquiries, forensic auditing, litigation expertise, etc.—be obtained from one source. He chose Kroll Lindquist and Avey, a world-renowned firm of investigators. At the peak of the commission's activities, the Kroll staff numbered as many as twenty people. In March 2004, the search for documents began and the first subpoenas were issued.

Gomery needed more time to consider how he was going to handle the media. For the first time in his career, he faced two very different challenges: on the one hand, there was the public nature of a commission of inquiry; on the other, the constraints of the quasi-judicial process and presentation of evidence. He based his decision on three criteria: openness, transparency and thoroughness.

Another concern was determining what task to assign to each commission staff member, or rather defining and limiting the scope of each person's prerogatives.

He knew that the hearings would subject his counsel to intense public exposure. He was also aware of lawyers' ambitions and their tendency to show off their best side in order to win new clients, rise in the ranks of their firms and even be considered for appointment to the bench. He feared three things: that counsel for the commission or lawyers for other parties might comment in enough detail to spark public argument over legal points; that they might engage in a competitive exhibition of legal skills for the television cameras; and that they might make inappropriate remarks that, if reported in the press, could seriously hinder the course of events at the hearings. But some among the counsel would have liked to speak directly to the media, and they made this known by showing off their communication skills and hinting at their well-placed contacts among journalists (without naming them, of course). Gomery knew that it would be essential to establish a code of conduct to protect the credibility of the commission and the integrity of the inquiry.

Finally, on an April morning, he made his decision: no one involved in the inquiry, not even himself, would talk to the press. The task would be assigned to a professional. He asked Sheila-Marie Cook to draw up a job description for a commission spokesman. This person would be bilingual and have a good knowledge of the media as well as the workings of the federal government. As one such candidate, I had met Cook while Gomery was on vacation. She sensed the media's eagerness to learn more about this judge who had left on a trip shortly after being appointed commissioner. Even before the work had begun, many people speculated about a premature political termination of the commission.

We met twice, and Cook asked me to prepare a few recommendations and warnings concerning the hazards of this commission of inquiry. My document summed up the political mood of the day and interpreted the media's attitude toward the inquiry. Cook decided that the commissioner should interview me.

At this point I must ask the reader to indulge me in sharing my personal impressions of my first meeting with John Gomery. I was already intrigued by this man whose integrity and values would become the trademark of the commission. He would constantly reassure a suspicious public, and his naive, candid approach to people and their motives would impress everyone. He is one of those extraordinary people who cannot be reduced to a common denominator, precisely because they are so uncommon. I have met some of them during the course of my career—clients, colleagues, interview subjects and others who made such an impression on me that I will never forget them. I fully appreciated every encounter. If by some magic I could gather all of these larger-than-life people in one room and address them, I would surely lose my voice. What I remember most clearly about many of them is the force and clarity of their thinking and of their actions, no matter what the context or the challenges.

When I entered John Gomery's office, I did not know whether I was there for an interview, a working session or an audience. I was guided more by humility than modesty. After all, who ever heard of a judge who asks for advice? Even expert witnesses don't tell him what to think or how to rule on a case, and no law school teaches consulting skills. Judges are not in the habit of having answers whispered to them, never mind having their answers called into question.

There he was, however, standing to greet me—an affable man with a lively, imposing personality, an authoritative man who can neverthe-less surprise interlocutors with his wit and candour. In our brief exchange of pleasantries, he conveyed solid self-confidence. "You know, I introduce myself as a part-time judge. I'm a farmer first of all. But this challenge was such that I couldn't resist. So I've asked my neigh-bour to take care of my cattle for the next eighteen months."

Right from the start, as he described his passion and long before we broached the actual subject of our meeting, I felt an energy, a subtle force at work. I quickly concluded that everyone wants to please John Gomery—not to be subservient in a calculated way, but because they are won over by an idea, a principle or a project that he has taken up. This response comes naturally and not just from his close circle of collaborators. Friends, children and relatives have all come under his spell. Some reporters have even tried to find out from me how he reacted to their articles.

I was no exception. I applied for my membership card at the precise moment when he hired me as media spokesman for the commission. On that matter, surprisingly, he rendered a decision on the spot, in the presence of Sheila-Marie Cook as well as Bernard Roy and Guy Cournoyer. They had all been invited to receive a clear and unequivocal message about what my role would be. He also encouraged them to help me out on judicial matters. In all, it took forty-five minutes to hire me.

Even before leaving the meeting in which we discussed the challenges of media relations at length, I gathered that the credibility of the commission, its image of transparency and integrity, would rest on its commissioner. It seemed strange that the scope of the mandate was known to all, yet the person responsible for it was yet to be known.

FIVE

WHO IS THIS JUDGE, ANYWAY?

IN AUGUST 1932, Montreal's West Island may not have been considered an anglophone stronghold in today's political terms, but it was a predominantly English-speaking neighbourhood, surrounded by boroughs with well-defined borders. John Gomery grew up in Montreal West, farther west and less well-off than Westmount, and a one-hour tram ride from downtown. Not until he entered the Faculty of Arts at McGill University at age eighteen did he encounter the francophone culture of Montreal for the first time. He completed a second degree— in law—in 1956.

Although his name is English, Gomery has never repudiated his deep Welsh roots. Determined and even tenacious, he is an independent man with ideas that are as well founded as they are carefully thought out. When he undertakes a project he devotes himself exclusively to it, never wavering or being distracted by other tasks. He does well enough financially, but that is not the point. He learned this from the experience of his own father, a stockbroker who lost everything during the Depression in the 1930s and had to start over again in a new business to feed his family. The stories and anecdotes that Gomery remembers from those times (he was the only male child) help explain the satisfaction he now derives from farming.

At the start of his career in the late 1950s, postwar circumstances helped him develop his expertise in family law, which was not a common specialty at the time and rather poorly regarded by the profession. In those days, one needed a decree from the Senate to obtain a divorce. Gomery showed up at the Parliament Buildings on many occasions on behalf of his clients, until a new justice minister by the name of Pierre Elliott Trudeau amended the law. Much later, one of Judge Gomery's decisions concerning joint custody helped set a judicial precedent. As a lawyer, he took advantage of all the tricks of the trade gleaned from his professors, many of whom he still loves to quote: "Someone who retains your services will already have a certain understanding of his rights and will obviously tell you what he expects. However, what he will be lacking is knowledge of procedure. That's why he will have chosen you, thinking you will be the best in what you so dislike to learn today—procedure." Or: "Through lack of experience, you will be tempted to sum up in your arguments all the details and aspects of the evidence you are presenting, making sure, of course, that nothing has been left out. You are likely to antagonize or overwhelm a judge—who, as it happens, has also studied law. Go to the heart of things, what you consider to be the core evidence. A choice of relevant arguments is what makes a good lawyer."

After several successful cases, he joined Martineau Walker as head of family law.

John Gomery had no interest in, or time for, politics. Quite unexpectedly, he was short-listed as a candidate for the bench, and in 1983 was appointed to the Superior Court by Mark MacGuigan, minister of justice in Pierre Elliott Trudeau's cabinet. He met the minister at a social event but never met the prime minister, whom he admired.

John Gomery likes lawyers, maybe because he is one of them, or maybe for their ideas and training. He doesn't hold all of them in high esteem, but always manages to find their good points or at least give them the benefit of the doubt. During the hearings, everyone saw him on live television, grilling one lawyer or the other for their weak arguments, inappropriate questions or delaying tactics. He was just as ruthless with his own commission's counsel, who were stunned by his manner. At no time, however, did he treat any of them with disrespect.

For instance, he allowed his counsel complete autonomy in their examination of witnesses. Just like television viewers, journalists and the audience in the room, he wanted to hear first-hand what the witnesses had to say.

•

IN RETURN FOR HIS natural spontaneity, he won the confidence of the public, who admired his responses. He applied this hard-and-fast rule right to the end, cutting me off whenever I alluded to the contents of future testimonies in my conversations with him.

This non-intervention in the preparation of the inquiry created a few operational problems for the legal staff. Differences of opinion, power struggles and contradictory instructions affected their working environment in many ways. Gomery was certainly aware of this but let it be known that it would be inappropriate to involve him in any disagreements. From beginning to end, he maintained his position— above the melee: "In my profession, serenity is not a concept. It is a necessary passage toward all thoughts."

With a few exceptions, all heard this dictum loud and clear. My role as spokesman, in which I was highly visible—often more visible than the legal counsel—made me the subject of many quarrels, and never once did the commissioner get involved in these internal squabbles.

In summary, the Gomery Code of Conduct was straightforward: meet the objectives, stay on schedule and come up with solutions rather than problems. As for ethics, it is the science of morals; we were all expected to be top students.

The respect that most of us have for this man is based on a complex combination of virtues and flaws. Although incomplete, the following portrait shows what the public was able to observe about John Gomery during the hearings, and what I learned about him as an insider.

Judges do not usually manage staff—it's just not the essence of their function. Gomery never just hired someone; he adopted people and was unfailingly loyal from then on. He didn't expect or foresee any problems, and to ensure that none arose, he built his team of close collaborators one by one, according to his needs. All of them had to overcome their irritations and resolve conflicts with their colleagues in the hope of pleasing him. We realized quickly that he was oblivious to confrontation and controversy. A critical remark or outburst from him was always short-lived; once it had passed, the reasons for it were quickly forgotten. Only on those occasions when he willed it, did his memory fail him.

Gomery expected everyone to act in good faith. Some reporters could hardly believe such trust and candour in a legal–political affair of this nature. (As we will see in the next chapter, however, this attitude only applied outside the hearing room, to those whom he did not already suspect.)

The media managed to win Gomery's respect. From the outset, he recognized their importance in maintaining the public's interest in the proceedings of the commission. Assigning them a permanent spokesperson was not just a way of fending off questions. He feared that their coverage of the evidence presented might be biased or interpreted wrongly. A mistake of this type would have been very costly for both Gomery's and my credibility. Besides, star witnesses, political parties and opponents of all sorts could use such mistakes to their advantage. For these reasons, the press had to be given all the support it needed.

Gomery would go through the press coverage on a daily basis, as if he were preparing for a major exam. He had very few questions for me, except when he tried to understand a reporter's point of view in an article. On some occasions he briefly discussed the subject of a column or editorial with me, using my reactions to gauge its consequences for the next day.

Gomery was hurtled from the shadows into the spotlight. Never have I seen a man become such a public figure in so short a time. The media helped out by reporting his quips, or by describing his signs of impatience, his annoyances and his sense of humour. What so impressed Canadians, however, were his quick reactions, his sharpness and his ability to ask the very questions that many of them would have liked to ask. They were convinced that he was on their side and that he would identify and denounce the looters of public funds.

The rise to fame was not without its pitfalls. Interviews in three national dailies on the eve of the Christmas holidays in 2004 turned out to be a tough lesson in humility. Happily, and against all odds, this difficult climb brought the commissioner to new heights in his approval ratings. With all the public curiosity about Gomery the man, and the fact that we were trying to raise his profile, I had recommended to the judge that he give interviews devoted to his origins, his family and his personal life.

I acceded to a request from a journalist who was unknown to me and who, unlike his colleagues from the *Globe and Mail* and *La Presse*, was not covering the inquiry on a day-to-day basis. Don Martin of the *National Post* had forwarded the request to Sheila-Marie Cook. Like her, he came from the West, where he had worked before being assigned to Parliament Hill. He proposed to conduct an interview with Gomery as part of a newspaper mini-series on the most influential Canadian newsmakers of the year. The article was to be published at the end of the year. I raised no objections.

The terms of the interview had been firmly established, but Don Martin was the first journalist scheduled to speak to Gomery, and the opportunity to get a scoop must have seemed irresistible. At 9:15 on the evening of the very day he conducted his interview, he left me a message on the commission's voice mail informing me that he had decided to publish an article the next day. It was only after reading his story that I retrieved his message.

Now I was in hot water with the *National Post*'s two competitors, but despite this, the commissioner's confidence in me was not shaken. To avoid overreacting, and in the interests of fairness, I persuaded him to go ahead with the other two interviews and to give those journalists the same information he had given to Don Martin, thereby diluting the effect of Martin's story. Whether or not the remarks were considered uncharacteristic, they opened up a whole new front for opponents of the commission.

What was going on in Gomery's mind at that point? What was he trying to project? A certain candour, of course, but also a desire to establish his unconventional approach and to introduce a human element that could be understood by all those who wanted to have their say concerning the squandering of public funds.

The commission's first reaction to the three articles was negative. The lawyers believed that the judge had dropped the ball and his spokesman was expendable. How could an experienced judge be seduced by the media in this way? Why did he take the advice of a man with no legal experience whatsoever? One of the lawyers even predicted that the commission's mandate would be terminated prematurely, before it resumed in January.

Once again, John Gomery preferred finding solutions to feeling sorry for himself. The three days that followed the article's publication seemed endless. One after the other, the two other interviews corroborated the spirit of the first, and they were followed by a deafening silence on the part of opinion makers, who must have been in shock. Occasionally, the media reported heckling by ex-Prime Minister Chrétien's supporters.

Then, suddenly, the wind shifted. Across the country, observers, analysts and editorial writers unanimously offered their unequivocal support for John Gomery. Of course, many reprimanded him for his remarks, but the incident spoke volumes about his integrity, his clear-sightedness and his independent spirit.

As soon as work resumed in mid-January, Jean Chrétien's lawyers attacked the commissioner, demanding nothing less than Gomery's recusal. The country's major dailies denounced the motion, accusing the ex-prime minister of trying to throw the inquiry off track. Gomery's reaction surprised many people: "The time when a judge had to remain stoic and expressionless like a sphinx is long past. Have these very experienced lawyers not noticed this?" That was the analogy he used a few days later, in his decision not to step down.

At the end of the day, Gomery turned to me and went even further: "I understand that my statement may have disturbed many people, and I regret what I said. However, if people found it threatening, they have no need to worry. After all, all they have to do is tell me the truth."

Much later, after the publication of the first commission report, Gomery said that he had few regrets about the course of his work, except maybe the three interviews he had given at the end of 2004.

Thus, even before past and present members of government appeared before him, John Gomery was invested with an authority that any elected official would envy—the full support and confidence of Canadians. In the last analysis, the incident was clearly to Gomery's advantage.

In a letter concerning the matter, Guy Pratte, the lawyer representing Jean Pelletier, chief of staff for former Prime Minister Jean Chrétien, asked me to confirm that the interviews with Gomery had been taped. Pratte intended to take the legal route to obtain the tapes. I told him, with some satisfaction, that no such recordings existed. In all things, it helps to have a little instinct and a lot of luck: I had previously decreed that the only recordings to be made of the commissioner would take place in the hearing room. The fact that no tapes of the interviews existed prevented an escalation of the war.

SIX

"BUT FIRST, TONIGHT'S HEADLINES . . ."

O NCE AGAIN, ISABELLE RODRIGUE must have been thinking, the long weekend had been far too short. For months, this wretched scandal had kept her working without a vacation; the rapid-fire sequence of events had allowed her only a few breaks of three or four days between work sessions. Early on that Monday morning in September 2004, she had no idea what to expect from her assignment. It was the first day of a public inquiry whose subject everyone already knew about. The scandal had started with the auditor general's devastating report, then was followed by a series of denunciations and accusations, a commotion fuelled by partisan rivalries that broke out as witnesses appeared before the Public Accounts Committee, and finally an election campaign that focused on the sponsorship affair right across the nation. Rodrigue had been writing up a storm, turning out revelations about this nasty affair week after week. At the outset, it was up to La Presse Canadienne to start the ball rolling on this commission of inquiry headed by an unknown judge.

Rodrigue threw her reporting paraphernalia into a backpack—her cell phone, digital recorder, battery backup, microphone, cables and wires, all jumbled up. Loaded like a sherpa, she headed for the old Ottawa City Hall rather than taking her usual route. Like everyone else in the capital, she enjoyed the lingering summer weather. After passing the governor general's gardens, she walked the footpaths along the Rideau River, then crossed the all-white Minto Bridges—two Lego blocks in the middle of a natural green setting. Rodrigue could not have guessed that she would be trudging the same path for the next hundred days or so.

Her immediate concern was to determine to what extent the commission's upcoming testimonies would be newsworthy. Aside from the star witnesses, was there any chance that revelations made by civil servants and non-political staff would create a buzz? Would they upset the predictable unfolding of the affair, adding a little pizzazz to a case that appeared to be open and shut? She planned to cover the story selectively, on a case-by-case basis, as there were only two Presse Canadienne correspondents in the Ottawa bureau and the government agenda for the fall was already looking very busy.

Her colleagues started arriving at the same time, in twos and threes. The motley crew were all after the same services: press room, document access, sound feed, translation services, Internet access, phone lines, scrum area. I made the rounds with them again and again, making sure everything was in place.

In the preceding weeks, I had read articles and reports by some of these same journalists on the creation of the commission—a pre-election gimmick by the government, according to some. Others were betting that we would never make it to the end of our mandate, given the Liberals' "thirst for power." Only the possibility of unveiling unknown or secret documents before the commission had improved our ratings on the daily news hit parade. Whatever their individual positions, I was willing to get to know the journalists assigned to cover the proceedings, and to catch up with a few colleagues from twenty years back.

On the busiest days of hearings presided over by John Gomery, there were more than forty reporters in the press room. Variously talented and informed, all of them worked with the same production schedule, and all were under the same pressure to come up with a headline. Then there were the "outside" reporters, based elsewhere in Canada or assigned to cover public affairs, who would phone in to catch the news. All journalists were driven by the same guiding principles. From my vantage point, I tried hard to help establish and enhance the credibility of the commission, its counsel and its method. The relevance of the proceedings, and especially the autonomy of the commissioner, had to remain my number-one priority. As a result, he and I became an inseparable team.

My experience of working with the journalists covering the inquiry turned out to be unlike any other. I worked closely with them every day of the hearings, not in order to dictate what they should report, but to collaborate with them in striving for fair and balanced coverage of the commission's work. This objective could only be achieved if we trusted one another, so it was imperative for me to speak frankly and to give them all possible access to documents and information. Any doubts about the commission's forthrightness must be dispelled. It was not enough that John Gomery and I believed in this candid, open approach; we had to prove that we meant it, in what we did and said every day.

The openness of my relationship with the journalists depended in part on a recognition of the two roles I had to play. In my primary role as communications director, I was to feed them all kinds of information and statistics on commission proceedings and procedures, the filing and presentation of evidence, and to guide them through the maze.

The men and women of the press were expected to distill this mass of data into short, succinct statements that would be heard and read across Canada every day. Sometimes several bulletins had to be filed in one working day. It was inevitable that these brief headlines and lead paragraphs summarizing the day's events would sound like verdicts on the commission's work. My daily task was to protect the credibility of the commission's activity by providing the journalists with the right materials and summaries, but not adding spin or hiding anything. They had to be free to write their own stories, and I had to deflect any biased interpretations of the facts.

Errors resulting from such misinterpretations were as worrisome as actual errors of fact, and it was very easy to make a mistake. On some days, as many as twenty-five volumes of documents relating to a single testimony were made available to reporters. Essentially, this evidence consisted of lists of all sorts—e-mails, letters, memos, invoices, cheques and contracts, which were potentially incriminating documents insofar as they raised the right questions. Each day's great jigsaw puzzle of documents became available early in the morning, and no reporter could possibly read, comprehend and process all of them in time to file a story before the end of the day. Therefore, I'd draw their attention to particular items, pages and documents that they could use as signposts and as references. My task was to ensure that the journalists had the information they needed, that they could pinpoint any document they required for reference, and that their "verdicts" represented accurately what had occurred that day, without misinterpretation.

To my great satisfaction, the effort to achieve a credible working relationship with the Ottawa correspondents was by and large well received. Each morning before the hearings got under way, the counsel involved that day would brief me on their examination strategies, and above all give me an idea of what they'd be trying to get from the witnesses. In this respect, Neil Finkelstein helped me out considerably, highlighting important passages or essential data right on the relevant pages. He even shared the order of the themes and questions that he would raise. In the minutes that followed, I could give journalists the key elements of the day's proceedings. Throughout this process, I had to keep in mind the necessity of offering fresh material regularly. News is ephemeral; reporters constantly needed new information or new aspects of the facts.

Each morning at 9:30, I produced the day's agenda for the media: "Hello, everyone. I won't tell you what to report today, any more than yesterday. But according to what I've heard and read, I can say that if I had to write a story today, these would be the main points. After the usual introductions and formalities, the examination-in-chief will begin with this question . . . This other point should not be raised until this afternoon; but you never know, it all depends on the memory and accuracy of the witnesses, right?"

I was very pleased to note that the flow of information could also run in the opposite direction. Reporters looking for more details or supplementary information sometimes asked me to intervene and ask counsel to put questions to the witnesses in order to elucidate certain matters or obtain auxiliary details. In many instances, this helped clarify the testimony while ensuring that the next day's story would be presented accurately.

The trust at the heart of my relationship with the journalists never faltered, though it was constantly tested. Reporters knew that the early-morning update prepared them in much the same way as the commission lawyers, who received the same documents. If any journalist was reluctant to accept my briefing, fearing some kind of bias, all of them nevertheless took advantage of the working relationship. Everyone was welcome to the information and guidance I provided, but they didn't have to take my word for it: they had full access to the documents. In this way, they avoided the agony of having to with-draw any incorrect statements—or, worse, having to face legal action. Luckily, there were no casualties.

My secondary role as commission spokesman was less conven-tional. A judge must, in the course of his work, take a vow of silence when it comes to the media, and suppress the urge to comment on or explain his decisions. In this situation, John Gomery had become a celebrity overnight, just after his appointment. Nevertheless, he main-tained that the inquiry was much more important than the attention he personally was attracting. This excessive modesty—or, perhaps, this mistaken conviction—did not affect his decision to hire me as spokesman. My task was essentially to speak on behalf of a commis-sioner who had chosen to remain silent. The press had to accept this distinction and realize that my responsibilities in this secondary role went well beyond media relations. In short, I had to make sure that my words expressed Gomery's thoughts. Reporters had to live with the fact that they would have just one official source, but after observing the closeness of my working relationship with Gomery, they tended to regard my statements as his.

The easy part for me was the questions I asked Gomery about proce-dural details, admission of evidence and motions. In these matters I could not have had a better coach. "I like it when you ask me these questions. I find it reassuring to see you going deeper into the subject, even though you probably don't need all of these details. If in the end you manage to pass your Law 101 course, I'll send you my bill!"

The trickier test had to do with Gomery the man, and with the values he held most dear. Questions raised about his judgment and impartiality, suspicions that he had indirectly given his eldest daugh-ter an unfair advantage, and gossip about contracts awarded to suppliers made for some passionate discussions. At the end of these talks, though, I had to prepare my public remarks and deliver them without emotion. It was a demanding exercise but a necessary one, given the intensity of our conversations.

After the golf-ball performance and Jean Chrétien's insinuations, Gomery remarked: "Whether or not he was involved in this affair, we will find out later. How can a former head of government take part in this vaudeville show! Everything was there, even the shills at the back of the room. His own lawyer looked uncomfortable. This show did not impress me. I feel sorry for my poor Sally, unjustly dragged into this."

My official response as spokesman was: "The commissioner regrets these allegations of conflict of interest in favour of his daughter Sally. Everything in this case is, of course, crystal clear. Sally Gomery and Bernard Roy, though working for the same law firm, have never practised in the same city and are not on an equal footing as associates of their firm. Mr. Roy was chosen for his experience and his skills. The proof of this has, I believe, been demonstrated."

As for the words Gomery used, often letting his amazement, disgust or impatience seep through, he had no regrets. "What do they think? That I just sit there all day, looking like I'm listening without really listening? Why don't you reassure them by telling them that I'm holding back a lot more than I'm saying? And judging from the lack of preparation of certain lawyers during cross-examination, they should probably do the same."

These were the constraints we had to live with. He was on the bench and I faced the microphones, each relying only on his own remarks without compromising the other. A spokesman is not there to act as a prompter; a commissioner does not wait for his cue.

For some reporters, especially those who were inquiry regulars and for whom the proceedings had become a specialty, the commission's work could be summed up in this way: to be assigned to Gomery is to cover the elements of a scandal, requiring first that fraudulent actions and those responsible for them be singled out; then, that the ringleaders be identified by working back up the chain of command. These leaders, however, are not part of a covert operation. They simply turned the Government of Canada into their headquarters. The number of copies sold, and audience ratings achieved, became a measure not only of public opinion but of the loyal following that certain journalists had acquired. Each morning, the news desks of all major national newspapers would select the Gomery Commission as one of the top five stories of the day. "It's very simple," said Claude Gervais, news editor for the Réseau de l'Information, the French-language counterpart of CBC Newsworld. "Depending on the revelations you come up with, Gomery is competing with Iraq, George W. Bush, the future of the Martin government and the state of the pope's health. The order may change, but you can bet you'll have one of the top spots in the news lineup."

This priority treatment by the national news media helped set a new record for the number of reporting hours on a single topic, and it generated a pile of press releases over three metres high. The news bulletins were essential for the public to gain a proper understanding of the facts and to maintaining everyone's interest in the intense commission proceedings, right to the end.

Outside the hearing room, other participants were helping keep public interest alive. Just behind the doors and in full view was the scrum area, where the witnesses' and participants' lawyers could air their opinions and frustrations at will as they left the hearing room. I had chosen this spot as a decompression chamber, where everyone could present the arguments and objections they had not managed to bring up before Gomery on behalf of their clients. It was also a news desk, where lawyers commented and answered questions on certain motions and procedures, and a rumour mill in which the value of certain testimony and evidence was assessed. But above all, it was the best place for lawyers to address Canadians directly about the latest revelations.

This pressure valve turned into a formidable tool for the commission. Many of the scenarios, responses and analyses that were tested in this venue helped me fine-tune our own messages and responses immediately, and to react on the spot. Certain high-profile lawyers representing notorious witnesses took ample advantage of this opportunity to respond to allegations and to issue statements intended to protect their clients' good reputations—in other words, they tried to inject their "enlightened" comments into the news reports of the day. All of this frantic activity was fed into the evening news bulletins, as the lawyers engaged in all-out assaults against the commission and a cutthroat competition for public opinion. It was as if they were fighting the ultimate battle every day. After a few weeks, it became easy to recognize the celebrities, even for those watching the proceedings on television. Pierre Fournier, representing Alfonso Gagliano, ex-minister and ex-ambassador; Guy Pratte, representing Jean Pelletier, ex-chief of staff for an ex-prime minister; Richard Auger, representing Charles ("Chuck") Guité, an ex-public servant; Peter Doody, representing the ex-prime minister; and finally, Sylvain Lussier, representing the current government. What an impressive lineup! These men were champions of the law profession, with whom I was to cross swords on more than one occasion, pitting statement against counter-statement. They showed remarkable skill and perseverance in handling their arguments, and they impressed me greatly. For reporters looking for a different angle, they were the silvering on the mirror, where one could glimpse a new perspective on the proceedings.

Of all of the participants, I had the greatest influence on the press. With a comment or suggestion, I could enhance a headline or improve an article, allowing certain reporters to set their work apart from the main lead story of the day. In reality, all journalists struggled to extract newsworthy items from the same mass of raw material. In this way they resembled a team of medical specialists poring over an X-ray and hoping to agree on a diagnosis. With a touch of collegial humour, they established an informal "lead committee" to help pinpoint a common editorial line at the end of the day. They realized that given the mountain of evidence involved, this was the best way to achieve consistency in their reporting. The approach, colour and flavour of the story remained each journalist's prerogative when they sat down to write. The trust they placed in me had to do with my understanding of, and respect for, individual treatments, which writers would sometimes show me when they required clarification or further information. In this way, I was often able to give the commissioner a preview of what he was going to hear or read the next day.

That working arrangement suited me. I grew worried about the move to Montreal, scheduled for February 2005, not so much because there the witnesses would be communications firms, political organizers, suppliers and so forth, but because there would be a changing of the guard among the journalists. Initially, many media decided to rely on local staff rather than sending the reporters who had covered the Ottawa hearings. They doubted that any further revelations would emerge; as well, they had to face budget considerations. I would have to start from square one—protocol, procedures, document usage, everything. In all honesty, I also worried about a decline in thoroughness and journalistic standards. Competition in Montreal was much fiercer than in Ottawa, because it was a much larger city with many more media outlets. I was very surprised when none of this happened. The press room contained triple the number of journalists, including many people from Ottawa as well as their Montreal colleagues, and the cohort of columnists, analysts and editorial writers who were making more and more frequent visits to the commission. The same collegial working environment that journalists had appreciated in Ottawa was established very quickly in Montreal, with the same concern for balanced reporting and fair play.

In many respects, a major event such as the proceedings of the Commission of Inquiry into Sponsorships, which spanned such a long time, reminded me of the working climate surrounding a lengthy election campaign—all of these people, living and working in their day-to-day lives, gathered around this single current event. In the Gomery microcosm, Emmanuelle got married, Gilles became a father and Christina became an adoptive mother, Louiselle lost her mother and Jean his employer, Gary went to Morocco, Kathryn signed up for French immersion, Daniel moved into town, Yves was transferred to Ottawa—and so on. The media team evolved and developed in step with the events of the commission.

SEVEN

WAR GAMES

THE PRIVY COUNCIL OFFICE gives the prime minister all the support of the public service and assists him directly in the exercise of his duties and responsibilities. At its head sits the clerk of the Privy Council, the country's highest-ranking civil servant, who also acts as secretary to the Cabinet. In essence, he is deputy minister to the prime minister, the guardian of the current government's documents and those of all preceding administrations. He plays a key role behind the scenes. In this capacity, Alex Himelfarb was the only person with sufficient authority to thwart the wishes—or at least dampen the eagerness—of the commission counsel. Although there were many attempts to hinder the proceedings, we were unable to trace the impetus back to the Privy Council. What is surprising is that there were so many such attempts, despite the fact that John Gomery had received his mandate from the prime minister himself.

In addition to attempts to withhold documents, there were efforts to misinform the public regarding the costs of the commission. These machinations, wherever they originated, only made it clearer to the press how unusual had been Paul Martin's decision to retain certain key civil servants after his election. Several of these people had occupied the inner circles of power, having been appointed or promoted within the public service by Jean Chrétien or Eddy Goldenberg, a loyal friend and advisor of the prime minister. Several of those promotions represented quantum leaps in career advancement; for example, Alex Himelfarb rocketed from deputy minister at Heritage Canada to clerk of the Privy Council. Some civil servants who watched his ascent describe him as an intelligent, crafty man, who learned how strings were pulled in government—a highly skilled tactician obsessed with getting results.

One morning in the spring of 2005, the news broke without making a ripple. A war cabinet had been created within the Privy Council itself to assess and control the impact of the Gomery Commission, and the government had invested more than a million dollars in the undertaking. For many people, this revelation confirmed that a concerted and secret effort was under way that could compromise the commission's credibility and efficiency. The operation's plan of action, budget and staff appeared on the front page of the *Ottawa Citizen*. According to the reporter, Jack Aubry, the war cabinet's objective was to minimize the collateral damage caused by the inquiry. The concern, among other things, Aubry wrote, was to protect the reputation of high-ranking civil servants, many of whom had been promoted to their positions during Prime Minister Chrétien's ten-year reign.

Even more disturbing was the fact that the war cabinet had been created in June 2004, months before the commission's public hearings began in September. Any keen observer would easily have connected the dots in a series of intentions, events and individuals that, in retrospect, were indeed cause for concern.

Within the commission itself, we had always treated each statement, propaganda assault or attack on the integrity of the commission and its staff on a case-by-case basis. We rejected all conspiracy theories.

It is clear today that each of these separate efforts—some subtle, some grotesque—was directly intended to weaken the impact of the inquiry. A few examples will prove the point.

When he unveiled his work plan during his opening statement on May 7, 2004, John Gomery described his strategy, schedule and procedure for presentation of evidence. This information was sufficient to to give fair warning to potential critics.

Moreover, because the media had reported the nature, scope and details of the government documents that had been requisitioned, anyone inconvenienced by the commission's existence could predict which stones would likely be turned over.

The commission's approach was simplicity itself, devoted to investigating the Sponsorship Program's origin and funding, political interference and the government administration's procedural maze. For five months, civil servants at every level were put in the spotlight, testifying as to how their processes functioned; i.e., what had been expected to be done as compared to what was actually done, but above all, on whose orders and according to which political agenda.

What was the real war that prompted the creation of the war cabinet? It was not a war being fought by Prime Minister Martin, who had yielded to pressure from his Ontario caucus and set up this commission in the hope that it would absolve his government. The only other enemies might have come from the Québec caucus, not all of whose members had welcomed the new leader. If they were the warmongers, who and what were they trying to protect?

Either way, the war waged against the Gomery Commission could not be fought out in the open. It had to be a covert operation, led behind the scenes with the help of rumours and middlemen. The warriors would have to be inconspicuous, discarding the high profile associated with power and ambition—simple messengers or go-betweens, links between certain civil servants and ministerial aides.

Others with heavily political agendas assumed more important roles on a completely different level, leading the charge with all-out attacks and provocative statements. These loyal members of a coterie now in plain view—all party officials and ex-members of political staffs—relentlessly denounced Gomery's ethical conduct as well as his counsel, haphazardly throwing stones from inside a glass house.

Of course, the war cabinet had no existence on paper. According to Aubry, the impetus officially came from a coordinating committee led by Guy McKenzie, who worked for the Privy Council Office and who operated under direct orders from Alex Himelfarb. In all, five individuals were assigned to the task. Ursula Menke, a lawyer and assistant supply officer with the Canadian Coast Guard who had also worked for the inspections unit of the Canadian Security and Intelligence Service, led the group and headed up its day-to-day operations. She was also a liaison officer between the Privy Council and commissions of inquiry.

Their mission was straightforward enough, although the means authorized to pursue it were unclear. The war was conducted in the media, using spot guerrilla tactics rather than conventional warfare. The objective was to produce a precise reading of the political fallout and potential threats resulting from the Gomery Commission's work—including public perceptions of and responses to the hearings. Once this work was completed, the task was to identify the initiatives that would limit the impact on the government, both current and previous.

According to the *Ottawa Citizen* article, the war cabinet was apparently in daily contact with the Prime Minister's Office and the office of the clerk of the Privy Council during the inquiry hearings. Paul Martin and Liberal MPS came under constant fire from the Opposition, yet for months on end they reiterated the party line—complete faith in John Gomery. It was as if the commission were the medicine prescribed in response to a crisis, and the dosage had to be measured carefully to avoid dangerous side effects.

Many people are involved in the process of ensuring that a commission of inquiry is being managed properly. For that reason, commissions report to the Privy Council Office, which in turn approves, among other things, budgets, professional service contracts and the financial considerations pertaining to these contracts. Once this overview is complete, the information is forwarded to the Treasury Board, which proceeds with its own review before giving approval.

Officially, this bureaucratic exercise ensures that the commissioner avoids pitfalls. Yet, like all commissioners, John Gomery was given full authority and independence in recruiting personnel and negotiating contracts as required, by virtue of the *Inquiries Act*. The level of autonomy granted him was required by the urgency of his mandate.

John Gomery took this sense of urgency very seriously. As early as mid-March 2004, only five weeks after being appointed, his work plan was established, his legal staff in place and his associates hired. As these decisions were made, budget estimates for the first year were prepared. At the same time, some government workers made their own projections. It was at this point, for the first time, that false information about the operating budget was leaked to the media.

Daniel Leblanc is a highly respected parliamentary correspondent. We owe to him and his colleague, Campbell Clark, the credit for unveiling the sponsorship scandal in the first place. Leblanc spent three years digging into the story and filing many official requests for access to information that was supposedly accessible. His articles in the *Globe and Mail* set the stage for an in-depth review of government actions in the affair, and he became a popular channel for anyone anxious to leak information that could damage the commission.

I had known Leblanc for only a short time—just a few weeks during the Ottawa hearings—yet we had already established a collegial relationship based on trust and professional respect. That shared respect never faltered during the course of events, but we did have to learn more about each other.

That day he caught me off guard. "When will you disclose the commission's budget, I mean the expenditure details? Sources tell me the amount could greatly exceed $50 million, and only for the first phase."

There are times when silence is golden—even for a spokesman. Sometimes you need a tactical break, even a few nanoseconds long, to come up with a response, a quote that everyone in the country will read in tomorrow's papers.

So I said to myself, where on earth did he get those figures? Only four people from the commission are aware of the budget. The only others work for the Privy Council. And what about the endless delays? They are already one month behind in their approval schedule. And I can't say a thing until the approval goes through. I can't just let him publish those numbers!

"Unfortunately, I can neither confirm nor deny the amount you mention," I said to Leblanc. "I can say, however, that it is way beyond the actual figures. In fact, it is more than twice the actual amount. I plan on releasing our budget estimates in detail as soon as the Treasury Board approves them. Of course, you're aware how long that could take, aren't you?" You bet!

In fact, neither the Privy Council nor the Treasury Board disclosed the budget they had approved for the Gomery Commission—no announcement, not even a rough estimate to compare with other commission budgets. By taking advantage of this lack of information, the informants had three months to set the media off on a spiralling escalation of numbers and budget forecasts. No fewer than thirty articles and stories appeared across the country, echoing the phony figures, each in its own way.

Among many variations on the theme were: why spend so much on an inquiry that the police can handle just as well? We will never recover the money this inquiry will cost us. Why waste public funds on an inquiry into facts that have already been revealed in the auditor general's report?

The pressure was mounting. An irritated John Gomery finally accepted my proposal: contrary to normal procedures, we would release our budget estimates ourselves, by announcing rather than publishing them. Gomery hoped that the authorities would then issue their own statement, which would put an end to the imbroglio.

This press release, however, was never issued—with good reason. When our opponents were unable to counter publicly the $20.4 million budget that the Gomery Commission had prepared—and that I explained in detail to reporters, including actual budget items and disbursements—they took advantage of the long official silence by taking another route.

On February 1, 2005, John Gomery rejected the demand by Jean Chrétien's attorneys that he resign for lack of impartiality. On the same day, several journalists got a phone call from the office of the minister of public works. The commission had adjourned for the day at 5:30 PM. Printing deadlines were inching nearer and nearer, but public servants had left their offices, making it impossible to verify information and sources. Susan Murray, press secretary to Scott Brison, told reporters that it would cost an additional $40 million just to meet the demands of the commission's counsel. This amount would essentially cover photocopies of the documents needed as evidence, as well as professional fees of lawyers representing civil servants who appeared as witnesses. There was no press release or document to back up the claim, no detailed breakdown of the costs and no other source to confirm the information, but we knew how the headlines would read the next day. Some newspapers even calculated their own numbers: the Gomery Commission would cost almost $100 million! And, to make matters worse, the sub-headline that day was: Commissioner Rejects Chrétien Allegations. He's Staying!

I managed to get Susan Murray's name from reporters, and called her and then her boss, Brison's chief of staff. In retrospect I rather regret my tone of voice that day, but I had been deeply shocked—not only by the allegations but by the way they had been divulged. How dare they throw out those numbers without either proof or explanation? After my somewhat lengthy speech, she confirmed that she had acted under orders.

"From whom?"

"Higher up."

"But from where higher up, exactly?"

"From the Privy Council Office."

"From whom at Privy Council?"

That ended our conversation, but not the situation itself. The budget saga was followed by revelations concerning fees paid to commission lawyers, but especially concerning the salary paid John Gomery himself. Unofficial sources even mentioned a fee of $300,000 for the judge—just for the first year! No one could identify the source of this fabrication, so once again I had to respond. "We would like to make it clear that only one employee of the commission is paid by the Department of Justice, and that is the commissioner himself. He receives the same salary as he would for his work at the Québec Superior Court, and no more." Once again, the Justice Department never corroborated the information we were putting forward.

Then, in an unprecedented assault on John Gomery's integrity, his family came under fire. The attack linked the hiring of Bernard Roy as the commission's chief counsel with the fact that Sally Gomery, the commissioner's eldest daughter, was also an associate of Roy's firm, Ogilvy Renault. According to some critics, the conflict of interest was made even worse by the fact that Sally Gomery would reap indirect financial benefits from Roy's mandate—because those benefits would also accrue to the Ottawa office, where she worked—all thanks to her father.

The story was offered to many reporters, but no one was taken in. At first the information was presented as an opportunity for a scoop. Eight reporters called with the same questions, worded in exactly the same way. Every one of them abandoned the story. After weeks of trying, the informants finally got results with a columnist at the *Vancouver Sun*, who mentioned the possibility of a conflict of interest. And that was it. In defence, I invoked the guidelines implemented by the Department of Justice concerning professional fees paid to commission counsel. The fee ceilings are well below those that apply to private practice, and Gomery, of course, took these guidelines into account. Once again, the government remained mute on the matter—no support and no corroboration of the facts.

As if that weren't enough, we caught another blow. On a February morning, almost a year to the day after his appointment, the headlines criticized Gomery for awarding a contract worth several million dollars to his investigators—Kroll Lindquist and Avey—without calling for bids.

At last, commission opponents had managed to make a slight incursion, and now they attacked openly. To make matters worse, they charged, the contract had been awarded and partially acted on before even being signed. What a disgrace!

My coffee maker was still bubbling in my hotel suite at 6:30 that morning when the phone rang for the first time.

"Hello, Mr. Perreault. Sorry to call you so early in the morning," blurted the research assistant. "Our program host would like to have your reaction to the Kroll story. We will be on the air in less than two minutes, if you would be so kind..."

What if I'm not so kind, I thought; would you make another call? How did they get my number? Let's go...just the two of us. At noon, the news will be stale.

Even the opening question was incriminating. "How do you explain the commissioner's action? Isn't this the kind of thing he suspects many of the witnesses appearing before him to have committed?"

"First of all, you must understand that the commissioner looked for a firm that had all five areas of expertise needed to fulfill his mandate: document management, inquiry, forensic auditing, litigation and expert witness support, in that order. Moreover, he had to make sure that no conflicts of interest were possible."

Touché! This "scoop" had given me an opportunity to dig in my heels. The entire Privy Council was aware of the choice of firms and agreed that Gomery's decision was the right one.

"Given the magnitude of the mandate, you'll understand why we also needed a few months to assess the scope of each of these tasks. Let me give you an example: the quantity of documents collected, compiled and analyzed amounted to seven thousand boxes in all."

Two days later, our credibility was re-established. It had taken a dozen interviews to deflect the manoeuvre.

EIGHT

CHRÉTIEN GOES THE DISTANCE

A s was his custom, rather than just arriving, Jean Chrétien appeared suddenly out of nowhere on the day of his testimony in February 2005. Walking briskly like a man who is perpetually late, and surrounded by an entourage of lawyers and cronies, he attempted to break through the wave of reporters, cameramen and photographers who had come to meet him. In the ebbing tide, a few dozen citizens watched the unfolding of this important event. A bold spectator looking for an autograph took advantage of the media scrum to press his request. His daring irritated the star witness, who, unable to restrain himself, ripped the marker from the poor man's hands and autographed his forehead in big red letters. Under the glass dome, a ruthless light made the gesture seem even more appalling. Chrétien's coterie guffawed as one man.

Resuming his brisk pace, the former prime minister tightened his grip on his attaché case, as if he were afraid someone would seize its valuable contents. He carried the case with the air of a magician holding a bag of tricks, and opened it during his testimony to reveal no letters, no documents, no evidence—only golf balls. The gesture was a reference to a published interview with John Gomery, in which the commissioner had remarked that golf balls printed with Chrétien's signature were "small-town cheap." Perhaps Chrétien was enjoying the memory of being out on the links with an American president, trying for a birdie. From Little Rock to Crawford, from Clinton to Bush, he might have compared their national security issues to his national unity concerns, which had the same urgency and the same priorities.

This time, the man who had devoted forty years of his life to getting re-elected was not looking for votes; he was campaigning to save his reputation. His ambition was to go down in history with an honourable mention, one up on his predecessors—Jean Chrétien, a great Canadian prime minister, a politician who had bequeathed an outstanding legacy.

Throughout his testimony, he looked extremely pleased with himself and defied anyone—especially the commissioner—to find fault in the least way.

"This was propaganda for my country," Chrétien declared. "If this is what happened. I will not apologize to anyone for doing this." And: "I have the impression that this commission is going to cost far more than the amount of money that was stolen." He even took the precaution of trying to dissociate himself from all embarrassing future revelations: "I'm proud of what we've done. If people have made mistakes, acted in bad faith, run away with the money, bring them to court and try them. I won't even send them oranges in prison."

The man was deeply hurt. His self-esteem had taken a beating in the days preceding his performance, when he was forced to submit to a preliminary interview. His lawyers had insisted on knowing how the interrogation would be carried out in order to be better prepared. For Jean Chrétien, Bernard Roy represented an enemy who had been in power before him, a Conservative and a friend of Brian Mulroney.

As for Roy, he enjoys politics but seems uncomfortable with politicians. He doesn't seem to appreciate their nearsightedness, opportunism or intermittent intellectual shallowness. And yet, during the 1980s, Roy accompanied his friend Brian Mulroney as he rose to power. He served as chief of staff for a full term and was a meticulous and thoughtful man of action.

Now, Roy's first encounter with his friend's successor turned into a face-off and a rebuff. Throughout, an aggressive Jean Chrétien treated the commission counsel like an adversary, and the chief counsel found it difficult to work in such a tense atmosphere. Their exchange amounted to a settling of scores with no one claiming victory; the questioner stated he was only doing his job, and the respondent insisted that was precisely what he had done.

Yet the former prime minister's closest associates had already provided background on the events under investigation. Marcel Massé, an intergovernmental affairs minister and experienced statesman— more experienced statesman than politician—confirmed the strategies and measures Cabinet had adopted for Québec. The clerk of the Privy Council, Jocelyne Bourgon, confirmed that she had warned Jean Chrétien about the inherent risks of a program of this nature that would be administered under direct orders from the prime minister. In a memo to Chrétien dated December 18, 1996, she expressed concern that he had assumed a big responsibility concerning money that was taken from the National Unity Reserve.

Chrétien did not answer the memo. In September 1997, Bourgon reiterated her concerns in a second communication. The only answer she got came eight years later, at the end of his testimony before John Gomery. "As prime minister, I received numerous memos from the Privy Council Office counselling me on all kinds of topics. In most cases, we followed the office's advice. I sometimes questioned this advice and my staff convinced me that the office was right. Sometimes

I convinced them that my judgment was correct. Sometimes I ignored their advice like any other prime minister. A prime minister, minister or chief executive officer cannot approve every memo that is submitted to him without discussion."

Many other accounts of Cabinet proceedings, classified e-mails and initialled marginal notes were disturbing. The tone they conveyed harked back to the crisis generated by the 1995 referendum, which the federalists won by a mere 54,300 votes. The province of Québec decided to stay—or rather, did not manage to leave—and as a result, Chrétien mobilized his ministers and his civil servants to fight the "separatists." This was *his* war, and everyone was called to the front for Canada.

In this warlike atmosphere, the good of the state was invoked to back up political motivations and means. The act of repeating the same arguments over and over became a way of making them valid. In the ultimate assault, at the end of the prepared statement he had been allowed to present within the context of his testimony, Jean Chrétien went back to work: "The Sponsorship Program did not favour any party in particular. It was not a Liberal Party entity. It was meant to increase Canada's visibility in Québec. There were, however, unexamined opinions concerning public relations agencies that were said to be 'friends' of the Liberals. We should be wary of such labels."

Why this favour? What made John Gomery give former Prime Minister Chrétien the right to add the statement to the testimony that he had just given?

For weeks on end, John Gomery had been the target of Chrétien loyalists. They had attacked his family, his ethical conduct, his impartiality—and, worse, his judgment. The energy expended denigrating Gomery increased in direct proportion to his public support. Chrétien's lawyers who, a few days earlier, had asked for Gomery's resignation, were suddenly demanding fair treatment by permitting their client to make a statement.

Gomery's staff was divided on the question. As chief counsel leading the interrogation, Bernard Roy was opposed to what he considered
a dangerous precedent for the testimonies of key witnesses later on. I
agreed, believing that the media would react negatively and could
assume that the commissioner had been intimidated by his opponents'
attacks.

For his part, Neil Finkelstein believed in the fair-play aspect of the
privilege Gomery had granted Chrétien. Finkelstein tried to convince
me of this so that I could serve it up to the media: "Since he was the
prime minister at the time, all suspicions are directed at him. Some
have already accused him. It is only fair that we hear his version of
the story."

I was in complete disagreement with him. "I thought his version
would flow naturally from his answers to Bernard Roy's questions," I
said, "or those asked during cross-examination. He will try to impose
his memory on ours. For that matter, Paul Martin could very well ask
for the same treatment. Why don't we give them all air time? We could
even find sponsors!"

In the end, Finkelstein was the one who could plead a case, and I
finally agreed. I was flabbergasted, though, when he insinuated that
he had seen the statement prepared for Jean Chrétien and that I had
nothing to worry about. I never asked him how he had managed to get
his hands on the text. I did, however, keep the question in the back of
my mind.

Finkelstein was present during Jean Chrétien's testimony: quite
unexpectedly he attended an examination-in-chief that he did not
conduct. He didn't sit at the commission counsel's table, preferring to
remain outside the range of the television cameras by taking a seat at the
back of the room. And when Chrétien had finished his statement and
was leaving the hearing room, Finkelstein spontaneously stepped forward
and shook his hand, ignoring the cameras, which were still running.

In any other situation, this would have been a simple act of courtesy, but in this instance it was much more significant. The extraordinary moment was captured by CPAC television cameras and made available to every national television network in the country. With avid interest I watched all the televised news bulletins that evening and read the newspaper columns the next day. Nothing came of it. John Gomery had just been publicly humiliated by Jean Chrétien showing off his collection of golf balls—apparently in a satirical retaliation against Gomery's "small-town cheap" remark—and one of the commissioner's counsel looked almost as if he were congratulating the former prime minister.

After compiling a press review, I asked for a meeting with Gomery. Finkelstein joined us. I felt a little embarrassed as I expressed my overall concerns about the incident of the previous evening. To my great surprise, Finkelstein did not seem to have reacted in the same way, nor did he appear to understand his commission colleagues' concerns. "As far as I know," he said, "no one has been accused or found guilty by this commission. My gesture was simply a mark of respect toward an ex-prime minister who agreed to play a very tough game."

Gomery showed no anger whatsoever. He held nothing against Finkelstein with respect to commitment or ethics. Perhaps he considered the gesture nothing more than an error in judgement. Moreover, if the incident had really been a misstep, it was likely to happen again the next day during Paul Martin's examination. "I have never demanded of my counsel that they submit their questions or interrogation tactics," said Gomery, "and I will not do it today. Apart from that, I know you've spent a great many hours with the prime minister to prepare his testimony. I therefore expect detailed questions that go straight to the facts and leave no room for complacency or falsehoods."

His remarks turned out to be well founded, and they pre-empted any reply.

These events took place during one of the most difficult weeks of the hearings, with many struggles and altercations. Only the referee kept his composure.

The natural inclination of a judge is to step back and observe, so that he can reflect on the big picture before rendering justice. Over the last twenty-three years, John Gomery has witnessed many dramatic scenes and seen many defeated human beings. For the most part, it sufficed just to listen to these people, who either incriminated or exonerated themselves. Gomery adopted the same attitude toward Jean Chrétien, moving beyond the cut and thrust and the shallow arguments to focus on the human element. This, not tactical considerations or weakness on Gomery's part, was the reason he allowed the former prime minister to speak. In the weeks that followed, no one really knew what impression Chrétien's words had made on the commissioner. The little black book containing his observations remained tightly shut. We had to wait for Gomery's fact-finding report in November to learn the rest.

NINE

ALONE AT THE HELM IN THE FOG

PAUL MARTIN HAD TO pass a test: he had to present himself before the Gomery Commission as a clean, honest, transparent statesman. Since the election on June 28, 2004, he had tried to control his minority government's agenda, a tough assignment given the attacks by Opposition parties on a variety of issues. Among the matters debated were the American missile defence program, same-sex marriage legislation and unspent budget surpluses, but also his sons' ships—the Canada Steamship Lines vessels based in faraway ports at which the taxman never called. The list of contentious issues went on and on. Now his government's survival had become even more uncertain because of John Gomery's work.

Martin's daily efforts to defend his record were regularly foiled during Question Period in the House of Commons, precisely as a result of the commission that he himself had created. Each day, the revelations of the previous day were picked up and bounced back on the floor of the House. Within his own caucus, MPs and ministers fearing for their political future begged Martin to put an end to the torture and revise the Gomery Commission's mandate. Martin carried on, though, convinced that he had set the best course. He must have believed it was the only way to avoid the trap that had been set on his electoral path: he had to declare his willingness to find the guilty parties in open forum, or his government would crumble.

A few months earlier, his rise to the top had been a close call, and since then his grip on power had been just as precarious. His testimony before John Gomery would give him a unique opportunity to convince Canadians of his innocence and his ignorance of the facts. The media hype, Gomery's sudden celebrity and the historic occasion of the appearance of a prime minister before a commission of inquiry—all of these factors guaranteed a large audience of very attentive listeners, without the interference and distortion added by the Opposition in the House. Martin intended to make airtight replies to the questions he was asked.

That Friday morning, instead of heading to his office in the Langevin Block, he left his residence, crossed Sussex Drive and headed for the old City Hall, just a few hundred metres away. He had asked for absolute secrecy and chosen a day when the commission was not in session for that very reason. His only escorts were two bodyguards from Security Services and two assistants. His guide was Brian Saunders, a lawyer from the Department of Justice. In order to accommodate his appearance, Sheila-Marie Cook had inquired about his requirements: a conference room for breaks, no public access, communication systems, and so on. She kindly let him tour Victoria Hall.

Paul Martin had not visited the hall just to take in the architectural refinements of this arched room bathed in light. He wanted to know where everyone would be seated—commission counsel, his own lawyers and those of the participants, the public and the media. He casually walked to the table and then to the witness's chair. After sitting down, he adjusted the height and angle methodically, as if he were thinking of buying it. Then, as he tried to find the best distance from the microphone, he memorized the locations of the fixed live cameras, as well as the risers for the mobile cameras that were used for news broadcasts. His gaze panned across the room just above the empty chairs, pausing subtly at certain angles, as if he were already on air.

The substance of Martin's remarks showed that he had done his homework. His support staff had been extensive at first, then was reduced gradually as the fateful day approached. It included lawyers, certain ministerial aides and assistants. It also included officials from all levels of government, and observers who had analyzed the preceding testimonies and would make certain that the prime minister would avoid mistakes and pitfalls. Together, these people reflected on the framework and guiding principles of the examination to come. Only a few of them focused on messages and ideas aimed more at convincing Canadians at large than the commissioner himself. It took weeks of preparation to explain first of all what Martin might have known about the Sponsorship Program when he was minister of finance in the Chrétien government—and especially what he didn't know. Having seen the extent of the damage to the Liberal Party's rank and file, committee members also took account of opinions and advice from grassroots party workers and regional organizers. While they were busy with this, others were guiding public opinion so that Canadians would interpret the facts in a way that was favourable to the testimony being put together for Martin. Jean Lapierre, minister of transport and the prime minister's political lieutenant for Québec, was heard inferring that illegal activities must have been the work of a marginal group whose existence was known to only a few. As a boon to taxpayers, he pledged that the government would recover the dirty money funnelled to the Liberal Party.

Still others on the sidelines of power were generating rumours and spreading them all over Ottawa, to the effect that Jean Chrétien had kept Paul Martin out of the picture. If Martin had known, they argued, he would have done something. He was never consulted. Disbursements under investigation amounted to $250 million over a ten-year period. How could Martin have detected this misappropriation of funds when he was managing billions, not to mention urgent monetary crises?

On the latter subject, Martin made a point of refreshing our memory—the peso crisis, followed by the yen crisis, and then the world economy. These serious concerns had kept him very busy, and he had been completely in the dark about the dollars being spent on sponsorships.

Opinion makers took considerable pains in aiming their message to the media. They behaved like lab technicians, relentlessly sharing their unique discovery: there might easily have been two groups of Liberals at the time, depending on which period we're talking about, each with its own DNA—the good Liberals and the bad ones, if you like.

To pass the test, all Martin had to do was suggest the themes—if not the questions themselves—that he wanted to raise during the examination. He had, after all, taken great care to prepare his statement. Martin set aside more than seven hours of his time to meet with commission counsel before appearing in front of Gomery.

Even before the hearings got under way in September, Neil Finkelstein knew he would be appointed as counsel for the commission to handle the prime minister's examination-in-chief. He wanted it that way and persuaded John Gomery to accept his proposal. First of all, the hearings had to open in Ottawa, the birthplace of the Sponsorship Program, where the initial decisions had been made. Phase 1A would be an opportunity to delve into the political responsibility of the participants in the sponsorship affair, as well as the accountability of the civil service.

The examination of Martin as a witness would be Finkelstein's greatest feat, the climax of a brilliant career in which his skill, intelligence and thoroughness had all been admired by his peers. For almost five months at the legal counsel's podium, he impressed all concerned with his sharpness and his talent. Within the commission, he was far and away the one who best understood the important role played by the media. He saw it as a tool to create added value—the value of the commission's work and its counsel's work. At nine each morning, he would ask me for my comments on the previous day's media coverage. Then he would show me his game plan for the current day, describing each witness, one by one, and what information he expected to extract from each of them.

Among the counsel, he was the one who was most keen to figure out what it was that reporters really wanted to know—or understand. In return, he expected their articles and other coverage to be fair and correct. "It's our responsibility, François," he told me. "If our task is to establish the evidence, theirs is to give a straightforward account of the results of our work and no more, without interpreting the facts in a way that would be detrimental to them as well as to us. We are governed by the same rules: integrity and credibility."

The reporters with the best attendance records were those who could read his facial expressions, signs of impatience and verbal tics—tics such as "Let's unpack this." Almost every time it was uttered, that particular expression was the signal that announced the next day's quote in the news.

Many people who were already won over by this method were eager to witness the Finkelstein–Martin face-off. But the face-off never happened.

What had become of Neil Finkelstein's skills in rooting out white lies and attacking half-truths? Why this sudden hiatus, just before a performance that would bring him the acclaim of so many admirers?

That day, a few hours before the hand-shaking incident with Chrétien and the subsequent meeting with Gomery, Finkelstein had shown me his blueprint for questioning the prime minister. Everything was organized and well structured, grouped by theme or event as Finkelstein had done before his other examinations—a considerable amount of work. This time, however, he said nothing about how he expected the witness to answer his questions. This time, I could not evaluate the appropriateness of his expectations.

One thing was certain, though. Nothing in this planning document pointed to an admission or revelation that Paul Martin might one day have to make. As for the dramatic crescendo, the rise in intensity expected during the testimony—none of this occurred.

Did we have the wrong witness? Without a real headline, all of the media would no doubt react in much the same way: Paul Martin invoked world economic events as an alibi, they would say; he was too busy elsewhere as finance minister to get mixed up in sponsorship matters.

However, an unforeseeable event confounded perceptions and expectations even further and helped defend Finkelstein's position in the matter. The day before his scheduled testimony, Paul Martin, speaking to members of his caucus, hailed Jean Chrétien's performance at the hearings and referred to him as a great Liberal who had defended his government's actions brilliantly. The caucus applauded this gesture, which brought about a truce between the two rivals. Yet this same Jean Chrétien had just told John Gomery that a National Unity Fund did in fact exist and that his finance minister had agreed to put $50 million into it each year. He declared confidently: "The Sponsorship Program was not created in a vacuum, and its significance cannot be understood out of context. Any serious review of the Sponsorship Program must take account of the circumstances that existed in Québec at the time it was created, and the corresponding political uncertainty during all the years it was operational."

Politics has its own code. Paul Martin wanted to reconcile those he had divided by his putsch against Jean Chrétien when he was prime minister. Martin needed to make this short harangue to unify the troops; he needed to honour someone he had elbowed out of office and who, despite the affront, had spared Martin the trouble of answering an embarrassing question about the existence of a National Unity Reserve Fund by discussing it proudly in his own testimony.

I refused to comment on the incident, except to say that the prime minister's support for the commission and its mandate had never faltered: "It's not our role at the commission to comment on Mr. Martin's appreciation of Mr. Chrétien's performance." Once again I had no explanation to offer concerning Martin's apparent approval of his adversary's unbridled arrogance, except to characterize it as opportunism. By sanctioning Chrétien's words in this way, wasn't Martin giving aid and comfort to John Gomery's opponents while reiterating his complete trust in the man each day? At the time, a few journalists speculated that the gesture might be part of an elaborate strategy.

In February 2005, Parliament was shivering. The Bloc wanted Québec all to itself and the Conservatives wanted the whole country. This commotion had little or no effect on Gomery. In his encounter with Prime Minister Martin, he maintained the same formal politeness and careful attentiveness that he offered all witnesses. In this instance, the judge was truer than ever to his real character.

A shared feeling of having witnessed a bungled finale spread among the media, who were wondering what impact the inquiry would make once it moved to Montreal. With regard to newsworthiness, the witnesses to be examined there were unknown outside public relations and advertising circles. What's more, the ongoing police investigations could prevent any important revelations from surfacing, because Crown attorneys were entitled to take a first look at the evidence in order to lay charges later.

In short, during the ten days that followed Phase 1 of hearings of the Commission of Inquiry into the Sponsorship Program, I took advantage of the commission's move to Montreal to touch base with the media and rekindle their interest in covering the hearings. Several reporters in Ottawa dropped out for financial reasons or shifts in priorities. Others were replaced by local colleagues. Most had planned to cover the Montreal hearings on a case-by-case basis. After all, there were such things as news agencies.

TEN

SCUFFLES BEHIND THE SCENES

As usual in February, Montreal's snowy streets and flooded inter-sections had been transformed into a slushy mess. Inside the car, the heat and slow beat of the windshield wipers had dulled the two men's senses; they had already spent forty minutes in heavy traffic travelling toward a neighbourhood in north end Montreal. Jean-Louis Gagnon and Jean-Pierre Witty were Gomery Commission investigators and had been among the first to be recruited by the Kroll agency.

The two men were very different from most of the young sleuths working on accounting fraud, spending weeks picking through bank statements, income-tax returns and invoices—in short, sorting through thousands of numbers on a computer screen. Gagnon and Witty were the real McCoy, always finding a lead, then following it.

They were two of a kind yet didn't belong to the same species. Witty came from the RCMP. There he had learned to keep a low profile as befitted his profession; he also learned to organize his work with a rigour that was almost military. After all these years, he was still every inch the cop, analyzing facts and interrogating suspects, always ready to tease out a confession. His partner Gagnon was different. He was a virtuoso intelligence officer who had worked in every aspect of the trade—undercover operations, liaison, data interpretation— including intelligence and counter-espionage duties. In the early 1980s he was involved in a commission of inquiry looking into activities of the RCMP Security Services, which later became the Canadian Security Intelligence Service (CSIS). Unlike Witty, Gagnon wasn't the type to interrogate a witness. He preferred to strike up a conversation and let it develop until it led inevitably to an admission of guilt. "Give me the time I need," he told Witty during their first meeting, "and they'll spill all the beans, even irrelevant stuff."

The security guard showed them where to park and which door to use to get to their meeting. The nondescript building squatted in an old quarry-turned-dump site. In the bleak winter landscape it looked like a polar weather station. No weather reports were posted on the bulletin board at the entrance, however—only the day's delivery vouchers and waste-handling slips. The two investigators had spent long hours assembling facts, statements and correspondence in order to wind up here. It was the final scene in a story like so many others at the heart of the sponsorship affair, a tale of wrongdoing.

Ill at ease in his large coveralls, the young man seemed nervous as he sat facing his two odd visitors. Witty slid an inventory slip onto the metal table. "Maybe this will jog your memory..."

Since their brief phone conversation the day before, the employee had been trying to remember the details of one ordinary day, four years back in time. It was tough, but the way his visitors kept at it, repeating their questions but wording them differently each time, refreshed his memory. Seeing his own initials on the bottom of the slip triggered something.

"At the time, I was assigned to reception, in charge of dispatching, for either processing or dumping. That's why my initials..."

"Why do you remember this delivery in particular?"

"Of course I remember this shipment...a container...I mean a quarter of a container, like it says...a special delivery. Just books."

"Did you take a look?"

"We always have to check shipments in case they try to sneak toxic substances by us. Some people try to get rid of them that way."

"So...?"

"I saw all these big red books, and I remember the title in gold letters: *The Canadian Encyclopedia*."

"Nothing else?"

"After I spoke to you yesterday, I remembered that a man turned up the next day. He had a BMW. He checked with the foreman to see if his shipment from the day before had been buried."

This line of questioning was getting them somewhere. Among the documents requisitioned from Jean Pelletier, Prime Minister Chrétien's ex-chief of staff, they found a simple letter from the publisher Alain Stanké, sent to Pelletier's avenue des Braves residence in Québec City. The missive went straight to the point, asking the federal government to support the production of a new luxury edition of the *Canadian Encyclopedia*. It was an ambitious but useful project, aimed mainly at primary schoolchildren. Witty and Gagnon had found another letter in the documents received by the commission, this one signed by Senator Serge Joyal in the course of which he hailed the merits of the important encyclopedia project to Deputy Prime Minister Herb Gray, in charge of Millennium Projects.

The investigators then got to the bottom of things. They sifted through correspondence from all of the familiar middlemen, who had left a trail of letters. Finally they hit the jackpot: a letter in which Ottawa recommended engaging the public relations firm, Lafleur Communication Marketing. Gagnon and Witty painstakingly worked their way back up the trail of bureaucratic paper pushers and insider contractors, whose knowledge of the subject was indeed encyclopedic. Some $2 million later, all that came of the project was a single volume, or rather directory—a book without illustrations that was clearly unattractive for grade fives. The publication turned out to be a hard sell, and a good chunk of it ended up at the dump.

Gagnon and Witty were convinced that with this case study in the bag, they could demonstrate the complete gamut of influence peddling, procedural abuse and misappropriation of funds that had so inflamed public opinion. According to the media, the Montreal phase of the hearings—about to get underway—would lead us down the money trail, and here was a good case in point.

In a commission such as this, however, investigators and lawyers rarely walk arm in arm. They often take very different paths while heading for a common goal. During the hearings in Ottawa, counsel Guy Cournoyer had already stated that as soon as the proceedings moved to Montreal, they would be conducted under his sole authority, implying that Finkelstein and his two young lawyers from Toronto would have nothing left to say or do.

When the encyclopedia report reached his hands, he intended to assume control of everything, thanks to the powers that Bernard Roy had delegated to him. Suddenly he presented himself as an expert in every field—administration, presentation of evidence, translation, media relations, even investigation procedures. "You've wasted too much time on this," he told Gagnon and Witty. "It will have no significance whatsoever for the evidence I want to establish. I've got everything I need from the accountants. I won't waste the commission's time on this during examinations."

Gagnon insisted. "This is exactly the kind of case that will ignite the public's indignation and reassure those who doubted that we'd find anything."

Cournoyer refused, as he had done many times before. "We're preparing a report, not a string of anecdotes. Besides, isn't it common practice to send out unsold books for pulping?"

In the end, after several people, including myself, continued to press the matter, he agreed to relegate the question to a sub-theme of an examination conducted by his colleague, Marie Cossette. Since the documents pertaining to this affair had been filed as evidence anyway, all I had to do was attract media attention and the encyclopedia incident made headlines across the nation.

Instead of subsiding, the conflict between Guy Cournoyer and other inquiry commission staff degenerated rapidly into a tug-of-war. One of the issues concerned the Bluenose Foundation generator, stored in Montreal and generously "donated" to the RCMP's C Division during the ice storm in 1998 by Gosselin Communication. In fact, the company had invoiced the government for expenses and fees amounting to some $12,000, without telling the RCMP. Once again, Cournoyer judged the theft too minor compared with other offences against the federal police force in the context of the Sponsorship Program. After sustained pressure, he finally included the incident in his examination of Gilles-André Gosselin. To his astonishment, the press picked up the story and ran with it.

Another illegal influence ring that was uncovered quickly concerned a system put in place to finance the Québec Liberal Party. Jean Brault, president of Groupaction, admitted later to the Gomery Commission that he had acted as a "stockbroker," transferring federal funds to the coffers of the party's provincial little brother. Even worse, Brault admitted covering up payments made to the Parti Québécois—an initiative that could hardly be interpreted as support for Canadian unity.

Well before Brault sat down for his first preparatory interview by Bernard Roy, Gagnon, Witty and their accounting colleagues had been following this particular lead. Roy discouraged them from pursuing it.

The investigators protested. "It shows the scope of misappropriations carried out by this same team of sponsorship suppliers," they pointed out.

"The donation to the PQ is not part of the Sponsorship Program," was Roy's answer. "Consequently it's not part of our mandate. We're going to steer away from this."

No matter. Like the investigators, the commission counsel had their preoccupations. When the hearings began in Montreal on February 28, 2005, Bernard Roy was worried and upset. His troubles had started with John Gomery's press interviews two months earlier and the subsequent motions calling for his resignation. This was followed by a campaign emanating from the Chrétien camp, relentlessly attacking Roy's past with the Conservatives, as chief of staff under Mulroney. Above all, though, he had to deal with the fact that both Jean Chrétien's testimony in defence of his sponsorship program, and Paul Martin's statement that he knew nothing about it, had failed to meet the media's expectations. Alec Castonguay from *Le Devoir* quoted Martin as saying: "It was hidden in the documents, under the line *other expenses*. No one showed it to me, and I never looked for it, either."

As for the discussions that Martin might have had with Chrétien on the use of the National Unity Reserve Fund, Martin said, "I simply said yes, and I put it in the budget. We had just had a referendum in Québec and introduced a stringent budget. I found it reasonable to leave $50 million at the discretion of the prime minister."

Bernard Roy, therefore, felt compelled to make a fresh start with Phase 1B of the commission's mandate—the money trail. Right from the outset, he was eager to call on the heads of public relations firms and Liberal Party workers to testify, though he worried that he might not find exactly what he was looking for. Roy is an intense, uncompromising man who prefers to place his bets where he thinks they can make a difference. To avoid wasting time and effort, he delegated day-to-day administration and preferred to work alone in his office, with the door closed.

One March morning, I entered his office and interrupted his reading—not difficult to do, as he read everything. His workspace extended well beyond his desk. In fact, he made full use of the sixteen square metres of office space he had. The credenza, visitor's chair, windowsill and entire floor were covered with paper, some of it piled up precariously and the rest simply scattered about. Walking through his door was like coming upon the scene of a recent tornado, but the documents were all arranged in a precise order that only he understood.

Roy's priority was Jean Brault. He had diligently and methodically prepared the interviews for this witness. He had put in long hours reading, verifying and cross-checking the documents against allegations heard in previous testimonies. He found it stimulating to pursue the case beyond what was already known because of the criminal charges laid against Jean Brault. In fact, that aspect of the investigation was out of bounds for Roy. He had to uncover new facts in order to prove that the commission was indispensable. The chief counsel was convinced that this witness was the key to success—both his own, and the commission's.

As usual, he came straight to the point, but on this occasion he had a hard time containing his self-satisfaction. I knew that he'd had his first meeting with Brault the day before and that it had lasted well into the evening. The deduction was simple enough. "Bernard, am I wrong or did the fox find the key to the chicken coop?"

"I saw Jean Brault last night. It's way beyond my expectations. He's ready to tell everything he knows—he wants to co-operate. He went even further than I expected. He surprised me. We're meeting again tomorrow."

"I won't ask for details at this point, but media-wise, what can I expect?"

"You'll have enough material to last a week!" And then, as always, with an undercurrent of concern in his voice: "However, we've seen witnesses deny their previous depositions from beginning to end, and once again we're powerless if that happens."

Bernard Roy prepared his interviews even more carefully than he did his examinations. In fact, the examinations often turned out to be abridged and streamlined versions of his long, thorough, elaborate pre-interviews. He would add, cross out and correct endless notes, which his assistant, Josée Lepage—the only living soul who could read this spider's web of scrawls and doodles—would type up for him. Despite this, he was meticulous and often worked until the last minute, then appeared on cue. We were lucky to learn what his legal strategy would entail before an examination, rather than at the moment Roy started speaking.

When he appeared before the commissioner to begin Jean Brault's examination, Roy knew that the lawyers for the witness would request an in-camera hearing, and he had already warned us about this, though he disagreed with the plan. He also knew that lawyers for Charles Guité and Paul Coffin would join forces to demand a ban on publication of their testimonies. They would argue that the trials, which were scheduled to begin in five weeks' time, wouldn't be fair: once the three attestations had been reported extensively, it would be very difficult to find neutral and objective jurors.

"I will listen carefully to each one of their arguments," Gomery had confided, "but I will find it difficult to agree to such a demand without knowing the contents of these testimonies up to the minute and to what extent they could be detrimental to the trials. We need to be cautious. It will be hard to maintain our transparency if we go with in-camera hearings. Remember, we need to establish clearly all of our substantial evidence here in Montreal."

That said, the commissioner knew, better than all of the judicial affairs columnists combined, that the court before which a trial is held has the last word in assessing what is or is not detrimental to a proper hearing of a case. He had to ensure that his decision was iron-clad enough to prevent lawyers from taking their arguments to Superior or Federal Court.

Some observers affirmed that John Gomery, over his career, had been more skilled as a practitioner of law and procedure than as a jurist. However, even if he rejected the request for an in-camera hearing, he still had to consider the rights of the accused. Since the hearings opened, he had insisted many times that neither commission counsel nor the lawyers representing the parties could under any circumstances raise questions or make statements related to the criminal proceedings under way. Nevertheless, the commissioner wanted to have an additional safeguard in place to block any motion that might silence the commission, so he ordered a complete ban on publication. This was a temporary measure, however, which could be lifted totally or partially depending on the revelation or the line of questioning. By taking such an unusual step in jurisprudence—for a commission of inquiry, at least—when no one knew what revelations were forthcoming from Jean Brault, Gomery had inadvertently put in place all of the essential ingredients of a blockbuster thriller. Everything coincided to make the situation uniquely newsworthy: an enigma, shadowy characters, gripping suspense and, above all, the pent-up fervour of journalists, who could hear everything but were forbidden to relate the contents of the testimony until the ban was lifted.

It was a turning point in the commission's work. Now nothing could cast any doubt on John Gomery's commitment to openness or, for that matter, the significance of the secrets that were to be revealed.

But a great number of those secrets came from documents that boggled the mind by their very abundance. In fourteen months, using subpoenas and requests, investigators sifted through some seven thousand boxes and catalogued 28.3 million pages. Almost 600,000 of these were entered into a document-management database and handed over to the legal team. These documents covered a ten-year period, from April 1, 1994, to March 31, 2004. In many instances, the commission's forensic accountants pulled the rug out from under the police, who were conducting their own investigations at the time. However, under the terms of reference of the commission's mandate, these documents could not be handed over. All the police could do was consult the papers as they were presented before Judge Gomery.

All of this information was densely packed and had to be analyzed, reconciled and presented in its proper context. For every payment or transfer of funds agreed upon, a corresponding invoice, progress report, proposal and purchase order had to be found. Even worse, the puzzle had to be put together with many of the pieces missing altogether. Among its discoveries, the Kroll firm concluded that government disbursements for sponsorships and advertising totalled $355 million and $1.1 billion respectively, compared to earlier estimates of $250 million and $800 million. With relentless determination, investigators mapped out the detours and shortcuts established by wrongdoers, their methods of distributing contracts and profits, and the routing of substantial amounts of money to hidden political accounts.

But the media, as well as the general public, wanted more, as with any other detective story. They had expectations on the scale of the Kroll firm's reputation. After all, this team of forensic accountants and consultants in corporate assessment and turnaround had been chosen to shed light on the Enron scandal in the United States, and had helped identify the hidden assets of Saddam Hussein. The press was counting on Kroll to open Swiss vaults, search offshore bank accounts and uncover third parties who had suddenly become multimillionaires.

That, however, was not Kroll's mandate. Rather, it had to establish clearly the business connections between public relations agencies, government and political activities. To put it plainly, the facts they reported to the commissioner represented the sum of all the evidence collected by the commission. How's that for a press line? I therefore devoted the weeks preceding the filing of the Kroll Report to deflating any expectations it might be creating.

On the big day, a new rift appeared among the counsel. On top of everything else, the Kroll Report—a complex document 450 pages long—had been added to the inquiry's duties. I planned to brief journalists on the important points during an in-camera session, but Guy Cournoyer argued against this initiative. No copies of the report were to be handed out by investigators or by his collaborators, and he also prohibited any prior press briefings before the report was unveiled.

If we'd listened to him, it would have been a serious blow to the commission's credibility and reputation for openness. I spent the night identifying newsworthy content and data, then made enough copies to distribute to the press. The report had been produced at the last minute, and only in English—circumstances that further complicated my job in a press room dominated by French-speaking reporters. Still, it was better to present them with the English report than to give them no information at all on the day the report was tabled.

Journalists who were disappointed by the report nevertheless hailed the commission's openness. As for the French translation, we had to wait more than a week, prompting one reporter from a radio station to say: "That's the way it is when it comes to the language of the tenants..." Harsh criticism for such an isolated incident.

The damage to the commission, caused by forces beyond our control, had been contained, but inside the commission, a lingering climate of distrust remained to be dealt with.

In spite of it all, the work of the Kroll specialists had been colossal. The bulk of the documents were compiled in a coil-bound volume almost two hundred pages long, and later they were appended to the commission's inquiry report filed on November 1, 2005. In hindsight, it goes without saying that apart from the talent and sharpness of the counsel, we needed to rely on reliable evidence and documents to conduct some 172 examinations. This was absolutely necessary to support the conclusions that Commissioner Gomery was to draw.

ELEVEN

THE SPIRIT OF THE LAW

THE LAWYERS ARRIVED with piles of documents teetering on small wheeled carts. The scene looked like a convention of obscure specialists that no one except themselves had even heard of, let alone recognized. These men and women possessed varying degrees of self-confidence and poise—qualities that were both a measure of their egos and incontrovertible proof that their clients had chosen the best. Whether they worked for major firms with countless names on their business cards or smaller, family-operated companies, whether they practised civil, common or criminal law, they all respected one another. After sounding out the commission counsel, I was convinced that an unusually high concentration of talent had paraded before me.

Watching them shake hands, smile at each other and catch up on news was like taking part in an old school reunion. The unspoken understanding between these professionals went beyond the legal proceedings during which they'd be testing each other's mettle. They already knew—all sixty-two of them registered with the commission— that many of them would be working exclusively on this important case for months. The convention had its own rules of courtesy and ways of acknowledging each lawyer's experience and success. Several were established champions; others, it was said, had declined offers to sit on the bench. Among the big guns were Pierre Fournier, Guy J. Pratte, Sylvain Lussier, Raphaël Schachter, Harvey Yarosky, Richard Auger, Richard G. Dearden, Peter K. Doody and Pierre LaTraverse (with apologies to the others). Some of them knew John Gomery; some had pleaded before him; others had only heard his name.

One day I made a remark to Gomery about the load of documents each lawyer dragged to the table reserved for counsel each day. He told me how, at the start of his career, he had unconsciously turned a weakness into an advantage: "Often lawyers, even those who are well prepared, go to court with all the documents related to the arguments they plan to present to the judge. It's only a precaution, in case they draw a blank. A fear of coming up empty, an insecure feeling that comes with the territory. When I started, I had many trials in French and found I had not sufficiently mastered the language. To be more at ease when pleading, I would prepare by writing out the main points, questions and sub-questions each time. I would arrive in court with a simple folder and nothing else. This would sometimes impress the judge, and it often threw the opposing counsel off guard. My French got better very quickly but I nevertheless kept this custom, if only for effect."

This anecdote illustrates the extent to which these lawyers would have to use all their cunning when pleading before this commissioner.

Meanwhile, the Conservative Party, Bloc Québécois and Liberal Party had all filed for full standing: access to documents assembled by the commission, prior information on testimony that witnesses had agreed to give, and especially the right to cross-examine or ask for other witnesses to be called. This question of full standing was a touchy one for Gomery, who intended to keep his commission well away from the

House of Commons. "This commission is not a parliamentary committee," he announced with characteristic candour. "The political forum will remain on the Hill; I will not allow Question Period to boil over into my hearing room. This inquiry must not be political; it concerns facts and individuals. As for the rest, once the exercise is over, politicians can do what they like."

The Conservatives and Bloquistes obtained limited participation rights; i.e., access to all documents but not the right to cross-examine. The Liberals, on the other hand, waited until after the proceedings began on September 13, 2004, to start making their demands. Charles Côté was the lawyer representing them: "Our intention is to participate actively in the proceedings of this commission during cross-examination... The Liberal Party of Canada was the party in power. It was the party that was allegedly at the heart of the sponsorship affair and its creation."

Gomery reacted immediately. "I thought the decision to create a Sponsorship Program was made by government," he said. "It was not the decision of a political party. Is there not a distinction here?"

"It is during cross-examination, Mr. Commissioner, that we will re-establish the facts, make it understood and demonstrate clearly that there is a real distinction between the political party and the government decisions that were made..."

Gomery was not surprised by the Liberal Party's request, only by its timing. He nevertheless took advantage of the opportunity to assert his authority once again. "I'm surprised to find you here at the beginning of September, when the debate over this question has been raging in the media for the last six months. I have two other political parties applying for participation rights, and the political party that was implicated most strongly in all this speculation was absent. I must say I was surprised not to see you earlier. Can you explain to me what this political party was thinking, if it was thinking, to keep them out of this process up to now?"

It was not the Liberals who engaged my attention at the start of the proceedings in Ottawa. For financial reasons, the Bloc Québécois and the Conservative Party had been allowed to send observers—people who were not lawyers but who would nevertheless have the same access to relevant documents. This decision opened up a channel of continuous news for the members of the Opposition, who used it to prepare questions for the House each day. I had to step in at one point, when some Opposition MPs decided to copy documents being used as evidence, tack on a partisan message and produce media material, which they would then distribute to journalists covering the hearings.

The commissioner gave me all the latitude I needed. He was prepared to review the status of political parties without appeal if they didn't put a stop to this practice. His only remark was: "It's true that these documents become public once they are filed, but tell me, are there no reporters following the proceedings of the House of Commons?"

Although from the start his authority was limited to the commission's business, John Gomery was able to impose his protocol, his rules and his efficiency on this room full of strong-minded individuals. Everyone noticed, perhaps to their disappointment, that he never once dozed off or lost track during the long months of hearings. Whether it was 9:45 AM or 4:15 PM, he intervened whenever he had to, with alacrity and sharpness. For example: "Counsel, correct me if I'm wrong, but I don't at all see the relevance of the path you are taking. It seems to me your questions have been off topic for almost ten minutes now, at least with this witness. I would like you to indicate your intentions clearly." Or, later in the day: "Allow me to say a word, sir. This witness has answered the same question reworded in different ways several times now. I believe he was clear in his first answer. Let's move on. I think we've wasted enough time as it is."

With each intervention, John Gomery added a new dimension to his public persona. People admired him immediately, although he was not aware of it. The spontaneity and openness he showed throughout the proceedings transformed that admiration into a profound trust. The lawyers themselves were among the first to adapt to this phenomenon. After reading the morning papers, they would search for the right tone to adopt with a commissioner of this calibre.

No matter how bright they were, these legal experts all had to report to their clients: they were the ones calling the shots. In accordance with the strategic alliances the clients forged amongst themselves, their lawyers joined forces on the battlefield. One could imagine the manoeuvring going on in the lawyers' room, where motions, objections and complaints of all sorts were prepared, by keeping track of the various strategies employed at the hearings. The bunker we had set up was an unusual venue, where anyone could consult with colleagues away from the commission's gaze. Topics included the day's strategy, or a motion they were preparing in response to a client's instructions. These warm-up sessions gave rise to informal alliances and supplementary arguments that added an air of formality to motions presented to the commissioner. Sudden changes in tone, mood and intensity could occur when it came time to make a point or to cross-examine. With respectfully worded statements, lawyers might take offence on command, flare up without real anger and deploy heated arguments while keeping their cool.

An example of this tactic that I found particularly stunning came from lawyers representing the Attorney General of Canada. Six of them stood in the line of fire, supported by an imposing phalanx from the government's legal claims department. Sylvain Lussier headed the team, watching over the rights of dozens of witnesses and the interests of a sole client. He amply demonstrated his formidable skills, keeping control while mediating between contradictory legal claims and subtly conflicting points of view. Thus, after a bitter dispute with the commission counsel on admissibility of evidence and the censoring of documents released by Cabinet and the Privy Council, he suddenly changed his tone to defend some other issue. Before top civil servants, deputy ministers and associates, he took pains to demonstrate the thoroughness and political neutrality of the public administration. As for the Privy Council Office, he defended its integrity. During the testimonies of Jean Chrétien and Paul Martin, he had said little. In the final analysis, depending on his performance in defending certain witnesses, one could guess which of them the political machine had chosen to abandon—or, worse yet, sacrifice.

Nothing was ever clear or definitive, however. For example, Lussier's approach and the tone of his questions during the Montreal hearings seemed to lend more credibility to allegations made by Charles Guité concerning public relations firms returning favours than had been the case in Ottawa, when Guité described the seats of power to which these same firms were paying visits. Indeed, these companies and their bosses became choice targets for Sylvain Lussier. He excoriated their greed relentlessly, in particular the commissions negotiated on each contract. Exasperated and disgusted, he shouted at Jean Lafleur: "Don't you ever answer questions people ask you? Answer me!" Even more astounding was Lussier's exchange with Michel Béliveau, a loyal Chrétien friend and ex-president of the Liberal Party of Canada, when he tried to discover whether Jacques Corriveau had given him $75,000 or $100,000, and whether the money had been placed in an envelope or a briefcase.

"Are you in a position to tell us if this money came in $20 or $100 denominations?...Was he carrying a briefcase?"

"...It was more likely an envelope, only thicker."

"You probably haven't seen $100,000 in cash very often, have you? And what about the 1993 rules concerning the laundering of the proceeds of crime and the financing of terrorist activities? Didn't you know that a financial institution receiving $10,000 in cash was required to register the transaction?"

Then, brandishing an envelope and an attaché case, both stuffed with enough paper to approximate $10,000 in bills, he lambasted the practice, which he attributed to the old Liberal regime. The exchange was caught on camera by all of the television reporters.

It made for a good show. But hard work had gone into preparing that appearance before the commission and all of the others. Each one of these lawyers had to prep one or several witnesses to answer questions related to their testimony, both in private with the commission counsel, and in public before John Gomery. In some cases, several meetings were needed. It could be an arduous task just to remember the sequence of events when the background to a conversation, letter or sponsorship was required. Some events had occurred six or eight years earlier. The documents requisitioned by the commission—thousands of pages in total—had to be sorted, assembled and filed as evidence before testimony was heard.

All of these bound pages were raw material for witness examinations, and for the lawyers who had obtained participant status for their clients and therefore had the right to cross-examine, received advance copies. Some fifty copies of every document had to be made and distributed—Roger Thomas would probably have agreed that printing a newspaper was a less stressful job. During ten months' worth of hearings, he photocopied nine million sheets of paper, more than five hundred memoranda and eighteen hundred boxes of paper! Thomas was semi-retired and had taken the job as his first freelance contract. He had worked for thirty-seven years, serving eight prime ministers from Lester B. Pearson to Paul Martin, and he had photocopied documents for federal-provincial conferences, federal budgets, economic summits and many more events. Yet he'd never had to manage such frenzied activity. Compared to his earlier achievements, the Gomery Commission was definitely in a class by itself.

The photocopy room was always warmer than anywhere else in Montreal. What with the number of witnesses involved and the many decisions on legal strategy that were made at the last minute, duplicating and assembling documents was a tricky business. The number of additions, deletions and changes made to the original list of scheduled witnesses, not to mention the discovery of new evidence, made it virtually impossible for Thomas to plan his work. Preparatory interviews often took longer than expected or were held the day before testimony, and document production went on through the night. Even so, lawyers complained that they couldn't get early enough access to the documents being filed. Several journalists had the same reaction, especially when it came to upcoming witnesses' order of appearance. In fact, this list was modified so frequently that a decision was made to reveal only three or four names at a time.

Even the commissioner himself, who was at the apex of the information pyramid, was often informed of the names of witnesses only twenty-four hours before he was to hear their testimony. This mattered little to him, as he preferred to have no inkling ahead of time about what he was going to hear. In the same way, he ignored the strategic deals being made in the lawyers' room. Even when he disagreed, he liked to be surprised.

TWELVE

WHAT DID THEY REALLY MEAN?

BY NOT SAYING what they meant or admitting what they knew, many witnesses inadvertently revealed a great deal about the sponsorship affair. Unforeseen memory lapses, expressions of impatience, displays of pent-up anger, even a convenient case of Alzheimer's by association showed us clearly what we were up against. Pointed questions often brought embarrassed responses. Outside the commission, cabinet ministers, columnists and others had their say as well. Some Canadians found their intelligence tested to the limit; to others the situation brought surprise, confusion, cynicism, anger, or even a good belly laugh.

During the ten months the hearings lasted, did we really understand what the politicians, public relations experts and party workers were saying? What sticks in the mind after all this time? Here are a few of the more memorable lines.

POLITICIANS

"Memory is a declining faculty."

—Alfonso Gagliano, former minister of public works

"I gave my consent, but I didn't approve."   —Alfonso Gagliano

"I'm looking forward to reading your report."
                              —Paul Martin, prime minister of Canada,
                                        former minister of finance

"The sponsorships were much more than just posters, flags and trade-marks."   —Jean Chrétien, former prime minister of Canada

"We were led to believe, as if it was gospel, that the ad agencies were close to the Liberal Party."   —Jean Chrétien

"How can a civil servant from Saskatchewan know what to sponsor in Québec?"   —Jean Chrétien

"Ten years ago, the ex-director of the sponsorship program, Charles Guité, would probably have been honoured as a model employee of government; he was unanimously praised for his work."
                    —David Dingwall, former minister of public works

"The problem in Québec is that every evening you have a soap opera on television called Gomery."
                    —Jean Lapierre, Prime Minister Paul Martin's
                              political lieutenant for Québec

"There are so many things crossed out on some of the documents that they look like a game of Mystery Word."
                    —Gilles Duceppe, Bloc Québécois Leader

"I feel like I'm in an old western where people are charged, convicted, and hanged without judge or jury."   —Alfonso Gagliano

"The big losers in this affair are the politicians in general. It's like taking a plane. There are hundreds of airplanes taking off every day; it's only when one of them crashes that everyone is afraid to fly."
—Claude Béchard, Québec minister of employment,
social solidarity and family welfare

"Stick with Corriveau; he will open doors for you."
—attributed by Jean Brault to Jacques Olivier, former mayor
of Longueuil, during Brault's testimony

"I still think Diane's age conveys such grace and beauty that youth still inhabits her. You should learn from her example."
—Paul Martin, writing to Claude Boulay on the occasion
of his wife Diane Deslauriers' birthday

"If you ever meet someone in bed between Jean Chrétien and his wife, it'll be Jacques Corriveau."
—attributed to David Dingwall by Charles ("Chuck") Guité,
former director of the Sponsorship Program

PUBLIC RELATIONS EXPERTS

"In the case of sponsorships, the state and politics were one and the same thing in many cases."
—Jean Brault, president of Groupaction

"We began to realize the secret recipe for getting lucky: we had to pay attention to whatever demands the party would make on us."
—Jean Brault

"Guité, he was like the central bank."
—Robert-Guy Scully, television host and producer

"Mr. [Jean] Pelletier is a charming man. We are the same age, we shared the same passions—a good meal, a glass of wine—but there was no agenda."

—Jean Lafleur, president of Lafleur Communication Marketing

"It seems easy today, but just visiting the Olympic Stadium and touring the place was a lot of work."   —Jean Lafleur

"What are you talking about! Honestly!"

—Jean Lafleur, infuriated by insinuations about his integrity. He later summed up the morning's testimony as follows: "I don't remember...I have no recollection of that... I can't remember...I don't know...I can't answer that... It probably happened...I presume...I would like to be of help, but...I'm not able to help you."

"I never would have expected such a bonanza."

—Gilles-André Gosselin, president of Gosselin Communications

"I run a company, not a charitable organization. I never said it would be free."   —Gilles-André Gosselin

"I'm tired, exhausted. I'm having trouble concentrating. I'm wondering what all this means."   —Gilles-André Gosselin

"If the people working with me had known that the goal was to promote Canada in Québec, I think I would have lost two-thirds of my staff."   —Gilles-André Gosselin

"Before I took on your client, I had never made out false invoices."

—Jean Brault, in a response to the Liberal Party lawyer

"Mr. Guité had a lot of influence. I used to bring projects to Minister Gagliano's office, and he'd glance at them but didn't say anything. He would operate through his chief of staff."

—Alain Renaud, former employee of Groupaction

"Jacques Corriveau was playing defence from day one of the Sponsorship Program."

—Jean Brault

"I'm not a vacuum-cleaner salesperson."

—Diane Deslauriers, Claude Boulay's wife, known for her skill at selling tickets for Liberal Party benefits

"You can catch a fish in an aquarium much quicker than that."

—Diane Deslauriers, describing Robert-Guy Scully's generosity

"I was stupid, perfectly stupid from day one of the Sponsorship Program."—Paul Coffin, former president of Coffin Communications

"I realize that I should have exercised better control." —Charles Guité

"I should never have told him I was responsible for that. Every three months after that, he'd come in and ask for candy."

—Charles Guité, commenting on Jacques Corriveau's behaviour

"When a campaign is over and a politician is elected, he wants to return the favour."

—Charles Guité

PARTY WORKERS

"At my age, it's easier to recall remote events than recent ones."

—Jacques Corriveau, former president of Pluri Design

"I never met Mr. Martin one on one. We never meet; I never make an appointment to see him. We meet at various functions."

—Claude Boulay, former president of Groupe Everest

"I presumed the money had been donated voluntarily. It's a judgment error on my part. This may be hard for me to admit, but that's the truth and I decided to say it."

—Michel Béliveau, former president of the Québec wing of the Liberal Party of Canada

"Still, red is a lovely colour."

—Michel Béliveau

"I felt I could trust him because, as everyone knew, Jacques Corriveau presented himself as one of Jean Chrétien's most loyal supporters."

—Daniel Dezainde, former director general of the Québec wing of the Liberal Party of Canada

"These incompetent, racist people were unable to organize anything better than broom-ball nights."

—Beryl Wajsman, former employee of the Québec wing of the Liberal Party of Canada, talking about Liberal Party staff

"Mr. Gagliano did not have the intellectual capacities or the charisma of Jean Marchand, but when he said something, he had clout."

—Beryl Wajsman

"He's not someone [Jean Brault] I can introduce to serious business-men, with his Elvis Presley haircut and tiny moustache."

—Beryl Wajsman

"I was born in 1939 in the northeast part of Italy. There are no godfathers who come from that region. I'm Venetian and proud of it."
—Joe Morselli, Liberal Party organizer and friend of Alfonso Gagliano, responding to disparaging remarks about his origins, including references to the Mafia

"I was accompanied by the person accompanying me."
—Tony Mignacca, Liberal Party organizer, speaking about a lunch he had with his friend Joe Morselli at Frank's Restaurant

A VICTIM AND A WITNESS

"When they offered us the generator, it was a godsend, it was marvellous."
—Odilon Émond, RCMP commanding officer during the ice storm of 1998

TO END OUR catalogue of quotations, recall the very apt remarks of columnist Lise Payette describing the national television broadcast of commission hearings. In her column on January 26, 2005, she wrote: "Even if they tried their hardest, television producers would never be able to put on a reality show like the one Judge Gomery is heading!"

THIRTEEN

CYBERBATTLE IN THE BLOGOSPHERE

BLOGGING IS THE equivalent of communicating by word of mouth, only it's all conducted on the Internet. Blogs are therefore an efficient way of spreading information—and misinformation. The blogger community spans the world, introducing topics for discussion and inviting comments, knowing perfectly well that the material passed back and forth may not be accurate.

Such a powerful communications tool would surely appeal to Chrétien partisans. As a Liberal activist, Warren Kinsella was obsessed with waging war against the Gomery Commission and all those who represented it. Little known beyond Parliament Hill, he had been an executive assistant to Public Works Minister David Dingwall before moving to Prime Minister Chrétien's office. Incredibly, this party militant played a modest supporting role in the sponsorship affair according to the first Gomery Report. He did, however, appear as a witness in Ottawa.

Both Dingwall and Kinsella denied they'd ever met Jean Lafleur, president of one of the agencies chosen by the Sponsorship Program. And yet, Charles Guité insisted that Lafleur had indeed been present when Dingwall and Kinsella introduced him to a "very close friend of the Prime Minister," with whom he would have to do business. The close friend was Jacques Corriveau, and John Gomery favoured Guité's testimony over theirs.

From the start of the commission proceedings, Kinsella turned his website—warrenkinsella.ca—into a forum for nasty gossip. He peppered the media and other public-opinion makers with e-mails that attempted to put John Gomery himself on trial. Most of these rapid-fire attacks on the commissioner focused on his appointment. They characterized Gomery as a "default choice" and denounced "his lack of credibility and integrity," his "favouritism in awarding contracts to suppliers of the commission," "favouritism toward his daughter Sally"—in short, an "ill-advised commissioner, a judge on a mission." Kinsella regarded the choice of Bernard Roy as chief counsel as a key element of the so-called mission—"an act that amounted to giving a thief the keys to the vault." He even went so far as to write to me, demanding that I supply him with copies of counsel employment contracts and disclose my salary. Each time he made a demand, he threatened to file an official access-to-information request, and each time I urged him to go right ahead and do so.

The concentrated attacks were not the work of one isolated sniper. The barrage was reinforced by other partisans, ex-hacks from the old Liberal regime. After the Martin team's putsch, these people managed to find jobs in the private sector, the civil service and even in the Senate. Now, united in a single cause, they looked to their in-house webmaster for headline ammunition to use in their press releases. Plundering Kinsella's site, they put together a chorus of catchy lines; then downloaded their song sheet.

Moreover, many political commentators were amused by the way Kinsella described the conduct of the commission—praising, of course, those witnesses he personally supported! In his zeal he went so far as to type up an account of the testimony of his former minister, David Dingwall, on his palm computer, live from the hearing room. Finally, as if live coverage weren't enough, his propaganda arsenal included exclusive previews, such as the script of Jean Chrétien's declaration at the beginning of his testimony. Half an hour before the former prime minister read his statement before the Commission, an account was already available on Kinsella's site. Most of the time, this eagerness for combat warned me that another assault was on the way.

Many other sites and blogs covered the commission, of course. Very few were openly opposed to the inquiry; instead, they represented a particular point of view or a professional interest. For example, the Association of Advertising Agencies, law and public relations students, political organizations and citizens' groups, all had their own sites. Some major media outlets offered their websites to interested readers, listeners and viewers. It was a good medium for conducting informal opinion surveys that gave an excellent feel for the scandal's effects on the general public.

In the blogosphere, that great melting pot of diverse opinions, the commission had set up its own flagship: gomery.ca. It was an ambitious undertaking, needing to address the specific requirements of different people who were themselves evolving and adapting with each new development. Over time, our initial reasons for choosing this Internet address became a source of ironic comment. Not only was it easier to remember than commissionofinquiryintothesponsorshipprogram-andadvertisingactivities.ca, but also we saw it as an opportunity to raise an unknown commissioner's public profile. Later, after the commission had received a blizzard of e-mails during the recusal crisis, John Gomery wisecracked: "To think that only recently I had to spell my name every time I made a reservation in a restaurant...Today the maitre d' already knows me—one M, with a Y at the end. I feel so popular!" It helped ease a tense situation.

Gomery.ca was our web diary, where we could find the upcoming testimony schedule, official decisions made by the commissioner and transcripts of day-to-day examinations. It became an instant and indispensable tool for lawyers, reporters and researchers. And it was also a barometer of the public mood, a way to find out how Canadians were reacting to new revelations or motions. Simply by counting the number of hits on the site, we could gauge the precise atmosphere of the proceedings or chart an emotional response curve. Our hits averaged twenty thousand per month.

Particular events sometimes boosted these figures, bringing a bonus flurry of e-mails. Each time we received a barrage of messages criticizing the reasons behind a motion or the attitude of a witness, or commenting on a shocking admission of guilt, media coverage reflected that reaction. The reverse was also true, when the public reacted to press reports. For example, following the first motion for recusal presented by lawyers for the former prime minister—a move that prompted a surge of e-mails—Les Whittington of the *Toronto Star* asked me to confirm the uptick.

"Of course, we got thousands more."

"And where did they come from—what were they all saying?"

"If I had to say what the gist was, I'd say . . . 'What is Jean Chrétien trying to do?'"

That remark won me a headline, an angry response from Jean Chrétien's lawyers, and a new wave of support.

With each passing day, no matter how intensely we experience the news, it eventually dies away, much like the rest of us. In this regard the Internet is ruthless. The sheer volume of available information accelerates the process of forgetting as it speeds up the rate of input. Thus, on November 1, the day the first Gomery Report came out, gomery.ca attracted more than 70,000 visitors. The number of simultaneous downloads of passages from the commissioner's findings—into digital memory!—reached 15,000 at one point. The next day it was 20,000; on November 3, the figure dropped to 6,600. Yet the infrastructure was here to stay. The commission had not skimped on facilities: three servers, three networks and three multiple-access software packages were used to ensure transparent, seamless access, regardless of the number of visitors and geographical locations. I don't think this was a sign of faltering public interest. Rather, each news item has to dissolve, making room for the next, a few hours or a few days later at most. It is a continuous chain of events. The momentum cannot be interrupted; if that happens, it only flares up again with a vengeance.

An incident involving the web forced us to confront this phenomenon. By issuing a publication ban on Jean Brault's testimony, the commissioner had, of course, not considered advanced technological means. No one in the room—journalists, lawyers, members of the public—was allowed to divulge the contents of this testimony. Edward Morrissey (known to bloggers as Captain Ed), however, an American with an accomplice in the room, bypassed Gomery's decision by publishing Brault's most important revelations on his website, captainsquartersblog.com.

Contempt of court! Contempt of commission! was the outcry. Legally, in fact, the commission could do nothing, dashing the hopes of those who wanted John Gomery to lash out at the parties responsible. I had to make a comment to the press: "Our courts have no jurisdiction over American law. It would probably be a case of contempt, though, if one of you reproduced these pirated excerpts."

Undeterred and intensely competitive, the national dailies gave their readers the website address. In this way they refrained from actually giving away commission secrets, while telling their readers where to find them. Over a period of four days, a million and a half people visited Captain Ed's "treasure island." Legal opinions piled up on Commissioner Gomery's desk as to whether or not he could impose sanctions on media accomplices. Nowhere in his official ban had he mentioned the Internet as a method of publication. What's more, the Canadian media had been scrupulous in obeying the order and, up to that point, had merely described the atmosphere in the room or the behaviour of those involved in the proceedings. They were also mightily impressed to see members of the public squeezed into the amphitheatre next door, or glued to the big screen, like a night out at the movies!

FOURTEEN

FINDING THE RIGHT WORDS

For two whole days, Chapter 11 of the Gomery Report was at a standstill. Alone in the room, facing two computer screens, Jean-Michel Gazet struggled for words. "Okay, right! *Culture of Entitlement...* what's that in French?... *culture de l'appropriation?* No, not really... *une société de l'acquis?* No, even worse." It was only after soliciting several spontaneous adaptations and comparing them that he finally decided on *la culture du tout m'est dû* ("the culture of 'everything is mine by right'"). Why not coin new words? After all, that's just about the last challenge left in translating this document!

With almost thirty years' experience as a translator, Gazet had never worked on a commission report with so rich a description of facts and subtle ways of assigning roles and attributing blame, yet all in such a direct, unequivocal style. This was nothing like a normal government document, he thought; it read more like a story. Take the reference, for example, to Jean Lafleur, president of Lafleur Communication Marketing: "It was obvious that the commission was hearing a witness who was quite prepared to appear slow-witted rather than give truthful answers." It would be hard to improve on that.

To help translate the text, Gazet had a secret weapon—his "little dragon," a software package called Dragon Naturally Speaking. As he studied the original English text on one screen, he translated it into French out loud, and the software simultaneously "wrote" his French adaptation on the second screen. He had taken great pains to tame the mythical beast, to help the program calibrate the tone, rhythm and speed of his voice. When the time came to start his work, everything was ready. In an intense, highly concentrated effort, he recited the commissioner's report out loud in its entirety, constantly reworking new expressions, complex concepts or unusual passages. Without altering the meaning of the text, his colleague Jean-Pierre Dany ran through the punctuation, consistency of numbers and gender, verb tenses—everything that might have escaped the "dragon's" attention. The translator's eloquence and differences between the two languages added sixteen pages to the French version. That version was a remarkable achievement for someone who "lent his voice" to so many celebrated people, for a few seconds at a time, on news and public affairs programs. Whether he was translating the words of a Chinese head of state, a German scientist or an American banker, his work was the same: the sound clip lasted a few seconds at best. This time, the author was prolific and also spoke French. Moreover, he was uncompromising when it came to variations in the emphasis or meaning of the words he used, leaving no room for misinterpretation. This strict approach was a matter of commitment and integrity for him, the kind of meticulousness that resisted interference with his written text. Gazet found it rough going at first: as far as John Gomery was concerned, this point was non-negotiable, and his attitude was based on many considerations.

Those who publicly attacked Gomery's integrity and impartiality only reinforced the commissioner's determination to draft the inquiry's findings by himself, to let no one else hold his pen or whisper in his ear—and with good reason. For one thing, a group effort would have been much more vulnerable to attack. One example was the many disparaging remarks aimed at Bernard Roy and his anti-Liberal political past. Another was the double-edged motion introduced during the final stage of hearings, on the afternoon of June 2, 2005, in the midst of a power struggle. The attack was led by one of Jean Chrétien's lawyers, supported by the lawyers representing Pelletier and Gagliano. The trio, made up of Peter Doody, Guy Pratte and Pierre Fournier, were making a last-ditch attempt to stir up doubts over the legitimacy of the proceedings. They referred to the sheer quantity of documents collected by the commission, of which only a fraction had been placed in evidence before the judge. Unlike commission counsel, they were not privy to the rest. They concluded that these other documents could have an impact when counsel contributed to the writing of the report. More precisely, they wanted assurances from the commissioner that he would not be influenced by his counsel when the time came to compile the commission's findings and write his report. For John Gomery, who was visibly irritated and eager to end the hearings, this was too much.

"I'm going to tell you what I've already told the commission counsel. Once all the evidence is heard, and I hope that will be today, I will tell them to leave. I'm closing the door and I don't want to hear them or talk to them for two weeks. I need to take a step back to clarify my ideas and prepare a framework for my decision... Once my work plan is established two weeks later, I will call on my counsel to look up facts and evidence heard. But the conclusions coming out of this will be mine only. I'm not aware of how this is done in other commissions of inquiry, but for twenty years now, I have been writing each and every one of my decisions and I plan on writing this one as well."

Once again a short break in the proceedings brought an opportunity to vent a few frustrations. For Gomery, the motion was not only long and convoluted, it was an insult to the entire magisterial profession, questioning its members' capacity to judge in an enlightened, independent fashion.

"What gall! And to think that some of these people that I've been listening to for months aspire to become judges one day!"

The motion was thrown out immediately. Meanwhile, commission counsel had just suffered a defeat of their own. For months they had preceded the commissioner like Roman lictors in pursuit of the truth. They had appeared on television six hours a day, standing before the podium, harassing witnesses. It was accurate to say they had given form to the commission, but the commissioner was the one who embodied it. Despite this, they had been keen to leave their mark on this document, the end product of a team effort. But the decision on June 2 left no room for doubt. There would be just one author of the Gomery Report.

The decision created a stir within the legal team. As soon as the Ottawa hearings ended, Neil Finkelstein and his close associates started writing a summary of evidence heard during the first phase in Ottawa. They were convinced that their work would find its way into the report almost verbatim. It was not meant as material for the commissioner; it was supposed to lay the foundations for a good many conclusions. It took them four months to write this valuable document, recording in sequential order all the evidence presented, as well as references by association and by contradiction analyzed during the Ottawa hearings. However, the commissioner used the document only to jog his memory and deliberately avoided his counsel's observations. For Bernard Roy the process was the same. He started writing a report that summed up the evidence heard in Montreal, and not a single passage made its way into the final report.

John Gomery's decision to work alone, however, entailed serious disadvantages. He alone would assume the responsibility for his judgment and he would have to abide by the production schedule unconditionally. As he'd promised, he picked up his pen toward the end of June.

His pen? Absolutely. Gomery wrote every page of his report by hand, single-spaced on a legal pad, all through the summer. Sometimes he wrote at the farm, sometimes in his Montreal office. He reviewed the notes contained in his five—not one, but five—black notebooks, in which we'd often seen him jot things down. Then he set out to reconcile the daily summaries of testimonies prepared by Laura Snowball. She was in large part responsible for the accuracy and relevance of the references and facts in the entire document, including the footnotes. She served as a contact person for counsel. The true value of her contribution was not always recognized.

Two other individuals, whose real names, Sadinsky and Gussman, conjured up memories of Starsky and Hutch, also had to prove their worth to Gomery. His report was so elaborately detailed that a summary had to be produced, containing a condensed version of the main findings derived from the evidence. Sadinsky and Gussman were in charge of the summary, which was crucial—it would be the first thing people read before tackling the full report. It was also the official condensed version of the report, which journalists would rely on. To say that Gomery wanted the document revised would have been an understatement. Gomery rejected the first draft outright, because in his view it failed to convey either the gist or the breadth of the report. At their second meeting, the three men put their heads together, agreed on a new approach and rapidly outlined a revision. The two writers completed their work smoothly as new chapters were received.

The deadline was set for September 15 but was constantly being extended—in fact, the ink was still drying on the document when it went to the printer.

Let's go back to Jean-Michel Gazet, though, and his reading of the text.

In addition to being efficient, Gazet's working method turned out to be ideal for such highly confidential material. There were no drafts and no printed copies, so the chance of a leak was reduced to a minimum. The many revised and improved versions were either deleted or encrypted on closely guarded CD-ROMs. On September 23 the countdown began, with only thirty-eight days to go before the report was to be submitted. That morning the choice of printers was announced: National Printers in Nepean, a suburb of Ottawa. Right up to the last minute, officials from the Department of Public Works tried to interfere with this decision. In fact, they would have preferred, as stipulated in their official procedures, to act as project coordinators.

Sheila-Marie Cook jokingly wondered what level of intelligence they attributed to members of the commission. "Maybe we could ask them to correct the proofs for us—after assuring us, of course, that none of it would be communicated to anyone else in government."

Public Works made another attempt when the time came to select translators. After all, they reasoned, why use freelancers when the best resources were right there, in their own department? There was no doubt that security measures were needed. So an agreement in principle was reached between the commission and the Privy Council, the former fearing "a leak" and the latter fearing that "its contents would be prematurely revealed." Special measures were established for round-the-clock security.

•

AS LONG AS THE weather holds out, Wanda Ariano must have thought. A light jacket was all she needed in this exceptionally warm October. She biked across Ottawa many times that month, speeding along like a messenger on a mission. She rode on a flat surface but her cardio rate was brisk, thanks to the invaluable contents of the package she was carrying to the printing shop in Nepean. With each delivery, another segment burned on the CD-ROM of the Gomery Report was printed. The first chapters held little interest for inquiring minds, containing only the decree creating the commission, biographical notes and a calendar of events surrounding the scandal. Then, a few days later, interest picked up, with findings taken from key testimonies. The race was on, and it would all have to be completed by November 1.

Ariano had been on the Gomery team from the very beginning. Like the rest of us, she was hired by Sheila-Marie Cook. She proved to be a true commando when it came to difficult missions. She had just returned from Botswana, where she had raised money for the University of Gaborone. For the commission, she was in charge of the organizational layout of the hearing rooms, logistics for document production and distribution, creation and updating of the website and, finally, the production of the two reports. She was one of a large pool of people living in Ottawa without steady jobs, who go from one contract to the next as they build up their experience. In this respect, government projects can be golden opportunities, and of all of these, the Gomery Commission was certainly high on the list.

The print shop was a hive of activity. The workers in the 9,000 square-metre building had been going full steam ahead for weeks. The project at hand was huge, but above all, secret. Surplus employees had been shut out, and those who remained had security clearance. Before starting, Anil Mehta, the founder of the company, met with his foremen. "With this contract, our reputation will grow immeasurably. But one leak, a single detail sent to the outside world, and we could lose it all. We've never worked on a project with such high visibility before."

Everything was done in-house to safeguard secrecy—design, layout, graphics—on computers that were disconnected from their networks to prevent hacking. It took six weeks to get the reports ready to print. Then, for ten straight days, the highly coveted pages raced through the press at high speed on oversized sheets of paper. Final corrections for the French version were submitted only three days before the first copy was delivered. The report consists of three volumes: the summary, the fact-finding report and the forensic audit. In all, eighteen thousand copies were assembled at breakneck speed.

On November 1, 2005, at 10:00 AM, the Speaker of the House announced the tabling of the Gomery Report. At the print shop, operations ground to a halt as almost sixty employees gathered around the television set to watch an event that rivalled the Stanley Cup playoffs for excitement. Within the hour, Anil Mehta proudly sent a letter to the commission expressing his thanks for having been associated with the enterprise.

FIFTEEN

IT'S IN THE BAG

AS THE HOURS went by and the big moment approached, Sheila-Marie Cook and I felt increasingly nervous. The waiting taxi would take us a mere four blocks away. Everything was ready. Two RCMP officers were expecting us at the corner of the Sparks Street pedestrian mall and Metcalfe Street, and they would accompany us on foot to the entrance of the Blackburn Building, the Privy Council's main office. It was barely a 200-metre walk, punctuated and brightened by the strobe effects of floodlights and camera flashes. In all, three television networks and a wire service had set up camp—not enough to give the impression that we were putting on a performance.

While waiting for Cook at the reception desk of her apartment hotel, I couldn't help reminiscing about the past twenty months, a time filled with many poignant moments, plenty of theatrical effects and even a few shouting matches. Everything had led inevitably to this day. In a few minutes, the Gomery Report would change hands and no longer belong solely to its author. I knew the contents, the strong points and the not-so-strong points. I could already hear the journalists drawing my attention to certain passages, asking for more information or even interpretations. Hours earlier, Neil Finkelstein and I had carefully mapped out the key chapters, the hard-hitting conclusions and the evidence to back them up. In short, we had tried to imagine how the report would be cut up into news bulletins and headlines.

Cook now stood before me, no doubt proud to have kept the report under wraps right to the end. Faced with a secret that they could not uncover, dozens of journalists had tried again and again to pass off their conjectures as hard facts. Articles and reports on October 31 all agreed—quite unexpectedly—that there had been no leaks. Emmanuelle Latraverse of Radio-Canada, interviewing me on the air, expressed surprise at being unable to glean even the tiniest bit of information. "How did you do it? Even a budget or throne speech is inevitably leaked to the press. We only had our imagination to go on."

My answer seemed to startle her: "Until six o'clock tonight, the report will be safely guarded, under the exclusive authority of the commission. After that, we can't guarantee anything. As for the 'revelations' obtained by some of your colleagues, I think we all have a little Gomery tucked away in the back of our minds that allows us to extrapolate."

It was 5:45 PM. The three-volume report was about to be issued officially. No one had seen the full-colour cover with its catchy title: *Who Is Responsible?* Sheila-Marie Cook intended to keep the secret right up to the private meeting with the media scheduled for 6:00 the next morning. She seemed relaxed, smiling like someone going on holiday. For the occasion, she had chosen to carry an elegant designer handbag, in which she had hidden her precious cargo. "I thought this would be just the thing for the circumstances. The lavender and gold pattern will look great on TV—it's a Ferragamo, can you believe it? A present from my daughters, back from Italy. You can only find these bags in Vancouver. After all," she laughed, "a handbag worth $1,200 for a report that cost a quarter-million to produce—the equation seems all right to me!"

"Easy, Raymond," she told the driver. "We don't want to arrive a single minute ahead of time. As it is, they've told us enough times already that we shouldn't be submitting the report sixteen hours before it's tabled in the House of Commons!"

She was referring to the contents of a disconcerting letter Gomery had received three days earlier. It was signed by the three leaders of the Opposition and warned of a political booby trap. Essentially, Stephen Harper, Gilles Duceppe and Jack Layton rebuked the Gomery Commission for its decision to submit an advance copy of the report to the Governor-in-Council, and eventually to Prime Minister Paul Martin, giving him a strategic lead to prepare an official public response. According to the leaders, this was unfair to the Opposition, who would be forced to wait until the following day to learn about the inquiry's findings. They demanded their copies of the report at the same time. Otherwise, they threatened, they would go public with their denunciation, file a complaint for collusion with the Prime Minister's Office, and so on. During the next hour, we held a summit meeting to discuss strategy. We reviewed all possible options, including submitting the report at 9:30 AM on Tuesday, November 1, and cancelling the lockup (closed-door meeting) with the press, which would probably delay the government's tabling of the report in the House. We decided to let the commissioner in on the situation. He was participating in the annual meeting of judges of the Québec Superior Court in Gatineau, not far away. Our recommendations comprised three main points: (i) avoid all political pressure and be prepared to change the schedule in order to do so; (ii) inform the Privy Council of the Opposition's request and see if the government would agree to it; (iii) prepare an immediate response that could be announced publicly in case the weekend press got hold of the story.

Gomery's response was brief, and it bore the stamp of a jurist. "We must give an answer, if only to tell them they are mistaken. As commissioner, I'm required to submit my report to the Governor-in-Council, not the prime minister. As parliamentarians, they should be able to tell the difference! As for the rest . . . think about it some more, but I'm submitting my report as expected on November 1 at the latest. Keep me informed."

A clarification is necessary here. "Governor-in-Council" refers to the Cabinet acting in its legal capacity. Officially, it represents the governor general, who acts on the advice of the Cabinet. Parliament therefore confers powers not to the Cabinet, nor to the ministers taken collectively, but rather to the Governor-in-Council.

The reaction at the Privy Council Office was even more pointed. "The decision is one the commission must make. However, in all cases we are the first and only ones that you should be submitting the report to. That's what the law says. We will take it from there. So, as far as submitting it simultaneously to the Opposition goes—when pigs fly!"

All we had to do was compose a response after reaching consensus on our strategy. Our letter, and its official translation for future publication, were ready for the commissioner's signature on Monday morning, October 31. In summary, it said: You are mistaken on the protocol we must follow concerning the submission of the report at 6:00 PM; status quo is maintained. By submitting our letter to the House, the Opposition would in a way be confirming the independence of the commission. Anyway, in a few minutes it would all be over!

The driver parked the car carefully, allowing time for the cameramen to get some footage. Guided by the lights, we walked the few steps into the building and toward the security desk. At the same time, a well-guarded delivery truck parked behind the building, ready to unload the boxes containing the report the moment we had officially handed over the first copy.

Robert Quinn's welcome at the elevator was in sharp contrast to the austere surroundings. He was a quietly powerful man with a big smile—an Irish giant with the kind of laughter in his eyes that could disarm any adversary. To describe the role he'd played on the sidelines of the commission from the beginning, you could say that he was an observer, an official reporter, an assessor of collateral damage caused by revelations, and an expert at gauging reporters' moods—all bundled up in one person. He was all that and more for the Office of the Privy Council, but especially for the clerk himself, Alex Himelfarb. Many journalists knew him already and didn't object to his presence. Some described him in a friendly way as a sympathetic "mole." Evidently he had served as a convenient official source for them. He and I had even joined forces to deal with various manoeuvres and motions presented before the commission as well as the Federal and Superior courts. By staking out a no man's land of constructive collaboration, he and I were able to ensure better follow-up on events and reached a common understanding of the situation.

A few storeys up, he led us to the office of the assistant deputy minister, Administrative Services. We were visiting the "department of departments." In all, we were there for a few minutes, just enough time for coffee. In another room, copies of the report were being numbered and coded to send to our counsel so they could familiarize themselves with it later that evening.

Seated before us, Quinn asked in a friendly way what we'd decided to do the next day. "Are the lockups for the press and the lawyers still set for six o'clock? You won't hold a press conference? Is the commissioner still planning to make a statement at 10:20? By the way, do you have a copy of this? It would help us prepare the statement the prime minister will make to the press later on."

I had no other options. "Unfortunately, his statement is not yet finalized and still subject to changes. I wouldn't want you to use an incomplete version."

Quinn knew how to read between the lines. He moved to another topic. "At any rate, it's strange to see such a hard-hitting report being submitted in such a low-key fashion. I'm looking forward to reading it. I mean, the commissioner did refuse to submit it personally to the prime minister, did he not? The PM would very much have liked a photo session for the press at this long-awaited moment."

We had moved almost imperceptibly from Practical Logistics to Applied Politics. "The commissioner was indeed uncomfortable with that idea, the point being that his report, commissioned by Mr. Martin, is essentially concerned with the activities of his government and party! Wrong message, wrong image—it was too much to fit into a single photograph!" I couldn't help adding: "As for Mr. Himelfarb, it was also too bad he couldn't receive the report from the commissioner in person—a scheduling conflict, no doubt!"

This was, of course, a euphemism. Indeed, columnists and other observers of the federal administration had mentioned to me many times how infuriated the clerk had been by the commission's very existence. Apparently several other top civil servants shared his irritation. Imagine: a judge who, with complete impunity, dared question the conduct and operations of the government! And to make an unacceptable situation even worse, he had been called not once but twice to appear before Gomery. His second testimony had taken place in Montreal, at the opening of Phase 1B concerning the money trail. Come on! As if he had been caught red-handed leaving something out or contradicting himself during his first testimony. It wouldn't have been so bad if the judge hadn't hinted at a possible conspiracy of silence between him and Jean Chrétien. No, given the possibility of such resentment, no such meeting between John Gomery and Alex Himelfarb could ever have taken place.

When we left, the pedestrian mall was deserted. The crowds and cameras were gone. The show was over. Fade out! We had to pick up the pace, as the to-do list was still long, and the deadline of 6:00 the next morning would come soon enough. Instinctively we turned toward the building, once a hotel and now offices for the Privy Council. At the top, a high-ceilinged ballroom had been converted into two storeys to make more room. On one of these brightly lit floors, a crowd of people were busy combing through the 454-page report, searching for the commissioner's conclusions and figuring out what they would tell the prime minister. At that very moment, Paul Martin was handing out candy to children who had come to his door at 24 Sussex. It was Halloween, and tomorrow was the day when the masks would come off.

Back at the commission offices, last-minute preparations were underway. Revisions were made to the press release confirming that the report had been submitted, and the statement the commissioner was about to make was reread. As for me, I returned to my hotel room to jot down and clarify my ideas in a few lines, something I could use to guide the media. I would have the advantage of being ahead of the game; the reporters and analysts would have only four hours to get to the bottom of things. My challenge was to persuade them to read the entire report and go beyond the findings' summary. Unlike many commission reports, this one had to be read cover to cover: it was much more an annotated account of an inquiry than a statement of work accomplished.

The clock radio murmured from the far end of the room, waking me from a light sleep that had felt more like a fall from consciousness. The night had been short-lived and terrible, and the whole room was cluttered with papers. I picked up Neil Finkelstein at the Château Laurier at around 5:30, and he wasn't in any better shape. He was worried about the interviews that his two colleagues, Bernard Roy and Guy Cournoyer, had promised to give to the media while I glanced with relief at the scant revelations obtained during the night by the *Globe and Mail*.

Victoria Hall, the place where the Ottawa hearings had taken place, resembles one of those university rooms where reputable faculties hold their entrance exams, filled with endless rows of tables. The perimeter of the room was reserved for television networks, which would do live commentary as soon as the disclosure ban was lifted. About three hundred journalists showed up, most of them for the opening at 6:00 AM. They would not be allowed to leave until four hours later, when the Gomery Report was scheduled to be tabled in the House of Commons, automatically becoming a public document. At that point, the contents of the report would also be made available on the website gomery.ca.

The early-morning influx of reporters at Old City Hall was cause for some concern, however. In addition to those journalists familiar with the inquiry and its accomplishments, there were many others without that experience, assigned to this unprecedented, crucial, long-awaited event. Neil Finkelstein and I tried to help them catch up. Each reporter had his or her own checklist of people likely to be singled out in the report. They wanted to check their lists first and then read the commissioner's comments. The same names appeared on many of the lists; only the order was different. To all of these first-time readers, the four hours allotted seemed far too short to absorb the whole document. At 10:00 AM, the telephone lines were opened, televisions and radios were plugged in and the Internet was connected.

The lawyers had equal time. Even though their briefing session was identical, I was opposed to having them join the journalists. There was too high a risk that the report would become secondary or incidental, pushed aside by the off-the-cuff remarks of certain individuals who would take over the headlines. I wanted the commissioner's findings to be centre stage for the media, at least for the morning. For the commission counsel, witnessing their colleagues' initial reactions might prove beneficial. For that reason, Bernard Roy, Guy Cournoyer and Marie Cossette took part in the briefing. Eighty-eight registered lawyers attended the lockup that we had organized in the same building to allow them to join the press as soon as the embargo was lifted. Once the doors were opened, no one was surprised to see the trio representing Chrétien, Pelletier and Gagliano make a beeline for the microphones.

The plan was that the commissioner would make his statement in the amphitheatre, which was used as a parliamentary press gallery. I was supposed to accompany him there, at the same time giving him a glance at the early media reactions, in case adjustments to his statement were needed. The press gallery's steering committee refused to let us in, however, claiming that only those taking questions from the press were permitted, not Commissioner Gomery, who intended only to make a statement.

But the exclusion turned to our advantage. We moved the event into a room right in City Hall, where I was able to control the setting and proper functioning of the event. The television networks had already set up their equipment there: we were sure to get direct coverage, with images of a confident and happy commissioner eager to share his thoughts on the work accomplished to this stage of the mandate. This live report would surely fill invaluable seconds of airtime in the coming news bulletins.

The rest of the day held few surprises. Each person in turn chose his or her turf, establishing a sort of hierarchy in order of appearance. By ensuring that the commissioner was the first to speak, I kept him out of the political battle—after all, many believed that his conclusions could lead to the government's defeat. In fact, I decided against holding any kind of press conference or exchange with the media precisely to avoid creating a stir. Since when was a judge in the habit of commenting on or explaining his decisions or how he had reached them? Others would be quick enough to exploit it for political reasons.

On November 1, the stage was set. The exonerated prime minister was delighted; the Opposition was looking for more material to bring down the government sooner; finally, the ex-prime minister continued to wage his private war to avenge an outrageous reproach. "Since Mr. Chrétien chose to run the Program from his own office," Gomery wrote in his summary, "and to have his own exempt [political] staff take charge of its direction, he is accountable for the defective manner in which the Sponsorship Program and initiatives were implemented. Mr. Pelletier failed to take the most elementary precautions against mismanagement—and Mr. Chrétien was responsible for him . . . since he is directly responsible for errors committed by Mr. Pelletier, he must share the blame for the mismanagement that ensued."

Fifteen days later John Gomery and I sat in his apartment on rue de la Commune, waiting for the Canadian bureau chief of *Time*. I had promised the magazine a long interview and photo session with the commissioner, who had been named Canadian Newsmaker of the Year. We took the opportunity to compare perceptions of how the media had judged the report. I especially wanted him to know about some of the impressions that our "regulars" had shared with me; their observations had been remarkably similar. "The summary is excellent, clear and precise . . . It lets us see the big picture right from the first reading of the report." Or: "There's no question the report is his, the style also. Why, though, did he insist again and again on exonerating Paul Martin?" And: "He pays too little attention to the advertising activities, even though a lot more money was spent there than on sponsorships. That's the document's only weakness."

But as far as John Gomery was concerned, the goal had been achieved. Not only had he delivered his inquiry report as promised, but also its content had generally been well understood. That morning he was more relaxed than usual, visibly relieved. Once again, he surprised me. "In general, I'm rather satisfied with the conduct of the inquiry. We got to the bottom of things. However, in retrospect, I would have preferred hearing certain witnesses, who made their appearance in the first months in Ottawa, only after taking note of the evidence presented to me in the spring, in Montreal. I realize now that some did not tell me the whole truth; they did not disclose everything they knew. But I managed to get the evidence necessary to unequivocally draw the essential conclusions. My counsel were free to establish the sequence and strategy of their examinations, and considering the size of the task, they did a good job."

These private thoughts were not regrets. They were the reflexes of a meticulous judge who, despite having finished his report, would not pass sentence on the guilty parties. As he reflected, he examined himself: "You know, François, at the end of this first report, I have to admit, after all I've heard of this affair, that I've lost much of my innocence."

What an admission, coming from a judge trained to hear every conceivable type of case, from executive management quarrels to crimes of passion to broken marriages! Confronted by human frailty, this clear-headed man had been stripped of his illusions. In one simple remark, he had just summed up the after-effects of a job well done.

There was a sudden knock at the door. To help regain our composure and rejoin the immediate present, I felt obliged to add: "Don't forget, this interview is supposed to be about you, not the inquiry. It's a portrait."

On November 28, Paul Martin's government was defeated in the House of Commons. The election campaign would focus on ethics and the moral authority of elected parliamentarians. At the same time, a confident John Gomery started writing his second report on governance in Ottawa.

SIXTEEN

INTERMEZZO IN A MINOR KEY

IN JUNE, AS THE Montreal hearings wound down, lawyers for clients with standing submitted their final defence arguments. To some, it seemed more likely that the lawyers were already gearing up for motions they would file upon release of the report that was yet to be written. We thought the storm had passed, but we were still in the eye of the hurricane.

In fact, on May 30, Jean Chrétien's lawyer, David Scott, announced that his client was withdrawing his motion for the recusal of Commissioner Gomery. The hearing had been set for June 7 in Federal Court. Scott insisted, however, that he wasn't excluding the possibility of another application for judicial review. Journalists covering the commission saw it as grandstanding, but we thought it was part of a larger strategy. Instead of tackling the commissioner head on, Chrétien and his lawyer planned to wait for the report and attack it again at an opportune time. For his part, John Gomery was relieved to have the leeway he needed to write up his findings without a hostile review hanging over his head.

Gilles Toupin of *La Presse* then published an excerpt from a letter written to Chrétien's lawyers by Brian J. Saunders, one of the legal team representing the government at the Gomery Commission. "We recognize that if he goes ahead [by withdrawing his motion], he will have the same right as all the other parties before the commission to submit a new application for judicial review once the commission files its report. We also recognize, in the event that your client asks for a judicial review of the commission's report, that he will have the right to bring forth the same arguments brought forth in the current motion and base his motion on the same alleged facts. In particular, we will not prevent him from bringing forth the argument of partiality if he so wishes."

John Gomery was surprised for two reasons. First, if this letter had never surfaced, he wouldn't have believed it. "François, you have to understand that a letter like that is quite extraordinary. This is a first for me in twenty years! It presumes the admissibility of a future motion notwithstanding any new circumstances that might occur. But, in addition, it looks like a veiled condition for Jean Chrétien to temporarily withdraw his motion!"

That was his immediate reaction as an experienced judge. Then came his reaction as the commissioner: "What game are those who gave me this mandate playing? Is Paul Martin aware of this little manoeuvre, or did he prepare a Plan B in case my report was too damaging for the Liberals? I'm going to force the issue. I'm going to insist on principle that the Federal Court hear Jean Chrétien's motion in any case."

As expected, Gomery's proposal was rejected. In his mind, he had just made it clear to everyone that he hadn't been fooled. Indeed, Brian J. Saunders was director general and senior general counsel at the Civil Litigation Section of the Department of Justice. As counsel for the government at the commission, he took his orders from the clerk of the Privy Council, Alex Himelfarb. The columnist Ian MacDonald of the *National Post* was the observer who best conveyed the content of my official response, in a column headed The Judge Is Angry! "We assume the Prime Minister's Office has nothing to do with this," he wrote, "given the undeniable support Mr. Martin has shown towards Judge Gomery until now."

Commission counsel discussed the matter amongst themselves. They felt that the commissioner had gone too far, and that right from the start I should have deflected the media's suspicion of a secret alliance between Martin and Chrétien. My private conversations with Gomery left me no choice. He had managed to stay out of the political game up to this point but was suddenly being sucked into it to defend his values and integrity. He insisted on letting the motion for his recusal be heard because he needed peace of mind to write his report.

This incident marked a turning point in the life of this commission of inquiry. From then on, we'd have to be more cautious in our surveillance of "outside forces." The alarm had sounded and we had counterattacked. From then on, we would defend the fort.

We also needed to get the second phase of the commission's mandate underway—a key mission in itself. Indeed, Gomery was to draw on the commission's factual findings in making recommendations to prevent the mismanagement of sponsorship and advertising activities in future. According to the Order-in-Council, the commissioner was also asked to pay special attention to bills or other measures that could be introduced to protect "whistle blowers" and to improve public access to information. Finally, the concluding phase of the mandate would not involve any hearings or testimony. The government apparently wished the second report to be based on a deeper study of the findings and their implications.

It was inevitable. After hearing 172 witnesses and admitting hundreds of documents as evidence, John Gomery intended to broaden the scope of the exercise. "The true legacy of this commission will be its second report. In it, I will obviously discuss ethics and values but from a practical point of view—the relationships, responsibility and accountability of those who hold power. Believe me, very little theory here, only case histories treated in a simple, straightforward way. And as I'm not an expert in this field, I will have to seek counsel."

Gomery launched the idea of consulting with experts in public administration without knowing how far the process would take us. We spent the whole summer preparing for it. What method would we adopt to remain credible, representative and realistic? Whom should we consult and according to what criteria? What principles would support the recommendations?

All of these questions were fundamental to our work but only increased the suspicions and wariness of senior civil servants. We heard from "generally well-informed sources" that discussions at the political level had turned toward new policies that would respond to the repeated attacks from the Opposition. Later, while we were still busy with our work, the government, as if by coincidence, announced a set of initiatives aimed at improving its administrative processes. No fewer than 158 concrete measures were proudly presented by Treasury Board President Reg Alcock: "This represents the most important set of changes ever applied to a government operation in the world."

Without providing details of his comparative research, Alcock added $40 million per year in the budget, solely for audits, external committees for auditing government auditors, publication of grants and funding allocations on the Internet and, finally, an "obligatory integrity pact" for government suppliers. This set of reforms, announced in the name of transparency, was described by the New Democrats as a "pre-emptive strike."

From the battlements, the pre-emptive strike looked more like an attempt to water down the impact and value of the second commission report, even though Paul Martin had promised to call an election after its publication, regardless of the contents. It was as if the government were saying, "It's a good report. In fact, we've already implemented over 60 percent of its recommendations. And we're off to a vote!"

For several weeks Gomery had been issuing instructions, sometimes from his farm, sometimes from his Montreal office. "The consulting process will be revealed only at the last minute. As for the planned round-table discussions, we'll announce the names of the participants only the day before each one was scheduled to take place."

Sheila-Marie Cook was the only commission member tapped to deal with the Privy Council. It was up to her to contain their impatience to know our plans. As the only other member of the commission authorized to speak to the outside world, I had to convince the media how essential this phase of our work was, despite the restrictions on information. This time, I would be seeking media attention, rather than managing it.

My target audience could wait no longer. It was clear that in their view, only one report really mattered. Once the summer holidays were over, journalists began calling to ask how the judge was faring and what the report was like—size, number of chapters, scope of responsibilities attributed, and so on. At that time, before the first volume had even been published, all I could do was describe the second report as the next volume of a saga.

Donald Savoie, professor of public administration at the University of Moncton, had full authority to identify the issues and establish the terms of reference of the consultations that would contribute to the second commission report. In fact, as director of research, he was responsible for defining the conceptual framework. He had outlined the main themes, identified the studies that would have to be commissioned and the list of questions that would be publicly debated. He too had received his orders. There was little doubt that this consultation would go well beyond the issues proposed by the government. With the caution of an academic, Savoie presented us with the "major issues to be discussed." To me this was like a game of Scrabble, using ideas instead of words. For the media's benefit I would have to place them in the right order, on triple-word-score squares, in order to set the scene for the coverage I wanted before the process really got underway.

Among other things, I told them: "Since the word *deficit* seems fashionable these days in Ottawa (we often hear people talking about fiscal or democratic deficits), I would like to suggest another possibility: the institutional deficit. This refers to the state administration apparatus, a concern of the commissioner that will be the main focus of Phase 2 of his mandate. For example, what is the real role played by parliamentarians in the monitoring and approval of government expenses? Where does ministerial responsibility lie, and what about the accountability of deputy ministers? Who should be required to account for his or her actions? Is too much power over government administration concentrated in the Prime Minister's Office? Judge Gomery would like to hear the opinions of several people on all that."

Throughout July and August, I pounded out my message in interview after interview. As my description of Phase 2 became clearer and more public, I suspected that people in certain other quarters were growing uneasy. I could imagine the conversations in the corridors of government buildings. What is he really up to? Our opinions are the ones that count, and we won't debate that in public. We are part of the most transparent administration there is. What more could you ask for?

In August, the powers that be decided that only one government memorandum would be submitted to the commission. It would come from the Treasury Board, in response to Prime Minister Chrétien's request in 1996 for additional sums of money to be placed in the National Unity Reserve Fund.

The interlude lasted well into the fall, and it contained negotiations and motions aimed at delaying the commission's work schedule. On October 12, Charles Guité, through his lawyer Richard Auger, requested a delay in the publication of the first report, and in a second motion, he asked to be the first person to see it! Yet another motion submitted to Superior Court requested that Guité's trial, which was to take place in the next few weeks, be deferred to prevent any risk of unfairness. This motion was rejected without appeal. The lawyer had taken the matter to the wrong authorities. It would be up to the Governor-in-Council to decide when to publish the report that would be in its hands on November 1.

In the period following the release of the report, it seemed to me that the commission's opponents, within the thirty-day time limit imposed, were preparing to go in for the kill. To extend the metaphor, I would say that the hunting horn had sounded three times—by Jean Chrétien; then by his ex-chief of staff, Jean Pelletier; but most loudly by one of his ministers at the time, Alfonso Gagliano. Certainly Gagliano had been reproached by the inquiry: "Contrary to his testimony to the effect that his participation was limited to providing political input and making recommendations about events and projects to be sponsored, Mr. Gagliano became directly involved in decisions to provide funding to events and projects for partisan purposes, having little to do with considerations of national unity."

On November 22, Gagliano asked the Federal Court for a judicial review, requesting essentially that "the report by the Commissioner of the Commission of Inquiry into the Sponsorship Program and Advertising Activities be declared null and illegal with respect to all matters concerning the plaintiff and that no blame be imputed to the latter." One of the arguments he presented in support of the request was that "the Commissioner, in the conducting of the commission entrusted to him, demonstrated an inappropriate attitude. The plaintiff is justified in believing that the evidence submitted to the Commissioner was not examined in a serious, serene, independent and detached fashion as required."

Then, in a second attack two days later, Jean Pelletier went to Federal Court to obtain a court order cancelling "any finding, speculation or insinuation concerning misconduct, inappropriate conduct, negligence or responsibility on his part." One of the arguments presented was that the commissioner had rendered a decision based on several incorrect factual findings, arrived at in an improper and arbitrary fashion, or without taking account of the elements at hand, or based on sheer speculation.

Finally, on November 30, the very day the Liberals launched their election campaign, their ex-leader Jean Chrétien put the Gomery report back on the day's agenda, describing it as "an incorrect, perverse, whimsical report." He then proceeded to attack the credibility and impartiality of its author more directly, demanding nothing less than the dismissal of the report.

The three motions rested on allegations of gross factual error, unfairness in the treatment of witnesses and lack of impartiality. The strategy was unambiguous: aim for the chief counsel Bernard Roy as the commissioner's alter ego, impugn Gomery's integrity and, incidentally, attack the commission's spokesman for certain remarks made to the media.

These motions would take several months to be heard, because of the time allowed to complete each court procedure. It was up to the court to assess their appropriateness, of course, and to determine whether they were well founded. It should be mentioned that the court's decision would be subject to appeal. In the meantime, I worried about handling the press on this subject and turned to John Gomery for advice.

"I think we shouldn't look surprised," he said. "All three, each in his own way, have made their intentions clear. It's up to the attorney general of Canada to defend the report, which is now in the hands of the government. As for me, in the event that the motions are heard, I'll assess to what extent I will have to respond to the accusations directed at me, and I'll see if I need to ask for standing. Until then, I have a second report to produce and I don't intend to deviate from this mandate. François, for the time being we have nothing to say. We must wait."

Despite the uproar, the commissioner once again demonstrated a consistent aspect of his character: *maintain your concentration and take on only one task at a time; that way you can make sure it's well done.* I couldn't suppress a smile when I left: Gomery would have made a great golfer in another life—he instinctively kept his eye on the ball. During our discussion, he was just as intense and thorough as he'd been during the inquiry.

SEVENTEEN

TIME TO CONSULT

GOMERY DID NOT intend to waste time. The hearings had already taken seven weeks longer than expected and delayed the second phase of his mandate. But the holdup didn't change his work routine. While he pressed on through the first chapters of his report with a farmer's stubbornness, the only matter on which we could interrupt him was the consultation—an essential activity, he had decided. It would give his second report a dimension that he alone as commissioner could not provide. Several months earlier, when he hired Donald Savoie, professor emeritus at the University of Moncton and a specialist in public administration, he chose a guide to help him find the best route: "I am a judge and my expertise is limited to that. Those who asked me to examine the state of governance knew full well I couldn't take on that task alone; my opponents are probably counting on it. So, if I want to ensure my work is not undermined, I'll have to base it on solid expert opinion—namely yours."

As a result, Savoie became director of the research program for a commission known essentially for delving into a scandal. He worked behind the scenes to develop a work plan and methodology, and to identify experts who could make contributions as required. An impossible summer for a farmer, thought John Gomery. Pierrette will be in charge of Havelock all by herself, if I'm to get this done.

The further he got in writing the first report, the more convinced he became of the importance of the second phase of his mandate. The description of Phase 2 provided by the government turned out to be incomplete. Indeed, the fact that the scope of recommendations had been circumscribed in advance made it impossible to develop recommendations that covered all of the factual findings of Phase 1. The terms of reference did ask for comments on the bill aimed at protecting whistle blowers in the public service, as well as proposed changes to the *Financial Administration Act*. They also mentioned the enforcement of the *Access to Information Act*, accountability measures, coercive measures and finally a report on ministerial and public service responsibility. Regardless of how long the list was, key elements were missing. Clearly the writers of the terms of reference had not foreseen all of the issues that would be raised or the consequences they would have. "I know enough today," Gomery said, "to understand that to assign blame to the political leadership is not necessarily to assign a general and unqualified blame to the public service as a whole."

Gomery wanted to go beyond the squandering of public funds for political purposes and measure the damage to democracy and the imbalance of power within parliamentary institutions that had allowed such misuse of authority to occur. In fact, the link between the greed of certain politicians and the wish lists of the public service seemed circumstantial. During the summer, he raised issues that some people would interpret as threats, simply because he'd raised them. With Savoie as his guide, he decided to base his study on practical considerations stemming from observations he'd made during the inquiry. He would limit the number of recommendations, but treat each one carefully.

John Gomery's knowledge of government operations was based on weeks of testimony given by civil servants at all levels. He had questioned them several times to make sure he grasped the bureaucratic procedures, administrative controls and lines of authority in place. Seated at the back of the room, I was struck by two things: the witnesses' firm grasp of the rules and the diversity of their interpretations of these same rules. By studying the answers provided by these civil servants and the decisions they made, one could understand how they related to and dealt with one another. The summary of the first report explained how Raynald Quail, deputy minister of public works during the sponsorship affair, was criticized by the Privy Council Office for some of his initiatives with respect to the normal chain of accountability and oversight: "Mr. Quail understood that his role in the Sponsorship Program had been reduced to ensuring that Mr. Guité's organization did not spend more money than it had available. As a consequence, the normal authority and oversight of the Deputy Minister virtually ceased. The involvement that the Deputy Minister would normally have in the formulation of a new program, its administration and its oversight did not occur, and his involvement was never sought. With the support and approval of persons at the highest level of the government, Mr. Guité was untouchable and beyond the control of Mr. Quail, in spite of the latter's obligation to manage his department."

It was inevitable that the many questions concerning freedom of action, jurisdiction and political intervention would lead John Gomery to ponder the ethics and values of senior civil servants one year later.

The inquiry uncovered a myriad facts and they helped Gomery to steer his vessel through one course open to him—the narrow, treacherous channel at the end of which integrity lies. His first questions concerned the jurisdiction of a minister and his or her deputy minister—what their responsibilities were and how accountable they were to each other. He also wished to understand the criteria used in deciding the responsibility for a bad management decision, or in pleading lack of knowledge.

On a higher level, he wanted a better understanding of the Privy Council Office's grip on the management of ministries. The link between them is more than just an organizational arrangement; many top civil servants worked for the Privy Council Office before being assigned to another ministry.

Finally, the study would look at the Cabinet and the collective accountability of its ministers. On this topic, Gomery wanted to disclose the rules governing the relationship between the executive branch, responsible for government affairs, and Parliament, which has the interests of all Canadians as its mandate.

It was a tall order, and Gomery needed all the help he could get. During his conversations with Donald Savoie, he constantly introduced new parameters, forcing Savoie to broaden the scope of investigation. In spring 2005, it was already apparent that a panel of experts was needed. To deflect the skepticism of the press and those opposed to the consultation, Gomery had to surround himself with the best—not only theoreticians, but people with experience in public administration and politics. Donald Savoie and Sheila-Marie Cook started looking for clear-headed candidates who had built on their successes and learned from their mistakes, who could improve what was good and eliminate what was bad by collaborating with others. Most important, those selected had to be universally acceptable, regardless of political affiliation, past policy positions and career milestones. The group had to be balanced and its members capable of joint action in recommending sound objectives.

The job took several weeks, and names were gradually added to the original list of candidates. Some declined to participate for health reasons, others for lack of interest or unavailability, and several people feared being associated with the explosive findings of an inquiry led by a popular judge whose impartiality had been called into question. In order to persuade them to join our team, while acknowledging their concerns, we promised them that the two phases of the commission's mandate would be scrupulously kept separate. "You will never have to comment on or discuss the findings or even the observations made by the commissioner in his first report," the commissioner told them. "Our meetings are meant to give me an overall perspective on the state of governance within the government. It will be up to me alone to recommend measures to ensure that the wrongdoing we have uncovered never happens again."

And the argument did make a difference. Raymond Garneau was the most insistent of the seven members hired on these conditions. He had his reasons: aside from his business success and past political work as Québec's finance minister under the late Robert Bourassa, he remained a close associate of Paul Martin. Gomery suggested that Garneau chair the committee, and as expected, Garneau completed his task with an open mind and an independent spirit, the qualities that had gained him respect throughout his career. However, the media continued to raise questions and my answer was always the same: "The commissioner wanted to call on experience. He believes that his panel consists of some of our most experienced public administrators. The criteria he used to make his choice have nothing to do with the political convictions or affiliations of any member."

No one doubted the judge's talent for establishing and maintaining freedom and objectivity among his extended team. Ten months spent observing his methods had been sufficient to convince them.

Roch Bolduc, former president of the Québec Public Service Commission; Bevis Dewar, former chairman of the Canadian Institute on Governance; John A. Fraser, the first elected speaker of the House of Commons; Constance R. Glube, nominated as chief justice of the Nova Scotia Supreme Court; John Hodgetts, professor emeritus, considered the founder of public administration studies in Canada, and finally Carolle Simard, professor and author of books, articles and research reports on public administration—all wished to be part of the commission proceedings but had no desire to deal with the political fallout.

Realistically, chances were slim that a concerted effort would be made to criticize their involvement. This advisory committee was above all a listening committee; their task was to present the commissioner with a summary of interesting opinions collected on issues that were essential to the report. As for ideas and recommendations, John Gomery continued to stand alone at the helm.

Where would the ideas come from? Donald Savoie wanted to ask the experts; i.e., people who had worked in public administration or who had taught others its principles. The commissioner disapproved of this compartmentalization of knowledge on a topic of broad public interest. "The question goes well beyond accounting and auditing standards. It raises ethical questions with respect to the way public funds are disbursed. You don't need to be an expert to have ideas on safeguards needed to maintain integrity."

According to Gomery, the inquiry had generated more than just a sustained interest. Witness the impressive media coverage, the large number of e-mails and letters of support, the size of the television audience, the results of opinion surveys and the crowded hearings. Canadians' interest in the inquiry was so intense that it had cast a shadow of doubt over all political leaders. The nation-wide interest must be sustained, Gomery thought. He dreamed of holding an even broader consultation, which would add the public's moral endorsement to the clinical observations of the experts.

However, he was forced to scale down his ambitions for two reasons. First, the mandate entrusted to him was urgent. The first report had marked the culmination of inquiry proceedings, but it was the second report that was supposed to propel the country into an election. Paul

Martin's commitment to do just that served to stir up the Opposition's impatience. Second, the commission had a limited budget. Expenses were well below the amounts "leaked" by commission critics—in fact, they were only a third of the false figures reported excitedly in the press—but the inflated numbers had wormed their way into the public memory and tainted their perceptions. Sheila-Marie Cook vowed never to relax in her stringent administration of the commission. "If we don't set an example, who will?" she asked. "I've taken part in so many consultations that turned into endless road trips for which costs were revised constantly. Our opponents—those who declare themselves and those who don't—would love to see us go over budget."

The compromise we reached was by far the best solution. We would submit straightforward questions to citizens on our website at gomery.ca. The number of questions would be limited so that respondents would not be discouraged. The proposal was a daring one: it presumed that Canadians were interested enough to visit the site and take the trouble to answer each question with more than a yes-or-no response.

From a public-relations perspective, the boldness of the project excited me. First, it would allow me to develop press material to present the initiative, highlighting the commission's openness and its eagerness to hear from the public. Second, I could use this mode of consultation to illustrate the importance of the entire process from the citizen's point of view. One detail bothered me, though: how would we ensure an acceptable response rate with no promotion or publicity campaign and no public notices, relying only on press coverage?

We gave the program two months to succeed. Even though it was summer, I gave as many interviews as I could, especially on the radio, inviting listeners to get to their computers right away and do their duty. But I found that my role as messenger was secondary—the interest was already there. In fact, one after the other, the radio hosts

I met were thrilled that taxpayers were being given the opportunity to vent their indignation over the sponsorship scandal.

The impact of the program went way beyond our wildest forecasts, exceeding our expectations threefold. In all, 4,106 Canadians from every province and territory completed the online questionnaire. Some people even embellished their answers with real-life public-service experiences. In terms of response rate, four provinces set themselves apart. Despite expectations to the contrary, Ontario, with 1,460 responses, was the overall winner, inching past Québec with 1,257. Clearly the questions being examined by the inquiry did not exclusively concern Québec and the 1995 referendum.

The commission asked only five questions, and the answers were enlightening.

Question One: *Should the government keep sponsorship and advertising programs shielded from all political influences?* Most respondents called for the creation of an independent committee or even one presided over by the auditor general of Canada. Curiously, though, a strong majority of respondents wondered about the relevance or value of such programs.

Question Two: *What protection should be guaranteed whistle blowers who witness unethical behaviour?* Opinion on this matter was deeply divided. A good number were in favour of maximum protection with financial compensation; others asked why civil servants should be rewarded for behaving ethically when it is an essential quality of their work.

Question Three: *On the subject of ministerial responsibility, implying that a minister be accountable for his or her actions before the House of Commons, should there be exceptions to this rule? If so, under what circumstances?* 72 percent of respondents (a proportion that exceeds the percentage of the popular vote any elected government can expect to receive) answered that no exceptions were acceptable. They declared that ultimately the prime minister and finance minister must be held accountable for the actions of their government.

Question Four: *What would you do to support greater accountability in the management and use of public funds?* It is interesting to note how strongly Canadians identify the stature and conduct of an institution with the individual at its head. Just as John Gomery's name has become associated with the upright behaviour expected of a public inquiry, Sheila Fraser's is associated with the incorruptible elements in government. To many respondents, not only was she the guardian of integrity, she was also the individual who should be invested with all the powers needed to deal severely with these problems.

Question Five: *Should a code of ethics and values specific to the public service refer explicitly to notions of responsibility and accountability? Should it be incorporated into a law?* Many respondents considered ethics and values a matter of individual responsibility. In fact, 84 percent believed that guidelines in this matter must be rigorous. At the time of hiring, a public servant should be required to adhere to strict rules of conduct.

Thus, Commissioner Gomery was satisfied not only with the number of responses to his questionnaire, but also with their quality. There was no doubt that this aspect of the commission's work would add credible moral heft to his report, making it hard for the government to downplay its importance. The concerns of Canadians would take their place alongside the opinions of experts. John Gomery did not want his recommendations to end up as grist for endless discussion within parliamentary committees. By proposing concrete measures to solve real problems, he intended to provoke a debate. He was convinced that many people across the country were already waiting for this debate to happen.

EIGHTEEN

MR. COMMISSIONER IS LISTENING

THE CANOPY AT THE entrance to the old courthouse barely protected us from the drizzle and autumn wind. Standing at the top of the steps, John Gomery controlled his impatience, making jokes while a photographer atop a stepladder gave him instructions. *Time* magazine was doing a photo session of the man it had chosen as its Canadian Newsmaker of the Year for 2005. To while away the tedium of trying different poses and facial expressions, Gomery chatted with the photographer in between flashes from the camera and reflectors.

"My hat should come out well...at least I hope it will. Pierrette will surely comment on it. She really hates it, but I can't part with it. It takes years before a hat gets comfortable."

"Left foot forward, please. Look in my direction this time, with the expression of a friendly, charming judge...that's it...there you go..."

"I see, you mean as if I were charmingly sentencing you to life imprisonment?"

The interview he gave to Steven Frank, bureau chief for the Canadian edition of *Time*, was a welcome break. He recognized that not every detail of his personal life would be interesting, but he was happy to relate anecdotes from his recent or distant past, before he had been appointed commissioner: his father's courage in spite of many setbacks, the attention he got from his mother and sisters as the only boy in the family, and other stories that he loved telling. It was like a recess break for the mind. His work plan and outline for the second report were already well established, and now he needed to let his ideas gel.

After rereading the summaries of the round-table discussions held in September and October for his consultation, he was once again amazed at the candour and intelligence of his guests. All he had intended to do in these discussions was to sound out a group of competent people involved at one time or another in public administration. What he got was a huge grab bag of thoughts and reflections that, once they were neatly organized, could easily have led to even more questions—all of them relevant but outside his mandate. Luckily, he thought, we decided to write summaries rather than taking minutes. This way I can refer to the contents of our discussions without attributing certain ideas to a particular person; realizing that, the participants will be much more open.

As it turned out, he wasn't disappointed.

These round-table discussions had been arranged months beforehand, as a compromise to avoid town-hall meetings, a type of gathering mentioned often by previous commissions of inquiry. Gomery's two main objectives were to arrive at a solid and well-thought-out opinion that reflected regional points of view from across Canada. That is why he chose to hold a meeting in each region—five round tables in the form of private work sessions. Moncton, Québec City, Toronto, Edmonton and Vancouver were the cities chosen, mostly because that is where the largest number of good candidates were living and working.

The media had little interest in this trans-Canada tour until we provided them with a list of participants: former Conservative and

Liberal Cabinet ministers, retired high-ranking civil servants who had been at the centre of events in federal and provincial politics, outspoken opinion leaders. The participants were divided into groups of ten and spent an entire day discussing their ideas. When they arrived, I felt they showed considerable respect for John Gomery. They respected his work, of course, but some were also nostalgic for the public recognition that had once been theirs. All of them had followed the proceedings of the inquiry but none knew anything about its findings. Of those sitting around the table, only the judge, who had now finished writing his first report, knew how important these discussions were, given the findings of Phase 1. The process was a rational follow-up to the fact-finding phase of the inquiry.

Each round-table participant had his or her own style and personality, but several also took advantage of the opportunity to share thoughts and frustrations that they may not have imagined they would ever express publicly. For example, a former Cabinet minister had this to say: "Once named, a minister becomes just one more amateur in power. No one is familiar with the public administration. In general, his boss—the prime minister—has chosen him for the riding he has won, the region he represents, the ethnic group he belongs to; rarely for his competence in managing his portfolio. This new minister immediately becomes the hostage of civil servants. They know all the ropes but show him only what he needs to know to avoid embarrassment to his department. In spite of this, he remains responsible for all decisions and initiatives taken. It was only much later that I realized how rudimentary my knowledge was of some issues I thought I'd mastered."

One of this person's old political rivals retorted: "It's true that ministers depend on the bureaucratic machine and senior civil servants, who are not accountable to Parliament, and use them as smokescreens. But things are no better inside the Cabinet. Since Brian Mulroney was elected, everyone fends for himself. Any observer will tell you that the collective responsibility of all ministers is a thing of the past. You're on your own."

In another city, retired senior civil servants picked up the thread on this question of accountability. "The candidates approached for the position of deputy minister know the public administration fairly well," said one. "They at least have a good idea of how it works. However, when you ask them to whom they are accountable, the answer is totally confusing. Some report to the prime minister, the clerk of the Privy Council, or directly to their ministers; still others answer to the governor general! This authority needs to be established clearly and explained to all concerned."

Others went further: "For a long time now, the Privy Council has unfortunately become a training ground for future deputy ministers, except in the Finance Department. This introduces an incestuous element to the system. Once promoted, they are staunchly loyal to the Privy Council. The minister inevitably takes second place."

Absorbing these comments from fifty veterans of public administration and combining them with his own reflections, Gomery was prompted to take a closer look at the Prime Minister's Office and the high concentration of power it embodies—a formidable political stronghold that has only grown more concentrated over time. Right from the start of the hearings, he had been surprised to learn that the PMO had authority to name deputy ministers. "Is that not a dangerous source of conflict of interest between the executive branch and the public administration?" he often asked.

On that subject, some round-table participants startled us once again: "Fifty metres from Parliament Hill, a member of Parliament is nothing. This is my way of telling you that the prime minister and his immediate associates very much dominate the entire government bureaucracy. This form of autocratic authority has been building up slowly but steadily over the last twenty years."

John Gomery had little to say during the round-table discussions. He took in everything that was said without trying to influence the course of the conversation. His black notebook still sat before him, but I had the feeling that he was memorizing faster than he could write. From one region of the country to another, he was fascinated to observe how perceptions and ideas varied. The East seemed more willing to punish those found guilty of abuse; the West was more interested in clarifying the power exercised by each institution.

Another issue emerged unanimously: the influential role played by political staff in the affairs of the state. Since 1984, this role has been growing in prominence. The Conservatives introduced this level of management into the machinery of government when they came to power. They established the hybrid position of chief of staff and executive secretary to the minister, which has long been a subject of concern. John Gomery added it to his list. In light of all he heard, he concluded that the existence of this influential position facilitates political interference with the decision-making authority of deputy ministers. When he was elected in 1993, Jean Chrétien perpetuated the practice, or at least gave the position similar status and authority. This can be gathered from the documents filed as evidence before the Gomery Commission, whether or not they were usable in the examination of witnesses. Grouped by event, time period or correspondent, they included internal memos and e-mails woven into a tight mesh that made them incomprehensible to outsiders. For example, on a list of proposed sponsorships drawn up by one person, you can read the disbursement authorizations for each sponsorship added by someone else. In general, the information these documents contained was only partially accurate, and references to dates, meetings and persons in attendance at meetings were often missing.

Many chiefs of staff come from extended political clans, and they are hired for their know-how and experience from previous volunteer assignments. Others are parachuted from the upper echelons of power into the hands of ministers who don't know them.

During the round tables, certain participants admitted to the commissioner that during their careers, they had no choice but to hire aides whose task was to ensure that a minister had the best possible relationship with his senior civil servants. "Many orders came directly through them. We never doubted where they were coming from."

Gomery was often shocked by the significant presence of these relationship weavers. It shattered his image of a public service that acted as a safeguard against all partisan intervention, regardless of which party was in power. One day in Edmonton, in the shuttle bus taking us back to the airport, he shared his disappointment with me: "I gather that a deputy minister, no matter how honest he is, does not have much clout if he wishes to oppose an order that he considers irregular. He can of course transmit his disagreement to the clerk of the Privy Council or even to the prime minister who appointed him. But such an initiative could lead to his resignation if what he is denouncing happens to have come from his bosses. Few people are willing to take it that far. As for their subordinates, blowing the whistle could sabotage their own career." It was the only time I ever saw him pick up his black notebook and scribble in it when he was not in a meeting.

In the days that followed, he focused on whistle blowing as a basic control mechanism for the sound management of the government. The Martin government's agenda for the inquiry had included a bill making it a duty to report improper activity and to protect those who did so. It was explicitly mentioned in the commission's mandate that such a law would be adopted once the judge had recommended the measures it should contain. The initial concept of the bill had been quite simple, but it took on a life of its own and grew complex in the process. If a law clearly demonstrated the will to clean up management practices, the means also had to be set out in no uncertain terms. In his numerous remarks on this question at the round tables, Gomery indicated that he intended to give whistle blowers rock-solid protection. "We need absolute confidentiality," he said. "Without such a guarantee, the threat of retaliation will never disappear and will discourage even those with the best intentions. The receiver of the confidential information will have to be shielded from all pressures; otherwise, you can't avoid having suspicions escalate to the point of being unbearable."

Similarly, he was concerned that this process might give rise to vendettas between colleagues or make senior personnel vulnerable to unfair attack. "Each accusation must be examined in depth, according to pre-established and well-known criteria; otherwise the witch-hunting season will be open year round. A kind of wisdom is needed to avoid guilty parties being brandished as trophies of the hunt, or those who denounced them becoming heroes of the day."

Gomery was surprised, as we all were, by the magnitude of the WorldCom, Enron and, closer to home, Norbourg scandals. In the same way, the FBI had made the headlines for failing to prevent the 9/11 terrorist attacks in 2001. In all of these cases, an informer had decided to talk and had instantly become a defender of ethical and moral values in our society, as represented by the media. The commissioner wanted to avoid this kind of publicity, which was like a land mine on the road to integrity.

I unwittingly added to his concerns when I asked him to do an interview with *Time* magazine for its end-of-the-year review. As an example, I had given him a copy of the December 2002 issue, whose cover page saluted three top news personalities of that year, "The Whistleblowers"— Cynthia Cooper of WorldCom, Coleen Rowley of the FBI and Sherron Watkins of Enron. Lengthy articles described the courage and tenacity of these women, as well as the way they went about salvaging their careers. Ironically, what I had wanted to show Gomery in this issue was the magazine's treatment of the Canadian Newsmaker of that year, Paul Martin.

If only past and present events were woven into our memory cells in a checkerboard pattern, news features would be much less surprising to us.

Some weeks later, while Gomery and his family were spending the Christmas holidays in a small Spanish town, another incident brought back thoughts about whistle-blower legislation. On the front page of the *Herald Tribune*, he read that a well-known Washington lobbyist named Jack Abramoff had pleaded guilty to charges of influence peddling and bribery involving members of the U.S. Congress. Three representatives and a senator were involved.

As Gomery unravelled the intricate mesh of financial transactions between the Department of Public Works and Government Services, Crown corporations and public relations agencies, one finding became crystal clear: the will to bypass the laws, in particular the *Lobbyists Registration Act*. There were many examples of this tendency, and in the summary of his inquiry report, he singled out the role played by Jacques Corriveau, president of Pluri Design. "From 1998 until the end of the Sponsorship Program, Mr. Corriveau obtained many sponsorships from PWGSC [Public Works and Government Services Canada] for Expour and Polygone. Pluri Design invoices do not reference a commission of 17.65%, but instead contain descriptions of services allegedly rendered. In almost all cases, the services described were simply not rendered and the invoices were designed to mask the commission agreement, probably to hide the fact that Mr. Corriveau was not registered as a paid lobbyist...Mr. Corriveau was at the heart of an elaborate kickback scheme, whereby at least some of the sums of money paid by Groupaction to Pluri Design were used by Mr. Corriveau to the advantage of the Liberal Party of Canada (Québec). Mr. Corrriveau was paid for his influence in obtaining sponsorship contracts..."

Jacques Corriveau contested the commissioner's findings right to the end. However, he never produced a plausible explanation as to why the invoices had been prepared as they were. Moreover, he claimed he wasn't terribly familiar with the rules governing lobbyists. The commission rejected this assertion, but did not let the matter rest there. In his *Fact Finding Report,* Gomery described the witness's attitude: "Mr. Corriveau presents himself to the world and to the Commission as a refined and cultured man with a patrician air, interested in and supportive of the arts... It was only when the full extent of his involvement in the Sponsorship Program was revealed as a result of the testimony of Luc Lemay that the Commission learned that Mr. Corriveau was as much motivated by an appetite for financial gain as by principle... He testified on two occasions, and in some respects contradicted his earlier testimony. I believe that these contradictions cannot be explained by a failure of memory but are due to an intention to mislead the Commission."

Through his remarks and some of the conclusions in his report, John Gomery missed few opportunities to express his contempt for premeditated deceit. In his view, an individual guilty of this offence deserves the maximum sentence, in other words, the withdrawal of any and all forms of respect. Even more shocking to Gomery is the immoral collusion of those in government who tolerate this kind of behaviour: "For an ex-minister or retired civil servant to act illegally by not fulfilling the requirement to register as a lobbyist or ignoring the time limits prescribed by law to partake in this activity, there must be others, ex-colleagues or associates still on the job, who have accepted the fact of this illegality."

When he told me this, I realized just how shocking the revelations of the last months had been, not only to the Canadian public but to John Gomery himself.

NINETEEN

ONLY THE WRITTEN WORD REMAINS

DARKNESS OVERCAME the farm quickly on that late December afternoon. At that time of day, the shadow of Covey Hill stretched toward the Adirondacks, which had disappeared from the landscape. For one last time—or so he thought—John Gomery broke his own rule about not letting his work invade his refuge.

He reread a recent summary of highlights and observations collected and annotated from the submissions sent to the commission. Part of Donald Savoie's research plan was to solicit the views of 103 organizations or individuals likely to be directly or indirectly concerned by questions of governance. Among them were the heads of eight federal ministries and organizations, five senior parliamentary civil servants, sixteen Crown corporation executives, representatives of the four political parties whose members were sitting in the House of Commons, and five universities.

Much to our surprise, a total of 251 submissions were sent to the commission, of which 124—almost exactly half—were relevant to the issues at hand. The commissioner could scarcely believe the breadth of the response. "I'm not the only one who feels as though something is very wrong," he commented. "Each of us in his own right has observed symptoms and wants to contribute to the cure...I really don't feel like I'm writing for a passive group of onlookers!"

It would probably have been much more difficult to generate this kind of active participation without the revelations of the inquiry. At the very least, public interest in the subject, hidden in the background, would not have surfaced with such force. The comments came from every direction, professional associations, the academic world, intellectuals and retired civil servants. Some entities chose not to respond. On the government side, for example, the Treasury Board was designated as the sole department authorized to co-operate with the commission. Of the four federal political parties, only the Bloc Québécois accepted the commission's invitation.

Virtually all the submissions noted that the sponsorship scandal signified the systemic cultural and moral malaise that was deeply rooted in government. Taken together, the experiences and observations described in the submissions made up an alarming catalogue of concerns. Cynicism, cowardliness, opportunism, lack of respect for rules and procedures, and lack of concern for inefficiency and waste were just some of the problems raised. Other people described a climate of deception, secrecy, tyranny and favouritism, as well as widespread contempt for Parliament and the public interest.

Two perceptions of the federal government as a whole emerged clearly in most of the comments. First, there was an impression that Ottawa does not enforce its own rules. Insiders will get what they want despite the rules, respondents wrote, and rules are applied arbitrarily or only when the public keeps a close eye on the situation. Second, the commission's unveiling of the internal operations of government had reinforced people's impression that incentives for good conduct are ineffective or non-existent. Respondents said that the disciplinary or political consequences did not seem at all proportional to the gravity of the acts committed.

Overall, the submissions were very skeptical about the possibility of instituting reforms through internal measures. Several people believed that only Parliament could reaffirm the primacy of the public interest within government.

Confronted by this array of candid thoughts and deep-seated convictions, John Gomery thought it better not to reveal the names of people or organizations whose contributions he would be using. I could just imagine a relentless media asking these people for more comments on their most negative views.

For example, on the grounds for shielding sponsorship or advertising programs against political meddling, positions ranged from one extreme to another. One person wrote: "...it should be illegal for Cabinet to ask the public service to call for tenders, proceed to reject the firm chosen legitimately by civil servants, and then allocate funds to the firm or firms it chooses. In the case of the Sponsorship Program, it was a sham government, not good government." On the same subject, another person offered this: "...I agree that political influences cannot be totally excluded...Another way of shielding these decisions is to entrust them to independent administrative organizations..."

On clarifying the division of responsibilities between ministers and deputy ministers, political staff and civil servants, everyone agreed that action was urgently needed. "...Between ministers and deputy ministers, there are so many points of contention in the system...measures need to be taken...Civil servants should not take orders from political staff...Political staff that are neither elected by Canadian citizens nor trained by our highly respected, professional public service should not be authorized to interfere in the management of the state."

On the question of where the ultimate responsibility lies: "...It would be too simplistic to say that ministers are responsible for everything going on in the department. In a pragmatic way, they should be held accountable for policies and positions they develop, and deputy ministers should be responsible for the implementation and efficient delivery of programs. Naturally, a minister cannot ignore management problems that come to light, but it is up to the deputy minister to take corrective measures."

Others assumed there would always be abuse: "...Senior managers in the public service who ask or order their subordinates to do something suspicious should always be required to give written instructions."

Based on the main points submitted for his review, Gomery confirmed the value of this type of consultation. Very few of the submissions bore partisan or ideological biases; the vast majority of respondents tried to be fair, an attitude that Gomery could spot right away. "This balance is admirable given the intense media coverage at the hearings," he said. "You can't blame those who tend to demonize certain individuals who testified. Their reaction is understandable but doesn't bring anything constructive to my study."

In truth, as 2005 drew to a close, even his first report seemed absent from John Gomery's thoughts. He had stopped talking about both the findings and the outcry they had provoked during the election campaign. The report had been a much-needed step toward the corrective measures he was developing for the future, but now he had evidently closed the book on it, focusing instead on the roles of parliamentary and government institutions and the improvements to the public administration he planned to recommend. He often told me that he considered his second report to be the true legacy of this commission of inquiry.

TWENTY

CHRISTMAS TRUCE

THERE HE WAS, standing right in front of me, smiling warmly, drink in his hand. He obviously wanted to talk to me and I guessed what the subject would be. The Christmas spirit reigned in this Westmount mansion, where forty or so guests, most of whom didn't know one another, made polite noises as they celebrated the season.

The man was still there. I reached out to shake his hand, betting that the conversation he was going to initiate would be more interesting than wandering through the gathering our hosts had organized, looking for a place to settle.

"Good evening. Maurice told me you're with Gomery...I've heard you often on the radio. My name is Robert Larue [not his real name]. I'm a stockbroker."

I had little to add. "François Perreault...pleased to meet you. You're right, I'm the commission spokesman."

We then got straight to the point.

"A lot of sound and fury, signifying little for $100 million. It was a good show while it lasted, but once the report came out, nothing concrete, no accusations. And then there's that guy, Coffin—he gets away with nothing more serious than having to deliver a few lectures. Lucky dog!"

Gotcha! I was knocked cold before I even stepped into the ring. While searching for a polite response, I became aware of a crackling fire and the sounds of a string quartet playing in the next room. What could I tell him? That I was impressed by the work we accomplished, that the way the two reports complement each other will give all Canadians food for thought? That he should talk about his vacation plans or shut up?

"You know, police investigations take time. By the way, it's $30 million...a lot of money, I agree, but we like to think that the final result will be worth it."

The ball bounced back one more time. "The fact remains that you have made them call a costly and useless election—the same characters will return to power, and we'll end up with another minority government!"

Luckily, a waiter appeared suddenly with a platter of hors d'oeuvres, distracting us just long enough to break Larue's stride.

Could we not lay down our arms temporarily, if not declare a truce, for Christmas? No, I guess not. Not even for Candlemas.

The election campaign was now well underway. As it happened, Prime Minister Martin did not manage to stay in power until the final report of the commission of inquiry was published. He had no choice but to call a mid-winter election, after the Opposition parties succeeded in passing a non-confidence vote that toppled his minority government. A few weeks of campaigning and two televised leaders' debates demonstrated the lessons learned from Gomery. The politicians spoke of morals, openness and clean government. It was a spic-and-span contest to see who would come out the whitest. Rarely had an election focused so tightly on cleanliness.

The race had two stages, with an interlude in between but no truce. While everyone watched the campaign battlefield, though, things were happening behind the lines.

For one thing, the diehard Liberal militant Warren Kinsella suddenly changed his tune. His blog now invited fellow militants to support the Conservatives and squeeze Paul Martin out of office. Others of the same opinion made the same arguments in Ottawa during chance encounters in restaurants and pubs, at private dinners and parties.

In its December 21 issue, the *Lawyers Weekly* expressed concern about the ruthless determination with which Jean Chrétien had accused the commissioner of bias. John Gomery admitted that he found the motions questioning his integrity both unpleasant and troublesome— adding that he'd managed to sleep very well anyway. In the same conversation he said he was more concerned about the impact of his recommendations on governance in Ottawa. "If they're all approved," he said, "the impact on the Canadian parliamentary system and democracy could be major and long-lasting, all modesty aside, as you'll see on February 1."

Mind you, he wasn't boasting; indeed, a major concession had just been won behind the scenes. After several high-level meetings, Sheila-Marie Cook, involved in producing the second report, won a concession from the Privy Council. The decree establishing the commission included a provision that forbade publication of any documents other than the two scheduled reports; but the prime minister had authorized publication of the seventeen expert studies commissioned by Gomery, with no idea of what they contained. In arranging the publication, Cook gave the second Gomery report a solid foundation and sheltered it from the political storm that the judge's recommendations might stir up. From now on, it would be impossible for the next prime minister, whatever his name or party, to ignore the contents of the second report.

After a few nibbles and a healthy quaff of white wine, Larue reappeared. "...Besides, the leaders have nothing new to offer," he continued. "Everything is so sadly predictable. Apart from the hundreds of billions of dollars in promises of all sorts, three of them are going to milk the sponsorship scandal while the other one shakes his sovereignty scarecrow. Everyone knows this corruption has always been going on. As for the sovereigntists, they blew their chances in 1995."

Right up until Christmas Eve, no political party had dared improvise in its campaign—except the Liberals, with their ill-advised ads based on a parody of the LNI improvisation theatre troupe. Paul Martin defended the virtues of a strong Canada supported by a strong central government, Stephen Harper became a friend of the provinces and Jack Layton supported the middle class. As for Gilles Duceppe, he presented himself as the sole champion of the interests of all Quebecers.

If an election is our society's ultimate democratic exercise, John Gomery, for his part, was now striving to restore the democratic balance in the administrative processes of government. The project appeared to be theoretical, but the task was highly practical.

Once again, however, the Liberals found themselves in an embarrassing position. An inflammatory book, published on the day of a televised leaders' debate, discredited all federalist forces put together. Invoices and cheques discovered by Normand Lester and Robin Philpot, the authors of *Les Secrets d'Option Canada*, supported the claim that the No Committee's activities had been illegally funded during the 1995 Québec referendum. The guilty party's name was simply Option Canada, but all this had yet to be proven. The authors demanded that public inquiries be held into the affair—still more inquiries!

Months beforehand, the commission had unearthed clues that led in the same direction. "François, we already knew about the existence of Option Canada," Bernard Roy was to tell me in January. "The scope of our mandate prevented us from taking this any further, though. Remember, in Ottawa? When he appeared on December 1, 2004, Roger Collet, ex-executive director of the Canada Information Office, said he was aware of a transfer of $5 million taken from the National Unity Reserve Fund and given to Heritage Canada. According to him, this same amount was relayed to Option Canada soon after, in 1995. Based on the allegations presented, that means that this reserve fund, which was under the authority of the Prime Minister's Office, was used for purposes other than the Sponsorship Program."

Pages 7,319 . . . 12,689 . . . 23,294 . . . As I jotted down the references to testimony transcriptions that Roy gave me, I couldn't help remembering how frustrated our investigators were, having to restrict their research to sponsorships and advertising activities. Indeed, they were much more intrigued by other examinations later in the proceedings. To begin with, there was Paul Martin. When Neil Finkelstein asked him whom he had consulted in preparing his testimony, the prime minister named five former assistants from Québec, including Claude Dauphin, ex-honorary president of Option Canada. Then, toward the end of the hearings, Yves Gougoux, president of the BCP agency, testified that he had been paid for advertising work commissioned by Option Canada during the referendum period of 1995.

At the end of our conversation Roy's last words sounded more like a wish than an order: "Make sure no one suspects us of not getting to the bottom of things and fulfilling our mandate."

Heaven knows we got to the bottom of things! Despite this, and even with the complete trust of Canadians, John Gomery probably disappointed many people in some respects. The inquiry was important for what it revealed to the commissioner, but it gave the public much to debate and speculate about. In exonerating Paul Martin in his first report, Gomery rested his case strictly on the evidence heard. This judicial rigour did not stop voters from making up their own minds on January 23, 2006. Indeed, if it was true that Gomery had inadvertently fired the starting gun for the election campaign by publishing his findings, it was also true that values and ethics remained one of the main planks in every party's platform right to the end.

The cocktail party was over at 8:00 PM and the guests began to leave—including Larue, who has since become an acquaintance. I had to admit that, fundamental as they may be, matters of integrity and transparency are only of passing interest to most people, something to fit into casual conversation. For those debating these questions thoroughly and openly, though, the truce stayed in place for a few more days.

During the following weeks, political storms broke one after the other, making the campaign an endless one for Liberals and a godsend for Conservatives. Opinion polls showed the wind shifting in early January, sweeping away previous survey results. Suddenly everything was up in the air. Which party would form the next government, and would it have a majority?

As in any close race, the federal administration perked up. Small groups of people in the major ministries began to examine the financial impact of the promises and commitments made by the Liberals and Conservatives—representing disbursements of over $100 billion—on existing programs. Based on the most realistic proposals, estimates were made of the budget allocations that the Treasury Board would need to approve.

As the election uncertainty grew, civil servants became increasingly anxious about a possible transfer of power and the urgent need to prepare background files on Cabinet and Privy Council ongoing business. In the same building where Sheila-Marie Cook and I handed over the first commission report, dozens of people were busy working on the future of the state—and theirs as well. Their efforts would be well underway come voting day.

John Gomery had extended his Christmas vacation in Europe by ten days, so it was impossible for him to keep abreast of the latest electoral developments. When he returned, he noticed immediately how volatile voters were about their intentions. This mattered little to him, though. He knew that public opinion is generally harsher or more lenient, depending on the case, than a judge rendering a decision. Having assigned the responsibility for the sponsorship scandal to certain individuals, he was not surprised when voters reacted on January 23 not to his findings, but to their own interpretation of them. His immediate concern was to gauge how Canadians would feel about his recommendations. In short, would his ideas make a difference? The scandal had helped launch a probing study into the balance and abuse of power. By decoding certain well-kept secrets, the commissioner had managed to shed light on the executive branch's ability to hide certain activities and keep the public in the dark. His inquiry now led him to the door behind which lie the keys to all of these powers: the office of the prime minister.

Over the last thirty years, the Prime Minister's Office has become the hub of decision making on all important issues. Its powers have become increasingly concentrated and far-reaching, to the point where the authority of other parliamentary institutions has been watered down.

In John Gomery's view, giving one office of government this much power alters the spirit and original design of our parliamentary system. As he finished writing his final report, Gomery shared his point of view with me. "Today, in Ottawa, the implementation of decisions becomes complicated insofar as the institutions responsible for approving the wishes of the executive branch have neither the resources nor the mechanisms needed to exercise any kind of control or study the matter. Take, for example, the budget of government expenditures in all its complexity, or program analysis. And what about the means provided to parliamentary committees? Do they really *have* the means? Once again, where are the control mechanisms?"

I told him it was my impression that the Canadian prime minister has powers that closely approximate those of an American president. "You know," he answered, "all the talk about our common interests with the president of the United States must have somehow coloured the way our recent prime ministers have used their power. A prime minister is not a head of state. That's the role of our governor general. And by the same token, he is not the counterpart of the American president."

And, with his signature grin, John Gomery added: "To get that far, he would have to trade in more than just golf balls, you know."

TWENTY-ONE

WHERE WAS PARLIAMENT?

THE VOTER TURNAROUND was firmly established, and the pace of the election campaign changed in its last few weeks. The volatile political mood of Canadians turned into a New Year's resolution for change, and opinion polls predicted a transfer of power to the Conservative Party. And the Gomery Commission's final report was scheduled to be submitted on February 1, only nine days after the election.

This prompted several questions from commission team. Would a new prime minister delay the tabling of the report? Would the report still be one of the government's priorities? Would Cabinet members be sworn in before the report was submitted? Would we have to wait until the House of Commons convened to release it? Each of these questions brought ten, fifteen or twenty different answers. Our meetings were devoted to imagining new scenarios and devising responses to them instead of planning our work. A few days before voters went to the polls, the commission made its decision and, with the assent of the Privy Council, confirmed that it would submit the report on the scheduled date of February 1. That day, the governor general of

Canada, Her Excellency Michaëlle Jean, would receive Commissioner Gomery's recommendations whether or not the new Cabinet was sworn in.

Over the course of these discussions, Sheila-Marie Cook and I tried to persuade the commissioner to meet the press. We thought the media deserved better than a simple statement marking the end of commission proceedings. From my point of view, there was much more at stake. The firm political will to follow up on the Gomery Report could be jeopardized by a change in government. With no guarantee that the new Cabinet would take action, we decided that John Gomery himself would have to present his report, *Restoring Accountability*. At the time, nothing was more important to us. We were beyond drawing up lists of party commitments made during the campaign. Our focus was elsewhere. Whether the winner was red, blue, tan or rainbow-coloured, our sole concern was what the government would do with the Gomery Report. Would all our work fade from memory, or end up on the table of a parliamentary committee responsible for debating the appropriateness and feasibility of its recommendations? The pessimists among us feared a "page turned, page forgotten" outcome.

Regardless of the new prime minister's intentions, I was convinced that an exclusive press conference given by the commissioner would, as a gesture of authority, represent a transfer of power in much the same way that political power would change hands in Ottawa.

To my surprise, the judge accepted my suggestion, but added a condition of his own. To make sure that reporters were fully prepared for the news conference, they must attend a lockup session on the report, much as we'd done when the first report was unveiled. This time, two hours would suffice, given the nature and treatment of the subject. I agreed, especially since this report, unlike the fact-finding report, did not contain the heavy concentration of evidence supplied by many individuals. On the contrary, the new document was concise, listing nineteen concrete recommendations on the functioning of government. However, the judge's outlook, approach and rationale in writing the report demanded careful reading if intelligent questions were to be asked. I had to temper my enthusiasm with one caution.

"I must remind you that the description of this part of your mandate stipulates that your recommendations should follow from the findings of your inquiry. To the press, I think it's essential that you refrain from referring to elements of your first report. Such caution is warranted by the fact that three motions against the commission and yourself are pending in Federal Court. As you know, even your sighs are being held against you in some of these motions."

He'd already considered the problem, of course. "I imagine you'll set a time limit on the press conference. For my part, I will discourage any references to last November's findings. I will stick to my recommendations, so that I don't put the new prime minister in an awkward position. What will you do with requests for interviews?"

"I couldn't agree more. Any additional remarks would likely be misinterpreted; given the sheer number of requests, we'd have to tour the country for months on end to grant them all! We can't do this on a case-by-case basis. It would be unfair, what with all the television and radio networks, each one with several shows, and the papers, magazines…"

Gomery slyly answered, "The commission will no longer exist on the very next day—February 2. Let's forget about touring the country, shall we?"

We then proceeded to prepare answers to the questions we expected journalists to ask, then developed a detailed press kit.

In restoring accountability, or recommending measures to make it possible, it is assumed that one knows *who is responsible*. The commission's academic approach to the seventeen studies it commissioned allowed John Gomery to identify measures needed to strengthen procedures and controls within the public service. With the precision of a neurosurgeon, he pinpointed the aneurysms in the administration, of which the sponsorship scandal was only a symptom. In his view, some existing laws and regulations could be modified; first, though, it was essential to enforce them. Moreover, the responsibility of civil servants assigned to programs, as well as that of deputy ministers and assistant deputy ministers, had to be better explained and, in some cases, clarified. A code of conduct or code of ethics would become a component of a public service charter and might even be included in the legislation. For those contravening the *Financial Administration Act*, the only sanction would be dismissal without financial compensation, once any wrongdoing was proven.

Beyond these practical considerations, the significance and value of the final report of the Commission of Inquiry into the Sponsorship Program and Advertising Activities is contained in the commissioner's recommendations. His analysis of the structures of our parliamentary democracy led him to a number of surprising discoveries.

"Where were the members of Parliament when sponsorships were swallowing up hundreds of millions of dollars? Do they not have the right and the duty to watch over government spending of public funds in all circumstances?"

Rather than accusing anyone of negligence, the judge pointed out that the distribution of powers and means between the executive branch and parliamentary institutions is unbalanced. The balance must be adjusted. How are the government and Parliament to work together? While we were preparing the press conference, John Gomery mentioned the adoption of budget expenditures as an example. "It takes months of work and preparation before a project is presented to Cabinet. Each department produces estimates, then modifies them according to the parameters received. Following this, the Treasury Board compiles and adapts the data, under the watchful eye of the

Privy Council. Once the Prime Minister's Office has approved it, the next step is to obtain parliamentary sanction. The schedule for this phase is very tight, leaving little time for revisions by the parliamentary committee and adoption by the House."

Two other measures are therefore urgently needed, Gomery believes. First of all, members of the Public Accounts Committee need to serve for a longer time and acquire more experience. Second, legislation is required to establish an official paper trail—a record of decisions made, including relevant documents. In short, parliamentary institutions need to put in place a process of storage and analysis that allows Parliament to review government activities without having to summon up another Gomery Commission.

These essential recommendations for improving the state management system, though, seem secondary compared to the deep unease that haunts the judge at his writing table. The Privy Council is apparently a nerve centre of conflicting roles, a bottleneck in the system that the clerk can tighten as he sees fit. His authority reaches far and wide—he is a power broker. He is secretary to the Cabinet, the prime minister's deputy minister and the head of the federal public service, entitled to oversee the hiring and posting of deputy ministers who, without exception, will be required to demonstrate their loyalty to him later on. For the commissioner, it's high time this stronghold surrendered to the forces of parliamentary democracy and gave up some of its prerogatives. According to Gomery, the Treasury Board should head up the federal public service. Similarly, the government should stop interfering with the boards of Crown corporations. If an independent committee were to oversee board appointments, all acts of favouritism would cease.

The sum of the proposed changes represents an unprecedented cultural upheaval of Ottawa's government system—the overthrowing of a highly centralized administrative regime.

As had been expected, many voters flirted with political change. On January 23, the Conservatives took power with a weak minority government, with 124 seats out of 308. The new prime minister can expect to run the country "under tight surveillance." This is the way Stephen Harper described the watchful eyes of the three other parties in the House, not to mention the Liberal stranglehold on federal institutions. At the outset, he drew up a list of priorities and set the transfer of power in motion. The Gomery Report probably did not top his list of immediate concerns. In any case, he would have to wait eight days before reading it. Yet on the evening of his election victory, he reiterated before his followers in Calgary that his government would give priority to ethics and transparency. His closest advisors had predicted a Conservative breakthrough in Québec on the heels of the sponsorship scandal, and Harper spoke French when he announced his intention to table legislation on accountability in the near future.

This statement, contained in Stephen Harper's first speech as prime minister, raised my hopes, and those of many other members of the commission team, that a quick, effective response to Gomery's recommendations would be forthcoming. Some of my other fears—that because the Conservatives had held power for far fewer years than the Liberals, they would have to nurture their working relationships with bureaucrats to gain their trust and co-operation— were also partly allayed. The Gomery Report deals with a situation that most civil servants in Ottawa would like clarified: the state of their working relationship with chiefs of staff. This key administrative position was instituted during the Mulroney years, and now another Conservative government would be called upon to respond to a judge's recommendations on the subject.

John Gomery recommends enforcing a code of conduct for political staff. For ministerial workers seeking a permanent position in the civil service, he recommends implementing a tightly run competitive process that is shielded from all political interference. He also recommends that when a deputy minister is to be selected, an official open competition be held until the appointment is made. Once hired, this person would be required to stay in the department for at least three years, to ensure management continuity. In accepting these two recommendations of the Gomery Report, I believe the government can get off to a good start in its dealings with its civil servants and allow the wounds opened by the inquiry to heal. But of course I'm expressing my own bias in favour of the commissioner.

Either way, Prime Minister Harper's resolve to act quickly was reassuring, as minority governments rarely last more than two years. The term in office is short and the task enormous until the next election.

As early as December 2005, well before opinion polls showed that voters' intentions suggested a Conservative victory, John Gomery decided that the measures he proposed would have to be binding. To be assured of a government's commitment, he believed, you often need a deadline. "No need to predict whether the January vote will be a majority or a minority win; the next government will, I hope, make my report a priority."

While rereading the document with this in mind, the commissioner added a nineteenth point to his eighteen recommendations, stating that twenty-four months was in his view sufficient time to implement the main recommendations in his report. The answer to this will come from Stephen Harper.

TWENTY-TWO

FINALMENTE, L'ITALIA E LE VACANZE!

"**G**OOD EVENING! I reserved a table for four. *Buonasera! Ho prenotato...
un tavolo...per quattro.*"

"Your friends are expecting you at the table at the back. *I vostri
amici...vi aspettano...al tavolo...in fondo.*"

Sporting earphones and deep in concentration, John Gomery
repeated the commonplace, if potentially useful, phrases in a meticulous, clipped voice. In a few days, they'll be in Sicily, with its mountain
landscapes and blue seas. The second half of the three-month trip will
take place in a villa between Tuscany and Umbria, where friends who
wish to drop in have been forewarned: this is strictly vacation time,
please! Gomery chose the place and the time to unwind so he could
avoid an abrupt return to work in September. This is not early retirement, he insists. Are you kidding? He intends to devote the last ten
months of his career to his work as a judge, something he still loves to
do. But until then, how do you recover from all this media coverage?
A complete withdrawal into anonymity seems unlikely. Invitations to
conferences and debates of all sorts have been pouring in for months.

Would everyone please let the commissioner just return to being a judge? From now on, he wants only one thing: to divest himself of the public persona he's had to adopt.

"What was the worst thing you had to deal with as head of this commission?" Given the number and variety of roadblocks he had encountered over the last two years, I was convinced this was a tricky question. The answer surprised me.

"Obviously, that I've lost my privacy. At first the attention was exciting, but I soon realized just how much I missed my life before the commission. Public recognition is flattering but unnatural. It was no doubt a condition of the job, but I wasn't prepared for it."

As I write the final pages of this book, I can appreciate one aspect of the man's personality that escaped me during those two intense years. He had accepted his mandate as a professional challenge, the crowning achievement of his career. He never expected the challenges presented by the high visibility of the commission and the heated political controversy generated by its work.

"Surely you found that some achievements were more gratifying than others."

"The way the commission fuelled the public's indignation. You know, a scandal can't be explained; it breaks out, and anyone can interpret it using ready-made concepts. With the media's help, our proceedings allowed people to vent their anger. When the inquiry was over, once those responsible for the wrongdoing were singled out, in a way we helped re-establish the reputation of the entire public service. They deserved it."

"Nothing more personal?"

"Recognition by my peers—that is important at the end of a career. According to several of my colleagues, the importance of my role and my performance as commissioner highlighted the value of judicial work. Let's face it, judges don't always come off as very dynamic. Yet

I acted as I always have, and I don't think I'm any different from my colleagues on the bench."

After submitting his second report, Gomery promised himself that he would no longer dwell on the sponsorship affair or its consequences. This is understandable, especially with that black cloud hanging over his head—the motions by Jean Chrétien, Jean Pelletier and Alfonso Gagliano, which he is watching out of the corner of his eye. It will take time for the Federal Court to render decisions on the motions alleging that Commissioner Gomery was biased or could be perceived as being biased. As the commission ceased to exist on February 2, 2006, the commissioner will not be able to defend himself. He will have to leave that task to government attorneys.

I know he is preparing a lecture that he will give at McGill University in the days preceding his departure. He plans to speak on the positive contribution of commissions of inquiry to Canadian democracy. He couldn't resist that invitation.

"Pros and Cons of Holding Commissions of Inquiry" is his chosen subject, in response to many comments from defence counsel criticizing the powers conferred on commissioners and the framework of procedures established for commissions of inquiry. Critics contend the pressure exerted by the media, the laxity of rules for the admission of evidence and the broad scope allowed for examinations can cause excessive damage to an individual's reputation.

"Defence counsel, more so than Crown attorneys, are used to presenting their points of view to the media," Gomery said, "and in a way I think the high visibility of my commission requires a response."

He would definitely respond, always attentive to the concerns of the public. His claim is that the four hundred or so provincial and federal commissions of inquiry created since Confederation have been beneficial for the most part, helping to maintain a balance between individual rights and the collective interest. Even though commission rules and procedures are such that a commission has more leeway to cut corners than a real trial, it speaks directly to Canadians and can help explain facts and events, transforming the public mood from exasperation to comprehension. Some commissions must deal with issues that are more political in nature, making it more difficult, but at the same time more important, to honour their mandate: "Take, for example, two commissions in the 1990s, the one presided over by Judge Gilles Létourneau, on the role of the Canadian Forces during the peace mission in Somalia, and the one presided over by Judge Horace M. Krever on the use of tainted blood products. Here were two extremely alarming public issues, two cases that had to be elucidated before measures could be taken to avoid a repeat occurrence. In both cases, only the proceedings of a commission of inquiry were able to reassure Canadians."

I had to agree with him. The crisis generated by the sponsorship scandal had turned our commission into a last hope for a majority of Canadians, who counted on John Gomery to uncover and clarify the facts. Even before the hearings began, public confidence could no longer be restored by one politician's rhetorical victory over another, nor could it recover through public debate in the context of such deep divisions. In fact, only our commission's work could reassure Canadians. The moral authority of the judicial system prevailed.

Several of the commissioner's counsel quietly criticized him for worrying too much about press coverage. They thought he was exaggerating and saw it as a weakness, a form of vanity. I watched him dissect many a news summary of the hearings, which in my view were a way for him to gauge the balance between legitimate public curiosity and the vulnerability of certain reputations. Some witnesses did suffer collateral damage, just because they happened to corroborate what others had already admitted. Simply being called before the commission was, temporarily, cause for suspicion. When revelations were plentiful, Gomery worried at least about the useless duplication of testimony. Dredging for facts was no excuse for succumbing to a form of McCarthyism. "One element of proof is enough. Can this next witness really bring something new to the same question?"

In searching for the truth, the whole truth and nothing but the truth, John Gomery ensured that the inquiry was fair, making sure that Canadians did not confuse the guilty with the victims. He always made a point of taking account of the evidence presented, nothing more.

Discussion surrounding the commission often confused the meanings of words, or blurred the distinctions between motives and causes, intentions and observations. Contrary to what some have written and said, the Gomery Commission was not responsible for overthrowing the government that created it. Rather, it was the scandal the commission investigated that hastened the government's fall. As the commission was not a court of law, it did not have the authority to launch legal proceedings. For that reason, it avoided all questions concerning legal proceedings that some of its witnesses were facing. Finally, the commission could not guarantee that its efforts in consulting experts and members of the public on good government would lead to real changes in the federal administration. All it could do was recommend.

Was the Gomery Commission necessary, then? In my view, it gave us what many other commissions have delivered: a rendering of the facts devoid of any bias, allowing us to comprehend why certain events occurred and how they were allowed to happen. In the case of a trial, the case is closed the day the judgment is handed down. In the case of the commission, we all learned from the experience and gave our own verdicts. The sponsorship affair will never be closed insofar as those who followed the inquiry will retain certain facts and keep an eye on the future. In many respects, the Gomery Commission tested our democratic values and our social and political systems. At the very least, it reminded us of how important those systems are.

As we met for the last time, and for no better reason than my wish to see him again in a few months, I asked John Gomery what his thoughts might be later on, with the benefit of hindsight. I interpreted his quick response as a positive one. With his contagious smile, Gomery now talked only about his holiday in Italy. Between the lines, I could appreciate the joy of a man returning to all he had been obliged to abandon for two years. The family reunions with grandchildren excitedly running about, his farm and its demanding chores, his friends, books and concerts, everything suddenly coming neatly back into place, in the harmony that he'd arranged long ago. As with music, life and ideas need silence to grow.

APPENDICES

APPENDIX I

MISSION AND GOALS OF THE GOMERY COMMISSION

THE COMMISSION OF INQUIRY on the Sponsorship Program and Advertising Activities was given a twofold mandate in February 2004. Following are the mission and goals of the commission as Justice John Gomery understood them and published them in his *Fact Finding Report* of November 1, 2005.

•

THE SCOPE OF the Commission is determined by the mandate, that I interpret as requiring me to accomplish two distinct but related tasks.

Firstly, in what I call Phase I, I must investigate and report on questions raised, directly or indirectly, by Chapters 3 and 4 of the November 2003 Report of the Auditor General of Canada to the House of Commons with regard to the sponsorship program and advertising activities of the Government of Canada, including the way and the reasons for which they were created, implemented and managed, as well as the way the corresponding funds were spent. As previously mentioned, Phase I will include public hearings in Ottawa and Montreal, followed by a report that I hope to submit to the Governor-in-Council on November 1, 2005 at the latest.

Secondly, following paragraph b of the mandate, I must make recommendations based on the findings of fact from Phase I, with a view to avoiding this type of problem. This will make up Phase II, during which I plan to ask experts to prepare studies on various subjects, and hear and receive the comments of people and organizations authorized to participate in Phase II. Moreover, I plan to hold public consultations to collect the comments of citizens. I hope to submit my second report containing my recommendations to the Governor-in-Council on February 1, 2006.

The issues that must be examined during Phases IA and IB, according to my interpretation of the mandate given to me, are listed below:

ISSUES LIST OF PHASE IA

1. the creation, purpose and objectives of the sponsorship program;
2. the role and responsibility of elected and non-elected public office holders and others in the government and Parliament of Canada, including Crown entities (collectively the "Government of Canada"), as well as others outside the Government of Canada, in the creation of the sponsorship program, the selection of communications and advertising agencies (including the creation, purpose and objectives of the advertising program), and the management of the sponsorship program and advertising activities of the Government of Canada (collectively the "activities");
3. whether Parliament was bypassed and, if so, by whom and on what basis;
4. whether there was political influence involved in the activities and, if so, by whom, to what purpose, and to what effect;

5. whether any person or organization in the Government of Canada gained an advantage financially, politically or otherwise from the activities and, if so, who, to what purpose, and to what effect;

6. whether the procedures, structures, reporting lines, systems for approvals and internal controls which were implemented by the Government of Canada in the activities were sufficient and, if not, why not and to what purpose and effect. This will involve an assessment of the normal procedures, structures, reporting lines, systems for approvals and internal controls, or other potentially applicable standards, for procurement programs and selections of service providers for activities of a similar nature, and whether there were deviations in the activities from normal procedures, structures, reporting lines, systems for approvals and internal controls;

7. whether there was compliance with normally applicable rules, regulations, standards and guidelines, including the *Financial Administration Act* and other relevant instruments and, if not, in what manner was there non-compliance, and to what effect;

8. whether the culture and structure in the Government of Canada discouraged whistleblowing;

9. the path of the funds, including the approvals and procedures in relation thereto, within the Government of Canada to the point that these funds were disbursed to non-Government of Canada sources.

ISSUES LIST OF PHASE IB

1. the identity of those who received the sponsorship, communications and advertising funds, including any commissions or fees payable with respect to them (hereinafter "the funds"), the purpose for which the funds were disbursed, and the extent of value for money received in return by the Government of Canada, the latter term as defined in the Issues List for Phase IA, item 2;

2. whether there was political influence on the distribution of the funds, including questions relating to whether there were direct or indirect political contributions or gifts made by recipients of the funds;

3. whether there were sufficient external monitoring and financial controls used by fund recipients described in 1 above; if not, why not and to what effect.

APPENDIX 2

THE GOMERY COMMISSION BY THE NUMBERS

- The Commission held 136 days of public hearings in Ottawa and Montreal.
- 172 witnesses were heard.
- From 1994 to 2003, the Government of Canada allocated $332 million to special and sponsorship programs, including $147 million in fees and commissions paid to public relations and advertising agencies.
- The federal government is one of the most important advertisers in Canada. Between April 1994 and March 2003, it awarded a total of $1.1 billion in advertising contracts.
- 62 lawyers were registered for the proceedings of the commission.
- Photocopies produced during 10 months of hearings amounted to 9 million sheets of paper, which filled 1,800 boxes.
- Transcriptions of hearings filled 28,000 pages.
- Contrary to several allegations, the total cost of the two years of proceedings of the Gomery Commission amounted to $30 million, as expected.

- Investigators handled 7,000 boxes of documents to prepare examinations and assemble evidence to be filed before the commission.
- The commissioner's notes taken during the hearings filled five black notebooks.

APPENDIX 3

ADVISORY COMMITTEE

IN JUNE 2005, Commissioner Gomery announced the appointment of an advisory committee to assist him with the second phase of his mandate. Following is the text of the press release issued for the occasion.

JUNE 22, 2005 (OTTAWA): Mr. Justice John H. Gomery announced today the appointment of an Advisory Committee to assist him with Phase II: the Recommendations Phase of the Commission's mandate. "My mandate authorizes me to establish an advisory committee of distinguished Canadians to provide advice and guidance for Phase II. I am called upon to make recommendations to the Government of Canada, based upon the findings of fact, to prevent mismanagement of sponsorship programs and advertising activities in the future," said Justice Gomery. The Commissioner is required to submit a report of his recommendations, which is separate from the report of Phase I: the Fact-Finding Phase.

The Committee will be chaired by Raymond Garneau, former Chairman of the Board of Industrial-Alliance Life Insurance Company, and includes the Hon. Roch Bolduc, Mr. D. Bevis Dewar, the Hon. John A. Fraser, the Hon. Constance R. Glube, Dr. John E. Hodgetts and Dr. Carolle Simard. Ex-officio members of the Committee are Sheila-Marie Cook, Executive Director and Commission Secretary, and Donald Savoie, Special Advisor and Director of Research.

The Committee will act primarily as advisors to the Commissioner but will also participate in the research programme and consultations. "These individuals bring a collective and specialized expertise in government, at both the political and bureaucratic levels, and from academia. They will contribute in a very substantial way to the fulfillment of my mandate," said Justice Gomery.

APPENDIX 4

EXPERT ROUND TABLE PARTICIPANTS

THE SECOND PHASE of the commissioner's mandate consisted in presenting solutions to clarify the distribution of responsibilities between the administrative and executive branches of government. To this end, the commission held round tables in five Canadian cities. Here is the list of participants in the round tables.

MONCTON

- Derek Burney, Chairman of the Board of Directors, New Brunswick Power; former chief of staff to Prime Minister Brian Mulroney.
- Spencer Campbell, partner in the law firm Stewart McKelvey Stirling Scales and former chief of staff to the Premier of Prince Edward Island.
- Honourable John C. Crosbie, Chancellor of Memorial University and, notably, former federal Cabinet Minister of Finance and Justice in the Mulroney government.
- Pierre Foucher, Professor, University of Moncton, School of Law.

- Paul Howe, former Research Director at the Institute for Research on Public Policy in Montreal.
- Dean Jobb, former reporter, editor and columnist at the *Halifax Herald*.
- Aldéa Landry, lawyer and businesswoman, former Cabinet Minister and Deputy Premier of New Brunswick.
- Honourable Donald H. Oliver, Senator and Counsel with Power, Dempsey, Cooper & Leefe.
- Wynne Potter, member of the Board of Genome Atlantic, formerly with the Atlantic Canada Opportunities Agency.
- Gordon Slade, Executive Director of ONE OCEAN and former Deputy Minister of Fisheries for Newfoundland and Labrador.
- Jennifer Smith, Chair of Political Science, Dalhousie University.

QUÉBEC CITY

- Denis Desautels, chartered accountant and former Auditor General of Canada.
- Alain Dubuc, former editor-in-chief of *La Presse* and former President and Publisher of *Le Soleil*.
- Honourable Marc Lalonde, former advisor to Prime Minister Lester B. Pearson and former Principal Secretary to Prime Minister Pierre Elliott Trudeau before serving as Minister of National Health and Welfare, Justice, Energy, Mines and Resources, and Finance.
- Vincent Lemieux, Professor Emeritus at Laval University and former President of the Canadian Political Science Association.
- Marcel Proulx, Director General of l'École nationale d'administration publique. He advises many departments and organizations in Québec on the topic of organizational dynamics and public administration.
- F. Leslie Seidle, Senior Research Associate at the Institute for Research on Public Policy and Senior Research Fellow for the Centre for Research and Information on Canada.

- Honourable Paul Tellier, Director of several Canadian companies, former Clerk of the Privy Council.
- Diane Wilhelmy, consultant in public administration and Director of a research centre at l'École nationale d'administration publique.

- Honourable Jean-Jacques Blais, counsel, former Solicitor General of Canada, Minister of Supply and Services and National Defence.
- Patrick Boyer, journalist, lawyer and teacher; he served as Parliamentary Secretary to the Minister of External Affairs and to the Minister of National Defence.
- Robert Giroux, Chair of the Canadian Council of Learning and Senior Fellow with the School of Public Policy, University of Ottawa.
- Arthur Kroeger, Chair of the Canadian Policy Research Networks and the National Statistics Council; he served as Deputy Minister for six federal departments.
- Claire Morris, President and CEO of the Association of Universities and Colleges of Canada; she also served as President of the Canadian Employment Insurance Commission.
- Honourable Barbara McDougall, Director of a number of Canadian corporations; she is also a former Minister of External Affairs, Employment and Immigration, Privatization and Regulatory Affairs and former President of the Canadian Institute of International Affairs.
- Honourable Gordon Osbaldeston, who has been in public service for over thirty years. After his retirement, he served on the Board of Directors of numerous Canadian companies.
- Lorne Sossin, Associate Dean of Law, University of Toronto; former Clerk to the Chief Justice of the Supreme Court of Canada.

- Hugh Winsor, visiting fellow to the Institute of Policy Studies at Queen's University, former Ottawa bureau chief for the *Globe and Mail.*

EDMONTON

- Honourable Harvie Andre, former federal Cabinet Minister of Supply and Services, and Consumer and Corporate Affairs, former Government House Leader; currently Chairman of Bow Energy Resources.
- Barry Cooper, Professor, Department of Political Science, University of Calgary.
- Gary Dickson, one of the foremost experts from the West on privacy; currently Information and Privacy Commissioner for the province of Saskatchewan.
- Rod Love, advisor for eighteen years to Prime Minister Ralph Klein of Alberta; currently works as a consultant.
- Robert Marleau, a specialist on parliamentary practice and procedure; advisor for over thirty years to seven Speakers of the House and Commons and to members of the House of Commons and the Senate.
- Ian McClelland, former Member of Parliament, former Member of the Alberta Legislative Assembly.
- David Smith, Professor Emeritus of Political Science at the University of Saskatchewan, a specialist in the structure of government, the Crown and federalism.

VANCOUVER

- Honourable Pat Carney, former federal Cabinet Minister of Energy, Mines and Resources and International Trade (in charge of negotiating the Free Trade Agreement). She also served as President of the Treasury Board.

- R. Kenneth Carty, former Head of Political Science, University of British Colombia, and former President of the Canadian Political Science Association.
- Honourable Herb Dhaliwal, former Member of Parliament, former federal Cabinet Minister of Revenue Canada, Fisheries and Oceans, and Natural Resources.
- Gordon Gibson, former Leader of the Liberal Party of British Columbia, former special assistant to former Prime Minister Pierre Elliott Trudeau.
- David A. Good, former federal Assistant Deputy Minister at the Privy Council Office, currently teaches at the School of Public Administration, University of Victoria.
- Rafe Mair, well-known political commentator, journalist and author from British Columbia who writes on political issues.
- Cynthia Williams, former federal Assistant Deputy Minister of several departments, in particular Cooperative and Community Development, Human Resources Development Canada and the Atlantic Canada Opportunities Agency.

APPENDIX 5

SUMMARY OF THE RECOMMENDATIONS
OF THE FINAL REPORT

O N FEBRUARY 1ST, 2006, Commissioner John Gomery filed his final report, Commission of Inquiry into the Sponsorship Program and Advertising Activities, *Restoring Accountability: Recommendations,* in which he presented the Canadian government with his recommendations to prevent any such wrongdoing in the future. Following is a summary of the recommendations.

•

RECOMMENDATION 1: To redress the imbalance between the resources available to the government and those available to parliamentary committees and their members, the Government should substantially increase funding for parliamentary committees.

RECOMMENDATION 2: The government should adopt legislation to entrench into law a Public Service Charter.

RECOMMENDATION 3: To enable the Public Accounts Committee to perform its responsibilities more effectively, the government should increase its funding substantially to provide the committee with its own research personnel, legal and administrative staff, and experts as needed.

RECOMMENDATION 4: In order to clear up confusion over the respective responsibilities and accountability of ministers and civil servants, the government should modify its policies and publications to explicitly acknowledge and declare that deputy ministers and senior public servants who have statutory responsibility are accountable in their own right for their statutory and delegated responsibilities before the Public Accounts Committee.

RECOMMENDATION 5: The government should establish a formal process by which a minister is able to overrule a deputy minister's objection to a proposed course of action in an area of jurisdiction over which the deputy minister possesses statutory or delegated powers. The decision of the minister should be recorded in correspondence to be transmitted by the deputy minister concerned to the comptroller general in the Treasury Board Secretariat, and be available there for examination by the Office of the Auditor General.

RECOMMENDATION 6: The government should adopt as a policy that deputy ministers and senior public servants are appointed to their positions for a minimum of three years, with the expectation that a standard appointment would normally have a duration of at least five years. In cases where it is deemed necessary to derogate from this policy, the government should be required to explain publicly the reason for such a derogation. The government should take the steps to apply the same policy to assistant deputy ministers.

RECOMMENDATION 7: Members of the Public Accounts Committee should be appointed with the expectation that they will serve on the committee for the duration of a Parliament.

RECOMMENDATION 8: The Public Accounts Committee should ensure that deputy ministers, other heads of agencies and senior officials are the witnesses called to testify before it. As a general principle, ministers should not be witnesses before the committee.

RECOMMENDATION 9: Special reserves should be managed by a central agency experienced in administrative procedures, such as the Treasury Board or the Department of Finance. The government should be required at least once a year to table a report in the House of Commons on the status of each reserve, the criteria employed in funding decisions and the use of the funds.

RECOMMENDATION 10: The government should remove the provision in the law and in its policies that enables exempt staff members to be appointed to a position in the public service without competition after having served in a minister's office for three years.

RECOMMENDATION 11: The government should prepare and adopt a code of conduct for exempt staff that includes provisions stating that exempt staff have no authority to give direction to public servants and that ministers are fully responsible and accountable for the actions of exempt staff. On confirmation of their hiring, all exempt staff should be required to attend a training program to learn the most important aspects of public administration.

RECOMMENDATION 12: The government should adopt an open and competitive process for the selection of deputy ministers, similar to the model used in Alberta.

RECOMMENDATION 13: The functions and titles of the clerk of the Privy Council should be redefined, by legislation if necessary. The title of this official should be "Secretary to the Cabinet," and his or her main role should be to represent the public service to the prime minister and the Cabinet. The designations "Clerk of the Privy Council" and "Deputy Minister to the Prime Minister" should be abolished. The Privy Council Office should be renamed the "Cabinet Secretariat." The secretary of the Treasury Board should assume the title and function of "Head of the Public Service."

RECOMMENDATION 14: The government should amend its current definition of "advertising" to conform to accepted advertising industry standards, and the new definition should be promulgated in the Government of Canada Communications Policy and related documents.

RECOMMENDATION 15: The registrar of lobbyists should report directly to Parliament on matters concerning the application and enforcement of the *Lobbyists Registration Act*, and the Office of the Registrar of Lobbyists should be provided with sufficient resources to enable it to publicize and enforce the requirements of the Act, including investigation and prosecution by its own personnel. The limitation period for investigation and prosecution should be increased from two to five years from the time the registrar becomes aware of an infringement.

RECOMMENDATION 16: The government should adopt legislation requiring public servants to document decisions and recommendations, and making it an offence to fail to do so or to destroy documentation recording government decisions, or the advice and deliberations leading up to decisions.

RECOMMENDATION 17: The *Financial Administration Act* should be amended to add a new section stipulating that deliberate violation of section 34 of the Act by an employee of the federal government is grounds for dismissal without compensation.

RECOMMENDATION 18: The chief executive officer of a Crown corporation should be appointed, evaluated from time to time and, if deemed advisable, dismissed by the board of directors of that corporation. Initial appointments to the board of directors of a Crown corporation should be made by the government on the basis of merit. Thereafter, the remaining directors should be responsible for filling any vacancies on a corporation's board.

•

IN ADDITION TO these recommendations, the Commission wishes to establish a reasonable timeframe for their consideration and implementation.

RECOMMENDATION 19: Within twenty-four months of receiving this report, the government should table before Parliament a report detailing how it has dealt with each of the commission's recommendations.

THE KOREAN WAR

Max Hastings, author of over twenty books, was editor of the *Daily Telegraph* for almost a decade, then for six years edited the *Evening Standard* in London. In his youth he was a foreign correspondent for newspapers and BBC television. He has won many awards for his journalism, particularly his work in the South Atlantic in 1982. He was knighted in 2002.

Also in the Pan Military Classics Series

ABSOLUTE WAR
Chris Bellamy

THE BATTLE FOR THE FALKLANDS
Max Hastings

BOMBER COMMAND
Max Hastings

COLDITZ
Major P. R. Reid

DAS REICH
Max Hastings

THE DAM BUSTERS
Paul Brickhill

DEFEAT INTO VICTORY
Field Marshal Viscount Slim

THE LONELY LEADER
Alistair Horne

OVERLORD
Max Hastings

MAX HASTINGS

THE KOREAN WAR

PAN MILITARY CLASSICS

PAN BOOKS

First published 1987 by Michael Joseph Limited

This edition published 2010 by Pan Books
an imprint of Pan Macmillan
20 New Wharf Road, London N1 9RR
Associated companies throughout the world
www.panmacmillan.com

ISBN 978-0-330-51365-4

Copyright © Max Hastings 1987

The right of Max Hastings to be identified as the
author of this work has been asserted by him in accordance
with the Copyright, Designs and Patents Act 1988.

13

A CIP catalogue record for this book is available from
the British Library.

Typeset by SetSystems Ltd, Saffron Walden, Essex
Printed and bound by CPI Group (UK) Ltd, Croydon, CR0 4YY

Visit www.panmacmillan.com to read more about all our books
and to buy them. You will also find features, author interviews and
news of any author events, and you can sign up for e-newsletters
so that you're always first to hear about our new releases.

To

Charlotte

Contents

List of illustrations

PLATES

31. (a) Chinese infantry making a night advance. (*Chinese National Army Museum*)

    (b) Chinese infantry laying Russian-made boxmines. (*Chinese National Army Museum*)

32. The air war: (a) Communist pilots being briefed. (*Chinese National Army Museum*)

    (b) The MiG 15. (*Jane's Defence Weekly*)

    (c) The Sabre. (*The Bettmann Archive*)

    (d) A flight deck mishap on HMS *Ocean* off Korea. (*Imperial War Museum*)

    (e) A North Korean bridge. (*Imperial War Museum*)

33. Exhausted men of British 29 Brigade, April 1951. (*Imperial War Museum*)

34. President Syngman Rhee with General James Van Fleet. (*National Archives*)

35. Troglodyte warfare: (a) A British mortar position. (*Imperial War Museum*)

    (b) Chinese soldiers in one of the network of tunnels on the communist line. (*Chinese National Army Museum*)

36. British soldiers help to bring in a wounded American. (*Imperial War Museum*)

37. ROK and American troops on the move. (*Imperial War Museum*)

38. Artillery in action:

    (a) UN. (*Popperfoto*)

    (b) Chinese. (*Camera Press*)

39. A British doctor treats a wounded Chinese prisoner. (*Imperial War Museum*)

40. Behind the lines:

    (a) British conscripts take a beer.

    (b) Australians take a shower. (*Imperial War Museum*)

41. Private William Speakman, V.C. (*Imperial War Museum*)

42. Helicopter casevac. (*Imperial War Museum*)

43. President-elect Dwight D. Eisenhower. (*Imperial War Museum*)

44. Chinese propaganda picture of UN prisoners. (*Chinese National Army Museum*)

45. Repatriation for communist prisoners. (*National Archives*)
    Copyright owners are indicated in brackets.

MAPS

KOREA

Foreword

In the past twenty years, the public fascination with military history has become a minor literary phenomenon on both sides of the Atlantic. It has centred overwhelmingly upon the Second World War. Indeed, at the extremities of the popular market, perceptions of the struggle between the Western Allies and the Germans long ago parted company with reality, and took on the mantle of fantasy borne a generation earlier by cowboys and indians. In the past decade, more surprisingly, Vietnam has also given birth to a major publishing industry. Some new books seek seriously to examine why the United States lost that war. Others, like the films they inspire, attempt to rewrite history, to present aspects of that sordid, doomed struggle in an heroic light.

How is it, then, that the other great mid-twentieth-century conflict with communism, Korea, remains so neglected? Popular awareness of the Korean War today centres upon the television comedy show M.A.S.H., which dismays most veterans because it projects an image of Korea infinitely less savage than that which they recall. The United Nations suffered 142,000 casualties in the war to save South Korea from communist domination. The Koreans themselves lost at least a million people. United States losses in three years were only narrowly outstripped by those suffered in Vietnam over more than ten. Korea cost the British three times as many dead as the Falklands War. Chinese casualties remain uncertain, perhaps even in Peking, but they run into many hundreds of thousands. Since 1945, only the Cuban missile crisis has created a greater risk of nuclear war between East and West. As some recent scholarly researchers have pointed out, notable among them Dr

Rosemary Foot in her fascinating *The Wrong War*, in Korea the American military displayed a far greater private enthusiasm for using atomic weapons against the Chinese than the Western world perceived, even a generation later. Korea remains the only conflict since 1945 in which the armies of two great powers – for surely China's size confers that title – have met on the battlefield.

Many Westerners were happy to forget Korea for a generation after the war ended, soured by the taste of costly stalemate, robbed of any hint of glory. Yet consider the extraordinary cast of American characters that came together to determine the fate of that barren Asian peninsula: Truman and Acheson, Marshall and MacArthur, Ridgway and Bradley. Then add the succession of great military dramas – the destruction of Task Force Smith, the defence of the Pusan Perimeter, Inchon, the drive to the Yalu, the shattering winter advance of the Chinese. A host of lesser epics followed, which may be allowed to include the stand of the British 29 Brigade on the Imjin in April 1951, an action relatively minor in scale, yet the ferocity of which caught the imagination of the world. The fascination of Korea centres, more than anything, upon the battlefield confrontation between the armies of China and the United States. But the tragedy of the Korean people, the principal sufferers in the three-year struggle across their land, deserves far greater attention than it has been granted.

Above all, perhaps, Korea merits close consideration as a military rehearsal for the subsequent disaster in Vietnam. So many of the ingredients of the Indochina tragedy were already visible a decade or two earlier in Korea: the political difficulty of sustaining an unpopular and autocratic regime; the problems of creating a credible local army in a corrupt society; the fateful cost of underestimating the power of an Asian communist army. For all the undoubted benefits of air superiority and close support, Korea vividly displayed the difficulties of using air power effectively against a primitive economy, a peasant army. The war also demonstrated the problem of deploying a highly mechanised Western army in broken country, against a lightly equipped foe. Many of the American professional soldiers who served under MacArthur or Ridgway did so later under Westmoreland or Abrams. When they reminisce about the campaigns of 1950–53, it is striking how frequently slips of the tongue cause them to substitute 'Vietnam' for 'Korea' in their conversation.

Yet because it proved possible finally to stabilise the battle in Korea on terms which allowed the United Nations – or more realistically, the United States – to deploy its vast firepower from fixed positions, to defeat the advance of the massed communist armies, many of the lessons of Korea were misunderstood, or not learned at all. For instance, Pentagon studies showed during Korea, just as they had during World War II, that it was America's lower socio-economic groups which bore the chief burden of fighting the war, and above all of filling the ranks of the infantry. Yet the same phenomenon would recur in Vietnam, and the serious shortcomings of the American footsoldier – the man at the tip of the spear – would once more have critical consequences. In Korea, the communists enjoyed the opportunity to learn a great deal about the limits of Western patience, the difficulties of maintaining popular enthusiasm for an uncertain cause in a democracy. By the time the armistice was signed at Panmunjom in August 1953, after a mere three years of hostilities, the Western Allies had become desperate to extricate themselves from a thankless war that offered so little prospect of glory or clear-cut victory. Yet in Korea, the communists had provided the most ruthlessly simple *casus belli*, the most incontrovertible provocation by aggression, to be offered to the West at any period between 1945 and this time of writing.

As in my past books, I have sought to explore the Korean War through a combination of personal interviews with surviving participants, and archival research in London and Washington. In the course of writing it, I have met more than two hundred American, Canadian, British, and Korean veterans of the conflict. Perhaps the most exciting aspect of my research has been the opportunity to talk to Chinese veterans, granted to me in 1985 through the good offices of the Peking Institute of Strategic Studies, and the help of the late and much-lamented Colonel Jonathan Alford of the International Institute of Strategic Studies in London. One of the possibilities that first attracted me to the project was that, in the new mood of détente between China and the West, it might be possible to gain some access to a Peking perspective upon the Korean War. After months of discussion and correspondence, this indeed proved to be so.

There are no German or Japanese triumphal museums commemorating World War II. It is an eerie experience for a Westerner to walk through the great halls of the Peking Military Museum, gazing upon the trophies of captured British bren guns and regimental flashes, American .50 calibre machine guns, helmets and aircraft remains. Yet if my visit was a measure of how much has changed between China and the West, it was also a reminder of how much remains the same. There is still a great display given over to America's supposed 1952 'bacteriological warfare campaign' against North Korea. China claims to have inflicted 1,090,000 casualties on the US armed forces in Korea, a figure one assumes was arrived at by adding a few thousands to the total Chinese casualties claimed by the US. I spent some fascinating days and nights in Peking and Shanghai, listening to Chinese veterans describing their battlefield experience in Korea. Yet it must be said that none deviated for a moment from strict Party orthodoxy in describing their enthusiasm for the war, and satisfaction with the manner in which it was conducted. There is no comparison with the experience of interviewing British and American veterans, whose views reflect such a wide and forthright range of opinion. In Peking, senior officers gave me some fascinating explanations of Chinese behaviour. At their Command and Staff College, I gained some glimpses of the PLA's military perspective upon various battles. But there remains, of course, no opportunity to check official assertions against archives or written evidence. In a totalitarian state, such as China remains, it is debatable whether even those at the summit of power can discover the historical truth about events in the recent past, even should they wish to do so. In the same fashion, when Mr Gorbachev claims in a speech that the Soviet Union won the Second World War effectively unaided, it seems rash to assume that he is perpetrating a conscious untruth. It may yet be that he, like the vast majority of his people, simply does not know any better.

During my researches in Korea, I must acknowledge an important debt to the US Commander-in-Chief there, General Paul Livsey, who also served during the war as a young platoon commander; to British and American officers who provided me with facilities to visit key locations such as Panmunjom and Gloucester Hill; and above all, to Brigadier Brian Burditt, who stayed on in Korea after the end of his tour of duty as British Military Attaché, to act as my mentor and guide, and to arrange some fascinating interviews with Korean veterans of the war. I made a decision from the outset to make no approaches to Pyongyang while writing the book. If truth remains an elusive commodity in China, in North Korea it is entirely displaced by fantasy. It seems impossible to gain any worthwhile insights into the North Korean view of the war, as long as Kim Il Sung presides over a society in which the private possession of a bicycle is considered a threat to national security.

General Sir Anthony Farrar-Hockley was himself writing the British official history of the Korean War while I was working on my own book. With characteristic generosity, he arranged for me to have access to some of the key official files in his care. He himself remains, of course, one of the most fascinating witnesses of the Korean drama. Not only was he awarded the DSO for his performance as adjutant of the Gloucesters in their stand on the Imjin in April 1951, but he returned from two years' Chinese captivity with a reputation for indomitable courage and determination. His official history will clarify much about British participation in the war, and no doubt add new revelations. He was good enough to read this narrative in proof, though naturally he bears no responsibility for my errors or judgements.

In Britain and the United States, I interviewed as wide a cross-section as possible of officers and men of all three services. I did not seek meetings with a handful of the most senior officers who survive, because of their great age. From past experience, I have found that very elderly veterans have long ago said and written all that they wish about their great campaigns. To discuss these again merely starts a conversational train running upon familiar railway lines. It becomes fraudulent to acknowledge their assistance, because it is so seldom that they wish to say anything of substance. After thirty-five years, with very rare exceptions the most helpful witnesses about the conduct of a campaign are those who held regimental and battalion commands, and staff officers who served under the principal commanders, whose memories are often remarkable. I shall always cherish the four-hour word portrait of MacArthur's headquarters at the Dai Ichi drawn for me by that great and wholly delightful American soldier who served there in 1950, Colonel Fred Ladd. Likewise, I am much indebted to Brigadier-General Ed Simmons, USMC, who is not only director of the Marine Corps Museum in Washington, but also a veteran of the Chosin campaign, and an uncommonly shrewd critic of the Korean experience.

This book, like those I have written upon other campaigns, does not purport to be a comprehensive history. The most scholarly account of pre-war Korea is that of Bruce Cumings. Even after twenty-five years, the British author David Rees' *Korea: The Limited War* remains the best-written overall narrative, above all about the American political aspects. More recently, Joseph Goulden has uncovered many new American archival sources for his *Korea: The Untold Story.* Dr Rosemary Foot of the University of Sussex, another distinguished researcher of the period, was characteristically generous in discussing with me her own reflections and sources about the political dimensions of the war. To all these authors and books, I acknowledge my indebtedness for important lines of thought. I have not attempted to emulate them. I have written relatively little about aspects of the Korean conflict, such as MacArthur's dismissal, which have been exhaustively discussed elsewhere. Instead, I have sought to paint a portrait of the war, focusing upon some human and military aspects less familiar to readers on both sides of the Atlantic. Because I am an Englishman, I have devoted more space to the experience of British servicemen in Korea than their proportionate contribution to the struggle justifies. But it seems reasonable to suggest that a British officer's or private soldier's recollection of the experience of fighting the Chinese is no less valid, as a contribution to understanding what the war was like, than that of an American, a Canadian, an Australian, a Frenchman. The ranks attributed to officers and men in the text are those they held at the dates concerned. I have retained old-fashioned spellings of Chinese names, which are likely to be more familiar to Western readers than the newer versions.

In one important respect, I must be numbered among the revisionists. Many writers about Korea in the fifties, not to mention politicians and voters, looked back on the war with bitter distaste for the long stalemate, the growing tensions between allies that it generated, and the inconclusive truce that brought it to an end. Misgivings about Western wars in Asia were intensified by the long misery of Vietnam. Yet whatever obvious criticisms must be made of MacArthur's excesses, of the West's handling of Peking, of the conduct of the first winter campaign, I remain convinced of the rightness of the American commitment to Korea in June 1950. The regimes of Syngman Rhee and his successors possessed massive shortcomings. Yet who can doubt, looking at Korea today, that the people of the South enjoy incomparably more fulfilling lives than those of the inhabitants of the North? Civil libertarians may justly remark that the freedom of the South's thirty-five million people remains relative. Yet few would deny that relative freedom, to pursue personal prosperity or private professions, remains preferable to absolute tyranny. North Korea is still among the most wretched, ruthless, restrictive, impenitent Stalinist societies in the world. South Korea is one of the most dynamic industrial societies even Asia has spawned in the past generation. The 1950–53 Korean War, which confirmed the shape of the two Koreas as they are today, remains one of the most significant, compelling clashes of arms in this century. Those who experienced it have long been irked by a sense of the world's neglect of what they endured, and of what they achieved. I hope this book will make at least a modest contribution towards remedying the omission.

Max Hastings
Guilsborough Lodge,
Northamptonshire.
January 1987

PROLOGUE: TASK FORCE SMITH

In the early hours of 5 July 1950, 403 bewildered, damp, disorientated Americans sat in their hastily dug foxholes on three Korean hills, looking down upon the main road between Suwon and Osan. The men of 1/21st Infantry had been in the country just four days, since the big C-54 transports flew them from Itasuki in Japan to the southern airfield at Pusan. Ever since, they had been moving north in fits and starts – by train and truck, sleeping in sidings and schoolhouses, amid great throngs of refugees crowding roads and stations. Some men were sick from the local water; Lieutenant Fox was injured on the train before they heard their first shot fired, by an inglorious stray cinder from the engine blowing into his eye. All of them were savaged by mosquitoes. They learnt that Korea stank – literally – of the human manure with which the nation's farmers fertilised their rice paddies. They watched earnest roadside rendezvous between their own officers and the smattering of US generals in the country. General William Dean, commanding the 24th Division, told the 1/21st commanding officer, Lieutenant-Colonel Charles 'Brad' Smith: 'I'm sorry – I just don't have much information to give you.'

They knew that the communist North Koreans had invaded the anti-communist South on 25 June, and had been striking ruthlessly southwards ever since, meeting little opposition from Syngman Rhee's shattered army. They were told that they themselves would be taking up defensive positions somewhere in the path of the enemy, as far north as possible. But after years of occupation duty in Japan, the notion of battle, of injury and sudden death, seemed infinitely remote. Their unit, like all those of the Japan occupation

1

army, was badly under-strength and poorly equipped. Their own A and D Companies, together with many of their supporting elements, were still at sea between Japan and Pusan. On the night of 4 July, they were ordered to take up a blocking position on the Suwon road, some fifty miles south of the capital, Seoul, which was already in communist hands. In a country of mountains, the paths open to a modern army were few and obvious. The enemy sweeping south must make for Osan. The 1/21st, the first unit of the United States Army available to be committed to battle in Korea, must do what it could to meet them. 'They looked like a bunch of boy scouts,' said Colonel George Masters, one of the men who watched the battalion moving to the front. 'I said to Brad Smith: "You're facing tried combat soldiers out there." There was nothing he could answer.'[1]

They moved forward, as most soldiers move forward to battle in most wars, in drizzle and darkness. The South Korean drivers of some of the commandeered vehicles flatly refused to go further towards the battlefield, so the Americans drove themselves. They unloaded from their trucks behind the hills that Colonel Smith had briefly reconnoitred that day, and began to climb, by platoons, through the rock and scrub amid much tired, muffled cursing and clanking of equipment. Their officers were as confused as the men, for they had been told to expect to meet a South Korean army unit to which to anchor their own positions. In reality, there was no one on the hill. Smith's company commanders deployed their men as best they could, and ordered them to start digging. At once, for the first time, Americans discovered the difficulty of hewing shelter from the unyielding Korean hillsides. For some hours, working clumsily in their poncho capes in the rain, they scraped among the rocks. Below them on the road, signallers laid telephone lines to their single battery of supporting 105mm howitzers, a thousand yards to the rear. A few truckloads of ammunition were offloaded by the roadside, but no one thought to insist that this was lugged up the hills in the dark to the company positions. Then, for an uneasy hour or two, most of the Americans above the road lay beside their weapons and packs, sodden clothes clinging clammily to their bodies, and slept.

Blinking and shuffling in the first light of dawn, the men of Task Force Smith – the grandiose title their little force had been granted in a Tokyo map room – looked down from their positions. They were just south of Suwon airfield, three miles north of the little town of Osan. They began to pick out familiar faces: 'Brad' Smith himself, a slightly built West Pointer of thirty-four with a competent record in the Pacific in World War II; his executive officer, 'Mother' Martain, now demanding some changes in positions chosen in darkness. Major Floyd Martain was a New Yorker who had served in the National Guard from 1926 until he was called to active duty in 1940, then spent the war in Alaska. Unkind spirits considered Martain something of a fussy old woman, hence his nickname. Yet he also earned it by looking after his men, many of whom felt a real affection for him. Corporal Ezra Burke was the son of a Mississippi sawmiller who was drafted in time to see a little action at the tail end of the Pacific campaign, then stayed on to share the heady pleasures of Japan occupation duty. Burke was one of many Southerners in the unit, young men whose home towns in the late forties could offer neither a pay check nor a lifestyle as attractive as that of MacArthur's army. Now, as a medical orderly, Corporal Burke and his team were laying out their field kits in a hollow behind the battalion position. They had 'figured to be a week in Korea, settle the gook thing, then back to Japan'. Now, uneasy, they were less confident of this timetable.

Lieutenant Carl Bernard, a twenty-four-year-old Texan, had served as an enlisted Marine in World War II. Quickly bored by civilian life when it ended, he enlisted in the 82nd Airborne Division, and was commissioned into the 24th Division in 1949. When the Korean crisis broke, as one of the few Airborne-qualified officers in the division, he spent some days at the airfield in Japan, supervising the loading of the transports. Now, he was put in command of 2 Platoon of B Company, where he knew nobody, after rejoining the battalion a few hours earlier.

Corporal Robert Fountain of the Communications Platoon watched Colonel Smith scanning the black smoke columns on the horizon through binoculars, his shoulders draped in an army blanket against the rain. The colonel looked like an Indian chieftain, thought Fountain. He himself, a nineteen-year-old farmboy from Macon, Georgia, was chiefly concerned whether the telephone lines would hold up. They had been unwound, used, spliced, rewound repeatedly on manoeuvres in Japan. Yet they were now the battalion's principal means of communication, with so many of the radios rendered unserviceable by the rain. Fountain had found the experiences of the past few days deeply bewildering. With his parents divorced and jobs hard to come by, he joined the army at sixteen because he could think of nothing else to do. He had never thought much about fighting. For himself, like many of the men, the flight to Korea was a first-ever trip in an aeroplane. In the days since, they had been strafed by presumed North Korean Yaks, which they later discovered were Australian Mustangs. They had watched an ammunition train explode, and a South Korean officer without explanation force one of his own men to his knees and shoot him in the back of the neck. There had been scares of enemy tanks which turned into friendly caterpillar tractors. Fountain and his comrades had left Japan under the impression that they would be away only five days: 'When the gooks hear who we are, they'll quit and go home.' They left clothes, possessions, money in their barrack rooms. Yet now the vainglory of their departure had faded. Fountain ate a can of cold C-rations, and asked if anybody had any water left in his canteen. He felt cold, wet and confused.

A few minutes after 7 a.m., Sergeant Loren Chambers of B Company called to his platoon commander: 'Hey, look over there, Lieutenant. Can you believe it?' Advancing towards them down the open plain from Suwon was a column of eight green-painted tanks.

Lieutenant Day asked what they were. 'Those are T-34 tanks, sir,' answered the sergeant, 'and I don't think they're going to be friendly towards us.' All along the crest line, men chattered excitedly as they peered forward at this first glimpse of the enemy. Officers hastened forward to confirm the threat. Captain Dashner, B Company Commander, said: 'Let's get some artillery on them.'[2] The Forward Observation Officer of the 58th Field Artillery Battalion cranked his handset. A few moments later, rounds began to gusher into the paddy fields around the road. But still the tanks came on. The guns of the 58th possessed negligible armour-piercing capability.

Lieutenant Philip Day and one of the battalion's two 75mm recoilless rifle sections manhandled their clumsy weapon to a position overlooking the road, and fired. Inexpert, they had sited on a forward slope. The round did no visible damage to the enemy, but the ferocious backblast slammed into the hill, provoking an eruption of mud which deluged the crew and jammed the gun. Urgently, they began to strip and clear it.

At the roadside, Lieutenant Ollie Connors clutched one of the unit's principal anti-tank weapons, a hand-held 2.36-inch bazooka. In 1945, the serious defect of the bazooka rocket was well known – its inability to penetrate most tanks' main armour. Yet even now, five years later, the new and more powerful 3.5-inch rocket launcher had not been issued to MacArthur's Far East army. As the first T-34 clattered towards the narrow pass between the American positions, Connors put up his bazooka and fired. There was an explosion on the tank hull. But the T-34, probably the outstanding tank of World War II and still a formidable weapon, did not check. It roared on through the pass, and down the road towards the American gunline. As its successors followed, with remarkable courage Connors fired again and again at close range, twenty-two rockets in all. One tank stopped, appearing to have thrown a track. But it continued to fire with both its main armament and coaxial machine gun. The others disappeared towards Osan, to be followed a few minutes later by another armoured platoon. A single 105mm

gun possessed a few rounds of armour-piercing ammunition. One
of these halted another T-34, which halted and caught fire. A
crewman emerged from the turret firing a burp gun as he came.
The communist's first burst, before he was shot down, granted one
of the gunners the unhappy distinction of becoming the first
American soldier to die by enemy action in Korea. Lieutenant Day's
recoilless rifle began to fire again, but its flash made it an easy
target. An 85mm tank shell disabled the gun, and left Day reeling
from blast, blood pouring out of his ears. Between 7 and 9.30 a.m.
some thirty North Korean tanks drove through Task Force Smith's
'blocking position', killing or wounding some twenty of the
defenders by shell and machine-gun fire. The Americans could
think of nothing to do to stop them.

Around 11 a.m., a long column of trucks led by three more
tanks appeared on the road from the north. They halted bumper
to bumper, and began to disgorge North Korean infantry who
scattered east and west into the paddies beside the road. Some of
the mustard-coloured tunics began to advance steadily towards the
Americans amid desultory mortar and small-arms fire. Others
worked patiently around the flanks. Since Task Force Smith occupied only a four-hundred-yard front, and no other American infantry units were deployed for many miles behind them, it was
immediately obvious that this action must eventually end in only
one fashion. As the hours passed, communist fire intensified and
American casualties mounted. Colonel Smith called C Company's
officers, west of the road, to the Company Command Post. The
entire force would now consolidate in a circular perimeter on the
east side, he said. The 150 or so men of Charlie Company left their
positions platoon by platoon, filed down to the road, clambered up
among the scrub on the other side, and began to hack foxholes
and fields of fire for themselves as best they could.

Smith's choices were not enviable. His unit was achieving very
little where it stood. But if he chose to withdraw immediately from
the position, put his men into their surviving trucks, and head
south, sooner or later the column was likely to meet the commun-

ist tanks that had gone before them. He would gain little, with his small force, by abandoning the high ground to launch a counter-attack against the enemy infantry. Yet if they remained in place, they could expect neither reinforcement nor relief. Here was an extraordinary situation. This was 1950, when vast economic wealth, possession of the atomic bomb and the legacy of victory in the Second World War caused America to be perceived as the greatest power the world had ever seen, mightier than the Roman Empire at its zenith, or the British a century before. Yet now, on a hill in Korea, the first representatives of United States military power to meet communist aggression on the battlefield were the men of a mere under-strength infantry battalion which faced annihilation as a military unit. Not all the B-29s on the airfields of the United States, nor the army divisions in Europe, the fleets at sea from the Taiwan Strait to the Mediterranean, could mitigate the absolute loneliness and vulnerability of Task Force Smith. Those in Tokyo or Washington who supposed that the mere symbolic commitment of this token of American military might would suffice to frighten the North Koreans into retreat were confounded. Subsequent interrogation of North Korean officers suggested that the encounter between their 4m Division and Task Force Smith provided Pyongyang with its first inkling of American intervention, which had not been anticipated. Neither side on the Osan road was troubled by political implications. The communists were using mortars now, to some effect. American small-arms ammunition was growing short, as men stumbled up the slippery paths worn into the mud to the forward positions, dragging crates and steel boxes. Among the boulders below the position, the wounded lay in widening rows, the medics toiling among them, hampered by lack of whole blood. Captain Richard Dashner, the Texan World War II veteran commanding C Company, said abruptly to Major Martain: 'We've got to get out of here.' Lieutenant Berthoff, commanding Headquarter Company, agreed. At first, Smith said there would be no immediate pull-back. But as the fire from the flanks intensified, he changed his mind. 'I guess we'll have to,' he told his officers. Then he added unhappily: 'This is a decision I'll probably regret the rest of my days.' C Company was to go first. Within minutes, the first of its men were slipping down the rear of the position and into the paddy fields beyond, stumbling and cursing at the stench and the enemy fire. There was no question of escaping along the road, open and vulnerable to raking machine guns as far as the eye could see. They could only scramble through the fields, balancing precariously on the intervening dykes, down the farm tracks as fast and as best they could, until they met friendly forces.

It was during the withdrawal of Task Force Smith that its imperfections as a fighting unit became apparent. There is no more testing military manoeuvre than disengagement in the face of the enemy. The Americans were softened by years of inadequate training and military neglect, bewildered by the shock of combat, dismayed by the readiness with which the communists had over-whelmed them, and the isolation in which they found themselves. As men saw others leaving the hills, they hastened to join them, fearful of being left behind. 'It was every man for himself,' said Lieutenant Day. 'When we moved out, we began taking more and more casualties ... Guys fell around me. Mortar rounds hit here and there. One of my young guys got it in the middle. My platoon sergeant, Harvey Vann, ran over to him. I followed. "No way he's gonna live, Lieutenant." Oh, Jesus, the guy was moaning and groaning. There wasn't much I could do but pat him on the head and say, "Hang in there." Another of the platoon sergeants got it in the throat. He began spitting blood. I thought sure ... For the rest of the day he held his throat together with his hands. He survived, too.'[3] The retreating Americans abandoned arms, equipment; sometimes even helmets, boots, personal weapons. Cohesion quickly vanished. The debris of retreat lay strewn behind them as they went. In ones and twos and handfuls, they scrambled south-wards through the fields.

C Company, first off the positions, fared better than B in hold-ing its men together. Captain Dashner reached Taejon after two days' hard marching with more than half his men still under command. Floyd Martain and the little team in the Battalion Command Post struggled to burn their confidential papers, but found them too wet to catch light. They dug a hole and buried them, then started walking, following the railroad tracks south. After some hours, Martain's little group saw some trucks, and hastily took cover. Then, to their overwhelming relief, they found that these were American vehicles, carrying some gunners – who had blown up their pieces rather than attempt to get them out, an action which infuriated some officers – and Colonel Smith himself. After a night of nerve-racking hide-and-seek with enemy tanks as they crossed country, they reached positions of the 34th Infantry at Ansong. Corporal Robert Fountain never heard any order to withdraw – he simply saw men streaming past him who glanced an answer to his shouted question about what was happening: 'We're pulling back.' Fountain joined them. He scrambled past an American sitting upright against a dyke wall, stone dead. Suddenly, he found himself face to face with two baled-out North Korean tank crewmen. The next man shot one, Fountain killed the other as he ran towards a house. Then the American stumbled away through the waterlogged paddies amid machine-gun fire from the positions the battalion had abandoned. In a wood, he met a group of sixteen other Americans. He took out a knife and cut off the tops of his combat boots so that he could get the water out. Two sergeants organised the group. They set off again, attempting to carry the wounded among them. One man, a Japanese-American, was shot in the stomach. When they reached a deserted village, they left him there, dying. Fountain found a turnip root and ate it. They walked on through the darkness for many hours, following a group of South Korean soldiers they encountered. They reached a Korean command post in a schoolhouse where they slept for a while. Then somebody shouted: 'Tanks coming!' They piled into a truck, and drove for some miles until the truck blundered into a ditch and stayed there. They began walking again, and eventually found themselves in the lines of the 34th Infantry.

Lieutenant Carl Bernard was still on the hill with his platoon of B Company when he sensed the fire from the other American positions slackening, and sent a runner to find out what was going on. The man returned a few minutes later in some consternation to report 'They've all gone!' Command and control frankly collapsed in the last stages of the action. Bernard, wounded in face and hands by grenade fragments, hastily led his men to beat their own retreat. At the base of the hill they found the medical orderlies still coping with a large group of wounded. They took with them such men as could walk, and left the remainder to be taken prisoner. The lieutenant divided the survivors of his platoon into two groups, sending one with a private soldier who had been a scout, and taking the other himself. He had no compass, but in an abandoned schoolhouse he found a child's atlas. He tore out the page showing Korea, and used it to navigate. In the hours that followed, his group survived a series of close encounters with enemy tanks. Bernard bartered a gold Longines watch that he had won playing poker on the boat from San Francisco for an old Korean's handcart, on which to push a wounded NCO.

Ezra Burke came off the hill with four of his medical team, two stretcher cases, and one walking wounded. As they staggered onwards with their burdens, they kept halting and glancing back, hoping to have outdistanced their pursuers. But all that afternoon, they could see files of North Koreans padding remorsely behind them. At last, they decided to split. Burke headed south-westward with two others. They were soaking wet, exhausted, and above all desperately anxious to be reunited with their unit and their officers, with anyone who could tell them where to go and what to do. They huddled miserably together through the hours of darkness, and at first light began to walk again. On a hill above Pyontaek, they met Lieutenant Bernard and his seven-strong group, and continued south with them. Thenceforward, they hid most of the day, and walked by night. Starving, they risked creeping into a village and bartering possessions with a momma-san for a few potatoes. They met two Korean soldiers, with whom they walked for a time. Then a South Korean lieutenant who talked to them declared his conviction that the men were communists. The two ran off across a rice paddy. Burke fired at them with a carbine and missed. Bernard caught them with a BAR just before they reached a wood.

They reached American positions on 10 July, five days after the battle at Osan, utterly exhausted, their feet agonisingly swollen. The next day Burke was found to be suffering from a kidney stone, and was evacuated by air from Taejon to Osaka. Carl Bernard spent some painful hours in a field hospital, where the grenade fragments were picked out of his face and hands. Then he slept the sleep of utter exhaustion for an entire day.

Most of Task Force Smith trickled back to American positions in something like this fashion in the week that followed their little action at Osan. 185 men of the battalion mustered after the battle. Some made their way to the American lines after epic adventures, like Sergeant William F. Smith, who escaped by fishing boat a fortnight later. Lieutenant Connors received a Silver Star for his brave endeavours with the bazooka by the roadside on 5 July. The official figures showed that Task Force Smith had suffered 155 casualties in the action at Osan. By the time they returned, they discovered that any shortcomings in their own unit's performance on 5 July had already been outstripped by far less honourable, indeed positively shameful, humiliations suffered by other elements of the American 24th Division in its first days of war, as the North Korean invaders swept all before them on their bloody procession south down the peninsula. And all this flowed, inexorably, from the sudden decision of the United States to commit itself to the least expected of wars, in the least predicted of places, under the most unfavourable possible military conditions. Had the men of Task Force Smith, on the road south of Suwon, known that they were striking the first armed blow for that new force in world order, the United Nations, it might have made their confused, unhappy, almost pathetic little battle on 5 July seem more dignified. On the other hand, it might have made it appear more incomprehensible than ever.

1 » ORIGINS OF A TRAGEDY

Seldom in the course of history has a nation been as rapidly propelled as Korea from obscurity to a central place in the world's affairs. The first significant modern contact between 'The Land of the Morning Calm' and the West took place one morning in September 1945, when an advance party of the American army, in full battle gear, landed at the western harbour of Inchon, to be met by a delegation of Japanese officials in top hats and tail coats. This was the inauguration of Operation Black List Forty, the United States' occupation of South Korea.

These first American officers found the city of Inchon, fearful and uncertain of its future, shuttered and closed. After a hunt through the streets, glimpsing occasional faces peering curiously at their liberators from windows and corners, they came upon a solitary Chinese restaurant bearing the sign 'Welcome US'. Then, from the moment the Americans boarded the train for Seoul, they met uninhibited rejoicing. A little crowd of Koreans stood by the tracks in every village they passed, waving gleeful flags. At Seoul railway station, the group had planned to take a truck to their objective, the city post office. Instead, on their arrival, they decided to walk. To their bewilderment, they found themselves at the centre of a vast throng of cheering, milling, exultant Koreans, cramming the streets and sidewalks, hanging from buildings, standing on carts. The Americans were at a loss. They had arrived without any conception of what the end of the Japanese war meant to the people of this obscure peninsula.[1]

*

Throughout its history until the end of the nineteenth century, Korea was an overwhelmingly rural society which sought successfully to maintain its isolation from the outside world. Ruled since 1392 by the Yi Dynasty, it suffered two major invasions from Japan in the sixteenth century. When the Japanese departed, Korea returned to its harsh traditional existence, frozen in winter and baked in summer, its ruling families feuding among each other from generation to generation. By the Confucian convention that regarded foreign policy as an extension of family relations, Korea admitted an historic loyalty to China, 'the elder brother nation'. Until 1876, her near neighbour Japan was regarded as a friendly equal. But early that January, in an early surge of the expansionism that was to dominate Japanese history for the next seventy years, Tokyo dispatched a military expedition to Korea 'to establish a treaty of friendship and commerce'. On 26 February, after a brief and ineffectual resistance, the Koreans signed. They granted the Japanese open ports, their citizens extra-territorial rights.

The embittered Koreans sought advice from their other neighbours about the best means of undoing this humiliating surrender. The Chinese advised that they should come to an arrangement with one of the Western powers 'in order to check the poison with an antidote'; they suggested the Americans, who had shown no signs of possessing territorial ambitions on the Asian mainland. On 22 May 1882, Korea signed a treaty of 'amity and commerce' with the United States. In the words of a leading American historian of the period, this 'set Korea adrift on an ocean of intrigue which it was quite helpless to control'. The infuriated Japanese now engaged themselves increasingly closely in Korea's internal power struggles. The British took an interest, for they were eager to maintain China's standing as Korea's 'elder brother', to counter Russian influence in the Far East. By 1893, Korea had signed a succession of trade treaties with every major European power. The Japanese were perfectly clear about their objective. Their foreign minister declared openly that Korea 'should be made a part of the

Japanese map'. Tokyo hesitated only about how to achieve this without a confrontation with one or another great power.

The Chinese solved the problem. Peking's increasingly heavy-handed meddling in Korea's affairs, asserting claims to some measure of authority over Seoul, provoked a wave of anti-Chinese feeling, and a corresponding surge of enthusiasm for the Japanese, who could now claim popular support from at least a faction within Korea. In 1894, Japan seized her opportunity, and landed an army in Korea to force the issue. The government in Seoul, confused and panicky, asked Peking to send its own troops to help suppress a rebellion. The Japanese responded by dispatching a contingent of marines direct to the capital. The Korean government, by now hopelessly out of its depth, begged that all the foreign troops should depart. But the Japanese scented victory. They reinforced their army.

The last years of Korea's notional independence took on a Gilbertian absurdity. The nation's leaders, artless in the business of diplomacy and modern power politics, squirmed and floundered in the net that was inexorably closing around them. The Chinese recognised their military inability to confront the Japanese in Korea. Tokyo's grasp on Korea's internal government tightened until, in 1896, the King tried to escape thraldom by taking refuge at the Russian Legation in Seoul. From this sanctuary, he issued orders for the execution of all his pro-Japanese ministers. The Japanese temporarily backed down.

In the next seven years, Moscow and Tokyo competed for power and concessions in Seoul. The devastating Japanese victory at Tsushima, a few miles off Pusan, decided the outcome. In February 1904, the Japanese moved a large army into Korea. In November the following year, the nation became a Japanese protectorate. In a characteristic exercise of the colonial cynicism of the period, the British accepted Japanese support for their rule in India in exchange for blessing Tokyo's takeover of Korea. Whitehall acknowledged Japan's right 'to take such measures of guidance, control, and protection in Corea [*sic*] as she may deem proper and necessary', to promote her 'paramount political, military and economic interests'.

Korean independence thus became a dead letter. In the years that followed, a steady stream of Japanese officials and immigrants moved into the country. Japanese education, roads, railways, sanitation were introduced. Yet none of these gained the slightest gratitude from the fiercely nationalistic Koreans. Armed resistance grew steadily in the hands of a strange alliance of Confucian scholars, traditional bandits, Christians, and peasants with local grievances against the colonial power. The anti-Japanese guerrilla army rose to a peak of an estimated 70,000 men in 1908. Thereafter, ruthless Japanese repression broke it down. Korea became an armed camp, in which mass executions and wholesale imprisonment were commonplace, and all dissent forbidden. On 22 August 1910, the Korean emperor signed away all his rights of sovereignty. The Japanese introduced their own titles of nobility, and imposed their own military government. For the next thirty-five years, despite persistent armed resistance from mountain bands of nationalists, many of them communist, the Japanese maintained their ruthless, detested rule in Korea, which also became an important base for their expansion north into Manchuria in the nineteen thirties.

Yet despite the decline of China into a society of competing warlords, and the preoccupation of Russia with her own revolution, even before the Second World War it was apparent that Korea's geographical position, as the nearest meeting place of three great nations, would make her a permanent focus of tension and competition. The American Tyler Dennett wrote presciently in 1945, months before the Far Eastern war ended:

> Many of the international factors which led to the fall of Korea are either unchanged from what they were half a century ago, or are likely to recur the moment peace is restored to the East. Japan's hunger for power will have been extinguished for a

period, but not for ever. In another generation probably Japan will again be a very important influence in the Pacific. Meanwhile the Russian interest in the peninsula is likely to remain what it was forty years ago. Quite possibly that factor will be more important than ever before. The Chinese also may be expected to continue their traditional concern in the affairs of that area.[2]

And now, suddenly, the war was over, and the Japanese empire was in the hands of the broker's men. Koreans found themselves freed from Japanese domination, looking for fulfilment of the promise of the leaders of the Grand Alliance in the 1943 Cairo Declaration – that Korea should become free and independent 'in due course'.

The American decision to land troops to play a part in the occupation of Korea was taken only at the very end of the war. The Japanese colony had been excluded from the complex 1943–45 negotiations about occupation zones between the partners of the Grand Alliance. The Americans had always been enamoured of the concept of 'trusteeship' for Korea, along with Indochina and some other colonial possessions in the Far East. They liked the idea of a period during which a committee of Great Powers – in this case, China, the US and USSR – would 'prepare and educate' the dependent peoples for self-government and 'protect them from exploitation'. This concept never found much favour among the British or French, mindful of their own empires. And as the war progressed, concern about the future internal structure of Korea was overtaken by deepening alarm about the external forces that might determine this. As early as November 1943, a State Department sub-committee expressed fears that when the Soviets entered the Far East war, they might seize the opportunity to include Korea in their sphere of influence:

> Korea may appear to offer a tempting opportunity to apply the
> Soviet conception of the proper treatment of colonial peoples,
> to strengthen enormously the economic resources of the Soviet

Far East, to acquire ice-free ports, and to occupy a dominating strategic position in relation both to China and to Japan . . . A Soviet occupation of Korea would create an entirely new strategic situation in the Far East, and its repercussions within China and Japan might be far reaching.[3]

As the American historian Bruce Cumings has aptly pointed out, 'what created "an entirely new strategic situation in the Far East" was not that Russia was interested in Korea – it had been for decades – but that the United States was interested'.[4] Yet by the time of the Potsdam Conference of July 1945, the United States military were overwhelmingly preoccupied with the perceived difficulties of mounting an invasion of mainland Japan. They regarded the Japanese armies still deployed in Korea and Manchuria as a tough nut for the Red Army to crack, and were only too happy to leave the problem, and the expected casualties, to the Russians. The Pentagon had anyway adopted a consistent view that Korea was of no long-term strategic interest to the United States.

Yet three weeks later, the American view of Korea had altered dramatically. The explosion of the two atomic bombs on Japan on 6 and 9 August brought Japan to the brink of surrender. The Red Army was sweeping through Manchuria without meeting important resistance. Suddenly, Washington's view of both the desirability and feasibility of denying a substantial part of Korea to the Soviets was transformed. Late on the night of 10 August 1945, barely twenty-four hours after the dropping of the Nagasaki bomb, the State-War-Navy Co-ordinating Committee reached a hasty, unilateral decision that the United States should participate in the occupation of Korea. The two officers drafting orders for the committee pored over their small-scale wall map of the Far East, and observed that the 38th parallel ran broadly across the middle of the country. South of this line lay the capital, the best of the agriculture and light industry, and more than half the population. Some members of the committee – including Dean Rusk, a future Secretary of State – pointed out that if the Russians chose to reject this proposal, the Red Army sweeping south through Manchuria could overrun all Korea before the first GI could be landed at Inchon. In these weeks, when the first uncertain skirmishes of the Cold War were being fought, the sudden American proposal for the divided occupation of Korea represented an important test of Soviet intentions in the Far East.

To the relief of the Committee in Washington, the Russians readily accepted the 38th Parallel as the limit of their advance. Almost a month before the first Americans could be landed in South Korea, the Red Army reached the new divide – and halted there. It is worth remark that, if Moscow had declined the American plan and occupied all Korea, it is unlikely that the Americans could or would have forced a major diplomatic issue. To neither side, at this period, did the peninsula seem to possess any inherent value, except as a testing ground of mutual intentions. The struggle for political control of China herself was beginning in earnest. Beside the fates and boundaries of great nations that were now being decided, Korea counted for little. Stalin was content to settle for half. At no time in the five years that followed did the Russians show any desire to stake Moscow's power and prestige upon a direct contest with the Americans for the extension of Soviet influence south of the Parallel.

Thus it was, late in August 1945, that the unhappy men of the US XXIV Corps – some veterans of months of desperate fighting in the Pacific, others green replacements fresh from training camps – found themselves under orders to embark not for home, as they so desperately wished, but for unknown Korea. They were given little information to guide their behaviour once they got there. Their commander, General John R. Hodge, received only a confusing succession of signals at his headquarters on Okinawa. On 14 August, General Stilwell told him that the occupation could be considered 'semi-friendly' – in other words, that he need regard as hostile only a small minority of collaborators. At the end of the month the Supreme Commander, General MacArthur himself, decreed that the Koreans should be treated as 'liberated people'.

From Washington, the Secretary of State for War and the Navy Co-ordinating Committee dispatched a hasty directive to Okinawa, ordering Hodge to 'create a government in harmony with US policies'. But what were US policies towards Korea? Since the State Department knew little more about the country than that its nationalists hungered for unity and independence, they had little to tell Hodge. As a straightforward military man, the general determined to approach the problem in a straightforward, no-nonsense fashion. On 4 September, he briefed his own officers to regard Korea as 'an enemy of the United States', subject to the terms of the Japanese surrender. On 8 September, when the American occupation convoy was still twenty miles out from Inchon in the Yellow Sea, its ships encountered three neatly dressed figures in a small boat, who presented themselves to the general as representatives of 'the Korean Government'. Hodge sent them packing. He did likewise with every other Korean he met on his arrival who laid claim to a political mandate. XXIV Corps's intention was to seize and maintain control of the country. The US Army, understandably, wished to avoid precipitating entanglement with any of the scores of competing local political factions who already, in those first days, were struggling to build a power-base amid the ruin of the Japanese empire.

The fourteen-strong advance party who were the first Americans to reach Seoul were fascinated and bemused by what they found: a city of horse-drawn carts, with only the occasional charcoal-powered motor vehicle. They saw three Europeans in a shop, and hastened to greet them, to discover that they were part of the little local Turkish community, who spoke no English. They met White Russians, refugees in Korea since 1920, who demanded somewhat tactlessly: '*Sprechen sie Deutsch?*' The first English-speaker they met was a local Japanese who had lived in the United States before the war. His wife, like all the Japanese community eager to ingratiate herself with the new rulers, pressed on them a cake and two pounds of real butter – the first they had seen for months. That night, they slept on the floor of Seoul Post Office. The next morning, they transferred their headquarters to the Banda Hotel.[5]

In the days that followed, the major units of XXIV Corps disembarked at Inchon, and dispersed by truck and train around the country, to take up positions from Pusan to the 38th Parallel. General Hodge and his staff were initially bewildered by the clamour of unknown Koreans competing for their political attention, and the disorders in the provinces which threatened to escalate into serious rioting if the situation was not controlled. There was also the difficulty that no Korean they encountered appeared to speak English, and the only Korean-speaker on the staff, one Commander Williams of the US Navy, was insufficiently fluent to conduct negotiations.

Amid all this confusion and uncertainty, the occupiers could identify only one local stabilising force upon whom they could rely: the Japanese. In those first days, the Japanese made themselves indispensable to Hodge and his men. One of the American commander's first acts was to confirm Japanese colonial officials in their positions, for the time being. Japanese remained the principal language of communication. Japanese soldiers and police retained chief responsibility for maintaining law and order. As early as 11 September, MacArthur signalled instructions to Hodge that Japanese officials must at once be removed from office. But even when this process began to take place, many retained their influence for weeks as unofficial advisers to the Americans.

Within days of the first euphoric encounter between the liberators and the liberated, patriotic Koreans were affronted by the open camaraderie between Japanese and American officers, the respect shown by former enemies to each other, in contrast to the thinly veiled contempt offered to the Koreans. 'It does seem that from the beginning many Americans simply liked the Japanese better than the Koreans,' the foremost American historian of this period has written. 'The Japanese were viewed as cooperative, orderly and docile, while the Koreans were seen as headstrong,

unruly, and obstreperous.'[6] The Americans knew nothing, or chose
to ignore what they did know, of the ruthless behaviour of the
Japanese in the three weeks between their official surrender and
the coming of XXIV Corps – the looting of warehouses, the systematic ruin of the economy by printing debased currency, the sale of
every available immovable asset.

To a later generation, familiar with the dreadful brutality of
the Japanese in the Second World War, it may seem extraordinary
that Americans could so readily make common cause with their
late enemies; as strange as the conduct of Allied intelligence
organisations in Europe, which befriended and recruited former
Nazi war criminals and Gestapo agents. Yet the strongest influence
of war upon most of those who endure it is to blur their belief in
absolute moral values, and to foster a sense of common experience
with those who have shared it, even a barbarous enemy. There was
a vast sense of relief among the men of the armies who still
survived in 1945, an instinctive reluctance for more killing, even
in the cause of just revenge. There was also a rapidly growing
suspicion for some prominent American soldiers – Patton notable
among them – that they might have been fighting the wrong
enemy for these four years. McCarthyism was yet unborn. But a
sense of the evil of communism was very strong, and already
outweighed in the minds of some men their revulsion towards
Nazism, or Japanese imperialism. In Tokyo, the American Supreme
Commander himself was already setting an extraordinary example
of post-war reconciliation with the defeated enemy. In Seoul in the
autumn of 1945, General Hodge and his colleagues found it much
more comfortable to deal with the impeccable correctness of
fellow-soldiers, albeit recent enemies, than with the anarchic rivalries of the Koreans. The senior officers of XXIV Corps possessed no
training or expertise of any kind for exercising civilian government
– they were merely professional military men, obliged to improvise
as they went along. In the light of subsequent events, their blun-
ders and political clumsiness have attracted the unfavourable
attention of history. But it is only just to observe that at this

period, many of the same mistakes were being made by their counterparts in Allied armies all over the world.

Hodge's State Department political adviser, H. Merell Benninghoff, reported to Washington on 15 September:

South Korea can best be described as a powder keg ready to explode at the application of a spark. There is great disappointment that immediate independence and sweeping out of the Japanese did not eventuate. Although the hatred of the Koreans for the Japanese is unbelievably bitter, it is not thought that they will resort to violence as long as American troops are in surveillance ... The removal of Japanese officials is desirable from the public opinion standpoint, but difficult to bring about for some time. They can be relieved in name but must be made to continue in work. There are no qualified Koreans for other than the low-ranking positions, either in government or in public utilities and communications.[7]

The pressures upon the Americans in Korea to dispense with the aid of their newfound Japanese allies became irresistible. In four months, 70,000 Japanese colonial civil servants and more than 600,000 Japanese soldiers and civilians were shipped home to their own islands. Many were compelled to abandon homes, factories, possessions. Yet the damage to American relations with the Koreans was already done. Lieutenant Ferris Miller, USN, who had been one of the first Americans to land in the country, and subsequently enjoyed a lifelong association with Korea, said: 'Our misunderstanding of local feelings about the Japanese, and our own close association with them, was one of the most expensive mistakes we ever made there.'[8]

In the months that followed the expulsion of the Japanese, the Koreans who replaced them as agents of the American military government were, for the most part, long-serving collaborators, detested by their own fellow-countrymen for their service to the colonial power. A ranking American of the period wrote later of his colleagues' 'abysmal ignorance of Korea and things Korean, the inelasticity of the military bureaucracy and the avoidance of it by the few highly qualified Koreans, who could afford neither to be associated with such an unpopular government, nor to work for the low wages it offered.'[9]

Before their enforced departure, the Japanese were at pains to alert the Americans to the pervasive influence of communism among South Korea's embryo political groupings. Their warnings fell upon fertile soil. In the light of events in Europe, the occupiers were entirely ready to believe that communists were at the root of political disturbances, their cells working energetically to seize control of the country. Benninghoff reported: 'Communists advocate the seizure *now* of Japanese properties and may be a threat to law and order. It is probable that well-trained agitators are attempting to bring about chaos in our area so as to cause the Koreans to repudiate the United States in favour of Soviet "freedom" and control.'[10]

The principal losers in the political competition that now developed, to discover which Koreans could prove themselves most hostile to communism, and most sympathetic to the ideals of the United States, were the members of the so-called 'Korean People's Republic', the KPR. In Korea in 1945, the phrase 'people's republic' had not yet taken on the pejorative association it would so soon acquire. The KPR was a grouping of nationalists and prominent members of the anti-Japanese resistance who, before the Americans arrived, sought to make themselves a credible future leadership for Korea. More than half of the eighty-seven leaders chosen by an assembly of several hundred at Kyonggi Girls' High School on 6 September had served terms of imprisonment under the Japanese. Also, at least half could be identified as leftists or communists. But prominent exiles such as Syngman Rhee, Mu Chong, Kim Ku, and Kim Il Sung were granted places *in absentia*, although few subsequently accepted the roles for which they had been chosen. It is significant that the men of the right nominated to the KPR leadership were, on average, almost twenty years older than those of the left.

It was not surprising that the Americans, on their arrival, knew nothing of the KPR. The chaotic struggle to fill the political vacuum in Korea was further confused by the arrival from Chungking of the self-proclaimed Korean Provisional Government, an exile grouping which included some nominated members of the KPR. In the weeks that followed, the military government's scepticism about the KPR – energetically fostered by the Japanese – grew apace. Here, there was more than a little in common with Western attitudes to Ho Chi Minh and his colleagues in Vietnam of the same period. There was no attempt to examine closely the communist ideology of the leftists, to discover how far they were the creatures of Moscow, and how far they were merely vague socialists and nationalists who found traditional landlordism repugnant. No allowance was made for the prestige earned by the communists' dominant role in armed resistance to the Japanese. Hodge and his men saw no merit in the KPR's militant sense of Korean nationalism – this merely represented an obstacle to smooth American military government. It would be naive to suppose that such a grouping as the KPR could have formed an instantly harmonious leadership for an independent Korea. The group included too many irreconcilable factions. But it also represented the only genuine cross-section of Korean nationalist opinion ever to come together under one roof, however briefly. Given time and encouragement, it might have offered South Korea its best prospect of building a genuine democracy.

But the strident tones in which the KPR addressed the American military government ensured that the group was rapidly identified as a threat and a problem. 'There is evidence [wrote Benninghoff on 10 October] that the [KPR] group receives support and direction from the Soviet Union (perhaps from Koreans formerly resident in Siberia). In any event, it is the most aggressive party; its newspaper has compared American methods of occupation [with those of the Russians] in a manner that may be interpreted as unfavorable to the United States.'[11]

It was another group, which could call upon only a fraction of the KPR's likely political support, that seemed infinitely more congenial to Hodge and his advisers: '. . . the so-called democratic or conservative group, which numbers among its members many of the professional and educational leaders who were educated in the United States or in American missionary institutions in Korea. In their aims and policies they demonstrate a desire to follow the Western democracies, and they almost unanimously desire the early return of Dr Syngman Rhee and the "Provisional Government" at Chungking.'[12] Barely three weeks after the American landings in Korea, official thinking in Seoul was already focusing upon the creation of a new government for the South, built around the person of one of the nation's most prominent exiles.

Syngman Rhee was born in 1875, the son of a genealogical scholar. He failed the civil service exams several times before becoming a student of English. Between 1899 and 1904 he was imprisoned for political activities. On his release, he went to the United States, where he studied for some years, becoming an MA at Harvard and a Ph.D at Princeton – the first Korean to receive an American doctorate. After a brief return to his homeland in 1910, Rhee once more settled in America. He remained there for the next thirty-five years, lobbying relentlessly for American support for Korean independence, financed by the contributions of Korean patriots. If he was despised by some of his fellow-countrymen for his egoism, his ceaseless self-promotion, his absence from the armed struggle that engaged other courageous nationalists, his extraordinary determination could not be denied. Through all his long years in the United States, Rhee learned nothing, and forgot nothing. His iron will was exerted as ruthlessly against rival factions of expatriates as against colonial occupation. He could boast an element of prescience in his own world vision. As early as 1944, when the United States government still cherished all manner of delusions about the post-war prospect of working harmoniously with Stalin, Rhee was telling officials in Washington: 'The only possibility of avoiding the ultimate conflict between the

United States and the Soviet Union is to build up all democratic, non-communistic elements wherever possible.'[13]

Rhee had gained one great advantage by his absence from his own country for so long. Many of his rivals disliked each other as much as the Japanese. But against Rhee, little of substance was known. He was free from the taint of collaboration. While the Americans struggled to come to terms with a culture and a society that were alien to them, Rhee was a comfortingly comprehensible figure: fluent in the small talk of democracy, able to converse about America and American institutions with easy familiarity, above all at home in the English language. Rhee was acerbic, prickly, uncompromising. But to Hodge and his advisers, this obsessive, ruthless nationalist and anti-communist seemed a plausible father-figure for the new Korea. On 20 October, the general was present at an official welcoming ceremony for the Americans in Seoul, stage-managed by the so-called Korean Democratic Party, the KDP – in reality a highly conservative grouping. On the platform stood a large ebony screen inlaid with mother-of-pearl. In a grand moment of theatre, the screen was pulled aside. The bony, venerable figure of Dr Syngman Rhee was revealed to the Korean people. The crowd cheered uproariously. Rhee delivered a rousingly anti-Soviet speech, and disconcerted even his sponsors by denouncing American complicity in the Soviet occupation of the North. The doctor was triumphantly launched upon his career as South Korea's most celebrated – or notorious – politician.

Overwhelmingly the strongest card that Rhee possessed was the visible support of the Americans. Roger Makins, a senior official in the British Foreign Office throughout the early Cold War period, remarks upon 'the American propensity to go for a man, rather than a movement – Giraud among the French in 1942, Chiang Kai Shek in China. Americans have always liked the idea of dealing with a foreign leader who can be identified and perceived as "their man". They are much less comfortable with movements.'[14] So it was in Korea with Syngman Rhee.

In an Asian society, where politics are often dominated by an instinctive desire to fall in behind the strongest force, Rhee's backing from the military government was a decisive force in his rise to power. When Benninghoff identified Rhee with the Korean 'Provisional Government' in Chungking, he blithely ignored the open hostility between the two which had persisted for twenty years, despite Rhee's continuing claim to be the 'Provisional Government's' representative in Washington. The State Department, with long and close experience of Rhee, regarded him as a dangerous mischief-maker. The return of Rhee to Seoul remains a murky episode. The military government firmly denied not only complicity, but prior knowledge of this. Yet all the evidence now suggests that General Hodge and his staff participated in a carefully orchestrated secret plan to bring back Rhee, despite the refusal of the State Department to grant him a passport. A former Deputy Director of the wartime OSS, one Preston Goodfellow, prevailed upon the State Department to provide Rhee with documentation. There appears to have been at least a measure of corruption in this transaction. Rhee came to know Goodfellow during the war, when the Korean mendaciously suggested to the American that he could provide agents for operations behind the Japanese lines. After the war, it seems almost certain that Goodfellow assisted and raised finance for Rhee in return for the promise of commercial concessions in Korea when the doctor gained power. The South Korean flew to Seoul in one of MacArthur's aircraft. Despite the vigorous denials of the US Army in the Far East, it seems likely that he met secretly with both the Supreme Commander and Hodge during his stopover in Tokyo. Rhee, it is apparent, was their nominee for the leadership of a Korean civilian government.

Why did not Washington, undeluded about Rhee's shortcomings, simply call a halt to the policies being pursued in Seoul? John Carter Vincent, director of the State Department's Office of Far Eastern Affairs, indeed sought to remind the War Department that the United States was seeking to avoid taking sides, far less promoting factions, in Korean politics. But his memorandum of 7

November on these issues provoked a response from John J. McCloy, the Assistant Secretary of War, which goes as far as any document of the period to explain the course of events in post-war Korea:

> Vincent's memorandum seems to me to avoid in large part the really pressing realities facing us in Korea ... From talking with General Hodge I believe that his concern is that the communists will seize by direct means the government in our area. If this were done, it would seriously prejudice our intention to permit the people of Korea freely to choose their own form of government. There is no question but that communist action is actively and intelligently being carried out through our zone ... It would seem that the best way to approach it in the over-all is to build up on our own a reasonable and respectable government or group of advisors which will be able under General Hodge to bring some order out of the political, social, and economic chaos that now exist south of the 38th Parallel and so provide the basis for, at some later date, a really free and uncoerced election by the people ... To get back to Vincent's memorandum – does it not add up to asking us to tell Hodge that we really repose little confidence in him, that we are not prepared to let him do the few things which, on the spot – and what a spot – he feels can be useful towards achieving our aims? Let us not only ask for his views on the communist problem and his thoughts as to how to keep it from wrecking our objectives, but let us also let him use as many exiled Koreans as he can, depending on his discretion not to go too far.[15]

The essence of McCloy's argument, which would serve as the justification for all that was done in Korea in the three years that followed, was that it was an idealistic fantasy to suppose that the United States could merely hold the ring, serve as neutral umpires while Koreans worked out their own destiny. Some Korean leaders must be singled out from the mob of contending factions, and assisted to win and retain power. It must surely be the men on the spot, Hodge and his staff, who were best qualified to decide which Koreans these should be. The American military rulers employed no further deceits to dignify the process by which they now set about installing a congenial regime. Just as the Russians, at this period, were securing control of North Korea for a communist regime, so the only credentials that the Americans sought to establish for the prospective masters of South Korea were their hostility to communism and willingness to do business with the Americans.

If this appears a simplistic view of American policy, the policy itself could scarcely have been less subtle. In October 1945, the Americans created an eleven-man Korean 'Advisory Council' to their Military Governor, Major-General Arnold. Although the membership purported to be representative of the South Korean political spectrum, in reality only one nominee, Yo Un-hyong, was a man of the left. Yo initially declined to have anything to do with the Council, declaring contemptuously that its very creation 'reverses the fact of who is guest and who is host in Korea'. Then, having succumbed to Hodge's personal request to participate, Yo took one look around the room at the Council's first session, and swept out. He later asked Hodge if the American believed that a group which included only one non-conservative could possibly be considered representative of anything. An eleventh nominated member, a well-known nationalist named Cho Man-sik who had been working in the North, never troubled to show his face.

The Council was doomed from the outset. It reminded most Koreans too vividly of their recent colonial experience – its chairman had been a member of the Japanese governor-general's advisory body, and an enthusiastic supporter of the Japanese war effort. Yet Yo Un-hyong's 'unhelpful' behaviour, contrasted with the 'cooperative' attitude of the conservatives who joined the Council, reinforced the American conviction that the conservatives – above all, the members of the Korean Democratic Party – were the men to work with. But what now was to be done about the reality in the countryside – that reports reaching Hodge declared that while the KPR was 'organised into a government at all levels', the KDP was 'poorly organised or unorganised in most places'?[16]

Hodge's answer was that the KPR must be fought and destroyed, to provide the KDP with the opportunity for survival and growth. On 10 November, as a warning to the Korean press, the most prominent Seoul newspaper sympathetic to the KPR was shut down, ostensibly for accountancy irregularities. On 25 November, Hodge cabled MacArthur about his intention to denounce the KPR: 'This will constitute in effect a "declaration of war" upon the Communistic elements in Korea, and may result in temporary disorders. It will also bring charges of political discrimination in a "free" country, both by local pinkos and by pinko press. If activities of the Korean People's Republic continue as in the past, they will greatly delay the time when Korea can be said to be ready for independence. Request comment.' MacArthur answered simply, like McCloy before him, confirming Hodge's absolute discretion: 'Use your own best judgement . . . I am not sufficiently familiar with the local situation to advise you intelligently, but I will support whatever decision you may take in this matter.'[17]

Throughout the winter of 1945–46, the military government waged a campaign to suppress both the KPR and resurgent labour unions, which were adjudged an inevitable focus of communist subversion. And even as this struggle was taking place, a new controversy was growing in intensity. In a fit of benevolent reforming zeal after their arrival, the Americans greatly eased the burdensome conditions of landholding for the peasants – a highly popular measure – and also introduced a free market in rice. The traditional rice surplus was the strongpoint of the Korean economy. Now, suddenly, by a measure introduced with the best of intentions, the Americans unleashed a wave of speculation, hoarding and profiteering on a scale the country had never seen. The price of a bushel of rice soared from 9.4 yen in September 1945 to 2,800 yen just a year later. Officials were making vast fortunes through rice smuggling and speculation. By February 1946, not only was the free market rescinded, but stringent rationing had been introduced.

Tough quotas were introduced for peasant farmers to fulfil, enforced by local police and officials.

In the winter of 1945, the Americans ruling South Korea harboured no delusions that they had made much progress towards creating an ordered and democratic society. They understood that they presided over a seething, unhappy country ripe for major disorders. They saw that the Koreans' hunger for unity and independence surpassed all other ideology and sentiment. They perceived that the drifting policies of the military government, contrasted with the coherent if ruthless socialisation now taking place north of the 38th Parallel, could only increase Korean respect for Soviet strength, and diminish still further American popularity. On 16 December, Hodge submitted a grim report to MacArthur in Tokyo, which subsequently reached the desk of President Truman. His summary of the situation he faced concluded: 'Under present conditions with no corrective action forthcoming, I would go so far as to recommend we give serious consideration to an agreement with Russia that both the US and Russia withdraw forces from Korea simultaneously and leave Korea to its own devices and an inevitable internal upheaval for its self-purification.'[18]

Hodge and his colleagues placed the overwhelming burden of blame for their difficulties upon the Russians: Soviet-directed internal policies in the North, and skilful subversion in the South. The Americans detected the organising hand of Moscow in a host of political groups in South Korea. In this, they greatly overestimated both Soviet will and capability in the South at this period. There is no doubt that communists throughout Korea wished to create a united nation under their own control. But many non-communist Koreans also incurred American animosity by their enthusiasm for national unification, merely because Hodge and his colleagues considered this unattainable under non-communist rule. The US military government in Korea – like its counterparts in other areas of the world at this period – dismissed the possibility that its own manipulation of conservative forces in a society was comparable, morally and politically, with the Soviets' sponsorship of communist groups in their own zone. The liberal view of history acknowledges the ultimate benevolence of American influence upon the post-war political settlement in the developed societies that came under their control, above all those in Europe. But in Korea, as in many other less developed nations, it was hard to discover any prospective anti-communist leadership possessed of the idealism, the commitment to tolerable moral and political standards, which rendered it worthy of the support of the United States.

On 27 December 1945, the Three-Power Foreign Ministers' Conference ended in Moscow with an important agreement. The Russians accepted an American proposal for Korea: the nation was to become the object of a Four-Power 'International Trusteeship' for five years, paving the way to independence as a unified state. Four-Power Trusteeship represented a concession by Moscow, cramping immediate progress towards a communist state in Korea. The Russians probably anticipated that the left in Korea was sufficiently strong to ensure its own ultimate triumph under any arrangement. But the Moscow Accords also reflected the low priority that Stalin gave to Korea. He was willing to appease Western fears in the Far East, no doubt in the expectation that in return, Washington would less vigorously oppose Soviet policies in Europe.

In the weeks that followed the Moscow meeting, there was political turmoil in South Korea. Right-wing factions expressed their passionate hostility to the trusteeship proposals, backed by strikes and demonstrations. So too did Hodge and his advisers, who raged against the unknown State Department 'experts' who had made the agreement with the Soviets. On 28 January, the general offered his resignation in protest. It was refused. More than this, the tide in Washington now began to turn strongly in favour of the American group in Seoul. No less shrewd a diplomat than Averell Harriman visited Korea in February, and returned to report most favourably upon Hodge's 'ability and diplomacy'. The Americans themselves now stood their own proposal on its head, and indeed revoked their assent to it. In the wake of the Moscow

meeting, President Truman determined that Secretary of State
Byrnes had given away far too much; that the time had come for a
determined stand against Soviet expansionism; that Stalin should
be confronted on a range of critical fronts. Of these, Korea was
now identified among the foremost. All Asia understood the nature
of the struggle taking place there. 'The Korean question', declared
an editorial in the Chinese newspaper *Ta-Kung-Pao*, 'is in effect the
political battleground for Russo-American mutual animosities, par-
rying and struggling for mastery.'

Hodge's new proposal was that an indigenous Korean political
body should be hastened into existence before the first meeting of
the American-Soviet Joint Commission, intended to supervise the
trusteeship arrangements. On 14 February, the Representative
Democratic Council held its first meeting in Seoul's Capitol building. Of its twenty-eight members, twenty-four were drawn from
rightist political parties. Syngman Rhee declared: 'Hereafter, the
Council will represent the Korean people in its dealings with
General Hodge and the Military Government.' Limited as were the
powers of the Council, it provided the Americans with a core of
acceptable Korean leaders to match the Russian-sponsored communist leadership now established in the North under Kim Il Sung.
When the Joint Commission began its meetings on 20 March, each
side focused its attention and complaints upon the lack of facilities
afforded to the sympathisers of the other for political campaigning
in their own zone.

American policy was now set upon the course from which it
would not again be deflected: to create, as speedily as possible, a
plausible machinery of government in South Korea which could
survive as a bastion against the communist North. On 12 December
1946, the first meeting was held of a provisional South Korean
Legislature, whose membership was once again dominated by the
men of the right, though such was their obduracy that they
boycotted the first sessions in protest against American intervention in the elections, which had vainly sought to prevent absolute
rightist manipulation of the results. A growing body of Korean

officials now controlled the central bureaucracy of SKIG – the South Korean Interim Government. In 1947, a random sample of 115 of these revealed that seventy were former office-holders under the Japanese. Only eleven showed any evidence of anti-Japanese activity during the Korean period.

The suspicions of many Korean nationalists about the conduct of the American military government were redoubled by the fashion in which the National Police, the most detested instrument of Japanese tyranny, was not merely retained, but strengthened. It was the American official historians of the occupation who wrote that 'the Japanese police in Korea possessed a breadth of function and an extent of power equalled in few countries in the modern world.'[19] The 12,000 Japanese in their ranks were sent home. But the 8,000 Koreans who remained – the loyal servants of a brutal tyranny in which torture and judicial murder had been basic instruments of government – found themselves promoted to fill the higher ranks, while total police strength in South Korea doubled. Equipped with American arms, jeeps, and radio communications, the police became the major enforcement arm of American military government, and its chief source of political intelligence. Such men as Yi Ku-bom, one of the most notorious police officers of the Japanese regime, who feared for his life in August 1945, was a year later chief of a major ward station in Seoul. A long rollcall of prominent torturers and anti-nationalist fighters under the colonial power found themselves in positions of unprecedented authority. In 1948, 53 per cent of officers and 25 per cent of rank-and-file police were Japanese-trained. By a supreme irony, when the development began of a constabulary force, from which the South Korean army would grow, the Americans specifically excluded any recruit who had been imprisoned by the Japanese – and thus, any member of the anti-Japanese resistance. The first chief of staff of the South Korean army in 1947 was a former colonel in the Japanese army.

Paek Sun Yup, who was to prove one of the few competent soldiers in Rhee's army in the 1950–53 war, rising to become its

Chief of Staff while still in his early thirties, was a typical product of the system. A North Korean landlord's son, he attended Pyong-yang High School, then Mukden Military Academy; he served as a young officer with the Japanese army in Manchuria. 'We thought nothing about Japanese influence,' he shrugged, years later. 'Every young man takes the status quo for granted. At that time, the Japanese were Number One. They were winning. We had never seen any British or Americans.'[20] Paek's unit was fighting the Russians when the war ended. He walked for a month to reach his home. He quickly disliked what he saw of the new communist regime in the North. On 28 December 1945, he escaped across the 38th Parallel, leaving his wife behind in the North. She joined him later. Two months later, he joined the constabulary as a lieutenant. He rose rapidly, to become director of intelligence in the embryo South Korean army, and a divisional commander a few weeks before the 1950 invasion. No man could have attained Paek's position without demonstrating absolute loyalty to the regime of Syngman Rhee, and all that implied. But in every Asian society, there is an overwhelming instinct in favour of serving the strong-est force. The worst that can be said of Paek is that he was a tough, ambitious product of his environment.

But many young South Koreans did express their hostility to Rhee, and paid the price. Beyond those who were imprisoned, many more became 'unpeople'. Minh Pyong Kyu was a Seoul bank clerk's son who went to medical college in 1946, but found himself expelled in 1948 for belonging to a left-wing student organisation. 'There was an intellectual vacuum in the country at that time,' he said. 'The only interesting books seemed to be those from North Korea, and the communists had a very effective distribution sys-tem. We thought the Americans were nice people who just didn't understand anything about Korea.'[21] Minh's family of eight lived in genteel poverty. His father had lost his job with a mining company in 1945, for its assets lay north of the 38th Parallel. Minh threw himself into anti-government activity: pasting up political posters by night, demonstrating, distributing communist tracts.

Then one morning he was arrested and imprisoned for ten days. The leaders of his group were tried and sentenced to long terms. He himself was released, but expelled from university, to his father's deep chagrin. Like hundreds of thousands of others, Minh yearned desperately for the fall of Syngman Rhee.

Kap Chong Chi, a landowner's son and another university student, felt far better disposed towards the Americans, and towards his own government, than Minh. But even as an unusually sophisticated and educated Korean, he shared the general ignorance and uncertainty about the politics of his own country: 'In those days, we did not know what democracy was. For a long time after the Americans came, we did not know what the communists were, or who Syngman Rhee was. So many of the students from the countryside, farmers' children, called themselves communists. There was so much political passion among them, but also so much ignorance.'[22] Korean society was struggling to come to terms with a political system, when it had possessed none for almost half a century. Not surprisingly, the tensions and hostilities became simplistic: between haves and have-nots; between those who shared the privileges of power and those who did not; between landlord and peasant; intellectual and pragmatist. The luxury of civilised political debate was denied to South Korea, as it was to the North.

*

Ferris Miller, the naval officer who was one of the advance party at Inchon in September 1945, left the country at the end of that year. But he was that rare creature – an American deeply attracted by Korea: 'Somehow, it had got into my blood. I liked the place, the food, the people.' In February 1947, he returned to Seoul as a civilian contract employee of the military government. He was dismayed by what he found:

> Everything had gone downhill. Nothing worked – the pipes were frozen, the electricity kept going off. The corruption was

there for anybody to see. A lot of genuine patriots in the South were being seduced by the blandishments of the North. There were Korean exiles coming home from everywhere – Manchuria, China, Japan. Everybody was struggling, even the Americans. The PX was almost bare of goods. Most of our own people hated the country. There were men who came, stayed a week, and just got out. There were Koreans wearing clothes made of army blankets; orphans hanging around the railway stations; people chopping wood on the hills above Seoul, the transport system crumbling. It was a pretty bad time.[23]

The conditions Miller discovered in Seoul might as readily have been observed in Berlin, Vienna, Hamburg – any of the war-ruined cities of Europe – that winter. Even in London and Paris, cold and shortages were a way of life in 1947. But whereas in Europe, democratic political life was reviving with remarkable vigour, in South Korea a fundamentally corrupt society was being created. Power was being transferred by the Americans to a Korean conservative faction indifferent to the concept of popular freedom, representative only of ambition for power and wealth. The administration and policing of the country were being placed in the hands of men who had been willing tools of a tyranny that a world war had just been fought to destroy. Their only discernible claim to office was their hostility to communism.

Between 1945 and 1947, the foreign political patrons of North and South Korea became permanently committed to their respective protégés. The course of events thereafter is more simply described. In September 1947, despite Russian objections, the United States referred the future of Korea to the United Nations. Moscow made a proposal to Washington remarkably similar to that which General Hodge had advanced almost two years earlier: both great powers should simultaneously withdraw their forces, leaving the Koreans to resolve their own destinies. The Russians were plainly confident – with good reason – that left to their own devices, the forces of the left in both Koreas would prevail. The

Americans, making the same calculation, rejected the Russian plan. On 14 November, their own proposal was accepted by the General Assembly: there was to be UN supervision of elections to a Korean government, followed by Korean independence and the withdrawal of all foreign forces. The Eastern bloc abstained from the vote on the American plan, which was carried by forty-six votes to none.

The United Nations Temporary Commission on Korea met for the first time in Seoul on 12 January 1948. The Russians and North Koreans utterly rejected UN participation in deciding the future of Korea. Thus it was apparent from the outset that any decision the Commission reached would be implemented only south of the 38th Parallel. The General Assembly's Interim Committee brooded for a time on this problem. Dr Rhee was strongly in favour of immediate elections for as much of Korea as was willing to hold them. But every Korean opposition party argued against holding a vote in the face of the communist boycott. Not only would this make genuinely 'free' elections impossible – it would doom for years, if not for ever, the national unity so many Koreans still cherished. It would be a formal recognition of the divided status of Korea.

The Australian and Canadian members of the UN Temporary Commission shared these misgivings. But a majority of its members – France, the Philippines, Chiang Kai Shek's China, El Salvador and India – supported elections in the South. The Interim Committee agreed that elections should go ahead. Campaigning for election to South Korea's first government was held in a climate of mounting political repression. William F. Dean, the American Military Governor, replied to a question from the UN Commission about political prisoners: 'I have yet to find a man in jail because his ideology is different from anyone else's.' Yet it was he who authorised the Korean police to deputise bands of 'loyal citizens' into 'Community Protective Organisations'. These quickly became known colloquially among Americans as 'Rhee's goon squads'. Their purpose was frankly terroristic – to drive not only communists, but any group unsympathetic to the right, from South Korean life. In the six weeks before polling, 589 people were killed in disturbances, and 10,000 'processed' at police stations.

On election day, out of a total population of 20 million, 95 per cent of the 7.8 million registered voters went to the polls. The UN Commissioners declared that the vote represented a 'valid expression of the free will of the people'. America's Ambassador to the UN, John Foster Dulles, told the General Assembly that the elections 'constituted a magnificent demonstration of the capacity of the Korean people to establish a representative and responsible government'. Syngman Rhee's 'Association for the Rapid Realisation of Independence' gained fifty-five of the two hundred seats in South Korea's new constitutional assembly. The Conservative Hanguk Democratic Party won twenty-nine, and two other right-wing groups gained twelve and six seats respectively. The right therefore commanded an effective majority of the two hundred seats. The left boycotted the election. The North Koreans, invited to send delegates, unsurprisingly made no response. Rhee and his supporters instituted a presidential system of government. He himself was inaugurated as South Korea's first elected leader on 24 July 1948. On 14 August, the third anniversary of VJ-Day, amid the wailing tones of the Great Bell of Chongno, the US flag was lowered over the Capitol building in Seoul, and that of the new South Korean Republic was hoisted. General MacArthur himself delivered a bellicose speech in which he told Koreans, 'an artificial barrier has divided your land. This barrier must and shall be torn down.'

In the months that followed, Syngman Rhee addressed himself to the creation of a ruthless dictatorship in South Korea. Any minister who showed symptoms of independence was dismissed. The President took steps to bind the police and constabulary under his personal control. Each new manifestation of left-wing opposition provided provocation for a renewed surge of government repression. There were frequent clashes along the 38th Parallel with North Korean border units, for which blame seemed about evenly divided. The most serious internal upheaval began on 19

October 1948, when an army unit sent to deal with communist rebels on Cheju island mutinied at Yosu, on the south-west tip of Korea. They won local civilian support by urging vengeance upon oppressive local police, and marched against the town of Sunchon. Here, they were checked. By the end of the month, the uprising had been defeated, at a cost of a thousand lives. But a climate of oppression, intolerance and political ruthlessness was deepening. Ferociously hostile radio propaganda from Pyongyang fed rumours of imminent invasion from the North. In November, press restrictions were imposed, and more than seven hundred political arrests carried out. Between September 1948 and April 1949, there were a total of 89,710 police arrests in South Korea. Only 28,404 of the victims were released without charge. Kim Ku, the seventy-four-year-old veteran of the 'Provisional Government' who had suffered grievously for his opposition to Japanese rule and still commanded widespread respect in South Korea as the President's most credible rival, was assassinated in his study by a creature of Rhee in June 1949. In the same month, the last United States occupation troops, excepting a five-hundred-man assistance and training group – the KMAG – left Korea. Rhee pleaded desperately for a continued American military presence. But the Russians had already pulled their army out of the North, and Washington was anyway reluctant to allow its forces to linger longer in Korea, whose occupation had cost so much pain and treasure. The United States had done all that it believed possible. With so many other demands upon America's resources as the Cold War intensified, its leaders were unwilling to allow Korea to assume a disproportionate importance. It was a measure of Washington's determination to limit the mischief that could come out of Korea, that Dr Rhee's new army was denied armour and heavy artillery. The intention was to provide South Korea solely with the means for her own defence, above all against mounting internal guerrilla activity.

The peaceful departure of the Red Army from North Korea diminished American fears of overt communist aggression in the peninsula. North of the 38th Parallel, the Soviets left behind a

ruthlessly disciplined totalitarian Stalinist society, in the hands of
their protégé, Kim Il Sung. Russian advisers helped to set up a
national network of 'people's committees', and a central government based upon a 'Provisional People's Committee'. In November
1946, the first election to membership was held, based upon a
single list of candidates, all members of a 'Democratic Front'.
Moscow reported that Kim Il Sung's grouping collected 97 per cent
of votes cast. In February 1947, a 'Convention of People's Committees' met for the first time in Pyongyang, and established the
'People's Assembly of North Korea'. The 'Democratic People's
Republic of Korea' was proclaimed on 9 September 1948. But North
Korea was an undeveloped society. The prospect that it might
embark upon a war without the direct support of its Russian
masters still appeared remote. Among those in the Pentagon and
the State Department conscious of Korea's existence, there were
considerable misgivings about what had been done and what had
been created in the South in America's name. Yet there was also
the feeling that the best had been made of an impossible situation.
Diplomatically, it was a considerable achievement that the United
States had been able to maintain the support of the Western Allies
for its anti-communist programme. The United Nations Commission on Korea, charged with pursuing the eventual objective of
supervising the unification of the divided nation, now maintained
a permanent presence in the South, monitoring the mutually
hostile activities of Seoul and Pyongyang, and seeking 'to observe
and report any developments which might lead to or otherwise
involve military conflict in Korea'. It is a backhanded tribute to the
vestiges of democracy that persisted in the South that, in the
elections for a new National Assembly in May 1950, Syngman
Rhee's bitter unpopularity was fully reflected. The parties of the
right gained only forty-nine seats, against 130 seats won by Inde-
pendents and forty-four by other parties.

*

With the advantage of hindsight, it is evident that United States policy in post-war Korea was clumsy and ill-conceived. It reflected not only a lack of understanding, but a lack of interest in the country and its people, beyond their potential as bricks in the wall against communist aggression. This failure, it may be suggested, lay close to the heart of the United States' difficulties not only with Korea, but also with China and subsequently with Vietnam. The occupiers' enthusiasm for the reproduction of American political and bureaucratic institutions in Asia held little charm for Koreans with different attitudes and priorities. Japan, alone in Asia, represented in the forties, as it represents today, the single glittering example of a society in which American political transplants took firm root. Only Japan was sufficiently educated and homogeneous to adapt the new institutions successfully. In Japan alone, the traditional leaders of society were not identified by their poorer compatriots with an intolerable measure of injustice, corruption and collaboration with foreign oppressors. The most powerful weapon in the communists' armoury in Asia was their appearance of commitment to personal honesty and selflessness, against the remorseless corruption and cupidity of their opponents. Many Asians discovered too late that the merits of private honesty were outweighed by the bitter cost of losing public freedom. In those parts of Asia where they exerted influence, the Americans honourably attempted to mitigate the worst excesses of landlordism and social oppression. But they never acknowledged how grievously these evils damaged their perpetrators as credible rulers in a democratic society. Again and again in Asia, America aligned herself alongside social forces which possessed no hope of holding power by consent. Chiang Kai Shek's followers, like those of Syngman Rhee, could maintain themselves in office only by the successful application of oppressive force.

Yet the United States is also entitled to argue before the bar of history, that a more idealistic policy in post-war Korea would have caused the country to fall to the communists. The local communists' credentials as fighters against the Japanese, their freedom from the embarrassments of landlordism and corruption, would almost certainly have enabled them to gain a popular mandate in 1945–46. Whatever their initial willingness to form a coalition with Koreans of the centre and right, would the moderates not have suffered the same inexorable fate of death or impotence that befell so many East European politicians of that period, not to mention those of North Korea? Diplomatic historians have convincingly shown that in 1945–46, contrary to American belief at the time, South Korea did not form part of the Soviet expansion plan. Yet how were the contemporary leaders of the West to know or to guess that this was so, that Stalin had indulgently decided to exclude Korea from the fate that had befallen Czechoslovakia, Poland, Yugoslavia, Rumania, Hungary, Austria? In the late forties it seemed, upon sufficient evidence, that the purpose of the Soviet Union was to test the strength of the West at every possible point, and to advance wherever weakness was detected. Dr Syngman Rhee and his followers appeared at least to represent strength and determination, at a period when these were at a premium. In historical assessments of the post-war period, it is sometimes forgotten that the Russians were as deeply feared by many Europeans as the Germans a few years earlier. The appeasers of Hitler had become figures of derision and contempt. Those who observed the Red Army's dreadful record of rape and pillage in Eastern Europe, the unquestionable readiness of Moscow to employ murder as an instrument of policy, felt nothing but scorn for the would-be appeasers of Stalin, in Europe or in Asia.

Nor did American manipulation of South Korean politics seem anything like as awful a matter, even in liberal circles, in 1945 as it might forty years later. In the course of the Second World War, none of the partners of the Grand Alliance had shown any greater sensitivity towards the human rights and feelings of Asian peoples than the chiefs of the military government displayed in Seoul from 1945 to 1948. If Korean policemen sometimes tortured or killed civilians, if their leaders accepted bribes, if their politicians behaved like mafiosi – was not this the way 'these people' had always done things? Was it not merely a higher form of Western arrogance to seek to impose Western ideas of humanity upon a society in which dog was a culinary delicacy – customarily strangled and depilated with a pine taper in the course of preparation – and where fried crickets and boiled silkworms featured prominently in local good food guides? The American record in Korea between 1945 and 1950 must be judged against the indisputable reality of Soviet expansionism, of Stalin's bottomless malevolence. No charge against the Rhee regime can blunt the force of one simple truth: that, while the United States deliberately declined to provide South Korea with the means to conduct armed aggression, the Soviet Union supplied North Korea with a large arsenal of tanks, artillery and military aircraft. The events that unfolded in the summer of 1950 demonstrated that American fears for the peninsula were entirely well founded, whatever the shortcomings of Washington's political response to these.

2 » INVASION

In the course of 1949, relations between North and South Korea, the tempo of mutual propaganda hysteria, rose sharply. In the South, constant military pressure eroded the strength of the communist guerrillas in the mountains. In April 1949, Pyongyang invited South Korea's anti-Rhee leaders to attend a 'coalition conference'. Of 545 delegates present, 240 were from the South. Rhee denounced them, not unreasonably, as 'communist stooges'. In August, a new communist 'Supreme People's Assembly' met in Haiju, just north of the 38th Parallel. At this, a 'People's Democratic Republic' embracing both North and South Korea was announced. A South Korean was its nominated foreign minister. But on the 38th Parallel, responsibility for border incidents was by no means a monopoly of Pyongyang. In May 1949, in one of the most serious incidents, South Korean forces penetrated up to two and a half miles into North Korean territory, and attacked local villages. In a climate of intense mutual mistrust, in December the British Foreign Office asked the War Office for a military assessment of the situation in Korea. It received a sceptical response:

> In the past [wrote Major J. R. Ferguson Innes] it has always been our view that irrespective of strengths the North Korean forces would have little difficulty in dealing effectively with the forces of South Korea should full-scale hostilities break out. This somewhat naturally (since they raised, equipped and trained South Korean forces) was not the American view. Recently, however, they have been coming round to our way of thinking regarding the capabilities of the respective

forces.... On the question of aggression by the North, there can be no doubt whatever that their ultimate objective is to overrun the South; and I think in the long term there is no doubt that they will do so, in which case, as you so aptly remark, the Americans will have made a rather handsome contribution of equipment to the military strength of Asiatic Communism. As to their method of achieving their object, short of World War III beginning, I think they will adopt the well-tried tactics of preparing the country from within rather than resort to open aggression, although 'frontier incidents' will doubtless continue.

... Regarding American policy, if in fact one exists, towards South Korea, I can only say we know little, and of their future intentions even less ... Whilst being in no doubt about future North Korean (or Soviet) plans regarding South Korea, we think an invasion is unlikely in the immediate view; however, if it did take place, I think it improbable that the Americans would become involved. The possession of South Korea is not essential for Allied strategic plans, and though it would obviously be desirable to deny it to the enemy, it would not be of sufficient importance to make it the cause of World War III. Meanwhile, we must accept an uneasy status quo and hope for the best.[1]

Brigadier-General W. L. Roberts, commanding officer of the American Military Assistance Group in Korea, not surprisingly took a more sanguine view of the South Korean army than the British officer quoted above. In a letter to General Charles Bolté, Director of Plans at the Pentagon, in March 1950, he urged that Americans should play a prominent role in stiffening ROK formations:

If South Korea is called upon to defend itself against aggression from the North, its ground army is capable of doing an excellent job. If American advisers are present (even on Regimental and Division level) it will do an even better job, for we have found the Americans are leaned on more heavily the rougher it gets. In other words, the advisers will almost command except in name.

Here, of course, was the root of many delusions that were to plague the US Army in Asia for the next generation. The belief that American officers could, in effect, officer Asian troops to the same effect that the British had achieved with their Indian army for two hundred years persisted into Indochina. Worse, there was the notion that they could temper control with politeness, by accompanying units merely as 'advisers'. Later, as the ROK army expanded in the course of war, this principle of giving Koreans American support would be extended, so that Korean sub-units were subordinated to American ones. The Koreans' knowledge of the absolute lack of confidence with which they were regarded by their allies and mentors contributed materially to justifying this. But in March 1950, despite his optimistic view of ROK capabilities, Roberts acknowledged that the strategic perspective did not favour Seoul's forces:

> All G-2 sources tell that the North Koreans have up to 100 Russian planes and a training program for pilots. You know and I know what 100 planes can do to troops, to towns and to transport on roads.
>
> So, if South Korea were attacked today by the inferior [sic] ground forces of North Korea plus their Air Corps, I feel that South Korea would take a bloody nose. Again then, knowing these people somewhat, I feel they would follow the apparent winner and South Korea would be gobbled up to be added to the rest of Red Asia.
>
> This is a fat nation now with all its ECA goods, with warehouses bulging with plenty of rice from a good crop even if their finances are shaky with great inflationary tendencies. It is getting into the position of an excellent prize of war; strategically it points right into the heart of Japan and in the hands of an enemy it weakens the Japanese bastion of Western defense.[2]

Washington's view of the importance of Korea to the anti-communist cause was changing. But the Administration's thinking remained confused, and so did the signals that it sent out across the world. The critical force in United States policy towards the Far East by the summer of 1950 was the deep bitterness and frustration of the American people about the 'loss' of China to the communists. The defeat of Chiang Kai Shek's American-sponsored nationalist armies was a profound shock and source of sorrow not only to the legendary 'China lobby', but to many Americans who had grown up all their lives with a sense of missionary commitment to China. The vast Asian society had been a central force in the lives of such men as Henry Luce, who put Chiang on the cover of *Time* magazine a record seven times. In the case of great industrialists such as Alfred Kohlberg, economic interest marched hand in hand with a real personal passion for China. America's cash investment in Chiang's creakingly corrupt regime had been enormous: $645 million in aid and $826 in Lend–Lease during World War II, followed by another two billion dollars in the years that followed. Asia in general, and China in particular, called deeply to many Americans in a manner that Europe did not. Europe was a fully-fashioned society, often ungrateful for American influence and aid. Yet Asia seemed to lie half-made, half-civilised, wide open for all the cultural, religious and democratic improvements that the United States could offer. Throughout the Second World War, America retained delusions about the virtue and power of Chiang Kai Shek's regime that were shared by none of her allies. When the State Department's admirable 'old China hands' warned persistently of the hopeless corruption and incompetence of the Nationalists, of the irresistible power of Mao Tse Tung's communists, their reports served only to damn them long afterwards. Davies, Vincent, and the others became, for conservative America, not the faithful prophets of disaster, but the agents who had contributed to bring this about. 'China asked for a sword, and we gave her a dull paring knife,' declared Senator Bridges of New Hampshire. Senator Taft damned the appeasers of the State Department, 'guided by a left-wing group who obviously wanted to get rid of Chiang, and were willing at least to turn China over to the communists for that purpose'. The fall of China to the communists, far from convincing Americans of the need to ensure that the regimes they supported possessed some validity within their own societies, merely persuaded much of the United States that anti-communist regimes must be sustained and supported, however unpopular with their own peoples. George Kennan sought to suggest that 'a certain sentimentality towards the Chinese' among Americans 'was both patronising and dangerously naive'. Dean Acheson, Truman's Secretary of State, was doing his utmost throughout 1949 to reconcile Americans to accepting the probable fall of Chiang's last bastion, the island of Formosa.

> The unfortunate but inescapable fact is that the ominous result of the civil war in China was beyond the control of the government of the United States [Acheson wrote, eminently sanely, in an August 1949 White Paper]. Nothing that this country did or could have done within the reasonable limits of its capabilities could have changed that result; nothing that was left undone by this country has contributed to it. It was the product of internal Chinese forces, forces which this country tried to influence, but could not. A decision was arrived at within China, if only a decision by default.

But this was now the day of Senator Joseph McCarthy. Gallup suggested that 39 per cent of Americans believed the Wisconsin Republican's Red witch hunt, his hounding of the State Department officials who had 'betrayed' China to the communists was 'a good thing'. In the words of McCarthy's best biographer, 'the political atmosphere in the spring of 1950 was such that evidence and logic were often avoided.' Senators Bridges, Knowland and McCarran issued a statement denouncing Acheson's China White Paper as 'a 1,054-page whitewash of a wishful, do-nothing policy which has succeeded only in placing Asia in danger of Soviet conquest, with its ultimate threat to the peace of the world and our own national security'. 'Growing numbers of Republicans were convinced that McCarthyism was their ticket to political power, and were determined to back Joe's Red hunt as long as the headlines continued to bombard the Administration.' By this mid-term of Truman's second Administration, he was already a beleaguered President, under immense domestic pressures for his alleged weakness in confronting the communist threat, at home and abroad.

Truman himself was increasingly convinced that the Soviets were risk-takers, opportunists who would press forward on every front where they detected weakness. In 1950, the memory of the thirties was not merely vivid, but a dominant force in the thinking of most Western politicians. At this historic period, when the closest advisers of the American President were men whose minds focused upon Europe as the cockpit of world affairs, the failure of the policy of appeasement of the dictators lay close to the heart of their political thought. 'We are losing the Cold War,' Bernard Baruch warned Truman in April 1950. John Foster Dulles accepted office in the administration that month only on condition that 'some early affirmative action' would be taken against 'the communist menace'. The joint State-Defense Study Group headed by Paul Nitze which produced the critical study of American foreign policy objectives, NSC-68, in the first months of 1950, urged much greater defence expenditure. It defined the Soviet purpose as 'the complete subversion or forcible destruction of the machinery of government and structure of society in the non-Soviet world, and their replacement by an apparatus and structure subservient to and controlled by the Kremlin'. George Kennan and 'Chip' Bohlen, two of America's most prominent experts on the Soviets, opposed the National Security Council's paper. They argued that Moscow was, in reality, far more cautious than the document suggested. But Acheson accepted NSC-68. Its principal conclusion – that the Soviets should be challenged wherever in the world they next embarked upon an assault on freedom – became part of the policy of the Truman Administration.

Yet whatever the validity of Washington's assessment of Soviet intentions, the gravest charge against the United States government in 1950 was that it made a precipitate commitment to an end, before it had begun to will the means. In the aftermath of World War II, the nation's armed forces had not merely been reduced – they had been allowed to crumble to the brink of collapse. Again and again between 1947 and 1950, the Joint Chiefs of Staff warned the President that he was extending America's diplomatic commitments beyond her military means to enforce them. Among the glittering cluster of intellects around the President, by far the least impressive was the Defense Secretary, Louis Johnson. A political operator, a fund-raiser, an electoral grandstander, Johnson had made much political capital from his dramatic savings in the military budget. Yet it was a direct consequence of Johnson's policies, approved by Truman, that by June 1950 MacArthur's divisions in Korea lacked 62 per cent of their infantry firepower and 14 per cent of their tanks; that 80 per cent of the army's sixty-day reserve was unusable, and the army in Japan possessed only forty-five days' supply of ammunition. It was in recognition of the desperate shortcomings of MacArthur's army that the Defense Department agreed that Korea could be removed from the general's theatre responsibilities.

The first and most obvious manifestation of the commitment to NSC-68 was that the United States began to give active support to the French in their struggle against the communist Vietminh in Indochina. Washington felt a growing concern that the Russians might consider some move against Japan, the centrepiece of the American defence of the Pacific basin. While Acheson remained unwilling to commit the United States to the protection of Formosa, his Assistant Secretary for the Far East, Dean Rusk, was increasingly anxious to do so.

Yet in June 1950, the hardening of attitudes within the Administration remained little understood within the United States, and scarcely at all outside it. NSC-68 has been cited as a classic example of a document whose secrecy destroyed its very purpose. Its conclusions remained unpublished for more than twenty years after they were drafted. The public signals reaching Moscow about

American intentions thus remained unchanged, and uncertain. Had the Russians possessed any inkling of the strength of Washington's newfound determination to seek a battleground upon which to challenge communist expansion, it is profoundly unlikely that Moscow would ever have allowed the North Korean invasion of June 1950 to take place.

*

To this day, there remains no explicit, trustworthy evidence about the circumstances in which Kim Il Sung made his decision to invade South Korea in June 1950. But the circumstantial evidence is strong that the Russians sanctioned, rather than instigated the attack. Plainly, it would have been impossible for Kim to act at all without the active assistance of Moscow in providing arms and supplies, and the connivance of Peking in allowing rail movements through Chinese territory. In addition, in the months before the invasion, many thousands of communist veterans who had fought with Mao Tse Tung's armies, but were Korean by birth, returned to their homeland in the north. In sending the Koreans back, the Chinese were almost certainly inspired more by their urgent need to demobilise their vast forces, rather than any desire to reinforce Kim Il Sung's divisions. But the effect was the same. Pyongyang's army was strengthened by large numbers of combat veterans.

The memoirs of Nikita Khrushchev, a heavily tainted source, nonetheless offer a plausible version of the events leading up to the invasion. According to Khrushchev, Kim Il Sung came to Moscow to seek Stalin's acquiescence in his plans for war, and the North Korean was successful in convincing the Russian that he could gain a speedy victory. Mao Tse Tung agreed that the United States would not intervene, 'since the war would be an internal matter which the Korean people would decide for themselves'.[3] The behaviour of Moscow in the months following the outbreak of war suggested Soviet reluctance to identify wholeheartedly with Kim Il Sung's adventure, to stake everything upon his victory. The Soviets appear to have satisfied themselves that the Korean could make his attempt to unify the country under communism without intolerable political or military risk to themselves. They were probably encouraged in this view by their knowledge of the widespread communist support within the South, which might be expected to rally when the Northerners swept across the country.

One of the foremost historians of this period, Allan S. Whiting, concludes that there was 'no agreement . . . nor . . . any direct evidence on the degree to which Communist China participated in the planning. It is possible that Stalin did not even inform Mao of the forthcoming attack during their weeks of conference in Moscow, although this is highly unlikely.'[4] The Chinese, the overwhelming probability suggests, were passive, if acquiescent parties to North Korea's intentions. Peking, that first summer after attaining final victory in its own civil war, had ample national problems at home, without seeking any share in those of Korea.

In the summer of 1950, a wave of intelligence reports reached both American headquarters in Tokyo, and the CIA in Washington, suggesting that the North Koreans were preparing an invasion of the South. One CIA report, of 10 March 1950, pinpointed June as the chosen date. Later that month, MacArthur's intelligence department even prepared a report, predicting a war in Korea by early summer.[5] Yet, as so often on the eve of twentieth-century crises, those at the summit of power showed no sign of expecting real trouble. MacArthur repeatedly declared his disbelief in the imminence of war. His absolute lack of attention to the combat training of his divisions in Japan can only be explained by his conviction that they would not be called upon to fight. The most serious contingency Far East Command recognised was likely escalation of the communist guerrilla struggle against Syngman Rhee, which had been in progress for many months.

But only historians can focus with such clarity on the intelligence warnings of war; the few flimsy sheets upon which these were provided reached the desks of MacArthur's officers and the Departments of Defense and State in Washington among a vast paper harvest of contradictory, confusing, often obviously unreliable information and analysis. It was the familiar intelligence problem, of distinguishing 'signals' from 'noise'. The 'noise', that summer of 1950, came in the form of communist threats that seemed to touch every quarter of the globe: on the occupation boundaries in Europe, at Trieste and in the oilfields of the Middle East, among the Huk guerrillas of the Philippines, on the borders of Greece and Yugoslavia. Korea was indeed recognised, in the war departments of the West, as a possible point of confrontation with the communists. But it lay near the bottom of a long list of prospective battlefields.

*

The devastating North Korean artillery and mortar barrage opened at 4 a.m. on the morning of 25 June 1950. In Washington, it was early afternoon on Saturday 24 June. The communist attack, masked by a skilful deception plan in the preceding weeks, achieved complete strategic and tactical surprise. The Korean People's Army possessed seven combat-ready divisions, an armoured brigade equipped with Russian T-34 tanks, three newly activated divisions and ample supporting artillery. Since Kim Il Sung's army was founded in February 1948, it had been welded into an intensely motivated, well-equipped fighting force of 135,000 men. The air force of some two hundred Yak-9 fighters and Il-10 ground attack bombers was negligible by Western standards, but sufficed to provide formidable close support for the North Korean assault, and to wipe out Seoul's pitiful handful of T-6 trainers on the ground in the first hours of war. Syngman Rhee's 95,000-strong army had been deliberately denied armour, anti-tank weapons, and artillery heavier than 105mm. In the summer of 1950 more than a third of the ROK army's vehicles was immobilised in want of repair. Spare parts were almost non-existent. There were just six days' ammunition reserve in the country. Only around a third of Rhee's army was deployed in the line confronting the communist

THE KOREAN WAR

The invasion of SOUTH KOREA
25 June–September 1950

assault on 25 June. Like its parent regime, the ROK army was a corrupt, demoralised body entirely devoid of the motivation that was so quickly apparent in the communist formations.

Four communist spearheads were soon driving south, led by their almost invulnerable armour, checked more by terrain and natural obstacles than by the ROK forces as they forged through the gaps in the hills. Ten communist divisions, supported by 1,643 guns, streamed over the Parallel. The town of Ongin fell within hours to the KPA 6th Division. The communist 1st Division drove for Kaesong, while in the east the 3rd and 4th Divisions took the Uijongbu corridor. Further eastward, the 5th Division mounted its own attack, supported by amphibious landings along the coast behind the collapsing ROK front. The fighting, such as it was in those first hours and day, involved only isolated stands by pockets of ROK troops. Faced by an assault of such formidable power and decision, Syngman Rhee's army was wholly unable to mount a coherent defence by formations. Reeling, its battered and broken companies began to straggle southwards, often abandoning their equipment, hastening to keep a brief bound ahead of the bleak, mustard-drab battalions of Kim Il Sung's victorious army. At 9.30 a.m., Kim himself broadcast the version of events along the 38th Parallel which would form the basis for the public posture on Korea throughout the communist world from 1950 until the present day:

> The South Korean puppet clique has rejected all methods for peaceful reunification proposed by the Democratic People's Republic of Korea, and dared to commit armed aggression . . . north of the 38th parallel . . . The Democratic People's Republic of Korea ordered a counter-attack to repel the invading troops. The South Korean puppet clique will be held responsible for whatever results may be brought about by this development.

Four hours after the North Korean onslaught began, it was evident in Seoul that this was no border raid. The American Ambassador in Seoul, John J. Muccio, cabled the State Department in Washington: 'North Korean forces invaded Republic of Korea at several places this morning . . . It would appear from the nature of the attack and the manner in which it was launched that it constitutes an all-out offensive against the Republic of Korea.'

3 » THE WEST'S RIPOSTE

1. Washington

Han Pyo Wook, the thirty-five-year-old First Secretary at the South Korean Embassy in Washington, was at home in Tacoma, Maryland, on Saturday night, 24 June, when a journalist acquaintance from United Press International telephoned him. 'Philip' – the name Han had long ago adopted for his American life – 'you know your country's been invaded?'[1] No indeed, 'Philip' did not know. He called the Associated Press to confirm the news, then the State Department. The Administration, like Han, had received its first news of the invasion from the agency wires. But this was now being confirmed from Muccio's office in Seoul. Han was told to come at once to Foggy Bottom with his Ambassador, whom he telephoned. Wretched and silent, the two men drove themselves into the city. Han had lived in America since 1938, and was a devoted adherent of Syngman Rhee, whom he had come to know well. He was embittered by the chronic criticism of his President in the State Department, the complaints that he was dictatorial. 'Sure, he's dictatorial compared with President Truman,' shrugged Han. He hated always to go to the Far East Department at State as a suppliant. In May 1949, when Rhee personally requested him to explain to the Americans that his army lacked ammunition to train, Han was deeply wounded when John Williams, on the Korean desk, answered lightly: 'Well, Philip, I guess you must be using too many bullets back there.'

This Saturday night, the two little Koreans were shown at once into the office of Dean Rusk, the Assistant Secretary of State. They found him standing grimly among a little cluster of his officials, all in dinner jackets. Rusk said: 'We have received cables from Ambassador Muccio, indicating that there is no doubt that an armed attack has occurred. Do you have any information?' The Koreans shook their heads. They made an immediate plea for American military assistance. Rusk's reply was inaudible, but plainly non-committal. The Koreans were merely thankful that the possibility was not ruled out. Twenty minutes after their arrival, they drove home through the darkness to the Ambassador's Residence. It was there, less than an hour later, that they took a call direct from Syngman Rhee in Seoul.

Rhee's voice was remarkably clear, but in the background they could hear a babble of voices from his Cabinet. 'The communists have invaded,' said the doctor calmly. 'Our soldiers are fighting courageously, but they lack weapons. Please ask the government of the United States to hasten the delivery of arms to us.' In reality, even as Rhee spoke he was preparing to flee with all the speed he could muster for the southern city of Taejon. But his representatives in Washington hastened to do his bidding. At 1 a.m. on Sunday morning, they were back in Rusk's office at the State Department, with the same group of American officials. 'This is plainly a serious matter,' said Rusk, 'a large-scale attack. This is a matter that should be the concern of the United Nations.' America's Ambassador to the UN was away in Vermont for the weekend, but his deputy had been contacted. The UN Secretary-General, Trygve Lie, had been requested to summon a meeting of the Security Council. But the Koreans still received no clear answer about military aid.

The next morning, they flew from Andrews Air Force Base to New York with two State Department officials, alongside whom they worked through the flight, preparing a short statement for the United Nations Security Council. At the UN's temporary home at Lake Success that Sunday afternoon, the Council met. Some members protested about the short notice, which had prevented them from receiving instructions from their governments. The Yugoslavs demanded that if the South Koreans were to be heard by the Council, no resolution should be passed until the North Koreans had also attended to put their case. They were outvoted. On 13 January, the Soviet delegate, Yakov Malik, had walked out of the Security Council in protest against the UN's refusal to seat communist China in place of the Nationalists. On 25 June, he was still absent. In these extraordinary circumstances, at 6 p.m. a UN resolution condemning the North Korean attack, and calling for the withdrawal of Kim Il Sung's forces south of the 38th Parallel, was passed by a 9–0 vote.

The UN resolution on Korea passed into history. It was a landmark event, probably never to be repeated in the history of this, or any other world body. Here, for once, was no mere vote for a peace-keeping force, a body to intervene between two warring parties; but unequivocal support for one combatant against another. Many times since 1950, nations have committed flagrant acts of armed intervention in the affairs of others: in many cases, the victim has appealed to the United Nations for military protection, and heard this refused. Whatever excesses states commit against their neighbours – Russia in Afghanistan, Libya in Chad, Israel in Lebanon – the issues are adjudged too confused, the tangle of international loyalties and hostilities too great, to achieve a consensus for international military action. The UN intervention in Korea was a fluke of history, made possible by the unique accident of the Russian boycott. In the absence of the Soviets, the United Nations in 1950 was still overwhelmingly the instrument of the Western democracies and their clients. In that last period before the rush of colonies to independence multiplied the UN's size and its dissensions, it possessed only fifty-eight members. Many of these cherished a sincere crusading enthusiasm that the new body should prove capable of more than the sterile debates of the inter-war League of Nations.

Most international disputes are shrouded in such a fog of claim and counter-claim, outrage and reprisal, that it is difficult to subject them to any absolute moral judgement. In less dangerous times, the questionable legitimacy and obvious unpleasantness of Syngman Rhee's regime in Seoul would have made many nations reluctant to come to his aid. There were few illusions about this in informed circles in the United States. 'The unpopularity of the Syngman Rhee government and the questionable political and military reliability of the army and police force', wrote Hanson Baldwin in the *New York Times* on 27 June, 'are the greatest weakness of the defending forces.' But it was not only the United States, in the summer of 1950, which saw in Korea an extraordinary opportunity to draw the line against communist aggression. In Europe, in Asia, in the Middle East, in Latin America, the advance of communism – nourished if not directed by the agents of Stalin – was seen not as an abstract problem, but an immediate physical menace. The spectacle of Eastern Europe, the heart of such gaiety and culture for centuries, disappearing into the dark fog of totalitarianism, had not only dismayed, but frightened a host of citizens of free nations. Not merely Greece, but France and Italy, seemed close to falling under communist rule. The vision of Russian armies storming across the post-war occupation lines to assault Western Europe appeared perfectly plausible. It was a British socialist Member of Parliament of that period who said, thirty-five years later: 'People have forgotten just how indescribably bloody the Russians were at that time. Because the Soviets have now become more reasonable, less frightening, we should not lose sight of how ruthless and immediate a threat they then seemed.'[2]

The miscalculation of Kim Il Sung was to launch so blatant an act of aggression that even the least bellicose spectators around the world found it difficult to take refuge in equivocation. The most cynical Stalinist takeovers in Eastern Europe had been protected by a cloak of legitimacy, however threadbare. The most successful communist acts of expansionism around the world, both before and after Korea, were achieved in a fog of moral and political confusion. Yet not even the tatters of a pretext had been erected along the 38th Parallel. Kim Il Sung set himself simply to seize South Korea by the exercise of naked military force. Even viewed from a communist perspective, it was a huge act of folly. A former senior South Korean officer remarked many years later: 'If Kim really wanted to get the South, by far his best course would have been to do nothing. His biggest mistake was to attack us.' The speaker meant, of course, that by 1950 Syngman Rhee's regime was in deep internal political trouble. A few more years of discreet subversion might well have ensured its collapse from within. But by precipitating his invasion, Kim gave Rhee what the South Korean President could never have gained on his own: a just cause and a banner of moral legitimacy. To these, the United Nations rallied on 25 June 1950.

*

Dean Acheson met President Truman at Washington airport on Sunday evening with news of the UN vote. Truman returned from his troubled weekend at home in Independence, Missouri, to host a dinner at Blair House attended by all his most senior defence and foreign policy advisers. For twenty-four hours, Acheson and his officials had been examining every aspect of the Korean thunderbolt. It continued to surprise and confuse them. For months, it had been thought likely that the Soviets would launch an operation to test the West's will. Korea had been listed as a possible, but not a probable, battlefield. Berlin, Greece, Turkey, Iran all appeared far more vulnerable. Korea was geographically easy for America to reinforce, difficult for the Soviets. Yet now the communists had gone to war for it. Acheson later wrote:

> Plainly this attack did not amount to a *casus belli* against the Soviet Union. Equally plainly, it was an open, undisguised challenge to our internationally accepted position as the protector of South Korea, an area of great importance to the security of American-occupied Japan. To back away from this challenge, in view of our capacity for meeting it, would be highly destructive of the power and prestige of the United States.[3]

If the first and last of these assertions were unchallenged by most of the President's advisers, Acheson's intermediate remarks were to be bitterly contested by his contemporaries, and by history. The Secretary of State was held largely to blame for sending the misleading signals to Pyongyang and Moscow, which made the communists believe they could attack with impunity. His statement to the Washington National Press Club in January 1950, when he so carelessly excluded South Korea from the defined perimeter of American vital interests in the Far East, has been fixed as a critical landmark on the road to war. Today, there remains no shred of evidence from either Russia or North Korea to indicate what influence, if any, Acheson's remarks had upon Stalin and Kim Il Sung. But Ambassador Muccio had warned for months from Seoul of the dangers of appearing to exclude South Korea from the declared interests of the United States. The withdrawal of American forces from South Korea, the visible lack of enthusiasm within the United States for Syngman Rhee's regime, the opposition of right-wing Republicans to financial aid of any kind for his country, combined with such public statements as that of Acheson to create an overwhelming impression of American indifference to Rhee's fate.

And beyond the misjudgements made in the past, there now also existed the utmost uncertainty among the military men assembled at Blair House concerning Acheson's easy assurance about 'our capacity for meeting' the North Korean threat. By the summer of 1950, the American armed forces were at the lowest point of the great post-war run-down undertaken by the Administration. Their numbers had shrunk from 12 million men in 1945 to 1.6 million. Spending was down from $82 billion to $13 billion, just 5 per cent of the GNP. Nearly every unit in the army was under-strength, under-trained, and under-equipped. Almost every regiment in the four divisions of MacArthur's occupation army in Japan had been stripped of a battalion or a battery, every company of a platoon, and so on. Their training and readiness for war – for whose shortcomings MacArthur would later seek to blame everyone but himself, their Supreme Commander – were lamentable. Admiral Forrest Sherman, Chief of Naval Operations, declared later: 'I was fully aware of the hazards involved in fighting Asiatics on the Asiatic mainland, which is something that, as a naval officer, I have grown up to believe should be avoided if possible.'[4]

Yet from the outset, Truman's Administration was determined to resist the North Korean aggression. 'The symbolic significance of its [South Korea's] preservation is tremendous, especially in Japan,' George Kennan told the British Ambassador in Washington, Sir Oliver Franks. The President and his advisers were convinced that, even if the communist invasion did not signal Moscow's readiness to risk all-out war with the United States, it represented a challenge to the will of the non-communist world that had to be met. 'The invasion of the Republic of Korea by the North Korean army was undoubtedly undertaken at Soviet direction,' declared a CIA report of 28 June, 'and Soviet material support is unquestionably being provided. The Soviet objective is the elimination of the last remaining anti-communist bridgehead on the mainland of northern Asia; thereby undermining the position of the United States and the Western Powers throughout the Far East.'[5]

At that first Blair House meeting, Truman made three immediate decisions. First, MacArthur would be told to evacuate the two thousand Americans in Korea, covering the operation with fighter aircraft from his command. Second, the Supreme Commander Allied Powers (SCAP) would be ordered to provide the South Koreans with every available item of equipment and round of ammunition that could be dispatched from Japan. Third, his area of command would be extended to include Formosa. The Seventh Fleet would deploy immediately between the island and the Chinese mainland, to 'quarantine' the Korean struggle, and discourage either Mao Tse Tung or Chiang Kai Shek from embarking upon a dangerous escalation of Asian hostilities. Throughout those first days of the crisis, Washington's thinking was profoundly influenced by fears that the communist powers were now embarking upon an orchestrated offensive, which might be scheduled to extend at any moment to other flashpoints around the globe. Seldom has mutual ignorance between the superpowers seemed so dangerous, or the absence of solid political intelligence posed a greater threat.

*

At noon on 26 June, the Korean mission in Washington received yet another call from Syngman Rhee, this time audibly shaken. 'Things are not going well militarily,' he said. 'Please see President Truman and ask him for immediate supplies of arms, for help of any kind.' That afternoon at 3 p.m., distraught and weeping, the Koreans were shown into the Oval Office at the White House to meet President Truman and his Secretary of State. Han was impressed by Truman. Like some Americans and many foreigners, he had formed a picture of a somewhat homespun president, a hick from the sticks. Instead, now, in the flesh he saw a smiling, self-assured statesman. 'We admire your people and their struggle in adversity,' Truman told the visitors. 'Your soldiers are fighting bravely. Please convey my appreciation of this to President Rhee. I tell you two things: many years ago, when Americans were fighting for their independence, at Valley Forge, our soldiers lacked food, medicine, clothing. Then some friends came and helped.' The Koreans, with a somewhat sketchy grasp of American history, were bemused by this. The President continued: 'In 1917, Western Europe was about to fall to pieces, Europeans were in despair, but some friends went over and helped them.' The meeting lasted thirty minutes, during which Acheson said nothing. But as Han and his Ambassador left, the Secretary of State handed them a statement, promising full United States support for the United Nations resolution. This the Ambassador read to the great throng of reporters on the White House lawn. But the Koreans went away confused and unhappy about the President's failure to give them an unequivocal assurance of American military support.

*

Early the next day, 27 June, the Korean Ambassador and his First Secretary were at Washington airport, preparing to take a commercial flight to La Guardia for another meeting at the United Nations, when they were paged to the telephone. They heard that President Truman had promised immediate United States air and naval support for the Korean armed forces. Then the Koreans wept once more. Douglas MacArthur later wrote:

> I could not help being amazed at the manner in which this great decision was being made. With no submission to Congress, whose duty it is to declare war, and without even consulting the field commander involved, the members of the executive branch ... agreed to enter the Korean War ... All the risks inherent in this decision – including the possibility of Chinese and Russian involvement – applied then just as much as they applied later.[6]

All this was perfectly true. The bewilderment caused in Moscow and Peking by the American intervention, which after all the signals the Administration had sent in the past two years suggested such a different attitude, was remarkable. The British Ambassador in Peking cabled to London a few days later: 'The strength and extent of American reaction has been a shocking surprise, and will prove a grave embarrassment to the People's Government.'

Of all the decisions taken by the White House in those days, it was the declaration of interest in Formosa – which caused little heart-searching for the President and his advisers – that was to have the most profound long-term consequences. At a stroke, it bound the United States more closely than ever before to Chiang and his Nationalists; and it signalled that commitment with dismaying clarity to Peking. The movement of the Seventh Fleet, and the extension of MacArthur's theatre to include Formosa, alarmed and angered Mao Tse Tung's government far more than the other early American decision, to provide air and naval support for the South Koreans.

At 10.45 p.m. on Tuesday 27 June, a resolution sponsored by

the US Ambassador, Warren Austin, was passed by the United
Nations Security Council, calling upon member nations to 'render
such assistance to the Republic of Korea as may be necessary to
repel the armed attack and to restore international peace and
security to the area'. It was carried by a vote of seven to one, with
Yugoslavia abstaining. At a press conference in the aftermath,
Truman agreed with a reporter who asked: 'Would it be correct to
call it a police action under the United Nations?' This was a phrase
that would later haunt Truman. Thousands of young Americans
fighting and dying in Korea through the years that followed, and
their families and friends at home, would laugh bitterly at the
suggestion that they were conducting a 'police action' against the
massed waves of communist infantry. But the immediate consequence of the United Nations vote on 27 June was that the
President prepared himself to provide whatever military resources
proved necessary to stem the communist invasion. Truman had
been accused of weakness in his stand against communism by his
Republican opponents. Suddenly, his beleaguered Administration
had been provided with the opportunity to demonstrate, once and
for all, the strength of its will. Truman seized upon this. The State
Department also began a hasty round of calls to its principal allies.
The British were contacted for the first time since the North
Korean invasion, with apologies from Acheson that there had been
no time to talk to them sooner. Would the British government
consider, as a matter of urgency, what forces it might commit to
the support of the United Nations? The earliest possible gesture
would be welcomed. In similar vein, Acheson's officials talked to
the Canadians, the French, the Australians and every other non-
communist power with the resources to make even a token commitment to a great armed demonstration in the cause of Freedom.

And MacArthur was to be their commander. In the light of the
Administration's subsequent difficulties with their general, it is
remarkable how great was its almost mystic faith, in those first
days of war, that SCAP could salvage the fortunes of the anti-
communist cause in Korea. If his appointment, as the man on the

spot, afterwards seemed entirely natural, even in those dramatic days there were sceptics, who predicted with remarkable accuracy the risks of placing the direction of the United Nations forces in his hands. '. . . at seventy,' wrote James Reston in the *New York Times*, 'General Douglas MacArthur . . . is being asked to be not only a great soldier but a great statesman; not only to direct the battle, but to satisfy the Pentagon, the State Department and the United Nations in the process.' MacArthur had never been regarded as an Eisenhower, with the Kansan's genius for international teamwork. SCAP, noted Reston, 'is a sovereign power in his own right, with stubborn confidence in his own judgement. Diplomacy and a vast concern for the opinions and sensitivities of others are the political qualities essential to this new assignment, and these are precisely the qualities General MacArthur has been accused of lacking in the past.'[7] It was impossible for anyone subsequently to suggest that the perils of appointing MacArthur had gone unnoticed.

But there was little doubt about the enthusiasm of the American people for the course their President had adopted. A leader in the *New York Times* on 30 June was headlined 'Democracy Takes Its Stand'. It praised Truman's 'momentous and courageous act', and welcomed the revision of the American policy in the Far East that 'helped to lose China'. Wall Street fell sharply in a fit of war nerves, and an unholy alliance of the *Daily Worker*, the *Wall Street Journal* and Colonel McCormick's *Chicago Tribune* opposed American intervention in another foreign war. But Washington and Middle America seemed uncommonly united in support of the Administration. 'The average American is pleased that the United States has for once boldly taken the initiative,' the British Ambassador, Oliver Franks, cabled to London, 'proud that it has called the Soviet bluff and "won't let them get away with it". Virtually all shades of opinion wholeheartedly support the President.' An hour after Truman's announcement of the American military commitment, Congress approved a bill extending the draft, by 314 votes to 4. On 30 June, the Military Assistance programme for Korea passed the

Senate by 66 votes to 0. Fuelled by the warmth of genuine outrage, the first American response to communist aggression in Korea enjoyed overwhelming popular support. 'I have lived and worked in and out of Washington for twenty years,' wrote Joseph Harsch in the *Christian Science Monitor* the morning after the announcement of American intervention in Korea. 'Never before in that time have I felt such a sense of relief and unity pass through this city.'

*

Oliver Franks, Britain's envoy, was a close personal friend of Dean Acheson. The two men spent much time together, at Acheson's house in Georgetown, or at Sandy Springs. If their business was very secret, they would talk it out in the midst of the fields, where in those innocent days they could not be bugged. Franks sometimes received letters from right-wing senators, disgusted with the anglophilia of the American Secretary of State and some of those around him, saying 'take your Acheson and your Marshall back to England with you'. By 1950, more and more conservative Americans were unhappy about an Administration which still revealed such a strong preoccupation with decadent Europe. But to a European, the quality of those men never seemed in doubt. More than thirty years later, almost the last living witness close to the very centre of events in the American capital in the summer of 1950, Franks remarked upon the extraordinary accident that, at this moment of history, such a group of Americans occupied the principal positions of power in the Truman Administration: The President himself – 'a man of wider outlook than you might think; he had read and enjoyed a lot of history, especially of Europe and of the American Civil War; he had a background of depth'; Acheson – 'a natural First Class in any university'; Marshall – 'he was looking at the big world all the time, a cool, definite mind which looked for solutions to problems rather than simply worrying about them'; Bradley – 'very, very high class'; Lovett; and in the second rank, George Kennan, 'Chip' Bohlen, Dean Rusk. Franks' strongest personal enthusiasm, of course, was for the Secretary of

State: 'He came to believe that the United States had an appointment with destiny, from which there was no way out but for the
nation to lead and bend its whole energies to ordering the world.
He could be irascible, romantic, short-tempered. But he was a blade
of steel.'[8] To that group of men, Kim Il Sung's invasion represented
a watershed.

> Their thinking [said Franks] moved from the Czech coup in
> February 1948, to the Berlin airlift, to Korea. These were seen
> as stages in Soviet risk-taking that would culminate in their
> armed forces crossing boundaries. It is hard now to remember
> the shudder about the Russian seizure of Czechoslovakia, and
> the ghastly memories that it evoked of 1938. There was the
> feeling 'we couldn't do anything in '38, and we find we can't
> do anything now'. There was the sense of not knowing where
> the Russians would break out next. I myself saw Korea as the
> last in a series of events. I favoured countering the North
> Korean invasion, because I thought that if any army could
> cross any frontier when it chose, then chaos had come. Look-
> ing back, I don't think I disagree with myself in 1950. It was
> one of those moments when *people* – the presence of that
> extraordinary group in the Administration – made a decisive
> difference to history.[9]

2. Tokyo

MacArthur first learned of the North Korean invasion when a duty
officer telephoned from his headquarters: 'General, we have
received a dispatch from Seoul, advising that the North Koreans
have struck in great strength south across the 38th Parallel.' To
the old warlord, it seemed an extraordinary rewriting of personal
history. Here he was once more, in the Philippines in December

1941; 'an uncanny feeling of nightmare ... it was the same fell note of the war cry that was again ringing in my ears. It couldn't be, I told myself. Not again! I must still be asleep and dreaming. Not again!'

> Barring urgent developments, the Supreme Commander said, he wanted to be left alone with his own reflections. Stepping into his slippers and his frayed robe, he began striding back and forth in his bedroom. Presently Jean stepped in from her room. 'I heard you pacing up and down,' she said. 'Are you all right?' He told her the news, and she paled. Later Blackie bounded in, tried to divert his master with coaxing barks, and failing, slunk off. Then Arthur appeared for his morning romp with his father. Jean intercepted him and told him there would be no frolicking today. MacArthur put his arm around his son's shoulders, paused, thrust his hands in the pockets of his robe, and renewed his strides.[10]

When MacArthur at last emerged from Olympian seclusion to drive to his headquarters and take up the web of vast new problems and responsibilities that now encircled him, his moods fluctuated. Some of those who saw him believed that ten years had fallen away, as a fresh crisis lent him new vigour. The extraordinary prospect that now, when it had seemed that the balance of his career could offer only dignified decline, he was once more to play a leading part in the destiny of the world, mantled him in serenity, almost euphoria. At first, he seemed slow to acknowledge that the North Korean action was more than a border incident. Even when events forced him to do so, he continued to declare his belief that the South Korean army could hold them. While the general was still wavering about the seriousness of the threat, it was John Foster Dulles, unconvinced by MacArthur's view that Rhee's forces could look after themselves, who cabled Acheson: 'Believe that if it appears the South Koreans cannot contain or repulse the attack, United States forces should be used even though this risks Russian countermoves. To sit by while Korea is overrun by unprovoked armed attack would start a world war.'

But if MacArthur was slow to grasp the climactic nature of the crisis, once he had done so he showed no further hesitation. For years, he had watched with dismay and disgust while the Administration focused its overseas attention overwhelmingly upon Europe. It had always been his fundamental conviction that America's destiny lay in the Pacific. He declared that he was almost as astonished that the Administration was showing the will to intervene in Korea as he was by the communist invasion. He was deeply gratified by Washington's decision, when it came.

Yet from the very beginning, the Supreme Commander entrusted with the execution of the American, and United Nations, response to the communist invasion revealed the gulf between his own attitude, and the policy of Washington. The Administration's purpose was to conduct a limited war. Communist aggression was to be repelled by whatever means proved necessary. But the struggle was to be confined to the Korean peninsula. The 'quarantining' of Formosa, the diplomatic signals sent to Moscow, were intended to demonstrate America's determination to prevent an Asian incident from escalating into a global conflict.

From June 1950 until his dismissal ten months later, MacArthur displayed a wholly different perception of the Korean conflict, which he never concealed from his superiors and scarcely at all from the world. He considered that it was the historic destiny of the United States, as the greatest capitalist power on earth, sooner or later to confront communism on the battlefield. He believed the immense advantage granted to America by her monopoly possession of effective nuclear forces could not last. It was therefore strongly in America's interests to conduct a decisive struggle against worldwide communism sooner rather than later. The conflict between Washington and MacArthur that was to become one of the most dangerous and divisive factors in the Korean War was essentially a simple one. MacArthur did not believe in the concept of limited war. He acknowledged the Thomist doctrine of just wars. As his biographer William Manchester has written, he 'believed that if the battlefield was the last resort of governments, then the struggle must be waged until one side had been vanquished'. Furthermore, and far more alarming in its implications, had Washington chosen to grasp them, MacArthur took the view that once hostilities had begun, the general in the field became the central force in decision-making. If he was being entrusted with the direction of United States forces in the Far East in time of war, he expected to be granted the widest discretion in determining their employment. In World War II, he enjoyed extraordinary policy-making powers in the Pacific. He now expected to exercise such powers again, in the age of the new superpowers, and of the atomic bomb.

From the beginning, some members of the Administration felt uneasy about MacArthur, the ageing titan, the 'overmighty subject', wielding power in Tokyo. It was unthinkable to replace America's greatest living field commander at such a moment. But given the convictions of the principal players in the drama, what was remarkable was not that Korea precipitated a crisis between the President and his principal subordinate in the theatre of war; but that the climax was delayed until the struggle was so far advanced.

*

Even the warmest admirers of General of the Army Douglas MacArthur have conceded his huge aberrations and defects of character. 'His paranoia was almost certifiable,' wrote William Manchester.[11] 'He hated an entire continent: Europe.' Another recent American study of MacArthur revealed some hitherto unknown details about his private life when Chief of Staff of the US Army before the Second World War: his penchant for histrionic threats of suicide; his enthusiasm for the platonic attentions of prostitutes, as an audience to boost his titanic ego. The author of this work suggests that, had these facts been widely known, they

President Harry S. Truman, who took the decision that the
United States should intervene in the Korean War.

Some key international figures in the Korean crisis:
(*above left*) US Secretary of State Dean Acheson; (*above right*) British Prime
Minister Clement Attlee; (*below*) British Foreign Secretary Ernest Bevin.

The Supreme Commander:
Douglas MacArthur.

American infantry on the march
in the first weeks of war, passing
a burning North Korean tank.

The face of defeat: men of the American 24th Division who lost even their boots in the headlong flight from the communists.

In the first weeks of the war, the world was shocked by revelations of North Korean ruthlessness, above all in the treatment of prisoners. This was one of the first photographs to be released, of a captured American soldier whose body was later found, bound and shot.

The face of tragedy: from the beginning, it was the civilian population of Korea that paid the heaviest price in the struggle.

The face of fear: political prisoners in the hands of the South Koreans, mustered at Pusan.

The hero of the Pusan Perimeter: General Walton H. 'Bulldog' Walker
with one of his divisional commanders.

The Royal Navy goes to war: the crew of HMS *Ocean* muster on the
flight deck to be addressed by Field Marshal Lord Alexander. Firefly
aircraft and the cruiser *Ceylon* in the background.

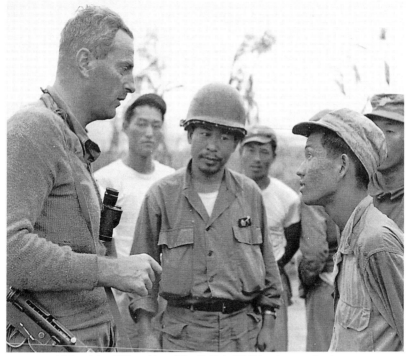

Major John Willoughby of the British 27 Brigade questioning a Korean soldier on the Pusan Perimeter.

Inchon: men of the 1st Marine Division grapple the seawall.

US Marine artillery in action.

would have provided sufficient evidence of instability to disqualify MacArthur from his command, either in World War II or Korea. This seems a hasty judgement. A moment's reflection upon great commanders of recent history shows that many have possessed eccentricities, to say the least: Patton, Montgomery, Stilwell spring to mind. Humility and the higher peaks of intellectualism are also doubtful assets. A sense of destiny may be shown to have been mistaken in the case of certain commanders, in whose ranks Hitler might be included. But the same attribute has guided others to marvellous achievements on the battlefield. MacArthur's role in the Korean War can be viewed as a tragedy; or as a case history of the overmighty subject in a democratic society; or as an example of unchallenged military authority leading to megalomania. But it is not enough merely to paint a portrait of an ageing general ruling a byzantine court in post-war Tokyo, and to argue that his nature and behaviour made all that followed inevitable. There was a greatness about MacArthur, which all his own efforts from the autumn of 1950 until his death have been unable to destroy.

Throughout his life, he acted on the assumption that the rules made for lesser men had no relevance to himself. Few commanders of any nationality could have borne so large a responsibility for the United States' military débâcle in the Philippines in 1941–42, yet escaped any share of it. Fewer still could have abandoned his doomed command on Bataan, and escaped to safety with his own court, complete even unto personal servants, and made good the claim that his own value to his country surpassed that of a symbolic sacrifice alongside his men. Even less so could they have escaped public censure for accepting a vast personal financial gift from the Philippines president, at the very hour when the battle for his country was being lost. There remains considerable controversy about MacArthur's achievement as Supreme Commander in the southern Pacific, forever struggling with the US Navy for greater personal authority, surrounding himself with sycophantic staff officers – 'the Bataan gang' – sometimes slow to grasp tactical opportunities.

Yet no one could deny his stature as a symbol of American authority and will to prevail, presiding over the vast military might deployed to destroy the Japanese empire in Asia. His military achievement in the Second World War was very real. Even his pomposity, his studied grandeur, suited the role in his country's affairs that he had been called upon to fulfil. Then, when the Japanese surrender came, MacArthur was the architect of that supremely imaginative gesture, the pardoning of Japan. Only a regal figure could have dared to do it, when the starving skeletons of the Allied servicemen who survived were still being released from Japan's prisoner-of-war camps, when the people of the United States had been impressed for four years with the baseness and animality of their Japanese enemies. By 1950, MacArthur was seventy years of age. He had gained heroic status in the eyes of the Japanese people, who believed – perhaps not entirely incorrectly – that he had saved them from slavery; while his unsuccessful flirtation with the 1948 Republican nomination for the Presidency failed to diminish his position in the eyes of America – the homeland he had not lived in since 1936 – as her greatest warrior of the Second World War.

For a young officer to join the staff of the Supreme Commander Allied Powers in Tokyo was an experience akin to becoming a page at the court of a seventeenth-century European monarch. His palace was the squat concrete mass of the old Dai Ichi insurance building. The restoration of self-government to Japan had scarcely diminished SCAP's authority over the nation he had first conquered, then resurrected. MacArthur remained the most powerful man in Japan, a legend not merely to Americans, but to the Japanese people who still crowded outside his headquarters each day to watch his ceremonious arrivals and departures. The ruler worked an unusual routine: arrival in the office at 10 a.m., departure at 2 p.m. for lunch at home, return at 4.30 p.m., when he might remain until 9 p.m. or later. Weekends and public holidays meant nothing to him. The more cynical members of his staff disputed his need for their assistance since, in the words of one, 'he made every goddam decision himself'.[12] But the 'Bataan gang' still dominated the court. Willoughby, his intelligence officer, was nicknamed 'Sir Charles' by the staff, for his pomposity. Of his key men, only General Almond, the Chief of Staff, was not a Bataan man, and very conscious of it. MacArthur liked and trusted Almond, for reasons unclear to some of his staff, who did not. They respected the Southerner's energy and dedication, but they disliked his fierce temper and arrogance. Almond could never take the liberties with the Supreme Commander that, say, Willoughby might. If Willoughby wanted to buttonhole MacArthur, he might lurk ready to catch him, apparently by chance, as he walked down the corridor past the honor guard to take the elevator.

'Well, Charles' – the deep, sonorous, actor's voice.

'Oh – you're going home?'

'Oh no, Charles' – taking Willoughby's upper arm in that characteristic gesture – 'come back in.'[13]

The curious group of men around the Supreme Commander could not be said to create a happy, relaxed atmosphere: rather, one of strained, ambitious professionalism. Almond never took time off, because MacArthur did not. Staff officers rode, shot skeet, played a round at the Far East Golf Club, worked out how many more months they must suffer on the rota before it became their turn to be allowed to have their wives come out to join them. But there was not a great deal of laughter, even at the big, formal parties of which there were so many, in a country where servants were two for a nickel, and any man with the right connections could buy a case of Canadian Club for $25.

Many of the staff were at just such a party, in the garden of one of the spacious villas every senior American in Tokyo possessed, late on the Sunday morning of 25 June 1950. MacArthur himself was not, of course, for he never attended mere social functions. He was already at the Dai Ichi. Almond called his aide, Captain Fred Ladd, and murmured discreetly to him: 'Get two or three of the cars lined up – we're going back to the office.'

'Are we coming back here?'

'No.'

They left the wives at the party, drove across the city, and took the elevator to the top floor of the Dai Ichi, where they found a ferment of conferences and briefings already in progress. What units were available? What could be done to bring them up to strength? What equipment did they lack? How could they be transported to Korea? The answers to all these questions were much less than satisfactory. The Supreme Commander developed an early rage on Monday afternoon, when he heard staff officers discussing the difficulties of finding quarters in Tokyo for some American personnel already evacuated from Seoul with their families.

'What do you mean – find space for the husbands? Why aren't they at their posts? I want them all rounded up – use the military police if you have to – and sent back to their posts in Korea where they are supposed to be.'[14]

While the evacuation aircraft were landing at Kyushu, all through Tuesday 27 June, the military reconnaissance party, detailed by SCAP to fly from Japan to Korea to make an urgent investigation of the military situation, waited at the airfield. At last, at twilight, the group of fifteen officers headed by Brigadier John Church boarded the transport, and took off for Korea. They were met at Suwon by the US Ambassador, John Muccio, standing with a cluster of Koreans alongside the abandoned Chevrolets of the Embassy evacuees. They drove to a nearby school, where they were briefed on the situation, as far as anybody knew it: 'The location of enemy forces was unknown, in short,' said Lieutenant-Colonel George Masters, an ordnance officer from Far East Command who was among Church's group. 'But it was reckoned that they would be in Seoul at any time.'[15] In reality, the enemy had taken the city that day.

The next day, the 29th, intermittent American aircraft landed at the strip. Some, from Japan, carried ammunition. Clusters of South Korean troops appeared from nowhere on the tarmac, hastily unloaded the cargo, and once more vanished. Two Japanese-based USAF B-26s set down, damaged while carrying out strafing runs. The crews were sent off to headquarters. A few minutes after they had gone, two communist Yaks appeared overhead, and machine-gunned the tarmac and the cripples before making off. Scarcely had these vanished when another aircraft arrived from Japan. This one carried MacArthur himself, together with a clutch of press correspondents. He had come to be photographed and reported inspecting the scene of battle.

MacArthur's brief visit was characteristic. His Constellation, christened the *Bataan*, was bounced in flight by a communist fighter, which had to be driven off by the escorting Mustangs. MacArthur alone of its passengers watched the drama with keen curiosity, unencumbered by fear. He landed to be met by Ambassador Muccio, a distraught Syngman Rhee, and Brigadier Church. In a nearby schoolhouse, Church briefed the visitors on the military situation. Then, for eight hours, MacArthur drove by jeep through the rear areas of the battlefield. He saw the great columns of terror-stricken refugees pouring south, streams of South Korean soldiers among them. He watched the smoke from artillery and mortar bombardment pockmark the horizon, gazed upon the distant buildings of Seoul, already in enemy hands. He later declared that it was there, at that moment, that he conceived the notion of a great amphibious landing behind the enemy flank. Then he drove back to the *Bataan*. On the airstrip, to the deep dismay of Brigadier Church's mission, he told the fourteen American officers that they were to remain 'and put some backbone into the Koreans'. Then he strode up the steps, and ordered his pilot back to Tokyo. He sat puffing his corncob pipe through the flight back, scribbling notes for his report to Washington. He declared unequivocally that the situation in South Korea could only conceivably be restored by the commitment of United States ground forces. Men must be thrown in as fast as they could be shipped aboard ships and aircraft. He acknowledged the shortcomings of his Occupation Army for immediate combat, but saw no possibility of waiting until they were trained or re-equipped. Days, hours, were now vital. He urged the Administration that the American commitment should be made on the most powerful possible scale: '... Unless provision is made for the full utilization of the Army-Navy-Air team in this shattered area, our mission will at best be needlessly costly in life, money, and prestige. At worst, it might even be doomed to failure.' Even now, MacArthur was not sketching a plan for the expulsion of the North Koreans from the South. He was demanding resources sufficient to inflict absolute defeat upon North Korea. He saw no lesser purpose for which it was worthwhile, or even conceivable, to wage war.

It was still the early hours of the morning of 29 June in Washington when MacArthur's report began to rattle off the printer in the Pentagon. The Army Chief of Staff, General Lawton J. Collins, 'Lightning Joe', who had been Bradley's ablest corps commander in north-west Europe, was woken from his makeshift bed in an anteroom to the Joint Chiefs' quarters. Collins proposed to see the President with the report as soon as the White House could decently be disturbed. No, said MacArthur. Truman must be seen at once. With every passing hour, the North Korean T-34s were driving deeper and deeper into South Korea. At 5 a.m., Truman was in the Oval Office, ready to act upon MacArthur's recommendations.

This was still 1950, less than ten years after Pearl Harbor and more than ten before the Tonkin Gulf resolution became the cornerstone of an impassioned debate about the rights of presidents to make war. Truman, like Roosevelt before him, considered it his function to make executive decisions in defence of the interests of the United States around the world, without need for prior reference to Congress. In his own mind, before MacArthur's report arrived, he knew what he would do. There was some discussion with Acheson about a proposal that had come in the previous evening, from Chiang Kai Shek. The Nationalist leader offered 33,000 men to the UN cause in Korea. Truman liked the idea of involving as many of America's allies in the war as possible. He wanted to accept. Acheson was appalled, recognising the likelihood that war with North Korea would at once become war with Mao's China. The Chiefs of Staff then cast a deciding vote against the proposal, on the purely pragmatic grounds that they doubted the training and usefulness on the battlefield of Chiang's divisions.

So it must be Americans, at first alone, who sought to check the communists. Truman approved MacArthur's request for authority to commit men drawn from the Occupation Army in Japan. From the White House, the order passed through Frank Pace, the Army Secretary, to Collins at the Pentagon, and thence back to the Dai Ichi. Its substance was declared to the world within hours: a naval blockade of the entire Korean coast had been ordered; the United States Air Force in the Far East was to be committed to the war against the communists. And, 'General MacArthur has been authorized to use certain ground units.' Within hours, the first men of the 24th Division were emplaning for Korea. American forces in Japan, jerked unceremoniously from the ease and, indeed, unashamed sloth of occupation life, began the painful struggle to adapt themselves to a war footing. MacArthur and his staff at the Dai Ichi immersed themselves in the huge task of intervention in a campaign against a ruthless and victorious enemy, with one of the least impressive forces the United States had ever put into the field.

*

An aide to Almond, MacArthur's Chief of Staff, Captain Fred Ladd later became one of the most respected American soldiers and advisers in Vietnam. Looking back on Korea many years later, Ladd believed that even in those first days of the war at the Dai Ichi, the roots of all the later disappointments and disasters were there to be seen:

All those officers, those generals: they really thought that they were going to go over there and 'stop the gooks' – just the same as in Vietnam. Just who 'the gooks' were, they didn't know, and didn't want to know. You could have asked any American senior officer in Korea: 'who commands the Korean 42nd division – ROK or communist – and what's his background?' He wouldn't have known what you were talking about. A gook is a gook. But if the Germans had been the enemy, he'd have known.[16]

Yet MacArthur would have asked: What was the choice? If he, or America, stayed their hands until the nation was militarily ready, South Korea would have been gone. Better, surely, to stake out and defend some claim upon the soil of South Korea, however precarious, than discuss from Tokyo how to recover a peninsula entirely fallen to the communists. And whatever the virtues of Kim Il Sung's hordes, the defects of the 24th Division and its sister formations in Japan, American soldiers could surely somehow prevail against a barefoot Asian army.

Whatever the next communist move, the Truman Administration was now committed to use such a measure of force as proved necessary to restore the independence and integrity of South Korea. It remained only to discover how many of America's allies and of the members of the United Nations would lend tangible aid for the cause to which they had voted commitment.

3. London

The British Cabinet met at 11 a.m. on Tuesday 27 June, to consider the integration of the French and German coal industries, white fish, grants for marginal hill land, and support for the United Nations in Korea. Clement Attlee and his ministers agreed, without recorded dissent, that 'it was the clear duty of the United Kingdom Government to do everything in their power, in concert with other members of the United Nations, to help the South Koreans to resist this aggression'.[17] Yet this gesture was to impose strains and stresses upon the sagging economic and military strength of Britain far beyond the proportionate cost that the United States' vast commitment imposed upon its own people.

The end of World War II left America with enormous new riches to enjoy, her people launched upon a frenzied consumer boom to compensate for four years of what had passed as austerity. Nothing remotely similar took place in Europe. For both the late victors and the late vanquished, there was only a struggle for survival. Germany and Austria expected nothing else. But for the British, who had exulted in their triumph in 1945, the pain of shortages, food rationing, and the deep economic and industrial difficulties that persisted into the fifties ran very deep. Clement Attlee's Labour government, in some respects a distinguished administration, was never a truly popular one. After its landslide electoral victory in 1945, it was reelected in February 1950 only by the narrowest of majorities. Its only audible messages to the British people were cries for yet more austerity, yet further sacrifices. Many Labour MPs were instinctively anti-American. They were compelled to accept the supreme irony that Britain's Welfare State, the richest jewel of socialism, was launched entirely with money borrowed from capitalist America. The war had cost Britain £7,000 million – a quarter of her national wealth. Post-war Britain needed at least £1,100 million a year of imports to sustain wartime standards of personal consumption. Yet her exports amounted to only £400 million. The only possible means of bridging this gap was by American loans. Yet Anglo-American relations were under considerable strain at the end of 1945, not least over the British conduct of their mandate in Palestine. When the Americans offered £3.75 billion on the tough terms of 2 per cent, the Labour left – Foot, Callaghan, Castle, Jennie Lee prominent among them – voted to reject the money.

The realists prevailed. The loans went through, and were followed by the extraordinary American gesture of Marshall Aid – $12 billion divided among the Western Allies of Europe. But one consequence of the dollar lifeline was to preserve the delusions of the British people through the late forties about their ability to continue to pay the costs of a Great Power. In 1946, Britain was still spending £1,736 million – one-fifth of her Gross National Product – on defence. There were still one and a half million men and women in the services and their supply industries. By 1948, defence spending had fallen to £700 million. But it then began to rise again: to £780 million in 1949–50; to a projected £1,112 million in 1950–51. If India and Burma had gone, vast areas of the maps in Africa and the Middle East were still painted imperial red, or remained under more discreet British control. Clement Attlee personally insisted that Britain should develop its own atomic bomb, for fear that America might suddenly isolate her leak-prone ally from nuclear secrets. His fiercely anti-communist Foreign Secretary, Ernest Bevin, overruled the objections of the economists.

The British had been dismayed, in the last two years of World War II, by the apparent naïveté of the Roosevelt Administration about the benevolent intentions of Stalin. With an instinctive distaste for excess, they were equally uneasy in March 1947, when the proclamation of the Truman Doctrine committed the United States to resist the spread of communism throughout the world. Yet the Cold War bonded the Atlantic Allies in a fashion hitherto unknown. In 1948, US B-29 bombers were deployed in East Anglia. The descent of the Iron Curtain; the 1949 Soviet blockade of Berlin; the communists' struggle for dominance in Greece; the perceived threat to British interests in the Middle East, combined to convince all but the extreme left of the Labour Party of the menace of Moscow, the vital need for the American alliance. Ernest Bevin has been called the most activist British Foreign Secretary since Palmerston.

Difficult as it may be to recall, half a lifetime later, in 1950 the status of Britain as a world force, as one of the 'Big Three', entitled to a seat at the top table with the United States and the Soviet Union, was not in question. Post-war life for most of the British people was still grey, cold, and bleak: it offered most of the discomforts of war, without any compensating sense of purpose in sacrifice. Yet 'Britain's standing as a great power', as a leading

British historian of the Attlee administration has written, 'so damagingly questioned, with self-fulfilling effect, after the Suez débâcle in 1956, was not in doubt in the 1945–51 period.'[18]

From the first Cabinet discussion about Korea on 27 June, the British demonstrated an anxiety which grew in the weeks that followed: they were unhappy about American proposals publicly to attribute responsibility for Pyongyang's act of aggression to 'centrally directed Communist imperialism', and to project it as a strand in Moscow's web of conspiracy across Asia.

> It had not been proved [record the Cabinet Minutes] that, in carrying out this aggression on South Korea, the North Koreans had been acting on instructions from Moscow; and it was suggested that there might have been advantage in seeking to isolate this incident and to deal with it as an act of aggression committed by the North Koreans on their own initative. This would have enabled the Soviet Government to withdraw, without loss of prestige, any encouragement or support which they might have been giving to the North Koreans. The announcement which the United States Government was proposing to make, by linking this up with communist threats in other parts of Asia, would present a major challenge to the Soviet Government; it would bring into controversy other issues which had not yet been brought before the Security Council; and its reference to Formosa might embarrass the United Kingdom Government in their relations with the Communist government of China, and might even provoke that government to attack Hong Kong or to foment disorder there.[19]

Here was the root of a difference of interpretation between London and Washington which was to persist throughout the Korean War. The Americans, still profoundly wounded by the 'loss' of China, regarded the Peking regime as an evil and sinister force, capable of infinite mischief, acting in close concert with Moscow. To the British, on the other hand, 'the communist Chinese were a fact of life,' in the words of the Washington Ambassador, Oliver

Franks: 'not a good fact of life, but a fact of life'.[20] The British had considerable doubts about the extent to which Peking and Moscow pursued a joint global strategy. Britain possessed no desire whatever to embark upon a confrontation with Peking. Yet when all the reservations had been entered, the risks assessed, the British government remained in no doubt of the necessity of supporting the United States, and the United Nations, in its resistance to North Korea's act of aggression: 'The Minister of Defence should arrange for the Chiefs of Staff to report to the Defence Committee what practical steps the United Kingdom could take to assist the Republic of Korea, in pursuance of the resolution which was being brought before the Security Council.'[21]

To the enormous relief of Washington, Britain immediately dispatched her Far East fleet – a light fleet carrier, two cruisers and five escorts – to join America's warships in operations against North Korea. The Ministry of Defence cabled to Air Marshal Lord Tedder, then leading a British delegation in Washington: 'We consider such demonstrations of solidarity are more important than the actual strength of the forces deployed, and we hope other members of the United Nations will quickly follow suit.' Public and press reaction in Britain was overwhelmingly supportive of the Americans. In the House of Commons only a handful of the Labour left – Sydney Silverman, Tom Driberg, S. O. Davies, Emrys Hughes – protested British involvement in Korea. *The Times* itself could scarcely have put the case for intervention more eloquently than the prominent left-winger Michael Foot, in the weekly *Tribune*. For Britain to decline to participate in United Nations action, he declared, would be an act of appeasement: 'The aggression of the North Koreans was, and remains, an international crime of the first order.'

By far the gravest uncertainty, in those first days, concerned the role of Moscow. Had Stalin directly instigated the invasion of South Korea? How far were the Soviets now prepared to press the issue in Korea: were they, for instance, even willing to risk global war? The British Ambassador in Moscow, Sir David Kelly, submitted a long appreciation on 30 June.

a) Attack was certainly launched with Soviet knowledge and almost certainly at Soviet instigation.

b) Campaign began well, and Soviet Government probably hoped for a walkover.

c) Security Council acted with unexpected speed, and prompt United States reaction had not been foreseen.

d) To judge from press presentation and comment, Soviet Government, although happy to exploit 'evidence' of US aggressiveness, is in no hurry to commit itself to North Korean cause.

e) Official statements . . . although uncompromising, have not so far been provocative by Soviet standards.

I think we can conclude that . . . North Korean attack was intended to exploit a favourable *local* situation, not to provoke a general conflict.

. . . Military intervention by United States was not expected, and Soviet Government either has no policy ready to deal with new situation, or has decided to sit on the fence until military situation is clearer.

. . . I would judge that Soviet Government are extremely anxious not to find themselves engaged directly with the United States.[22]

Subsequent events suggest that Kelly's assessment was remarkably shrewd. He presented three alternative scenarios for the next phase: either the Soviets or Chinese might increase tension by starting another incident elsewhere – in Berlin, Yugoslavia, or Persia; or the communists might climb down, and order a North Korean withdrawal; or the Soviets might offer the United States a North Korean climbdown, as a *quid pro quo* for allowing the Chinese back into the United Nations.

Even in these first days of the struggle, other diplomats and soldiers foresaw dilemmas which would become increasingly acute as the war progressed. On 30 June, Britain's Ambassador to the United Nations, Gladwyn Jebb, cabled to the Foreign Office:

The Americans appear to be endeavouring to achieve at the same time two separate and probably irreconcilable objectives.

In the first place the delegation here . . . is much concerned to correct any impression that the American people are fighting a lone battle in the struggle which is now going on between the two factions in Korea. It is very desirable therefore to make out that the United States is only one of a band of brothers who are all participating in the struggle, so far as their resources permit, under the banner of the United Nations. On the other hand, some Americans – and more particularly I believe the State Department – are much concerned with the reactions on Capitol Hill to any suggestion that the American troops are being forced into battle at the behest of some outside body, and notably of the Security Council, and that once so engaged they will not be under exclusively American command.

This problem was partly resolved, in the event, by the lesser powers of the United Nations forces in Korea deferring, on almost every occasion, to American command and policy. In these first days, the Foreign Office assumed – in a cable to the Washington Embassy – 'that the American intention is to clear the territory up to the 38th Parallel'. But from the outset, the British Chiefs of Staff foresaw one notably difficult issue.

It might be suggested by the Americans [they minuted at a meeting on 28 June] that in the event of their participation being insufficient to restore the situation in Korea, an atom bomb should be dropped in North Korea. If the proposal should be made, ministers would wish to know the views of the Chiefs of Staff. There was general agreement from the military point of view that the dropping of an atomic bomb in North Korea would be unsound. The effects of such action would be world-wide, and might well be very damaging. Moreover it would probably provoke a global war.

These remarks must rank among the more notable exercises of military understatement in history. But the Chiefs of Staff were almost as unhappy about the prospect of being asked to commit British troops to the struggle. Anticipating an American request for ground support, they registered 'strong military objections to sending land and air forces'. Like their American counterparts, they were in no doubt that Kim Il Sung's onslaught represented a calculated play by Moscow. 'It may be assumed,' they concluded at a meeting on 5 July, 'that the invasion of Korea is another example of the Soviet technique of "a war by proxy", and we consider that this action is a deliberate move in the cold war on the part of the Russians . . .' But they feared that Korea was planned by Moscow as a diversion at the very extremities of Western interests; that another and much more deadly thrust might be imminent, closer to home. It was for this reason that they were so reluctant to commit British air or ground forces to Korea. Even when the political pressure from the Americans became irresistible, for the deployment of at least a token force, the British Chiefs of Staff found it difficult to see where the men might come from.

Two generations later, looking back on the British order of battle of those days, their heart-searchings may appear absurd. In July 1950, the Royal Air Force still possessed 120 squadrons of aircraft. The army deployed two infantry brigades and one airborne brigade in the United Kingdom; one infantry and one armoured division in Germany, together with seven armoured regiments, one artillery regiment and two infantry battalions; there was an under-strength infantry division in the Middle East, plus three artillery and two armoured regiments; a Gurkha division, a British infantry brigade and a commando brigade in Malaya; an infantry division and supporting armoured and artillery regiments in Hong Kong; an infantry brigade in Austria; two infantry battalions and an antitank regiment in Trieste.

These deployments reflected the costly combination of residual imperial responsibilities, post-war hangovers, and new Cold War perils that burdened the British in 1950. There had been pitifully little money to spare for new equipment since 1945. Many of the formations listed above were seriously under-strength. For the British to find even a single brigade to go to Korea represented a desperate drain on the nation's overdrawn resources. Yet, in the first debate on the Korean crisis in the House of Commons on 5 July, the Prime Minister said: 'I hope the House will not spend very much time on the legal subtleties, but will concentrate on the realities of the situation. I think that no one can have any doubt whatever that here is a case of naked aggression. Surely, with the history of the last twenty years fresh in our minds, no one can doubt that it is vitally important that aggression should be halted at the outset.'

Winston Churchill, for the Opposition, congratulated Attlee. The Conservative Party, he said, would give full support to the government in this matter. One of the more remarkable aspects of the House of Commons at this period was the level of courtesy and understanding Government and Opposition showed to each other, an echo of their wartime coalition experience, when so many among the Labour and Conservative leaderships worked together. A few sceptics such as the Labour MP Tom Driberg, who later served as a war correspondent in Korea, sounded a discordant note. Driberg wrote with disgust in his column in *Reynolds News* of the 'substantial number of back-bench Tories who, true to their jungle philosophy, cannot help baying at the smell of blood in the air'.[23]

It is in danger of being forgotten today that at this period in Britain, as well as in America, there was intense fear in government circles, bordering upon paranoia, about communist penetration of national institutions. As the Korean crisis escalated, the British government was fearful that communist-led dockers would sabotage troop and munitions movement, and reacted nervously to evidence of minor incidents at the ports. Attlee addressed the British people about the need to stand alongside the Americans in the Far East – 'The fire that has been started in distant Korea may burn down your own house.' But in a recruiting speech, he made direct reference to dangers of treachery at home: 'I would ask you all to be on your guard against the enemy within. There are those who would stop at nothing to injure our economy and our defence.'

The direct consequences of Korea for Britain included the

extension of National Service to two years, and a mounting balance of payments deficit as a result of rearmament. But even most left-wing socialists conceded the justice of the American cause in Korea. There was almost a euphoria among MPs about the raising of the banner of the United Nations. 'I should like to remark,' said Mr Harry Hopkins, the member for Taunton, 'that we are, in fact, witnessing something quite unique in the enforcement by arms of collective security by a world organisation . . . That is something that has never before occurred in the history of the world and it is, at least, a consolation that we are moving along the lines towards an international police force.' Thus, full of wordy ideals as well as economic and strategic fears, the British made their modest commitment to the cause of South Korea.

4. Seoul

At 7 a.m. on Sunday morning, 25 June, Major-General Paek Sun Yup, the thirty-year-old commander of the South Korean 1st Division, was telephoned at home by his Operations officer to be told that the ROK forces on the west bank of the Imjin had been overrun. He himself had been away from his formation for ten days, attending a course at the army command school. Now, he took a taxi at once to ROK army headquarters, in the old Japanese headquarters building in Seoul. The atmosphere there was still surprisingly calm: there was no understanding of the scale of the communist offensive. Colonel Rockwell, his senior American adviser, took Paek in his own jeep to collect one of his regimental commanders who was at home in Seoul for the weekend. Then the three men drove north, up roads still peaceful, because the Korean public had been told nothing of the crisis.

At the divisional command post, they found that half the men were away on weekend leave. Officers trickled in. Paek's units were digging in south of the Imjin, but they had no wire, and they had already lost contact with one regiment north of the river. The commander and some stragglers escaped south a few minutes ahead of the North Koreans. It was learnt that the engineers had failed to blow the Imjin bridges behind them. On Monday 26 June, the division held its ground south of the river. But they learned that the 7th Division, on their right, had collapsed completely. They received a bitter blow when Colonel Rockwell and their other American advisers announced that they had been ordered to leave the front. Some of the Americans shed tears in their embarrassment. The Koreans were utterly dismayed. Paek said, 'We thought that it was for this kind of situation that they were there, to help us.'[24] Then the American KMAG jeeps drove away southwards, leaving the Koreans alone.

The next day, they began to retreat. That afternoon, Paek received orders from one of his superiors immediately to pull back to the south bank of the Han river, south of Seoul. That order was hastily countermanded by the army chief of staff. But the ROK 3rd and 5th Divisions, committed piecemeal to the battle, were being rolled back by the communists. Everywhere the line was crumbling. On the afternoon of the 28th, the North Koreans broke through on their right flank. By now, American aircraft were overflying the front, looking for targets. But the ROKs possessed no forward air controllers, and no contact with the planes. They were compelled to watch many unloading their ordnance on empty paddy fields. Far worse, hundreds of tons of bombs were unloaded upon ROK troops by the USAF in those first, chaotic days. One of Paek's regimental commanders announced that he knew a place where they might get a ferry across the Han. Paek told his men to make their way out as best they could, and head for a rendezvous north of Suwon. Then, in small groups, they made for the river, crossed at the ferry, and started walking south – colonels, generals and privates alike. After one week of war, Syngman Rhee's army could account for only 54,000 of its men. The remaining 44,000 had merely disappeared, many of them never to be seen again. 'South Korean casualties as an index to fighting have not shown adequate resistance capabilities or the will to fight,' MacArthur signalled bluntly to Washington, 'and our best estimate is that complete collapse is imminent.'

*

Ferris Miller, the American who had first come to Seoul as a naval officer in 1945, and was now an economic aid adviser working from an office in the Banda Hotel, spent the night of Saturday 24 June playing mahjong at the Nationalist Chinese Embassy across from the Catholic Cathedral. On Sunday morning, he rose late, heard the news, and hastened to wake up a Korean politician friend. 'It's only a skirmish,' he told Miller casually. 'It won't amount to much.'[25] Through the hours that followed, Miller watched the tempo of panic rise: vehicles careering through the streets at reckless speed, radio appeals for military personnel. From a hotel room, he watched communist planes strafing. Yet still Miller could not escape a sense of ridicule, of fantasy, about what he was seeing.

That evening, he attended a long-scheduled dinner party at the US Army compound. Here, he found growing signs of nervousness. By Monday night, looking out of his apartment window, he could see the gunflashes on the northern horizon. Then he heard on the US Armed Forces radio that the situation was stabilising. Emergency feeding arrangements would be suspended. As from Tuesday, all US personnel would once again be required to pay for meals in the mess. Miller went to bed somewhat reassured.

But in the early hours of the morning, there was a fierce banging on his door. An American officer told him to bring a toothbrush and pyjamas to US headquarters in the Banda Hotel. Amidst a total blackout, he packed his possessions in two footlockers, and drove to the US Embassy. Here, he found chaos: men burning documents in great heaps on the street outside, Koreans besieging the building for help in making their escapes. Inside,

Miller saw a Korean woman sobbing helplessly, amid officials hastening to and fro. 'Help me, help me,' she begged him. 'My husband is in the States.' Miller could do nothing. At dawn, buses
came to take the staff out to Kimpo for evacuation. Miller was
one of the last to leave. He felt guilty, as he pushed his footlockers
into the hold of a C-47, conscious of all the men and women
around him who had salvaged nothing. The Ambassador's secretary climbed aboard with a dog under one arm, a bottle of
scotch under the other. Then they started the engines, and taxied
bumpily across the tarmac for take-off. Only when they landed in
Japan did they discover holes in the fuselage from stray communist ground fire. Only later did they learn of those left behind: the
mining adviser who overslept in his billet, and was never heard
of again; the party of Americans who had been attending a wed-
ding in Kaeson, and became prisoners in North Korea for three
long years.

*

Lee Chien Ho, a twenty-one-year-old tax collector's son studying
chemical engineering at National University, was in a barber's
shop having his hair cut on the morning of 25 June, when the
news of the North Korean invasion came through on the radio. His
father was away in Inchon. Unlike many Koreans, Lee was eager to
take some part in the defence of his country. He and a few score
like-minded students spent much of the next two days at their
university campus east of the city, pathetically standing guard
armed with broomsticks. On the second night of their vigil, South
Korean army stragglers began to come through from Uijambu.
'What do you kids think you're doing?' demanded one. They told
him they were defending the university. 'You're out of your minds,'
the soldier said. 'Go home.' Bewildered, they drifted away in ones
and twos towards the city, among the dejected military fugitives.
He slept that night at the School of Liberal Arts, by the streetcar
terminal. Walking out the next morning, he saw a long row of
large, shiny government cars abandoned neatly in front of the

railway station. It was his first tremor of understanding of the scale
of the disaster.[26]

Lee went home and told his mother that he was sure they
should leave. At first, she was bitterly reluctant to abandon all
their household possessions. The banks were closed, so they had
no means of recovering their money. But at last, he persuaded her.
On Tuesday afternoon, carrying a sack of rice on his back and
leading his two younger brothers, Lee led his mother through the
streets towards the Han river bridge. Curiously enough, he found
few others going their way, and many re-entering the city from
the south. They laughed at the family, burdened with their belong-
ings: 'What are you so worried about?' That night, they slept in a
schoolhouse, disturbed by the thunder of heavy rain on the roof,
and distant guns. The next morning, as they walked on southwards, they heard the huge explosion as the Han river bridge
was blown by Rhee's retreating army. They struggled on, amidst
a growing army of panic-stricken soldiers and frantic civilians, a
confusion of abandoned possessions on the road and low-flying
aircraft sweeping overhead: the wreckage of defeat.

*

To Suk Bun Yoon, a thirteen-year-old middle school pupil, the son
of a merchant, the North Koreans looked more like a defeated
army than a victorious one as they straggled into Seoul.[27] Suk and
his family had spent much of the previous two days hiding in a
sewage pipe. On the 27th, they struggled through the seething
mass of refugees towards the Han river. But the press, the hysteria,
the screaming mass of humanity fighting to reach the ferries, was
too great. Despondent and frightened, they returned home to
await their fate. On the morning of the 28th, as the first communists arrived, civilians in red arm bands hastened through the
streets, urging the watching citizens to cheer their liberators. Some
did so. But most of the older people slipped away to their houses,
from whose windows they peered nervously out into the street at
the solemn, olive-clad files padding past, some still wearing

camouflage foliage in their helmets. Many hundreds of thousands of the small men and women of Korean society, whose names featured on no lists, whose lives had merely been a struggle for survival, were unsure what to make of the communists' coming. Won Jung Kil was a peasant's son who had grown up in Inchon as the breadwinner of a family of eight. Their father was dead, Won had no fixed employment: 'We thought about food – nothing else.'[28] Inchon was a stronghold of communist sympathies of a primitive kind: Won and his kind hated Syngman Rhee because he did nothing for the working man, and loathed the police for their privileges. He himself was in Seoul the day war broke out. He hastened home, uncertain what to think. He found the local communists running exultant through the streets, preparing a grand welcome for the North Korean army. The family talked. They decided that it was safer to go. There might be fighting in the town. They gathered up saucepans, blankets, children, and began walking southwards. They expected that it would be safe to come home in a week. In reality, they were embarking on a three-year odyssey that would be shared by millions of their fellow-country men; that would cost them their home – a shack carelessly destroyed by the warring armies; their freedom – for the young men of the family were conscripted, and spent three years barely subsisting in uniform; and enormous hardship for the women, who would exist chiefly upon American milk powder and herbs picked from the mountains until many months after the war ended. For the nations of the West, the war that had now come to Korea represented a challenge to the principles of freedom and anti-communism. The democracies were to endure huge anxieties and frustrations in the course of seeking to meet this. But for the people of Korea, three years of unspeakable tragedy, privation, and sacrifice had begun, from which scarcely a family in that unhappy land would be spared.

4 » WALKER'S WAR

1. Retreat to the Naktong

South of Seoul, Kim Il Sung's army paused. The North Koreans needed time to regroup, and allow their logistic 'tail', such as it was, to catch up. Yet the week that they lingered, however essential to enable them to consolidate their hold on the capital and prepare for the next thrust, was critical in the development of the war. When their advance began once more on 5 July, the communists encountered Task Force Smith north of Osan. Smith's battalion, committed under the most unfavourable circumstances, inflicted only the merest check upon the communists. But behind the 1/21st Infantry, the remainder of the US 24th Division was deploying.

Major-General William Dean, its commander, a big man of fifty-one with a reputation as something of a martinet, set up his headquarters in Taejon as the South Korean army appointed its third chief of staff in less than three weeks of war. For all the South Korean assertions that their army was fighting desperately, the Americans could see evidence only of chaos and retreat. Subsequent evidence from communist sources suggests that, in reality, in those weeks some South Korean units inflicted substantial damage and important delay upon the invaders. But the only useful intelligence about communist movements came from the American aircraft now flying constant interdiction missions. These in turn were critically hampered by lack of general knowledge of the North Korean forces, and specific information on targets. No effective system of Forward Air Control existed. In those first weeks of war, the USAF poured thousands of tons of bombs on to Korea. There is little evidence that these proved more than an irritant to communist operations in the first stage of the war, however important they became in August and September.

The next unit of the 24th Division to face the enemy assault was the 34th Infantry, moving up behind Lieutenant-Colonel Smith's battalion. 1,981 men strong, devoid of tanks or effective anti-tank weapons, it was transported from Japan in conditions of haste and confusion, and was no more prepared in mind, training, or equipment to arrest the North Korean advance than Task Force Smith. But Dean could only give its commander the simplest and most straightforward of orders: to deploy his men in blocking positions across the key routes southwards, at Ansong and Pyongtaek. It was to these positions, late on the night of 5 July, that the stragglers and survivors of Task Force Smith began to drift in, bearing their bleak and confused tale of being overrun by a communist armoured host. The disarray within the 24th Division was compounded by almost total lack of communications: telephone wires were repeatedly cut, radios were defeated by distance and mountains between units. In the rain and mist of early morning on 6 July, the 1/34th found itself facing North Korean infantry and armour swarming south across the shallow river line they were defending.

The brief action that followed was considerably more inglorious than that of Task Force Smith. The Americans engaged the communists with mortars and machine guns, but quickly found the enemy closing in upon them. The battalion commander, Lieutenant-Colonel Harold Ayres, saw no alternative to retreat if his men were not to be isolated and cut off. He had earlier been advised by General George Barth that, come what might, he was 'not to end up like Brad Smith', left irretrievably exposed behind the communist advance. A few minutes ahead of the enemy's T-34s, amid a frenzied stream of Korean refugees, their carts and baggage and animals, the Americans hastened southwards, discarding equipment as they went. By the time General Dean had learned that his point battalion was in full retreat, and hurried forward in his jeep to check the movement, the 34th Regiment was south of Chonan. A furious scene ensued between the divisional commander and the senior field officers of the 34th. They had offered no significant resistance to the enemy, and had withdrawn without orders. Dean expressed his disgust. He now had no alternative but to order them to dig in where they stood. He also relieved the commanding officer of the 34th Infantry, and replaced him by an officer with experience of regimental command in World War II. It was the first of a long procession of sackings in the field which proved necessary in those early, traumatic weeks. Martin, the 34th's new commander, survived just forty-eight hours before his death in action at Chonan.

> As daylight broke on July 8 [recorded PFC Robert Harper of the 34th Infantry's Headquarters Company], we heard this loud clanking noise off on the left. We understood now what was happening – their tanks were coming. Eventually I could see them dimly, moving through the morning mist. I counted them. When I got to nine, an order was given to pull back off the railroad tracks and set up in the first row of houses behind the sewage ditch. From there I saw the North Korean infantry moving to my right across the field in front of the railroad depot. I could hear occasional small-arms and machine-gun fire. Mortar rounds began falling nearby. The tanks continued to roll down the road toward us. We had no way of stopping them. They came to the end of the road and I could hear them firing. I did not know which of our companies were down there but knew they were catching hell. We were ordered back to a narrow street, where we waited to see what would happen next. I heard the new CO, Colonel Martin, tried to take on one of the tanks with a bazooka. The tank scored a direct hit on the colonel, and he was killed on the spot. We began receiving real heavy mortar and tank fire ... We ran down some alleys and met some more GIs who said orders had been issued to

evacuate the town. I could hear a lot of small-arms and mortar
fire behind me. We went to the east edge of town, worked our
way through rice paddies and got to the road. There were quite
a few civilians still on the road. We joined them in heading
south. We drew heavy artillery fire and began to lose a lot of
people.[1]

'Resistance had disintegrated, and now our troops were bug-
ging out,' wrote Dean.[2] Through the wretched weeks that followed,
among the gloomiest in the history of the United States Army, the
pattern of Chonan was repeated again and again. An uncertain and
unhappy American infantry unit would be hustled into a defensive
position, its officers unwilling or unable to conceal their own
confusion and dismay. The flood of refugees slowed to a trickle,
then halted altogether. There was a tense silence, men peering up
the empty road, until they heard the tortured squeal and clatter of
advancing armour. The North Korean tanks crawled forward until
they met American fire; then they halted, to allow infantry to
swarm past them, infiltrating the American positions and working
around their flanks. The Americans then withdrew, often in undignified haste, abandoning vehicles and equipment as they escaped
as best they might, amid the swelling columns of civilian refugees.
'We knew that we weren't doing very well,' Major Floyd Martain,
one of the survivors of Task Force Smith, declared wryly. 'But we
kept saying to ourselves: "Well, here we are, and we've been here
a month, and where the hell is the rest of the United States
Army?"'[3] They felt profoundly lonely.

The essential criticism of the performance of the 24th Division
at this period centres not upon the fact that its units repeatedly
withdrew; for had they not done so, they would assuredly have
been bypassed and eventually destroyed. It was their failure to
inflict significant damage or delay upon the enemy before disengaging that so embarrassed their commanders. Neither MacArthur
nor his subordinates could reasonably have expected the scant
American forces deployed thus far to halt the communist invasion.

But well-handled regimental combat teams could have hit and run: punished the North Koreans for a few hours with mortar and machine-gun fire, then pulled back to the next obstacle suitable for defence. In reality, American officers seem to have had neither will nor skill to create anti-tank obstacles, to use mines even when these became available, or to employ the support weapons they had against the North Korean infantry. Terrain, logistics, poor communications and refugees did more to delay the North Korean advance in the first weeks of July than the American infantry in their path.

*

On 10 July, General Douglas MacArthur was formally appointed Commander-in-Chief of the United Nations Command. The United States rejected the UN Secretary-General's proposal that the war should be directed by the 'Committee on Co-ordination for the Assistance of Korea' as the British, French and Norwegians seemed to favour. Since the US was bearing the overwhelming burden of war – and directly contributing most of its cost – Washington insisted upon direct military control, and got its way with its allies. 'In the military field,' the principal diplomatic historian of the UN has written, 'the control of the United States government was complete; in the political field, consultations with the United Nations and some contributing members were more frequent. On occasion the UN made various recommendations. In the final analysis, however, a large range of political decisions was taken by the United States government, as the Unified Command.'[4] This was to be a war overwhelmingly directed by American soldiers and American politicians. On 13 July General Walton Walker, a corps commander under Patton in north-west Europe, established his Eighth Army headquarters in Korea, with operational responsibility for UN ground forces in the field. The stubby, rugged, impatient little Texan could scarcely enthuse about the material he was being asked to work with. His forces were exclusively now, as they would remain principally for many weeks, men of the

American occupation army in Japan. The only available reinforcement for the crumbling forces of Syngman Rhee must come from
Japan, where the 25th and 1st Cavalry Divisions were being hastily
mobilised for war. Until they came, it was essential for Dean's 24th
to delay the communist advance, to give ground only yard by yard,
between Osan and the next natural defensive line, forty miles
southwards on the Kum river.

The North Koreans brushed past the two regiments of Dean's
shaken force deployed along the Kum with almost contemptuous
ease. At its low, almost barren summer level, the river presented
no significant threat to T-34s. The 19th Infantry found itself compelled to fight its way out of encirclement, with the loss of almost
one man in five, more than half of its 1st Battalion. With his flanks
turned, Dean was driven back into Taejon. The communists began
their assault on the city on 19 July. Dean directed its defence with
furious energy. Anti-tank teams armed with the newly arrived
3.5-inch bazooka scored a string of successes against the communist T-34s. Dean himself led one team, stalking a tank through the
streets for more than an hour before successfully destroying it. But
within a few hours, North Korean armour and infantry had broken
through, and the survivors of the 24th were retreating southwards
once more. Dean himself remained a fugitive in the hills for a
month before he was captured, the senior American officer to be
taken by the communists in the Korean War.

It was a period when there was a desperate need for heroes,
and Dean was represented as one across the United States. At the
end of the war, he was decorated with the Congressional Medal of
Honor. His courage was never in doubt. Yet some expert soldiers
in Korea were dismayed, even disgusted, by the collapse of leadership in the 24th Division even before the Taejon battle. 'Why any
general would tolerate the chaos at his headquarters in the fashion
that Dean did, I never understood,' said Colonel John Michaelis, a
distinguished World War II combat veteran who witnessed it.
'There was a sense of hysteria. Nobody seemed to want to go and
kick somebody in the butt. I never knew what Dean thought he

was doing, as a divisional commander, to grab a bazooka and go off hunting tanks.'[5] Michaelis was among those who considered Dean's behaviour the negation of his responsibility as a commander. He was not alone in his opinion. 'Dean was very personable,' said Lieutenant-Colonel George Masters, 'but he still did not know what war was. Fundamentally, he was a silly man.' If these seem harsh judgements, they are those by men who watched the agony of the 24th Division. It was difficult to pass any less cruel verdict upon the performance of most of the American units in the battle. 'We had the conceited opinion that we were trained soldiers,' said Colonel Masters. 'Yet what we did in Korea, as we do quite frequently in our history, was to try to use civilians as soldiers and expect them to be combat-effective. We are usually disappointed.'[6]

Between 10 and 15 July, the US 25th Division landed in Korea. On 18 July, the 1st Cavalry – paradoxically, an infantry division – came ashore at Pohang-dong. By 22 July, they were deployed. The remains of the battered, indeed almost ruined, 24th Division was able to withdraw through their positions and at last catch its breath. In seventeen days, it had lost some 30 per cent of its strength, more than 2,400 men reported missing in action. Yet the reinforcing formations gave little ground for confidence on their first appearances in action. On 20 July, the 24th Infantry of 25th Division broke and fled after their first few hours in battle at Yechon. The 24th was an all-black unit, a relic of the US Army's ill-fated segregation policy. The pattern of the 24th's first action was repeated in the days that followed, with men streaming towards the rear as soon as darkness provided cover for their desertion. An inexplicable panic overcame the 1st/24th on 29 July, after facing a communist mortar barrage. It became necessary to set up roadblocks behind the 24th's positions, to halt deserters and stragglers leaving the line. The US Army's official history castigates the regiment for its habit of abandoning arms and equipment in the field, lack of leadership by officers, chronic unreliability: 'The tendency to panic continued in nearly all the 24th Infantry operations west of Sangju . . .' By the end of

July, Walker recognised that it was possible to use the 24th only as an outpost force, a tripwire in the face of communist assaults. It proved necessary to maintain another regiment in reserve behind the front, to conduct serious resistance when the 24th broke. In Washington, Collins, the Army Chief of Staff, recognised the failure of the concept of all-black units. At the earliest possible moment, black soldiers must be integrated into white units. But there was no time for that in Korea in July.

Even for the better American regiments, the first encounter with the communist manner of making war in Korea was disturbing, confusing, demoralising, brutalising. It was a common experience to see a herd of refugees shuffle towards an American position, swept aside at the last moment to reveal the North Korean infantry sheltering among them. Even for GIs who had seen combat against the Japanese in the Pacific in World War II, it was a frightening experience to meet a North Korean enemy willing to hurl away his life in suicidal 'human wave' charges at point-blank range. Later, when the Chinese came in, these tactics would be translated to a vastly greater scale, even more unnerving in its fanaticism. The communists acknowledged no claim of treachery or breach of the rules of war in their use of soldiers in civilian clothes, or pretended surrenders to mask attacks. Most shocking of all to American sensibilities in Korea and at home in the United States, the communists proved ruthlessly indifferent to the taking of prisoners. A shudder of revulsion ran through the American nation at the discovery, in Korea, of the first groups of American prisoners shot dead by the roadside, their hands tied behind their backs with barbed wire. It rapidly became apparent that the North Koreans served prisoners in such fashion whenever they had no explicit need for them alive, for propaganda or intelligence purposes.

Bleakly, American commanders perceived a certain advantage, when news of communist atrocities spread through their formations. Some soldiers who had hitherto made little show of wanting to fight were now brought face to face with the likely consequence of capture. There was no salvation to be sought in a comfortable

PoW compound. Yet, conversely, fear of being outflanked and cut off became an obsession in many units. 'Bug-out fever', the urge to withdraw precipitately in the face of the slightest threat from the flank, was already a serious problem. 'I saw young Americans turn and bolt in battle,' wrote Marguerite Higgins of the New York *Herald Tribune*, 'or throw down their arms cursing their government for what they thought was embroilment in a hopeless cause.' Americans trained and conditioned to fight as part of a large army of mutually supporting elements were deeply ill at ease holding isolated positions with their flanks in the air, with the knowledge of perhaps twenty or thirty miles of mountain between themselves and the next Allied formation in the line.

Beyond this, the terrible shocks of the first weeks of war, the sense of facing a merciless Asian enemy, caused many Americans to extend their fears and suspicions to the entire people of Korea: 'the gooks' meant not merely the communists, but all Koreans. Communist atrocities provoked callousness in many Americans, fighting a desperate struggle for survival, towards the Asians around them, creatures from another planet whose language they could not understand, whose customs bewildered them, whose country seemed most vividly represented by the universal stench of human excrement manuring the fields.

Yet whatever the shortcomings of the American military performance in those weeks, it narrowly sufficed. And for all the bitter criticisms of the South Korean army, the ROK, whose battered and demoralised remnants were falling back alongside the Americans, its struggle had not been in vain. Amid the pain of withdrawal and defeat in July, America and her allies were disposed to dwell upon the sufferings of their own armed forces. Yet in those first weeks of fighting, surprised and facing overwhelming odds, the South Koreans and their American allies inflicted heavier losses upon the communists than was understood at the time. It later emerged that the North Koreans suffered some 58,000 casualties between 25 June and early August. At the moment when the confidence of Walker and his army was at its lowest ebb, when they saw defeat staring them in the face in south-east Korea, the UN forces in Korea by now outnumbered their communist enemies.

The 25th Division held its positions in the centre of the country until 30 July before being compelled to begin falling back. The 1st Cavalry, outflanked around Yongdong, began retreating on 29 July towards Kumchong. And even as the Americans fought the threat from the north, in the west an even more dangerous communist movement was under way. A North Korean division had hooked around Taejon, and hastened through the defenceless countryside southwards. By 1 August, its leading elements were near Masan, just thirty miles short of the south-eastern port of Pusan. If the North Koreans could reach Pusan, the Americans would be encircled with little chance of escape. Their predicament was desperate. Walker was able to rush units of the 25th Division down to Masan with hours to spare, to block the advance. By now, Eighth Army's commander knew that both his men and the North Koreans had run out of room for grand manoeuvres. The defenders must stand and fight. On the high ground behind the great loop of the Naktong river, they would command positions of great natural strength. In the first days of August, the long files of dusty, exhausted Americans and their overloaded vehicles trudged doggedly south and east, to the new line. Here, on the last mountain mass before the sea, the fate of Walker's army, of the United Nations in Korea, would be decided.

2. Dressing Ranks

Even as the men from that soft, ill-prepared American occupation army struggled to improvise a perimeter against the communist assault, the Western powers were gathering forces to reinforce them. From the outset, it was apparent that MacArthur would need every man who could be spared from the democracies' worldwide commitments if he was to hold the North Koreans. At the Pentagon, the War Office in London, the war departments of Canada, France, Australia and New Zealand, Turkey and a clutch of smaller countries, politicians and staff officers pored earnestly over orders of battle and staff tables, seeking to determine what could be spared for Korea. From far and wide, reservists were being recalled from civilian occupations and tranquil domestic lives; draftees hustled through basic training; cadre formations built up to strength with whatever men could be found to fill their ranks, and equipment to stock their inventories. Only five years after the end of World War II, the victors found themselves embarrassingly pressed to find the means with which to fight a limited war in Asia.

MacArthur's initial optimism about the scale of resources required to halt the communists in Korea was replaced, by mid-July, with demands for men on a scale that thoroughly alarmed the Joint Chiefs in Washington. On 5 July, he sought – and received agreement for – the commitment of the 2nd Infantry Division, a regiment of the crack 82nd Airborne, and the 2nd Engineer Special Brigade. On 20 July, four National Guard divisions were activated. Within days of the outbreak of war, Congress rushed through a one-year extension of the newly lapsed Selective Service Act. The Defense Department declared a requirement for 50,000 conscripts in September, the same again in October, 70,000 in November. Caught in the contemporary mood of war fever, Congress voted the President an $11 billion emergency defence appropriation. Yet even the vast economic strength of the United States did not make it possible, by a mere national act of will, instantly to transform a demobilised, almost decayed military machine into an instrument of war capable of fighting effectively in Korea, while maintaining combat readiness for a greater struggle elsewhere in the world. For months to come, as America mobilised, her military effort in the Far East would be a patchwork of expedient and improvisation.

*

Some young Americans, matching the mood of the time in their country, saw the war in genuinely idealistic terms, as an opportunity to take an heroic part in the crusade against communism; that – and perhaps a hint of boredom with post-war life in a small town. Bill Patterson was the tall, lanky, twenty-year-old son of an industrial worker in Stillwater, New York. He and a group of friends became passionately excited by the cause – forty-five of them marched in a group to enlist: 'They had a problem over there. We wanted to do something about it. And I guess I didn't have a lot to do at home. We started preaching around the town, saying – "Come down to Albany! Join the service!" I remember driving one kid of seventeen home to his parents to sign the papers.'[7]

Private Warren Avery was a bus driver's son from Virginia, a high school drop-out who had 'bummed around' for a year before joining the army in June 1949. He volunteered for Korea because the war sounded exciting. He was issued with a brand-new M-1 rifle, pushed on to a Pan Am airliner to make the first flight of his life to the Far East, and posted to the 29th Infantry on line on the Pusan Perimeter just ten days after he put in his name for Korea.[8]

Corporal Selwyn Handler was called to active duty with the 1st Marines after two years as a reservist, a few days after returning from summer camp. He found the intense, purposeful bustle at Camp Pendleton entirely romantic: 'To me, it was a great adventure.'[9] A few reservists with young families were unhappy, but most exulted in the intensive training that continued every day on the ships on which they sailed for Japan. Marine Bill Sorensen had always bitterly regretted missing World War II, not least because his idolised elder brother had won the Congressional Medal of Honor as a sergeant. He was thrilled to be recalled from the reserves and shipped to join the 7th Marines. As they practised firing their rifles over the fantail of the transport in mid-Pacific, the young man from Michigan enthused like a schoolboy about the prospect of combat. But an old sweat said to him: 'Sorensen, as soon as that first shell goes over your head, you'll wish you'd never seen a war.'[10] And, of course, it was true.

But many men still believed that whatever was happening in Korea – and whatever Korea was – it would 'never be any big deal'. Private Clyde Alton, an Indianan World War II veteran of thirty, found himself drafted to a battalion of the 2nd Division alongside the same top sergeant with whom he had gone through the North African campaign. He and Alton agreed that Korea was unlikely to amount to much: 'This is going to be no war, 'cos these people are natives.'[11]

*

Until well into September, the British Chiefs of Staff remained gravely doubtful about the ability of the United Nations army to sustain its position in the peninsula. 'Whether the Americans succeed in keeping a foothold in South Korea or have to go back again after a withdrawal,' they noted on 20 July, 'the subsequent campaign, if conducted on ordinary lines' – a polite euphemism for eschewing the use of nuclear weapons – 'cannot fail to be long, arduous and expensive in human life and material.' They believed that it might take six to nine months to mobilise the resources for a full-scale combined operation to reinvade Korea, once the communists had been allowed to consolidate their hold on the country.

> We may well be faced with the situation that the Koreans as a whole will urge us not to return. In any event, the people who would mainly suffer from any kind of normal campaign of 'liberation' would be the South Koreans, whose villages, roads and railways would be destroyed and their country turned into the usual squalid battlefield.

If the peninsula had to be evacuated, the British urged a sustained air offensive against North Korea's communications and industry. They admitted that this might not be successful in bringing Pyongyang to the negotiating table, but

we shall be no worse off if it did not. We assume there will be
no question of using the atomic bomb in Korea. This weapon
must in our view be kept in reserve for use in the proper place
in the event of a major war with Russia. Anyway there are
no suitable objectives for it in North Korea. This is a United
Nations police action, and we do not want to kill thousands of
civilians and create a radio-active shambles, but with the minimum loss of life and expense on either side, to restore the
status quo and the integrity of South Korea.

This assessment, cabled to Air Marshal Tedder in Washington,
admirably exemplified London's policy of cautious prevarication,
which so greatly taxed the patience of the Americans in the
months that followed. The British Chiefs of Staff, perhaps even
more than their government, feared becoming engulfed in a
bottomless morass in Korea, at great cost in men and treasure,
only to discover the Soviets striking elsewhere in the world, at
the moment of greatest Western weakness. To the Americans,
on the other hand, whatever threats tomorrow might bring, Korea
was the communist challenge of today. They sought to confront it
with a wholeheartedness that was always lacking on the part of
the British. The British decision that a token land force must be
dispatched, at least a brigade in strength, was reached with the
greatest reluctance. So too was the necessity, with manpower in
such desperately short supply, to recall men to the colours to fill
the ranks of units for the war.

Many British reservists were enraged to find themselves
recalled to duty. Through thousands of British letterboxes that
summer, unwelcome summonses fluttered: 'In accordance with
the terms of your reserve liability, it has become necessary to recall
you to active military duty. You are accordingly required to report
to duty on 9 August 1950 to OC 45 Field Regiment RA'; or it might
be the 5th Fusiliers, the 1st Ulsters, the 1st Gloucesters. No hint of
logic, far less compassion, was discernible in the manner in which
the War Office selected men for service. Hundreds were former

wartime PoWs in Germany and the Far East. Some had not even been classified medically A1. A recalled Fusilier who had spent five years as a prisoner after being captured at Dunkirk went absent without leave from the depot at Colchester. His wife had urged him: 'No one's going to blame you.' But they did. He was caught and sent to Korea. There were extraordinary scenes at the depot: an enraged housewife pushing three snivelling children before her into the orderly room, shouting at a bewildered young officer: 'You've taken their father – you can look after this lot!' One man was taken whose wheelchair-bound wife was entirely dependent upon him. He was later flown home from Hong Kong.

A few men were quite keen: 'We thought it would be like Europe – lots of looting and women,' said one of their number sheepishly, long after. For ambitious professional soldiers like Captain Anthony Farrar-Hockley, adjutant of the Gloucesters, a war – any war – promised the chance of distinction – 'the chance to sort out the soldiers from the time-servers.' Captains James Majury and Bill Anderson of the Ulsters went out and made themselves gloriously drunk to celebrate the thrilling news of their departure, only to receive a stony welcome home from their wives, both of whom were nursing newly born babies. Even among the recalled reservists, there were enthusiasts. Some were anyway fed up with civilian life, or had failed to readjust after World War II. Some simply liked fighting.

But most did not. Each morning at Colchester, welfare clerks interviewed a long procession of compassionate cases, demanding release. Bill Cooper was a twenty-three-year-old management trainee in Leicester when the recall letter came. He had only been out of the army two years, and was married just a month. A friend who was also summoned fled to France to escape duty. But reluctantly, Cooper himself reported to Bury St Edmunds, driven by the thought: 'What would people say if I didn't go?'[12] The call-up was generally chaotic, with many men's pay and allowances adrift for weeks.

In Cooper's battalion, the 5th Northumberland Fusiliers, there was a mutiny. One evening, the men returned from training to be confronted by a mess of corned beef which they declared to be 'off'. Cooper, as Orderly Officer, was summoned to taste it. He agreed. The men in the mess hall then staged a sit-in. All their resentments and bitterness about their predicament were boiling over. The adjutant arrived to rebuke Cooper for condemning the corned beef without first consulting the medical officer. As weightier and weightier 'brass' arrived to attempt to control the situation, some regulars slipped away, to escape involvement in the escalating situation. But even after repeated appeals and orders from senior officers, a dozen recalcitrant mutineers remained, who defied all orders to move. They were eventually removed for court-martial. The atmosphere in the battalion remained poor, with a succession of chaotic training exercises, and a feeling among reservist and National Service officers that the regulars lacked sensitivity in handling the men in their unwelcome predicament. 'Haven't you got a sword?' demanded a fellow-subaltern when Lieutenant Stan Muir abandoned his labours as a traveller in ladies' underwear to report to 45 Field Regiment. 'No? Oh my God. You know we do ceremonial guard-mounting here?' But at least Muir and his colleagues found little difficulty in readjusting to the ways of their 25-pounder guns after a two or three years' absence: 'It's like riding a bicycle or playing a musical instrument. You never really forget.'[13]

One British group went eagerly. Early in August, the Royal Marines were ordered to mobilise as rapidly as possible a group of commando volunteers for service in Korea. The Americans urgently needed some coastal raiding specialists. Major Douglas Drysdale, a highly experienced officer who had led a Commando in the Far East in World War II, was hastily restored to his old rank, and ordered to put together '41 Independent Commando, RM', and take off for Japan. Drysdale had the pick of Marines eager to see some war service. Within three weeks, he had assembled some 150 officers and men, including contingents of swimming, demolition and heavy weapons specialists. Then, under melodramatic and wholly ineffective security restrictions which compelled them to travel in civilian clothes, they flew by BOAC Argonaut to the Far East. Here, they were joined by a further 150 men 'kidnapped' from a draft in transit to 3 Commando Brigade in Malaya. At a base camp in Japan, they were issued with arms and equipment, American in everything except their cherished green berets, and began three weeks' intensive training before they started operations. Yet even among the Marines, it was necessary to qualify the press reports of their enthusiasm for Korean service. A certain Sergeant Molony found himself in deep trouble with his wife in England, when she picked up her newspaper to discover that he was being described as 'an eager volunteer' for the war. 41 Commando spent the early autumn conducting a series of modest hit-and-run raids on the coast of North Korea, where parties landed by the US Navy blew up sections of coastal railway and caused some alarm to communist outposts, with considerable satisfaction to themselves, and only one man killed.

Lieutenant-Colonel 'Jumbo' Phillips of the 8th Hussars preserved every cliché of the British cavalry going to war. While his unit prepared their Centurion tanks for embarkation, Phillips issued his own hints to officers about their preparation. He suggested taking fishing gear; four rolls of lavatory paper; and a shotgun – 'though not your *best* gun' – and ammunition, 'because Eley cartridges may be difficult to obtain'. The CO himself embarked with a vast load of personal equipment – 'them's Jumbo's fooking handkerchieves,' a disgusted trooper explained, sweating to load the boxes aboard. Meanwhile, his officers struggled to deal with their huge draft of disgruntled reservists. 'They were very angry – it really was quite a tricky situation,' in the words of Captain St Clair Tisdall. 'Come to that, I think we were all fairly horrified. Most of us were heavily married, with young children.'[14]

Above all, many men remained uncertain why they were going to Korea, or why they should be expected to fight for the United Nations. Bill Cooper said: 'The general feeling was that we shouldn't be going, that it was nothing to do with us. There was an undercurrent that the Yanks had got themselves in a mess again, and we were being sent to bail them out.' But at last, like so many soldiers that summer wailing *I'm going to take you on a slow boat to China*, they boarded the trucks for the docks, to take the troopship to Korea. Major Gerald Rickord of the Ulsters, like most of his fellow-officers, 'knew no more about Korea than I read in the *Daily Telegraph*'. A bachelor, he was embarrassed to be presented by an aunt before he departed with two pairs of long Johns. He took them rather crossly. Before a month was gone, he was desperately grateful.[15]

The voyage out, for most of the British, was an idyllic exercise in nostalgia, cruising comfortably from waystation to waystation on the great imperial route to the East. At Port Said, Lieutenant Patrick Kavanagh of the Ulsters was astonished to be frustrated in his quest for Egypt's legendary dirty postcards: 'No, sir! No good, sir! King Farouk very clean man!' A young National Serviceman on the bank of the Suez Canal shouted up to the deck of the troopship the immortal veterans' cry: 'Get your knees brown!' Private Albert Varley of the Ulsters, who had served through five campaigns in World War II, and for whom recall for Korea had been a most unwelcome shock, shouted back: 'We got them brown in 1941!'[16]

There was already considerable cynicism about their equipment. Newspapers briefed by the War Office declared 29 Brigade to be 'the best-equipped military force ever to leave Britain'. This was rubbish. On their arrival in Korea, the British contingent found themselves at a lamentable disadvantage to the Americans in the quality and quantity of their equipment and transport – above all, their clothing. The British in Korea in the first year of the war suffered privations of almost Crimean proportions. It would have been comic, were it not so wretched, that just five years after the end of World War II, herculean efforts were required to de-mothball sufficient transport from the army's vast stocks to give them roadworthy vehicles.

And beyond equipment, what were men to be told that they

were going to Korea to do? The names of Kim Il Sung or Syngman Rhee meant nothing to them. The 38th Parallel possessed no more reality than the rings of Saturn. Malcolm McDonald, the British Commissioner-General in South-East Asia, made the best of an almost impossible task when he addressed 27 Brigade as they embarked for Pusan:

When you get to South Korea [he told the men crowding the flight deck of the carrier *Unicorn*], the troops opposing you will be North Koreans. But their weapons, strategy and training were supplied by the Russians. The aggression in Korea is part of the attempt by Russian Communism to conquer the world. In Korea you will be fighting in defence not only of Asia and of Europe, but also of Britain, as surely as if you were fighting on the fields of France or the beaches of England itself . . . The enemy has committed an act of unprovoked aggression. That aggression is being resisted by the United Nations. The Americans and South Koreans fighting there are fighting not only as Americans and Koreans, but also as soldiers of the United Nations – that fraternal association of peoples set up to banish military aggression and establish the rule of law in international affairs. It is the first time in history that the peoples of the world have been mustered in arms under the auspices of the United Nations . . . May good fortune attend you and victory be yours.

On the other side of the Pacific, thousands of young Americans were embarking for Korea, taking with them similar ringing declarations of purpose, based upon the best efforts of their government to make a faraway country and a confused cause relate to their own land and experience. Yet on the hills of Korea, survival, fear of personal disgrace, loyalty to the man in the next foxhole – the most powerful motivations of soldiers throughout the ages – would mean far more than the strange new concept of fighting for the cause of world order.

3. The Pusan Perimeter

The six-week series of actions that came to be known as the battle of the Pusan Perimeter began on the night of 31 July, when the last of Walker's retreating army crossed the Naktong eastwards. 'There will be no more retreating, withdrawal, readjustment of lines or whatever you call it,' Eighth Army's commander declared, in a ringing order of the day following the fall of Chinju. 'There are no lines behind which we can retreat. This is not going to be a Dunkirk or Bataan. A retreat to Pusan would result in one of the greatest butcheries in history. We must fight to the end. We must fight as a team. If some of us die, we will die fighting together.' If it was corn, this was an hour when corn, as well as courage, was called for.

The Naktong river itself created an obstacle between a quarter and half a mile wide in its lower reaches defended by Eighth Army, but was shallow enough to be forded in many places. More important for Walker, it was commanded by steep hill ranges on both banks. Half the length of the UN perimeter lay along the river line. On the south side, the Americans were now dug into positions of great natural strength. Armour, heavy artillery and support equipment was being unloaded in quantity at Pusan. As the fighting stabilised, forward air control and clearer identification of positions made fighter-bomber strikes increasingly effective against communist concentrations. Walker's most serious problems, his chronic difficulties throughout the Perimeter battle, were the poor morale and training of many of his men; together with the shortage of manpower which made it impossible for him to hold his entire 130-mile front in strength. At the end of July, Walker disposed of a paper strength of some 95,000 men. Most of his 47,000 American combat troops were deployed in three infantry divisions of the Japan occupation army, some of whose units were already badly mauled. Week by week, this number was increasing as reinforcements reached Korea – the Marine Brigade, the British 27 Brigade. Walker could also call upon 45,000 South Koreans, though the combat value of these men was very limited indeed. Most were entirely untrained levies, dragged at gunpoint from their villages days before being sent to the front.

In August 1950, the men on the Pusan Perimeter saw themselves as a beleaguered army, clinging to the United Nations' last toehold in Korea, amid the onslaught of massed ranks of communist fanatics. Walker's army indeed was beleaguered. But it is a measure of the psychological dominance the communists had achieved at this time that most Americans would have been frankly disbelieving had they been told that the UN forces by now outnumbered the North Koreans significantly, and outgunned them overwhelmingly. The ferocity and suicidal recklessness of the massed attacks of Kim Il Sung's units, night after night through those weeks, gave the defenders the impression of an Asian horde with limitless supplies of manpower. In reality, the North Koreans were squandering their dwindling reserves of armour, ammunition, and trained men. But again and again, the communist gamble came close to success. Enemy attackers broke through Walker's line, began pushing forward to open a chasm in the front, and were halted only by the last-ditch movement of one of his handful of reliable 'fire-brigade' units to stop the gap.

The battle for the Pusan Perimeter was marked by an almost daily succession of crises for Eighth Army, in which disaster was averted by the narrowest of margins. Kim Il Sung and his commanders fully grasped the urgency of smashing through to Pusan before the UN build-up made their task impossible. The North Korean 4th Division mounted one of the first big attacks against the US 24th: the battle of the 'Naktong Bulge'. On the night of 5 August, they successfully pushed forward across the river with tanks and guns, overrunning American outpost positions. In the days that followed, they built up strength on the east bank, gaining ground steadily.

On 17 August, the Marine Provisional Brigade was committed to counter-attack. Two days later, after bitter fighting, the communists were driven back across the Naktong. And even as the 24th Division was being hard pressed, further north the 1st Cavalry and ROK 1st and 6th Divisions faced a succession of thrusts aimed to break through to Taegu, where Eighth Army headquarters was sited. By 15 August, they had come within fifteen miles of the town. Three communist divisions were poised for the assault. But when two further enemy formations, the 3rd and 10th Divisions, sought to force the Naktong eastwards to link up with the assault, in a week of intense action between 8 and 15 August, they were thrown back with massive losses. American air and artillery concentrations hammered their crossing points by day and night. The Naktong's defensive value was diminishing, as the river fell to its lowest summer level. Some of the 1st Cavalry's forward positions east of the river were overrun. But the North Koreans proved unable to reinforce their leading elements. The attack was repulsed. Walker could turn his attention to the north-western threat to Taegu.

The 25th Division bore the brunt of the fighting in 'the Bowling Alley', as it became known, the sheer-sided valley in which a week-long tank battle – one of the rare armoured encounters of the war – raged as the communists strove to break through. The defenders watched in awe as the glowing armour-piercing shells of the T-34s streaked down the valley through the night, searching out the American Pershings. Again and again the communists pushed forward, yet each time their assaults broke upon the barrier of American firepower. By 24 August, the north-western thrust had burnt itself out. The sector was left in ROK hands, while the 25th Division was withdrawn.

At the north-eastern end of the perimeter, the ROK 3rd Division was pushed back through Yongdok to Changsa-dong. On 10 August, the North Koreans worked through the mountains to cut the road south behind the South Korean positions. The 3rd Division was successfully evacuated by sea, but the town of Pohang-dong was lost, and Walker's resources were stretched to the limit to fill the hole in his line. Scratch American task forces were dispatched to support ROK units in the north-eastern sector. To their relief, they began to perceive that the communist effort and manpower in the area were almost spent. Pushing cautiously north again, by 20 August they had retaken Pohang-dong. Walker was confident that he faced no further serious threat in this quarter.

*

Most men's first impression of Korea was of the stench, drifting out from the land to the sea: of human excrement and unidentifiable oriental exotica, mostly disagreeable. Replacements and new formations filed down the gangplanks at the pierside amid the disturbing spectacle of casualties being loaded alongside. There was no shortage of black jokes about the most likely fashion of leaving the country. Pusan was a grossly overcrowded shambles of corrugated iron, street markets, refugees, military convoys, beggars, prostitutes and organised crime. Most American units had been organised and reorganised, stripped of specialists and reinforced with drafts so often since early July that officers, NCOs and men scarcely knew each other. 'We realised something was radically wrong the moment we arrived,' said Lieutenant Clyde Fore of the 29th RCT. 'We could see our advance party sitting on the quay, silent and unmoving. Our unit really was unfit to go at all. We had been told we would have three or four months in country to train before we were committed to combat. Instead, on the quayside we were just told to uncrate the weapons and get ready to go in the line.'[17]

When Lieutenant-Colonel Robert Taplett, commanding the 3/5th Marines of the 1st Marine Provisional Brigade, landed on 1 August, 'everything seemed in turmoil – there were too many people with a wild stare in their eyes. The whole story of the army at this period is a very unsavoury one.'[18] The Marines were dismayed by meeting army units which had abandoned their dead, and even wounded, on the field; by units which, indeed, did not linger to fight at all. There were tales of officers who had found it convenient to make their own way back to Japan, and of the black battalion of the 9th Infantry which had failed to distinguish itself, to put the matter politely, by its determination in combat.

When Private James Waters reported with two other replacements to the 1/35th Infantry of the 25th Division on 28 August, his company commander welcomed them bluntly: 'This isn't a police action – it's a war. You'd better get it into your heads that you can get killed at any second.'[19] Waters' companions were indeed killed within weeks. The seventeen-year-old Missourian found the nervous strain of the night battles, the constant uncertainty about where and when the enemy would come, almost intolerable. He and his comrades came to hate even the cowbells tinkling in front of the positions, for the North Koreans sometimes used them to mask their movements. The low moment of the day came towards evening, when section by section they filed back down the hill to the chow jeep, knowing that night was approaching. The high moment broke at early morning, when once again they went to get their chow, knowing that they had survived the hours of darkness.

'Everything I had read about Bataan, I felt in the first few hours after landing at Pusan,' said Sergeant John Pearson of the 9th Infantry. 'People were just completely demoralised. We were told right off that the front had collapsed. As we were taken forward on the train, we could see GIs on flatcars, without weapons, going the other way – stragglers getting out.'[20] Pearson was dismayed to learn that his raw recruits would not even be given time to zero their weapons. They were dumped out in the countryside by trucks which turned and drove back towards the city at once, to fetch more men. They were filling their canteens in a stream when a furious officer drove up in a jeep, jumped out, and began demanding what they were doing. It was Walton Walker himself. They said they were taking on water. 'What are you thinking of?' shouted the Eighth Army commander. 'I want your asses forward.'

Without reconnaissance, they were launched into a counter-attack to recover a lost position, advancing in skirmishing line across open paddy fields towards high ground held by the enemy. Their battalion commander was wounded within a few minutes, while men dropped right and left from the communist fire. But they reached their objective. In the early days that followed, Pearson began to marvel at the incompetence of the North Koreans, as much as at the shortcomings of his own side: 'They just threw their tanks away, coming at us head on again and again.'

Pearson was twenty-seven, a veteran of the Pacific campaign who had found life in the post-war army an anticlimax – 'I couldn't stand all the peace and quiet.' He had married a German girl while stationed in Frankfurt, and the very night after that first action in Korea, he received a letter reporting her safe arrival in New York. Pearson was the son of British immigrants, and a keen student of military history. On the wall at home, he cherished a sepia photograph of his uncle Charlie, a Lancashire Fusilier in the First World War. In Korea, he was dismayed to see how far the US Army had declined since 1945: 'Somehow, the whole thing had come unglued.' There were too few West Point officers, too few trained men. They became accustomed to the sudden appearance of North Korean infiltration parties behind the front, to sudden movements from position to position to meet communist night attacks, to the chronic shortage of tank and artillery support on their own side. One morning, Pearson was an awed spectator as the 1st Provisional Marine Brigade launched its legendary assault in the battle of No Name Hill. 'They went up in column of companies. They came back on stretchers in column of platoons,' he said. 'It was a magnificent thing, but out of another era – a typical Marine frontal attack.'

That night, the 9th Infantry were committed to the battle. After fighting all through the hours of darkness, the men stood up on their positions and cheered as the Australian P-51 Mustangs came in rocketing and machine-gunning the North Korean trenches at first light. Again and again as the infantry met communist attacks and approached their last reserves of ammunition, they were saved at the last moment by resupply from the patient files of Korean porters, trudging up the reverse slopes, their backs bent over their A-frames laden with ammunition. 'We couldn't have fought the war without those Korean litter-bearers,' said Pearson. 'There were a lot of complaints about them, but I guess there were a lot of complaints about Gunga Din, too.'

Sergeant Pearson was walking the line of his platoon's positions when a new communist assault began, and he was slow jumping for a foxhole. A bullet entered his thigh, turned on his message book and stopped at the base of his spine. He suffered instant trauma, and lay thinking himself dead, wondering dimly what would happen to his wife. Then a man gave him a drink from his canteen, which made him feel even worse. Semi-conscious, he endured the agony of being bumped and jolted down the hill on a stretcher, along an endless track by jeep. At the aid station, the orderly who stripped off his boots asked if he could keep them: 'You won't be needing them.' He made the first helicopter trip of his life to an operating table from which he looked up at an exhausted, blood-spattered surgeon who said: 'This is not going to hurt. We'll give you a spinal.' Then he pulled Pearson's bowels up, and the sergeant was torn by excruciating pain. They left the bullet and the scraps of his message pad inside him. Next he remembered a train, and hearing a grenade explosion and the hammer of quad .50 calibre machine guns. Was this the reality of a guerrilla attack, or a comatose fantasy? He never knew. In Pusan, a priest gave him the last rites. He murmured that he was an Anglican. 'That's all right,' said his comforter reassuringly. 'It all counts upstairs.' A British hospital ship bore him to Japan. Thence, after almost six months of medical care, he was returned to the United States in March 1951.

*

It was only with the deepest reluctance that the British government and Chiefs of Staff at last agreed to send a token ground force to Korea. In response to Washington's urgent pleas, 27 Brigade, part of the Hong Kong garrison, were dispatched post-haste to join the defenders of the Pusan Perimeter.

On Sunday 20 August, the orderly room of the 1st Middlesex was roused by an unexpected telephone call. The CO, Lieutenant-Colonel Andrew Man, gave orders to begin rounding up his officers and men from 'the Duchess of Richmond's ball' – the local water sports. The unit was badly under-strength. It was hastily reorganised into three companies, and reinforced within a few hours by volunteers from other garrison units. Company commanders sat with their sergeant-majors, hastily slotting new arrivals into sections: 'Anybody who's got a mucker – say so'; 'Is there a man here who can fire a two-inch mortar?' 'Any bren-gunners?' The men were rushed down to the range for a token musketry course before they embarked. But many had spent their time in Hong Kong on administrative or ceremonial duties: 'As a fighting unit, we were virtually untrained,' said Major John Willoughby, one of their company commanders.[21] They sailed on Friday morning, the 25th, aboard the carrier *Unicorn*, with all the trappings that Britain's empire in the Far East could still muster. The brigade's second battalion, the Argyll & Sutherland Highlanders, travelled aboard the graceful cruiser *Ceylon*.

This first British contingent became known as 'the Woolworth Brigade', because of the pathetic shortcomings of its equipment and clothing. They possessed not a scrap of specialist gear for warfare under extremes of cold and heat, no sleeping bags, only a handful of vehicles. Such winter clothing as they owned, and left on the dockside when they marched out from the port of Pusan for the Perimeter, was comprehensively looted before they saw it again. There was some tension in the Middlesex between their CO, an officer of administrative rather than combat experience, and Major Willoughby, who had at one stage been his senior officer. Willoughby himself was 'terribly concerned about what would happen when we went into action. I was also worried about fighting alongside the Americans – I had seen them in the Pacific, and I knew what a mess they could get themselves into.' The officers began the uphill struggle to indoctrinate their men about the small routines of war: after years in barracks, where rifles were secured except on parade or on the range, soldiers must now be nagged and prodded into carrying their weapons everywhere – everywhere.

The brigade's arrival at Pusan was not auspicious. Their briga-dier, a sound, steady, competent professional named Basil Coad, was met by an American officer with the cheerful greeting: 'Glad you British have arrived – you're the real experts at retreating.' When Coad and his staff were taken on an introductory tour of the line by an American general, the British were disconcerted to find that their movements were stage-managed for the benefit of the accompanying photographers. They were staggered by the lack of military security, above all by the freedom with which men could telephone on civilian circuits from the Perimeter to girl-friends in Japan. And the British had ample problems of their own. Many of their men were young conscripts, bewildered to find their service abruptly extended to go to war.

> They seemed in a state of shock for many weeks after we arrived [said Major John Willoughby]. They accepted any order without hesitation. There was no question of imposing World War I discipline: if you found a man asleep on guard, you knew for certain that he was exhausted. When I found a sentry unconscious in his sleeping bag, I just picked it up and bumped him. What was the point in charging him? I simply said: 'Wake up, you bugger! All your mates could get killed!' When they marched, I had to go round with the sergeant-major to find the entrenching tools they had hidden to avoid carrying them. Yet you could only deal with these things on a fatherly basis.[22]

The British were rushed into the line west of Taegu for the first time on 12 September, in the face of a sudden communist push.

They spent their first night in a river bed under pouring rain. D Company of the Middlesex were detailed to hold some four and a half miles of front with a handful of tanks and AAA guns in support. They decided instead that the only sane course was to concentrate their men within reach of each other. They found themselves sharing the position with 230 Korean policemen whose commander appeared, reeking of brandy, and announced that his men would not remain unless they were given some weapons. The British reluctantly handed him a bren gun, and their own sanitary orderly as 'liaison officer', on the grounds that he could speak Japanese. In the days that followed, the British defended their sector by sending out parties at dawn to light fires at intervals along the ridge line, to deceive the communists. Their first patrol was fired on by their own men: 'Baptism of fire my eye, it's A Company!', in the words of a disgusted NCO. A stray rifle shot at night was liable to panic the entire unit into opening fire. It became essential to reassure every position by telephone the moment an alarm was given.

For some days, such was the silence from the far bank of the river that they doubted whether the enemy was there. From time to time, without warning the darkness was broken by a casual incoming shell. There were constant rumours of imminent enemy attack: 'I used to pray for the dawn,' said Willoughby. 'That first grey in the sky was very important there.'

*

For many South Koreans, the process of discovering the meaning of communist liberation was extended through the four months that Kim Il Sung's army occupied their country. It is difficult to overemphasise the importance of this period in the subsequent history of Korea. In the years between 1945 and 1950, many of those living under the regime of Syngman Rhee were dismayed and disgusted by the corruption and injustice that the old President came to represent. For all the rumours filtering down from the North, about land reform and political education, there seemed no reason to imagine that life under Kim Il Sung was any worse than under Syngman Rhee. The two vicious totalitarians appeared to have much in common. Even when the invasion came in June 1950, in the words of the young bank clerk's son Minh Pyong Kyu, 'we still did not realise that this was a catastrophe for us.'[23] Syngman Rhee's creatures conducted some odious killings of alleged communist sympathisers as they fled south. Yet the behaviour of the North Koreans in their four months of dominance of the South, their ghastly brutalities and wholesale murders of their enemies, decisively persuaded most inhabitants of the country that whatever the shortcomings of Syngman Rhee, nothing could be as appalling as communist tyranny. In 1950 and in the years that followed, some distinguished Western journalists such as the British James Cameron were so disgusted by the excesses of Rhee's lackeys that they became opponents of the UN presence in Korea. Not a few UN soldiers were appalled by the acts they witnessed, committed by South Korean soldiers and police. Yet the attitude of such observers as Cameron reflected a Western liberal conscience that shrank from facing the relative moral issues that Korea posited. Something will be said below about the crimes of Syngman Rhee's minions. But to this day, not a shred of evidence has been discovered of crimes by the Seoul regime on the scale which the North Koreans committed during their rule in the South: the awful mass murders, of which the 5,000 bodies discovered in Taejon alone were only a sample. The UN Command later estimated that some 26,000 South Korean civilians were slaughtered in cold blood by the North Koreans between June and September 1950. The arrival of the communists unleashed a reign of terror, which gave the United Nations' cause in Korea a moral legitimacy that has survived to this day.

*

Young Minh Pyong Kyu and his family lived near the West Gate prison in Seoul. They watched the arriving communist army unloose its doors, spilling out into the streets thousands of captives, common criminals and political prisoners who ran forth yelling, 'Long Live the Fatherland!' Minh said: 'In the beginning, it was an atmosphere of unrestrained happiness, of true liberation. Everybody was running through the streets, leaping for joy.' Minh's family found themselves penniless. But they had relations in the country. His father decided to travel to visit them with his younger brothers, in the hope of getting food. Minh himself went back to his medical school. He found most of the teachers still in residence, having declared decisively for the cause of socialism. Minh and other students who had been expelled for political activity were readmitted. But there were no classes. Only the hospital was functioning, under North Korean military supervision. Minh was impressed by the communists' tough discipline. They kept themselves to themselves, they committed no excesses. 'Then, in the days that followed, we heard that the communists were rounding up "reactionaries". Slowly, the atmosphere of terror set in.'

Kap Chong Chi, a twenty-two-year-old student, knew from the beginning that as the son of a landowner, his position and that of his family were perilous. He spent the night after the communist seizure of Seoul deep in thought about what he should do. He had still reached no decision the next morning, when he walked out into the street to see the bodies of two policemen, their identity cards laid neatly upon their chests. Yet foolishly, he went to the house of a friend in the police force, to ask his advice. The man had gone, but two strangers carrying rifles stopped Kap by the door, and demanded to know who he was. His answers did not satisfy them. He was taken away to police headquarters near the Capitol building, and held alone with his fear all that day and night. Early the next morning, he was marched through the courtyard, past the bodies of men already executed, and taken up to the third floor. He joined a long procession of men and women awaiting interrogation, their wrists tied together with strips of cloth. After an endless, wretched wait, he found himself before the People's Court. The judges, in white civilian clothes, were themselves newly released from Syngman Rhee's prisons. To his dismay, he identified one as an acquaintance of his older brother. This man said: 'I know your family. Landowners. Your life is finished.' Kap was taken away to join some thirty others, mostly South Korean soldiers or policemen, in a basement cell.

The captives said little to each other through the hours and days that followed, each one fearful of willing his own death by identification with another. A succession of different communist officials took their names and asked further questions. Kap, in desperation, tried a new tactic. He told his interrogators that, like his cousin, he had always been a secret sympathiser. His answers to new, probing questions about his communist convictions sounded pathetically unconvincing. But one of his interrogators proved surprisingly sympathetic. He prompted Kap with some ideological answers. At last, at 4 a.m., five days after his arrest, this official gave him a chit to present to the desk officer responsible for the prisoners.

The little student suffered a further agonising delay in the central hall of the headquarters building, sitting amid a throng of officials, guards and prisoners coming and going, while his papers were processed. He shrank against the wall, hiding his face, terrified of being identified by a new denunciator. But at last, he was casually told that he might go. He walked home through the early morning Seoul streets, decked with huge posters of Stalin and Kim Il Sung. For a few hours he hid, listening to Voice of America, desperate to discover what was happening in the south of the country. Then, ravenously hungry, he went to the house of a fellow-student. He found his friend in the same case as himself. They discussed what to do. No young man could leave the city, yet somehow they must. They considered stealing a boat, rowing out to the American fleet. They lingered for days, not daring to venture on to the streets. Only when they became convinced that if they remained, they must face rearrest, did they summon up the courage to join the great throng of refugees crowding the approaches to the improvised ferry crossings south across the Han river. They had forged themselves crude passes to get past the communist checkpoints. In the confusion at the river, they bluffed their way through.

Like hundreds of thousands of Koreans in those days, they walked for weeks, hither and thither amid the communist troop columns and incessant American strafing which killed many hundreds of civilians, along with the North Koreans. They sought in vain to get through to the UN perimeter in the south-east. Despairing of this, they set out for the family home at Kwangju. Kap was arrested again, held overnight, and escaped during a bombing raid. From a friend outside Kwangju, he heard that all his family had been arrested, and were believed to be dead. Kap could think of nowhere else to go: 'I began to travel aimlessly, merely waiting for something to happen.'[24]

Thousands, even millions of South Koreans lived on the brink of animality in those months, roaming the countryside; fighting off fellow-strugglers for survival with increasingly ruthless desperation; existing partly on peasant charity, but more generally by plundering the fields of whatever crops and scraps and domestic animals they could reach in darkness. Suk Bun Yoon was a thirteen-year-old middle school pupil, the son of a Seoul merchant. Many of his fellow-students, urged by their teachers to volunteer for Kim Il Sung's army, did so. But Suk's father knew that sooner or later, the communists would find his name on the rolls of several Rhee-sponsored political organisations. The family hid in their home for weeks while Suk and his younger brothers walked out into the countryside to buy food, each trip a longer search becoming necessary, sometimes twenty, thirty, forty miles; then they struggled back to the city. One day, Suk was stopped on the road and pressed into joining an army forced-labour group, humping ammunition. It took the boy twelve hours to carry his huge load six miles to the station where it was wanted. Then he was detained to dig slit trenches, a task interrupted by repeated flights to a nearby sewer during air attacks. Once, he found himself within a few yards of a bridge which blew up before his eyes, beneath the bombs of a B-26. At last, he was able to slip away, and walk home to the city. He found that his father had gone, seeking refuge in the countryside. The rest of the family lingered in the house, exhausted by hunger and fear. They could think of nowhere to go, but they knew that if they remained, sooner or later the communists must come for them. They prayed for a miracle.

There are those who might argue that the families of such young men as Suk Bun Yoon or Kap Chong Chi had willed their own misery, by their support for the regime of Syngman Rhee; that their own terrors at the hands of the communists were matched by those of left-wing sympathisers in the hands of Rhee's police in the years that went before. Yet if Rhee's regime had been a relative tyranny, that of Kim Il Sung proved absolute. There are no more striking testimonials to the political development of Korea at war than those of such young men as Minh Pyong Kyu, who were avowed left-wing sympathisers before the North Korean invasion; yet who abruptly ceased to be so, when they saw the manner in which the regime of Kim Il Sung exercised its power.

*

The men of Eighth Army strung out along the mountains above the Naktong were entirely ignorant of the terrors and nightmares of many South Koreans at the hands of their occupiers. They could measure something of the reluctance of thousands of people to join the ranks of Kim Il Sung by the vast drift of refugees into the Perimeter. But the Americans had come to this war too speedily to have any chance of indoctrination about its higher purposes, and their cause still lacked any remotely grand grievance in the manner of Pearl Harbor. They were told that they were fighting Asian communism at the gates of the Pacific. Most were only aware of the desperate need to survive against the cluster of 'gooks' working up the defile below them, the T-34 grinding down the road towards their position. The struggle for the Pusan Perimeter only attained its historical coherence to those who wrote about it afterwards. In those autumn weeks of 1950, it was an interminable series of short, fierce, encounter battles in which the defenders' units had known each other, had fought together, for too brief a period to be called an army in any meaningful sense.

> There was no point where the line began [wrote the British correspondent James Cameron], because naturally there was no line – except at rear on the briefing-room map; a doubtful chalk-mark between established positions; it had no meaning on the ground. What line there was, was this road, winding up from security in Taegu northwards into the hills until it stopped, only for fear of its own length. A mile or two outside town no part of it was safe; you would meet nothing on the road, but the hillsides were full of invisible people, and when you turned back along the track there would be a barrier between you and your rear. It might be only a machine-gun roadblock, but for a while it would dislocate the whole crawling vertebrae of the column, which could move only in one plane, forwards or back, and never to the side. One drove trying to look behind; the dangerous place was always one corner away, at the back of your head.
>
> Bit by bit the front materialised, the tanks squatted on the flats of the river-beds, the road grew dense with traffic, and soon, where it ran in a kind of cutting between wooded slopes, were the groups of men, like picnickers, crouching on the verge with automatic guns, huddling in the dust of the passing wheels among a litter of ration-cans ('The Ripe Flavour of Nutty Home-Grown Corn Enriched with Body-Building Viadose') or heads buried under the hood of a jeep. The air was alive with a tinny whispering from field-telephones and the radios of tanks, a thin erratic chattering like insects, the ceaseless indiscriminate gossip of an army. Up and down the road, weaving through the traffic, bare-legged Koreans humped loads of food or mortar ammunition on their porters' frameworks of wood, like men with easels on their backs.[25]

'In many ways, it seemed a tougher war than Europe,' said Lieutenant Walt Mayo, an artillery forward observer with the 8th

Cavalry. Mayo had fought as an enlisted draftee with the 106th Division at the Battle of the Bulge.

> Things were so disorganised and depressing – I remember going back to the battery and get some clean clothes, to find them evacuating our ammunition dump. We were rationed to twenty-five rounds a tube a day, and one was constantly fighting to get extra rounds – it became a game as to which FOO could lie best to the Fire Direction Officer. There were days when one lay there for hours on end under incoming mortar fire, but could get no rounds at all to send back. You fought for a hilltop; you lost it; you got it back. There was none of that excitement of being on the move. Men were kept going just by a crude feeling of 'To hell with it, those bastards aren't going to beat us.'[26]

Many men's service on the Naktong was painfully brief. Lieutenant David Bolté of the 2/8th Cavalry, son of the US Army's Chief of Plans, arrived in Korea straight from West Point. Many of his men, he learnt, were slow to understand that here, the penalty for failing to behave like a soldier was death. The shortages even of basic equipment were a constant source of frustration. Bolté found himself wrestling with a machine gun under heavy communist fire, lacking the tool for removing a ruptured barrel. He himself had been compelled to take over the gun when he saw it standing abandoned. One of its crew had been wounded, and the others had seized the familiar excuse to take him to the rear. There were chronic problems with men drifting away out of the line in darkness: 'They just didn't want to be up there at night.' Bolté saw a man blow himself to pieces, clumsily dropping a primed grenade into his own foxhole. He himself lasted just ten days in Korea, before a bullet smashed into his shoulder as he peered at the communist lines through his binoculars. In the days that followed, as he lay in a Japanese hospital where plaster was so short that they could not put a cast on his arm, he remembered his last night before embarkation, watching three smart young paratroopers celebrating in the Top of the Mark Hopkins hotel in San Francisco. An excited woman said: 'Oooh, it's just like World War II all over again.' Bolté looked back from the perspective of a man who would never be fit to see a battlefield again: 'One had this great romantic ideal, of an adventure in which people don't bleed.' In that Japanese hospital where the halls were crowded with stretcher cases, where nurses were working twelve-hour shifts to cope with a thousand-patient overload, Bolté's youthful ideal died.

*

The difficulties of defending the Pusan Perimeter were caused, above all, by inadequacies of training and leadership in the American formations thrust into the line after five years' chronic national neglect of the armed forces. Some of Walker's formations were in desperate condition. After its terrible mauling in July, the 24th Division was scarcely battleworthy – 'a completely defeated ragtag that had lost all will,' in the words of Colonel Paul Freeman of the 23rd Infantry. Like most American officers, Freeman could also find little to say in favour of the ROK army's contribution to the campaign: 'It was pitiful. But it wasn't their fault. They lacked the training, the motivation, the equipment to do the job. Whenever their units were on our flanks, we found that they were liable to vanish without notice.'[27] Nor were some of the American reinforcement units much better. The men of 1st Cavalry Division were scornfully nicknamed 'MacArthur's pets' for their supposedly decorative, rather than active function in Japan. The 1st Cavalry would suffer terribly in the autumn and winter of 1950 for their shortcomings of training and competence.

The line could not have been held at all without the ruthless professionalism of a handful of outstanding officers, among whom must rank Colonel John Michaelis of the 27th Infantry. 'Iron Mike' was a thirty-seven-year-old 'army brat' who graduated from West Point in 1936. By 1945, the tall, slim Californian had become one of America's outstanding combat soldiers, commanding the 502nd Airborne regiment, a twice-wounded veteran of D-Day and

Arnhem. Michaelis was posted to the Operations Section of Eighth Army in 1949, where he was dismayed to find so many of the best officers being diverted from regimental duty to administrative and staff jobs. He assumed command of the 27th 'Wolfhounds' when its CO was abruptly relieved in the field. His second-in-command and two of his battalion commanders were likewise drafted in haste. With his ranks filled with so many green, frightened young soldiers, Michaelis resorted to drastic measures to raise their confidence. One of his master sergeants took post behind a wall while their own guns dropped 105mm shells in front of it, to demonstrate the effectiveness of cover. The 27th had lost many of its best NCOs, who were sent to stiffen the 24th Division when it was first committed to Korea. Michaelis was acutely conscious of the shortcomings of leadership at platoon level. He was ruthlessly frank about the difficulties of taking into battle men with pitifully little tactical or weapons training. At the height of the battle in August 1950, when many heroic myths were being circulated about the fighting qualities of Eighth Army, Michaelis told an interviewer from the *Saturday Evening Post*:

> In peacetime training, we've gone for too damn much falderal. We've put too much stress on Information and Education and not enough stress on rifle marksmanship and scouting and patrolling and the organisation of a defensive position. These kids of mine have all the guts in the world and I can count on them to fight. But when they started out, they couldn't shoot. They didn't know their weapons. They have not had enough training in plain, old-fashioned musketry. They'd spend a lot of time listening to lectures on the difference between communism and Americanism and not enough time crawling on their bellies on manoeuvres with live ammunition singing over them. They'd been nursed and coddled, told to drive safely, to buy War Bonds, to give to the Red Cross, to avoid VD, to write home to mother – when somebody ought to have been telling them how to clear a machine gun when it jams ... The US Army is so damn roadbound that the soldiers have almost lost

the use of their legs. Send out a patrol on a scouting mission and they load up in a three-quarter-ton truck and start riding down the highway.[28]

If it sometimes appears, in the course of this narrative, that a British author is adopting too critical an attitude towards the professional conduct of the US Army in Korea, it is worth recalling the brutal professional strictures of Michaelis, echoed by other objectively minded observers. In September 1950, even as the colonel talked to his interviewer at his command post in the chemistry laboratory of a Korean middle school, there was a shot outside, followed by a report that a man had killed himself cleaning his pistol. 'See what I mean?' said the colonel. 'They still don't know how to handle their weapons without blowing their own brains out. They've had to learn in combat, in a matter of days, the basic things they should have known before they ever faced an enemy. And some of them don't learn fast enough.'[29] The colonel's comments on the shortcomings of Eighth Army remained equally vigorous, thirty-five years later.

The 27th Infantry became a vital ingredient in Walker's defensive operations, the Perimeter's 'fire brigade', held in reserve to be rushed from point to point as enemy attacks developed. Again and again under Michaelis' ruthless leadership, the Wolfhounds proved the force that stemmed the tide. Their morale soared from this knowledge. It was a Korean officer, Paek Sun Yup, who remembered watching Michaelis lose his temper after a neighbouring ROK unit broke off an action and withdrew without informing the Americans. 'If we lose this battle, we may not have a Korea,' the furious colonel of the 27th told the hapless ROK battalion commander. 'We have nowhere else to go. We must stand and fight.'

Throughout the struggle for the Perimeter, Syngman Rhee's army was being reinforced by the most ruthless means. Each day, police combed the city and the countryside for any male capable of bearing arms: boys, teenagers, grandfathers were relentlessly rounded up, given a few hours' rudimentary weapon training, and herded into the line to join a unit. 'It was never at any time possible to obtain a firm or official figure for the number of South Korean troops in the field,' wrote a British correspondent.[30] 'They were at most times heavily outnumbered, and their casualties were enormous. The intake was vast, the training almost unbelievably cursory. The man was drafted at the age of eighteen. On the Sunday he might be at work in the paddies or the shop; by the following Sunday he was in the line; in next to no time he was either a veteran or a corpse.'

Lee Chien Ho, the young Seoul chemical engineering student who had sought to defend his campus with a broomstick in the dying days of June, reached Pusan on 4 August after an endless, painful journey by train, oxcart, and shoe power. He went to the temporary Ministry of Education building and asked where he might go to continue his schooling. An official looked at him in astonishment: 'Your country is at war.' Then he learned that Lee spoke a little English: 'The Americans need interpreters.' He was sent to the 1st Marine Brigade, and soon felt relieved to be fed, clothed – to belong somewhere. He remained with the Marines through all the battles of the six months that followed.

As the struggle continued, American and South Korean units began to learn – or rather, relearn from history – painful tactical lessons. It was fatal to seek to defend a sector by spreading men in penny packets along its length: defend everything, and you defend nothing. Units must concentrate on key positions. If the enemy outflanked a position, the defenders must hold their ground while reserves were brought forward to counter-attack. Every battalion, every company, every platoon must site its foxholes for all-round defence. These were principles essential to survival. Some units had still failed to learn them by November 1950, with tragic consequences. But there were enough – just enough – men of Eighth Army who did so in August and September, to hold the Pusan Perimeter.

*

In the last ten days of August, there came a lull in the fighting along the entire Pusan front. The communists were reorganising and regrouping their shattered formations. They acknowledged the mistake they had made by attacking successively at different points, enabling the Americans to rush reserves to meet each thrust in turn. This time, it would be different. They would mount a co-ordinated assault. The North Korean 6th and 7th Divisions would attack in the south, by Masan, on the US 25th Division front. The 2nd, 4th, 9th and 10th would strike at the Naktong Bulge, against the US 2nd Division. The 8th and 15th Divisions, in the north, would seek to cut off Pohang-dong and the ROK units covering the line of communications from Taegu. The 5th and 12th Divisions would strike directly at Pohang-dong. Underwater bridges were constructed across the Naktong, log and sandbag constructions intensely difficult to detect even from the air, in the muddy water. Each night, there was intense activity on the communist front: guns and ammunition being moved forward, such tanks as remained being concentrated, small armies of men labouring with shovel and mattock. Walker knew for certain that the communists were coming. He was in doubt only as to when.

The onslaught, the last great North Korean effort of the battle, was unleashed on the night of 31 August. In the south, the attackers broke through the defences of the 25th Division to threaten Masan. Further north, the 2nd Division was almost cut in two by KPA troops overrunning some of its forward positions, sweeping on to leave others completely isolated. Around Taegu, the US 1st Cavalry lost Waegwan, and Walker was compelled to transfer his own main headquarters to Pusan, so imminent seemed the threat to EUS AK HQ at Taegu. Pohang-dong fell once more. By 5 September, Walker was obliged to consider a general withdrawal. Almost everywhere along the line, the will and ability of his army to sustain their positions seemed in serious doubt.

Yet over the next hours and days, reports reaching Eighth Army first hinted, then confirmed that the communist advance had run out of steam. On every sector of the front, the fighting was withering away. Desultory North Korean movements were checked with little difficulty by the defenders and their air and artillery support. The communists had reached the limits of men, guns, supplies, ammunition. The Pusan Perimeter held, and more than a few of its defenders now heard the astonishing rumours of a great operation for their relief already being mounted from Japan. The spirits of Eighth Army rose perceptibly, and with it their respect and gratitude to Walker, the fiercely energetic little Texan who had made their survival possible. Walker would not go down in history as a military intellectual, a man of ideas. But he would be remembered for bringing to the battle for the Pusan Perimeter the qualities that made its survival possible: ruthless dynamism, speed of response, dogged determination. He was leading one of the least professional, least motivated armies America had ever put into the field. Even many of its higher commanders seemed afflicted by 'bug-out fever', a chronic yearning to escape from Korea and leave the thankless peninsula to its inhabitants. Walker kept his men at their business by sheer relentless hounding, goading, driving, and the support of a handful of exceptional officers and units whose competence decided the day. Eighth Army's performance at Pusan narrowly maintained the United Nations presence in Korea. It remained to be seen whether the achievement of survival on the battlefield could now be translated into outright victory over the communists.

An American doctor tends a Korean civilian casualty of the Inchon bombardment.

Refugees under questioning by South Korean and American military police.

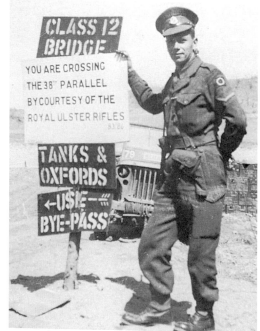

Above: The road north: a British jeep surrounded by the customary crowd of curious villagers and children.

Right: The five-year-old frontier between North and South Korea becomes a mere military tourist attraction.

Opposite page: Marshal Peng Te Huai, commander of the Chinese People's 'Volunteers' in Korea, with North Korea's leader Kim Il Sung.

CLASS 12 BRIDGE

YOU ARE CROSSING THE 38" PARALLEL BY COURTESY OF THE ROYAL ULSTER RIFLES

TANKS & OXFORDS ←USE—"' BYE-PASS

The coming of the Chinese; (*above*) the bugle that signalled so many communist assaults; (*below*) the supply route across the frozen Yalu.

Chinese 'Volunteers' in Korea.

Americans surrender to Chinese infantry. This is almost certainly a posed propaganda picture, but its reality became grimly familiar in the winter of 1950.

Back from the reservoir: US Marines rest in the midst of their desperate march down the thin thread of frozen road between Chosin and the sea.

General Edward M. Almond, commander of the US X Corps.

Chinese infantry enter the ruins of Seoul.

Men of the Royal Ulster Rifles move forward with sten guns and grenades.

A column of porters wind their way up a Korean hillside. The porters, all conscripted civilians, provided vital assistance for the UN forces.

5 » INCHON

For all its undisputed Korean provenance, the name of Inchon possesses a wonderfully resonant American quality. It summons a vision of military genius undulled by time, undiminished by more recent memories of Asian defeat. Inchon remains a monument to 'can do', to improvisation and risk-taking on a magnificent scale, above all to the spirit of Douglas MacArthur. So much must be said elsewhere in these pages about American misfortunes in Korea, about grievous command misjudgements and soldierly shortcomings, that there is little danger here of overblowing the trumpet. The amphibious landings of 15 September 1950 were MacArthur's masterstroke. In a world in which nursery justice decided military affairs, Operation CHROMITE would have won the war for the United States.

From the early stages of the conflict, as Eighth Army struggled to maintain fighting room in the south-east of Korea, MacArthur's thoughts had been fixed with almost mystic conviction upon a possible landing at Inchon. In July, he told General Lemuel Shepherd, Fleet Marine commander, as they pored over the map in his office: 'If I had the 1st Marine Division, I would make a landing here at Inchon, and reverse the war.'[1] By all manner of improvisations and expedients, 1st Marine Division was indeed being assembled and hastened across the Pacific. But six weeks of acrimonious, passionate debate preceded Inchon. On one side were ranged the Joint Chiefs of Staff, all the key naval officers in the Far Fast, and an overwhelming proportion of army, marine and amphibious specialists. For this, it must be recalled, was still the immediate post-war period, when the middle and upper ranks of America's armed forces were still thickly populated with officers who had planned and carried out opposed landings from end to end of the Pacific. These men understood from experience every subtlety of tides, beach gradients, unloading capacity, fire support plans. They examined MacArthur's concept with acute professional care and, almost unanimously, declared against it.

When the G-3 of 1st Marine Division, Colonel Alpha Bowser, first arrived in Tokyo in the first days of September, he was greatly dismayed by the uncertain mood he encountered: 'It seemed very "iffy" to me. The feeling about whether we could go on holding at Pusan fluctuated from day to day. They appeared to be in a dreamworld at MacArthur's headquarters. I could not understand how they could be so sanguine about what was happening to them. It scared the hell out of me.'² Lieutenant-Colonel Ellis Williamson, G-3 of X Corps, also found the atmosphere 'pretty dismal' when he arrived in Tokyo from California. When first he heard talk of Inchon, he was among those staff officers who feared that the landing was being conducted on the wrong side of Korea. But MacArthur said to them: 'It will be like an electric fan. You go to the wall and pull the plug out, and the fan will stop. When we get well ashore at Inchon, the North Koreans will have no choice but to pull out, or surrender.'³

Inchon was the only plausible target for an amphibious envelopment. Kunsan was so close to the besieged Pusan Perimeter that to make a landing there would be meaningless. Chinnampo, Pyongyang's port, was too far north. Posung-Myon, below Inchon on the west coast, offered inadequate scope for a break-out inland. Yet Inchon's thirty-two-foot tidal range was one of the greatest in the world. Only on three plausible dates – 15 and 27 September and 11 October – would the tides be high enough to give the big landing craft three brief hours inshore, before the coast became once more an impassable quagmire of mud. Beyond this problem, beyond the fierce current up the Flying Fish approach channel, there was no hope of achieving tactical surprise at the seawall where the main landing force must go ashore. Before the Americans could even assault Inchon, they must unmistakably signal their intentions eleven hours in advance, by seizing the offshore island of Wolmi-do, which commanded the approaches. Thereafter, the problems became worse: the limited cargo-handling facilities, the imminence of the typhoon season, the steep overlooking hills from which a competent enemy could pour a devastating fire on to the beachhead. Finally, the tide times dictated that the main landings must take place at evening, leaving the assault force just two hours of daylight in which to gain a secure perimeter ashore, amid a city of 250,000 people.

The memory of Anzio still bulked very large in military memory, when just such a grand envelopment as Inchon had landed – in Churchill's memorable phrases – not 'a wild cat to tear out the heart of the Boche', but 'a stranded whale', an invasion army besieged under heavy fire in a strangled perimeter. Why now take such vast risks, when the commitment of the two available divisions to Eighth Army at Pusan should make possible a break-out by more conventional means? The Marines' General Shepherd opposed Inchon, because he perceived the North Koreans as a fanatical enemy capable of mounting as fierce a resistance to the Americans as the Japanese on Iwo Jima six years earlier.

Arrayed against all these arguments, and their proponents glittering with brass, MacArthur stood alone. He, too, admitted a fear that Inchon was a long march from the Pusan Perimeter. Yet he also saw the deeply demoralised state of the UN forces in Walker's command. To commit the last readily available reinforcements at Pusan risked a disastrous strategic stalemate. MacArthur was determined upon a grand gesture, reaching out for strategic freedom, a war-winning thrust. Against all the reasoned arguments of admirals and generals and staff officers, he deployed only the rocklike, mystic certainty of his own instinct.

No man who was present ever forgot the conclusive 23 August meeting on the sixth floor of the Dai Ichi between MacArthur and America's foremost commanders in the Far East. Stratemeyer was there, and Radford, and Collins and Sherman from Washington;

there was Shepherd, Fleet Marine commander, Struble and Doyle for the US Navy. Collins spoke openly of the army's fears about the consequences of withdrawing the Marine brigade from Pusan for the landing. Sherman advocated a safer landing at Kunsan. Then other naval officers, led by Admiral Turner Joy, outlined the overwhelming difficulties, as they saw them, of putting an amphibious force ashore at Inchon. It was Rear-Admiral James H. Doyle who summarised the navy's attitude, concluding bleakly: 'The best I can say is that Inchon is not impossible.' Then Mac-Arthur stood, puffing on his corncob pipe.

> He spoke with that slow, deep resonance of an accomplished actor [recalled one of the officers who heard him]. 'Admiral, in all my years of military service, that is the finest briefing I have ever received. Commander, you have taught me all I had ever dreamed of knowing about tides. Do you know, in World War I they got our divisions to Europe through submarine-infested seas? I have a deep admiration for the navy. From the humiliation of Bataan, the navy brought us back.'
>
> Then – literally with a tear in his eye – he said: 'I never thought the day would come, that the navy would be unable to support the army in its operations.'[4]

It was a great theatrical performance. MacArthur's peroration embraced the communist threat to Korea: '. . . It is plainly apparent that here in Asia is where the Communist conspirators have elected to make their play for global conquest. The test is not in Berlin or Vienna, in London, Paris or Washington. It is here and now – it is along the Naktong River in South Korea . . .' He summoned up the ghost of his hero, General Wolfe, whose assault upon the heights of Quebec had also been opposed by his staff. He asserted the very implausibility of his own plan as its strongest argument for surprise, and thus success: 'The very arguments you have made as to the impracticabilities involved will tend to ensure for me the element of surprise. For the enemy commander will reason that no one would be so brash as to make such an attempt.'

Then, finally: 'I can almost hear the ticking of the second hand of destiny. We must act now or we will die ... We shall land at Inchon, and I shall crush them.' The deep voice fell away to a whisper. After forty-five minutes of oratory such as the world seldom sees save from the stalls of a theatre, the Supreme Commander returned to his chair. The Chief of Naval Operations stood up and declared emotionally: 'General, the navy will get you to Inchon.'

This was not the end of the debate, for many of the most senior officers present left the briefing room unconvinced. But it was the turning point. Shepherd and Sherman made one more vain private attempt to convert MacArthur to a landing at Posung-Myon. But in the absence of a flat rejection from Washington, MacArthur continued to make his plans. On 28 August, he received the formal consent of the Joint Chiefs of Staff to the Inchon landings.

Yet even as the plans for the landing were finalised, the doubts persisted. The Chiefs of Staff in Washington gained the written sanction of the President for the operation, a step that was militarily quite unnecessary, but reflected their anxiety to ensure that they were not saddled with sole responsibility for disaster. Faced with the new communist drive against the Pusan Perimeter early in September, General Walker showed deep unhappiness about releasing forces from his front for Inchon. It was decided that the Marine Brigade would be taken out of the line and sent to sea only at the last possible moment; and that a regiment of the 7th Division would be kept in Pusan Harbour as a floating reserve to deal with a possible Eighth Army crisis, until it became essential for it to sail for Inchon.

The planners were irked to discover that, throughout the three-year American occupation of Korea, nothing had been done to assemble raw information about the geography of the country. Even the dimensions of the Inchon tidal basin were unknown. In haste, Tokyo set about remedying the yawning deficiencies in SCAP's knowledge. Agents put into the Inchon area reported that there were only some 500 North Korean troops on Wolmi-do, and a further 1,500 around Inchon. But just a few hours' warning would be necessary for the North Koreans to move major reinforcements from the south-east. In an effort to keep the enemy in confusion until the last possible moment, a British naval task force was committed to carrying out a deception bombardment against Chinnampo, while a British frigate landed a raiding party at Kunsan. A courageous US naval officer, Lieutenant Eugene Clark, was put ashore at Yonghungdo, fifteen miles south of Inchon with similar coastal conditions. He returned to confirm the navy's worst fears about the waist-deep mud, the shallow water extending three miles offshore, the high harbour wall against which the Marines must land.

Lieutenant-Colonel Robert Taplett, a tall, steady South Dakotan commanding the 3/5th Marines, was more worried about the prospect of the landing than most of his officers, 'because I knew more about it. I thought it would be a very rough affair. I received an extraordinary message stating that once we were committed to the landing, we would continue with the operation until we had suffered 82.3 per cent casualties. I thought: "God, what kind of idiot would write an order putting in a decimal point like that?"'[5]

Yet, against the background of such fears, it has been a mistake by some historians to presume that Inchon represented a great triumph for the underdog of the Korean campaign, against all odds. Rather, the mood of apprehension and outright dismay in which the landing was prepared showed how low the morale of the UN armies in Korea had sunk, and how great was the psychological dominance the enemy had achieved over their commanders, with the critical exception of MacArthur. The strength of the North Koreans' continuing thrusts against the Pusan Perimeter masked the enormity of their losses since the war began. Allied intelligence was seriously overestimating the size of the forces facing Walker's divisions. The staff continued to believe that the North Koreans possessed numerical superiority. Yet in reality, Kim Il Sung's ruined regiments besieging Pusan could now muster only some 70,000 men, against a total of 140,000 in Walker's command. The Allies possessed absolute command of the air and sea, and overwhelming superiority of firepower. The ferocity and effectiveness of the enemy's assault troops should not be permitted to mask the immense handicaps under which the communists laboured, lacking sophisticated logistic and technical support. Their intelligence gathering, for instance, was as lamentable as the American army's security. The intention to land at Inchon was one of the worst-kept secrets of the war, the subject of open discussion among thousands of men in Japan and Korea. Yet miraculously, no word leaked through to Pyongyang. Not a man was moved to strengthen the communist defences in the last critical days before the armada sailed.

*

At Walker's headquarters in Korea, pessimism continued to prevail, not only about Eighth Army's predicament, but about the western landing. It was MacArthur's knowledge of this spirit, or lack of it, that must have contributed significantly to his decision to appoint his own Chief of Staff, Lieutenant-General Edward M. Almond, to command the Inchon landing force, designated X Corps. So much criticism was subsequently heaped upon Mac-Arthur for his decision to divide military authority between two separate commands in Korea, which would have important and unhappy consequences later, that it is worth examining his motives for doing so. The most obvious, and the least admirable, was that Almond was the Supreme Commander's protégé, a ferociously ambitious soldier who had played a somewhat undistinguished role as a divisional commander in Italy in World War II, and now hungered for a more promising battlefield command. Almond was not a man who inspired much affection among his subordinates. O. P. Smith, the 1st Marine Division commander whose poor relations with his corps superior would become a serious blight upon the campaign, was antagonised by their first meeting before Inchon, when Almond dismissed the difficulties of amphibious operations: 'This amphibious stuff is just a mechanical option.' Smith then 'tried to tell him a few of the facts of life. But he was rather supercilious and called me "son", which kind of annoyed me.'[6]

Yet there was an entirely legitimate case for placing the conduct of the Inchon landings in hands other than those of General Walton Walker. MacArthur well knew the low morale that existed in Eighth Army headquarters, and it presented him with a difficult dilemma. Walker had conducted a stubborn defence of Pusan. But there was grave reason to doubt his ability now to lead the sort of imaginative and dynamic operations MacArthur planned. MacArthur considered, and rejected, the possibility of relieving him of his command. This would have been a most unpalatable step to the American public. As is often the case in desperate situations, the figure of 'Bulldog' Walker had been exalted by publicity to heroic proportions. MacArthur's compromise was to entrust the amphibious operation to Almond. Whatever his Chief of Staff's vices, he was an undoubted driver of men. MacArthur was supremely confident that this one great effort would be decisive. Once it had succeeded, issues of command would no longer be important. He told O. P. Smith: 'I know that this operation will be sort of helter-skelter. But the 1st Marine Division is going to win the war by landing at Inchon.'[7]

Among the senior officers of the Marine Division, there was never a moment's doubt of the importance of the landing, not only for the cause of the United Nations, but for their corps's survival. Since the end of World War II, they had been compelled to watch its remorseless shrinkage to a shadow of its wartime might. Many naval officers made plain their belief that the Marines should be confined to a role providing token shipboard contingents with the fleet. No less a figure than General Omar Bradley had declared his conviction, at the 1949 Congressional hearings on the B-36 bomber, that in the nuclear age there would never again be large-scale amphibious operations. 'The Marine Corps was fighting for its very existence,' said General Lem Shepherd.[8] In Korea, and above all at Inchon, he and his fellow-Marines perceived a supreme opportunity to show their nation what the corps could still do.

1st Marine Division's commander, O. P. Smith, was in many ways the least likely of Marine heroes. A slim, white-haired Texan of fifty-seven, of professorial manner, unfailing courtesy – even diffidence – Smith was a cautious commander who believed that 'you do it slow, but you do it right'. But many of his subordinates in this big, heavy division of some 20,000 men were cast in more exotic mould. Ray Murray of the 5th Marines was perhaps the outstanding regimental commander, who would become one of the critical figures of the campaign. Colonel Homer Litzenburg of the 7th Marines was slower and less impressive. Colonel Lewis B. 'Chesty' Puller of the 1st Marines was already a legend of his corps, a bombastic officer who led from the front, beloved of his men – perhaps less so of his seniors, who were sometimes exasperated by his tactical carelessness. All these men, and many of their subordinates, possessed immense combat experience in World War II.

The first slow convoy of Admiral Struble's armada of 260 ships sailed from Yokohama on 5 September. It was a makeshift transport fleet that carried the Americans to Inchon. Of the bigger ships, thirty-seven LSTs were World War II veterans that had been transferred to the Japanese merchant service, and were now recalled to duty with their Japanese officers, supplemented by American personnel flown in from the United States. Some ships smelt vividly of fish. There was much wisecracking speculation about the personal histories of their inscrutable deck officers. 'Everybody believed,' in the words of a Marine, 'that he was being ferried to Inchon by a Japanese who had been an admiral at Midway.' There were constant breakdowns of aged machinery: 'The whole thing was a rusty travesty of World War II amphibious operations.'

Few men found the voyage to Inchon agreeable, crammed aboard old ships devoid of creature comforts. Many were violently seasick as the convoy plunged and heaved amid Typhoon Kezia, whose 125 mph winds wreaked havoc with the nerves of the naval commanders, and the stomachs of 70,000 hapless Americans below decks. On some ships, tanks and vehicles broke loose, demanding desperate struggles to resecure them as they smashed hither and thither on the cargo decks. The men lay in their bunks, or played cards incessantly. There was little left to prepare. The plans were all made. The command ship *Mount McKinley* sailed from Sasebo in the small hours of 13 September, the anniversary of Wolfe's triumph at Quebec. The ship's captain gave up his own cabin to MacArthur, and had a shed built for himself on the bridge wing. The convoy was maintaining radio silence, but Almond demanded that dispatches should be air-dropped to him each day. To the glee of his enemies on the staff, the first day's attempt ended with the bag falling in the sea, and X Corps commander in a rage.

*

Lieutenant Jim Sheldon of the 17th Infantry, 7th Division, felt desperately anxious for the invasion and the war to be over, because Korea smelt so awful, and he found his own platoon so dismaying. Sheldon was a rebellious twenty-year-old who had been dismissed from the US Navy for misconduct, then enlisted in the army, and was commissioned from the ranks the day the Korean War broke out. He arrived in Japan as an officer replacement, and was abruptly given a fifty-four-man platoon, composed partly of Koreans, of whom some were wholly untrained civilians, ranging in age from the mid-teens to mid-sixties: 'They were a pretty unhappy group of people for a twenty-year-old lieutenant to have to cope with, with their strange eating and sanitation habits. I couldn't do anything to stop them sneaking out after dark and crapping in the middle of the compound.' In four weeks, with the aid of a handful of experienced American NCOs, he had instilled the rudiments of tactical training in them. Then they were shipped to Pusan, where as part of the deception plan they were required to disembark from their ships, march out into the country, and re-embark three times in succession. At last, to their astonishment, they were told that they were on their way to take part in an amphibious landing. Sheldon and his platoon were not impressed.[9]

Just before dawn on 15 September, the *Mount McKinley* and the transport convoy attained the Inchon narrows. It was the fifth day of air and naval bombardment of Wolmi-do island. The commanders had gambled heavily upon the success of the diversionary operations to blind the defenders to the real significance of the barrage. At 6.33 a.m. after a final storm of rockets and napalm from the carrier strike aircraft, a last deluge of shellfire from the cruisers offshore, the first Marines hit Wolmi-do.

Throughout the voyage from Japan, the Supreme Commander himself had remained invisible in his cabin. Only now, as the first men clambered down into the landing craft amid the rolling thunder of the naval bombardment, did MacArthur betake himself to the bridge of the *Mount McKinley* in his grandeur. This was his creation, his hour, his last great moment of martial glory before the worm of disappointment, disillusionment, defeat began to gnaw into that enormous ego and reputation. He took the captain's high seat on the bridge, to sit flanked by his reverential courtiers in all the stage properties of majesty: the corncob pipe; the massive peaked cap laden with brass; the proud chin and protective sunglasses. And there the photographers caught him for posterity, the master of ceremonies sitting high above the sea, watching the unfolding of his last triumph.

Ellis Williamson, G-3 of X Corps, did not trouble to beg a place in a landing craft, as had some staff officers. He remembered the British officer who said to him before D-Day in 1944, when he was still an impatient young lieutenant: 'When you get over there, you'll find there's enough war for everybody.' Williamson had been wounded five times in north-west Europe: 'By Inchon, I was no longer overly curious.'[10]

Until a late stage of planning, Almond had opposed the sacrifice of surprise for the seizure of Wolmi-do island. But the Marines insisted that they could not assault the main beaches with the approaches unsecured. Their will prevailed. Now, Litzenburger's

5th Marines swept ashore at 'Green Beach' on Wolmi-do with almost contemptuous ease. Two Marine tanks smashed through a feebly defended North Korean roadblock on the causeway to the mainland. The Stars and Stripes was raised 300 feet up on Radio Hill, dominating Inchon Harbour, at 6.55 a.m. The entire position was secure an hour later. Marine bulldozers wrote a macabre footnote, by entombing a handful of defenders who declined to surrender, alive in the caves in which they had taken refuge. From the bridge of *Mount McKinley*, MacArthur signalled Struble: 'The Navy and Marines have never shone more brightly than this morning.'

At noon, with half of the CHROMITE operational plan success-fully completed and only desultory firing coming from the shore, the long, wretched interval began before the next act. As the tide swept back to reveal miles of dull, flat mud between the invasion fleet and the shore, the men in the ships waited, impotent, for the sea to return. The Marines on Wolmi-do, entirely isolated from the fleet, lay over their weapons, willing the enemy to maintain his silence. They requested, and were refused, permission at once to continue their advance across the causeway. They contented them-selves by firing mortars and machine guns at the shore whenever they observed activity. Fighter-bombers roamed the roads for miles behind the coast, ready to strike at any communist attempt to reinforce their coastal positions. Yet astonishingly, none came. At 2.30 p.m., the cruisers resumed their fire upon the main water-front.

> The guns began erratically [wrote the British war correspond-ent James Cameron]: a few heavy thuds from the cruisers, an occasional bark of five-inch fire, a tuning-up among the harsh orchestra. At what point the playing of the guns merged into the final and awful barrage I do not know; so many things began to take place, a scattered pattern of related happenings gradually coalescing and building up for the blow.
>
> All around among the fleet the landing-craft multiplied

imperceptibly, took to the water from one could not see exactly where, because the light was failing now – circled and wheeled and marked time and milled about, filling the air with engines. There seemed to be no special hurry. We could not go in until the tide was right; meanwhile we lay offshore in a strange, insolent, businesslike serenity, under whatever guns the North Koreans had, building up the force item by item, squaring the sledge-hammer. The big ships swung gently in the tideway, from time to time coughing heaving gusts of iron towards the town. It began to burn, quite gently at first. What seemed to be a tank or a self-propelled gun sent back some quick, resentful fire, but it soon stopped. Later we found that one ship had thrown a hundred and sixty-five rounds of five-inch ammunition at the one gun: the economics of plenty.[11]

At 4.45 p.m., the first landing craft pushed off from the transports, laden with Marines, headed towards the smoke-hung skyline of the city of Inchon. At 5.31, the first Americans sprang up the ladders on to the seawall, covered by grenades from the men who followed. After a brief scamper, the British Consulate was taken, and a platoon reached the foot of Observatory Hill, overlooking the harbour. Amid the sharp firefights with pockets of defenders, it became rapidly apparent that most of the surviving communists were still stunned and dazed by the bombardment. In the industrial suburbs south of the city, where the 1st Marines were landing on Blue Beach, the regiment overcame difficulties with mud and natural obstacles, to establish themselves securely ashore in the first hours of the darkness.

The makeshift manner of the operation persisted even as the Marines descended into the landing craft. Major Ed Simmons, commanding the Weapons Company of the 3/1st Marines, was a twenty-nine-year-old from New Jersey who had seen action in the Pacific as an engineer, where every landing was intensely rehearsed and meticulously timed. Now, he found himself clambering aboard an amphibious tractor, as a young naval lieutenant pointed towards the shore and shouted almost hysterically through a bullhorn: 'There's your beach! Go find it!' A landing craft loaded with Koreans pulled alongside, and somebody called: 'Here's your interpreters!' Two Koreans climbed on Simmons' tractor as it got under way. Neither proved to speak English. The Marine asked the driver where the compass was. The man shrugged: 'Search me. Two weeks ago I was driving a bus in San Francisco.' Simmons set off towards the point on the shoreline where the smoke seemed thickest, aided by his own compass.[12] The carefully planned landings by waves of craft were forgotten. They merely headed in columns for the beach, where they found a modest firefight in progress. Visibility was very poor, amid the smoke and drizzle. Most men's clearest memory of Inchon was of struggling ashore in soggy clothing, which still hung clammily about them as the light began to fail. Officers and men hastened hither and thither, searching for headquarters and company positions in the darkness, broken by occasional gunflashes and the flames of burning buildings. As the sounds of battle died away, they were replaced by the insistent patter of operators murmuring into radio handsets, struggling to gain contact with straggling units. But already, the vital moves of the day were complete. The seal was set upon the American triumph when eight LSTs grounded side by side against the seawall on Red Beach. As the tide fell, they remained there, 'dried out', and from their cavernous holds poured forth a stream of tanks, trucks, jeeps, stores, laying vital flesh upon the bones of the beachhead.

Through the hours of darkness, the Marines dozed over their weapons, apprehensive of a counter-attack that never came. Astoundingly, two regiments were established ashore in Inchon at a cost of just twenty killed among a total of less than two hundred casualties. If the landing on the west coast of Korea was a make-shift, amateurish affair by the standards of 1944 or 1945, it had proved formidable enough to overcome the primitive legions of Kim Il Sung. In the days that followed, as the men of 7th Division and the 7th Marines followed the vanguard ashore, MacArthur and his officers exulted. The gamble had triumphantly succeeded. All the Supreme Commander's instincts about the conduct of the North Koreans had been justified. He had driven his spear deep into the flank of the enemy, who now reeled stricken before him.

First light on 16 September revealed Korean civilians picking their way among the shattered debris of the Inchon waterfront, among the fallen power lines and flickering fires and broken walls.

> There was quite a lot of Inchon still standing [wrote James Cameron]. One wondered how. There were quite a number of citizens still alive. They came stumbling from the ruins – some of them sound, some of them smashed – numbers of them quite clearly driven into a sort of numbed dementia by the night of destruction. They ran about, capering crazily or shambling blankly, with a repeated automatic gesture of surrender. Some of them called out as we passed their one English phrase, as a kind of password: 'Sank you!' 'Sank you!'; and the irony of that transcended the grotesque into the macabre.[13]

The 1st and 5th Marines linked up ashore early on the morning of 16 September. They began at once to drive eastwards, towards the capital, leaving the ROK Marines to mop up Inchon in characteristically ruthless fashion. Belatedly, a column of North Korean armour and infantry appeared, to be swept aside by air strikes and ground fire. The 5th Marines now led the advance on the north side of the Inchon-Seoul road, while the 1st took the southern side. Smashing through sporadic communist resistance, by the night of 17 September they held much of the big Kimpo airfield complex. By the evening of the 19th, the 5th had cleared the entire south bank of the Han river on their front. The 1st Marines had meanwhile seen some heavy fighting in more difficult country, meeting a regiment of the North Korean 18th Division deployed in their path. But on the 19th, they were on the outskirts of Yongdungpo, the suburb of Seoul on the south bank of the Han.

The raw relations between the army and the Marines became increasingly apparent on the road to Seoul. Smith's men displayed a lasting bitterness about the haste urged upon them by Almond,

From INCHON to SEOUL
15-22 September 1950

obsessed with fulfilling a promise to MacArthur that he would
liberate the capital by 25 September. This would be three months
to the day since the communist invasion. 'He wanted that commu-
niqué,' said the disgusted Smith. 'I said I couldn't guarantee
anything – that's up to the enemy.'[14] But some army officers, in
their turn, declared their dismay at the headlong tactics of the
Marines. 'The Marines were always too keen on frontal attacks,'
argued Colonel John Michaelis of the 27th Infantry.[15]

> The Marines are a product of their history [said Colonel Ellis
> Williamson]. They are trained, indoctrinated, to go from ship
> to shore, then keep running forward until they have taken the
> pressure off the beach head. The thought of outflanking a
> position would horrify a man like 'Chesty' Puller. We used to
> call the Marines 'the nursery rhyme soldiers' because their
> motto was: 'Hey diddle diddle, right up the middle'. On that
> march to Seoul, I saw Marines doing things no army outfit
> would think of. I watched them crossing that great sweep
> of wide open ground in front of Kimpo airfield, hundreds

of young men rising up and starting across the flats in open order. They took far more casualties than we considered appropriate.[16]

It is interesting that Williamson's perception of the US Marines, as a soldier, is that shared by most army officers around the world about their amphibious brethren. It is probably true that the Marine Corps places greater emphasis upon headlong courage than upon tactical subtlety. Even their own General Shepherd afterwards challenged the sluggishness of O. P. Smith's move into Seoul: 'If a man who is in command of a pursuit is someone who likes to have his ranks dressed all the time, you might just as well not pursue.'[17] It was agreed by most senior marines that 'Chesty' Puller had been overpromoted to regimental command, and was saved from making disastrous mistakes only by the professional competence of Major Robert Lorigan, his Operations Officer. Yet in Korea, the courage and determination of the Marines remained unchallenged through three years of war, while many army units proved disturbingly lacking in morale and professional skill. If the senior officers of the 1st Marine Division could not be described as intellectual warriors, between Inchon and Panmunjom O. P. Smith and his men would earn great gratitude from their country.

Twenty-year-old Corporal Selwyn Handler of the Weapons Company, 2/1st Marines, found the advance from Inchon to Seoul an intoxicating experience. In checks and starts, the long files of men moved forward, jeeps carrying the heavy equipment, ahead the sound of spasmodic artillery and small-arms fire as the point companies cleared the road. The local Korean civilians seemed delighted to see them. They scurried hither and thither across the battlefield, looting rice stores and abandoned equipment, hastily removing their families and possessions from the immediate line of fire. Once, they found some North Korean stragglers hiding in a cave. Two men were detailed to escort them to the rear, but they soon returned. They said: 'Prisoners are too much of a bother, right now.' Like most men on most battlefields, Handler retained brief snapshot glimpses of those days: leaping into a foxhole under shellfire, to be cursed by a man already sheltering in it, whom he had last seen in high school in California; watching a child scuttling past, bent under the burden of a rice sack larger than himself; Marines filling themselves with beer in a brewery they occupied in Yongdungpo; watching a Corsair hit overhead, diving into the ground and blowing up. Korean children swarmed around them, even as they fought. One said incessantly: 'North Korean! North Korean!' as he tugged at the American's leg and pointed. Exploratively, Handler tossed a grenade into the rubble. Nothing moved, but still the child gestured furiously. The Americans threw two more grenades, and were rewarded with the bodies of two communist soldiers.

*

As Almond's X Corps drove east, on 16 September in driving rain Walker's Eighth Army launched its long-awaited break-out. It began sluggishly: the Americans were not across the Naktong in strength until the 19th. MacArthur suffered a period of serious concern that even now, the North Koreans could hold in the southeast. For four days, the weather severely hampered the air forces' ability to support the UN advance. But as it cleared sufficiently to enable the bombers to operate, once the communist front had been broken open it collapsed with extraordinary speed.

The British contingent suffered a wretched little tragedy, indicative of the indifferent air–ground liaison of the period. On 23 September, the Argyll & Sutherland Highlanders had just fought their way up Hill 282, on the left flank of the push across the Naktong. They called for air support, and laid out their recognition panels. A flight of Mustangs swung in to attack with cannon and napalm, which they laid with terrible accuracy on the Scots positions. The survivors retreated in confusion from the summit. But Major Kenneth Muir, second-in-command, determined that they must retake it. He led thirty men towards the crest, and reached his objective with fourteen. 'The gooks will never drive the Argylls off this hill,' he said, as he fell mortally wounded by automatic fire. Muir won a posthumous Victoria Cross. The Argylls lost seventeen killed and seventy-six wounded.

But this was the bitter small change of war. All along the front, the enemy was collapsing. North Korean units began to melt away, thousands of fugitives throwing away weapons, equipment, clothing. On the 26th, at Osan, men of the 1st Cavalry driving north from the Perimeter met men of the 7th Infantry, pushing south from Inchon. ROK units advanced up the east coast, meeting negligible resistance. Everywhere, the North Koreans were breaking in flight, surrendering in hundreds, or taking to the mountains to maintain guerrilla war.

Further north, 1st Marines were obliged to fight hard for three days for Yongdungpo. Meanwhile, after a setback to their first attempt on the night of the 19th, on 20 September Puller's 5th made a successful assault crossing of the Han river. By 25 September, both Marine regiments were committed to the bitter, desperate street battle for possession of Seoul, which devastated great areas of the capital, and continued for three days. Even as air reconnaissance revealed the main body of Kim Il Sung's army fleeing northwards, communist rearguards fought on to delay the advance of Smith's regiments, extracting their price yard by yard, at each rice-bag barricade.

The battle for Seoul became a source of lasting controversy, and deep revulsion to some of those who witnessed it. It provided an example of a form of carnage that would become wretchedly familiar in Indochina a generation later – allegedly essential destruction in the cause of liberation. It was passionately argued by some correspondents and not a few soldiers that the civilian casualties and wholesale destruction could have been avoided by an effective enveloping movement, rather than a direct assault supported by overwhelming air and artillery support. But MacArthur and Almond wanted Seoul fast. In their path stood some 20,000 still resolute communist troops. 'The slightest resistance brought down a deluge of destruction blotting out the area,' wrote an eyewitness, R. W. Thompson of the *Daily Telegraph*.[18] In the words of the historian David Rees, 'at the heart of the West's military thought lies the belief that machines must be used to save its men's lives; Korea would progressively become a horrific illustration of the effects of a limited war where one side possessed the firepower and the other the manpower.'[19]

The Marines advanced into the capital from north, south and west, while a regiment of 7th Division and the 187th Airborne RCT covered their flanks. Some men were appalled by the evidence of atrocities they encountered. Selwyn Handler was among those who entered a jail compound in which they found several headless bodies, and the sword that had obviously been used for the executions. Ed Simmons of the 3/1st saw a group of Marines clustered around a trench. A lieutenant waved him over. The trench was filled with dead Koreans – men, women, children, hundreds of them: 'It was a ghastly sight. The stench was unbearable. For days, civilians were coming out from the centre of Seoul in the hope of identifying them.'[20] Colonel Taplett of the 3/5th was less troubled by the evidence of the communist occupation. 'That's the way these people treat each other,' he shrugged, a view that would be repeated through foreign UN contingents again and again in the years to come.

Darkness in the streets, still possessed of so many unknown perils, brought hours of acute tension to the Marines in the forward positions. On the night of 25 September, the 5th Marines were appalled to receive a sudden order to launch an attack at 2 a.m. It was made clear that this was the direct consequence of General Almond's obsessive determination to control all Seoul within the deadline he had promised MacArthur. Major Simmons had assumed temporary command of a rifle company in place of its commander, who was hiding in a cellar. 'I can't do it! I can't do it!' the officer cried, amid the stress of battle. 'Take my bars! Take my bars!' Simmons was horrified to discover that a supporting artillery bombardment would be put down in the area to which he had just dispatched an eight-man patrol. But the American attack was pre-empted. Long before H-Hour, the Marines heard the grinding clatter of armour advancing towards their own positions. The North Koreans had launched their own movement. All night, the artillery poured fire in front of Puller's men, breaking up the communist infantry concentrations. An immobilised communist tank stood stalled in front of Simmons' company position. The major feared what it might still do to them with its gun when daylight came. He ordered up a 75mm recoilless rifle, and told its gunner to fire as soon as he had enough light to aim. At last, in the first glimmerings of dawn, he said: 'I can see it!' and fired. The Marines were so absorbed in the enemy that they forgot the backblast of their own weapon, which bounced off a house behind, blowing them off their feet and showering them in mud and debris. But the communist impetus was spent. American tanks moved up, and they began to advance again. The Marines found their own patrol intact, having taken refuge in a culvert all night, their fatigues concealed beneath civilian clothing stolen from a washing line.

*

The 5th Marines reached the Capitol building only on 27 September, two days after Tokyo had announced the liberation, in relentless accordance with the Supreme Commander's schedule. To the chagrin of the visitors, soon after they had hoisted the Stars and Stripes, they were diplomatically ordered to lower their nation's colours, and raise the blue flag of the United Nations. Two days later, MacArthur himself presided over the solemn ceremony in the shattered Capitol building, marking the liberation of Seoul and the return of the government of Syngman Rhee. The Joint Chiefs in Washington sought in vain to prevent the ceremony, because of their reluctance to identify the United States so closely with the controversial South Korean President. They were unsuccessful. MacArthur was determined to savour his moment of ceremony, indifferent to the cynicism of his own troops who had made it possible. 'If the Inchon landing had been as carefully planned as that ceremony, it would have been marvellous,' said Ed Simmons acidly. Immense labour and resources had been diverted from the battle to build a pontoon bridge across the Han that would enable MacArthur and his cavalcade to drive direct from Kimpo airport into Seoul.

In the midst of the ruined Capitol, the Supreme Commander unleashed a characteristic flood of rhetoric for the throng of soldiers, naval officers and correspondents gathered around himself and Rhee: 'By the grace of merciful Providence, our forces fighting under the standard of that greatest hope and inspiration of mankind, the United Nations, have liberated this ancient capital city of Korea . . .' The Lord's Prayer was interrupted by the crash of glass and masonry from the damaged dome a hundred feet above. MacArthur appeared not to notice. He turned to address Rhee: 'Mr President, my officers and I will now resume our military duties and leave you and your government to the discharge of the civil responsibility.' The two men shook hands. Rhee seemed overtaken by the emotion of the moment: 'We admire you,' he murmured to the general. 'We love you as the saviour of our race.' The Supreme Commander flew home to Tokyo mantled in his own serene sense of destiny fulfilled, imbued with an aura of invincibility that awed even his nation's leaders. He was confident that the war for Korea had been won, and that his armies were victorious. Now it was just a matter of cleaning up.

6 » TO THE BRINK: MACARTHUR CROSSES THE PARALLEL

When MacArthur came out on to the deck of the *Mount McKinley* the morning after the Inchon landing, his first question to the Marines' General Shepherd was: 'Have we seen or heard anything of the Russians or the Chinese?'[1] It was an inquiry he repeated, insistently, each day thereafter as his army drove deep inland. The Supreme Commander was perfectly aware of the political embarrassments and military implications of killing, capturing, or even encountering Chinese or Russian advisers or troops. Yet as each day passed with no word of their presence, MacArthur's assurance grew. Peking and Moscow had backed off. This was a struggle between the United Nations and the crumbling divisions of Kim Il Sung. The communists had reached out for their easy victory in South Korea, and come within a hairbreadth of achieving it. Yet when the will of the United States – the will, indeed, of the nation's supreme representative in Asia, Douglas MacArthur – was tested and shown to be strong, that of the enemy crumpled. In MacArthur's perception, strengthened by each day of triumph after 15 September, the crisis had passed.

Since 25 June 1950, the key figures in Tokyo, Washington, London, and indeed throughout the Western world, had explored a remarkable range of emotions. The shock of Kim Il Sung's invasion was succeeded by alarm about its global implications. Truman and his allies and generals overcame these fears, in their determination that the communist onslaught must be resisted. Then, through July and August, as defeat followed defeat upon the battlefield, it appeared that the only fruit of their efforts would be a massive humiliation for Western arms. Yet now, after the miracle of Inchon, the great burden had been lifted from their shoulders. From the brink of defeat, MacArthur's genius had brought them to the verge of overwhelming military triumph. Fears that the North Korean invasion signalled a worldwide communist offensive had proved unfounded. The Russians, considered prime movers in Kim Il Sung's invasion, now appeared anxious to distance themselves from the Korean adventure, and certainly unwilling to commit their military power to Kim's support. The balance of advantage in Korea lay firmly with the UN, with the Western powers. The wider dangers had receded. The leaders of the Truman Administration, who had been so sensitive to the global risks of the original communist invasion, were overtaken by something close to euphoria. Firmness had paid off. The communists were in full retreat. No new world war would start in Korea.

The chief problem that now exercised Truman and Acheson, their allies and military commanders, was that of how the utmost political and strategic advantage could be extracted from military victory. The starting point for the debate was the view, held instinctively by many citizens of the Western powers, that it would be intolerable if Kim Il Sung proved to have been able to launch and retreat from the failure of his monstrous adventure without cost to his own regime. Beyond his unprovoked invasion of a neighbouring state, the atrocities his forces had inflicted upon the people of South Korea compounded the original outrage. If the North Koreans were now permitted to withdraw behind their original frontier, the 38th Parallel, and remain there unmolested, the huge efforts and sacrifices of the United Nations – and of the South Korean people – would seem hollow indeed. It would be absurd, said Acheson, 'to march up to a surveyors' line and stop'. It seemed equally inappropriate for MacArthur's army to pursue the North Koreans into their own land merely to complete the destruction of the enemy's forces, then withdraw, leaving Kim Il Sung's regime in place.

The United Nations' mandate for war was based upon the General Assembly vote of 27 June, calling on members to 'furnish such assistance to the Republic of Korea as may be necessary to repel the armed attack and to restore international peace and security in the area'. The Soviet Union, which returned to its seat on the Security Council on 3 August, argued in vain that the conflict did 'not come under the definition of aggression, since it is a war, not between two states, but between two parts of the Korean people temporarily split into two camps under two separate authorities'. Once the Russians were back at the UN, the possibility of directing the war through the forum of the Security Council, rather than at the behest of Washington, finally vanished. But weeks before Inchon, there was intense private debate in Washington as to whether the occupation of North Korea was a legitimate United Nations – or, more frankly, American – war aim. The Defense Department believed that it was. So did some senior officials in the State Department, led by Dean Rusk and John Allison of the Far Eastern Division. The Policy Planning Staff raised serious doubts as to whether it was possible to invade North Korea without precipitating a wider war with China or the Soviet Union, and expressed doubt whether other UN members would support such a move. But even the PPS concluded in late July that a decision about invading North Korea or integrating it with the South could be postponed until these became more immediate military options.

Characteristically, while others havered, MacArthur alone harboured no doubts. In mid-July in Tokyo, he told Collins and Vandenburg that his war aim was not merely the repelling of Kim Il Sung's invasion, but the destruction of his army, for which the occupation of North Korea might prove necessary. There is no evidence that the two Chiefs of Staff disputed MacArthur's view, although they were perfectly aware that he had no authority to make such a decision for himself. When Collins returned to Tokyo in mid-August, he told the Commander-in-Chief that he personally favoured crossing the 38th Parallel, but warned that Truman had not yet reached a decision on the issue. From the outset, while the

State Department expressed serious reservations about the feasibility or desirability of sustaining Syngman Rhee as ruler of all Korea, MacArthur made it plain that he strongly supported this course. On 1 September, the National Security Council circulated a frankly inconclusive working paper, NSC 81, which rehearsed the arguments for and against taking the Korean War to the enemy's homeland. It took note of the danger that the Russians would intervene to prevent the loss of their suzerainty over North Korea, but contrarily suggested that Moscow was unlikely to risk the wider war that could result from intervention. Finally, NSC 81 proposed a compromise: any crossing of the Parallel should be conducted only by ROK forces, and solely in pursuit of tactical objectives. It proposed that MacArthur should be required to 'request new instructions before continuing operations north of the 38th Parallel with major forces for the purpose of occupying North Korea'.

The Joint Chiefs of Staff condemned the 'unrealistic' approach of NSC 81. They were determined that the military should have the flexibility it needed to complete the destruction of the North Korean People's Army, wherever its elements took refuge. An amended version – NSC 81/1 – was agreed between Acheson and the Joint Chiefs at an NSC meeting on 9 September, almost a week before Inchon. The passage in the original, specifying that UN forces 'should not be permitted to extend into areas close to the Manchurian and USSR borders of Korea', was redrafted. Now, it was agreed merely that they should not cross those borders. NSC 81 decreed flatly that only ROK troops should operate near the Russian and Chinese borders. NSC 81/1 declared only that it should be 'the policy' not to deploy other UN forces in these sensitive areas. The paper restated Washington's determination that the US 'should not permit itself to become engaged in a general war' with China. But it also reaffirmed the position consistently adopted by the Administration since the war began – that if Chinese forces intervened in Korea, the US would defend itself by whatever means it possessed, not excluding the bombardment of targets on the Chinese mainland. The political future of North Korea was not discussed in NSC 81/1, perhaps chiefly because the Administration regarded this as a matter of detail rather than new national policy: on 1 September, Truman had publicly declared the right of all Korea to be 'free, independent and united', committed the United States to do its part to see that all Koreans gain that right 'under the guidance of the United Nations'.

There was an interval of almost three weeks between the drafting of NSC 81/1, and the promulgation of a formal JCS directive to MacArthur based upon its conclusions. A measure of confusion overtook the Pentagon during this period. The Defense Secretary, Louis Johnson, was sacked by Truman, and replaced by General George Marshall. Meanwhile in Korea, the distant military hopes that underpinned Washington's discussions in early September had been translated into triumphant reality. The victorious UN forces were streaming northwards, the broken remains of Kim Il Sung's army in full retreat before them.

Now, the JCS told MacArthur:

> your military objective is the destruction of the North Korean armed forces. In attaining this objective, you are authorised to conduct military operations, including amphibious and airborne landings or ground operations north of the 38th Parallel in Korea, provided that at the time of such operations there has been no entry into North Korea by major Soviet or Chinese Communist Forces, no announcement of intended entry, nor a threat to counter our operations militarily in North Korea. Under no circumstances, however, will your forces cross the Manchurian or USSR borders of Korea and, and as a matter of policy, no non-Korean ground forces will be used in the northeast provinces bordering the Soviet Union or in the area along the Manchurian border. Furthermore, support of your operations north or south of the 38th Parallel will not include air or naval action against Manchuria or against USSR territory.

Although the directive cautioned MacArthur that changing military and political circumstances might make modification of these instructions necessary, a secret 'eyes only' signal from Marshall to MacArthur on 29 September explicitly declared Washington's commitment to an advance into North Korea, but explained the desirability of avoiding public advance announcements of the crossing of the 38th Parallel, which might precipitate a new vote in the United Nations.

America's allies, Britain prominent among them, had publicly expressed their support for a move into North Korea. They were overtaken by the same euphoria that gripped Washington, the same belief that with the war almost over, it remained only to ensure that the maximum advantage was extracted from victory. But the Soviet Union was back at the Security Council. If there was a UN vote about crossing the 38th Parallel, the Russians would certainly veto it. There might then be serious questions about the legitimacy of the actions of MacArthur's army. On 30 September, the general responded from Tokyo to Marshall's message. He would take care, he said, to caution General Walker against saying anything too specific about operations around or north of the Parallel. He made it clear that the only delay in ordering his forces to advance beyond it was not political, but logistical. The army would drive north as soon as it was ready: 'My overall strategic plan is known to you. Unless and until the enemy capitulates, I regard all of Korea open for our military operations.' On 2 October, MacArthur made a broadcast to North Korea, calling upon the communist forces to lay down their arms. He neither expected, nor received, any response. He continued his preparations for the drive north across the 38th Parallel.

MacArthur's strategy was guided by two principal considerations. First, he wanted forces moving fast north-eastwards up North Korea, to cut off communist forces retreating towards the Manchurian border. Second, the Taebaek mountain range running up the spine of North Korea made west–east movement across the country intensely difficult. The principal road and rail routes up

Korea are determined almost entirely by the lines of the north–south river valleys. MacArthur was one of the great twentieth-century exponents of amphibious operations. At Inchon, he had exploited the flexibility and resources of American seapower to cut short a land campaign across difficult terrain. Now, he proposed to do the same again. He would withdraw Almond's X Corps from South Korea through Inchon, load it aboard his shipping, and transport it direct to North Korea's east-coast port of Wonsan, from whence the Marines and the army's 7th Division could strike north towards the Manchurian border. Meanwhile, Walker's Eighth Army would drive directly north from Seoul, for Pyongyang and Kim Il Sung's western dominions.

MacArthur's plan roused immediate opposition from Eighth Army. First, Walker considered it absurd to subject X Corps to the immense upheaval of withdrawal from Seoul, and sea movement to Wonsan, when the ROK army was already driving up the east coast in the face of negligible opposition. Second, Eighth Army's commander was disgusted by MacArthur's determination to maintain a divided command, with Almond continuing to report directly to the Commander-in-Chief. It seemed a deliberate insult to Walker, the defender of the Pusan Perimeter, the saviour of American arms in the first desperate weeks of war, to withold X Corps from his command, when all military logic demanded a unified ground authority.

Here were the seeds of serious difficulties ahead. Many of those in Korea believed that MacArthur was once again exercising his notorious weakness for favourites – granting his own Chief of Staff, Ned Almond, a privileged opportunity to gain independent glory. Yet in MacArthur's defence, there were good reasons to doubt the ability of Walton Walker and his staff to conduct a vigorous major offensive on their own. The doubts about Walker's fitness for high command that were raised before Inchon persisted at the 38th Parallel. Visitors to his headquarters were often unimpressed by the confusion and lack of direction that they found there. MacArthur felt ill-disposed to increase Walker's authority in the field. But there was no incentive to remove Eighth Army's commander when the war was almost won, the spine of communist resistance broken. The detailed administration of the drive into North Korea against a foe in utter disarray scarcely seemed momentous. After the event, MacArthur's critics heaped devastating criticism upon the casualness, the military unsoundness, of the command arrangements for the drive into North Korea. It is difficult to dispute these charges. Yet the critics, in their turn, ignored the real grounds for doubt about the capabilities of Walton Walker. They also discounted the mood of the time. If MacArthur allowed himself to lapse into complacency about the imminence of undisputed victory, he succumbed to a failing shared by many of his peers in Washington who allowed themselves to think too narrowly of the military realities.

On 28 September, ROK troops advanced north of the Parallel. American units waited impatiently for the signal to follow them, to complete the wretched task upon which they were embarked, and go home before winter. Yet still the political and diplomatic manoeuvring in Washington continued. Abroad, America's allies were growing ever more uneasy. The British were alarmed by the signals now emerging from Peking, although their Foreign Secretary had earlier been a prominent supporter of reunifying Korea. How was the British government to explain to its own people the new situation? 'It would . . . be necessary,' Attlee told his Cabinet on 26 September, 'to present clearly to public opinion the reasons justifying a military occupation of the whole of Korea, its temporary character and limited objectives.'[2] The British government would dearly have liked to hold back its own contingent in Korea from crossing the 38th Parallel, but recognised that this was impracticable if the rest of Eighth Army was moving into the North. Bevin, the ever-robust Foreign Secretary, 'felt there was insufficient foundation for their apprehension that China or Russia might thereby be provoked into active intervention', but he suggested that the President of the UN General Assembly might make one more appeal to the North Koreans to lay down their arms before Walker's army entered their country. The British Chiefs of Staff recommended holding back MacArthur's army for a week or so, while offering the North Korean army one further chance to surrender. This uneasy message, drafted amid much private wringing of hands, the British communicated to the Americans.

In reply, Bradley told Tedder, Britain's senior military representative in Washington, that UN forces on the Parallel were already making just such a final appeal to reason to the communists. The British, their fears a little abated, sought to strengthen the American diplomatic position by securing the passage through the UN General Assembly, on 7 October, of a resolution calling for 'all appropriate steps . . . to ensure conditions of stability throughout Korea', and the formation of a unified government elected under UN auspices. This passed by forty-seven votes to five, with seven abstentions. Its purpose was to provide a cloak of UN support for military operations in North Korea, while preserving some vagueness about what form these operations would take. A growing body of moderate opinion in the West believed that action by Syngman Rhee's army operating alone in the North, confining the conflict to an encounter between rival bodies of Koreans, presented a much lesser threat of Chinese or Russian intervention than a Western presence. In this, they probably deluded themselves. Given the doubtful military abilities of the ROK army, the communists could almost certainly have driven Rhee's unaided forces out of the North, with or without Chinese intervention. The dilemma for Washington and its allies would then have been even worse.

But to Acheson's dismay, MacArthur now declared openly and directly to the North Koreans that unless they laid down their arms, he would take 'such military action as may be necessary to enforce the decrees of the United Nations'. Yet again, the general had swept aside diplomatic niceties, ignored critical political sensitivities, overridden fundamental constitutional limitations upon his own powers. And yet again, however unhappily, the Administration in Washington muffled its own doubts and fears. The insuperable difficulty of containing or controlling MacArthur remained the same as ever: the general commanded in Tokyo upon his own terms, as he always had. Either MacArthur was endured, or dismissed. Yet how could he be removed without devastating damage to the image and authority not only of the Truman Administration, but of the United States? Now, he was not merely the Pacific victor of World War II, but the sole begetter of triumph at Inchon, heroic arbiter of the destinies of a free Korea. It is not only with hindsight that it is apparent that MacArthur's gigantic hubris could lead only to tragedy. Many men in Washington and Tokyo also perceived this in the autumn of 1950. But they could see no realistic means of ridding themselves of this old man of the sea. The play must be acted out to the end.

Washington continued to share with Tokyo the most funda-mental misconceptions about the enemy's behaviour and inten-tions. The Administration based its policy now, as from the outbreak of war, upon the conviction that the communist powers were acting in concert. Available intelligence about Chinese think-ing was negligible. It was much more plentiful, both from covert and diplomatic sources, about Moscow's frame of mind. By the winter of 1950, it was apparent that the Russians greatly regretted the North Korean adventure, were eager to distance themselves from it, and to prevent any widening of the war. Soviet signals to this effect were received, and understood, in Washington. Yet these entirely blinded the Administration to the danger of unilateral action by Peking. For the first, but by no means the last time in Korea, a preoccupation with ideological confrontation deflected the attention of the leaders of the United States from the national-istic considerations at play. They simply did not entertain the prospect that the Chinese might act in Korea for their own reasons, quite heedless of Soviet wishes or policy.

On 9 October, Eighth Army at last advanced in full force across the 38th Parallel. For almost a week, they encountered serious resistance. Then the North Koreans broke, and fled north in full retreat. The 1st Cavalry and 24th Infantry began a headlong pursuit, the long convoys' road race interrupted only for spasmodic small unit actions against isolated enemy rearguards.

*

At this moment, with military victory imminent and Eighth Army heavily committed, MacArthur was astonished to receive a message from Washington, informing him that the President sought his presence at a personal meeting on Wake Island, in the mid-Pacific between Tokyo and the west coast of the United States. On the morning of 15 October 1950, nursing acute disgust for what he regarded as a piece of political grandstanding by Truman, the general and his staff took off from Haneda aboard his Constellation.

Truman wrote simply in his memoirs that a moment had come at which he considered his lack of personal contact with MacArthur a handicap: 'I thought that he ought to know his Commander-in-Chief, and that I ought to know the senior field commander in the Far East.' Yet there is little doubt that for once, MacArthur's scepticism about Washington's motives was justified. Truman was politically beleaguered at home, under fire from the right for supposed softness towards the communists. There were indeed good reasons for President and Supreme Commander to meet. But the timing was such that it remains difficult to doubt Truman's desire to associate himself in the public mind with victory in Korea, and with the victor.

MacArthur was anyway the least tractable of men. The consequence of this apparently blatant political act by the President was to cause him to approach the meeting in a mood of cynicism bordering upon contempt. He flew to Wake Island on 15 October, unreceptive to frank discussion of serious issues. When Truman stepped down on to the tarmac the following morning to be greeted by his theatre commander, the general did not salute. He shook hands, as an equal. 'I've been a long time meeting you,' said Truman. 'I hope it won't be so long next time,' said MacArthur with historic triteness. The two men talked alone for an hour in a quonset hut on the edge of the airstrip. Both Acheson and Marshall had declined to join Truman on the trip. Acheson afterwards shook his head about the folly of private talks, 'the sort of lethal things which chiefs of state get into', that lead to disastrous misunderstandings about points of view and decisions. On this occasion, according to Truman's subsequent account, MacArthur assured him that the Chinese would not attack; that victory was imminent; that he himself had no political ambitions. Then the two men emerged into the mounting Pacific heat, and drove across to an airport office building for a full-dress meeting with their entourages.

Even at this, no formal record was taken. MacArthur told the gathering that 'formal resistance will end throughout North and South Korea by Thanksgiving'. He planned to withdraw Eighth Army to Japan by Christmas, leaving X Corps as an occupation force. He reiterated his view that even in the unlikely event that the Chinese intervened, 'now that we have bases for our Air Force in Korea, if the Chinese tried to get down to Pyongyang there would be the greatest slaughter.' If the Russians provided the Chinese with air support, their competence was so limited 'that I believe the Russian air force would bomb the Chinese as often as they would bomb us'. There was some desultory discussion about the political future of Korea, in which MacArthur warmly supported Syngman Rhee's claims to primacy. Truman agreed: 'We must make it plain that we are supporting the Rhee government, and propaganda can go to hell.' An hour and a half after it began, the meeting broke up. Truman invited MacArthur to stay for lunch, but the general demurred. Urgent military business called him to Tokyo. To his surprise, he found himself facing a brief awards ceremony, at which Truman presented him with his fifth Distinguished Service Medal. Amid eager public protestations of goodwill towards his commander in the field, Truman took off from the airstrip, declaring to reporters, 'I've never had a more satisfactory conference since I've been President.'

MacArthur left for Tokyo in a rage. He considered himself diminished by the summons to be cross-questioned by a group of political hacks for whom he felt only contempt. 'Who was that young whipper-snapper who was asking questions?' he demanded insistently, until his staff divined that he referred to Dean Rusk, the Assistant Secretary of State. 'That conference,' wrote MacArthur later, 'made me realize that a curious, and sinister, change was taking place in Washington. The defiant, rallying figure that had been Franklin Roosevelt was gone. Instead, there was a tendency towards temporizing rather than fighting it through.'[3]

With hindsight, the Wake Island conference can be seen as a disastrous landmark in the Korean conflict, as fatal to the interests of the Truman Administration as to those of the tenant of the Dai Ichi. Before Wake, Washington had been given ample grounds to doubt the tractability and judgement of MacArthur. Having summoned the general to meet the President, however, the Washington delegation signally failed to use the opportunity to drive home to MacArthur his responsibility to accept instructions from his own government. Instead, they allowed themselves to be profoundly impressed by his charisma, his sublime assurance, his omniscience about unfolding events in the Far East. They went home reassured that Chinese or Soviet intervention in Korea were not significant dangers. MacArthur, meanwhile, returned to Tokyo with all his antipathy towards the leaders of the Administration confirmed. Whatever Truman and his party had done at Wake, this would have been unlikely to deflect the victorious MacArthur from his chosen course. Yet, by failing to use the opportunity to pursue a serious, prearranged agenda; by causing the Supreme Commander to fly 2,000 miles from his headquarters in the midst of a campaign merely to exchange banalities, Truman and his associates diminished, rather than reasserted, their authority over the general. It is difficult to regard Truman's initiation of the Wake meeting as other than a serious error of judgement, prompted by uncharacteristically frivolous political considerations. Its cost to his stature in dealing with MacArthur, his weakening of his own position in the months that followed, are hard to overestimate.

*

On 19 October, Pyongyang fell. General Paek Sun Yup led 1st ROK Division into the city, the infantry clinging to the hulls of American armour. They swept aside the flimsy communist barricades, and clattered through almost empty streets. Most of the civilians had fled, or were in hiding. Paek felt 'utterly exhilarated. I had left five years earlier as a refugee. Now, I was back with 10,000 men, 100 guns and a battalion of M-46 tanks.'[4] Kim Il Sung and his government had fled into the northern fastnesses. Fascinated, the South Korean and American officers poked among the chaos of his abandoned office in the old Japanese provincial governor's residence. There was an orgy of mutual souvenir photograph-taking, for this was the first war in which every soldier – among the UN forces at least – carried a camera in his pack. An American civil affairs officer, Colonel Archibald Melchoir, chose a council of 'representative non-communist citizens' to run the enemy's capital, from North Koreans plucked almost arbitrarily from the streets. 'We thought the war was over,' said General Paek. 'The North Koreans were now completely wiped out, throwing away their weapons as we met them.' On 20 October, from MacArthur's headquarters Colonel Charles Willoughby circulated an intelligence summary throughout Far East Command:

> Organized resistance on any large scale has ceased to be an enemy capability. Indications are that the North Korean military and political headquarters may have fled into Manchuria. Communications with, and consequent control of, the enemy's field units have dissipated to a point of ineffectiveness. In spite of these indications of disorganization, there are no signs, at the moment, that the enemy intends to surrender. He continues to retain the capability of fighting small scale delaying actions against UN pressure . . .

While Eighth Army pushed north from Seoul, X Corps was in motion in the east. 1st Marine Division had embarked at Inchon. Alongside the Marines, 7th Division was assigned to move south to Pusan to embark for Wonsan. Spirits in the formation were not high. The 7th's limited experience of combat during the advance from Inchon had done little to convince them of their own effect- iveness. Lieutenant Jim Sheldon and his platoon of the 17th Infan- try were sent on a motor patrol to secure an ammunition factory, which they found deserted. But a few hours after their arrival, they were dismayed to encounter a column of North Koreans arriving to replenish their stocks, which provoked a little firefight in which the Americans lost four wounded. There was much wild firing at shadows in the darkness that night. In the days that followed, a succession of successful minor skirmishes with communist strag- glers began to persuade them that they were quite competent soldiers. Their commanders thought otherwise, and embarked upon a hasty field training programme. This ended abruptly when sixteen men were killed and eighty wounded by white phosphorus bombs from their own 4.2-inch mortar company during a demon- stration exercise before spectators. It was in the aftermath of this grim fiasco that they were ordered to move to Pusan: 'Morale in the regiment was pretty low,' said Sheldon.

*

On the LSTs, ploughing north towards Wonsan, the Marines cleaned their weapons and equipment, talked and slept with little sense of stress. O. P. Smith was exultant about the showing of his men in the battle for Seoul, optimistic that even when the war was over, the division had staked a formidable claim to be retained under arms. Smith's Operations Officer, Al Bowser, nursing a bad cold, was chiefly preoccupied with the problem of where the formation might spend the winter. He had no thought for the far northern mountains or the Yalu, but merely for some coastal location where conditions might be made endurable if they had to remain. But with luck, they would not. With the North Koreans in headlong retreat, the war could be over in a matter of weeks. If that was the case, the Marines had already been told that two regiments would return at once to the United States, leaving only one for garrison duty in Japan.

The Marine landing at Wonsan was seriously delayed by communist mines blocking the harbour entrance. On 12 October, two minesweepers were lost, impacting on Russian-built mines. It took two weeks, and cost three more minesweepers, before the field was cleared. To the intense irritation and discomfort of Smith and his men, they wallowed offshore in the transports while the navy bustled hither and thither. Then, to their embarrassment, the Americans learned that the South Koreans were there before them. The ROK 3rd and Capital divisions had entered Wonsan on 10 October, after a dramatic two-week dash from the 38th Parallel. The Capital Division was already fifty miles northwards, and still going. 1st Marine Division staged its amphibious landing at Wonsan on 25 October, twelve days after its own advance and technical parties had arrived by land and air. Even Bob Hope was there before them. To their profound chagrin, by a stroke which entered Marine legend, the entertainer staged a USO show in Wonsan the night before the division stormed ashore to take possession. The 7th Division suffered even more acute delays and counter-orders before being put ashore at Iwon in the last days of October and first of November. X Corps was at last deployed, in time for MacArthur's last act. Men's thoughts were chiefly addressed to going home.

*

The men of Eighth Army exulted in their triumphal drive north, the road race towards the Yalu. The British were astonished to see a senior officer of 1st Cavalry Division riding his jeep past their column, seated astride a massive cowboy saddle. Amid negligible resistance, the chief peril lay in carelessness about the position of the enemy. On 17 October, the Argyll & Sutherland Highlanders were approaching the industrial town of Sariwon. They had expected it to be strongly defended, but found instead only bombed and burning buildings. The supporting tanks opened fire with their machine guns on a distant group of enemy who appeared on the skyline, but otherwise the town appeared abandoned. The colonel was conducting an Orders Group in its midst, his officers gathered among their cluster of vehicles, when they saw a large truck laden with men tearing towards them. Suddenly, they perceived that it was North Korean. There was a long moment's silence. Then a fierce gun-battle began, terminated by a grenade thrown into the truck by an Argyll. Peace restored, young Lieutenant Colin Mitchell was sent off westwards in a bren carrier, to reconnoitre a new base. His party drove cheerfully down a long column of Korean infantry – North Korean. One officer fired a pistol at them. The remainder of those beaten men had no stomach for combat: 'Some looked up at us. Others just plodded on. After four miles of this inspection of the enemy, we had reached their rear echelons and baggage trains, and were gratified that they moved their bullock carts out of our paths as we kept going.'[5] Once clear of the enemy, prudence once more overtook the British party. They hid in a ditch through the night.

*

As Eighth Army's drive north continued, MacArthur made plain his contempt for the carefully drawn niceties of Washington and the UN, about restricting movement near the Chinese border to South Korean forces. He responded witheringly when he heard of a British proposal for the establishment of a buffer zone south of the Yalu, jointly policed by China and the UN:

> The widely reported British desire to appease the Chinese communists by giving them a strip of North Korea finds its historic precedent in the action taken at Munich on 29 September 1938 ... To give up any portion of North Korea to the aggression of the Chinese communists would be the greatest defeat of the free world in recent times. Indeed, to yield to so

immoral a proposition would bankrupt our leadership and
influence in Asia, and render untenable our position both
politically and morally.[6]

When he issued orders, on 20 October, for 'all concerned'
within his command to prepare for a 'maximum effort' to advance
rapidly to the border of North Korea, the Joint Chiefs made no
attempt to interfere. Fear of Chinese intervention had sunk so low
that on 23 October, at a joint meeting in Washington of the British
and American Chiefs of Staff, Bradley declared soothingly: 'We
all agree that, if the Chinese communists come into Korea, we
get out.' On 24 October, MacArthur's new directive removed
all remaining restrictions on the movement of American troops
towards the Yalu. Walker and Almond were 'authorized to use any
and all ground forces as necessary, to secure all of North Korea'.
The Joint Chiefs in Washington queried this order, which was 'a
matter of some concern here'. MacArthur brushed them aside.
General Collins and his colleagues were in no doubt that they were
being flatly disobeyed by the commander in the field. In the same
week, they requested MacArthur to issue a statement, setting at
rest fears in the UN Security Council that the Chinese might move
across the Yalu to protect their vital Suiho electrical generating
plant, unless this was declared safe from UN military action.
MacArthur declined to give such an assurance, unless he was sure
the plant was not powering communist munitions production. Yet
again, with the war almost over, the Joint Chiefs showed their
unwillingness to precipitate a confrontation. Washington resigned
itself to playing the hand against the communists MacArthur's
way.

'We are going to go ahead and force the issue now,' a Department of State spokesman told a correspondent in Washington.[7]
The decision to advance north across the 38th Parallel was a classic
example of military opportunity becoming the engine of action, at
the expense of political desirability. No rigorous debate was carried
to a conclusion about UN, or US, objectives in occupying the North.

The very great political and diplomatic hazards were submerged by the public perception of the prospect of outright military victory. At the root of American action lay a contempt, conscious or unconscious, for the capabilities of Mao Tse Tung's nation and armed forces. The Chinese communists were considered a sinister ideological force in Asia, but not a formidable military one. Far greater courage and determination would have been required from the Truman Administration for a decision to halt Eighth Army at the 38th Parallel than was demanded for acquiescence in MacArthur's drive to victory. If there remained a measure of apprehension within the Administration about entering North Korea, there was also the powerful scent of triumphalism among many prominent Americans. Harold Stassen declared in a speech in support of Republican candidates on 5 November that the war in Korea was 'the direct result of five years of building up Chinese communist strength through the blinded, blundering American-Asiatic policy of the present national administration . . . five years of coddling Chinese communists, five years of undermining General MacArthur, five years of appeasing the arch-communist, Mao Tse Tung'. Now Mao was to be appeased no longer. American arms were being carried to the very frontier of his vast land.

7 » THE COMING OF THE CHINESE

On the evening of 1 November 1950, Private Carl Simon of G Company, 8th Cavalry, lay in the company position with his comrades, speculating nervously about the fate of a patrol of F Company, which had reported itself in trouble, 'under attack by unidentified troops'. As the darkness closed in, they heard firing, bugles, and shouting. Their accompanying Koreans could not identify the language, but said that it must be Chinese. When a wave of yelling enemy charged the Americans out of the gloom, firing and grenading as they came, no effective resistance was offered. 'There was just mass hysteria on the position,' said Simon. 'It was every man for himself. The shooting was terrific, there were Chinese shouting everywhere, I didn't know which way to go. In the end, I just ran with the crowd. We just ran and ran until the bugles grew fainter.'[1] The war diaries of 1st Cavalry Division, of which 8th Cavalry was a part, present the events at Ansung in a somewhat more coherent, less armageddonist spirit than PFC Simon. But since his uncomplicated perception – of a thunderbolt from the night that brought the entire ordered pattern of his army life down about his head – was to become common to thousands of other young Americans in Korea in the weeks that followed, it seems no less valid than that of his superiors.

The twenty-year-old New York baker's son had joined the army to see the world. He was in transit to Japan when the war began, and had to look on a map to discover where Korea was. When he saw the place for himself, he liked it not at all. His unit had been uneasy, unhappy and uncomfortable since it crossed the 38th Parallel. Simon himself had been slightly wounded in a skirmish soon after entering North Korea. The only moment of the war he had enjoyed was the Bob Hope Show in Pyongyang, though he was so short that he had to keep jumping up and down among the vast audience of soldiers, to catch a glimpse of the distant stage. Simon was one of many thousands of men vastly relieved to find the war almost over, impatient to get home.

Yet now, he found himself among thirty-five frightened fugitives, in the midst of Korea without a compass. The officers among them showed no urge to exercise any leadership. The group merely began to shuffle southwards. Most threw away their weapons. They walked for fourteen days, eating berries, waving their yellow scarves desperately but vainly to observation planes. Once, in a village, they got rice and potatoes at gunpoint from a papa-san. At night, they gazed at the curious beauty of the hills, on fire from strafing. For a time, they lay up in the house of a frightened civilian, who eventually drove them out with his warnings of communists in the area. They were close to physical collapse, and to surrender, when one morning they thought they glimpsed a tank bearing a 'red carpet' identification panel. They ran forward, and found on the ground a London newspaper. Then they saw British ration packs, and at last, far below them in the valley, a tracked vehicle moving. They determined to make for it, whatever the nationality of its occupants. To their overwhelming relief, they found themselves in the hands of the British 27 Brigade.

*

PFC Simon and his companions were a small part of the flotsam from the disaster that befell the US 1st Cavalry Division between 1 and 3 November, which also inflicted desperate damage upon the ROK II Corps. The South Koreans were the first to be heavily attacked. The Chinese 116th Division struck against the 15th ROK. Then, on 1 November near Ansung, about midway across the Korean peninsula, it was the turn of the Americans. Strong forces hit them with great determination, separating their units, then attacking them piecemeal. Batteries in transit on the roads, rifle

THE CHINESE INTERVENTION – November 1950 to January 1951

companies on positions, found themselves under devastating fire from small arms, mortars and katyusha rockets. The 3rd Battalion of the 8th Cavalry was effectively destroyed. The regiment's other battalions were severely mauled, and elements of the 5th Cavalry damaged. Yet when the 1st Cavalry Division's action ended, activity across the Korean battle front once again dwindled into local skirmishes.

Herein lies one of the greatest, most persistent enigmas of the Korean War. More than three weeks before the main Chinese onslaught was delivered with full force, Peking delivered a ferocious warning by fire: we are here, said the Chinese, in the unmistakable language of rifle and grenade, in the mountains of Korea that you cannot penetrate. We can strike at will against your forces, and they are ill-equipped in mind and body – above all, in mind – to meet us. We are willing to accept heavy casualties to achieve tactical success. The armies of Syngman Rhee are entirely incapable of resisting our assaults.

Yet this message, this warning, MacArthur and his subordinates absolutely declined to receive. They persisted in their conviction that their UN armies could drive with impunity to the Yalu. They continued to believe that the Chinese were either unwilling or unable to intervene effectively. They showed no signs of alarm at the evidence that not only the ROK divisions, but their own, were at something less than peak fighting efficiency. They had created a fantasy world for themselves, in which events would march in accordance with a divine providence directed from the Dai Ichi building. The conduct of the drive to the Yalu reflected a contempt for intelligence, for the cardinal principles of military prudence, seldom matched in twentieth-century warfare.

*

The first ROK forces reached the Yalu on 25 October, and sent back a bottle of its intoxicating waters to Syngman Rhee. Some soldiers, like their American counterparts, equally symbolically chose to urinate from its bank. On the same day, the ROK II Corps, driving north on the western axis of the UN advance, was strongly attacked, and in the action that followed, almost destroyed. The ROKs reported that the agents of their disaster were Chinese, and sent some Chinese prisoners to the Americans. General Paek Sun Yup, probably the ablest South Korean commander, was at this time transferred to temporary command of II Corps, and demanded to see the PoWs personally at his Command Post. He himself spoke fluent Chinese, and immediately established that the prisoners were indeed from the mainland, with southern accents. They wore Chinese reversible smocks. Paek asked them: 'Are there many of you here?' They nodded. 'Many many.' Paek reported the conversation directly to I Corps's commander, 'Shrimp' Milburn. But Milburn was no more impressed by the Korean than by his own intelligence officer, Colonel Percy Thomas, who was also convinced that there was now a serious Chinese threat. General Walker himself sought to explain away the presence of some Chinese among the North Koreans as insignificant: 'After all, a lot of Mexicans live in Texas . . .' II Corps fell back as the enemy advanced under cover of vast makeshift smokescreens, created by setting fire to the forests through which they marched. When the US 1st Cavalry passed through the ROKs to take up the attack, the division was savaged. Meanwhile in the east, the ROK 1st Corps moving north from Hamhung was stopped in its tracks on the road to the hydroelectric plants of the Chosin reservoir. As early as 25 October, the ROK 1st Division found itself heavily engaged, and captured a soldier who admitted that he was Chinese. The next day, more prisoners were taken, who were identified as members of the 124th Division of the Chinese 42nd Army. By 31 October, twenty-five Chinese prisoners had been taken, and the strength of the communist force at the foot of the Chosin reservoir was apparent.

The Argyll & Sutherland Highlanders, of the British 27 Brigade, took part in a skirmish near the Chongchon river, which cost them five killed and six wounded. They advanced cautiously forward to examine the scattered bodies of the communists on the hillside.

'They were unlike any enemy I had seen before,' wrote Lieutenant Colin Mitchell. 'They wore thick padded clothing, which made them look like little Michelin men. I turned one body over with my foot, and saw that he wore a peaked cap with a red star badge. These soldiers were Chinese. I then turned over another and, as I looked down at him, he opened one eye and looked up at me. I shot him with my Luger, shouting to the platoon, "they're alive!" It was quickly over, and all the enemy lay dead.'[2] Yet still the UN Command could not bring itself to recognise the simple truth – that the Chinese had entered the Korean War in force.

Bradley, in Washington, speculated uncertainly as to whether Peking was merely seeking to make a face-saving gesture in support of its defeated North Korean allies. There was renewed debate about the merits of bombing the Yalu bridges. On 13 November, the State Department sought opinions from London, Canberra, Ottawa, Delhi, Wellington, Moscow and the Hague about possible overflights of Manchuria by UN aircraft in 'hot pursuit'. US ambassadors in each capital reported that reaction to such an initiative would be highly unfavourable. CIA reports continued to give uncertain guidance: on 8 November, the Agency estimated that there were 30–40,000 Chinese already in Korea, with 700,000 more poised across the border in Manchuria. The reports suggested that Peking considered itself to possess full freedom of action, and might move in strength. But Washington remained obsessed with the belief that the communist world acted in concert, to a pre-arranged plan; that Peking would not or could not operate independently of Moscow, and that the evident unwillingness of Moscow to see the war extended would preclude Chinese action. Bedell Smith, the CIA's director, urged the National Security Council on 9 November that MacArthur should be given a freer hand in North Korea, because 'the Kremlin's basic decision for or against war would hardly be influenced by this local provocation in this area.'[3]

At a joint State–Defense meeting on 21 November, Vandenburg and Forrest urged that, if MacArthur's advance to the Yalu was checked by the Chinese, Peking should be told to 'quit, or we would have to hit them in Manchuria'.[4] No evidence of dissent from this view by Marshall or any others present is recorded. Washington interpreted Chinese warnings and probes in October as evidence of weakness and reluctance to fight. The Administration's instinct was to call the Chinese bluff. Although Washington had some reason to be exasperated by MacArthur's public declarations and threats, the private mood in the capital, the confidence in imminent victory and lack of apprehension about Chinese intentions, mirrored that in Tokyo.

And if the American assessment of Peking subsequently proved bitterly mistaken, the circumstantial evidence indeed supports the view that the Chinese moved with caution and circumspection into Korea, and committed themselves to all-out war only when it became apparent, first, that the UN forces were not entirely formidable foes; and second, that unless they were defeated on the battlefield, they were committed to an advance to the Yalu. Some of the Chinese soldiers who took part in the first actions against the ROKs and 1st Cavalry described how afterwards they were marched back across the Yalu, and moved eastward to cross the river into North Korea once more, for the main offensive that followed. For an army as scantily provided with transport as that of China, this was scarcely an economical approach to deployment. It can be most readily explained by a measure of caution and indecision in Peking, as the Chinese leadership measured the military capability of the UN forces. In November 1950, General MacArthur thundered to the United Nations that the Chinese intervention was 'one of the most offensive acts of international lawlessness in historical record'. This was absurd. The Chinese had been given much to alarm them. It may never be possible to piece together the precise decision-making process in Peking that led to the order to enter Korea. Almost all the key participants are dead, and among the living there is no reliable body of records to make it possible to establish the objective truth about recent Chinese political history. But the evidence is overwhelming that in 1950,

Mao Tse Tung and his colleagues were deeply reluctant to engage the United Nations – or, more precisely, the forces of the United States – in Korea.

China had scarcely begun to recover from her civil war. In 1949, an estimated forty million of her population were affected by natural disasters. To famine was added the new problem of local guerrilla war: the traditional phrase 'kung fei' – 'communist bandits' – was now transferred to the Kuomintang. Over a million were rounded up or killed between May 1949 and May 1951, most of them south of the Yangtse. In the country, secret societies had grown up to resist land reform. There was widespread dissent in the cities. China was still seeking to secure what she considered to be her own borders. In October 1950, the People's Liberation Army moved into Tibet, and completed its occupation of the country only the following year. Meanwhile in the east, Peking's attentions were overwhelmingly focused upon eliminating Formosa as the base of Nationalist opposition. Throughout the summer of 1950, invasion barges were being built, some 5,000 junks assembled, airfields prepared to support the assault on Chiang's stronghold, which the 3rd Field Army's deputy commander, Su Yu, declared would be 'an extremely big problem, and will involve the biggest campaign in the history of modern Chinese warfare'. Yet amidst all this, Mao had been seeking to demobilise vast masses of his unwieldy army, to return soldiers to the factories and fields and workshops where they were so badly needed. It was a problem that Peking had failed to resolve by the autumn of 1950, when China still possessed some five million men under arms.

Peking must have been well aware of Kim Il Sung's invasion plans – the railway system of north-east China played an important part in moving Soviet supplies and equipment into North Korea. But there is no evidence that China played a significant role in the North Korean decision to go to war. The Sino-Soviet Treaty of Friendship, signed in Moscow on 15 February 1950, went some way to heal the longstanding rift between Mao and Stalin. But it provided China with disappointingly little material assistance. It was reported that Stalin had demanded, and Mao rejected, the wholesale appointment of Soviet advisers as a condition of major equipment aid. The People's Liberation Army was still equipped entirely with arms captured from the Japanese, or supplied by the Americans to the Kuomintang. Despite considerable skill in field-craft, it lacked the communications or the training to operate cohesively much beyond regimental level. The PLA remained, in large measure, a guerrilla army, lacking the advantage of the heavy weapons – and the handicap of the impedimenta – of a modern Western army. Both for reasons of domestic political stability and military preparedness, in the autumn of 1950 it appears that many key figures among China's leadership were most reluctant to see their country exposed to war with the West, with all the uncertainties this entailed.

But Washington's linkage of the invasion of South Korea with the threat to Formosa in June 1950 had an immediate influence on China. Truman's statement on 27 June, declaring that 'the occupation of Formosa by communist forces would be a direct threat to the security of the Pacific area and to US forces performing their lawful and necessary functions in that area', created – incidentally and almost casually – an entirely new and firm commitment to keeping Formosa out of the hands of Peking's communist rulers. This was a much greater blow to China's perceived national interest than Washington seemed to recognise at the time. Premier Chou En Lai adopted a far tougher public attitude towards the American blockade of the Taiwan Strait than towards American intervention in Korea. Henceforward, as a leading historian of the PLA has written, 'the struggle to liberate Taiwan began to be linked to the struggle against US imperialism as such, and the achievement of the former was now seen in the more long-term context of the latter.'[5] After years in which Chiang Kai Shek had been considered the foremost enemy of communist China, with astonishing rapidity the United States took on this role. 'The American imperialists fondly hope that their armed aggression against Taiwan will prevent us from liberating it,' Kuo Mo-Jo wrote in the

People's Daily in August. 'Around China in particular, their designs for a blockade are taking shape in the pattern of a stretched-out snake. Starting from South Korea, it stretches to Japan, the Ryuku Islands, Taiwan and the Philippines and then turns up at Vietnam.'[6] Westerners, and Americans in particular, sometimes made the mistake of allowing their scorn for propagandist rhetoric such as this to blind them to the very real Chinese fear of encirclement. Throughout the Korean War, Washington persistently sought the communist ideological logic behind Chinese actions. It might have been more profitable to consider instead historic Chinese nationalist logic. Korea had provided the springboard for the Japanese invasion of Manchuria only a generation before. As the Americans drove north after smashing Kim Il Sung's armies in September 1950, Peking was appalled by the imminent prospect of an American imperialist army on the Yalu.

Chinese alarm was intensified by the visibly strengthening relationship between the United States and Chiang. The warm words spoken by both sides during MacArthur's July visit to Formosa were widely publicised, as were Chiang's offers of Nationalist troops to fight alongside the United Nations in Korea. The communists would have been even more disturbed had they known how close Truman came to accepting Chiang's offer of 33,000 men, when MacArthur's armies were desperate for reinforcements.

In late September and early October, the Chinese issued increasingly forceful warnings, both in public statements and in private remarks to the Indian Ambassador in Peking, about their attitude to the American presence in North Korea. In the first weeks of fighting in Korea, the Chinese press scarcely reported the war. Yet now, a growing crescendo of anti-American propaganda was printed and broadcast: 'Resist America, Aid Korea'; 'Preserve Our Homes, Defend the Nation'. Mass meetings denounced the 'bloodstained bandits', 'murderers', 'savages'. The People's Republic did not intend, General Nieh Jung-Chen, China's acting Chief of Staff, told Sardar K. Pannikkar, 'to sit back with folded hands and let the Americans come to their border . . . We know what we are in for, but at all costs American aggression has got to be stopped. The Americans can bomb us, they can destroy our industries, but they cannot defeat us on land.' On the danger of American nuclear reaction, Nieh said: 'We have calculated all that . . . They may even drop atom bombs on us. What then? They may kill a few million people. Without sacrifice, a nation's independence cannot be upheld . . . After all, China lives on the farms. What can atom bombs do there?'[7]

At the State Department in Washington, a handful of officials took heed, and sounded a note of caution. John Paton Davies warned that a combination of 'irredentism, expansionism, Soviet pressure and inducements, strategic anxieties, ideological zeal, domestic pressures and emotional anti-Americanism' might lead China to intervene. Edmund Chubb, director of the Office of Chinese Affairs, expressed the conviction that China would fight. But his persistent pessimism on this issue had undermined his credibility. As late as 12 October, the CIA argued that 'despite statements by Chou En Lai, troop movements to Manchuria, and propaganda charges of atrocities and border violations, there are no convincing indications of an actual Chinese Communist intention to resort to full-scale intervention in Korea.' Dean Acheson found the logic against Chinese intervention irresistible: they would lose all hope of their coveted UN seat; they would need to become clients of the Russians, dependent upon Moscow for air and naval support to be able to wage war at all; the PLA was too poorly equipped to compete convincingly with MacArthur's armies; the Chinese government must be daunted by the expectation of devastating American reprisals if Chinese forces were committed against those of the UN. The United States was convinced that its policies in the Far East presented no threat to any legitimate Chinese interest. Washington therefore persuaded itself that Peking would reach the same conclusion.

Peking did not. On 2 October, Premier Chou En Lai summoned Pannikkar, the Indian Ambassador, and directly informed him that if the United Nations crossed the 38th Parallel, China would intervene in the war. Truman, when he learned of Chou's message, dismissed it as 'a bald attempt to blackmail the UN . . . The problem that arose in connection with these reports was that Mr Pannikkar had in the past played the game of the Chinese communists fairly regularly, so that his statement could not be taken as that of an impartial observer.' The absence of any direct link between Washington and Peking was a significant force in preventing the Americans from achieving even the tenuous level of understanding they possessed with Moscow. The lack of diplomatic relations, together with the absolute ignorance of the Peking regime about how these might profitably be conducted, ensured that Washington never received the sort of signals from Peking which, if believed, could have averted a confrontation on the battlefield. On 8 October, the day after American troops crossed the 38th Parallel, Mao issued the order for 'Chinese People's Volunteers' to 'resist the attacks of United States imperialism'.

For many years, it was believed that the reinforced 4th Field Army which entered North Korea a week later was under the command of Mao's close associate, Lin Piao. The Chinese today assert most firmly that this was not so. And while Lin's political disgrace might provide a motive for deceit on the issue, there is sufficient corroborative evidence to take seriously the modern Chinese claim about Lin. Military sources in Peking say that, in the autumn of 1950, Lin was indeed urged by Mao and the Central Committee to accept command of a Chinese army to fight in Korea, and was their first choice to do so. Yet he himself argued strongly against immediate military intervention. He believed that the PLA was not yet ready to take on the army of the United States. He urged delay, if necessary for a year or more, until the army could be retrained and re-equipped. He was especially concerned about the impact of US air power on an unprotected Chinese army. Marshal Peng Te Huai, on the other hand, declared that he could not see that China would be any better placed to fight in 1951, or for that matter in 1952, than in 1950. He believed – to resort to contemporary cliché – that 'imperialists could be shown to be paper tigers'. A big, forceful, talkative man, Peng told his staff robustly that will and motivation could compensate for any short-comings of equipment. One of his former officers says that Peng, from beginning to end, treated the struggle in Korea merely as an extension of the Liberation War against the Kuomintang.[8] According to a memoir published under Peng's name in 1981, on 4 October he found himself suddenly summoned from his head-quarters, as commander-in-chief in north-west China, to fly to Peking to attend a conference, and arrived to discover the Central Committee already in session, debating the dispatch of troops to Korea. At the next session the following day, he was appointed to command them. The simple fiction of describing the Chinese forces in Korea as 'volunteers' was designed to prevent all-out war with the United States, above all to diminish the danger of massive American retaliation against the mainland.

China's initial force in Korea was organised as XIII Army Group, and comprised four armies, each of three 10,000-man infantry divisions, a regiment of cavalry, and five regiments of artillery. They crossed the Yalu bridges by night. Their first objective was to establish a wide enough bridgehead on the south bank to give themselves room to deploy. Had they permitted the United Nations to close up to the Yalu border along its length, they would have been confronted by the intolerable initial task of conducting an opposed river crossing before they could join battle. The 42nd Army came first, to block the road running north-west from the Chosin reservoir. The 38th Army was to deploy across the road north from Huichon. The 40th Army advanced from Sinuiju towards Pukchin. The 50th and 66th Armies followed.

It was an extraordinary achievement of modern warfare: between 13 and 25 October, the intelligence staffs of MacArthur's armies failed to discern the slightest evidence of the movement of 130,000 soldiers and porters. A combination of superb fieldcraft and camouflage by the Chinese, together with their lack of use of any of the conventional means by which modern military move-ment is detected – wireless traffic, mechanised activity, supply dumps – blinded the UN High Command to what was taking place on its front. Above all, perhaps, the generals were not looking for anything of this sort. They had persuaded themselves that the war was all but over. Their senses were deadened to a fresh consideration.

*

On the night of 5/6 November, after the disaster to the 8th Cavalry and the crumbling of so many major ROK units, the UN Command was briefly sufficiently disturbed by the situation to consider a major withdrawal. Yet on the morning of 6 November, it was found that it was the communists who were disengaging all along the front. After ten days in which they had dramatically seized the initiative and forced back UN forces in a succession of battles, they chose to break off the action. Once more, their motives and intentions are not entirely clear. Military sources in Peking today declare that there were problems of supply and co-ordination; that having thus warned the Americans of their will and capability to intervene, the Chinese were prepared to linger for a time, to discover whether their message was needed. Both these assertions seem at least plausible. The Chinese also claimed that their purpose in withdrawing was 'to encourage the enemy's arrogance'.[9] But it became immediately apparent that MacArthur, far from being deterred by the first Chinese offensive, considered that the communists had striven their hardest to overcome his forces, and failed. Peking, he believed, had shot its bolt, and most unfrightening this had proved. The UN offensive, the drive for the Yalu, would resume forthwith. The Chinese, in their turn, prepared to meet it.

So who were they, the men of these 'fanatical hordes' who were about to force upon the United States Army one of the most humiliating retreats in its history? It is sometimes forgotten that after twenty years of war, many Chinese soldiers were men of exceptional military experience. 'My first memories as a child were of the Japanese burning and destroying,' said Li Hebei, a twenty-

two-year-old infantry platoon commander who crossed the Yalu
with the 587th Regiment on 25 October. Li had served first with
local guerrillas, armed only with a home-made rifle, then graduated to the PLA and a captured Japanese weapon when a unit
passed through his devastated village when he was sixteen. Like
thousands of politically aware young Chinese, he called the PLA
'the big university', for it was in its ranks that he learned to read
and write. Between 1943 and 1947, he saw his family just once. He
learned to march . . . forever. Mile upon mile he and his unit could
walk or even trot, in their quilted cotton uniforms and tennis
shoes, up mountain tracks hauling all that they possessed in the
world: personal weapon, eighty rounds of ammunition, grenade,
spare foot rags, sewing kit, chopsticks, and perhaps a week's
rations – tea, rice, a little sugar, perhaps a tin of fish or meat.
Thirty-five years later, Hebei grinned at the memory: 'We had a
saying – Red Army's two legs better than than Kuomintang's four
wheels. Life was very hard, but the atmosphere was very good,
because we were full of hope.'[10] A Chinese soldier required just
eight to ten pounds of supply a day, against sixty for his UN
counterpart. Thus, to sustain fifty divisions in combat, Peking
needed to move only 2,500 tons of supplies a day south across the
Yalu. This compared with 600 tons for a single US Army division,
700 tons for 1st Marine Division. Each of the tens of thousands
of porters supporting the Chinese drive into Korea could carry
80–100 pounds on his shoulder pole or A-frame. Thus did the
impossible become possible.

Yu Xiu was one of the men who stormed the 8th Cavalry's
positions on 1 November, exulting to discover the success of their
techniques of hard-hitting night assault. Yu was a twenty-nine-year-
old from Chungsu province, brought up in the French sector of
Shanghai, who joined the 4th Field Army when his father was
killed by a Japanese bomb in 1937. A deputy political commissar of
his regiment, he said that the overwhelming lesson the PLA
learned from its first brushes with the Americans was of the need
for speed. 'In the Liberation War, one might take days to surround

a Kuomintang division, then slowly close the circle around it. With the Americans, if we took more than a few hours, they would bring up reinforcements, aircraft, artillery.'[11]

Li Hua was twenty-three, from Shandung province, a veteran of 8th Route Army since he was sixteen, a peasant's son who had been trained at one of the PLA's officer schools. On the train south to the Yalu in October, he and his comrades were told nothing of their destination, 'but everybody guessed: we were going to support the Koreans against their invaders. We felt pretty confident, because we had just beaten the Kuomintang, with all their support from the Americans. We expected to do the same to Syngman Rhee's people. We weren't very wrong. They were a pushover compared with the Japanese.' They walked across the Yalu bridge by night in their long files, then fifty miles onwards to their initial contact near the Chosin reservoir. Li, the propaganda officer of his company, examined his unit's first American prisoner at much the same time, and with much the same curiosity, as Eighth Army were studying its captives from the PLA: 'This young American, he fell on his knees and begged for mercy. We felt sorry for him. He obviously didn't want to fight.'[12]

Americans who found North Korea an alien land might have reflected that it was almost equally so to the Chinese. The men of the PLA found the Korean peasants at first cold and unfriendly, the weather and the mountains unyielding and vicious. They were guided across country only by a few old Japanese maps – one to a regiment. Yet this initial wave of PLA veterans, in the months before massive casualties caused their replacement by less promising material, possessed some notable advantages over the Americans. For all their lack of equipment and sophistication, these Chinese soldiers were among the hardiest in the world. Many had known no other life but that of war since their teens. Most were genuinely enthused by the spirit of revolution, the sense of participation in a new China that seemed to offer brighter promise than the old land of tyrannical landlordism and official corruption. In Korea, in the months to come, the PLA would suffer its own difficulties with shaken morale and growing disillusionment in its ranks, matching those of its enemies. But in the winter of 1950, the spur of early success outweighed the impact of high casualties in Peng's divisions.

*

On 15 November, the *Korea Times* described life in liberated Seoul as 'returning to normal'. Food queues were said to be fading. The government had just declared 'Epidemic Prevention Week'. A statement from ROK Army headquarters declared: 'Our army is continuing its exterminating drive against the enemy, who are taking refuge (remnants) in the mountains.' Over 135,000 communist PoWs were said to be in UN hands. Total North Korean casualties were estimated at 335,000.

24 November was Thanksgiving Day – bleak and blustery. Immense logistic efforts had been made to ensure that the men of Eighth Army enjoyed their turkey dinner. By truck and even by air drop, the traditional Thanksgiving trimmings were shipped to the army that was still assured by its commanders that it was victorious. The British and other allies mocked the idea of bringing domestic comforts into the forward areas. 'I could not stop asking myself what on earth it had all cost,' said one British soldier,[13] faintly ashamed of his own small-mindedness. Yet he and his compatriots were also secretly impressed by a nation capable of such a feat in the midst of a campaign. The enemy were nowhere much in evidence. In the forward areas, the troops were uneasy, yet they clung to MacArthur's promise: home by Christmas. In some units, work had begun to clean up vehicles and equipment, to crate surplus stores for shipment to Japan or Stateside. The cold was already intense, though not as bitter as it would become. In a thousand positions among the barren valleys and hillsides of North Korea, American soldiers huddled around flickering fires fuelled from the wreckage of local huts and imported packing cases, and made what seasonal cheer they could. Afterwards, they looked back on that day as a hollow echo of a celebration, when they had

seen what was to come. The clothes that Colonel John Michaelis of the 27th Infantry was wearing on Thanksgiving Day, he did not take off until 16 February.

*

On 25 November, Walker's Eighth Army and Almond's X Corps began to move forward once more. The men of B Company of the 1/9th Infantry, 2nd Division, were approaching the crest of yet another faceless, meaningless geographical feature – Hill 219, on the east bank of the Chongchon river on the road to Kanggye, when they were hit with fierce grenade and small-arms fire. By nightfall, fighting was in progress throughout the area. The 9th Infantry were in no doubt that they were engaged against the Chinese. But poor communications and extraordinary command lethargy hampered 2nd Division in rousing itself to meet a major new threat. In camps and vehicle concentrations along the length of the Chongchon Valley, Americans found themselves wakened in their sleeping bags by a terrifying cacophony of bugles, drums, rattles, whistles – and gunfire. Again and again, Chinese assault groups smashed through ill-prepared perimeters, overrunning infantry positions, gun lines, rear areas. By the night of 26 November, 2nd Division had been driven back two miles south-west down the Chongchon. The Command Posts of the 9th Infantry's 1st and 3rd Battalions were overrun. Shortly before midnight, the 2nd Battalion was heavily attacked and forced back, losing most of its equipment. Some men waded the Chongchon in their flight, to find their clothes and boots turning to ice as they climbed the southern bank. Not that the Chinese possessed any magical means of walking upon water: that first night, the 23rd RCT captured a hundred communist soldiers, stripped as they forded the river. On the 2nd Division's left, 25th Division was also under pressure. Amid individual acts of great bravery, the collective American response was feeble. From Army Command to the meanest hilltop foxhole, men seemed too shocked and appalled by the surprise that had overtaken them to respond effectively.

Eighteen-year-old Private Mario Scarselleta and other men of the mortar company, 35th Infantry, had been less than happy for some days – the cold, the shortcomings of their 'shoepacks', the jamming of their weapons, and the rumours of the Chinese had already eaten deep into their morale. When the shooting began around them on the night of 26 November, their first thought was to pull back. Their somewhat elderly lieutenant declared doggedly: 'I'm not leaving until I get the word from battalion,' which upset his men greatly. Then the shooting closed in around them, and somebody shouted 'Every man for himself!' 'Then there was really chaos. Everybody just bugged out,' said Scarselleta. They ran a few yards along the hillside, met a Chinese with a bugle whom they killed, then dashed for their trucks, and began to drive away. To their astonishment, they found that the Chinese appeared to be seeking to capture, rather than to kill them. There were some extraordinary hand-to-hand fights. Scarselleta saw a friend laid out by a blow on the jaw from a Chinese. The man rejoined the unit a month later. They abandoned the hopeless effort to load the vehicles, and started walking. They walked for four days, among a great throng of ill-assorted Turks, Koreans, fellow-Americans. 'There was a complete loss of leadership,' said Scarselleta. 'It was a nightmare, really. Many times, I felt that we'd never make it out of there, that to survive this would be a miracle. Those Chinese were just fanatics – they didn't place the value on life that we did. To this day, I still think about it – the bodies blown up, the Americans run over with tanks, the panic and shooting in the nights.'[14] He and his comrades did not reorganise as a unit until they were a few miles north of Seoul.

*

Yet the setbacks to IX Corps were insignificant, compared with the absolute disaster taking place on the right of Eighth Army: the whole ROK II Corps, three divisions in strength, had collapsed almost literally overnight, and was falling back in chaos, abandoning guns, vehicles, equipment. Not a gap, but a chasm eighty miles wide had thus been opened in the Allied line – if the United Nations deployment before the Chinese attack could be dignified as such – between Eighth Army in the west of the country, and X Corps in the east. An attempt by the Turkish brigade to move to the support of the ROKs was halted abruptly at a Chinese roadblock at Wawon, well behind the American flank. Eighteen communist divisions of the Chinese XIII Army Group were now committed. Eighth Army faced a desperate danger of being cut off from the south. Walker ordered his forces' immediate retreat. But while they moved as best they could down the western side of the country, the 2nd Division around Kunu-ri, just south of the Chong-chon, must hold open its own line of withdrawal, and prevent the Chinese from bisecting Korea to the south.

General Keiser, 2nd Division's commander, only began his move back to Kunu-ri early on the 28th. By the next morning, Chinese troops were already attacking road movements south of the formation, between Kunu-ri and Sunchon. Yet still there was a reluctance in the higher command to grasp the deadliness of the threat, to understand that the retreating units faced not roadblocks, but enemy forces in strength. This, although as early as 24 November PoWs had been reporting massive Chinese concentrations in the area. When 'Shrimp' Milburn of I Corps telephoned Keiser that morning of the 29th, to ask how things were going, Keiser replied: 'Bad. Right now, I'm getting hit in my CP.' Milburn promptly urged Keiser to bring his men out westwards, via Anju. But the 2nd Division commander was unwilling to undertake such an extended diversion. He preferred the short road – directly south, to Sunchon. As Keiser's men were falling back in disarray around Kunu-ri, infantry were struggling to sweep the enemy out of range of the Kunu-ri to Sunchon road – and failing. Yet even this did not convince their commanders of the seriousness of the threat on their line of retreat.

In the first two days of the Chinese offensive, there was the bizarre kidglove quality of a drawing-room game about their behaviour. Though the men in the line might detect nothing frivolous about the communists' assault, how could they rationally explain the repeated episodes when Americans who might easily have been killed were taken prisoner, then turned loose to return to their own lines? American officers returning to command posts that had been overrun discovered to their astonishment that nothing had been touched by the enemy. Colonel Paul Freeman was one of many commanders who were later convinced that the first days had been a test of American strength and will: 'They came tongue-in-cheek at first, to see what we would do. Then they found what a thin line we had, how easily the South Koreans cracked. They saw what a pushover we were – that we would not even bomb across the Yalu. Then they became very aggressive, very bold – and stayed that way.' The most savage American experience of the Korean War now began.

*

Major John Willoughby of the 1st Middlesex of the British 27 Brigade had spent the afternoon of 26 November soaking ecstatically in his first bath for weeks. The brigade was in reserve. He was still in the bath when an orderly brought in a signal reporting that four unidentified horsemen had been spotted near Brigade HQ, who galloped off when challenged. They were Chinese, of course. Later, when the British grasped their symbolic importance, they called them 'the four horsemen of the apocalypse'. That night, they were warned to be ready to move, and the next morning they were moved north in a piercing wind – still lacking winter clothing – to Kunu-ri. They could see icefloes forming on the rivers they crossed as they drove.

Willoughby accompanied Brigadier Coad to IX Corps headquarters, where they found an atmosphere close to panic. The position of several American formations was marked on the big perspex map overlay with an enigmatic question mark following their numbers. In the centre, pointing south, a great red arrow had been chinagraphed in, marked '2 MILLION?' The British were uncertain whether this was satirical. 27 Brigade was directed to take up position north of Sunchon, on the road from Kunu-ri. There was no available transport to move them, so the men began to march the twenty-two miles back to the positions. It was a long, exhausting hike in the icy wind, hearing unexplained bursts of firing from time to time up the valleys around them. The young soldiers were tiring. Willoughby found himself carrying five rifles for a time. After ten miles, to their enormous relief, trucks arrived to carry them the last stretch. At 4 a.m., they lay down to sleep for an hour in the frozen paddy.

The next morning they were ordered to move north once more, towards the pass through which they had marched unscathed the previous night. There was talk of an ambush. A few miles up the road, they met an American jeep coming the other way, a colonel hanging dead over the side of the vehicle, two other corpses lying in the back. The British dismounted, and began to deploy. Suddenly, at the far edge of the paddy, they saw a cluster of white-clad figures leap up and begin running into the hills. There was absolute silence around them. Yard by yard, expecting a volley at any moment, the Middlesex advanced towards the southern end of the pass in front of them. At last, inevitably, the Chinese opened fire. The Middlesex began a battle which continued all day of 30 November, and cost them some thirty casualties. And as they fought, they watched a great tragedy unfold in the pass before them.

*

At 1.30 p.m. on 30 November, with his shrinking perimeter around Kunu-ri under violent pressure, General Keiser ordered his men to run the road south, whatever was in their way. The leading elements of 2nd Division's great nose-to-tail vehicle convoy drove south from Kunu-ri into a storm of mortar and machine-gun fire. The horrified British onlookers to the south watched trucks keel over and catch fire, men mown down as they ran for their lives from the communist machine-gunning, occasional jeeps slewing crazily into the 27 Brigade positions laden with survivors, dead and wounded. The Middlesex suffered several casualties from the fire of shaken Americans, driving forward unable to understand that they had passed into safety. The 'death ride' of the 2nd Division through the pass below Kunu-ri become one of the grimmest sagas of the Korean War. Through six miles of enemy fire, vehicles sought to smash their way past the blazing wreckage of those that had gone before. Infantrymen ran among them, seeking their own salvation, and rarely finding it. A dreadful paralysis of command and discipline overtook the division. Major Walt Killalie, commanding the division's mobile anti-aircraft battalion, saw men sitting motionless in their vehicles, incapable even of rousing themselves to return the hail of Chinese fire, merely waiting for death. Clusters of soldiers struggled to push wrecked vehicles off the road, falling as they did so. Others screamed and shouted in pain or fear. And the unemotional communist mortaring continued. Nightfall brought infantry attacks from the Chinese, ending in desperate close-quarter fighting among the shambles of vehicles and casualties on the road. Only a handful of men like Colonel James Skeldon, commanding the 2nd/38th Infantry, kept their heads and maintained their units' cohesion sufficiently to maintain an effective defence, and lead their survivors to safety.

Bill Shirk, a young gunner with the 15th Artillery, was newly returned to duty after a month in Osaka hospital recovering from a bullet wound he had received on the Pusan Perimeter, where he found himself in a convoy which was ambushed and almost wiped out. After that experience, he was reluctant to return to Korea. He hated the country. When the word came in late November to begin cleaning up the guns to return home, 'like everybody else, I felt really happy to be getting out of this stinking place.' But Korea had hardly started on the nineteen-year-old Ohian. In the pass at Kunu-ri, 'the order came – "Every man for himself". We dropped phosphorus grenades down the gun barrels, then we set about getting out.' Shirk started off with a group of eighteen men, hastily shedding his gaiters to move faster. By dawn, he was running clumsily in his overcoat, alone with an unknown major. They were trying to hide in a cluster of cornstacks when the Chinese reached them, and they were herded away into a large cave where they found some two hundred other American prisoners already assembled. A bitterness about the war, a sense of betrayal by his own superiors, was born in Shirk which remained undiminished by the ensuing two and a half years of captivity.[15]

Some men escaped in small groups, by taking to the hills. A few vehicles and even gun teams got through that night, or early the next morning, when American fighter-bomber support belatedly made some impact upon the enemy positions in the hills. The division's rearguard, the 23rd RCT commanded by Colonel Paul Freeman, was successfully diverted to the Anju road. But in that one afternoon, 2nd Division lost 3,000 men and almost all its transport and equipment, on the road from Kunu-ri. The division's history speaks of 'a magnificent stand ... Even in defeat, the "Indianhead" division proved to be a rock which held fast, giving other units an opportunity for survival.' The truth was sadder, and more bitter. Much of 2nd Division fell apart in those days. It was months before the formation was considered capable of fighting effectively again in Korea. 'In general, to achieve quick decision,' wrote Mao Tse Tung, 'we should attack a moving and not a stationary enemy.'[16] At Kunu-ri, the PLA ruthlessly implemented his dictum.

At last, quiet fell on the pass, and 27 Brigade understood that no more Americans would be coming that way. They left the great graveyard of MacArthur's hopes, and pressed on southwards, under increasing fire. American air strikes sought to blast the hills around the road into silence, but still the shooting went on. Major Willoughby remembered an insanely irrational moment when he saw machine-gun fire striking the road around his vehicle, and opened the door to let it pass through. Yet it was somewhere on that road that they heard a news broadcast in which it was reported that the British Prime Minister, Clement Attlee, had declared that Britain 'has no quarrel with the Chinese'.

On the road to Pyongyang, a growing element of panic was

overtaking the whole of Eighth Army. Rumours multiplied – of 20,000 Chinese straddling the line of retreat, of a communist regiment at a ford where a patrol discovered only two dead farmers and three dead horses. A British officer was shocked to attend a briefing at which his American regimental counterpart warned his subordinates: 'Remember – if you see a red Verey light, just get together everybody you can and head south.' Private David Fortune of the 2/35th Infantry felt 'numbed, stunned by the situation. We had believed that it was all over. Yet now we knew the war would end no time soon.' Fortune was captured on 2 January when his company was cut off. 'You guys better get out while you can,' a fugitive shouted to his platoon as he 'bugged out'. 'There's no end to them – the more you kill, the more they come.'[17] Fortune spent two and a half years in captivity.

Private James Waters of the 1/35th Infantry, 25th Division, had joined the army 'because I felt I had to get out of Joplin, Missouri'. On the morning of 26 November, his unit was marching in long files up a road some forty miles south of the Yalu, when the company commander was called to a battalion O Group. He returned two hours later. The word was passed from man to man, sitting stunned and disbelieving by the roadside: 'The Chinese are in the war, and they're behind us.' There was no firing that day, but when they made camp on a hilltop, they lay awake, jumpy and watchful. An elderly NCO, Sergeant Jennings, confided sadly to Waters in the darkness: 'I don't think I'm going to make it. I've just about had it – I'm not young any more.' Many men were taking counsel of their fears that night. The next morning, they began to walk south before dawn. Each soldier seemed to be trying to tiptoe, fearful that a rash sound would bring the communist hordes upon his head. At last, the stillness was broken. They heard the quad .50 calibre machine guns on a half-track firing, heard the shouts and screams of Chinese attackers. But still Waters' company marched on in darkness, past an abandoned field hospital, with a jeep full of dead medics lying beside it. Daylight brought Chinese mortaring, and casualties. Most were left behind. They quickened their pace, shedding sleeping bags, tents, heavy equipment to ease their burden. There were occasional brief scuffles with the enemy.

That day, and each day and night that followed, the sense of fear and desperate danger grew. They had no resupply, until one morning a jeep halted by the column, to disgorge cooks bearing hot chow. They had abandoned even their messkits, and held out their helmets to be filled with a mess of cereal and powdered eggs. The cooks' impatience to be gone – shouting 'Hurry up! Hurry up!' as the men queued before them – heightened their own fear. As they neared Pyongyang, Waters and his companions found themselves marching among a growing host of retreating Americans: 'Somewhere along that road, an orderly withdrawal became a disorderly withdrawal.'[18] A glimpse of oriental faces became sufficient to cause a local panic, until the men were confirmed as ROK troops. Their feet were lacerated and bleeding, young officers hobbling like old men. Men lost their units, and grew frightened in their loneliness amid a mob of soldiers and refugees harbouring so much fright.

The Argyll & Sutherland Highlanders marched south in style, each company led by its piper. The British had been fortunate enough to escape a mauling from the Chinese, but they were no less prey to hunger and exhaustion than the Americans. Officers urged on stragglers: 'The next man down this road will be Joe Stalin.' The men called their move from Kunu-ri to Sunchon 'the death march'. Sometimes they covered twenty miles in a night, amid the havoc of retreat all around them. Lieutenant Colin Mitchell used a map torn from the *Daily Telegraph* to brief his men – it was all he had. He and the other officers were under no delusions: 'Under these conditions, it was pointless to stand and fight. The almost inevitable result was to be overrun.' Even the toughest men were shattered by the experience of that withdrawal:

> I remember one of my company headquarters, a quiet, reliable chap, who was sitting on the ground near me, about to open a tin of baked beans. He suddenly stood up and screamed. He ran

wild-eyed into the middle of a paddy-field ignoring the sergeant-major's shouted orders to come back. I walked after him and he stood there waiting for me, holding the tin of beans like a grenade, shouting, 'don't come any nearer!' I did, and he flung the tin at me, but missed. When I came up to him, I just told him that I knew exactly how he felt, because I felt like that too, but we were all in this together and just had to stick it out or go under. At this he broke down and sobbed, then walked back with me to our position and resumed his place with the battalion.[19]

The men of Eighth Army, plodding south, were awed by the great pillars of flame and smoke from the supply dumps of Pyongyang, fired to keep them from the hands of the enemy. Private Waters met a tanker by his ditched monster, who told them sardonically: 'This vehicle requires a new part that costs $5. We do not have one. Therefore we must blow up this vehicle.' Pyongyang was abandoned on 5 December, leaving behind vast quantities of stores and equipment. Having lost 11,000 casualties dead, wounded, and missing in the first days of the Chinese offensive, Eighth Army was now in full retreat by land, sea, and air, its men fleeing from North Korea by every means available. It was fortunate for the reputation of United States arms that, while Walker's army hastened southwards in disarray, almost incapable of organised resistance, further east other Americans were salvaging at least a portion of honour from one of the most inglorious moments in their nation's military history.

8 » CHOSIN:
THE ROAD FROM THE RESERVOIR

On the drive north of the 38th Parallel, MacArthur had deliberately separated Eighth Army, under Walker, from the operations of X Corps, under his own Chief of Staff, General Edward Almond. The two divisions of X Corps – 7th and 1st Marine – landed on the east coast and moved north, miles out of ground contact with Eighth Army. Thus it was that, when the enemy struck, Almond and Walker's formations endured entirely separate nightmares, divided by the central spine of the North Korean mountains. All that they possessed in common were the horrors of weather, isolation, Chinese attack – and the threat of absolute disaster overtaking American arms.

Relations between General Almond and O. P. Smith of 1st Marine Division had been frigid since they came ashore at Inchon. Smith was thoroughly unhappy about the dispersal of X Corps strength on the advance north: 'I told Almond we couldn't make two big efforts. I said: "Either we go to the Yalu by Chosin, or by the north-west route, but not both." ' Almond, whatever his other shortcomings an undisputed driver of men, was exasperated by the sluggishness – even obstructionism – that he perceived in the Marines. Smith in his turn, profoundly suspicious of Almond's lust for glory, feared that sooner or later the corps commander's impatience would inflict a disaster upon his men: 'What I was trying to do was to slow down the advance and stall until I could pull up the 1st Marines behind us, and get our outfit together.'[1] The Marines' advance to the Chosin reservoir, and up its western

arm, had indeed been slow, because Smith insisted that at every
stage reserves of ammunition and supplies should be brought
forward and stockpiled: meanwhile, Almond urged haste to prevent the Chinese from destroying the vast dams at the reservoir,
which intelligence believed to be the communist intention.

By 25 November, two of Smith's three regiments – 5th and 7th
– had reached Yudam-ni at the western extremity of the reservoir,
and were scheduled to jump off on the 27th towards a link-up with
Eighth Army's northern movement at Mupyong. Thereafter, they
would strike for Kanggye and Manpojin on the Chinese border.
The 1st Marines were deployed along the main supply route
between Hagaru and Koto-ri, alongside some army elements. The
corps's rear coastal area was the responsibility of 3rd Division. On
the Marines' right, three battalions of 7th Division were moving
up the east side of the reservoir. The bulk of 7th Division was more
than sixty miles northwards, the most advanced American formation, behind the very banks of the Yalu.

Residual communist strength in North Korea was reported
by GHQ to be around 100,000 men – about the same as the UN's
front-line numbers – while some 40,000 communist guerrillas
and stragglers were believed to remain behind the front. In reality,
over 100,000 Chinese troops were already deployed on X Corps's
front alone. Whatever delusions persisted in the rear, the marines
who visited North Korean villages to raid for food, who talked to
villagers about the masses of men that had passed through, were
in little doubt about the scale of enemy activity. When Lieutenant-
Colonel Robert Taplett, commanding the 3/5th Marines, flew forward in a helicopter, he could see a maze of tracks and foxholes in
the mountain snow. 'Those damn holes are just crawling with
people,' said his pilot wonderingly.

1st Marine Division began to move forward on the morning of
27 November. That night, the Chinese launched violent assaults
not merely upon their leading elements, but for thirty miles down
their main – indeed, only – supply route to the coast, seventy-eight
miles to the south. To Marine officers in command posts among

Retreat from the
CHOSIN RESERVOIR

the positions at Yudam-ni, it seemed that every unit in the two regiments was reporting itself under attack that night. A Chinese grenade knocked out the switchboard of the 3/5th Battalion CP. One of its company commanders 'froze' in his position, and his men could not be moved until another officer was hastily dispatched to take his place. All through the hours of darkness, the Chinese hurled themselves again and again upon the company positions of the two Marine regiments. It is a remarkable tribute to the quality of units reconstituted only three months earlier, heavily manned by reservists, that they mounted so dogged a defence under the most appalling conditions. Almost every man who returned from the hills above the Chosin reservoir brought with him a little epic story of close-quarter combat, amid the flares, mortaring and grenade and small-arms duels. Although the Chinese broke into a succession of positions and inflicted severe casualties, nowhere did they succeed in causing the Marine companies to collapse.

By morning, the Marines were holding three isolated perimeters: at Yudam-ni, furthest north; at Hagaru, on the base of the reservoir; and at Koto-ri, another ten miles south. There was brief discussion among the Americans about continuing their own offensive. 'But I told Ray Murray: "Stop",' said General Smith. 'It was manifest we were up against a massive force out there.'[2] It was apparent to the Marines that their predicament was precarious. They were facing very large Chinese forces: some twelve Chinese divisions, it later emerged, were deployed in X Corps's area of operations. Hagaru, with its airstrip and supply dumps at the junction of the only escape route south, was defended only by one Marine battalion and such local army elements as could be scraped together to man a perimeter on the surrounding hills. The formations of X Corps were dispersed among hundreds of square miles of barren mountains. Many of the American positions were accessible only by a single track or road, appallingly vulnerable to isolation by an enemy who moved at will among the mountains. As soon as the scale of the Chinese offensive became apparent, there was only one prudent option open to Almond's forces: withdrawal to the coast. Yet for this to be possible, it was necessary for the Main Supply Route, the MSR, to be held open. And in those last days of November, the lonely track through the passes from Hungnam to Yudam-ni was a snowbound thread liable to snap at any moment. X Corps commander was always ready to find reason to attack O. P. Smith. Almond believed that he had ample cause for anger with the Marine general, in the weakness of the Hungnam garrison. X Corps had correctly perceived that the junction at the base of the Chosin reservoir was a vital position which must be held in strength. Now, Almond raged. Why had Smith left so few men to defend it? The Marine answered that he could never have pursued Almond's cherished advance from Yudam-ni with less than two regiments. Smith was furious that, even now, Almond was unwilling to recognise the urgency of their plight, and call off his offensive. It was two days before the Marines at

Yudam-ni received orders – or rather, consent – to withdraw. Meanwhile, Smith laboured by every means to strengthen the garrison at Hagaru.

*

The 235 men of 41 Independent Commando, Royal Marines, arrived at Koto-ri on 28 November, with orders to operate under X Corps. When transport and equipment had been found for them, it was intended that they should act as a reconnaissance group. But it now became a matter of urgency to reinforce the Hagaru perimeter with every available man. On the morning of 29 November, the Royal Marines, together with a company of US Marines and another of infantry, 922 men and 141 vehicles in all, were ordered north under the command of Lieutenant-Colonel Drysdale. There was no chance to feed the men before they marched. The British had just time to remove a section of 81mm mortars and .30 calibre Brownings from the crates in which they had been brought up from Hamhuing, before 'Task Force Drysdale' moved north.

They met resistance almost immediately. The British and American Marines deployed from their vehicles, and began painfully to clear the high ground overlooking the road. Yard by yard, under constant fire, they pushed forward, aided by a company of tanks which had arrived to support them. By 4.15 p.m., with darkness falling, they were only four miles north of Koto-ri. Drysdale radioed Hagaru to ask General Smith whether he was to keep coming. Smith answered that he needed every man he could get into the perimeter. After a delay while the tanks refuelled, the column pressed on into the darkness. To Drysdale's fury, the armoured company commander – 'an opinionated young man' – flatly rejected his request to distribute his seventeen tanks along the length of the convoy, and insisted that they should punch through in a body, at the front. As a result, when 'Task Force Drysdale' was ambushed by the Chinese in a defile known as 'Hellfire Valley', above the Changjin river some five miles from their starting point, the soft-skinned vehicles were unprotected. When the Chinese hit back in the midst of the convoy around 10 p.m., those in the rear were cut off. Some of the US Army company in the rear retired to Koto-ri without displaying much enthusiasm for a night battle against powerful enemy forces. Pockets of British and American Marines fought all night beside the road.

A mortar bomb hit the truck ahead of that carrying Marine Andrew Condron, a twenty-two-year-old radio operator from West Lothian. He and the others in his vehicle jumped down, and lay in the monsoon ditch beside the road, watching the dim shapes of Chinese soldiers flitting to and fro in the darkness. His carbine jammed at his first attempt to fire it, and he picked up an M1 rifle from a dead American lying nearby. They exchanged desultory fire with the enemy around them until, about 1 a.m., an officer ran up, and urged them to join him in an effort to break out. They collected some ammunition and grenades, and began to work their way across open ground. Condron was appalled to pass an American in agony by the roadside, on fire from burning phosphorus, screaming for someone to shoot him. The Marine lost track of his officer early on, and found himself with two other British rankers, wading an icy stream. There was a sudden shot, and the leading man fell. They heard American voices, at whom the outraged Marine with Condron shouted: 'You've killed my mate!' When the emotional temperature had cooled, the little group of British and Americans lay together in silence, listening to the firing and explosions among the convoy, now some half-mile distant. Condron hung his socks in a tree to dry, where they promptly froze. He put a beret on one foot, a camouflage net on the other under his boots. Condron was dressing the wound of a comatose Marine shot in the hip, when he glanced up to see a South Korean standing above him, wearing a snowcape and carrying a Thompson gun. The man grunted aggressively. 'Bugger off,' Condron grunted back. An American shouted hastily to the Scot: 'Hey buddy, you'd better drop that rifle fast – we've surrendered.' The 'South Korean' was a Chinese soldier.

Condron's brother was a Japanese prisoner-of-war in World War II. He had told the young Marine to ensure that he always carried the vital essentials of life on the battlefield, in case he himself was captured. Condron took heed, and stowed in his pack an emergency kit of razor blades, waterproof matches, vitamin pills, and two books of poetry – Burns and Fitzgerald. But all these things still lay in the distant truck. Like most of those who suffered the same fate in Korea, Condron passed into captivity with only the clothes on his back.[3]

Around fifty British and American soldiers and Marines, in all, surrendered at first light. Some others escaped back to Koto-ri. A few, like the British heavy weapon section, eventually got through to Hagaru in desperate straits from frostbite. Captain Pat Ovens also made good his escape on foot to the Marine lines. The leading elements of the survivors pressed on in their vehicles until, within sight of the American engineers working under floodlights to improve the runway inside the Hagaru perimeter, they were hit again. An abandoned tank blocked the road, and Chinese mortaring ignited a succession of vehicles. After another fierce firefight, the tank company and the surviving infantry struggled into Hagaru around midnight. The armour came first, smashing headlong through the defending American roadblock, crushing a jeep. The British, according to one of the Marines manning the road position, appeared looking more like a raiding party than a military unit: 'Don't shoot, Yank!' Colonel Drysdale himself was slightly wounded by a grenade fragment in the arm, and less than a hundred of his Royal Marines were still behind him. 'I never thought I should be so glad to see an American,' said Lieutenant Peter Thomas wryly. Thomas brought in the last two vehicles of the convoy, both loaded with wounded. Sixty-one British Marines had been lost on the road from Koto-ri, out of Task Force Drysdale's total of 321 casualties and seventy-one vehicles destroyed. 41 Commando became garrison reserve, under the command of Ray Murray of the 5th Marines.

*

The little town of Hagaru lay in a cleft in the mountains that otherwise appeared to the Marines to occupy the entire surface of North Korea. For those brief winter weeks of 1950 when it was held by the Americans, Hagaru resembled a nineteenth-century Arctic mining camp. Snow coated the peasant houses, the Marines' tents, the tanks and trucks, the supply dumps and artillery pieces and command vehicles. The local sawmill was kept in perpetual motion by the engineers, cutting timber to strengthen positions and assist the vital labour of airfield construction. Thin plumes of smoke from a hundred fires and stoves curled upwards on rare days when the air was still. More often, they were whipped aside by the driving wind that stung every inch of exposed human flesh. At first, men marvelled at the depths to which the thermometer could sink: -10, -14, -20 at night. Then they became as numb to the misery of the cold as to everything else. Many said that it was not only their capacity for physical activity that diminished, but even their speed of thought. General Smith himself found it increasingly difficult even to move his jaw to speak. The simplest action – loading a weapon, unbolting a steel section, rigging an aerial – became a laborious, agonising marathon. The jeeps were kept running continually. In some cases, their headlights were run on cables into key positions such as the sickbay and operations tents, to supplement the feeble coleman lanterns. To start an engine required hours of work – thawing its moving parts, persuading its frozen oil to liquefy. Blood plasma froze. Medical orderlies were obliged to carry morphia syrettes in their mouths, to maintain their fluidity. For the men, the miraculously effective space heaters in the tents became the very focus of life. All this, before the enemy had even begun to take a hand.

The battle for Hagaru was a strange affair, like so many of the actions of that first Korean winter. By day, there was little enemy activity, and the Americans could move with almost complete freedom, while their own air strikes hammered the communists' presumed positions. Then, with the coming of night, the struggle began in earnest. All through the hours of darkness, the defenders fought back the Chinese attacks, glimpsing their enemy briefly by the light of flares and gunflashes, perceiving him above all by the eerie sounds he brought with him – the bugles, the whistles, the banshee yells. For many men, the greatest fear was that when the moment came, when the communist wave broke upon their positions, the cold would have jammed their life-saving weapons. After the first November battles, rumours swept the UN armies that some men – allegedly of 1st Cavalry Division – had been surprised by the Chinese in their sleeping bags, and bayoneted where they lay, unable to extricate themselves in time. Thereafter, most men on the line were either themselves unwilling, or were forbidden by their officers, to zip up their bags to sleep.

On the forward positions, the cold was so appalling that an extraordinary improvisation, perhaps unique to this campaign, became necessary: the introduction of 'warming tents', a few hundred yards behind the front, where every two or three hours men retreated to thaw themselves a few degrees, to restore circulation to their deadened limbs, in order that they might be capable of resistance when the Chinese came again. How the Chinese themselves coped, lacking any such refinements yet presumably at the same extremities of human tolerance, men marvelled to speculate. When the garrison received an occasional night air strike in support, they marked the pilots' aiming points by firing solid tracer. The optical effects of battle below zero were astonishing: mortar bombs flew through the sky like rockets, leaving fiery trails in the ice-cold air.

The garrison was a hotchpotch. There were two companies of the 1st Marines; some gunners conscripted as infantry; an army engineer company sent to build a command post for General Almond, but now pushed into the line; a ragtag of American and South Korean line of communication personnel, deployed on the hills as reluctant riflemen. It was a matter of pride to a platoon of army signallers that, during one Chinese attack, they successfully held their positions while the engineers broke. One night, East Hill was lost, overlooking the vital airstrip. A scratch force of two hundred cooks, drivers, and stragglers was ruthlessly rounded up from all over the perimeter and herded forward to counter-attack at dawn, protected by an air strike. Only some seventy-five were still present when they mustered at the start-line – the remainder had simply drifted away into the darkness. But they regained part of the hill, and G Company of 3/1st Marines completed the job. One night, a company clerk standing in as a heavy machine-gunner was appalled to see a file of Chinese advancing upon his roadblock. Ignorant even of how to elevate the barrel of his gun, he could only lift the legs of the gun's tripod to bring fire to bear upon them. Fortunately, the company runner then woke up and took over, to more effect.

The Americans seemed to enjoy the company of their little British party of 41 Commando. They found Colonel Drysdale himself somewhat reserved, although the effects of exhaustion and his wound undoubtedly influenced his demeanour. The two nations set about reconciling their military inconsistencies – the British habit of calling a mortar-round a bomb, while the Americans called it a shell; the instinctive British parsimony with ammunition, when the Americans believed in intensive bombardment if the rounds were there. A Marine rifle company commander sought to illustrate his approach to fire support to Drysdale: 'Suppose we were going up that hill over there – we'd expect to put in two hundred rounds before we left the start-line.' The British officer ruminated for a moment, then remarked drily: 'We wouldn't go up the hill at all. We'd go around it.' The British insisted upon shaving each morning, in the interests of morale and discipline. Most Marines preferred to cultivate a stubble. The Commandos found the Americans' carelessness about showing lights at night almost incomprehensible. Their formidable Regimental Sergeant-Major, Jim Baines, tore a ferocious strip off a dim figure whose cigarette he saw glowing in a nearby foxhole, and was embarrassed to find an American officer hastily stubbing out his butt. But if the Commandos and Marines found some of each other's habits incomprehensible, they also formed a deep admiration for the tenacity and determination common to both corps. 'I felt entirely comfortable fighting alongside the Marines,' said Colonel Drysdale.

Each day, as the men on the hills watched the C-47s taxi along the frozen airstrip to collect their loads of wounded, it was impossible not to feel a deep pang of envy for those who would be safe in warm beds, far out of range of enemy fire, within a few hours. It was too much to expect, in those circumstances, that they should count their blessings: while the Chinese deployed immense numbers of infantry, well supported by mortars, they possessed virtually no artillery. The centre of the perimeter was thus almost immune to direct fire. The predicament of X Corps would have been incomparably worse, had their enemies possessed the normal support weapons of a modern army.

*

Among a host of tragic spectacles that MacArthur's forces were to behold that Korean winter, the arrival of the survivors of the 7th Division's 'Task Force Faith' at Hagaru remained one of the most vivid. Across the great sweep of ice covering the reservoir, the Marines on the perimeter saw handfuls of men stumbling, limping, even crawling. Some were without weapons. Most had lost their equipment. Many were at the extremities of frostbite. 'Some of these men were dragging themselves on the ice,' wrote a Marine officer, 'some had gone crazy and were walking in circles. It was pitiful.'[4] The Marines hauled sledges out on to the reservoir, and brought in all the soldiers they could find. But only 385 of the thousand survivors from a force of 2,500 were considered sufficiently fit to take their place in the line at Hagaru.

Yet as late as 27 November, the day that the elements of the 7th Division east of the reservoir at Sihung-ni first met the Chinese, General Almond had flown in by helicopter personally to emphasise his determination that the American offensive should not be deflected. 'We're still attacking and we're going all the way to the Yalu,' he said. 'Don't let a bunch of Chinese laundrymen stop you.' In the days that followed, X Corps only slowly began to understand the disaster that was unfolding east of the reservoir. 'We didn't see it as a tragedy, because we had no idea at all how terrible their losses were, until they came out,' said one of Almond's staff. Yet from the night of 27 November until their withdrawal in ruins three days later, the men of 'Task Force Faith' – as 32nd RCT became when their original commander was killed – found themselves under constant attack from the Chinese, who drove them back down the east bank of the Chosin reservoir, bleeding terribly as they marched.

*

Private Don McAlister was the son of a Kansas farming family who had spent his teens trying any job that would earn a buck: dishwashing, sawmilling, farmwork. It was a grindingly hard life. After spending the winter of 1949 clearing a hedgerow, he and his cousin decided to join the army, and try to get a training in the engineers. McAlister was still in basic training in June 1950. He found himself abruptly shipped to the 1/32nd Infantry, 7th Division. He felt an instinctive sympathy for the South Korean farmers, whose poverty seemed only a degree or two worse than that from which he himself had come. He greatly admired his battalion commander, Don Faith, who walked every battlefield with a cane rather than a weapon. He had much less confidence in some of the other officers, and sometimes suspected that the battalion commander did, too. On the night of 27 November, McAlister was on an outpost position when the Chinese attacked, in overwhelming strength. The BAR team and Browning gunners fired for as long as they could, but at last the Chinese swept over the position. The American survivors ran back to their own company front as fast as they could go. They fought all night. McAlister at one point found himself physically wrestling with two Chinese soldiers for possession of his BAR. The company commander was killed, the hillside littered with the bodies of dead Chinese and Americans. At dawn, when the attacks stopped, he and his section were sent back to their outpost. To their astonishment, lying in the bottom of a foxhole they found two of their own men, alive and unharmed. They had successfully played dead when the position was lost.

All that day, Marine and Navy aircraft flew strikes against enemy concentrations in front of the Americans. But that night, the Chinese came again. Their second assault pushed back McAlister's A Company halfway down their hill line. They hung on only with urgent support from their neighbours of B Company. As they fought from foxhole to foxhole, American fortunes see-sawing through the night, McAlister lost his pack, his sleeping bag and extra rations. The bag had been important not merely for sleeping, but to stand in through the long hours in freezing holes. About 4 a.m., the battalion began to withdraw. Many of the machine-gunners covering their departure were lost, as the Chinese raced forward in pursuit. The 1st Battalion reached the positions of their own gunners and other infantry to find that they too had been attacked and surrounded. It was now that Colonel Faith assumed command of all the survivors.

That day, like its predecessor, the Americans spent stamping their feet in the desperate cold, trying to improve their positions for the night, and watching the air strikes. The Chinese harassed and sniped at them. That night, they lost their positions in one attack, and were compelled to counter-attack to retake them, all the time losing men. The following morning, 30 November, supplies and ammunition were air-dropped to the perimeter.

Retrieving them was difficult [wrote McAlister], because the Chinese wanted them as much as we did, and some were dropped far out of reach. Of what we got, we found that a lot of the belts and clips were damaged, and we had to work in the cold refilling the BAR magazines. That night my BAR assistant got hit by rifle fire in the eye and had blood all over his face. He was still alive and in a lot of pain. I called the medic and pushed him down in the hole, because I had to keep firing as the enemy was almost on top of us. After a while the medic came and took him to the rear, and I never saw him

after that. Later I ran out of ammo, and reached for the rifle
that my buddy had left. There was no ammo in it either. I was
reaching for my .45 when a grenade was thrown into the hole.
The next thing that I remember, I was back in the centre by
the artillery, but all I could see around me was men that had
been wounded or killed.

I left the area on a truck with the rest of the wounded. We
were being fired on constantly by enemy machine-guns. Our
planes were trying to help by dropping napalm between our
troops and theirs. As a result some of our men got burned
pretty bad and were put aboard the trucks with us wounded.
I will never forget the smell of human flesh after that. A lot of
them died before too long.

McAlister himself was hit shortly afterwards by a stray bullet
which rendered his right arm useless. Then the trucks were halted
by a Chinese roadblock. Their captors ordered the occupants out.
When those who could walk had climbed down, to their sick
horror they watched North Korean soldiers run along the line,
setting fire to the vehicles, together with those who remained
aboard them. For several days that followed, McAlister and his
comrades were held captive close to the road. Then, numb and
at the limits of exhaustion, they were gathered together, to be
marched north. McAlister sat down on the running-board of a
burned-out American truck. He could not bring himself to move
when a Korean guard ordered him to his feet. He was hit twice,
hard, on the head, and passed out.

When I came to, I was alone. I guess they figured I was dead. I
stumbled around for what seemed to be hours, and finally got
back to the lake. I could only walk for a few minutes before
falling down. My feet were frozen and I couldn't use my hands
much. Somehow I got started towards Hagaru-ri. At last I met a
'big ole Marine colonel' who carried me to a truck, and onto
an aid station from which I was flown to Japan. I had frostbite
in both feet and hands, shrapnel in the head, and my right
wrist was almost severed. I was in hospital until 31 May, 1952.[5]

When the predicament of Task Force Faith became apparent, General Almond blamed O. P. Smith for the Marines' failure to leave a force at Hagaru strong enough now to send a relief force to the 7th Division's aid. At Almond's insistence, an attempt was made to cut a path up the east side of the reservoir to link up with the retreating units. But this rapidly encountered heavy opposition. It was abandoned. Colonel Faith spoke to Hagaru for the last time through a Marine air liaison officer's radio link: 'Unless someone can help us, I don't have much hope that anybody's going to get out of this.' He was told: 'We are bringing in an awful lot of air support, but that's all we can give you. We just don't have enough people here to risk losing our hold on the foot of the reservoir.'

'I understand,' said Faith.

This was his last contact with Hagaru. Air support could do nothing by night, when the fate of Task Force Faith was sealed, and its courageous commanding officer killed. 'Whenever I hear the words "task force", I shudder,' said a distinguished Marine veteran later.[6] In Korea, all too often, the phrase became an apology for a makeshift collection of vehicles and men, committed to disaster.

A staff officer who entered the general officers' mess at Hungnam the evening of the arrival of the news of the destruction of Task Force Faith found inside it, alone by the stove, General David Barr, the 7th Division's commander. He was sobbing quietly. 'Barr was a nice man,' said the officer later, 'but he had no personal magnetism, and should never have been permitted to command a division at war. He was too old, and too soft. The Chosin campaign finished him.' Barr was relieved of his command and sent home.

If General Almond's chief preoccupation in mid-November had been to seize North Korean real estate, at whatever cost to the dispersal of his corps, by the end of that month he had become as hasty in his anxiety to get his command back to the coast. As the weight of Chinese forces confronting X Corps and threatening its Main Supply Route became apparent, those privy to the intelligence reports felt a growing, gnawing fear that they were close to the brink of a great disaster for American arms. 'I really thought we'd had it,' said Colonel Al Bowser, G-3 of 1st Marine Division. 'We did not know the detail of what was happening to Eighth Army, but we knew that there was only eighty miles of open flank on our left. We knew the size of the Chinese forces against us – and we didn't at that time understand their shortcomings. I would not have given a nickel for our chances of making it. Fortunately, a lot of people down the line could not see the overall position as I could see it, and continued to conduct themselves as if they were going to get out.'[7]

Fresh argument now broke out between the army and the US Marines, precipitated by the newly acute sense of crisis: the soldiers favoured abandoning all heavy equipment and artillery, and pulling back south as fast as 1st Marine Division could march and ride. O. P. Smith, however, was determined to conduct what he termed 'an orderly and honourable withdrawal'. He would bring out all his vehicles and guns. 'Don't worry about your equipment,' Almond told Smith impatiently one morning at Hagaru. 'Once you get back, we'll replace it all.' Smith said: 'I'm not going to do that. This is the equipment we fight with.'

'Okay,' said Almond wearily. 'I just wanted you to know that we would replace it.' When the two men parted, Smith turned to Colonel Bowser: 'This guy is a maniac. He's nuts. I can't believe he's saying these things.'[8]

On this occasion, it was Smith's will which prevailed, that formed the basis for the legend of the retreat from Chosin, perhaps the only really creditable American military performance of that winter campaign of 1950. On 1 December, the 10,000 men of 5th and 7th Marines began their epic fourteen-mile fighting retreat from Yudam-ni to Hagaru, battalions leapfrogging each other southwards, pressed at each pass by the Chinese, who were machine-gunning and mortaring every point upon the road upon which their weapons would bear. The Marines could move forward only by clearing the ground commanding the road in front of mem, yard by bitterly contested yard. The 3/7th, leading the assault, became bogged down, and Taplett's 3/5th were ordered to pass through and take up the lead. When night came, with the men utterly exhausted by wading in snow up to their hips on the hillside, Taplett asked if his battalion might halt, at least for long enough to establish its own precise location. Permission was refused: 'Attack, keep attacking,' he was told. Item Company of Taplett's battalion was almost wiped out on the first day. Taplett himself lost four runners attempting to pass messages to its commander. A single tank led the column, followed by Taplett's command jeep, directing the infantry on the shoulders above the road. Ray Murray appeared at Taplett's jeep and demanded to know why the attack was stalled.

'We can't even get artillery support,' said Taplett.

'We've got trouble behind us, too,' explained Murray.

'If you want to get out of here,' said Taplett flatly, 'you'll give the guys at the front the support.'[9]

In a sea of mountains reaching to the horizon, it was impossible for the infantry to reach and command the higher ground. They could seek only to hold the shoulders and suppress the Chinese small-arms fire while the great regimental train crawled along the road below. It was fortunate for the Americans that the Chinese now appeared to have outrun the artillery they had brought down on the marines at Yudam-ni. The Marines could see communist troops swarming on the hills around them. Without the dedicated support of the Marine air wings, few men believed they would ever have made it. Even Marine pilots who were tasked to fly interdiction missions against targets further north kept a bomb, a rack of rockets, or a few seconds of cannon ammunition to expend in close support of their own people, on the way home. Men marvelled at the great gusher of snow, the black impact on the hillside, as each Skyraider unloaded its ordnance. Prosaically it reminded Major Ed Simmons 'of a giant bird taking a crap'.[10]

On the one day when blustering snow and low cloud made air support impossible, the column scarcely moved. Every few hours, a group of Chinese succeeded in breaking through to the road, disabling a vehicle, blocking the route. Then the Americans were compelled to counter-attack, to shift the wreckage, before they could get movement started again. Even without the intervention of the enemy, mechanical failure or a moment's carelessness by a driver would block the road with a stranded or ditched vehicle. There were difficult decisions: whether to keep the artillery moving, or suffer the delays of causing guns to unlimber on the road, to provide urgent support for the infantry. It was an agonisingly slow business, by day and by night, for men crippled by exhaustion and the weather, the inescapable elements. The cold seemed to gnaw into their bodies, sapping reserves of strength, making every movement painfully slow and clumsy.

The first men of 1st Marine Division entered the perimeter at Hagaru on the afternoon of the 3rd, the last on the evening of the following day. Taplett's battalion was reduced to 326 effectives out of some 2,000 whom he had commanded at Yudam-ni. Many of the casualties were suffering only from frostbite, but the serious cases still required evacuation from the overworked airstrip. It was also found necessary to introduce rigorous security on the runway, to prevent stragglers from sneaking aboard one of the C-47 casevac aircraft that could offer them a priceless passage to safety. The aircraft that flew out wounded brought in supplies and some replacements, many of them men wounded on the Naktong or in Seoul. 'The feeling now was – "let's get the hell out of this",' said Taplett. ' "This is too much for us with our resources". It was hard to take, for men who had been told that the war was won, who were looking forward to that big parade we had been promised in San Francisco.'

*

The performance of 1st Marine Division in desperate circumstances began to command the attention of America, so hungry for heroic news at a moment when there was so little to be had. O. P. Smith captured headlines all over the country when he told correspondents who flew into Hagaru on 4 December: 'Gentlemen, we are not retreating. We are merely advancing in another direction.' His remark was interpreted as a magnificent defiance of reality. Yet as he said afterwards, it was also tactically accurate, as the great military historian S. L. A. Marshall perceived: '"Slam" was the only one who understood that what we were doing really was attacking in another direction, because you couldn't withdraw when you were completely surrounded,' said Smith.

The feud – for it was nothing less – between Smith and Almond became a focal point of controversy both during the campaign, and in the recriminations after it ended. At times, the Marines almost seemed to relish the X Corps commander's misjudgements. During the struggle to hold the Hagaru perimeter, Smith took bleak pleasure in the discovery of a group of big treadway trucks with winches, which Almond had dispatched to prepare his Corps Command Post, when he believed that he was presiding over an administrative advance to the Chinese border. Officers who flew down to Hamhuing returned with scornful tales of the china, napkins, fresh fruit and meat flown in from Japan for the corps commander's table.

Almond seemed to lack any instinct for identifying himself with the men of his command in their brutal predicament. One morning, he flew into Hagaru from his headquarters, and sought to make himself agreeable to some of the Marines on the perimeter. 'Well, men, and how are you today? Pretty cold, isn't it.' The bearded, muffled scarecrows peered out at him from the inch or two of exposed flesh around their eyes. 'Do you know I wear a plate?' persisted Almond conversationally. 'When I got up this morning, there was a film of ice on the glass by my bed.' 'That's too f-ing bad, General,' said one of these men who could not dare to dream of ever seeing a bed again. Almond strolled on, oblivious of the impression he had made. It was a soldier, a member of Almond's staff, and not a Marine, who recounted witnessing that incident.[11]

Yet some able officers retained great respect for the X Corps commander's abilities: 'I consider Almond was an excellent corps commander,' said General Lemuel Shepherd, commanding the Fleet Marines. 'He was energetic, forceful, brave, and in many ways did a good job under most difficult conditions. He and O. P. just didn't get along.'[12] Ed Rowney and Al Haig, both officers who served on Almond's staff in Korea and rose to high rank in the US Army, retained a lifelong respect for their old commander. Lieutenant-Colonel Ellis Williamson, Almond's G-3, took an ambivalent view: 'O. P. Smith wasn't a team player at all. He just wanted to do what he wanted. Ned Almond was one of the most energetic, dedicated officers I have ever known. He was so energetic, that at times he was tactically careless. He could not visualise himself being wrong. He was almost as bad as MacArthur in this. Once he had made up his mind that something was so, he was just not listening any more.'[13] The evidence is overwhelming that O. P. Smith was indeed a slow and cautious commander. Likewise, his habit of lapsing into sturdy silence when confronted with Almond's tantrums precluded any possibility of understanding between the two men. Smith was disgusted by Almond's obsession with achieving a personal triumph on the battlefield. If fortune had fallen otherwise, if Almond had been granted his opportunity to lead a Patton-like pursuit, a dash for victory, he might indeed have earned his place in military history, while Smith would have been remembered as a plodding encumbrance. Instead, however, on the road back from Chosin, Smith's dogged, imperturbable leadership not only saved the honour of 1st Marine Division, but the reputation of American arms in Korea. Almond, on the other hand, was branded by many as the commander whose impatience and overweening personal ambition came within a hairbreadth of creating a catastrophe.

*

Although the first great danger to 1st Marine Division had been overcome by the successful withdrawal to Hagaru, there were no delusions about the difficulties of the next stage. At Koto-ri, when officers of the 1st Marines were briefed about the plan for the movement of the 5th and 7th, there was obvious concern about its feasibility. But 'Chesty' Puller, whose capacity for histrionics had markedly not been diminished by circumstances, climbed on a ration box beside the space heater in the briefing tent, and harangued his team: 'I don't give a good goddam how many Chinese laundrymen there are between us and Hungnam. There aren't enough in the world to stop a Marine regiment going where it wants to go! Christ in His Mercy will see us through.'

On 6 December, 1st Marine Division set out on the eleven-mile journey from Hagaru to Koto-ri. It was intended that the entire formation should be clear of the base of the reservoir by nightfall, but the slow progress of the vanguard caused the rear elements to linger at Hagaru into the darkness, fighting off the Chinese who began to descend from the hills and bring down fierce fire on the road. Finally, sluggishly, the last Americans pulled out. They left behind vast dumps of stores, burned or destroyed to keep them from the Chinese. Yet one cargo the Marines insisted upon taking with them, to the renewed exasperation of X Corps staff: their own dead. Some British Marines found it macabre to advance alongside trucks from which the frozen limbs of the corpses protruded, uncovered. Smith's men were merely determined that, dead or alive, the entire division should make it back. 'We were grateful for what the cold had done to those bodies,' said Robert Tyack, a British Marine. 'You were looking at a chunk of frozen meat, rather than a messy, stinking corpse.'[14] The march took thirty-eight hours through the snow, under constant harassment from the Chinese. Not every Marine was a hero. When the Chinese broke through close to the road, it proved essential for American officers to stay close to their men, to drive them to respond. Lacking immediate leadership, some exhausted men were prone to lapse into a ditch, and lie huddled, too numb to trouble to fire back. Robert Tyack remembered vividly a moment when his mate fell asleep on a hillside as they scraped a position with their bayonets, and furiously shook off every attempt to rouse him: 'Leave me! If I don't wake, what the hell?' Stragglers had to be kicked, pushed, cajoled. Those who stopped never started again.

When they were not under direct fire, men plodded wearily beneath the ice-laden telegraph poles, their helmets and weapons and clothing decked in crusts of snow. It was better to feel the pain in their feet. The thousands of men who no longer possessed any sensation in their boots were suffering from various extremes of frostbite. Once again, as on the withdrawal from Yudam-ni, while the thousand-vehicle convoy crawled along the road, leap-frogging battalions cleared the high ground above. When they passed the dozens of burned-out vehicles from Task Force Drysdale's battleground, they gathered up the frozen dead, and to their utter astonishment found one wounded man in a hut by the road, still alive.

Clearing the road from Hagaru to Koto-ri cost the Marines another 103 killed and 506 wounded; also, the loss of all but 13 of the 160 Chinese PoWs they were marching south. When the PoW contingent came under fire from the hills, they broke and ran from the road, causing the Marines to shoot them down. Their arrival at Koto-ri, the reunion with the garrison on its perimeter, was another emotional landmark, celebrated with bear-hugs between men clumsy in their layers of clothing, rejoicing to have survived another desperate stage of their journey. Men who had been fighting at Koto-ri searched the ranks of those from Hagaru for friends and even relations. Corporal Selwyn Handler of the 2/1st looked for his brother Irwin among the men of B Company, 5th Marines. For hours, he stood hunched by the road as the gaunt files marched in, peering between raised collars and lowered helmets for the familiar face he had last seen at Wonsan. Irwin was eighteen, and planned to be an optometrist. He was one of those who never made it down the road from Yudam-ni.

Among the few scrubby trees and the forest of tents in the overcrowded perimeter at Koto-ri, the dead were at last buried in a grave blasted from the iron-frozen earth. There was an old-fashioned little squabble when General Smith insisted that the indomitable *Herald Tribune* correspondent Marguerite Higgins should be evacuated by air, despite her enraged protests of sexual discrimination: 'There are a lot of good Marines who are getting frostbite,' said O. P., 'and if you march down with these Marines, you will probably get frostbite, and then somebody is going to have to take care of you. I am sure these Marines will see that you are taken care of, and we haven't got men for that kind of business.' Smith's chivalrous concern almost misfired when the aircraft carrying Higgins and General Lem Shepherd came under heavy Chinese fire as it took off. 'My God, Maggie,' said Shepherd as they sat hunched together watching the tracer pass beneath them, 'won't it be an awful scandal if the two of us are found crashed together?'

With 15,000 men and almost 1,500 vehicles crowded into the perimeter at Koto-ri, there was precious little room for movement. The new arrivals blasted themselves foxholes with C-3 demolition sticks, and stripped every house in the little town to provide roofing and firewood. There was a moment of raw comedy when the 'recreation packs' air-dropped to the division were discovered to include contraceptives: 'What the **** do they think we are doing with those Chinese?' If the pressure of enemy attack had diminished, that of the cold never did so. Men carried C-ration tins under their armpits, wore one of their two canteens under their clothing, to keep it usable.

A new and serious difficulty developed when it was learned that the bridge over the gorge in the Funchilin Pass, a few miles south of Koto-ri, had been destroyed by the Chinese for the third time in the battle, this time irreparably. The only conceivable means of getting Smith's Marines through was to air-drop and lay a new treadway bridge. Could it be done? Lieutenant-Colonel John Partridge, the divisional engineer officer, overflew the gap, making notes about the equipment that would be needed to bridge the thirty-foot culvert: 'I got you across the Han river,' he told Smith reassuringly. 'I got you the airfield here. I'll get you a bridge.' In the south, a young engineer captain experimented with parachuting a bridge section, which smashed on impact. 'It's okay – we'll use bigger parachutes and the next rehearsal will go fine,' he reassured the Marine headquarters. 'We don't have time for a next rehearsal. Next time is for real,' he was told bleakly. Eight bridge sections were parachuted into the perimeter at Koto-ri. Six were recovered intact. The culvert was bridged.

The routine – if such a word does not diminish the nature of the ordeal – for the march from Koto-ri to Hamhung was identical with that from Hagaru. Some men trudged along the road, among the vehicles, while others took their turn 'ridge-running', sweeping the shoulders of the high ground above the column. When the snow squalls came, it was sometimes impossible even to see the man a few yards in front. And still, every few hours, parties of Chinese managed to work close enough to put in fire somewhere on the column. 'Aw, quit horsing around,' said Corporal Handler of the 2/1st in some exasperation, when his buddy, 'a kid named Freudenberg', began to pull wounded men out of a truck that suddenly came under fire, only to topple over sideways into the snow. But Freudenberg was dead.

Not all the memories of that march were heroic. Colonel Taplett of the 3/5th had a ferocious argument on the road with an army officer who suddenly sought to get his men into the column in front of Taplett's battalion. The Marine was disgusted, since he knew that the army officer had been instructed to bring up the rear, behind the 5th. At the rear of the great snake of Marines and their 1,400 vehicles, some 3,000 refugees struggled with their carts and pitiful possessions. It was critical for the American rearguard to maintain a clear field of fire between themselves and the Koreans. Desperate measures became necessary in order to achieve this. Finally, the divisional engineers blew a bridge behind the Marines. The Koreans were left on the other side, gazing hopelessly into the chasm.

*

On 10 December, the first men of the great Marine column began to trickle into the port of Hamhung. The first ships of a vast amphibious armada awaited them. Many Marines, including their most senior officers, believed that they could easily have held a perimeter around the port through the winter, a formidable enclave deep in North Korean territory. But by now, the Dai Ichi had no stomach for such dangerous gestures. Rather than a stronghold, a perimeter at Hamhung could become a vast beleaguered fortress. Unit by unit, 100,000 men of the US Army, the Marines, the ROKs boarded the ships and sailed away for Pusan. Behind them, an orgy of looting and destruction was taking place, as one of the greatest supply dumps in Korea was stripped by civilians, or blown up by engineers. Pillars of black smoke plumed along the horizon behind the waterfront. As the last Marines departed, thousands of civilian refugees boarded the ships behind them, taking a last chance to escape the return of Kim Il Sung. On 24 December, with the evacuation completed, the US Navy unleashed a huge bombardment on the abandoned port, blasting its facilities and remaining dumps into wreckage. It was more a gesture of frustration, of embittered anger and disappointment, than of military utility. The Marine performance had been heroic. They had retired from the Chosin reservoir in column of units, with virtually all their heavy equipment and transport intact, maintaining the cohesion of the division to the end. But X Corps's battle was lost. The Marines alone had suffered 4,418 battle and 7,313 non-battle casualties, the latter mostly minor cases of frostbite. From subsequent PoW interrogations and captured documents, the Chinese were believed to have suffered some 37,500 losses in the Chosin campaign, many of these from the cold. The communist army endured privations more dreadful than those of the Americans. In the last stages of the American march to the coast, and through the evacuation, X Corps suffered scarcely at all from Chinese intervention. The enemy, too, was spent. He had outrun such supply lines as he possessed, and his men were at the extremities of misery from hunger and cold. But the formations of the People's

Liberation Army who inherited the wreckage of Hamhung in the last days of 1950 could at least exult in the certainty of strategic achievement. They had driven the US X Corps headlong out of North Korea.

9 » THE WINTER OF CRISIS

1. The Big Bug-Out

As Walker's Eighth Army reeled before the Chinese offensive in the first days of December, one morning Colonel Paul Freeman of the 23rd Infantry turned bitterly to his executive officer: 'Look around here,' he said. 'This is a sight that hasn't been seen for hundreds of years: the men of a whole United States Army fleeing from a battlefield, abandoning their wounded, running for their lives.'[1] Freeman was among those few senior soldiers in Korea who never lost their grip, who remained bewildered to the end of their lives about the fashion in which their commanders and their comrades allowed the collapse of the American army in North Korea in the winter of 1950. Freeman watched with pride his own 1st Battalion, holding the Chinese on the Chongchon for thirty hours; his regiment undertaking thirteen successive redeployments without losing a man. Suddenly, he received an air-dropped message from 2nd Division 'to extricate ourselves as best we could', and retired under cover of a powerful artillery barrage. Only then did he begin to discover what was happening to the rest of the army: in 25th Division, only the 27th Infantry held together effectively. In 2nd Division, Freeman's regiment remained the only combat-effective unit by the turn of the year.

Private Pete Schultz, a platoon runner in A Company of the 1/23rd, had been feeling somewhat dejected about the promise of MacArthur's 'home for Christmas': 'Here I was, full of life, eighteen years old, fresh out of basic training, and about as green as they come. I wanted to see some action.'[2] He spent the night of 25 November crouching in a foxhole listening to the intense firing all around him, without the remotest idea what was going on. A small-town boy from Kansas, Schultz found the action that he wanted in the next few days. The memories merged into a blur: picking among abandoned supply dumps as they retreated; manning a .30 calibre machine gun, watching the tracer arch towards a cluster of Chinese on the next ridgeline; running to clamber up on the hulls of their supporting tanks when they heard the engines rev up, a sure sign that they were about to move. They feared above all being left behind, finding themselves last out. 'A lot of men convinced themselves that each was the last man left in Eighth Army,' said Lieutenant Carl Bernard of 21st Infantry.[3]

Lieutenant Karl Morton of the 5th RCT found the first reports of the retreat incomprehensible, for his unit had scarcely been engaged. The first symptom of defeat was the absence of transport to carry them back. They began to walk. And as they walked, day after day their morale sunk. They did not fight, but they heard rumours. Faster, faster, they were constantly warned, lest you be cut off by the Chinese. Morton's thighs became raw, agonising, with the constant slapping of wet fatigue cloth against them. One of his corporals walked with a toilet roll on his rifle barrel, in permanent misery from diarrhoea until they somewhere found him a packet of cornstarch to solve the problem. One day, they watched from a roadblock as men of the 2nd Division moved past, 'in awful disarray'. Only one black battalion, led by a ramrod-straight, white-haired colonel, still appeared to possess all its equipment. As they marched on, and on, they discarded gear to lighten their burdens: rocket launchers went first; then spare clothing, ammunition, even sleeping bags. One evening at dusk, they saw a solitary soldier pedalling manically past them on a bicycle. They tried to stop him: 'Hey, what's going on up there?' The cyclist did not check, but shouted back over his shoulder: 'Hell of a lot of Chinamen!' As the supply system cracked, men grew desperate in their hunger. Morton saw two soldiers discover an

US infantry amid a characteristic Korean winter landscape.

General Matthew Ridgway with one of his divisional commanders.
Note the grenade on his webbing, which became a personal hallmark.

A soldier of the Gloucesters with communist prisoners. The lack of tension among all concerned suggests that this, like so many 'frontline' pictures in all wars, was staged.

A patrol of the British 29 Brigade. Its composition vividly illustrates the mixed nationalities which operated together – here, British, American, Korean and Belgian.

A British soldier points out the hills on which the Gloucesters fought out their bitter battle in April 1951. He is standing on A Company's position.

Men of the Gloucesters at a church parade taken by Padre Sam Davies before the Imjin battle.

The officers commanding the two British brigades in Korea in April 1951:
(*left*) Tom Brodie of 29 Brigade; (*right*) Basil Coad of 27 Brigade.

Lt. Col. J. P. Carne, commanding 1st Gloucesters at the battle of the Imjin.

Chinese infantry making a night advance and (*below*) laying
Russian-made boxmines.

The air war: (*above*) Communist pilots being briefed for a mission over Korea.

Below: The MiG 15, the first communist jet fighter, whose intervention in Korea in November 1950 sent ripples of alarm throughout the West.

Bottom: The Sabre, the outstanding fighter of the Korean War, which made a succession of US pilots 'aces'.

A flight deck mishap on HMS *Ocean* off Korea. The victim is a Sea Fury. Accidents remained almost as great a peril as enemy action throughout the war's intensive carrier operations.

One of the North Korean bridges which remained critical targets of UN air attack throughout the conflict.

Exhausted men of British 29 Brigade, April 1951.

President Syngman Rhee of South Korea with (on his left) General James Van Fleet, successor to Ridgeway as commander of Eighth Army.

abandoned, half-empty can of peas coated in days of dust. They simply scraped off the dust with a bayonet and wolfed the remains. The young lieutenant found this spectacle, of thousands of men on the margins of panic, very frightening.[4]

As Captain Fred Ladd drove north to a divisional headquarters, against the endless stream of traffic fleeing southwards, to his astonishment he saw among the files of marching men a leathery NCO whose face was instantly familiar. Sergeant Davis had served with his father, half a lifetime ago in the 15th Infantry. Davis faced Ladd with tears in his eyes: 'This just isn't the goddam American Army – running away. We ought to be taking up positions.' Ladd could find no words of comfort for the old NCO: 'I know, I know,' he nodded helplessly. Then he drove away, and Davis trudged on, shrunken, southwards.[5]

In ten days, the men of Eighth Army retreated 120 miles. By 15 December, they had crossed the 38th Parallel and the Imjin river, and still they were moving south. Since the destruction of 2nd Division south of Kunu-ri, they had scarcely even been in contact with the Chinese. Yet while the Marines conducted their measured, orderly retreat from Chosin despite acute difficulties of terrain, in the west Walker's army astoundingly collapsed.

Few men ever forgot the sights of those days. They looted what they could carry from the vast supply dumps in Pyongyang – alcohol, tobacco, sugar – but acre upon acre of equipment was put to the torch. The great pillars of smoke from the fires were visible for miles to the retreating army. An officer of the 8th Royal Irish Hussars, a British Centurion tank regiment, recorded:

> The march out of Pyongyang will be remembered mainly for the intense cold, the dust and the disappointment. Nothing appeared to have been attempted, let alone achieved. Millions of dollars worth of valuable equipment had been destroyed without a shot being fired or any attempt made to consider its possible evacuation. Seldom has a more demoralising picture been witnessed than the abandonment of this, the American

forward base, before an unknown threat of Chinese soldiers –
as it transpired, ill-armed and on their feet or horses.[6]

Yet everywhere they expected the Chinese to catch up with
them. It was almost as if they were tiptoeing away. As the British
armour clattered noisily across the bridge south of Pyongyang,
Captain James Majury of the Ulsters found himself desperately
wishing that the vehicles would make less noise. A young troop
commander's tank knocked over a ROK soldier in the long files
trudging along the roadside. A track ran over the man's leg. The
horrified young officer jumped down to aid the Korean. But even
as he knelt, the ROK platoon officer pulled the Englishman's pistol
from his holster, and put a bullet in the mangled man's head.

On the road south of the North Korean capital, General Paek
Sun Yup of the ROK 1st Division met the 27th Infantry's commander, Colonel John Michaelis, whom he greatly admired. The
Korean was deeply depressed by the loss of Pyongyang, his home
city which he had entered in such triumph a few weeks earlier.
Now, he asked the American what was happening. 'I don't know,'
said Michaelis. 'I'm just a regimental commander. But we may not
be able to stay in the peninsula.'[7]

A patrol from A Company of the British 1st Gloucesters came
upon a huddled mass of Korean civilians lying in a river bed.
Some were dying – of exposure, weakness, hunger, exhaustion.
Others were merely too weak to climb out. The British soldiers
formed a human chain to pull them up. 'Thank you very much,'
said a woman, in perfect English. 'I teach English at the university,'
she explained, answering their surprise. The Gloucesters asked if
there was anything more they could do for her. 'Haven't you done
enough already?' she demanded bitterly. 'Just all go away and leave
us with what's left of our country.' She turned on her heel and
walked away across the hill.[8]

As early as 5 December, Brigadier Basil Coad, commanding the
British 27 Brigade, dispatched a signal to the British Commander-
in-Chief, Far East, General Sir John Harding, painting a grim

picture of the state of his own brigade, and the difficulties of continuing to operate effectively with the Americans.[9] 'This, I must say, rather shocked me,' Harding told the War Office. He replied to Coad in the sharpest terms, making clear the absolute need for the British contingent to hold firm, whatever the difficulties:

> It seems clear to me that the present situation in Korea is one in which everyone, whatever their difficulties or deficiencies, must continue to do their utmost with what they have ... If you are given any specific task which, in your considered opinion, does risk your troops to an extent exceptional in war, and the peculiar circumstances in which the United Nations forces in Korea are now placed, you should make a formal written protest to your immediate superior commander ... I need hardly impress upon you the grave importance of being absolutely certain of your ground before making any such formal written protest.[10]

In other words, for the solidarity of the UN and Anglo-American relations, 27 Brigade must somehow stick it out. Coad and his men did so.

*

The Korean people were, of course, the principal victims of the Chinese winter offensive, as they were of every phase of the war. As Eighth Army straggled south in disarray, everywhere around them a great human tide of refugees surged and stumbled. When the army monopolised the road, the civilians fled along the railway line. Many scarcely knew where they were going, or why; only that they had lost whatever they had owned behind them, and sought to attain something fresh in front, if it was only shelter from the battle. But Moon Yun Seung and his family knew why they were on the railway embankment south from Pyongyang: to escape the communists. Moon was eighteen, and until 1945 his family had owned a silk mill in the north. When they lost that, they moved to Pyongyang and became silk traders. But in the autumn of 1950, as the communists fled from their own capital, they left behind them an epidemic of grim rumours. Moon was assured that the Americans proposed to drop an atomic bomb on Pyongyang. He and his family moved hastily back to the village where once they had owned their mill, and it was there that they saw their first Americans, advancing north at the height of their triumph. Then, when the Chinese came and the retreat began, Moon and his family began walking. 'There were too many people,' he said. 'We could not keep together. When the American fighters came, machine-gunning the roads, everyone scattered like beanshoots.' He never saw his family again. For eighteen days, he walked towards Seoul, scavenging scraps of food from abandoned houses, pathetically waving a South Korean flag when the F-86s strafed the refugee columns, as he saw them do repeatedly. In Seoul, Moon had expected to find refuge with a friend of his father. But this man, like three-quarters of the population after their dreadful experience the previous summer, had fled. Moon kept walking south. He was picked up in one of the ROK army's periodic round-ups of conscripts, but after three months rejected as unfit – this, despite the bleak United Nations joke that a ROK medical examination merely involved holding a mirror to a man's mouth to check that he breathed. Moon was a scavenger in Pusan when he was run over and his leg broken by an American army truck. A Scandinavian medical team rescued him. He spent six months in a Swedish hospital, a year on crutches. Finally, he got a job as a longshoreman at the docks. He was merely another stray scrap of flotsam, amid a great sea of such private tragedies in the winter of 1950.[11]

*

Lieutenant Bill Cooper and a couple of brother officers of the 5th Northumberland Fusiliers left their positions guarding the Han bridges to drive into Seoul on Christmas Eve. It seemed fantastic to shake off the snow and refugees, the strong sense of imminent disaster outside, and walk into the brightly lit Chosan Hotel, where a ferociously drunken party was in progress. Men of all ranks lurched around the corridors clutching their Korean bargirls. If there was no food to be had, everybody was helping themselves to drink. At last, the British walked out once more to their jeeps in the darkness, into the reality of Korean figures scuttling urgently through the snow, of acute desolation and apprehension. Cooper had spent much of the voyage out from England attempting to diminish the bloody-mindedness of his platoon, largely recalled reservists, about their commitment to Korea. He told them: 'It's going to be no good sitting on top of some mountain saying "I shouldn't be here" while some bugger blows the top of your head off.' For all his efforts, he felt that throughout their time in Korea, 'there was still that undercurrent of resentment.' Yet now Cooper's men, like the rest of the British 29 Brigade, were warned to be ready to move.[12]

On New Year's Day, as 29 Brigade moved forward to take up positions in support of 1st ROK Division, they were dismayed to encounter its commander and his staff 'trotting briskly towards the rear'. Americans moving south shouted to the British tank crews as they drove forward to take up position: 'You're going the wrong way, buddy!' On the night of 2 January, the British found themselves defending positions in 'Happy Valley', north of Seoul. It was their first major action since arriving in Korea a few weeks earlier. Unlike 27 'Woolworth' Brigade, which had come from Hong Kong in the midst of the Pusan Perimeter crisis lacking the most elementary necessities, 29 Brigade was alleged to lack for nothing. Its three battalions and supporting armoured regiment possessed the best that the British army, in those days of austerity, could provide. Yet nothing diminished the shock of that first night of heavy action. A straggling stream of refugees had been coming through the British positions. Suddenly, the men in their hastily scraped foxholes and sangars heard an NCO's cry: 'Watch your front!' Seconds later, the bugles and burp guns were upon them. The Chinese were driven out of the battalion headquarters of the

Northumberland Fusiliers only after hand-to-hand fighting. Both the Fusiliers and the neighbouring Ulster Rifles were compelled to give ground.

It was a night of confusion. Some Chinese worked to within a few yards of the Ulsters' position, advancing led by a man with a white flag shouting 'South Korean – we surrender!' Private Albert Varley of the Ulsters was a regular veteran of half a dozen World War II campaigns, recalled as a reservist for Korea. Now, he found himself lost on a hillside with his nineteen-year-old platoon commander and platoon sergeant. A voice shouted out of the darkness in English: 'I'm wounded! I'm wounded!' Varley went to investigate, and found a Chinese lying groaning among the rocks. He shot him. Then the three men walked a lonely two miles until they were challenged by their own sentries. 'It was a proper shambles, a right cock-up,' in Private Varley's estimation. Like many men, Private Henry O'Kane was dismayed by lying all night listening to the cries and groans of the wounded of both sides.

All next morning, Cromwell and Churchill tanks of 'Cooperforce', led by Captain Donald Astley-Cooper, were firing in support of 29 Brigade's counter-attack. Lieutenant Bill Cooper and W Company of the Northumberland Fusiliers advanced from their start-line around midday. Cooper was without his platoon sergeant, York, a dour, solid, grizzled regular, a simple man with high standards and six children who had been borrowed by the mortar platoon of Support Company. It was Support Company that had borne the brunt of the previous night's casualties. When W Company reached their positions, they found them littered with British dead. Sergeant York was sitting against a rock, looking surprised. He had been hit six times in the chest and stomach, and was quite dead. Lieutenant Cooper had lost eight of his platoon in his first battle: 'I was shaken by the speed at which it all happened: the red in a stream with bodies in it, the great trails of blood in the snow as if a snail had crawled across it.'

Yet that evening, soon after the British battalions had painfully recovered their lost ground, they learned belatedly of a general

withdrawal south of the Han. A liaison officer from the neighbouring American unit arrived at the Ulsters' battalion headquarters to
announce graphically: 'Colonel, we are buggered. We've gone.' The
British were on their own. There was no time to lose. To the open
dismay of Astley-Cooper, brigade decreed that the tanks were to
form a rearguard, moving out in darkness with a single platoon of
infantry for close protection.

Twenty-year-old Lance-Corporal Robert Erricker, co-driver of
Lieutenant Godfrey Alexander's Cromwell, thought of his mother
and father at home in Surrey. In England, it was lunchtime on
early closing day. They would be pulling down the shutters on
their little shop. The track down the valley through which they
departed was barely wide enough to carry a tank. Even as the
infantry withdrew in front of them, they came under fire from the
hills overlooking the road. Astley-Cooper saw to his dismay that a
village along his line of retreat was already ablaze. He sought a
detour by a river bed to the right. The tanks ground and battered
their path along it, cutting up the darkness with their tracer in
every direction, infantry clinging to the hulls and being shot off as
they drove. Alexander's tank found itself blocked. It could go no
further, and hastily turned round, in search of another escape
route. A wounded Ulster Rifleman threw himself aboard. Then
Chinese mortar bombs began to fall on the hull. Johnnie Healey,
the Besa gunner, shouted: 'The guvnor's hit.' They pulled their
officer down into the turret, and found that he had been killed by
a mortar fragment in the head. The tank swerved off the road.
They had thrown a track. Another tank halted alongside. 'All right,
spike your gun and get out of it!' shouted the commander. He
hastened on, while the crew climbed on the back of their own hull
to remove the wounded Rifleman. Then there were Chinese
soldiers all around them, motioning them down. They were put
against a wall, hands in the air. 'This is it,' muttered Erricker
miserably. 'Don't worry, Bob, we'll be all right,' Bob Healey, the
driver, said sturdily. Suddenly, another tank was upon them,
spraying tracer. Captors and captives dived for cover. When the

firing stopped and the Chinese began reassembling their prisoners, Healey and Bates, the wireless-operator, had vanished. They made good their escape to the British lines. Erricker found himself among a hundred unhappy British prisoners.[13] The most fortunate man of the night was the mortar platoon storeman of the Ulsters. He was in an Oxford carrier which ran into a haystack and was at once overrun by the Chinese. The man was bayoneted, and made to kneel with the rest of the carrier crew. When the prisoners were herded away, they carried the mortarman until the Chinese ordered them to abandon him. The next morning, an American helicopter pilot found him. He survived.

Astley-Cooper's tank cast a track on the rough ground. His crew bailed out and escaped. Their commander was never seen again. Lieutenant Bill Cooper and his platoon of the Northumberlands marched out alongside the unit's Oxford carriers, all of which had been christened with names beginning with 'D'. Someone with an advanced sense of the macabre had decreed that the carrier loaded with the unit's frozen corpses should carry, neatly white-painted on its flank, the word DEATH. The Royal Ulster Rifles suffered a total of 208 casualties in the Happy Valley battles, while five tanks were lost. The rest of the British brigade made good its withdrawal across the Han, and thence to Suwon, blowing the bridges behind them.

Major Tony Younger, the British sapper charged with some of the demolition tasks, was dismayed to see a train jammed with refugees, sitting on carriage roofs and clinging to every projection, halt just south of one railway bridge. He urged them to move. They refused. He fired the charges, and watched the spans collapse into the river. Scores of Koreans leapt from the train and ran towards the little engineer party, who feared that they were about to be attacked by a furious mob. Instead, the refugees seized them and shook their hands in strange gratitude. The train at last puffed away, and Younger's squadron followed the infantry towards Suwon.

*

When the North Koreans held Seoul in the summer of 1950, thirteen-year-old Suk Bun Yoon's father had a miraculous escape. Denounced as an anti-communist, he was taken to a hillside outside the city along with a group of others, and shot. But the wound was not fatal. He crawled away and eventually found his family, and convalesced with them through the winter. His son became the most important male in the household, which did not cost his education much, since by the end of the year almost all his teachers had been recruited or taken prisoner by one side or the other. But his father was still a sick man on 3 January 1951, when the family determined that they must flee Seoul. That evening, they made their way among thousands of Koreans on a similar mission, towards the frozen Han river. It was a terrible spectacle, a terrible night. Shellfire broke the ice in some places, and the boy watched struggling refugees sink helpless into the river, while thousands more ran hysterically past them. Somewhere in the darkness and the panic-stricken crowds, their grandfather disappeared: 'We simply lost him. We never saw him again. Maybe he froze to death.' In the days that followed, the family crawled south with their possessions. They had gone only twenty-five miles when they were overtaken by the Chinese. That night, in an abandoned house, they held a family conference. It was decided that as they were, they stood no hope of breaking through to the UN lines. They left their grandmother and Suk's three younger brothers and sisters aged ten, seven, and three, in the village, reliant upon the charity of the peasants. Suk and his parents struggled on through the darkness, amid the gunflashes and refugees and wailing infants, until at last they crossed into the ROK lines.

To a Westerner, the decision to abandon the very old and the very young seems almost fantastic. But as the UN armies so often observed, the people of Korea seem to draw their character from the harsh environment in which they live. This was the kind of parting, the kind of decision that was commonplace in hundreds of thousands of Korean families, that created the legions of starving orphans and infant beggars that hung like flies around every UN camp, supply dump, refuse tip. Behind the UN lines, for the next two months Suk and his parents lived with an aunt deep in the countryside. Only when Eighth Army at last moved forward again did the boy return to the village in search of the rest of the family. They found the children. Their hair was dropping out. They were in rags; their bodies were lice-ridden; they could not readily digest food. But they were narrowly alive. Thanks to canned food begged and stolen from the armies, they survived. Their grandmother was dead. The surviving family was ruined, destitute, homeless. But like millions of other Koreans that winter, they clung tenaciously to the margins of existence and waited for better times.

*

As Eighth Army retreated, mile by mile and day by day on the road southwards, as men abandoned equipment and lost their officers, allowed themselves to be washed along with the great tide of American and Korean humanity fleeing south away from the communists, the withdrawal became 'the big bug-out'. The impulse to escape not only from the enemy, but from the terrible cold, the mountains, from Korea itself became overwhelming. In December 1950, most of Eighth Army fell apart as a fighting force in a fashion resembling the collapse of the French in 1940, the British at Singapore in 1942. 45 Field Regiment RA were reduced to hysterical laughter by an American intelligence report announcing that the Chinese were employing large numbers of monkeys as porters. Rumour of every kind, the more dramatic the better, held sway over the minds of thousands of men. 'Everything the Chinese were showing they could do, their aggressiveness, was strange to us,' said Major Floyd Martain. 'What we knew of the Chinese in America was so different – they were so submissive.'[14] Most Americans expected Chinamen to be dwarves. They found themselves assaulted by units which included men six feet and over. Yet the enemy wreaking such havoc with Eighth Army was still, essentially, fighting a large-scale guerrilla war, devoid of all the heavy fire-power every Western army considered essential. It was a triumph not merely for the prestige of communism, but for that of an Asian army.

From Walker's headquarters, to Tokyo and on to the Joint Chiefs' offices in the Pentagon, there was bewilderment and deep dismay about the collapse of Eighth Army. For public consumption, the sheer surprise and weight of the Chinese offensive were emphasised. But professional soldiers knew that these were not enough to explain the headlong rout of an army that still possessed absolute command of sea and air, and firepower on a scale the communists could not dream of. The Chinese victories were being gained by infantry bearing small arms and regimental support weapons – above all, mortars. The Americans had been subjected to very little artillery fire, and no air attack whatever. The mobility of the Chinese, moving across mountain ranges without regard for the road network, was achieved at the cost of carrying very limited supplies of arms and ammunition.

Chinese peasants might be better attuned to hardship than Western soldiers, but they were not superhuman. The men of the UN complained of the difficulty of fighting the ferocious cold as well as the enemy. But the winter was neutral. The Chinese were far less well equipped to face the conditions than their opponents, possessing only canvas shoes and lacking such indulgences as sleeping bags. Marshal Peng's casualties from frostbite dwarfed those of the Americans. And the Chinese could expect no ready evacuation or medical care. UN soldiers told terrible stories of taking prisoners with whole limbs blackened and dead in the cold. Chinese veterans later declared that 90 per cent of the 'volunteers' in Korea suffered from some degree of frostbite in the winter of 1950. Their 27th Army suffered 10,000 non-combat casualties: '. . . A shortage of transportation and escort personnel makes it impossible to accomplish the mission of supplying the troops,' declared a 26 Army document of November 1950, later captured by the UN. 'As a result, our soldiers frequently starved . . . They ate cold food, and some had only a few potatoes in two days. They were unable to maintain their physical strength for combat; the wounded could not be evacuated ... The firepower of our entire army was basically inadequate. When we used our guns, there were often no shells, or the shells were duds.'[15]

The Chinese could achieve great shock power, but only the most limited ability to sustain an attack, whether at company or army level. They missed dazzling opportunities to annihilate, rather than merely drive back MacArthur's army in Korea in the winter of 1950, because they could move only as fast as their feet could carry them, and their radio communications were so poor that they could not co-ordinate large-scale movements effectively. Some PLA units were out of contact with their higher formations for days on end. The key to tactical success against the Chinese was to create all-round defensive perimeters, and not to allow panic to set in when it was discovered, as it so frequently was, that the communists had turned a unit's flank. If UN firepower could be brought to bear in support of a counter-attack, this was almost invariably successful. But in those weeks of November and December, Peking's armies achieved psychological dominance not only over UN units at the front, but over their commanders in the rear. After the first battles of November, the flimsiest rumour of the men in quilted jackets being observed on a main supply route behind the front was enough to spark fears of encirclement, and often outright panic. The undoubted Chinese skills as tacticians, night-fighters, navigators, masters of fieldcraft and camouflage, caused even many senior officers to forget the enemy's huge disadvantages in resources and firepower. Worse, the leaders of the UN forces in Korea found themselves facing the stark fact that, man for man, most of their troops were proving nowhere near as hardy, skilful, and determined upon the battlefield as their communist opponents. It is difficult to overestimate the psychological effects of this conclusion upon strategic and tactical decision-making.

Yet even at this phase, the struggle was not entirely one-sided.

The Chinese were learning bitter lessons about the potential of air power. They discovered that their truck drivers could not move by day, because they could not hear the sound of enemy aircraft. Every infantry movement had to be completed before dawn, the men deeply covered by the snow into which they dug themselves, before the prowling Mustangs, Corsairs, Panthers found them. A nationwide system of air-raid precautions was created, sentries stationed at intervals of two hundred yards along every mile of the Chinese supply routes, ready by whistle and rifle-shot to warn of impending air attack the moment engines were heard. Hung She Te, the Chinese officer responsible for all logistics inside Korea, performed miracles with his legions of porters and oxcarts. But throughout that winter campaign of 1950, the overwhelming limitation upon the Chinese was not manpower, of which their reserves were almost unbounded, but supply. Chou En Lai exhorted every family in China to fry flour for the volunteers. Great columns of men and trucks moved south across the Yalu each night, backs bent and springs groaning under their burdens. They learned to place wide brooms on the front of vehicles to sweep aside the puncture nails dropped on the roads by US aircraft. They organised emergency repair parties to replace broken bridges and ruined roads within hours. But the Chinese were never able, in that first campaign, effectively to deploy artillery in support of their advance. Probably the most critical contribution of American air power in the Korean War was the interdiction of supply routes during the winter battles of 1950. This alone, it may be argued, prevented the Chinese from converting the defeat of the UN forces into their destruction.

How could Marshal Peng and his staff organise their own intelligence about UN movements effectively, when they lacked equipment to intercept American communications, or aircraft to conduct effective reconnaissance? Thirty-five years later, the face of Hu Seng, one of Peng's secretaries, cracked into a craggy grin at the memory: 'It was very easy to get intelligence, in the beginning. There was no censorship in the West at that time about troop movements. We gained much vital information from Western press and radio.'[16] Daily from July, from the agency wires in Seoul clattered details of the landings of the Marines, the arrival of new foreign contingents, the assault on Inchon – ten hours before this took place – the deployment of the first F-86 Sabre fighters. At the end of December, Ridgway introduced censorship of all disclosures concerning the UN Order of Battle. Western correspondents introduced private codes to evade this. Eighth Army asked for a press blackout on the UN evacuation of Seoul until this was completed. The story was broken in the US within hours, by a correspondent who simply did not submit his copy for censorship. Restrictions on reporting were never, of course, enforced on the media outside the Korean peninsula.

The impetus of the Chinese advance could only be sustained into 1951 by the vast captures of arms and supplies on the drive south. Thousands of Chinese picked up new American weapons, learned to eat C-rations and handle some American heavy weapons. 'We quickly got used to American biscuits and rice,' said Li Xiu, a regimental propaganda officer with the 27th Corps, 'but we never cared for tomato juice. We were particularly glad to get carbines, because we found rifles so heavy to carry. Without the American sleeping bags and overcoats that we captured, I am not sure we could have gone on. Two-thirds of our casualties were from the cold that winter, against one-third from combat. The main difficulties were always: how to avoid American planes and artillery, and how to catch up with the Americans in their trucks.'[17]

'The chief problem was to gather all the prisoners,' said Li Hebei of the 587th Regiment. 'On New Year's Day, an order was issued for our troops to compete to see which unit could collect most prisoners as a New Year gift for Chairman Mao. American prisoners at first didn't understand the "lenient policy" of our volunteers towards them. But after a period of contact, they began to believe it. We gave them whatever we could offer to eat. One or two were very stubborn, and would not admit that their action was aggression. Because of our poor weapons and equipment, they didn't take us seriously. So we did some work to persuade them: we told them, "the US is far from Korea, but the Yalu river is the border between Korea and China. If you cannot accept this, let us settle it on the battlefield." Always the problem was, how to win the battle with less advanced weapons than the enemy.'[18]

*

For all the shame and humiliation of the precipitate American flight from North Korea in the winter of 1950, the simple truth remains that the very speed of the retreat saved many units from annihilation, and left Eighth Army with forces that could be rebuilt to fight another day. It was plainly, bitterly apparent that where the Chinese could catch American troops at that time, they could almost invariably defeat them. But American mobility was not entirely useless. It enabled many thousands of men, who would not otherwise have done so, to outrun their pursuers and escape to fight better another day.

Yet nothing could diminish the dismay both in Korea, and in the capitals of the West, about the performance of Eighth Army in the retreat from the Yalu. After the winter battles, the British General Sir Robert Mansergh, C-in-C in Hong Kong, visited Korea, and delivered a devastating secret report to the British Chiefs of Staff upon the situation that he discovered there.

> I doubt whether any British really think that the war in Korea will be brought to a successful conclusion. The reason for this is primarily because of the American lack of determination and their inability, up to the time of my visit, to stand and fight. Most Americans sooner or later bring the conversation around to an expression of the view that the United Nations forces ought to quit Korea. The British troops, although sympathetic to the South Koreans in their adversity, despise them and are not interested in this civil war . . . I would judge the American morale as low, and in some units thoroughly bad. They appear to think that the terrain is unfavourable for American equipment and methods . . . It must be remembered that many

thousands of the Americans joined the army for the purpose of getting a cheap education after their service and that they, at no time, expected to fight. Their training is quite unsuited to that type of country or war and, in spite of lessons learnt, they will not get clear of their vehicles ... Their rations, supplies, and welfare stores, are on such a scale as to be comic if they were not such a serious handicap to battle ... Regular American officers have been a high proportion of those lost. As a result, the problems of replacement of men with experience is becoming very difficult.

... They have never studied or been taught defence. They appear only to have studied mechanised and mechanical advances at great speed. They do not understand locality defence in depth or all-round defence. They do not like holding defensive positions. They have been trained for very rapid withdrawals. Americans do not understand infiltration and feel very naked when anybody threatens their flank or rear.[19]

Mansergh expressed respect for American artillery, whose gunners the British had also found more courageous than the infantry, and for the performance of the US Marines. But he was highly critical of the staff work within Eighth Army.

They do not understand the importance of reconnoitring ground. Units in action almost invariably overestimate the enemy against them, the casualties inflicted, and the reasons for their rapid withdrawal; this I have known in our own units in war, but it appears worse here and more frequent. At night, main headquarters blazed like gin palaces ... Roadblocks, car parks, dumps etc were as crowded as Hampstead Heath on a bank holiday.[20]

Mansergh summarised his conclusions about the problems of the US Army in Korea: 'a) training on wrong lines b) bad staff organisation c) low quality infantry d) disinterest in the war in general e) weak and inexperienced commanders at all levels'. The general's views must certainly have been influenced by those of

Brigadier Basil Coad, commanding the British 27 Brigade in Korea since September. Coad at about this time submitted an unhappy report of his own, citing the lack of liaison with American higher commanders, and the general inadequacy of direction:

> Since the withdrawals started, the behaviour of some senior staff officers and Formation HQs was, at times, quite hysterical and resulted in the issues of impossible orders which, if obeyed without question, would have resulted in unnecessary loss of life. American commanders frankly tell me that they have never taught defence in any of their military schools. The American soldier did not like being attacked, especially at night, and with exceptions will not stand and fight. I think their [the British contingent's] attitude to the American infantry is largely one of contempt.[21]

'Standards of discipline in the US Army in Korea, never very high, are now lower than I have ever known them,' wrote the military assistant to the British Ambassador that December. 'Officers told me quite openly that it is useless ordering their troops to attack, because they simply won't go. The US Army is still road-bound, and it is very difficult to describe their tactics, since it seems that tactics in the normal sense of the word do not exist. In an advance, motorised columns headed by a few tanks are sent up the roads making use of what is described as "prophylactic fire". This seems to consist of everyone who has a weapon blazing away on either side of the column into the blue.'[22]

In assessing the justice of these British opinions, it is necessary to discount something for the chronic scepticism of one nation towards another's methods of making war. Throughout the twentieth century, there has been a measure of jealousy in the British Army, traditionally accustomed to fight on short commons, towards the vast weight of resources available to the Americans. Yet the evidence of such able American professionals as John Michaelis and Paul Freeman supports the British view of US performance in the winter of 1950. Matthew Ridgway himself, on his

arrival, wrote of the remarkable difference between the demeanour of the American and British troops under his command. A
problem which was already familiar from World War II reasserted
itself in Korea, as it would again in Vietnam: the disproportionately
low percentage of the nation's best manhood which served the
infantry regiments of the United States.* Because the American
instinct for war favours a technological, managerial approach, far
too many of the ablest men are diverted to technical and managerial functions. At the time of Korea, indeed, overwhelmingly the
most talented section of America's young manhood remained in
colleges at home, as a result of the workings of the Selective
Service Act. Yet in this war, as in every war, it was upon the
infantry that the greatest burden of battle, and of casualties, fell.
As in America's other major Asian war a generation later, terrain
and the circumstances of the enemy made it difficult to employ
technology and firepower anywhere near as effectively as upon a
European battlefield, against a European enemy. From beginning
to end in Korea, the United States Army laboured under grave
disadvantages in fitting itself to meet the enemy on favourable
terms.

It is well-nigh impossible for any man to retain a vision of
United Nations action in Korea as a great and essential experiment in international relations [wrote a British correspondent
on 27 December, in a private report to the War Office in Lon-
don] should he be subjected for long to the atmosphere of
Korea. Inefficiency and squalor among the civil population
make some contribution to the overall feeling of disillusionment. But the major fault lies with the morale of the armed
forces. Men of the United States Army so completely dominate
the scene, numerically, that their attitude is all-important. It
can be very simply expressed: 'How soon can we get t'hell out
of this goddam country?' That is the one question in the minds

---

* This problem is discussed at more length in the author's *Overlord: D-Day and the Battle for
Normandy* (London and New York, 1984).

of every GI and almost every officer up to the rank of colonel encountered in Korea. Half has no thought beyond the single objective of escape. Of the remainder, a few felt that crossing the 38th Parallel was a mistake, either tactical or moral. But far more took the view that the United States should stop consulting anybody, and should use the atomic bomb. They did not wish it employed against the North Koreans, or even, to any great extent, against the Chinese communists. Their emotional reaction to the whole problem was that the Russian is solely responsible, and that therefore the logical thing to do is to atom bomb Moscow . . . Offensive thinking amongst junior officers and men was confined almost entirely to the Marines. It was prompted mostly by a drive for revenge for the losses inflicted on them at the Chosin reservoir, and was accompanied by a distrust and contempt for higher leadership almost more frightening than the lack of fibre of their army compatriots. There can be few occasions in history when officers and men of a fighting force have expressed themselves so freely and violently, in public, on the subject of their commanding officers.[23]

Dear Folks [PFC James Cardinal of the 3/5th Cavalry wrote home to his parents in the Bronx on 7 January 1951] . . . We are now about 60 miles NW of Taegu, holding a mountain pass thru which the entire 8th Army is moving headed south. It looks like the beginning of the end. The Chinese are kicking hell out of the US Army, and I think we are getting out, at least I hope so. I think they are going to evacuate all UN troops from Korea soon, as it's impossible to stop these Chinese hordes. There's just too many of them for us to fight in Korea. If the big wheels in Washington decide to fight here it will be the biggest mistake they ever made, as I don't think we can hold the Chinks. Anyway, let's hope they decide to evacuate us.

When you get complaining and bitching letters from me, remember every soldier over here feels that way. The troops over here are mad, mad at America, Americans and America's leaders. We all feel we've been let down, by our incompetent blundering leadership, from the White House down. It seems to me to be – to hell with the troops in Korea. If we must fight communism, let's do it in Europe which is the cradle of western culture and our own civilisation. It seems to me that's more worth fighting for than some barren oriental wasteland, with uncountable hordes of savage warriors. It's about time that all of you back home awakened to the truth of the matter, and let your voices be heard thru letters to your congressmen. That's the only way to get direct action. Well, folks, that's all for now. I'm in the best of health and spirits and hope that you all and the rest of the family are too. Love, Jimmy.[24]

The American army had reached its lowest point of the Korean War. Corporal Robert Fountain, late of Task Force Smith, gazed around the schoolhouse at Chonan in which he found himself sheltering in the depths of the retreat, and recognised the very same building in which he had taken shelter in July, in the midst of the first traumas of the war. It was too much to bear: 'We had fought all the way south, and all the way north. I thought – "Look what we have suffered, and we are back where we began. I have nothing in this country, and I never will." '[25] Corporal Fountain was not alone in his dismay. Defeat on the battlefield had also provoked a crisis of confidence among statesmen and politicians at home which now threatened, for a time, to escalate the Korean War into a nuclear conflict.

2. Washington and Tokyo

On the morning of 28 November, Truman informed his personal staff in his office at the White House: 'General Bradley called me at 6.15 this morning. He told me a terrible message had come in from General MacArthur ... The Chinese have come in with both feet'. This was the day, he wrote later, 'when the bad news from Korea had changed from rumours of resistance into certainty of defeat.'[26]

At the meeting of the National Security Council later that day, the President, Marshall and the Joint Chiefs agreed that all-out war with China must be avoided. Acheson said he believed that if the United States bombed China's airfields in Manchuria, the Russians would come into the war. Yet none of this caution prevented Acheson from denouncing Peking's action the following day as 'an act of brazen aggression ... the second such act in five months ... This is not merely another phase of the Korean campaign. This is a fresh and unprovoked aggressive act, even more immoral than the first.' Dean Rusk declared, at the 28 November meeting of the National Security Council, that the Chinese intervention 'should not be on our conscience, since these events are merely the result of well-laid plans, and were not provoked by our actions'. To a remarkable extent, Washington still failed to consider exclusively Chinese motives for intervention, and focused upon Russian reasons for inciting Chinese action, and the new interpretation that must be placed upon Moscow thinking. The CIA predicted that the Russians would give the Chinese maximum support. Bedell Smith said there was now 'a much better case than they previously thought for believing Russia plans for war soon ... They probably do not plan on war now, but are willing to have it if they can bog us down in Asia.'[27]

MacArthur now issued a desperate plea for reinforcements. But Frank Pace, the Army Secretary, said that the only available unit was the 82nd Airborne Division. MacArthur again demanded to be allowed to use men of Chiang Kai Shek's Nationalist army. His request was once more refused. He also wanted more air and sea power, and some additional forces were dispatched. All the senior soldiers were now increasingly bitter about the political restriction upon bombing beyond the Yalu. Bradley wrote on 3 December:

'We used to say that an attack on a platoon of United States troops meant war. Would anyone believe that now if we don't react to the Chinese attack?'[28] No one wanted war with China, he said, but if Eighth Army was driven out of Korea, the United States should retaliate by hitting China's cities.

In Tokyo, from the first moment of the Chinese intervention, MacArthur issued a flood of bulletins and statements which drifted further and further from reality as each day went by. First, he declared that his own drive to the Yalu had forced the Chinese hand, interrupting plans for a grand communist offensive which would have been disastrous for the United Nations. He rejected utterly the suggestion that his forces were engaged in a retreat. He castigated 'ignorant' correspondents for their inability to distinguish between a planned withdrawal and a 'full flight'. His flights of Olympian rhetoric contrasted ever more grotesquely with the reality of what was taking place within his command: 'Never before has the patience of man been more sorely tried nor high standards of human behaviour been more patiently tried and firmly upheld than during the course of the Korean campaigns.' He cast direct blame upon the Administration in Washington for imposing restrictions upon bombing and military operations beyond the Yalu – 'an enormous handicap, without precedent in military history'.[29] Harry Truman wrote: 'Now, no one is blaming General MacArthur, and certainly I never did, for the failure of the November offensive . . . But . . . I do blame General MacArthur for the manner in which he tried to excuse his failure.'[30]

When the British General Sir Robert Mansergh met MacArthur in Tokyo at this period, he found him intensely emotional:

> At these times, he appeared to be much older than his 70 years . . . Signs of nerves and strain were apparent . . . When he emphasised the combined efforts and successes of all front-line troops in standing shoulder to shoulder, and dying if necessary in their fight against communism, it occurred to me that he could not have been fully in the picture. I cannot believe he

would have made these comments in such a way if he had been in full possession of facts which I would inevitably learn later, that some Americans had been far from staunch. It occurred to me then, and was emphasised later, that the war in Korea is reproduced in Tokyo with certain omissions of the more unpalatable facts.[31]

And if MacArthur was prey to powerful private delusions about what was taking place within his command, he was also entering perilous political waters with his public statements about the course of things to come. His enigmatic comments, when questioned by a magazine interviewer about the desirability of employing the atomic bomb, left little to the imagination.

> Question: Can anything be said as to the effectiveness or ineffectiveness of the bomb in the type of operations in which you are now engaged?
> Answer: My comment at this time would be inappropriate.
> Question: In the type of warfare now going on in Korea, are there large enough concentrations of enemy troops to make the bomb effective?
> Answer: My comment at this time would be inappropriate.[32]

But if MacArthur was alone in declining to deny publicly the merits of employing atomic weapons, a large company within the military were privately thinking furiously about the possibilities. On 20 November, J. Lawton Collins told colleagues it was conceivable that the JCS would be called upon to present views about the use of atomic weapons.

Then, at a press conference on 30 November, President Truman allowed himself to be trapped into making a statement on the atomic bomb which reverberated around the world, caused consternation among America's allies, the repercussions of which were never entirely stilled for the remainder of the Korean War. Truman declared that the United States would take 'whatever steps are necessary to meet the military situation'. A reporter inquired: 'Will that include the atomic bomb?'

Truman said: 'That includes every weapon we have.'

'Mr President, you said, "every weapon we have". Does that mean that there has been active consideration of the use of the atomic bomb?'

'There has always been active consideration of its use . . .'

Among America's allies, above all in Europe, unease had been mounting for many months about developments across the Atlantic. The stridency of conservative Cold War rhetoric; the rise of McCarthy; increasing fears in government circles, prompted by diplomatic reports from Tokyo about the extravagances of MacArthur, coupled with the Administration's inability to control him, had combined to create the gravest unease about the course on which the United States might be headed. For the most part, real fear of what the Russians might attempt, matched by nervousness about any statement that might encourage American isolationism – above all a possible American retreat from Europe – encouraged discretion in Allied public statements about Washington policy. The British had never been enthusiastic about the commitment to Korea. Henceforward, they were the most reluctant partners in the war. As early as 13 November, the Cabinet's OS Committee reported its view:

> that it was no longer practicable, without risking a major war, to attain the original objective of occupying the whole of North Korea and placing it under a UN regimen. They were doubtful whether the UN forces could reach the northern frontier without making air attacks on targets in Manchuria, and even if the frontier could he reached, it would be a difficult task to hold it along a line of about 450 miles in mountainous country. Korea was of no strategic importance to the democratic powers; and further operations there should now be conducted with a view to preventing any extension of the conflict and avoiding any lasting commitment in the area. The Chiefs of Staff favour shorter lines along the 40th Parallel.[33]

Bevin, the Foreign Secretary, said 'he was anxious to prevent the US Government from being led by their military advisers into policies which would provoke further intervention by China. He was also anxious to do everything he could to allay the reasonable fears of the Chinese lest the Western Powers should occupy large areas of Asian territory under a plea of military necessity.' By 29 November, Bevin was adopting a more phlegmatic view in Cabinet: 'If we had to fight the Chinese, it was much better, from both the political and military point of view, that we should do so in North Korea ... his conclusion was that, although the situation was serious, it was not out of hand.' But he remained apprehensive that MacArthur would press his demand to be allowed to bomb north of the Yalu. It is interesting that, in all the British Cabinet debates about Korea, there is virtually no evidence of discussion about the interests of the Korean people, beyond a remark of Bevin's in October that 'there was little doubt that the Koreans on both sides had conducted the war in a barbarous fashion'. To the British, as to the Americans, Korea was a battlefield upon which the will of the West was being tested, and a vital principle being reluctantly upheld. No more, no less.

Public support for the war in Korea had been waning rapidly in Britain through the autumn. In a passionate speech to the Labour Party Conference on 2 October, Bevin sought to chastise the fainthearts and the waverers. It was ludicrous to suggest, he declared, that there had ever been an alternative to intervention in Korea:

Do you think we like it? Do you think, after all the years of fighting we have done in the Labour movement in the hope of getting a peaceful world, that we like having to do it? Is there any Minister who likes to go down to the House of Commons to ask for £3,600 million for war? ... Is there any delegate in this conference who would go back to his constituents and say we are doing wrong in paying the proper insurance premium now for our security? We blamed the Conservatives for knowing Hitler was on the move and not making adequate preparations ... because they would not go in for collective security ... We are in office now, and shall we refuse to do what we called upon others to do which would have prevented the 1939 war if they had only done it.[34]

The Americans recognised Bevin as the only British Cabinet Minister after Attlee of real international stature. Yet the Foreign Secretary, a tired and sick man, received no ovation or vote of thanks. The defence chiefs were now declaring that they would need at least £3,800 million, which Britain did not have, to fund the rearmament programme. On 29 November, the House of Commons showed real irritation with Bevin's evident ignorance of what was happening in Korea. British fear, frustration and uncertainty about where the Allies were being led by MacArthur were becoming daily more acute. The Americans, in their turn, were exasperated by Allied hand-wringing about the possible consequences of UN actions, when faced with the immediate reality of defeat on the battlefield. Britain could have it one way or the other, Washington felt: she could accept responsibilities as a major ally and first-class power, and be treated accordingly; or she could bow to the economic need to withdraw from those responsibilities, and acknowledge the eclipse of her influence upon the United States.

But it would be many years before the British people were ready to face the issues in such bald terms. Truman's statement of 30 November, publicly declining to exclude the nuclear option in Korea, provoked the British to new ecstasies of uncertainty. In a debate that evening in the House of Commons, Foreign Secretary Ernest Bevin made it apparent that he had no clear idea of American intentions towards China, or indeed of any change in American policy in the Far East. The Tory front bencher R. A. Butler said:

I want to come immediately to some circumstances which have arisen this evening, and which have caused many of us great concern and anxiety ... I want to express, at any rate on my own behalf, and I believe on behalf of a great many other Hon. Members, my very great disquiet – the horror that many of us would feel at the use of this weapon in circumstances which were not such that our own moral conscience was satisfied that there was no alternative.

Attlee, the Prime Minister, expressed his wholehearted sympathy and agreement with Butler. Even Churchill, whom no one had accused of lack of zeal in the confrontation with communism, declared in the House of Commons: 'The United Nations should avoid by every means in their power becoming entangled inextricably in a war with China . . . the sooner the Far Eastern diversion . . . can be brought into something like a static condition and stabilised, the better it will be . . . For it is in Europe that the world cause will be decided . . . it is there that the mortal danger lies.' Attlee concluded the debate by announcing that he proposed himself to fly to Washington to meet the President.

If Britain was always the most junior of partners with the United States in the struggle to defend South Korea, in 1950 she also remained indisputably the second non-communist power on earth, the most important ally of the United States. Attlee's meeting with Truman in December 1950 provided both sides with a valuable opportunity to articulate their private convictions about the state of the global confrontation. As had been the case since the Korean War began, British views were coloured by fear that American strategic attentions were being diverted from Europe, towards the Far East. The British were also profoundly opposed to confrontation with China, given their own vital trade interests in the Far East. Attlee arrived in Washington as 'more than the spokesman of the United Kingdom and even the USA's allies in NATO'. He also represented 'the fears and doubts of all the states which had supported the original decision by the UN to resist the North Korean attack'.[35] Truman, meanwhile, came to the conference table as leader of an Administration which was even now suffering humiliating defeat upon the battlefield; and which stood beleaguered by its political critics at home. Senator McCarthy was demanding the resignations of Acheson and Marshall, and threatening impeachment proceedings against the President himself. Attlee's very coming provided more ammunition for Truman's Republican critics, for it supplied fresh evidence of the unwelcome influence of enfeebled Europeans upon American policy, the very force that they alleged had done so much to 'lose' China for the United States. Even had Washington been immersed in torrential downpours, the British were wise to arrive with no umbrellas at the airport.

The discussions that began on 5 December, and included both British and American Chiefs of Staff, were held under the shadow of real fear that the United Nations might be compelled to evacuate the Korean peninsula. One of Field-Marshal Slim's first questions to the American delegation was whether MacArthur had been ordered to withdraw. Marshall told him that no such order had been given, but that the Supreme Commander had been told that 'the security of his command is his first consideration'. Probably the chief significance of the discussions was the reassurance that Attlee gained from Truman, that the United States was *not* actively considering the employment of nuclear weapons in Asia. Much discussion also centred upon British economic and financial difficulties in sustaining their programme of rearmament, which Washington strongly supported. At this time, the United States possessed an extraordinary proportion of the world's stockpile of vital metals and other strategic materials. The British made it clear that, without greater access to these, their defence build-up could not continue.

Sir Oliver Franks, the British Ambassador in Washington whose close friendship with Acheson made him a key participant in the talks, believed that the Administration never seriously considered the use of nuclear weapons in Korea. In this, he may have underestimated the pressures that would have closed in upon Truman, had the Americans been driven out of Korea with heavy loss. And even Franks, like Attlee, acknowledged fears about what the

Americans might do 'if their backs were to the wall. There was a fear of the consequences of hot pursuit into China, or bombing across the Yalu. There was a fear that War, with a capital W, might break out in the Far East. The last thing that we wanted to see was the United States getting bogged down with China, because we saw no end to it.'[36]

The most interesting feature of the discussions was the clarity with which they emphasised the differing British and American attitudes to communist China. The British pressed their view that all-out war with China must be avoided at all costs. They remained convinced that communist access to China's UN seat must be held out as a possible negotiating card with Peking. This the Americans strenuously resisted. Acheson asserted that 'in his view, the central moving factor in this situation was not China but Russia. Some promise of support must certainly have been given by them before the Chinese intervened. There would not be many who would advise the President to embark upon an all-out war with China on land, sea, and air. But on the possibility of negotiations, they were far less optimistic ... This was the very worst moment at which we could seek to negotiate with the communist forces in the world.' Acheson, traditionally the Europeanist, sharply reminded the British at the Washington meetings of the United States' global responsibilities, and made plain his belief that the British position towards China was founded upon self-centred political and commercial considerations. If the US gave up now in the Far East, 'we are through. The Russians and the Chinese are coming in, and other Far Eastern peoples would make their best terms with them.'

The Americans agreed that it was doubtful whether MacArthur's army could hold on in Korea. They would willingly settle for a ceasefire based upon the restoration of the pre-war position, but saw no real prospect of attaining this. Truman said that he wished it to be on record that he could not agree to voluntary withdrawal from Korea: 'We must fight it out. If we failed, we should at least fail honourably.'

Attlee replied sturdily that the British would stand shoulder to

shoulder with the Americans in the bridgehead. But he then turned
to the much more contentious issue of China. He believed that
Britain and the United States had different appreciations of the
new China. It was a mistake to think Peking the pawn of Moscow.
Western policy should be to detach the Chinese from the Russians.
The West could look with considerable satisfaction upon other
societies whose nationalist aspirations had been indulged – India,
Pakistan, Burma. Acheson declared that he agreed with Attlee's
overview, but could not see how it helped to determine an immediate policy. When the British expressed their concern for the risk
to their interests in Hong Kong, Malaya and Singapore if the
Chinese mainland was attacked, Bradley inquired sarcastically
whether a Chinese attack on Hong Kong would mean war, when it
was not considered war for the Chinese to attack American troops
in Korea. Field-Marshal Slim asked whether a limited war against
China would be likely to provoke the invocation of the Sino-Soviet
Friendship Treaty. Marshall said that it would, and Truman
acknowledged his concern about this possibility. Slim remarked
that if the Soviet Air Force intervened in the war, 'we should have
to say goodbye.'

At a session following dinner at the British Embassy on 7
December, the vexed question of MacArthur was raised, and Attlee
voiced British anxieties. Truman agreed that some of the Supreme
Commander's statements had been unfortunate. Acheson said
there were two questions: 'First, whether any Government had any
control over General MacArthur, a point on which he desired to
express no view; and secondly, the question of what arrangements
should be made for consultation in future.' Marshall declared that
wars cannot be run by committee. Yet the British were determined
to emphasise their grave misgivings about direct military action
against China. Their greatest cause for concern when they left
Washington after the summit was that they seemed 'not to have
convinced the Americans of the need to make a serious effort to
reach a political settlement with the Chinese, and not to have

shaken them in their intention to undertake some form of "limited war" against China'.[37]

As from the beginning of the war, the chief British motive for supporting America in Korea continued to be fear that if she did not do so, America's sense of betrayal by her Western allies might have disastrous political and strategic consequences for Europe. It was not that the British did not sincerely share Washington's dismay at North Korean aggression: merely that they feared that the political and military costs of preserving Syngman Rhee's shoddy dictatorship in South Korea were in danger of exceeding any possible gains. This apprehension would persist to the very end of the war.

On the American side, President Truman and his advisers clearly perceived, as much of the American public did not, that the legitimacy of US policy in the Far East rested heavily upon maintaining the concept that a wider cause and greater principles than mere US national interest were being contested in Korea, and were being upheld by a family of nations. If Attlee and his delegation failed to gain many explicit assurances in Washington, certain implicit understandings were achieved: above all, that Britain and other major allies would be consulted before any major step was taken to expand the war. This concession to British sensitivities, as it became known in the upper reaches of the US military, caused disgust at the Dai Ichi and among other officers who believed the moment had come for a showdown with communism. It was knowledge or suspicion of what had been said between the British and American governments in Washington in December 1950 that sowed the seeds of belief in an Anglo-American conspiracy against the Supreme Commander in the MacArthur camp during the crisis of the following spring.

The British delegation might have returned to London in less tranquil spirits had they been aware that, even if the President did not lie to them, he certainly did not disclose the extent of American nuclear contingency planning. Since mid-November, the Army

Plans and Operations Division and the Joint Strategic Survey Committee had been conducting studies about the possible use of nuclear weapons in Korea. On 28 November, Plans and Ops recommended that the armed forces should ensure their readiness to make 'prompt use of the atomic bomb . . . as, if and when, directed by the President'. On 7 December, Acheson correctly predicted that the British would demand consultation on any planned American use of nuclear weapons. He recorded that he would promise to move 'in step with the British . . . but will agree nothing that will restrict his freedom of action'.[38] As the Chinese entered Pyongyang, the Joint Chiefs dispatched a memorandum to all commands giving their view 'that the current situation in Korea has greatly increased the possibility of general war. Commanders addressed should take such action as is feasible to increase readiness, without creating an atmosphere of panic.'[39] Throughout December and into the New Year, a groundswell of opinion within the United States demanded that the country's armed forces should no longer be compelled to endure punishment at the hands of the communists if this could be prevented by the ultimate expression of American technology, the atomic bomb. The national commanders of the four largest veterans' organisations petitioned the President to use 'such means as may be necessary' to check the communists.[40] On 24 December, MacArthur submitted a list of 'retaliation targets' in China and North Korea, requiring twenty-six atomic bombs in all. He requested four bombs for use against communist forces in North Korea, and four on 'critical concentrations of enemy air power'; the remainder were destined for enemy installations and industrial concentrations.[41] Such politicians as Senator Owen Brewster and Congressman Mendel Rivers pointed out publicly how effectively the atomic bomb had been used against the Japanese.

Yet if Truman and his advisers talked very toughly to the British about their refusal to concede defeat as the price of a ceasefire with the Chinese, they also underlined the extraordinary change in American objectives in Korea brought about overnight by the Chinese intervention. In a few short days of battle and retreat, Washington had tacitly renounced any prospect of presiding over a unified, non-communist Korean state. The Administration was now willing to consider a peace proposal based upon restoring the prewar status of Korea, divided at the 38th Parallel. This was a momentous change of heart, and one which proved entirely unwelcome when it became known at the Dai Ichi.

And if the Americans were often impatient of what they considered crude displays of self-interest by the British, in the aftermath of Attlee's visit, they brooded to considerable effect about what the British delegation had said. First, the British had cast some penetrating doubts upon the likely effectiveness of limited war with China. Nothing could be worse for the United States than to launch a blockade of the Chinese coast, or even a bombing offensive against industrial targets, only to find that these made no impact upon Peking's behaviour. Acheson also declared at the National Security Council meeting of 12 December that the Anglo-American talks had emphasised how important a close relationship with Britain remained, 'since we can bring US power into play only with the cooperation of the British'.

In the weeks following the departure of the British delegation, the domestic debate about policy in Korea raged with increasing bitterness in the United States, in both public and private forums. The Administration's standing with the electorate fell to unprecedented depths. An 8 December Gallup poll found 49 per cent of respondents disapproving of Truman's leadership, and only 20 per cent of those who had heard of Acheson thinking well of him. It was a paradox of the period that right-wing Republicans alternated between demands for all-out war with China, and immediate withdrawal from Korea. A January opinion poll found 49 per cent of Americans believed that US entry into Korea had been mistaken, and 66 per cent considered that the US should now abandon the peninsula. These confused responses would become wretchedly familiar a generation later, in the midst of another Asian war. In 1950, they represented the impotent political thrashings of a public opinion unaccustomed to frustration of its will at home or abroad; to military defeat – least of all at the hands of a primitive people; or to the exercise of patience. Grassroots America had only the dimmest perception of what was taking place in Korea, but it understood with disagreeable clarity that little glory or happiness was being won there. It was incomparably easier to understand the rhetoric of Republicanism, demanding that America's full might should be employed to bring the Asians to heel, than the uncertain pleading for restraint from the Administration. Why should the United States be called upon to exercise restraint, when the enemy was plainly displaying none?

It was in the hope of focusing public understanding on the importance and seriousness of what was taking place in Korea that Truman declared a state of national emergency on 16 December. The Administration now believed that Korea could be held – following the return of General Collins from a fresh visit on 8 December – and should be held. Kennan and Rusk recalled the defiant example of the British in 1940: to abandon South Korea now 'would set a poor example of what it means to be a friend of the United States'. Truman and his advisers had determined to resist the calls of the Allies for an immediate ceasefire, and to resist any such a resolution in the United Nations. They were determined that MacArthur's army must improve its military position, regain some lost ground, to be able to negotiate from reasonable strength. To appease world opinion, Washington felt obliged to take a desperate diplomatic gamble, supporting a United Nations resolution calling for an immediate ceasefire in Korea proposed by a clutch of Asian states on 11 December. The Americans, who wanted no such thing, counted upon the Chinese rejecting it.

Fortunately for the Administration's hopes, the Chinese indeed dismissed the resolution, since it included no call for the removal of all foreign troops, or for the withdrawal of the Seventh Fleet from Taiwan, or for the recognition of Peking at the UN. Washington now forced through its own resolution, against the deepest misgivings of Britain and the other allies, branding China an aggressor. Even such a moderate man as Bradley believed that, if the United States suffered the humiliation of military expulsion from Korea, she should retaliate with air attacks upon the Chinese mainland.

As the military position in Korea continued to deteriorate into the New Year, a growing divide became apparent between America's political and military leaders about possible responses. Admiral Sherman, consistently the most bellicose of the Joint Chiefs, demanded early in the New Year that America should stop equivocating and recognise a full state of war with China. On 12 January, the Joint Chiefs recommended hitting China with 'damaging naval and air attacks' if the communists attacked American forces outside the Korean peninsula. They also favoured sponsoring guerrilla action in China, allowing the Nationalists to invade the mainland, and 'aerial reconnaissance' of Manchuria and the Chinese coast. If the UN did not agree, said Admiral Sherman, 'the time has come for unilateral action by the United States'. When Acheson and the National Security Council proved unenthusiastic, Bradley emphasised that the JCS were not advocating a large-scale invasion of the Chinese mainland. But he remarked that there was 'heavy popular pressure for the United States to do something', unilaterally if necessary. Marshall took the point, but suggested that the United Nations would deteriorate into a mere forum for debate if the United States acted alone in Korea. Truman postponed any decision by referring back the whole subject of direct action against China for further study.

Then, through the last days of January and early into February, imperceptibly the mood began to shift in Washington. As it became evident that military disaster was no longer imminent in Korea, as the choices before the Administration became less stark, so passions cooled and the more dramatic options receded. State Department analysts argued strongly against the view that the Chinese intervention in Korea represented a Soviet build-up to a new world war. Washington was at last beginning to look much more closely at narrower, more nationalistic reasons for Chinese behaviour. In the eyes of the 'hawks', MacArthur notable among them, the change of mood in Washington represented a weakening of the American position, influenced by the feeble fears of the Allies, and above all the British. Yet the British might legitimately claim that events increasingly supported their interpretation of Chinese behaviour. Acheson told Bradley: 'We are fighting the wrong nation. We are fighting the second team, whereas the real enemy is the Soviet Union.'[42] Increasingly, senior members of the Truman Administration and the State Department began to develop the view that would become dominant in the months that followed: that the United States was fighting the wrong war against the wrong communist power in Korea. On 30 January, Peking attempted to get a letter through to the US government, a gesture Marshall declared should be treated with 'the utmost seriousness'. CIA estimates of Chinese casualties suggested cause for growing concern in Peking. Washington began to adopt a more attentive attitude to straws in the wind that suggested possible Chinese interest in a ceasefire. On 12 February, C. B. Marshall of the Policy Planning Staff suggested to Paul Nitze that stabilisation in Korea would save 'two sets of faces.'[43] Acheson, more than any other man, may claim credit for having discouraged the President's most bellicose advisers, arguing constantly for further discussion and delay. A 23 February paper from the State Department summarised his arguments against any escalation or change of policy in the Far East:

a) the capability of the Moscow-Peiping axis to inflict a decisive defeat upon United Nations forces if they make the decision to do so; b) the risk of extending the Korean conflict to other areas and even into the general war at a time when [the United States was] not ready to risk general war; c) the heavy additional drain on American manpower and resources without a clearly seen outcome of the effort; d) loss of unity among [America's] allies and in the United Nations in support of the Korean effort, and e) the diversion of additional United States effort from other vital requirements.[44]

It is easy to focus attention upon Washington and London's misjudgements in the winter of 1950–51, and to forget those of the other side. If, at the end of 1950, Peking had shown itself ready to negotiate a ceasefire based upon the *status quo ante* in Korea, Mao Tse Tung's government would have been in an overwhelmingly strong position to gain its seat at the UN, and to divide America from her allies if Washington proved reluctant to negotiate. MacArthur was not alone in his hubris. Peking deluded itself that absolute military victory, the reunification of Korea under communist rule, lay within its grasp. Between December and May, when repeated defeats at the hands of the UN gradually convinced the Chinese that total victory was not attainable, they showed themselves entirely intractable until their moment had passed, and threw away a commanding political advantage. In December, as the first communist power to inflict a great defeat upon the West, China's worldwide prestige was at its zenith. Had Peking accepted a negotiated end to the struggle with its own armies victorious, China's military standing for a generation to come would have been immense. Instead, however, by continuing the war, the communists gave time for the West to reassert its own military might, to demonstrate that even the greatest peasant army could be repulsed and defeated. If Washington had made a devastating miscalculation in the autumn of 1950, by driving for the Yalu, Peking's error that winter was equally great, in reaching out for a victory beyond its powers.

Pragmatic considerations almost certainly weighed far more heavily than moral ones, in bringing about America's decision against extending the war to China in the winter of 1950. There were grounds for overwhelming doubt as to whether bombing China, unleashing Chiang's Nationalists upon the mainland, or enforcing a blockade would have a decisive impact upon China's capacity to continue the war in Korea, or upon the stability of Mao Tse Tung's regime in Peking. However, any of these options created a real danger of Soviet intervention. If this took place, the Pentagon was doubtful whether American forces in the Far East could hold their ground, or even whether a third world war could be avoided. Any major initiative against China by the United States would cost Washington the support of the United Nations – more serious, that of the Western Allies. President Truman and his advisers were scarcely enthusiastic about, or even satisfied with, the policy of waging a limited war for limited objectives, to which they became tacitly committed in the winter of 1950, after seeing imminent victory slip from their grasp. But their debate, and its conclusion, had a decisive influence upon the struggle with General Douglas MacArthur, which reached its climax three months later. For MacArthur attempted to pursue an argument about the war, and about its extension to China, which had been effectively concluded in Washington before the Supreme Commander made his play.

How close did the United States come, in the winter of 1950, to employing atomic bombs against the Chinese? Much closer, the answer must be, than her allies cared to believe at the time. If Truman and the fellow-members of his Administration recoiled from bearing the responsibility for so terrible an act, America's leading military men, from the Joint Chiefs downwards, were far more equivocal, and seemed far less disturbed by the prospect. All those at the seat of power in Washington drew back from discussion of the nuclear option as the military situation in Korea improved. But had the Chinese proved able to convert the defeat of the UN forces into their destruction, had Eighth Army been unable to check its retreat, and been driven headlong for the coastal ports with massive casualties, it is impossible to declare with certainty that Truman would have resisted demands for an atomic demonstration against China. The pressure upon the politicians from the military leaders of America might well have become irresistible, in the face of strategic disaster. The men who reversed the fortunes of the UN on the battlefield in Korea in the first weeks of 1951 may also have saved the world from the nightmare of a new Hiroshima in Asia.

3. The Arrival of Ridgway

On the Korean battlefield, the United Nations entered the New Year of 1951 still losing ground, still in desperate straits. Yet more than a week earlier, an event took place which was to have an overwhelming influence upon the turning of the tide of the war in Korea. On the morning of 23 December, General Walton Walker was driving from his headquarters to that of 27 Commonwealth Brigade. Walker, the doughty little hero of the Pusan Perimeter, was a weary, almost broken man. His quarrels with Almond, the collapse of his army, the knowledge that MacArthur was consider-ing his replacement, had reduced the morale of the Eighth Army commander and his staff to an ebb as low as that of their troops. At Eighth Army headquarters, officers spoke openly of evacuation as the only course; talked without shame of the need for every unit to have its 'bug-out route'. Walker was indisputably a brave man. But he was not a clever one. He had given all that he could offer to the cause of the United Nations. Now, a ROK truck turned across the road in front of his jeep. The general was thrown out in the collision, and suffered head injuries from which he died, on the way to hospital.

General Matthew Ridgway was sipping an after-dinner highball at the home of a friend when he was summoned to receive a telephone call from the Army Chief of Staff, Lawton Collins. Walker was dead. MacArthur had asked for Ridgway to succeed him. To lull his companions' curiosity, Ridgway lingered drinking for a few minutes before driving home with his wife. The next morning, Saturday, he paid a quick call at the Pentagon to collect his papers, chat briefly with Sherman, Chief of Naval Operations, and left that night for Tokyo without an opportunity to see his family again. He arrived at Haneda airport just before midnight on

Christmas Day. The next morning at 9.30 he called upon MacArthur at the Dai Ichi. The Supreme Commander had no hesitation in expressing his enthusiasm for an attack on mainland China by the Nationalist Chinese, as a means of relieving the pressure upon South Korea. He showed his acute concern at the 'mission vacuum' in which he considered the army was operating, while the politicians decided where they wanted to go. He painted a bleak picture of the military situation, before assuring Ridgway of his support in whatever he decided to do: 'The Eighth Army is yours, Matt. Do what you think best.' At 4 p.m. that afternoon, 26 December, Ridgway was shivering on the apron at Taegu, being met by Eighth Army's Chief of Staff, General Leven Allen.

Matthew Bunker Ridgway was fifty-six. At the beginning of World War II, he had been a lieutenant-colonel in the Plans Division of the War Department, where he remained until 1942. He then became, first, assistant commander, soon commander of 82nd Airborne Division, which he led with distinction in the Sicilian and Normandy landings. In August 1944, he took over 18 Airborne Corps, which he commanded in the Ardennes campaign. He was regarded not only by his fellow-countrymen, but also by their British allies, as one of the outstanding American soldiers of the war. Had he, rather than Browning, commanded at Arnhem, the outcome of that operation might have been astonishingly different – or certainly, less disastrous. He possessed almost all the military virtues – courage, brains, ruthlessness, decision. He made the grenade and field dressing on his shoulder straps familiar symbols, as much his own trademarks as Montgomery's beret or Patton's pistols. It has been cruelly but appositely remarked that Walton Walker's death, making possible the coming of Ridgway, was the salvation of Eighth Army. It is difficult to overstate the importance of the contribution that Ridgway made to the United Nations cause in Korea, and to the achievement of a tolerable outcome of the war.

Ridgway arrived on 26 December full of hope that with the Chinese impetus temporarily spent, he might be able to organise a rapid counter-offensive. But within a few hours, visiting his formations, 'I had discovered that our forces were simply not mentally and spiritually ready for the sort of action I had been planning . . . The men I met along the road, those I stopped to talk to and to solicit gripes from – they too all conveyed to me a conviction that this was a bewildered army, not sure of itself or its leaders, not sure what they were doing there, wondering when they would hear the whistle of that homebound transport.'[45]

The new commander was dismayed to discover the shortage of essential winter clothing and equipment, the poor food and lack of amenities available to the troops. 'The leadership I found in many instances sadly lacking, and I said so out loud.' Ridgway was unimpressed, to put it politely, by 'the unwillingness of the army to forgo certain creature comforts, its timidity about getting off the scanty roads, its reluctance to move without radio and telephone contact, and its lack of imagination in dealing with a foe whom they soon outmatched in firepower and dominated in the air and on the surrounding seas'.[46] He met Sir Robert Mansergh, and told him, according to the British general, that 'training was needed, and touched on the problem of pampered troops. I said that all ranks felt the absence of information and were in a vacuum. He said he could tell me nothing, because he knew nothing except "Stand And Fight".'[47]

The transformation of Eighth Army after the coming of its new commander astonished and profoundly impressed all those who witnessed it. 'It was incredible, the change that came over the Americans and their discipline,' said a British gunner officer.[48] 'They started to wash their vehicles, and things like that.' Colonel John Michaelis of 27th Infantry called it 'magic, the way Ridgway took that defeated army and turned it around. He was a breath of fresh air, a showman, what the army desperately needed.'[49] From the outset, Ridgway demanded a new attention to terrain, and the assessment of key features which must be defended. There would be a fresh focus upon defence – and attack – in depth, with unit flanks secured against infiltration. Above all, the army must get off the roads, must be willing to reach for and hold high ground – some British officers had been bewildered to see American units digging in to defend roadside positions at the base of prominent hills, where they were totally exposed to incoming fire. Ridgway was unimpressed by the performance of the corps and divisional commanders. He wrote to Collins in Washington, urging the need to awaken Americans both in government and across the land to what was taking place in Korea, the demand for 'a toughness of soul as well as body'. He had no patience with the preoccupation among Eighth Army – and at the Dai Ichi – with evacuation of the peninsula. Ridgway did not believe this should be remotely necessary. The only contingency for which he was willing to prepare was withdrawal to a new Pusan Perimeter: but this one would be dug and prepared on an unprecedented scale. A senior engineer officer and thousands of Korean labourers were soon working day and night, creating a powerful defensive line in the south-east.

Ridgway – and soon MacArthur also – realised the immense advantage of his own shortening supply lines, while those of the Chinese were now extended to the limits of their fragile logistics system. MacArthur told the British Brigadier Basil Coad on 26 January that on the Yalu, the Chinese might be able to support a million men under arms; but at a line through Pyongyang this figure fell to 600,000; at the 38th Parallel, it became 300,000; forty miles south of Seoul, it became only 200,000. This was one of the Supreme Commander's less fanciful judgements. Prisoners were reporting that as much as 50 per cent of the Chinese front-line length was afflicted by frostbite. 'While we wished to continue to push the enemy, we could not open our mouth too wide,' said Hu Seng of Marshal Peng's staff. 'China was unprepared for the new military situation created by the deep advance. We were now in a position where we could not continue to reinforce our army in Korea, because we could not supply more men.' The Chinese offensive had exhausted its momentum. After inflicting a devastating shock upon the UN Command and the nations from which this was drawn, the initiative in the Korean War was once more about to change hands.

10 » NEMESIS: THE DISMISSAL OF MACARTHUR

In December 1950, by a remarkable paradox, it became General Douglas MacArthur's purpose to persuade his political masters in Washington, not only that the war in Korea could not be won, but that the absolute defeat of the United Nations was imminent. To this end, his headquarters launched a propaganda campaign of doom-laden pessimism. They exaggerated the numbers of Chinese troops now believed to be in Korea, or capable of being committed. They proclaimed their insistent doubts as to whether the UN armies could confront the enemy successfully. The Supreme Commander's belief that the war against the communists in Korea should be extended across the border into China had become an obsession. In a long series of letters and cables, he pursued his argument with the Chiefs of Staff about the bombing of the Yalu bridges and beyond.

It will never be certain how far MacArthur's affronted personal hubris influenced his attitude to the Chinese, how far he became instilled with a yearning for crude revenge upon the people who had brought all his hopes and triumphs in Korea to nothing. But there can be no doubt that in the winter of 1950, the sense of destiny which had guided MacArthur from Corregidor, back across the Pacific, to the reconstruction of Japan, the salvation of South Korea and the landing at Inchon, now persuaded him that he should confront the power of communist China. It seems probable that he did not consider it beyond his own powers to reinstate Chiang Kai Shek's Nationalist regime in Peking. Certainly, his enthusiasm for committing Nationalist troops in Korea in the largest possible numbers seemed to go beyond any direct military considerations in the peninsula. If Nationalist divisions were deployed in Korea in strength, if they could drive Mao Tse Tung's legions back to the Yalu, would not the momentum to allow them to go further become irresistible? Given the strength of militant anti-communist feeling in the United States, if the Chinese Nationalists got as far as the border of their own country, would not the pressure upon the Administration be overwhelming, to allow them to reverse the 'loss' of China, which had caused so many prominent Americans so much grief? 'Brave, brilliant, and majestic,' one of MacArthur's biographers, William Manchester, has written, 'he was a colossus bestriding Korea until the nemesis of his hubris overtook him. He simply could not bear to end his career in checkmate.'[1]

In an attempt to curb the extravagant statements emerging from the Dai Ichi, on 6 December Truman had issued his presidential order to all US theatre commanders, warning them to exercise 'extreme caution' in their public pronouncements, and to clear all of these with the State or Defense Departments. But MacArthur continued his propaganda campaign, merely issuing his threats and demands 'off the record' to correspondents. There was a real danger, he warned, that if he was compelled to continue the war under the present restrictions imposed by Washington, the evacuation of the entire peninsula would become necessary.

His play was called. On 29 December, a new directive from the Joint Chiefs of Staff confirmed that he could expect no further major reinforcements, and that Washington remained convinced that Korea was the wrong place to precipitate a major war. MacArthur was called upon to maintain a front as best he could in 'successive positions'. If his armies were forced back to the Kum river, then the United States would indeed be obliged to preside over an evacuation. But the JCS reminded SCAP, somewhat limply, that 'a successful resistance to Chinese-North Korean aggression at some position in Korea, and a deflation of the military and political prestige of the Chinese Communists would be of great importance to our national interest . . .' In other words, MacArthur must continue to do his best with what he had, upon existing terms.

The general disagreed. On 30 December, he dispatched a reply to Washington, bitterly protesting the flagging will for victory that he perceived in the Administration, and the attempt to make himself a scapegoat for disaster. He made four demands of his own. First, for a blockade of the Chinese coast; second, for an onslaught on China's industrial capability for making war, by air and naval bombardment; third, for the reinforcement of the UN forces in Korea by Chinese Nationalist forces; fourth, for all restrictions imposed upon Chiang Kai Shek's forces to be removed, enabling them to launch direct attacks upon the Chinese mainland. This programme, MacArthur declared, would not only save Korea, but inflict 'such a destructive blow upon Red China's capacity to wage aggressive war that it would remove her as a further threat to peace in Asia for generations to come'.

Once again, amid acute dismay in Washington, MacArthur's proposals were rejected. The stakes in Korea, he was informed, had risen as high as the Administration intended that they should go. If the peninsula could not be held within the existing framework of UN operations, then it must be conceded to the communists. MacArthur's tone towards Washington now became increasingly distraught. He accused the Joint Chiefs of crippling his authority, and suggested that the morale of his men was suffering acute damage from 'shameful propaganda which has falsely condemned their fighting qualities'. This assertion alone suggested a disturbing measure of ignorance, or wilful fantasy, about events during 'the big bug-out'. He spoke of 'extraordinary limitations and conditions' imposed upon his own command, and ended with an armageddonistic flourish: Eighth Army could hold, he said, 'if overriding political considerations so dictate for any length of time up to its complete destruction'.

Many years later, General Charles Bolté, Chief of Plans at the Pentagon, freely conceded the nervousness even the Joint Chiefs suffered, in dealing with MacArthur: 'We were all rather scared of him. When you considered what he had been . . .'² Yet if, in the past, the Administration and the Pentagon had sometimes havered in their handling of MacArthur, they did so no longer. His threats and bombast received a response of exemplary dignity. A new JCS directive on 12 January reasserted American policy. The following day, in a personal letter, President Truman sought to restore some heart to MacArthur for continuing the struggle in Korea. Even if the mainland was lost, he urged, the struggle might continue from the offshore islands. Even if evacuation became necessary, it would be made clear to the world that this 'is forced upon us by military necessity, and that we shall not accept the result militarily or politically until the aggression has been rectified'. MacArthur's credibility suffered a serious blow a few days later, when Collins, Vandenburg and Bedell Smith reported back to Washington after a tour of the front in Korea. They discovered the remarkable change of mood that Ridgway was already creating, the growing optimism that the line could be held. If Ridgway lacked the status of Mac-Arthur, he was a battlefield soldier of great distinction. The new commander of Eighth Army offered Washington hopes and judgements incomparably more acceptable than those emerging from Tokyo.

In one respect, however, MacArthur correctly perceived an undeclared, radical change of policy by the Administration. There was no longer either hope or expectation of achieving a unified non-communist Korea. Washington's hopes now centred upon exerting sufficient military leverage to cause Peking and Pyong-yang to negotiate upon the basis of a return to the pre-war division of Korea. The United Nations' objectives from the spring of 1951 to the end in 1953 were plainly limited. At an acceptable cost in casualties to Eighth Army, Ridgway's forces sought to kill sufficient communists and defend sufficient real estate to secure peace.

That was all, and for many soldiers it was not enough. In the two years that followed, it became progressively more difficult to define the war aims of the UN in terms comprehensible, far less acceptable, to the men on the line. Even some higher commanders never entirely came to terms with the new, undeclared circumstances. Month after month throughout 1951, long after the peace talks began, army and corps planners devised elaborate schemes for airborne or amphibious envelopments, for full-blooded thrusts to the Yalu. None was ever to be implemented.

Ridgway's achievement in the first weeks of 1951 was that despite all this, despite the political congealment that disgusted and infuriated the chief inhabitant of the Dai Ichi, Eighth Army's commander successfully motivated his beaten and battered forces to make important gains, and decisively to demonstrate their ability to turn the tables on the Chinese. The enemy entered the New Year with the very problem that so afflicted the UN two months earlier: a long and vulnerable supply line. Communist casualties had been enormous, not least from the winter weather. There were still believed to be some 486,000 Chinese and North Korean troops in the country, against around 365,000 under the flag of the United Nations. But the raw figures masked the immense UN superiority of resources, above all air power. The balance of advantage had shifted sharply away from the communists.

Eighth Army now undertook a series of cautious probes, to test the enemy's mood. In mid-January, the 27th RCT pushed north to Suwon without meeting significant resistance. There were no major Chinese formations more than a few miles south of Wonju. A second reconnaissance by IX Corps on the 22nd also found itself treading empty space. On the 25th, Ridgway launched a more ambitious operation on a two-division front. The Chinese 38th and 50th Armies fell back, offering only sporadic resistance. By 9 February, the ruins of Inchon and Suwon were back in UN hands, and a fine attack by the 25th Division had regained Hill 440, north of Suwon. Ridgway's men lost just seventy killed, while they counted over 4,000 dead Chinese on the battlefield. I Corps pushed steadily onwards to the line of the Han river.

Further east, there were now two weeks of much heavier

switchback fighting. An advance by X Corps was met by a counter-attack against three ROK divisions on 11 February. The Americans were forced to give ground in order to hold their line. In mid-February, there was a fierce battle for the town of Chipyong-ni, where the 23rd Regiment of 2nd Division under Colonel Paul Freeman found itself encircled together with the French battalion. But they held on, sustained by air-dropped supplies. The Americans were vastly encouraged to see the effects of their firepower upon headlong night attacks by massed Chinese infantry, the awesome 'human wave' technique. 'We could see them tumbling down like bowling pins,' wrote Corporal Pete Schultz, a machine-gunner with the 1/23rd. 'As long as the flares were up we never had trouble finding a target, and the flares also slowed the advance as the Chinese took what cover they could to avoid being seen ... As soon as it got light enough some Boxcars came flying in, and those beautiful parachutes with more supplies came falling down. I will never forget that sight. It was just beautiful. As it turned out, we did not need it. We had held, and tanks from 5th Cavalry Regiment broke through to our positions. The Chinese had left.'[3]

The Chipyong-ni battle represented not only a fine perform-ance by American units, but also an important stage in the rehabili-tation and revival of the morale of 2nd Division, which had been so crushingly handled at Kunu-ri. After a week of hard fighting, in which North Korean forces broke through close to Chechon, expos-ing the X Corps's flank, the communist offensive ran out of steam. It was a decisive moment of the war, of incalculable importance to the spirits of the UN forces. They had confronted the strongest offensive that the Chinese could throw against them, and they had driven it back. Formations that, only a few weeks earlier, possessed no thought beyond escape from Korea on any terms, now found renewed energy and will. The 'gooks' could be beaten. Americans had done it once, they would do it again. A British observer, Air Vice-Marshal C. A. Bouchier, reported exultantly to London: 'The myth of the magical millions of the Chinese in Korea has been exploded. In the last United Nations offensive, the Americans have learned how easy it is to kill the Chinese, and their morale has greatly increased thereby.'

Ridgway's army jumped off on the next phase of his advance, Operation KILLER, on 21 February. By 1 March, they had closed up the UN line south of the Han, driving back the Chinese with huge casualties, by the progressive, massive use of firepower. The advance of the seven American divisions now in the line was the twentieth-century successor to the Roman 'tortoise': instead of long columns, exposed to surprise attack, Ridgway's formations deployed at every stage for all-round defence in depth, securing themselves against infiltration while they waited for the massed artillery and air strikes to do their work upon the Chinese positions. On 7 March, KILLER was succeeded by RIPPER, a measured advance to a new phase line, IDAHO, on the central front. Ridgway successfully dissuaded MacArthur from providing his customary signal to the enemy of an impending offensive, by visiting the front to be photographed 'firing the starting gun' with the formations involved. The envelopment of Seoul that followed the success of RIPPER made the communist evacuation of the capital inevitable. On 14 March, the victors recovered a devastated city, a metropolis of ruins and corrugated iron, in which only the Capitol and the railway station survived, of the principal buildings. An attempted airborne envelopment of the retreating enemy by the 187th RCT at Munsan – the only major parachute operation of the war – was unsuccessful. Another disappointment was the extraordinary escape of the North Korean 10th Division, which had been fighting since January in the south of the country as guerrillas, far behind the UN lines. Now, seeing the protracted shift in the strategic situation which was taking place, the 10th broke through the ROK lines near Kangnung, to rejoin the communist armies. The British General Sir Richard Gale reported to London: 'The enemy has conducted his withdrawal methodically and with no little military skill. He knows how to make the best use of the terrain, both on a large scale and on a minor tactical scale.'[4]

In a shrewd letter to London on 12 March, the British Military

Attaché, Brigadier A. K. Ferguson, drew attention to local problems which, at theatre level, were precisely those which so irked General MacArthur:

I foresee difficulties in maintaining morale indefinitely in present circumstances, in view of the ill-defined task set for the United Nations forces. You have no doubt heard of General MacArthur's remark of some months ago, when he said he was fighting 'in a political vacuum'. It seems to me that the reputed objective of UN forces in Korea which is 'to repel aggression and restore peace and security to the area' is much too vague under present circumstances to give the Supreme Commander in the field a military objective, the attainment of which would bring hostilities to a close. While it is outside my province to discuss the political issues, I consider the question of the maintenance of the morale of the troops to be a matter for serious consideration. For the past ten days, 'Operation Killer' has been conducted in Korea with the publicly pronounced intention of 'killing Communists'. While this no doubt gave the US 8th Army a limited objective, it is neither a desirable nor lasting objective which will appeal to any educated individual. Already many British and American officers and other ranks have asked such questions as 'When will the war in Korea end?', 'When do you think the UN forces can be withdrawn from Korea?', 'What is our object in Korea?' Such questions tend to make me believe that, unless the British and American forces in Korea are given some definite goal at which to aim, the commander in the field will have the greatest difficulty in maintaining morale. I have only included British and American troops, because generally speaking the relatively small numbers of troops of other western nations which are represented are adventurous mercenaries who are as content to serve as part of an international fighting brigade in Korea as elsewhere.[5]

On 27 March, another landmark was passed when the first UN troops – ROK I Corps – once more crossed the 38th Parallel. They took the town of Yangyang four days later. The Americans kept pace with them, driving north from Uijongbu. But this time, there was to be no headlong race for the Yalu. Ridgway's objective was merely to reach the 'Iron Triangle', south of Pyongyang, the heart of the communist supply and communications network. By 9 April, the UN armies had reached the KANSAS line. Here, with their positions anchored upon the barriers of the Imjin river in the west and the Hwachon reservoir in the centre, they could pause and gather breath before embarking upon the next phase. The line from coast to coast had shortened to just 115 miles. In the days that followed, I and IX pushed forward a few miles further, and a new advance to the WYOMING line was being planned. 'We now had a tested, tough, and highly confident army,' wrote Ridgway, 'experienced in this sort of fighting, inured to the vicissitudes of the weather, and possessed of firepower far exceeding anything we had been able to use on the enemy heretofore. The only development that could possibly cause us to withdraw from the peninsula was, I felt sure, massive intervention by the Soviets. In the spring of 1951, such intervention was not altogether an impossibility.'[6]

But the next move belonged not to Moscow, or Eighth Army, but to Peking and Washington: Peking, where a massive spring offensive by nineteen Chinese armies was being prepared, in an attempt to undo all that Ridgway had accomplished in his astonishing four months in Korea; and Washington, where patience had at last expired with the dangerous military majesty of the Dai Ichi.

*

President Truman's dismissal of General Douglas MacArthur has been the subject of millions of words of narrative and analysis. It is unlikely that any important new evidence will emerge to alter historical perceptions of events in Washington and Tokyo in the spring of 1951. In a primarily military study of the war in Korea, it is redundant to rehearse once again much familiar detail. Here, it is relevant only to summarise the arguments and the events that culminated in the Great Fall of 11 April.

Ten months of crisis in Korea had exercised a powerful influence upon the domestic politics of the United States. They had witnessed the growing ascendancy of the right wing of the Republican party, convinced that the United States faced a co-ordinated external and internal communist conspiracy, of which North Korean aggression was merely one manifestation. Republicans found it intolerable to behold the spectacle of United States military power lurching ineffectually to maintain a tenuous grip in Korea against the communist hordes. If their opposition to deep entanglement in European alliances was founded upon a dislike of the restraint that European liberals thereby sought to impose upon American foreign policy, their enthusiasm for a 'forward policy' in the Pacific and the Far East assumed an American freedom of manoeuvre in the hemisphere which events in Korea seemed to deny. It was only five years since the United States had emerged from a war in which she triumphantly projected her huge power across five continents, and emerged with an apparently unchallengeable primacy in world affairs. Yet now, America seemed unable to impose her will upon a nation of tinpot dictators and cotton-clad communists. In the 1980s, this frustration of power seems a commonplace. But in 1950–51, it was a repugnant revelation to much of the American people. It seemed intolerable that American boys should be suffering and dying in thousands in an odorous Asian wasteland, fighting a war with goalposts set by Pyongyang and Peking. Prominent Republicans such as Senator Taft demanded that America should fight for her interests in Asia upon terms that would enable her to use her vast technological superiority. Implicit if not explicit in much conservative rhetoric of this period was the conviction that American policy should not exclude the use of nuclear weapons, America's greatest technological advantage of all. The Republicans also exploited the charge that President Truman had acted unconstitutionally by sending American troops to Korea without the formal assent of the US Congress, an issue which may have possessed some substance.

The most conspicuous consequence of Senate pressure upon

the Administration for a more vigorous brand of anti-communism was the commitment of hundreds of millions of dollars, and firm guarantees of American support, for Chiang Kai Shek's regime on Formosa. Dean Rusk declared: 'We recognise the National Government of the Republic of China, even though the territory under its control is severely restricted . . . We believe it more authentically represents the views of the great body of the people of China, particularly the historic demand for independence from foreign control . . .' And matching the United States' new commitments to the anti-communist cause in the Far East, four further divisions were dispatched to reinforce the US Army in Europe.

But these developments of the Cold War were peripheral to the central debate, about what was to be done with America's hot war against communism in Korea. From Tokyo, MacArthur maintained constant pressure on the Administration, to commit the United States to the defeat of communism in Asia. On 13 February, MacArthur declared that 'the concept advanced by some that we establish a line across Korea and enter into positional warfare is wholly unrealistic and illusory'. He had now conceived a plan to cut off Korea from China by massive air attack. Even more ambitiously, he proposed to create an impassable boundary between the forces of communism and those of freedom, by sowing a no-man's-land with radioactive waste. He discussed amphibious and airborne envelopments of enemy forces on a scale that would have dwarfed Inchon. 'MacArthur believed even more deeply than before,' wrote Courtney Whitney, one of those closest to his confidence, 'that Red Chinese aggression in Asia could not be stopped by killing Chinese, no matter how many, in Korea, so long as her power to make war remained inviolate.'[7] On 7 March at Suwon, MacArthur proclaimed loftily: 'Vital decisions have yet to be made – decisions far beyond the scope of the authority vested in me as the military commander, but which must provide on the highest international level an answer to the obscurities which now becloud the unsolved problems raised by Red China's undeclared war in Korea.'

Truman, in Washington, was making it clear both in public and in private that with the armies close to the line from which the war had begun, it was time to discuss a peace on these positions. MacArthur at once declared his profound disagreement with the President's view, by issuing his own statement:

> The enemy must by now be painfully aware that a decision of the United Nations to depart from its tolerant effort to contain the war to the area of Korea, through an expansion of our military operations to its coastal areas and interior bases, would doom Red China to the risk of imminent military collapse . . . The Korean nation and people, which have been so cruelly ravaged, must not be sacrificed. This is a paramount concern. Apart from the military area of the problem where issues are resolved in the course of combat, the fundamental questions continue to be political in nature, and must find their answer in the diplomatic sphere. Within the area of my authority as the military commander, however, it would be needless to say that I stand ready at any time to confer in the field with the commander-in-chief of the enemy forces in the earnest effort to find any military means whereby realisation of the political objectives of the United Nations in Korea, to which no nation may justly take exception, might be accomplished without further bloodshed.

A constant stream of propaganda now flowed out of the Dai Ichi, directed as much against the Administration in Washington as against the communists. Above all, the general and his entourage were disgusted by the attitude of America's enfeebled and compromising allies. MacArthur's staff spread word of a conspiracy by the British, to induce the United States to give Red China Chiang Kai Shek's seat at the UN. The constant refrain from Tokyo was that any truce, any botched-up compromise in Korea which left the Chinese militarily undefeated, would be a national disaster for the United States.

It was ironic that in this crisis between the civil and military power, President Truman and his close advisers found themselves in much closer accord with America's allies than with their own people. There is no evidence to support the view – later widely propagated in the Dai Ichi – that the British 'conspired' with Truman, or indeed, had a decisive influence upon his decision, to dispose of MacArthur. But they left no doubt of their fears about where his excesses might lead, and certainly strengthened the will of the Washington Administration to act. On 9 April, that eminently sensible soldier Sir William Slim, Chief of the Imperial General Staff, presided over a meeting of the British Chiefs of Staff at which he expressed a characteristic European view:

in his opinion, General MacArthur personally wanted war with China . . . As he had proved in November and December last year, he had few scruples about colouring both intelligence and operational reports to suit his own ends. In present circumstances, it would be most inadvisable to delegate to the United States Joint Chiefs of Staff responsibility for deciding what constituted 'a massive air attack' [around the Yalu]. They were scared of General MacArthur; his definition of the scope of air attack would be what they would work on, and this definition might well be coloured to suit his own wishes.[8]

In a long message about Anglo-American attitudes to Korea, the Foreign Secretary cabled to the British Ambassador in Washington:

Our principal difficulty is General MacArthur. His policy is different from the policy of the UN. He seems to want a war with China. We do not. It is no exaggeration to say that by his public utterances, he has weakened public confidence in this country and in Western Europe in the quality of American political judgement and leadership. Here we seem to have a case of a commander publicly suggesting that his policy is not the stated policy of his government, not subject to the control of his own government, and whom his own government is, nevertheless, unwilling and unable to discipline.[9]

No more. The intense debates among the British and other allies about MacArthur were redundant when this cable was sent. London was given no hint or forewarning. But Truman had already determined that MacArthur must be sacked: 'I could no longer tolerate his insubordination.' On 5 April, a letter was read on the floor of the House of Representatives, from MacArthur to Representative Joe Martin, answering his request for the Supreme Commander's comments on Martin's demand that Chiang's Nationalists should be permitted to land on the mainland of China.

> It seems strangely difficult for some [wrote MacArthur] to realise that here in Asia is where the Communist conspirators have elected to make their play for global conquest, and that we have joined the issue thus raised on the battlefield; that here we fight Europe's war with arms while the diplomats there still fight it with words; that if we lose this war to Communism in Asia the fall of Europe is inevitable; win it and Europe most probably would avoid war and yet preserve freedom. As you have pointed out, we must win. There is no substitute for victory . . .

The yawning chasm between Washington and the Dai Ichi was now entirely apparent to the governments and peoples of the United States and her allies. Senator Wayne Morse remarked that the nation possessed two foreign policies, 'that of General Mac-Arthur and that of the President'. There was open speculation in the American press about the general's sacking, although Washington still doubted Truman's will to carry it through. 'MACARTHUR RECALL RULED OUT', headlined the Washington Post. 'REPRIMAND IS STILL SEEN POSSIBLE'. On Friday 6 April, Truman presided over a meeting of his closest advisers at the White House, to discuss the future of General MacArthur. He did not tell them that he had already made the decision to dismiss his Supreme Commander. Averell Harriman said he believed that MacArthur had given ample grounds for his own removal two years ago, by his high-handedness in opposing aspects of the Administration's occupation policy in Japan. Marshall opposed precipitate action, and asked for time to consider. Bradley believed that MacArthur must go, on the plain grounds of insubordination. Both he and Dean Acheson urged ensuring that the White House had the support of the Joint Chiefs of Staff, before taking any action. But all the men in the room knew that the need for secrecy was paramount, to prevent MacArthur's supporters, in Congress and the country, from mobilising. At a second meeting later that morning, Truman asked Marshall to review all the messages that had passed between Washington and the Dai Ichi in the previous two years. The next day, Saturday, the five men met once more. Marshall declared that, having read the papers, he considered that he shared Harriman's view: MacArthur should have been sacked two years earlier. Truman now asked Bradley to give him the recommendation of the Joint Chiefs on the future of the Supreme Commander by Monday.

At 2 p.m. on Sunday afternoon, the Joint Chiefs met in Bradley's office at the Pentagon. After almost two hours of discussion, the Chiefs went up to the office of the Secretary for Defense. They gave Marshall their unanimous recommendation that MacArthur should be sacked 'on purely military considerations'. It was Bradley who provided the simplest and best reason for MacArthur's sacking. SCAP had provided overwhelming evidence that he was 'not in sympathy with the decision to try to limit the conflict to Korea . . . it was necessary to have a commander more responsive to control from Washington.'

On the afternoon of Tuesday 10 April, the President and his advisers met once more to examine Bradley's draft of the order for MacArthur's removal and replacement by Ridgway, and to consider the press release by which the decision would be announced. It was decided that it should be broken to MacArthur at 10 a.m. on the 12th, Tokyo time, 8 p.m. on the 11th in Washington. But that evening of the 11th, Bradley hastened to Blair House with disturbing tidings: there had been a leak. The *Chicago Tribune* would break the story of MacArthur's removal the following morning. It had become essential for the White House to rush its timetable. The order for MacArthur's relief went out on the Pentagon teletype half an hour after midnight, Washington time, on 11 April. The White House press corps was summoned to a press conference at 1 a.m. for a 'special announcement'. On their arrival, reporters were handed a copy of the President's order for MacArthur's relief, the announcement of Ridgway's promotion, and a statement from Truman:

> With deep regret I have concluded that General of the Army Douglas MacArthur is unable to give his wholehearted support to the policies of the United States government and of the United Nations in matters pertaining to his official duties. In view of the specific responsibility imposed on me by the Constitution of the United States, and of the added responsibility which has been entrusted to me by the United Nations, I have decided that I must make a change of command in the Far East. I have, therefore, relieved General MacArthur of his commands, and have designated Lieutenant-General Matthew B. Ridgway as his successor.
>
> Full and vigorous debate on matters of national policy is a vital element in the constitutional system of our free democracy. It is fundamental, however, that military commanders must be governed by the policies and directives issued to them in the manner provided by our laws and Constitution. In time of crisis, this consideration is particularly compelling.
>
> General MacArthur's place in history is fully established. The Nation owes him a debt of gratitude for the distinguished and exceptional service which he has rendered his country in posts of great responsibility. For that reason I repeat my regret at the necessity for the action I feel compelled to take in his case.

From the perspective of thirty-five years later, respect for the political courage of Truman, Acheson, Marshall and the others who saw the need to limit the war in Korea, and to sack MacArthur, may make it hard to understand why so many Americans recoiled from the action of the Administration. Above all, perhaps, it can be difficult to grasp the lack of awe with which the atomic bomb was viewed by many Americans in those days. For a large part of the nation, it remained merely a weapon: a greater weapon than any other, perhaps; but nonetheless, a legitimate extension of American military power. Flight-Lieutenant John Nicholls, a young RAF pilot who served in Korea with a US Sabre squadron, was struck by the difference in attitude he perceived between that of his American comrades, and that of Europeans, towards the atomic bomb: 'Americans seemed to take the view that it was a weapon which was there to be used, if necessary. Yet we had been brought up with the view that it was there *not* to be used.'[10] It is striking to observe how many senior American veterans of Korea, looking back thirty-five years, still believe that nuclear weapons should have been employed to inflict outright defeat upon the Chinese. Colonel Ellis Williamson, G-3 of X Corps, was one of the soldiers in Korea who supported the nuclear option: 'I favoured using one bomb in one unoccupied area – say, The Punchbowl. Pop it off. Say to the communists: "Come off of this stuff and get out." The Korean War was our first real national vacillation, the first evidence of the great decline in our will as a nation to make a real hard decision.'[11] Colonel Paul Freeman said: 'We should have knocked the Chinese out, whatever it took. My senior officers were certainly in favour of using atomic weapons. But some of the European nations were scared we were going to start something.'[12]

Yet if views such as this were widely expressed in the middle and even upper reaches of the US Army, it is surely significant that America's most distinguished soldiers – her outstanding commanders of the twentieth century – were at one in their conviction that MacArthur had to go. Beyond Marshall and Bradley, Ridgway had quickly wearied of the Supreme Commander's posturing and egocentric fantasies. The Eighth Army's commander was far too big a man to allow his historical judgement on MacArthur to be clouded by the promotion that he gained by his superior's fall. After Ridgway planned Operation RIPPER, he was compelled to endure

the spectacle of MacArthur flying into Korea on 20 February, and
announcing to the press that the new offensive was entirely his
own conception and decision. Ridgway later wrote of his deep
regret at the undignified manner of MacArthur's sacking. But he
minced no words in his judgement of the Supreme Commander's
plan for extending the war to China.

> [It] entailed the very considerable risk of igniting World War III
> and consequent overrunning of Western Europe, with the loss
> of our oldest and staunchest allies sure to follow ... It was an
> ambitious and dangerous program that would demand a major
> national effort ... It is clear that the nation's top civilian and
> military leaders, using a wider-angle lens, with deeper sources
> of information on the atomic situation in the Soviet Union,
> and with more comprehensive estimates of the possible conse-
> quences of general war in Europe, had a much clearer view of
> the realities and responsibilities of the day.[13]

The dignity of Truman's action was marred by the clumsy haste
with which it proved necessary to inform MacArthur, to forestall a
press leak. Just after 3 p.m. on the afternoon of 11 April, a
messenger delivered a personal signal for MacArthur to Blair
House, from Bradley in Washington. It announced his relief from
all his commands, minutes after the news had been broadcast to
the world. Reporters were already gathering at the general's gates.
The calls of sympathy quickly began to flow in. MacArthur did not
conceal his hurt, his anger at being 'publicly humiliated after fifty-
two years in the army'.[14] Early on the morning of 16 April 1951,
the general flew out of Tokyo in his Constellation, bound for the
United States, amid scenes of deep emotion among his staff and
many Japanese, who still regarded him as their saviour.

The circumstances of his return to America have passed into
national legend: the ticker-tape parades, the address to Congress,
the Senate hearings at which he sought to establish once and for
all the justice and constitutionality of his actions. Among the press,
from the beginning, the *Washington Post*, *New York Times*, *Herald*

Tribune and other liberal organs sided decisively with the President. But among ordinary people, it was not only conservatives who felt a wave of revulsion against Truman for his action. Many Americans, with their instinctive emotional enthusiasm for a man larger than life, a national symbol, a hero, were bitterly grieved to see him brought low. Yet MacArthur himself, exalted by the warmth of his reception in his own country, failed to grasp its ambivalence. He believed that his prestige and the case he sought to argue were inseparably entwined. In reality, even many of those who cheered his passing through their cities had no stomach for embarking upon another great war, such as he believed necessary. If Truman's personal popularity was deeply wounded by his sacking of MacArthur, in the months that followed it became apparent that only a small minority of Americans doubted its constitutionality. Many regretted that MacArthur the man had been humbled; but few in the end doubted that Truman, the elected President, was obliged to curb MacArthur the general.

The shock and emotion in the United States about MacArthur's dismissal was in marked contrast to attitudes in Korea. Many senior officers had long since lost faith in SCAP's judgement. Even among junior ranks, his standing had never recovered from the disasters of the winter, for which so many men held him personally responsible. One UN officer wrote: 'MacArthur's departure made as much impact on the soldiery as would have, say, the replacement of Scipio Africanus on a Roman outpost in the wilds of Mauretania.'[15] In the same mood, Lieutenant Jim Sheldon of the 17th Infantry said: 'MacArthur was too distanced from us for his going to make much impact. The only sort of thing we noticed was the food getting better after Ridgway took over.'[16] Colonel Paul Freeman echoed the ambivalent attitudes of some senior officers who could not forget MacArthur's past great deeds: 'I thought his sacking was disgraceful. Sure, he had it coming. He should have been relieved. But it should have been done in a dignified way. He was an actor and an egoist, but he had been a very great man.' Colonel Ellis Williamson thought MacArthur's removal 'absolutely necessary. I think the world learned a lesson – when you leave a man in a position of authority too long, he stops looking for ideas different from his first thoughts.' Williamson added, in a moment of compassion common to thousands of Americans in Korea: 'He was a pompous old bastard; but a great soldier.' Almond's aide, Captain Fred Ladd, said: 'I think he went out like he would like to have gone. How would it have been if he stayed, and eventually gone like Admiral Rickover, just told to retire because he was too old? This way, he went in a blaze of glory.'[17]

The surge of relief at MacArthur's dismissal among most of the world's democracies served, if anything, to enhance the anger and strengthen the isolationist impulses of right-wing Americans. The President was compelled to console himself for the abuse he received at home with the enthusiasm his action inspired abroad. The British Ambassador in Tokyo gave an acid description of MacArthur's departure, 'after a brief ceremony that, possibly appropriately, was marked by all the traditional discourtesy and casualness to the Diplomatic Corps to which we have become so used . . . To me personally, MacArthur's departure is a tremendous relief as it is, I think, to nearly all my colleagues.'[18] Many Asian newspapers welcomed the news: 'Truman has earned the gratitude of all peace-loving peoples everywhere, by eliminating the greatest single opposition to peaceful efforts and policies in the Far East,' enthused the *Civil & Military Gazette* of Pakistan. The British Ambassador in Paris reported that Premier Schuman 'referred at once to General MacArthur's dismissal in terms of heartfelt thankfulness . . . He had the impression that the United States Administration had almost lost control of the situation.'[19] Outside the United States, many Western newspapers greeted MacArthur's fall with something close to exultation. The general had deeply frightened the allies of the United States. They saw in his pronouncements the threat of nuclear war. The impunity with which he spoke suggested that he was a military commander so powerful that he might be capable of action beyond the control of the civilian power. Whether or not these fears were fully justified, they were sincerely held in Europe. The relief at MacArthur's departure was matched by pleasure at the succession to the Supreme Command of Matthew Ridgway, whose abilities and judgement commanded immense respect. General James Van Fleet, a wartime divisional commander under Eisenhower in the European theatre, was appointed to direct Eighth Army in Ridgway's place.

MacArthur's memory faded with remarkable speed in Korea. Ridgway proved to be all that was hoped as Supreme Commander. He took with him to Tokyo the military skills he had already displayed in full measure in the peninsula, and showed in addition the discretion and political judgement that so conspicuously eluded MacArthur. If the paratroop veteran was no more able than his predecessor to produce a magic formula for extricating the United States, and the United Nations, from the Korean morass, he nevertheless ensured that throughout his tenure of command, no new crisis of authority developed between his headquarters and Washington. Ridgway was unyielding in his opinion that only a display of firmness on the battlefield could force the communists to make peace. But he shared the Administration's conviction that Korea was not the theatre in which to embark upon a major war. Civilian authority to determine policy in Korea was never challenged again.

Thus far, history has supported Truman's view of the Asian battlefield in 1951, rather than that of MacArthur. Some conservative writers continue to argue that, had the West displayed the will to achieve decisive victory in Korea – with or without the use of nuclear weapons – there need have been no war in Vietnam, and communism could have been driven back across Asia. This seems highly doubtful. In Korea as in Vietnam, America showed itself militarily at a loss about the conduct of a war amid a peasant society. The will simply did not exist, in the United States and far less among its allies, to treat Kim Il Sung's act of aggression in Korea as a pretext for all-out war against Asian communism. And had it done so, it remains doubtful whether MacArthur's policy was militarily practicable, even with the support of nuclear weapons. If MacArthur had had his way, the cost to the moral credibility of the United States around the world would almost certainly have been historically disastrous.

Truman's greatest difficulty was that his own political authority was too weak to explain to his own people the realities of the new world in which they lived, where immense military power could not always be translated into effective foreign influence. Perhaps more than any other conflict in history, the outcome of World War II could be claimed as a simple triumph of good over evil. Yet in 1951, only six years later, such clear-cut decisions already seemed obsolete. Americans were learning to come to terms with a world of constant crises, of problems chronically resistant to solutions. The finest minds in the Administration understood all this, but it was a wholly unwelcome message to convey to Middle America – or to such a man as Douglas MacArthur. It was Truman's misfortune that MacArthur chanced to be commanding in Tokyo when the Korean conflict began. The accident was compounded by the hesitation and weakness with which Washington handled this Olympian figure through the months that followed. Inchon was indeed a masterstroke, but it was a perverse tragedy for MacArthur and those around him, because its success prevented them from confronting the fact that his judgement was gone. He was too remote, too old, too inflexible, too deeply imprisoned by a world vision that was obsolete, to be a fit commander in such a war as Korea. It was fortunate that his removal was achieved before he could inflict a historic military, moral, or political disaster upon the West's cause in Asia.

Acheson and Truman endured phlegmatically the emotional scenes that followed MacArthur's recall. The Secretary of State told a story, of a family with a beautiful daughter living just outside an army camp. Her mother worried constantly about her daughter's virtue, and nagged her husband incessantly about the perils to which she was exposed. One day, the daughter came home in tears and confessed that she was pregnant. The father mopped his brow and said: 'Thank God that's over.'[20]

Troglodyte warfare (*above*). A British mortar position, dug deep into the sort of bunker occupied by both sides once the conflict stabilised in the summer of 1951.

Chinese soldiers in one of the great network of tunnels that honeycombed the communist line from 1951 until the armistice.

British soldiers help to bring in a wounded American.

ROK and American troops on the move. Notice the age of the young Korean in the centre. He was not untypical.

Artillery in action: (*above*) UN (*below*) Chinese.

A British doctor treats a wounded Chinese prisoner.

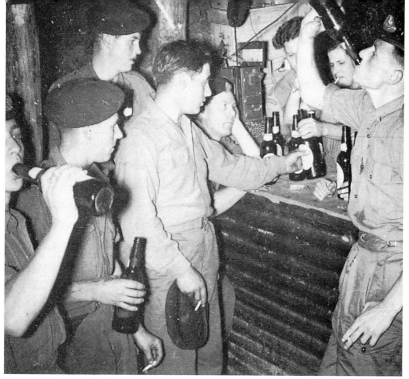

Behind the lines: (*above*) British conscripts of the Duke of Wellington's Regiment take a beer. Australians take a shower.

Private William Speakman, of the King's Own Scottish Borderers, who won the Victoria Cross in November 1951.

Helicopter casevac: this was the first 'war of the whirlybirds' which saved the lives of so many wounded men and shot down aircrew.

'I shall go to Korea.' President-elect Dwight D. Eisenhower on the fleeting visit which confirmed his determination to negotiate for an armistice.

Propaganda: a Chinese picture designed to show the world that UN prisoners in communist hands were enjoying good treatment. A PoW in home-made Santa Claus outfit distributes gifts.

Repatriation: the last, grotesque act of thousands of communist prisoners being shipped to Panmunjom for return to China and North Korea was to hurl away the clothing and boots with which they had been supplied by their UN captors.

11 » THE STRUGGLE ON THE IMJIN

On Sunday 22 April 1951, the new commander of Eighth Army, General James Van Fleet, held his first press conference. 'General,' a correspondent demanded, 'what is our goal in Korea?' Van Fleet replied, memorably: 'I don't know. The answer must come from higher authority.' Yet the most obvious goal of the United Nations forces – survival in the face of enemy assault – required no definition. That same Sunday, the Chinese launched their fifth offensive of the Korean War. Eighth Army was well advised of its coming, and anticipated that the enemy's main attack would fall upon the centre of the front in the Pakyong–Chunchon area, against IX Corps. For three weeks, the United Nations had been pressing cautiously northwards with the intention of securing a line of commanding ground around the 38th Parallel – the KANSAS Line. The Chinese proposed to arrest the UN advance, and throw Van Fleet's army back southwards. Chinese prisoners declared that their commissars were promising the celebration of May Day in Seoul.

The 1st Marine Division in the so-called 'Iron Triangle' between Chorwon, Pyongyang and Kumhwa received two hours' tactical warning of the Chinese assault, which fell most heavily in the west, against the 7th Marines, who were engaged a few minutes into the darkness of 22 April. Their position deteriorated rapidly when the ROK 6th Division, on their left, collapsed and began streaming to the rear, impeding the advance of American supplies and reinforcements. The Marines were compelled to hinge back their line, to cover the open flank to the west. By the morning of 24 April, they had been obliged to give substantial ground. But they had broken the impulse of the Chinese advance, and inflicted the usual huge casualties on the enemy's massed frontal assaults.

The gunners of the 16th New Zealand Field Regiment, who were firing for 6th ROK Division, found themselves in a desperate position when the South Korean infantry broke in front of them. DC Corps insisted that the New Zealanders must continue to support the ROKs. But they gained permission to take a British battalion, 1st Middlesex, to protect their positions. For a few perilous hours, the two units held their ground. Then, when it became apparent that the ROK collapse was irreversible, they were allowed to pull back down the Kapyon river. Here, they were joined by the rest of 27 Commonwealth Brigade, brought out of reserve to fill the gap opened by the Koreans' precipitate departure. Between the nights of 23 and 25 April, the British, Australian and Canadian battalions fought a fine defensive battle against repeated attacks by the Chinese 118th Division. For almost twenty-four hours, the men of Princess Patricia's Canadian Light Infantry were surrounded and cut off, dependent on air-dropped supplies and ammunition. Their achievement has been overshadowed by the bloodier and even more dramatic action that took place further west at this time. But 27 Brigade won much professional admiration from their allies for the fashion in which they broke the communist attack north of Chongchon-ni. It is a typical irony of history that, because their battle ended in success at small cost in Commonwealth lives, it is little remembered. There, at the centre of the UN front, the line stabilised, and held. The surviving attackers withdrew. One arm of the Chinese offensive was shattered.

But even as 27 Brigade and the US Marines were fighting their battle, twenty-five miles further west on the I Corps front, another action was taking place, which passed into the legend of Korea. The British 29 Brigade – three infantry battalions with a fourth, Belgian unit under command – was holding positions along the line of the Imjin river, just over thirty miles north of Seoul. Throughout the war, the contribution of the lesser United Nations contingents was dwarfed by the dominant role of the Americans.

But just once, the British played a part which captured the imagination of the Western world: the battle of the Imjin river in April 1951.

*

To an inexpert eye, the hill range south of the Imjin offers a defensive position of such overwhelming strength that it appears almost impregnable. The highest peak, Kamak-san, rises to 2,000 feet. The river bows north in front of the British line, almost every yard of its banks plainly visible from the high ground. The ROK 1st Division occupied positions to the west. The American 3rd Division stood to the east. Yet the Imjin position was by no means as strong as at first appeared. The river at this point was shallow enough to be easily forded, and thus to offer little difficulty to an attacker. The brigade relied for fire support upon the 25-pounders of 45 Field Regiment, RA, but lacked ready access to medium or heavy artillery, always in chronic short supply. Any position is only as strong as the force that defends it. 29 Brigade possessed pitifully small numbers to cover almost seven and a half miles of front. If they were to do so, indeed, there was no possibility of holding a continuous line. Brigadier Tom Brodie determined to deploy his men in separate unit positions, centred upon key hill features. He placed the Belgian battalion on the far right, north of the river. On the south bank, the Northumberland Fusiliers took the right flank, with the Gloucesters on the left, the Royal Ulster Rifles in reserve. Up to two miles separated each of the Northumberlands' company areas from its neighbour. Their positions were neither deeply dug, nor wired, nor mined, because the British did not expect to hold them for long. They were merely a springboard from which the advance to the KANSAS Line would be continued. Though some work had been done to clear fields of fire, the thick scrub covering the hillsides throughout the area offered plenty of useful cover to an attacker. It is difficult to overstate the influence of the lack of defensive preparations upon the British difficulties that were to follow. Infantry with good overhead protection, and minefields and wire to impede assaults, can achieve miracles even against overwhelming enemy forces, especially when these lack artillery support. Infantry without these things are critically handicapped in their own defence.

Some officers were most unhappy about the scattered deployment of the small force, when 29 Brigade's position lay across the historic route southwards to the Korean capital. They argued in favour of concentrating the battalions where they could provide effective mutual support, for instance on the dominant heights of Kamak-san, where there were superb natural defences and ready access to water. Major Tony Younger, commanding the British engineer squadron, was in Japan on leave when he saw speculation in the US Army newspaper *Stars and Stripes* about a possible Chinese thrust towards the Imjin. He flew hastily back to Seoul, and rejoined the brigade. He was dismayed to find that no special precautions were being taken: 'We were not really in a defensive frame of mind. We had been crawling forward, probing forward for months. We didn't even really know exactly where on our front the Imjin was fordable.'[1] Major Guy Ward of 45 Field Regiment, the gunner battery commander with the Gloucesters, found the atmosphere 'relaxed. Too relaxed'. Despite all the intelligence indications of an imminent Chinese offensive, the extraordinary absence of enemy activity in front of Brodie's men suggested that the blow would fall elsewhere. The Imjin position was deemed safe.

During the days following their arrival in the line on 5 April, the British probed north in search of the enemy. On the 14th, the Belgians and tanks of the 8th Hussars skirmished with a Chinese patrol four miles north of the river, and took a prisoner. On the 16th, the Northumberland Fusiliers and the British Centurions carried out a reconnaissance in force nine miles into no-man's-land. Again, they met only token Chinese fire. Their officers carried out laborious interrogations of local villagers through interpreters. 'In a language which required eight minutes to say "perhaps",' wrote one of the participants irritably, 'battleground interviews of this nature were often more exasperating than instructive'. On

63rd Chinese Army
187, 188, 189 Divisions

Imjin River

Hill 194

Belgian
Battalion

'Ulster'
crossing

Y
Company

Z
Company
Hill 257

X
Company

Royal
Northumberland Fusiliers

W
Company

45th RA

HQ
8th Hussars

Hill 398

Tac HQ

Crossing

A
Company

D Company

B
Company

Gloucesters

C
Company

HQ
Hill 235

▲ Hill 314

▲ Kamak-san Hill

Royal
Ulster Rifles

N

CHINESE advance

Initial deployment

UN Retreat

Re-formation

Approximate scale
0   1   2 km
0   1 ml

29th Brigade main HQ

The BATTLE OF IMJIN RIVER

To UIJONGBU

20 April, yet another 'armoured swan' drove eighteen miles north. 'Lowtherforce', led by the CO of the 8th Hussars, again skirmished with a small Chinese force which withdrew at once under pressure. Aerial reconnaissance reported no sign of significant enemy forces on the British front. All the evidence suggested that the Chinese possessed only a few observation posts, keeping a cautious eye upon 29 Brigade.

On the morning of 22 April, patrols of the Gloucesters and the Northumberland Fusiliers north of the Imjin reported the astonishing news that major enemy forces were on the move on the British front. By afternoon, the Gloucesters' CO was at 'Gloucester Crossing' on the river bank, personally directing mortar fire on Chinese parties moving on the north side. By 6 p.m. that evening, the Belgian battalion also reported contact with the enemy. The brigade adopted a 50 per cent stand-to for the night hours. But the Chinese were still expected to open the battle with their customary local probing attacks, before committing themselves to a major assault. At 10 p.m., on Brodie's orders the Ulsters' battle patrol was sent hastily forward in Oxford carriers to secure the bridges at Ulster Crossing, the ford by which they had been passing the Imjin for three weeks, and to protect the Belgians' line of retreat.

Few young men had gone to as much trouble to arrange their own presence on the Imjin as Lieutenant P. J. Kavanagh, the battle patrol's twenty-year-old second-in-command. The son of a well-known comedy scriptwriter, Kavanagh found the tedium of National Service at the regimental depot intolerable, and volunteered for Korea. Once in the country, he lobbied incessantly for a transfer from the rear areas to a fighting battalion. His wish had been granted a few days earlier. Now, he stood with the patrol commander, Lieutenant Hedley Craig, peering warily into the darkness north of the river.

> 'Looks a bit fishy.'
> 'Yes.'
> 'Better push on a bit, though.'

'Right.'

He screwed his eyes up so tight he saw stars, private semi-voluntary comment on fatuousness [Kavanagh wrote later]. Slowly they move off again, pressing into the tautening membrane of the night. Grind, whirr, whine go the tracks, the engines, a defined envelope of noise in the white moon-silence.

Penetration! The membrane snaps. Flames, rockets, yells, a thousand Cup Final rattles, Guy Fawkes, one of the carriers in front goes up, whoosh! Christ! Fifty of us have run into a bloody army! Weapons, helmets, wireless sets, all go flying in the mad scramble to get out, back into the womb of the dark away from the red bee-swarms of the tracers.

'Come back,' he shouted. Not quite sure why, except that he didn't particularly fancy being left sitting there alone. Anyway it annoyed his schoolboy sense of order to see them running off into nowhere. Run home by all means, I'll come with you except the river's in the way, but not into the meaningless no-direction dark.

'Stop!'

Some do uncertainly. A few run on, never to be seen again, ever. He dismounts gingerly from his lonely chariot.

'Lie down, face your front and return the fire.'

Good notion that, keep us occupied for a bit. Irregular spiritless bangs begin around him.

'Get that bren gun going.'

'There's something wrong with it, Sorr.'

'Mend it.'

Splendid stuff this. And will the First Cavalry, just in the nick, pennants a-flutter come riding riding . . . No. He wished he wasn't there.

'I can find nothing wrong with this bren, Sorr, known to God or to man.'

Oh, the Irish, the irresistible cadence, unresisted.[2]

In the chaotic loneliness of the night, Kavanagh struggled to push a morphia syrette into a wounded man, scrambled alongside

Craig to restore some control to the ruin of the patrol after the Chinese ambush. They began to straggle back on foot towards the river, losing men as they went. A few hundred yards on, they paused for the survivors to regroup.

'Sir, Leary's got hurt on the way across. Can I go and get him, Sir?'

'No.'

'But he's my mukker, Sir!'

Blank consternation. Greater love than this ... Another face, contorted, is thrust into his –

'Sir, there's one of 'em moving about just down there. Shall I kill him? I'll throw this at him.'

Brandishing a grenade, hopping up and down. You'd have his head in your knapsack, too, wouldn't you, you blood-crazy little bastard. Takes people different ways, apparently.

'Shall I kill-kill-kill um, Sir?'

'No.'[3]

The Ulsters' survivors were bewildered that they were allowed to withdraw, when the Chinese seemed to have the patrol utterly at their mercy. Communist infantry were moving all around them. Lieutenant Craig and ten men covered the withdrawal of Kavanagh, wounded in the shoulder, with the remainder. Craig himself was briefly taken prisoner, but escaped to find his way back to the British lines two days later. Kavanagh rejoined the battalion in the early hours of the morning with five men. That brief, ferocious glimpse of battle was the young officer's first and last. He was evacuated to hospital in Japan. He was one of the lucky ones, the men who escaped the carnage that now overtook 29 Brigade.

Lieutenants Bill Cooper and Jimmy Yeo of the Fusiliers' W Company had taken a jeep down to Yongdungpo that Sunday, to visit the 8th Hussars. For Saint George's Day, every Fusilier had already been issued with the regiment's traditional red and white roses, specially flown in from Japan. Yeo, a regular in the East Lancashires who had volunteered for Korea to get in some active service, met a friend from Sandhurst, with whom they shared a pleasant tea. They drove back to their own positions for evening stand-to, lying in silence in their slit trenches gazing out into the dusk. Nothing happened. Stand-down was called. Then, as they cooked the usual Sunday stew, they began to hear grenades and gunfire further west, towards the Gloucesters' positions. Once more, the word was whispered down from trench to trench by running NCOs: 'Stand to!' They lay straining their ears, momentarily unnerved by the sound of many feet running near them. Yet even as they cocked their weapons, the alarm was dispelled: the feet were British. For two more hours they waited, passive. Flares erupted from time to time to their left, but strict standing orders specified that they should keep silent, and remain in their slits.

Then brief bursts of fire opened in front of them, and shuffling movements began in the darkness. The Chinese were probing towards them. There was an explosion, then the muffled thud of a mortar illuminant bursting before them. Cooper and Yeo's neighbouring platoons began to fire across each other's fronts, exactly as they had planned. But the Chinese did not throw their weight against W Company that night. They were fully occupied elsewhere. Throughout the hours of darkness, wave after wave of attackers threw themselves upon the Fusiliers' X and Z Companies, and the Gloucesters' A and D. The absolute unsuitability of the brigade deployment for meeting an all-out attack by large forces now made itself clear. Each company was compelled to meet the Chinese alone. X Company of the Northumberlands, nearest the river on the left, was impossibly exposed, and withdrew towards the battalion position before first light. To the alarm of the Fusiliers, however, at 6.10 a.m. on the 23rd, the Chinese gained a key hill position overlooking a major road junction held by Z Company. The enemy had been able to bypass Y Company, nearer the river, and strike at the positions behind it. Z Company's commander, Major John Winn, won a DSO for his superbly courageous direction of the defence of his line that day. But the Northumberlands were compelled to fall back. Of all the actions at this period, that in which the Northumberlands lost vital ground so early in the battle had most serious consequences, and is most open to criticism. The British were dismayed to find Chinese infantry now firing upon their artillery positions, and already establishing themselves upon the untenanted high ground of Kamak-san. Centurions of C Squadron, 8th Hussars, covered the retreat of the Fusiliers' Y Company. The Ulsters, hastily moved forward from their reserve positions, were now committed to clearing and holding the high ground east of the vital road to the rear.

On the left flank, the battle began well for the Gloucesters. Their standing patrol on the river bank, commanded by Lieutenant Guy Temple, poured devastating small-arms fire into the first Chinese attempting the night river crossing. 'Guido' Temple, nicknamed for his swarthy Italian looks, had been considered a somewhat feckless young officer back in England, repeatedly in trouble for late return from nightclub outings. Yet now, in the words of a fellow-officer, he proved 'a good man in a difficult time', lying with his men over their weapons looking down on the moonlit river. Four times, the Chinese came, and on each occasion they were repulsed. Then, with their ammunition expended, Temple's platoon withdrew into C Company's perimeter on the hillside more than a mile to the rear.

The Chinese were now crossing the river in force at a dozen places. In the hours before dawn they launched repeated attacks on the Gloucesters' A and D Companies. Lieutenant Philip Curtis won a posthumous Victoria Cross for leading a counter-attack to recover A Company's Castle Hill position. Although wounded early in the action, he struggled on to the summit, wiping out a Chinese machine-gun team with grenades seconds before he fell dead from the effects of their fire. The company commander, Pat Angier, spoke by radio to Colonel Fred Carne, the Gloucesters' CO: 'I'm afraid we've lost Castle Site. I want to know whether I am to stay here indefinitely or not. If I am to stay, I must be reinforced as my numbers are getting very low.' Flatly, Carne told him that the position must be held – at all costs. Angier signed off reassuringly:

'Don't worry about us; we'll be all right.' He was killed fifteen minutes later. By mid-morning only one officer of A Company remained in action. All the others were dead or wounded. Yet still Carne was compelled to order the survivors to hold on. If A Company's ground was lost, the remaining battalion positions also became untenable. Again and again, with their customary indifference to casualties, the Chinese assault groups crawled to within yards of the British trenches under cover of withering long-range machine-gun fire, then threw themselves forward with their burp guns and grenades, their screams and bugle calls. Each party was eventually destroyed. But each assault knocked out a bren team here, killed the occupants of a slit trench there, removed an officer or NCO with grenade splinters. Major Pat Angier was one of the last Gloucester casualties whom a handful of his comrades and the padre could spare time to bury with the hasty rituals of the Church. His batman followed his body in tears.

Meanwhile, further east, Colonel Kingsley Foster of the Fusiliers concluded that he must counter-attack to recover Z Company's lost hilltop, from which the Chinese were bringing down fire across the entire battalion area. W Company clambered doggedly up the hillside covered by heavy machine-gun and tank fire, taking pains to keep their line, hardly losing a man until they came within fifty yards of the crest, for the Chinese rounds were flying above their heads. Then, as they neared the objective, the enemy defenders began to hurl down grenades and satchel charges. Brian Millington, the mortar observation officer, was wounded in the back by a grenade exploding below him as the Fusiliers gained the crestline. There was a moment of exhilaration as the Chinese manning it turned and fled. Then, beyond them, another Chinese unit rose from the ground and charged at the British. W Company's assault collapsed, men turned and ran back down the hill for their lives.

Bill Cooper was shocked to hear clearly the 'thwack!' as bullets slammed into his own men. He saw his radio operator collapse to his knees, mortally wounded, as the set on his back disintegrated. Halfway down the hill, he saw that Millington was missing, and scrambled up again until he found him lying in the scrub. Urgently, he asked if the young officer could move. 'No, I think I'm dead,' muttered Millington. 'It's no good. You'd better leave me.' Cooper picked him up in a fireman's lift, and staggered down the hill, pursued by desultory Chinese fire. Back at the start-line, the doctor examined Millington for a moment, then shook his head: 'He's moribund.' About half the men who had taken part in the counter-attack had failed to return. Deeply despondent about their failure, the survivors of W Company trudged back to their old positions. Cooper became even angrier later, when somebody told him that they had never been expected to gain the hill. Their attack was chiefly a diversion, to keep the Chinese busy while the Belgians withdrew from the north bank of the Imjin. That evening, with some American tank support, the Belgian battalion success-fully disengaged from its positions, crossed the bridges at the junction of the Imjin and Hantan rivers, and began moving to take up new positions alongside Kamak-san, to the rear of the Glouces-ters and Northumberlands. The British liked the men of their attached unit, a tough, swashbuckling bunch with a proud '*Vive La Belgique*' banner displayed behind their positions. On the Imjin, the Belgians fought as hard as any battalion in 29 Brigade.

That afternoon, Padre Sam Davies of the Gloucesters listened grimly to the news over the radio that Chinese elements were already attacking the brigade's rear echelon: 'Standing in the sunny hollow where main Headquarters lay, I tried to realise the position. We were isolated by Chinese hordes intent on the kill. It was simply a matter of hours before darkness fell, and the lonely battalion would be assaulted on all sides in the nightmarish moonlight. Gloucester was 11,000 miles away. I longed to be able to say "Stop" to the rushing minutes: to prolong this quiet, sunny afternoon indefinitely.'[4]

By evening on 23 April, it was apparent that the forward bat-talions of 29 Brigade must concentrate, or be wiped out piecemeal. Around 8.30 p.m., the survivors of the Gloucesters' A and D Com-panies withdrew from their positions, and filed through the darkness into the battalion headquarters area to redeploy, Korean porters moving their heavy equipment. During a lull in the renewed Chinese attacks that night, Major Paul Mitchell's C Company was also pulled back. But it proved impossible to disengage Major Denis Harding's B Company. Between 11 p.m. that night and dawn the following morning, Harding's men faced seven major assaults.

The company commander himself was a thirty-six-year-old veteran with great experience in World War II. That morning, one of his NCOs had led a patrol to explore the ground around the company positions, and returned to report bleakly: 'There's not just dozens of them down there – there's thousands.' Yet Harding still felt confident of his company's ability to hold its ground. He had spent much of the day with his artillery observation officer, calling down fire on enemy concentrations whenever they could see them. Then he fell asleep for a time, and while he rested ammunition and food were brought up to the company area from the battalion echelon. The officer who brought them, Captain Bill Morris, should then have returned to the rear with the carrying party. But he was reluctant to wake Harding, and stayed to cover for him. By evening, it was too late for him to go anywhere. Morris remained, to share the fate of the battalion.

All that night, amid the cries and orders and bugles from the darkness, B Company grenaded and poured fire into the Chinese with rifle, bren and sten. By dawn, one platoon's positions had been entirely overrun. Sheer weight of numbers had driven in Harding's perimeter. At first light, the survivors withdrew to join the rest of Carne's men on Hill 235 – the height that was to become known to the British Army as Gloucester Hill. There were only Harding himself, his sergeant-major, and fifteen others. Their ammunition was virtually exhausted. The remains of B and C were merged to form a single weak company. The Gloucesters had begun the battle with some seven hundred infantrymen holding a front of over 12,000 yards. Now, both their numbers and their perimeter had shrunk dramatically. Yet one of Support Company, hearing from the colonel that they were to concentrate on the higher ridge for the last round, declared cheerfully: 'We shall be all right, sir, 'twill be like the Rock of Gibraltar up here.'

The quality about the Gloucesters' stand upon which all the survivors focused in their later accounts was the confidence: the serene conviction of most officers and men that they could cope, even as their casualties mounted, their perimeter shrank, and their ammunition dwindled. Infantrymen are often impressed by the magical fashion in which a gunner battery commander can use his telephone to drop fire within yards of their own positions. But Guy Ward and his officers from 70th Field Battery were acknowledged as supreme wizards. Ward was astonished to see Chinese cavalry in the valley below him. To a professional gunner, 'they were magnificent targets'. 25-pounder shells poured down on them. The 4.2-inch heavy mortars of 170 Battery, RA, compounded the communists' dreadful losses. Chinese infantry concentrations were shattered again and again by devastating British artillery fire: 'The slaughter we did was absolutely tremendous,' said Ward, although like most of his companions, he was astounded by the fashion in which the enemy still kept coming.

That day of the 24th, efforts were made to pass a column of the 8th Hussars' Centurions down the narrow, winding valley road to the Gloucesters' positions. Infantry cover was provided by a Filipino battalion, who were responsible for sweeping the high ground on either side. The operation failed. One of the three Filipino light tanks leading the column was knocked out, blocking the road; it could not be dislodged by its successor. There is little doubt that the infantry advanced too close to the road, and did not climb high enough to have any chance of keeping the armoured column out of range of the Chinese. But the track was anyway almost impassable by the big, heavy Centurions. And with the limited forces available, it is not unlikely that the relief column would itself have become trapped with the Gloucesters, even had it been successful in making contact.

*

Some of those most intimately concerned with the Imjin battle believed that it revealed the fatal disadvantages of committing an independent national brigade group in a major war. Brigadier Tom Brodie found himself bearing the brunt of an assault by two Chinese divisions, with important implications for the safety of Seoul. Yet as a British officer under temporary American command, he could not be expected to achieve the clear understanding with higher formations that would have been possible with his own fellow-countrymen. A British officer at Brigade HQ believed that the Americans did not understand until much too late how desperate was the predicament of 29 Brigade: 'When Tom told Corps that his position was "a bit sticky", they simply did not grasp that in British Army parlance, that meant "critical".' Brodie was twice told by American Corps headquarters that he could not withdraw his brigade, and he felt that he had no choice but to obey. Those around the brigadier said that he found the strain almost intolerable, commanding a brigade that was being shattered beneath his eyes. The Imjin battle confirmed the urgency of bringing into being the planned Commonwealth Division, commanded by a major-general with the rank and authority to safeguard the interests of his command.

It was not that Brodie blundered, but that his position was exceptionally difficult, as a British officer naturally anxious to 'keep his end up' with the Americans. 29 Brigade had dug and wired rear positions weeks earlier. On Gloucester Hill, the battalion adjutant Captain Tony Farrar-Hockley repeatedly asked himself why they had bothered to prepare such a fall-back line, if not for just such a situation as this. Knowing that his men were asking the same question, and demanding why they were receiving such limited air support, he told them that another big battle was being fought elsewhere. 'Higher Sunray' – higher command – 'have insisted we stay.' There were other difficulties: although 45 Field Regiment's 25-pounders were fine guns, they possessed limited killing power. There was a desperate need for the support of heavier metal. Yet the Gloucesters' American artillery liaison officer had been withdrawn a few days before the battle, and they possessed no means of calling in 155mm fire. The British battalions' establishment of automatic weapons was inadequate to face the sort of devastating attrition battle in which they were now engaged. Above all, perhaps, the brigade was able to call upon too little close air support, too late. That first bloody day, the Gloucesters received none whatever. Even in the days that followed, it was apparent that 29 Brigade was not being given high priority.

Once the assessment had been made that the British faced a major Chinese assault, which they could not possibly hope to overcome in the dispersed positions they held, rapid disengagement and withdrawal were by far the most prudent military options. This was a classic case for 'rolling with the punches'. Like so many sacrificial actions which pass into military legend, that which was now unfolding on the Imjin should never have been allowed to take place.

In the next twenty-four hours the men in the British trenches, and even their officers, possessed astonishingly little notion of what was happening beyond the knowledge of wave after wave of Chinese attacking their positions. Rumours filtered through that the brigade would soon be fetched out. The brigade-major told the Gloucesters' adjutant on the radio that an American infantry-armour column in brigade strength would be moving to the battalion's relief later that day. Lieutenant Bill Cooper's company commander in the Northumberlands told him that 'the idea is to make the Chinese deploy, then withdraw on to the Americans behind us, who need more time'. The Fusiliers had received a hasty reinforcement of National Servicemen, thrown overnight from a transit camp in Japan into the midst of the battle. Cooper's quota of seven replacements were understandably appalled and bewildered by their new circumstances. In the darkness, the platoon commander was exasperated to see one of the new arrivals yet again defying the order to stay in his trench. 'Bloxham!' he called furiously. 'Get back in your trench!' Then he saw that the man was a Chinese. Cooper was not holding a weapon and found himself thrashing on the ground, hand to hand with the communist soldier, until an NCO ran forward and shot the man in the head.

At dawn, nervous and uncertain, the Northumberlands were ordered to withdraw and redeploy, some eight hundred yards to the rear. To their immense relief, the Chinese did not interfere. That day, they lay in their positions, suffering little from the enemy, but listening to the fierce struggle further west, where the Gloucesters were under desperate pressure. They cursed the feebleness of their air support, the sluggishness of the reinforcements alleged to be preparing the blocking positions behind them. The tempo of battle was leavened by a moment of black comedy, when inquiries were made about charges against a Fusilier who had stopped dead in the midst of an assault, because he claimed that 'the Lord Jesus had instructed him to take no part in the attack'. He was sent for court-martial.

Men were constantly asking their officers: 'What happens next, sir?' 'When can we get out?' They received repeated bland reassurances about help on the way. Ammunition was running short, above all grenades. The Fusiliers met one Chinese attack with a barrage of tins of compo cheese, to deceive the enemy into putting their heads down. The incoming mortaring intensified. The weariness showed above all in men's eyes, red and raw and aching from their tiredness. Yet still they remained unaware of the huge risk that they would not get out at all.

During the night of 24/25 April, orders at last reached 29 Brigade to withdraw from the Imjin to new positions north of Seoul. Infiltration parties were now deep behind the British flanks. Chinese snipers were firing on transport four miles behind 29 Brigade's front. Yet the Ulsters were bemused and dismayed by the order. Throughout the battle, their acting CO, Major Gerald Rickord, a highly experienced officer who ended World War II in command of an airborne battalion, felt less than happy with the level of information reaching him from Brigade HQ. He knew nothing of the Belgian withdrawal, of the exposure of the brigade's right flank, of the increasingly desperately predicament of the

Gloucesters. His men had thus far repulsed the Chinese wherever they met them, and suffered very few casualties. Above all, Rickord was dismayed by the plan for the withdrawal, which called for his companies to leave their positions on high ground, and descend to the valley road. The Ulsters would have vastly preferred to walk out along the ridges, keeping the enemy below them. But Brigadier Brodie decreed otherwise. While the OC 29 Brigade had been given an impossible task, holding a difficult area of front with a small force against overwhelming odds, there was considerable criticism after the battle of his tactics, from some of those who survived.

*

At 8 a.m. on the 25th, the retreat began in a thick ground mist, commanded by Colonel Kingsley Foster of the Fusiliers. There is no more difficult operation of war than disengagement when closely pressed by the enemy. Chinese infantry were now deployed on high ground from which they could overlook every stage of the British movement. As soon as they understood what was taking place, they hastened forward to exploit their success in forcing 29 Brigade back.

Most of the Northumberland Fusiliers got away intact down the road south, past a vital defile held by B Company of the Ulsters and a troop of 55 Squadron Royal Engineers. Their worst enemy was now their own exhaustion: '. . . the infantry, after seventy-two hours of fighting, were in no state to do more than walk out, fate being willing, on their own feet', in the words of a Hussars officer.[5] The British began their descent from the high ground in textbook fashion, counting their men through checkpoints, moving by bounds. But as the Chinese swarmed forward in their wake, the Ulsters and the Belgians became engaged in a desperate piecemeal scramble for safety. In the words of Major Henry Huth of the 8th Hussars, it was 'one long bloody ambush'. After so many months in which the tanks had languished idle, without a role in impassable country, along the valley road from the Imjin to Uijongbu they found their moment. They fought in troops and half-troops: some tanks providing direct fire support for infantry defending stretches of hillside, others crashing down the road to safety laden with exhausted and wounded survivors, others again covering their departure. Their 20-pounders and Besa machine guns raked the hillsides. When Chinese infantry began to scramble on to the hulls, Captain Peter Ormrod and Gavin Murray resorted to machine-gunning each other's Centurions to sweep them off. Sergeant Jack Cadman drove his tank through a Korean house, to dislodge a Chinese battering on his turret hatch. All that day, the Centurions fought along the road with a continuous rain of small-arms fire splattering against their armour, driving off periodic rushes of Chinese seeking to dash near enough to ram pole charges through their track guards. Major Huth, C Squadron commander, won a DSO for his direction of the tank actions during the retreat, and for the personal example he set: his own was the last Centurion out of the valley.

A runner reached Bill Cooper's platoon of the Fusiliers around 11 a.m., with news of the withdrawal. They were told to 'leave the heavy stuff, but bring all the ammunition you can'. There were believed to be enemy across their line of retreat, and they must be prepared to cut their way through. The Gloucesters would be moving independently. Cooper and his weary men reached the pass held by the Ulsters and Engineers, to see Colonel Foster standing among a clutch of Centurions and a half-track ambulance clustered by the roadside under increasingly heavy fire. Foster stopped him: 'I can't order you to do this,' he said, 'but I would be very grateful if you would stay and see the wounded out on the half-track.' Cooper's subsequent memories were a confused blur of grenades and mortaring, of a boy named Angus screaming after a tank ran over his legs, of a Chinese grenade that blew him off his feet and knocked him out. He awoke to find a Chinese searching his body. He sat up, causing the astounded enemy soldier to spring backwards. It was dusk. His elbow was shattered, he had splinter wounds from his knee to the top of his thigh. He was led to join a group of fellow-prisoners, lying and sitting by the roadside. Suddenly, an American aircraft swung low past them, and a napalm tank fell away from its belly, to land by the crippled Centurion it had been sent to destroy. For the watching British captives, this was the last glimpse of friendly forces for many months to come.

Colonel Foster followed his Fusiliers down the road in his jeep. At the pass held by the Ulsters, their company commander urged him to take to his feet – the route was under heavy fire, and a jeep was instantly vulnerable. Foster declined, and was killed a few moments later by a Chinese mortar bomb, which destroyed his vehicle. The commanding officer of the Belgian battalion was terribly burned by phosphorus, pouring from a tank grenade discharger as he stood alongside it when it was hit by a chance Chinese bullet.

Private Albert Varley of the Ulsters had been slightly wounded by fragments in the eye early in the battle, when a bullet struck his bren. The Regimental Aid Post sent him back to his company, as they lacked means to evacuate him. His platoon was one of those on the high ground, swarming with Chinese, which received the order: 'Every man for himself!' He and his 'oppo', a National Serviceman from Bristol named Ronnie Robinson, stumbled down the hill towards the road. Robinson was supporting a man with a shattered arm, who kept pleading to be allowed to stop and give himself up. Varley paused every few moments to turn and fire a brief burst towards their pursuers. He was convinced that they would never make it. But at last, they staggered thankfully on to the road, and clambered on to a Centurion, Varley casting away the pieces of his bren. They bucketed off down the road, Ulsters clinging desperately to every hull projection, the tank crew firing their Besa continuously until its ammunition was exhausted, then bouncing high-explosive shells off the road in front of them. A clutch of Americans appeared from somewhere, who also boarded the Centurion. One fired his bazooka at a hut surrounded by Chinese, who were also overrunning a stranded Centurion by the roadside. The surrounding hillsides now seemed infested with running, standing, crouching Chinese, firing down upon the hapless British below.

Varley was one of the lucky escapers. Many of the wounded and survivors of the Ulsters who crowded on to the tank hulls for that last desperate ride out of the valley were shot off as the Centurions drove back through the Chinese. On the radio set, the retiring tank crews heard their doctor, left behind them on the road with his charges, reporting bleakly: 'I am about to be captured . . . I have been captured.' It was now a race between the retreating British, struggling along the road and over the hills, and a mass of thousands of Chinese, moving with astonishing speed across country, unmoved by the losses inflicted upon them at every turn by tank gunfire.

Private Henry O'Kane of D Company had scarcely fired a shot during the preceding days, which he remembered chiefly for the confusion of moving from position to position every few hours, apparently without reason. As the withdrawal lapsed into a chaotic struggle for personal survival amid the milling rush of Chinese, he was hit in the leg by a mortar fragment. He collapsed into a ditch by the roadside for a moment. Then he unbuckled his equipment, threw it down, and limped along the road until somebody pushed him up on to a tank already crowded with men. He lost consciousness, then woke to find himself once more in a ditch beside the Centurion, which was slewed disabled across the paddy. Chinese soldiers scuttled up and thrust pole charges through its track guards. Those of the British who could still move, now ran. Those who could not, such as O'Kane, lay exhausted as the battle lapped past them. Another Ulsterman put a field dressing on his leg, and gave him a swig of rum. The sound of gunfire receded, while Chinese infantry ran heedless past, still intent on pursuit. At last a Chinese officer wearing a wooden Mauser holster stopped, gazed down on the motionless huddle of men, nursing their pain, and said in careful English: 'I think it is a good fight.' O'Kane and the other walking wounded were gathered and led away, hands on their heads. They never saw the stretcher cases again. They were given 'safe-conduct passes', declaring that they had been 'liberated by peace-loving peoples'. Then they passed into the bleak cycle of marches, makeshift political lectures, weary pauses in peasant huts, and the diet of sorgum, peanuts and beanflower that was their introduction to captivity.

The survivors of 29 Brigade reached safety behind the protection of a blocking position established by the US 25th Regimental Combat Team. Word was passed from the 8th Hussars to Brigade Headquarters: 'Everybody's come down who's coming.' The road back from the Imjin lay strewn with the wreckage of the British retreat: wrecked vehicles, abandoned equipment, bodies and shell cases. Fire still flickered from the remains of one of the abandoned Centurions, demolished to prevent its use by the enemy. Tom Brodie seemed vastly relieved, and frankly surprised, to see Gerald Rickord and the Ulsters B Company who had provided the rearguard. They were told that they must expect to fight another battle, that they must begin to dig in again at once. 'It was odd to hear that old clink of picks and shovels going again,' said Rickord. But late that night, fresh orders came. It was recognised that the brigade was exhausted. Sufficient American forces were now in the line to hold it against any new Chinese pressure. The men were coaxed and prodded a few miles further down the track, to a rendezvous with transport. Then they were driven away, overwhelmed with relief at their own survival, to recover from the ordeal.

*

For one group, of course, there was no escape from the ridge above the Imjin: the survivors of 1st Battalion, Gloucestershire Regiment. Attempts to resupply them by air achieved little – most of the drops fell outside their perimeter. Since the first day, helicopters had been unable to reach them to evacuate wounded. Contact with the outside world was fading as their last wireless batteries died. They knew at 6 a.m. on the morning of the twenty-fifth that they were doomed to death or captivity. At that hour, Brigade informed Colonel Carne's headquarters that the other battalions were withdrawing, that no further attempts to break through to their rescue were possible. Brodie could only tell Carne to stand his ground. 'I understand the position quite clearly,' said the colonel. 'But I must make it clear to you that my command is no longer an effective fighting force. If it is required that we shall stay here, in spite of this, we shall continue to hold.' Carne left the radio set to tell his adjutant: 'You know that armour/infantry column that's coming from 3 Div to relieve us?'

'Yes sir.'

'Well, it isn't coming.'

'Right, sir.'[6]

The natural comradeship of war is surpassed by the bond between men who find themselves doomed to share disaster. Colonel Fred Carne was a taciturn, in the eyes of some, almost inarticulate officer who had never in his army career been regarded as a 'high flier', despite experience of commanding an infantry battalion in Burma in World War II. Yet Carne, with his pipe and unshakeable calm in the face of tragedy, assumed heroic stature on Gloucester Hill. Early that morning his adjutant, Captain Anthony Farrar-Hockley, met Carne coming down the hill with two regimental police, a driver, his pipe and a rifle, after a brutal little firefight.

'What was all that about, sir?'

'Oh, just shooing away some Chinese.'[7]

Farrar-Hockley himself was an exceptionally tough, clever and ambitious officer who had enlisted under age in World War II and served as an airborne soldier. His ruthless single-mindedness and commitment to discipline did not make him universally beloved. Yet in the Imjin battle, he was able to show what the same uncompromising purpose and stubbornness could do to the Chinese. Farrar-Hockley it was, in the early dark hours of the 25th, who responded to the nerve-stretching bugles of the communists, gathering for yet another assault, by ordering Drum-Major Philip Buss to return their calls on his own bugle. The moment when Buss stood at attention on the position, playing in succession 'Reveille', 'Cookhouse', 'Defaulters' and 'Officers Dress For Dinner' passed into the legend of the Imjin battle.

There were others: Sergeant-Major Jack Hobbs; Padre Sam Davies; Denis Harding; Guy Ward of 45 Field Regiment; Captain Bob Hickey, the doctor; and a rollcall of officers and other ranks whose names became familiar throughout the British Army. There are those who have claimed, since the war, that the ranks of the Gloucesters were filled with exceptionally keen and dutiful soldiers. This does the regiment no service. In reality, there were as many disgruntled reservists and brassed-off regulars on Gloucester Hill as in any other unit of 29 Brigade. It was this that made their fate and their performance the more moving: they were a typical, perhaps a little above average county battalion, who showed for the thousandth time in the history of the British Army what ordinary men, decently led, can achieve in a situation which demands, above all, a willingness for sacrifice.

Brodie left it to Carne's discretion whether his battalion should attempt to break out; or whether, if this was impossible, they should surrender. Soon after 9.30 a.m. on 25 April, the colonel was informed by Brigade that within the hour he would lose all artillery support as 45 Field Regiment were compelled to pull out their guns. He gave the order to his company commanders to make for the British lines as best they could. Most of them had not eaten for forty-eight hours. When the men checked their ammunition, they found that each rifleman possessed just three rounds, the bren gunners a magazine and a half. They had begun the battle with more than fifty refills a magazine. 'I'm afraid we shall have to leave the wounded behind,' Carne told Bob Hickey. 'Very well, sir,' said the doctor. 'I quite understand the position.' Hickey and the chaplain, along with some of the medical staff, stayed with the eighty casualties on the position. 'This looks like a holiday in Peking for some of us,' remarked Padre Davies to the RAMC sergeant.[8] He and the others were taken prisoner soon after. Major Mike Harvey led the survivors of D Company by a circuitous route, first north towards the river, then west and south again. They encountered only one group of Chinese, whom they killed. Thereafter, they survived intact until, two days later, they exposed themselves before a group of American tanks, which promptly opened fire, inflicting some casualties. When they at last identified themselves, Harvey and his thirty-nine men were carried in safety into the UN lines. They, alone of their battalion, came safe home.

Some men, too weary to face a desperate march in doubtful pursuit of freedom, lay down on the battalion position to await capture. The men of A, B and C Companies who set off directly southwards immediately encountered heavy Chinese machine-gun fire. It fell to Farrar-Hockley, of all men, to call on them to lay down their arms and surrender: 'Feeling as if I was betraying everything that I loved and believed in, I raised my voice and called: "Stop!" '9 This did not prevent him from making three escape attempts in the days that followed.

Like many men that week, throughout the battle Major Guy Ward had sustained a curious conviction that in the end, 'it would all be all right'. Even after the order was given to make for the British lines independently, he did not lose this faith. Then, as he walked, 'I suddenly saw hundreds and hundreds of Gloucesters in a corner surrounded by Chinese. I thought: "Oh my God, here we go again." ' Guy Ward had been a prisoner of the Germans from 1941 to 1945. Colonel Carne, RSM Hobbs and a handful of others evaded capture for twenty-four hours. Then they, too, joined the rest of the battalion 'in the bag', where thirty more of them were yet to die. It was weeks before the survivors of 29 Brigade even knew that more than half the Gloucesters were alive and in enemy hands. A large part of Brigadier Brodie's personal trauma stemmed from the conviction of himself and his staff that all but Major Harvey's party had perished. 'The Brigadier seemed shattered by the whole experience,' said one of his officers.

The Imjin battle has been the subject of some controversy in the past thirty years. Men of the Ulsters and the Northumberland Fusiliers have been irked by the massive tide of publicity that flowed over the Gloucesters in the days and years after the destruction of Carne's battalion. They point out that the overwhelming majority of the Gloucesters' casualties were taken prisoner – the battalion also suffered sixty-three killed and perhaps thrice as many wounded. It is invariably the case that decorations and eulogies are heaped upon the survivors of military disasters, to make both themselves and their nations better able to endure sadness and dismay, less likely to ask The Reason Why. There is a quality about 'Last Stands' which draws painters and poets. Intelligent soldiers are more inclined to demand, sceptically, whether it should have been necessary for any last stand to take place. In the cold accountancy of war and history there may be headlines to be extracted from defeat, but there is no virtue.

29 Brigade's battle is unlikely to find a place in any manual of military instruction, except as an example of how not to hold a difficult position. If the brigade had been prepared for a big defensive action, its men had ample time to surround themselves with obstacles covered by fire, the first resorts of the infantryman in defence. They could have concentrated their forces either to cover the eastern or western passes through their sector. They had insufficient forces to do both. The communist attackers did not hold all the cards. They possessed ample mortars, which they used to great effect, but no air or artillery firepower. It is a remarkable tribute to the limitations of air support that, with the vast air forces at the disposal of the UN, tactical air strikes could not be used to more effect to break up the Chinese attacks. It was a tragedy – worse than that, it was a blunder somewhere in the UN chain of command – that the brigade was not pulled back from the Imjin positions as soon as the scale of the Chinese assault became clear. In the Korean campaign from the beginning of 1951 to the end, there was no other instance of the UN Command permitting a substantial force to be isolated and destroyed piecemeal over a period of days. Campaign histories attribute losses of 10,000 killed and wounded to the Chinese, against 1,000 29 Brigade casualties in the battle, around a quarter of the British front-line

strength. 169 of 850 Gloucesters mustered for rollcall with the brigade after the battle. The estimated communist loss figure is an arbitrary one, based upon the minimum that seemed credible to the British, given the weight of their own fire they saw take effect upon their enemies.

Major Rickord, the Ulsters' acting CO, came away from the Imjin 'feeling devastated'.

> I believed that we had lost the battle, had suffered a disaster. But I was afterwards reassured that it was by no means a disaster. The morning after we came out, the soldiers were singing Irish songs, playing a banjo. I told the quartermaster to get them a bath and their green tropical uniforms. He said: 'It's much too cold for that.' But I said – 'No, go on, do it. It'll make all the difference in the world to them to get a change of clothes.' And forty-eight hours later, they were fit to fight again, which was a wonderful feeling. I think they felt very proud of the fight they had put up. We felt no particular animosity towards the Chinese. Indeed, I think we felt great respect, even liking for them. But the regiment's old motto – *Quis Separabit* – was something we felt very strongly about.

The Northumberlands, the Belgians, the Gloucesters, the gunners and mortar crews would have said the same. If Rickord's words might sound to a cynic like the bromides of a professional soldier, the sentiments are none the less powerful and valid for that. When all the sceptical comment has been made, when all the exaggerations of time and regimental pride have been discounted, the British can still reflect with pride that they broke one arm of the communist spring offensive in those three days on the Imjin. If it was always unlikely that the Chinese could have got through to Seoul, they might have expected at least to drive south further and faster, and at much lower cost. There were repeated instances in Korea of UN units crumbling remarkably easily in the face of pressure, giving ground which had to be regained later in bloody and painful counter-attack. On the Imjin, the Chinese discovered the price of meeting efficient, determined footsoldiers who cared little for the Cold War, for the glory of the United Nations or the survival of Syngman Rhee; but to whom the regiment, the unit, a man's 'oppo' in the next trench, were everything. The most political army in the world encountered the least political – and was savagely mauled to gain its few sterile miles of rock and paddy. Across the breadth of the Korean front, Peking's spring offensive had failed. Never again in the war did the communists mount an all-out assault which appeared to have the slightest prospect of strategic success.

12 » THE STONY ROAD

1. Towards Stalemate

While the British 29 Brigade stood on the Imjin, Van Fleet hastened
to create a reserve position north of Seoul – the 'No Name' Line –
where Eighth Army had no difficulty holding the communists, the
momentum of their offensive spent. Yet the Chinese continued to
reinforce failure. On 15 May, Marshal Peng launched a new assault
with twenty-one Chinese and nine North Korean divisions. Once
again, the ROK III Corps collapsed, as it had done with monotonous
regularity throughout the war. The communists pushed forward
as much as thirty miles in some places. The ROK 5th and 7th
divisions gave way. But on the right, the ROK I Corps held its
ground. Despite sustaining some nine hundred casualties, the US
2nd Division also stood firm. One of its batteries fired more than
12,000 rounds of 105mm ammunition in a single twenty-four-hour
period. The 38th Infantry stemmed repeated attacks on the night
of 16 May. 'Artillery, crashing into the ground forward of the lines,
took a terrific toll of the attackers,' recorded the divisional history,
'while other hundreds died in the minefields checkered with
barbed wire. The groans of the wounded, screams of the attackers
and the blast of bugles mingled with the clattering roar of battle
as waves of Chinese pushed against the lines . . . Searchlights were
turned on to illuminate the battle area and aid the defenders in
locating and slaughtering the onrushing Chinese.'[1] The divisional
commander, Major-General Clark Ruffner, played a prominent
front-line role in organising the defence and concentrating his

units for counter-attacks, surviving a helicopter crash as he flew between positions.

The US 3rd Division and the 187th Airborne RCT plugged the gap on the right of the 2nd Division opened by the ROK collapse. By 20 May, the Chinese offensive was spent, and the UN was estimating that it had cost the communists 90,000 casualties. Even if this figure was exaggerated, like so many 'guesstimates' on the battlefield, there was no doubt that the enemy had been decisively worsted. The US Army, above all the 2nd 'Indianhead' Division, had displayed heartening determination in holding the line. On 22 May, Van Fleet opened his own counter-offensive, designed to exploit the exhaustion of the Chinese. The ROK I Corps moved up the coast against negligible opposition and gained the town of Kansong. The 187th RCT and 1st Marine Division reached the Hwachon reservoir. On the left, I Corps regained the old Imjin line, including the positions from which the British 29 Brigade had withdrawn in April.

There was little doubt that, had the political will existed, the communist front now lay open. The morale of the Chinese armies in Korea was shattered. After all their exhilarating successes of the winter, they were now compelled to confront the new face of the UN armies, the careful deployment of men and firepower which the communists could no longer break through. But Washington and its allies possessed no inclination to press the crumbling enemy northwards, to extend the UN front and put at risk all that had been gained. The objective declared by the Joint Chiefs was to bring about 'an end to the fighting, and a return to the status quo; the mission of Eighth Army was to inflict enough attrition on the foe to induce him to settle on these terms.' In the words of a British gunner officer, 'everybody could see that we had reached stalemate, unless someone started chucking atom bombs.'[2] Ridgway wrote: 'We stopped on what I believe to be the strongest line on our immediate front.'[3] In the first half of June, Van Fleet mounted limited operations to consolidate his positions – an exact repeat of the movement Ridgway began in April, but found frustrated by the Chinese spring offensive. This time, Operation PILEDRIVER successfully gained Chorwon and Kumhwa, the base line of the 'Iron Triangle'. X Corps cleared 'the Punchbowl', another important communist fortified zone. On the new front, give or take a few miles at various points, the United Nations would hold its ground for the remainder of the war.

The Chinese were compelled to concede stalemate. At vast cost in lives, they had demonstrated their inability to break through the revitalised divisions of Eighth Army, whatever local gains they could still achieve against the vulnerable ROKs. However limited the war aims of the Chinese in November 1950, there is no doubt that their early triumphs opened up, in the eyes of Peking, illusory visions of absolute military victory in Korea, of an all-embracing communist success. Now, once again, the prospect for Mao Tse Tung had narrowed dramatically. Chinese hopes of unifying Korea had died. The economic cost of the war to China was proving crippling, with the Russians insisting upon payment for the arms and ammunition which they supplied to Marshal Peng's army. The West had convincingly demonstrated its determination to defend South Korea, at whatever cost in lives and treasure. Yet, from a Western perspective, the war had thus far proved an unhappy and divisive experience. America's relationship with her allies had been deeply strained by the behaviour of MacArthur, the real fears in Europe that American desperation might provoke the use of nuclear weapons and even a third world war, in defence of another 'far-away country of which we know little'. As a leading political historian of the period has written, 'alarm that Britain might be dragged into war sharpened anti-Americanism, always latent in the Labour Party, and as a study of the Press shows, soon began to undermine confidence in American leadership.'[4] Many Westerners in Korea, above all many Europeans, were dismayed by the brutal injustice and corruption of Syngman Rhee's government, which they were being asked to uphold, and of which more will be said below. 'We felt a great hatred of being there, of the country,' said Captain St Clair Tisdall of the 8th Hussars. 'We seemed to be doing nothing very useful.'⁵ The costs of rearmament, above all for Britain, were proving almost insupportable. Even the modest British contingent in Korea was a very serious financial burden.

On 1 June 1951, the UN Secretary-General Trygve Lie declared his conviction that if a ceasefire could be achieved roughly along the 38th Parallel, the resolutions of the Security Council would have been fulfilled. The next day, Dean Acheson made a speech in which he reaffirmed the objective of a free and independent Korea; but he spoke of the prospects for peace resting upon the defeat of communist aggression, and the creation of suitable guarantees to prevent a repetition of that aggression. On 7 June, he told a US Senate committee that UN forces in Korea would accept an armistice on the 38th Parallel. The world was learning to live with an acknowledgement of changed military and political realities in Asia. On 23 June, when Yakov Malik, the Soviet delegate to the United Nations, proposed a ceasefire in Korea, his olive branch was received with overwhelming relief in the Western world. The Peking *People's Daily* endorsed the Russian initiative. At last, the end seemed in sight. Some compromise could be agreed, and the armies could go home. 'I . . . believe,' Ridgway had concluded a report to the Joint Chiefs on 20 May, 'that for the next sixty days the United States government should be able to count with reasonable assurance upon a military situation offering optimum advantage in support of its diplomatic negotiations.' On 10 July, communist and UN delegations met for the first time in the town of Kaesong to open ceasefire negotiations. It was fortunate for the peace of mind of the governments of the West that they had no inkling of the two years of struggle and bloodshed that still lay ahead. The communists were about to teach the world yet another bitter lesson in Korea: that war can be waged as doggedly and painfully at a negotiating table as with arms upon the battlefield.

2. Panmunjom

From the outset, Ridgway urged upon his government the toughest possible posture towards the communists in negotiations: 'To sit down with these men and deal with them as representatives of an enlightened and civilised people,' he wrote to Washington, 'is to deride one's own dignity and to invite the disaster their treachery will bring upon us.'[6] If the UN Commander's remarks would have been considered embarrassingly bellicose, had they been known to some of America's allies, they were bleakly justified by the events that began to unfold at Kaesong.

At the front, on the first day of talks with the communists sixteen men of the UN forces were killed, sixty-four wounded, fifteen missing. In Seoul, Western correspondents provoked a near-riot in Seoul because of the UN Command's initial refusal to allow them to attend the truce meetings. Ridgway himself had to leave his headquarters to pacify them. Floyd Park, the Pentagon's Chief of Information, issued a defensive statement:

> Arranging for an armistice during the progress of actual fight-ing is one of the most delicate negotiations in human affairs and must necessarily be conducted in strictest secrecy. More-over, ultimate success must depend in some measure upon the willingness of the public to await concrete results, and especially to refrain from violent reaction to incomplete or unfounded reports and rumours.

Yet within weeks, all these sensible considerations would be buried without trace, as the peace talks began their rapid deterioration into a public circus.

The UN Command perceived no special import in the commun-ists' proposed choice of a site for talks until these began on 10 July.

The UNC delegation was led by Vice-Admiral Turner Joy of the US Navy, the communist group by the North Korean General Nam Il. The significance of the fact that Kaesong was firmly in communist hands became rapidly apparent: the Chinese and North Koreans were not seeking the give-and-take of armistice negotiations. They had come to receive the UN's capitulation, or at least to score a major propaganda triumph. It had been agreed that the UN party should fly to the talks under a white flag which the Westerners regarded as an emblem of truce. They quickly discovered that the communists were presenting this symbol to the world as a token of surrender. Joy's delegation found that across the conference table, they had been seated in lower chairs than their communist counterparts. Every speech from the North Korean and Chinese team was punctuated with propaganda phrases about 'the murderer Rhee', 'your puppet on Formosa'. Every exchange was delayed by interminable adjournments demanded by Nam IP's delegation. Every procedural detail, the most basic discussion of an agenda, was dragged down into a morass of ideological rhetoric and empty irrationality. One of the most urgent UN demands, for the Red Cross to have access to prisoners in communist hands, was unhesitatingly brushed aside. A low point in negotiations was attained on 10 August, when the two delegations stared across the table at each other in complete silence for two hours and eleven minutes, a communist gesture intended to display their rejection of the preceding UN statement. An extraordinary catalogue of ludicrous, indeed often fantastic complaints was presented against the UN Command.

By 22 August, the talks had got nowhere. The communist delegation had wrung every conceivable propaganda advantage from the meetings, while talking for long enough to see that the UN delegation had not the slightest intention of yielding on acceptable terms. Nam Il therefore broke off the talks, claiming that UN forces had attempted to murder his delegation by air attack.

The communists had gained an immensely useful breathing space. Ridgway's forces had passively held their own positions during the five weeks of talks, and the Chinese were able to reinforce their own formations strongly with artillery. The UN battle for its next important objective, the Hwachon reservoir which provided both water and electricity for Seoul, proved bitter and costly. The names of Heartbreak Ridge and Bloody Ridge, dominating the reservoir, entered the unlovely vocabulary of the campaign. These features changed hands again and again between August and October. But on 14 October they fell to the US 2nd Division for the last time. Meanwhile, further west, UN forces advanced up to nineteen miles north of the 38th Parallel. Chinese casualties were enormous. There was little doubt that the tide of war had turned once more against the communists. On 7 October, they proposed a resumption of negotiations. This time, there seemed little doubt that the military pressure was forcing them to parley in earnest.

Talks began once more on 25 October 1951, at the genuinely neutral site of Panmunjom, in the no-man's-land between the armies. On 12 November, Van Fleet, Eighth Army's commander, was ordered to desist from major offensive action and restrict his forces to the defence of their existing front, to be known as the MLR – Main Line of Resistance. Local attacks were still permissible, but no operation in greater than battalion strength could be mounted without authorisation from Ridgway. This was the prelude to a striking negotiating bid by the UN delegation at Panmunjom: if the communists signed an armistice within thirty days, Joy's group told the Chinese and North Koreans, the existing front could be frozen into the final demarcation line between the two sides.

This was a move designed to show the communists, and the world, that the UN had no interest in further territorial gains in Korea. It was also intended, of course, to hasten Peking and Pyongyang towards the rapid ending of a war of which Western opinion was becoming increasingly weary. The communist negotiators hastened to ratify the proposal on 27 November. Then, for thirty days, they talked empty nothings at Panmunjom. And while they talked, immune from major UN military action, on the mountains their armies dug. Day by day, yard by yard, they sunk their trenches and tunnels into the hillsides. For 155 miles from coast to coast of Korea, through December 1951, they created a front of defensive positions almost impregnable to artillery fire and assault, manned by 855,000 men. Successive lines were interwoven into a fortified belt from fifteen to twenty-five miles in depth. By 27 December, when it was amply apparent at Panmunjom that the communist delegation had merely been playing for time, their armies were dug into the positions that, with only minor variations, would form the final armistice line nineteen months later. The communists could feel entirely satisfied with their progress. They were well aware of the growing war-weariness with Korea among the Western democracies. Granted that they had been compelled to forgo the immediate prospect of a military takeover of South Korea, they could hold their existing positions confident that it was most unlikely that the governments providing the UN contingents would tolerate the casualties that would be necessary to break the Chinese line. Peking and Pyongyang, facing the real risk of complete defeat in June 1951, had now achieved a virtual no-lose position. They could settle down at Panmunjom with a sense of time on their side, to wear down the fragile patience of the democracies, with only occasional injections of offensive action at the front, to keep up the drain of casualties and maintain pressure on the UN.

*

Yet if the December semi-truce was an error by the UN, throughout this period its military commander remained undeceived by and unyielding towards the communist strategy. The secret communications between Washington and Matthew Ridgway which have now been released for historical scrutiny underline the American general's qualities. Unlike MacArthur, Ridgway never allowed his private rhetoric to escape into public bombast. But he displayed a commitment and sense of purpose of the highest order, at a moment when the will of the United States was being visibly sapped by the frustration of stalemate.

Already in the press and radio [he wrote to the Joint Chiefs in July 1951], such expressions as the following are beginning to appear: 'Let's Get the Boys Back Home' and 'The War-Weary Troops'. I can hardly imagine a greater tragedy for America and the free world than a repetition of the disgraceful debacle of [running down] our Armed Forces following their victorious effort in World War II. We can never efface that blot on the record of the American people on whom the responsibility squarely rests. Within my authority and in the light of common sense and my best judgement, I shall seek to the limit of my ability to eliminate among all US military personnel in this theatre the type of thinking indicated by the use of such expressions. If this be 'Thought Control', then I am for it, heart and soul. To condone it would be a cowardly surrender of everything for which we have fought and plan to fight. It would coincide completely with the line the Communists would wish us to take.[7]

But if Washington's patience and resolve were being tested by events at Panmunjom, in Tokyo, Ridgway remained certain that there must be no indication of weakening will. 'I have a strong inner conviction,' he wrote in September, 'admittedly based on the Korean as contrasted with the world situation, that more steel and less silk, more forthright American insistence on the unchallengeable logic of our position, will yield the objectives for which we honorably contend . . . With all my conscience I urge that we stand firm.'[8]

Between July and the end of November 1951, the United Nations Command suffered almost 60,000 casualties, more than 22,000 of these American. Communist resistance in the air was strengthening, with the appearance of the first Tu-2 light bombers. The war in Korea had entered its longest and most frustrating period – of stalemate on the ground and sterile attrition at the negotiating table. The United Nations Command had renounced any military objective beyond the defence of the MLR, and spasmodic local operations, designed to sustain morale and demonstrate its army's continuing will to fight. For many months, the airmen had been urging the Chiefs of Staff in Washington – as airmen so often urged commanders throughout the twentieth century – that they could pursue the Allies' strategic objectives at far lower cost in lives by a sustained bombing campaign. From the last months of 1951 until the end of 1952, while the negotiations at Panmunjom dragged interminably on, the USAF waged a massive campaign to bring pressure upon the communists by bombing, of which more will be said below. Yet by December 1952, the communists had been able to increase and supply forces in Korea that numbered 1,200,000 men of seven Chinese armies and two North Korean corps. And through all those weary months, on the mountains of Korea the UN armies alternately baked and froze, fought fierce little local actions, whiled away the weeks in their foxholes and bunkers – in the name of a cause whose meaning and purpose had long been forgotten by most of those 'at the sharp end', if they had ever understood it.

3. The Cause

From beginning to end of the Korean conflict, most United Nations soldiers found considerable difficulty in reconciling the ideals that they were alleged to be fighting for with the unattractive conduct of the regime of Syngman Rhee. As early as 18 July 1950, the British chargé d'affaires in Korea, Henry Sawbridge, wrote to the Foreign Office from Pusan:

> It appears from here that this war is being fought *inter alia* to make Korea safe for Syngman Rhee and his entourage. I had hoped that I might find it otherwise. I may be wrong, but I fancy that the inexperience, incompetence, and possibly corruption of the present regime are in some measure responsible for this crisis.[9]

'Nor is there any real soul to this war,' the Australian Richard Hughes wrote in the London *Sunday Times* on 5 September. 'No powerful sympathy or even warm liking exists between the Americans and the South Koreans. The soldiers of the United States and Britain notoriously have little abstract opinion or articulate comment on why they are fighting, but they can usually detect in any war a menace to their country or their homes. They can perceive nothing of that sort in this war.'

Through the months that followed, American and British soldiers constantly witnessed dreadful acts of brutality by the South Koreans towards their own people. In the early stages of the war, Washington and London sought to brush aside disturbing reports from Seoul. 'Newspaper reports of atrocities,' noted a disdainful Foreign Office hand, 'have usually been based upon "spot" observations, and some have been written by inexperienced, biassed, or apparently highly emotional reporters.'[10] But what was the Foreign Office to make of such a cable as this, from their Minister in Korea on 8 January 1951?

Besides two instances of mass executions reported in my telegram No 197, a third occurred near Seoul on the evening of 20 December, within half a mile of 29 Brigade Headquarters. It was stopped by British troops on orders from Brigade Headquarters when 20 persons had already been shot, but the execution of 38 more was prevented, and they were sent back to the gaol whence they came. It transpired afterwards that the South Korean military authorities were responsible in this case ... As the threat to Seoul developed, and owing to the destruction of the death house, the authorities resorted to these hurried mass executions by shooting in order to avoid the transfer of condemned prisoners south, or leaving them behind to be liberated by the Communists. However deplorable their methods, one can readily grasp their problem ... The ordinary Korean finds it hard to understand our logic in this matter. He sees that the UN have sent troops to fight the Communists in Korea, and is therefore bewildered at the violent reaction evoked when

South Koreans themselves give practical proof of their anti-Communist sentiment by publicly eliminating persons who are, in their eyes, traitors convicted by law of helping the Communists in one way or another. As for the methods used, what we regard as brutality is only normal treatment expected from those in authority, I should say.[11]

But others would not say. Many British soldiers were repelled by the behaviour of the regime for which they were alleged to be fighting. One man, a Private Duncan, wrote to his MP after the 20 December incident:

40 emaciated and subdued Koreans were taken about a mile from where I was stationed and shot while their hands were tied, and also beaten unnecessarily by rifles. The executioners were South Korean military police. The whole incident has caused a great stir and ill-feeling among the men of my unit. We have heard of lots of other occasions of the same happening. I write to tell you this, as we are led to believe that we are fighting against such actions, and I sincerely believe that our troops are wondering which side in Korea is right or wrong.[12]

John Ellis of the Gloucesters was talking one day to Ronnie Littlewood, the Transport Officer, about an incident he had witnessed, in which retreating ROK troops systematically mowed down refugees in their path. 'What the hell are we doing here, propping up this old bandit Syngman Rhee,' asked Littlewood, 'if they're doing things like this?'[13] Ellis, the younger man, like many junior officers merely brushed aside higher moral issues. He was there, in the long tradition of British soldiers fighting far-flung campaigns, because he was there. But very many UN soldiers asked themselves the same question as Littlewood. 'The locals so plainly didn't want us there,' said Lieutenant Chris Snider of the Canadian Brigade. 'They didn't want outsiders of any kind. When you were very close to the front line, the locals would smile at you and bring you water. But further back, behind the front, Koreans made it plain you were just a nuisance, an intrusion.'[14] Lieutenant Stan Muir of 45 Field

Regiment, RA, found it chronically difficult to harden his heart to the need to turn back refugees appearing in front of the British positions, lest they be masking infiltrators. 'Sometimes, one could hear them out there in no man's land, howling in the night. Everything we saw of the Korean people was sad.'[15]

In the spring of 1951, a wave of outrage swept through the ranks of the British 29 Brigade, following the publication in the London *Sunday Times* of a statement by Syngman Rhee, denouncing the alleged British role in the dismissal of MacArthur, and declaring: 'The British troops have outlived their welcome in my country.' This was one of Rhee's notorious tantrums. He told an Australian Embassy official: 'They are not wanted here any longer. Tell that to your government. The Australian, Canadian, New Zealand and British troops all represent a government which is now sabotaging the brave American effort to liberate fully and unify my unhappy nation.'[16]

The publication of these remarks, within weeks of the bloody battle on the Imjin, was too much for British soldiers yearning above all to shake off the dust of Rhee's terrible country from their feet. Bombardier A. Humphreys of C Troop, 170 Independent Mortar Battery, wrote to the Foreign Office:

Dear Sir,

A few hours ago *The Sunday Times* dated 6 May 1951 arrived at the battery, and the first article that was read by myself was headed 'South Korean President Denounces Britain'. I take it, Sir, that you have read this article, and ask you to put yourself in my position. I am a reservist, called back to the armed forces, parted from my family, to take part in a conflict which my whole train of thought said was wrong when the UN forces crossed the Parallel for the first time. The stand of the 29th British Brigade is so very fresh in my mind. Am I to go into the next conflict, and possibly become a battle casualty, for a cause one is not in full agreement with? Knowing that President Syngman Rhee decries the efforts we have made, tells the world that the British are unwelcome, and the sacrifices made thought so very little of . . . My own personal opinion: bring the British forces back, and use them where their efforts would be fully appreciated.

Yours Faithfully,

Humphreys

A Foreign Office hand annotated the soldier's scrawl: 'This a very moving and sane letter, and deserves a good reply.' Other letters in the same vein reached Britain, either direct to Ministers, or through soldiers' Members of Parliament. British diplomats in Korea sighed, and sought to take refuge in an urbane view of Syngman Rhee's deficiencies. After the British Minister in Korea had seen the President, he wrote to London on 16 June:

The South Koreans – as is perhaps to be expected at their stage of national development – are going through one of the more acute stages of the 'awkward age'. It is their misfortune, and their allies', that this should coincide with the obligation to fight for the survival of their newly acquired independence. When they show themselves, as they often do, uncomprehending and intolerant of other people's views, their extreme inexperience is an extenuating circumstance that has to be taken into account when evaluating the irresponsible statements made by people in prominent positions. Chief among these is the President himself.[17]

This line of reasoning, of course, offered little consolation to the men on the line, such as Bombardier Humphreys. And even some UN officials took a far less sanguine view than the British Minister of the South Korean government's behaviour. 'At least many hundreds [of alleged communists] have been shot,' reported the Australian delegate to the UN Commission for Korea, James Plimsoll, on 17 February 1951. He described how the prisoners had been compelled to dig their own graves, then 'rather clumsily and inexpertly shot before the eyes of others waiting their own turn'. In fairness to the Seoul regime, Plimsoll pointed out the immense bitterness and yearning for revenge among South Koreans for the dreadful atrocities committed by the communists during their occupation: 'The members of the Korean government and the Korean police are literally fighting for their lives. Any one of them or of their families who fell into enemy hands would be killed. They therefore do not take quite the detached view of the situation that persons overseas can take . . . Even allowing for all this, the executions remain shocking. The picture is not a pretty one, even when due weight is given to the special conditions of war and of a relatively primitive country.'[18]

It was made even less pretty by such scandals as the creation of the so-called National Defence Corps by the South Korean government in December 1950. This was intended to act as a paramilitary militia. In the months that followed, it became evident to foreigners in Korea that something was going wrong, when they glimpsed bodies of starving beggars in the streets, and when it was learned that thousands of wretched members of the NDC were dying of cold and exposure, kept confined in barracks unfed and deprived of warmth. Even the Seoul government could not indefinitely resist demands for an investigation. It was discovered that the NDC commanding officer, one Kim Yun Gun, had embezzled millions of dollars intended to clothe and feed the militia. He and five of his officers were shot outside Taegu on 12 August 1951. Yet every Allied government knew that this case was only the tip of the iceberg of official corruption.

Throughout the war, Rhee conducted his own dictatorship without reference to Allied sensibilities, almost indeed as if the war did not exist. The National Assembly fought a long series of political battles with him, and lost all of them. The last, and most dramatic, came in May 1952, when the Assembly voted to overrule Rhee and lift martial law in the Pusan district. On 27 May, the Assembly building was surrounded by military police. Some 50 Assemblymen in shuttle buses were towed by army trucks to a military police station. Four were jailed, although their arrest in mid-session was blatantly illegal. Rhee then wielded power as if the legislature did not exist. 'Spontaneous' demonstrations were organised in his support. Coercion of the anti-Rhee Assemblymen became outrageous.

At midnight on 4 July, eighty were dragged into the Assembly hall under police guard to prevent their escape. None were allowed to leave until constitutional amendments had been passed, placing all effective power in South Korea in Rhee's hands. Thus armed, he called a presidential election on 5 August, at which he was declared elected with 72 per cent of the vote. Thereafter, official corruption in Korea ran entirely unchecked, and meaningful political debate was at an end. The United States and her allies were deeply embarrassed. Rhee made it plain that he could not care less.

Captain Ves Kauffroth arrived in Korea in December 1950 from New Orleans, to serve as an air traffic controller. Driving towards Kimpo, 'the truck was stopped by Korean police while a procession of Korean prisoners marched across the road directly in front of us. The procession was led by a long line of men wearing pointed, conical hats that even covered their faces. The long lines were four abreast and were followed by women who were also roped together. The women's heads were not covered, and several looked up to us in the truck in a most beseeching manner as they were dragged along. I asked the driver what was happening, and he said they were communists being taken away for execution. He said that now the Chinese had entered the war, all communists were being "gotten rid of".'[19]

Here was a pattern that was to become bleakly familiar in Indochina: of two opposing authoritarian regimes, each waging war *à l'outrance*, each committing acts of extraordinary brutality by Western standards. In Seoul, as in Saigon later, it could be argued that the scale of atrocities committed by the anti-communist forces was far less great than that attributable to the communists. Yet nothing could change the fact that the process of law scarcely existed in Seoul, any more than in Pyongyang. The vengeance of Syngman Rhee and his officials upon their perceived enemies was quite as casual and ruthless as that of Kim Il Sung. The communist guerrilla activity in South Korea, which remained a constant feature of life there until the end of the war, required unceasing military activity to contain it, and provided the Seoul regime with an alibi for all manner of brutalities to its own people, 'suspected of assisting the enemy'. Western soldiers were struggling to believe that they were fighting in Korea to defend certain principles of justice and freedom, which they witnessed daily being flouted, indeed trampled under-foot, all around them.

*

Throughout the first year of the war, Washington conducted a tire-less diplomatic offensive to broaden to the utmost the participation of foreign contingents in the struggle. If the concept of the war as a United Nations crusade, rather than a narrow pursuit of American national interests, was to remain plausible, the member nations of the UN must be seen to contribute on the battlefield. Yet the very insistence of the Washington Administration that the Korean War must be regarded as one front in the worldwide struggle against communism made many nations reluctant to flock to the standard. It might have been easier to persuade them to fight against North Korean aggression than to participate in a confrontation in which, they were told, Pyongyang was merely acting as the tool of Moscow and Peking. In the first year, the towering shadow of MacArthur, together with his pronouncements, deterred some governments. It was embarrassing enough to be invited to send troops to fight as subordinate partners of the American army. But when there was also serious doubt whether the Washington Administration could control its own theatre commander, when the spectre of a third world war hung heavy over the battlefield, even greater fears came into play. Many nations were still in deep economic difficulties in the aftermath of World War II. Their men in the field had to be clothed, armed, equipped, ammunitioned, even fed by the United States. Each country was supposed to repay the US government $14.70 per man per day in the field – though settlement was deferred until the armistice. Individual nations also paid for some of their supplies. Once when a Filipino artillery battery was called upon to lay down a heavy barrage in support of the Turkish brigade, it is claimed that the following morning, the Filipino commander protested to his American divisional commander about the cost to his poor country of all that ammunition. Yet, for all the great and sincere efforts that were made by senior Americans to cloak their efforts in Korea in the mantle of the United Nations, from beginning to end the conflict could never be other than Washington's war, to which other states provided token contributions chiefly for the diplomatic appeasement of the United States.

Among the most prominent contributors, the Turks sent a much-respected infantry brigade, whose men were evidently uninterested in higher tactics or sophisticated military skills, but possessed much rugged courage and willingness to endure. The Philippines, Thailand, Holland, Ethiopia, Colombia, Belgium and Greece each contributed infantry battalions with some supporting elements. South Africa provided a fighter squadron. The more cautious Indians, Scandinavians and Italians provided medical units. The French, whose military resources were strained to the utmost in Indochina and North Africa, provided a token infantry battalion which was exceptionally well regarded. The French unit, like those of all the other small nations, was incorporated into an American formation. But by far the most important non-American contribution was that of Canada and other nations of the British Commonwealth. The major Commonwealth countries all provided significant air and naval forces. Canada dispatched three destroyers and an air transport squadron soon after the outbreak of war, and maintained a significant naval presence until the end. In addition, on the ground the British provided two infantry brigades, an armoured regiment, and supporting artillery and engineers. The Canadians sent a reinforced infantry brigade. In June 1950, their armed forces totalled only 20,369 men of all ranks, and thus assembling a contingent posed great problems. Their initial unit, the 2nd Princess Patricia's Canadian Light Infantry, proved to include much unsatisfactory material and many men who had to be sent home. But after that first shake-out, the 'Princess Pats' were welded into a fine fighting unit. The Australians also sent two exceptionally good infantry battalions, the New Zealanders an artillery regiment. In

July 1951, all these elements were combined to form the Commonwealth Division, under the command of Major-General James Cassels. In the two years that followed the formation achieved an
outstanding reputation in Korea. 'There was enormous enthusiasm
for the ideal,' said the division's first artillery commander, Brigadier
William Pike. 'There was tremendous competition between the
units, because nobody wanted to be thought less good than the
others.' The genuine excitement within the division, about proving
that the experiment of an integrated Commonwealth fighting force
could work, gave its senior officers, if not its men, reasons for being
in Korea that seemed to many more worthwhile than defending the
regime of Syngman Rhee. 'You must remember that at that period,
we still assumed that the Empire would go on,' said Pike.[20]

*

And among all the UN formations fighting in Korea, there were
the Koreans themselves. The decision to provide a contingent of
'Katousas', Korean Attached Troops, to every Allied sub-unit was
partly a desperate expedient to bring some UN formations up to
strength, and partly a reflection of the UN Command's lack of confidence in the ROK troops' ability to fight in formations. Thus,
almost every American and Commonwealth platoon possessed its
handful of Koreans. Some were adopted as much-beloved mascots,
some were respected as memorable comrades. Others were treated
with callous contempt. As a system of reinforcement, it left much
to be desired, because few Koreans became sufficiently integrated
in the units to which they were attached to be fully accepted and
trusted. Meanwhile, the ROK army's formations continued to cause
chronic concern to the commanders of Eighth Army. Faced by a
communist offensive, they collapsed with monotonous regularity.
Knowing themselves to be untrusted by their foreign sponsors, the
Koreans repeatedly showed themselves militarily untrustworthy.
Until the end of the war, the worst excesses of corruption were
commonplace in the ROK army. Officers neglected their men, sold
their rations on the black market, paid phantom soldiers to line

their own pockets, neglected even to give the men in their ranks the pittance of pay to which they were entitled. The only consolation for being an ROK soldier was that, for some men, life was marginally more endurable than for their civilian counterparts. The South Koreans, from beginning to end of the war, suffered an eternity of hardship and injustice, modified only by the efforts of foreign refugee organisations who did their best to feed and clothe the worst sufferers. 'The whole country seemed to have become a quagmire,' said Lieutenant Chris Snider of the Canadian Brigade. 'Everything had been beaten down to the lowest level. There seemed no society but peasant society. The place was a huge armed camp, strewn with homeless children and devastation.'[21] To every foreigner, the poverty was almost unbelievable. President Rhee's official salary was US $37.50 a month; that of a ROK army colonel, $10.75. The Bank of Korea claimed that the average salary of a Korean was $5, yet the average spending in a family of 4.6 adults was $32. The Koreans suggested, denying the vast influence of the black market, that the difference was made up by families selling odd valuables, putting children in street stalls, and 'calling on Confucius for aid'. The equation was distorted by foreign largesse: every Korean employee of EUSAK was paid $17.50, and the average houseboy received $30 to $60. It was a web of hardship interwoven with corruption and foreign free spending which was to wreak equal havoc with the moral fabric of Vietnamese society a decade later.

*

Suk Bun Yoon, the fourteen-year-old schoolboy who had twice escaped from Seoul under communist occupation, was living with the remains of his family as suppliants upon the charity of a village south of the capital in the spring of 1951. A government mobilisation decree was suddenly thrust upon the village: twenty able-bodied men were required for military service. Suk's family was offered a simple proposal by the villagers: if the boy would go to the army in place of one of their own, they would continue to feed his parents.

An American army truck bore him and the other bewildered young men first to Seoul, and then on up the dusty road towards the front. They spent a night in an old station warehouse, where they were given chocolate and a can of corned beef. It was the first meat the boy had tasted for six months, and was impossibly rich. He was sick at once. Next morning, after five hours on the road, he and a cluster of others were deposited at the camp of the Royal Ulster Rifles. He was not to be a soldier, but a porter under military discipline. He found himself joining a unit of some forty porters attached to the battalion. His first job was to carry a coil of barbed wire up to the forward positions. It was hopeless. He was too young, and too weak. The corporal in charge took pity on him. He was assigned to become a sweeper and odd-job boy at the rear echelon. Yet life remained desperately hard. Each night, the porters were confined to their hut, yet they were sometimes awakened amid the sound of the gunfire to carry ammunition or equipment forward. One day, they found themselves hastily ordered back to a new position. Suk scarcely understood what was happening, beyond the confusion of retreat. Gradually, he and the others understood that there had been a battle, and heavy casualties. Around half the porters had disappeared, captured or killed.

After the battle, the porters' conditions seemed to improve. Suk became more accustomed to the life, and determined to educate himself. As he learned a little English, he questioned the soldiers incessantly: What was the longest river in the world? Which was the highest mountain? How was England governed? Since in later life he became a professor of economics, this experiment cannot be considered a complete failure. The soldiers called him 'Spaniard', because he had a reputation for hot temper. Yet when the Ulsters were relieved and he found himself attached to the Royal Norfolks, conditions deteriorated again. He was caught scavenging for food, roughly handled, and sent for a spell in a barbed-wire cage. He was then sacked from his job as a porter at battalion headquarters, and sent to the pioneer platoon, where he spent several more months.

'I was very homesick,' he said. 'By February 1952, I was on the verge of a mental breakdown. The only letter I had sent to my family was returned undelivered. I was missing them desperately.' That month, he was given leave to Seoul. He reached the capital determined not to go back to the front. He contacted some of his old schoolmates, and in April was able to arrange to return to school – a school without books or desks. His only asset was a strong command of the English language which he had acquired on the hills behind the Imjin.[22]

*

The men of the UN forces sometimes behaved with dreadful callousness towards South Koreans. Eighth Army was compelled to issue a forceful Order of the Day in the summer of 1951:

> Many soldiers seem to take a perverse delight in frightening civilians by driving very close, and then suddenly blaring their horns at the unsuspecting. Others make repeated attempts to drive the Koreans off the roads and into ditches. Americans are notably impatient, and too often drivers direct vile and belittling profanity towards those who slow their progress. Swearing at the driver of an oxcart will not make the ox move faster. It will cause the owner of the cart to resent the impertinent discourtesy of the soldier who curses him. We are not in this country as conquerors. We are here as friends.[23]

Some of these 'friends' were extraordinarily gentle and generous to Koreans, adopting and educating orphans, raising large sums for Korean charities, giving all the food and clothes they could spare from their units. Yet many never overcame their chronic suspicion of the 'gooks', and carried this to savage limits in moments of stress. One morning in February 1951, Private Warren Avery of the 29th Infantry was out on 'chicken patrol' with a handful of other men in a local town, searching for fowls for the platoon pot. They were stopped at a Korean military police checkpoint: 'One of them said something to Gibson, and they all put a round in the chamber. We didn't know whether to believe they were South Koreans or North Koreans. When I heard a bolt snick, I just turned around with the BAR and wiped them off the f***ing crossroad.'[24] There is no reason to doubt the truth of the story, for such episodes were commonplace. 'Unless you were an anthropology student,' said Marine Selwyn Handler, 'Koreans were just a bunch of gooks. Who cared about the feelings of people like that? We were very smug Americans at that time.'[25] Talking of Eighth Army's treatment of refugees approaching the UN lines, Lieutenant Robert Sebilian of 5th Marines said: 'We probably shot some people who were innocent – but how could you know which side they were on? The military problem was simply: Do you let these people filter through?'[26] The answer, very often, was a ruthless negative.

UN soldiers' sense of alienation from the Koreans was intensified by observing their brutality towards each other. 'One had a hard time thinking of them as civilised human beings,' said Major Gordon Gayle, executive officer of 7th Marines. 'I was impressed by their absolute absence of Christian spirit. The ROKs thought it was funny to see some other guy over the hill being shelled.'[27] Americans were told not to interfere when the ROK CIC were interrogating prisoners. 'We found it hard to watch a man being beaten to death,' said Major Ed Simmons of 1st Marines.[28] When Sergeant William Norris was sent to join the KMAG training mission, he was horrified by the Korean army's discipline: 'I saw a deserter shot; a kid who lost a rifle – an $87 rifle – was made to stand in a barrel of water all day in January. Men were beaten with pine saplings. Whole cities were roped off to collect people for the draft. And Americans could do nothing about it. You have to understand the Asian way.'[29] The young Canadian Chris Snider complained about one of the Korean Katcoms in his platoon who persistently fell asleep on duty. The Korean liaison officer came down from battalion headquarters to deal with the matter. Snider was awoken to be told by one of his men that the visitor, along with a Korean senior NCO, had taken the offender out and ordered him to dig a grave. The man was shot before the Canadians could intervene. The liaison officer and NCO were replaced, but the episode had a traumatic effect on the whole platoon. The Canadians were astounded that men of any society could behave in such a fashion to each other. Yet almost every UN veteran of Korea saw South Koreans do such things. Indeed, arbitrary execution appeared the foundation of ROK army discipline. The South Korean army officer, wrote a KMAG adviser – Lieutenant Colonel Leon Smith of I ROK Corps – in a scathing report to the Pentagon,

> in almost all cases has no love or respect for his superiors – only homage – and no love, respect, nor sense of responsibility for his subordinates. He will browbeat his juniors, steal from all. He spends his time and effort on 'eyewash', rather than the actual correction of conditions. He works hard at building his own ego to the point where he believes himself infallible, but when times really get rough, he comes back to his adviser for strength and decision.[30]

Upon such a foundation of mistrust and contempt for the nation in whose interests the war was being fought, did the UN seek to make the ROK army an effective instrument, and South Korea a viable political entity.

13 » THE INTELLIGENCE WAR

In the aftermath of World War II, it was not merely America's uniformed armed forces that were abruptly run down and demobilised. William Donovan's intelligence organisation, the Office of Strategic Services, built up almost from scratch over five years of intensive wartime activity, was reduced to a tiny bureaucracy in Washington, operating a handful of field agents. In the summer of 1950, this was the extent of the renamed Central Intelligence Agency and its resources. 'The Company' maintained a small office in Tokyo, but its operations in the Far East were chronically crippled by the hostility of MacArthur. Ever since World War II, when he had refused to allow clandestine activities by any of the intelligence 'private armies' in his theatre, the general cherished a distaste for such practices. Only in May 1950 was the CIA allowed to set up its first Tokyo station. And only later that summer, under the desperate pressure of work, was this expanded into an active operational network. William Duggan's Office of Special Operations was responsible for Far East intelligence-gathering. George Aurell maintained liaison with SCAP's headquarters with some difficulty. An outlandish Danish-American named Hans Tofte, whose enthusiasm for behind-the-lines adventuring took him into the OSS in the last stages of World War II, set up a new unit named the Office of Policy Co-ordination to organise covert activity. Meanwhile, back in Washington, as the Administration became brutally aware of the consequences of attempting to conduct foreign policy with inadequate intelligence about enemies actual and potential, the Director of the CIA, Admiral R. H. Hillenkoetter, was sacked. On the strong recommendation of General Marshall, Truman replaced him with General Walter Bedell Smith, Eisenhower's wartime Chief of Staff in north-west Europe. Bedell Smith's appointment gave the CIA almost overnight a credibility and claim upon resources in Washington that provided the motive power for the Agency's massive expansion in the next three years.

Yet throughout the war, the United Nations' intelligence about Chinese and North Korean strategic intentions remained very poor. There is still no evidence to suggest that Washington possessed any highly-placed agent in either Pyongyang or Peking. By far the most important and effective sources of operational intelligence, as in World War II, were decrypts of enemy wireless transmissions by the signals organisation established outside Washington for the purpose. But the available quantity of 'sigint' was restricted by the enemy's shortage of sophisticated communications equipment. From 1950 onwards, a variety of organisations were established in South Korea to provide 'humint' – intelligence based upon agent observation behind the communist lines – and to sponsor covert guerrilla operations. None were notably successful, and all paid a frightful toll in lives – most of these Korean. But their efforts have a place in any portrait of the war.

When America entered the Korean conflict, a CIA station was hastily established in the peninsula, initially at Pusan, under the direction of a veteran paratroop commander from World War II, Ben Vandervoort. But Vandervoort had little special operations experience, and seemed unhappy in his role. He was replaced by a big, formidable ex-FBI man who had spent many years in South America, Al Haney. Jack Singlaub was an ex-World War II paratrooper who had served with the Office of Strategic Services in Indochina, and thereafter in OSS's successor organisations, the Special Services Unit, the Central Intelligence Group, and finally the newly created Central Intelligence Agency. Until the Nationalists were driven out of mainland China, Singlaub was CIA Station Chief in Mukden. When the Korean War began, he was a lieutenant-colonel, building a Ranger organisation at Fort Benning. He volunteered for Korea in the hope of being given a battalion command. Instead, he was seconded to the CIA, to serve as Haney's deputy Station Chief.

A complex chain of command was established to preside over intelligence-gathering. At its summit stood JACK – Joint Advisory Commission, Korea, which was in turn part of CCRAK – Combined Command Research and Activities in Korea – controlled from Tokyo by Willoughby, MacArthur's G-2. They were primarily concerned with the parachute insertion of parties of locally trained Koreans to gather intelligence behind the lines. The accident rate was high. The recovery rate was low. Yet in the customary empire-building contest between service bureaucracies, a multiplicity of covert operations groups developed in Korea. The US Navy was sponsoring coastal raiding parties of its own. The British were landing Royal Marine hit-and-run assault groups. There were outposts on the offshore islands controlling escape and evasion organisations for downed pilots, or monitoring enemy movement. By a characteristic irony, the only interested body not known to be sponsoring intelligence operations in the North was the government of South Korea. Syngman Rhee's intelligence organisation confined its attentions to keeping a close watch on its own society.

The CIA was determined to maintain its independence of CCRAK, and was largely successful in doing so. A strict edict was issued that no Americans were to be dispatched into the North. But the Seoul station, based upon the Traymore Hotel, rapidly expanded to a strength of more than a hundred officers, training Koreans to land in enemy-held territory by small boat from the coast. In the first year of the war, some 1,200 recruits were trained at Yong-do, an island off the southern tip of Korea where a marine named Colonel 'Dutch' Kraemer ran the programme.

Initially, the purpose of putting agents into the North was to discover whether there was any basis upon which a local resistance movement might be built up. A few Koreans were sent for long-term training. Most were merely given the most rudimentary instruction before being pitched ashore on a hostile coast with a radio set. Some, perhaps to their controllers' surprise, sent back remarkably optimistic messages giving rendezvous at which more agents and supplies could be dropped. It was many months before the Americans began to perceive that almost all these operators had been captured, 'turned', and were transmitting under communist instruction. Slowly and reluctantly, the CIA recognised the ruthless efficiency of the communists' control of their own countryside. North Korea was simply too small, too overcrowded with troops, militia, and police, to make covert movement readily possible.

*

But the lesson was learned the hard way, at tragic cost in lives. There were fewer stranger stories of behind-the-lines operations in Korea than that of Major William Ellery Anderson of the Royal Ulster Rifles. Anderson, an Englishman, played a major role in one of the early attempts to wage war behind the lines in Korea, under the auspices of the US Army. He was an architect's son, commissioned into the British Army in 1940. He saw considerable service as a paratrooper, was wounded in Sicily, and in 1944 survived for some weeks in occupied France, having being dropped after D-Day with a Special Air Service party, to support the Resistance. When the war ended, Anderson spent some months as a war crimes investigator, then accepted a regular commission in the Ulsters because he had a friend in the regiment. He found the routine of peacetime soldiering intolerable, and by 1950 when the battalion was sent to war, he was barely on speaking terms with his colonel. As soon as they arrived in Korea, Anderson was sent off to a 'Battle Training Team', and it was made clear that the colonel hoped not to see him back.

Anderson was a natural adventurer, and he was bored. There was an exciting rumour that the SAS were to send a squadron to Korea, which he hoped to join. But then it was learned that MacArthur, with his intense dislike of special operations, above all foreign ones, had quashed the idea. One day in early 1951, Anderson was complaining to the correspondent René Cutforth about

the lack of imagination of the High Command in failing to organise guerrilla operations behind the communist lines. Cutforth said
he had heard something of that kind was in the wind. Anderson
at once asked for an interview with General Van Fleet. He got as
far as seeing the Eighth Army commander's G-1. He was then
passed on to Colonel John Magee of Eighth Army's Operations
staff. Magee welcomed Anderson's enthusiasm, and invited the
Englishman to join the embryo organisation, Combined Command
for Intelligence Operations, Far East. Indeed, Anderson found himself running his own little section of it. From a quonset hut in
a reinforcement depot, Anderson began to recruit Koreans. ROK
officer cadets were invited to volunteer, with the promise of
commissions if they survived. Within a few days, Anderson had
twenty recruits. One of them was Lee Chien Ho, the chemical
engineering student who had escaped from Seoul as a refugee, and
become an interpreter with the 5th Marines. Jimmy Lee, as he now
called himself, developed great respect for Anderson's skills as a
special operations officer, and indeed contrasted them favourably
with those of some American officers with whom he subsequently
served.[1] With the aid of an American Ranger officer, one British
and two American NCOs, Anderson began to put the Koreans
through classic commando training. At a simple ceremony, Colonel
Magee presented the Koreans with their parachute wings, on
completion of their jump training. In March 1951, Anderson felt
ready to lead their first simple operation. They were to blow up a
railway in a tunnel.

Anderson took four Koreans and two Americans. One of their
Koreans had already acquired an American name, John. They
rechristened the other three Matthew, Mark and Luke. On the
night of 17 March, they parachuted uneventfully from a Dakota.
All the next day, they laid up in paddy fields, some fifteen miles
south of Wonsan. The next night, they marched some eighteen
miles to reach the Kyongwon railway line, between Osan-ni and
Huchang-ni. On the night of 19 March, covered by a heavy snowfall
they climbed down into the railway tunnel and laid their charges

and pressure switches. Then they lay and dozed, waiting for the sound of a train.

It came in the early hours of the morning. In an agony of suspense they waited, and waited. Then there were two heavy explosions. The little group of men on the hillside leapt with glee like schoolboys. Their exhilaration faded somewhat an hour later, when they made radio contact with their base to learn that the US Navy could not pick them up from their intended rendezvous on the coast. A lot of walking lay ahead if they were to get home. They marched for three nights: 'each man was silent,' wrote Anderson afterwards,

> lost in his own thought, plodding along mile after mile, wet, cold and hungry or, during the day, escaping reality in brief snatches of troubled sleep. The map meant nothing in this area, and many times I felt that we were heading for a hopeless wilderness. My compass showed that we were still moving in the right direction, but at times I doubted it. I sensed a feeling of resentment behind me as we walked mile after stumbling mile. Perhaps I should never have committed these men to such an ordeal. At times I even toyed with the idea of surrender. After all, perhaps we would never find the place we were looking for; perhaps we might wander for weeks about these hateful rain-soaked mountains without food or shelter. Perhaps the war would end and nobody would think of us again.[2]

Somehow, they survived. They evaded the North Korean troops whose paths they crossed. But they suffered another disaster when Matthew and Mark, two of the Koreans whom Anderson dispatched to steal food from a peasant house, did not return. They were never seen again. Anderson himself was feverish, and his spirits were not improved by difficulty making radio contact with their base. But at last, when they had almost despaired of rescue, they were given a new rendezvous. Two helicopters closed in under powerful fighter cover. One by one, they were winched into the sky and away to safety. 'We were over the moon – we felt as if we'd won the war,' said Anderson.[3]

He now began to plan his next operation. His American parent organisation at Taegu was expanding fast. He was excited by the idea of creating long-term bases deep in the mountains of North Korea, from which his teams could sally forth to attack communications and dumps. Above all, they would seek to create an indigenous resistance movement in North Korea, on the familiar lines of the French maquis. This time, he would be more ambitious. He planned to take twenty men, to form a nucleus for a guerrilla army. In a mood of high excitement, he and his reinforced team prepared to drop once more into North Korea: 'The very fact of belonging to a "secret" operational unit is exciting in itself,' Anderson wrote, with frank delight. 'All active-minded men the world over are boys at heart, be they generals or privates, and there are few things more stimulating or conducive to high morale and self-confidence than the knowledge that you have been chosen to do something about which others know nothing and which calls for a high standard of efficiency, integrity and courage. Basically, I suppose, it is conceit – a buccaneer complex.'[4]

That conceit was soon to be brutally shattered. But for the time being, they revelled in their fantasies. Anderson concocted one plan, to find and kidnap a Russian adviser. Colonel Magee was appalled: 'My God, Bill, don't do that for heaven's sake!' he said. 'I admit it seems quite feasible, but Washington would go mad if they suddenly found a Russian officer on their hands.' To Anderson's consternation, only a few days before they planned to leave, he received new orders from Eighth Army: no British or American personnel were to engage in operations behind enemy lines. In future, these would be conducted exclusively by Koreans. But Anderson drove to headquarters, and persuaded them to allow himself and his British and American colleagues to go. There was another setback when the shortage of aircraft compelled Anderson to reduce his Korean contingent for the operation to fourteen men.

The remaining six, desolate, signed a petition in their own blood, demanding to be allowed to go. But the space problem was insoluble.

There was a momentary embarrassment at the airfield from which they departed, when the guerrilla party queued at the Red Cross canteen for coffee and doughnuts. 'Say, are those Koreans in your party?' asked the Red Cross helper behind the counter. 'Well, I'm sorry, we don't serve Koreans.' The Koreans smiled sadly. The whole party took off without their coffee. They landed this time in the centre of North Korea, near Isang-ni. One of the Koreans, John, a veteran of the earlier operation, was severely injured in the drop. Uneasily, Anderson watched a North Korean patrol moving across the valley near their position. Then a young, ragged Korean peasant walked into the midst of their group. He told them that the police had seen their parachutes the previous night. He said that he himself was hiding from conscription for the army. Anderson's party debated what to do with the boy. Eventually the Englishman let him go, with the promise of food if he brought some of his friends to help them. This, after all, was what they had come to do – to recruit North Korean sympathisers for a local guerrilla force.

The boy, named Lim, led Anderson to a nearby valley where he pointed out some hundreds of North Korean and Chinese soldiers bivouacked. Anderson thought the concentration big enough to justify an air strike. He radioed the co-ordinates of his position back to base. Sure enough, within a few hours aircraft strafed and rocketed the area. Then they let Lim go.

Now matters rapidly began to go wrong. The parachute landing of a reinforcement party was botched – they were dropped two miles from their landing zone. A supply drop resulted only in smashed equipment and radios littered across the mountainside. Anderson requested a helicopter to take himself out, to return to base to grip the situation. The helicopter came under fire as they climbed away, but Anderson felt confident that his party's location would not be discovered. He returned to Taegu to find that a new draft of Korean recruits had arrived to be trained. Anderson personally checked the parachutes and cargo nets for that night's supply drop.

But three days later, disastrous news came. In a garbled radio message from his British wireless operator in the field, Anderson learned that his party had been surprised by the communists, and was heavily engaged. That night, Anderson overflew the area in an American aircraft, and established voice contact with his party. They told him that the situation was hopeless. 'It's no good, sir,' said the voice of the Northumberland Fusilier on the ground. 'They've got us – we'll try and make our way out as best we can. Over.'

Anderson urged the wireless operator to light a fire or otherwise show his position to a helicopter. But the Englishman said finally: 'There's just me and Sergeant Monks, sir. But he's hurt and I can't leave him. We'll be all right, sir, but there is no place a chopper can put down here and I think the place is lousy with the bastards. I'll stay here with the sergeant, we'll be all right. Out.'

Neither the English Fusilier nor the American sergeant were ever heard from again. Wretched with the burden of responsibility and guilt, Anderson flew back.

Most of his party were killed. Ten days after Anderson lost contact with the group, two Koreans, his American Ranger officer and NCO walked into his office and saluted. They told a bitter story. In an act of criminal folly, a supply aircraft had arrived over their position in broad daylight, and dropped a string of parachutes which brought the communists hastening down upon them. When the party scattered, the four men had been able to make their escape. They walked south through the mountains, miraculously got through the communist lines, and swam the Imjin river to reach the American lines.

In the months that followed, a growing ruthlessness was evident in the American approach to covert operations in the north. No more Americans or British were to go, but there was an ample supply of Koreans. To his astonishment and dismay, Anderson found himself asked to train Koreans by a new American

commanding officer, to be parachuted into the North seven days
after their induction.

'Seven days!' exclaimed Anderson. 'Good God! I can't even train
them to shoot straight in that time, let alone give them parachute
training and practice jumps.'

'There won't be any time for practice jumps, just ground
training and weapons training. Sorry, but there it is – that's the
assignment. The air force know where to drop them.'

Anderson was told that this was to be a new scheme – dropping
Koreans in pairs some fifty miles behind the lines, with orders to
make their way back with whatever information they could gather:
'That way we can cover a hell of an area and get some really good
information.' He smiled at Anderson. 'You don't seem too happy
about it. What's worrying you?'

'How many do you think will get through, sir?'

'Maybe four or five. Hell, it's their war, too, isn't it?'

Bitterly unhappy, Anderson accompanied the first party of
Koreans to their drop zone: 'Never before had I taken unprepared
men into battle and now I was about to do something far worse. I
was sending untrained men into the most frightening and lonely
of battles – a battle within a battle in which one's own mind
becomes the field of conflict, where hope, discipline and courage
must fight against loneliness, fear and panic.'[5]

The British officer asked to be relieved of further involvement
in the programme. At the behest of a British intelligence officer
serving under diplomatic cover at the Seoul Embassy, Anderson
made some further attempts to run intelligence-gathering teams
into North Korea from the island of Chodo. But after the loss of his
surviving British officer and most trustworthy Korean during a
Chinese raid on their base, he withdrew. Anderson was posted
back to England, where for some months he worked on small boat
operations in the Adriatic for the A19 intelligence organisation.
They discussed and planned the setting up of a unit to aid prisoner
escapes from North Korea, burying supplies and inflatable boats
along the coast. But by now, the talks at Panmunjom seemed likely

to succeed. And by 1953, the heart had gone out of both American and British enthusiasm for covert operations in the North. There had been too many tragic accidents such as Anderson's Operation Vixen.

The United Nations never established successful covert activities in North Korea. The Royal Marines' coastal raiding parties could inflict minor pinpricks on the enemy at small cost, with the heavy air and naval support they could call upon. But any operation which demanded the support of local North Koreans proved doomed to failure. The communist control of the countryside was too ruthlessly effective. From the spring of 1951, even the peasants of North Korea understood how very unlikely it was that the UN forces would ever reoccupy their country. The realities of power, or rather, of personal survival, demanded obedience to the regime of Kim Il Sung. It remains difficult, today, to believe that the information brought south by the small numbers of South Korean agents who survived justified the cynical squandering of so many lives by the various intelligence organisations in the South.

*

Yet as the Korean War progressed, like the Japanese economy and the regime of Chiang Kai Shek, the Central Intelligence Agency became one of its principal beneficiaries. Korea put the CIA on the map. Its principal officers were eager, ruthless, and ambitious for their organisation. They acquired control of forty old C-47s in the markings of CAT – 'Civil Air Transport', a forerunner of Air America and Air Continental which they sponsored in Vietnam. Their network of offices and bases extended throughout Japan and Korea. Hans Tofte even sponsored the shooting of a full-scale propaganda feature film in Japan, about the experience of Japanese prisoners in the hands of the Soviets, which became a local box-office success.

Later in the war, the CIA attempted ever more elaborate and ambitious operations. Hans Tofte claimed to have organised the interception of a Norwegian freighter loaded with medical supplies donated to the Chinese by the Indian government. Nationalist Chinese gunboats with CIA agents aboard boarded the ship north of Formosa, seized its cargo, and left the freighter adrift, apparently the victim of piracy. According to one historian of the operation, 'the nurses, doctors, and other medical personnel were never heard of again, and he [Tofte] does not speculate as to their fate.'[6] Yet such dubious adventures plainly impressed somebody. Resources continued to be lavished upon the Agency's Far East operation. A hydrofoil was built to its specifications in a Japanese yard, to which a junk upper deck was fitted, to provide a high-speed covert landing vessel. A succession of Korean teams were dispatched to try to contact American prisoners in the Yalu camps. All failed. A major base was established on one of the islands in Wonsan Harbour, from which to land parties on the mainland. A technique was developed for snatching men off the ground from a moving aircraft, which was employed to recover a handful of agents from North Korea. But the sum result from all these efforts was pathetically small.

The CIA operation, as its veterans readily admitted later, was disturbingly amateur. They experimented with recruiting some ex-Rangers from Fort Benning. But they discovered – in another foretaste of Indochina – that by the time these men had grasped the job, they were due for rotation back to the United States. The CIA's first generation of direct recruits were young and green; many had volunteered in order to avoid being drafted into the army. Perhaps most serious of all, the quality of the intake of Koreans was poor. CIA recruiters constantly trawled the refugee camps, searching out North Koreans sufficiently motivated to return to their country. But the drop-out rate in training was very high. And the casualty rate among agents dispatched into North Korea was appalling, perhaps 80 per cent. The Agency's officers also chafed under the difficulties of gaining access to the navy's ships and the air force's planes for moving its men and supplies. This problem was increasingly solved by the creation of their own sea and air fleets.

In the view of Jack Singlaub, the greatest single cause of the Americans' difficulties in running effective operations in the North was that almost every anti-communist in the country had long left it. When Eighth Army retreated south in the winter of 1950, North Korean refugees followed in their hundreds of thousands: 'The lesson was – "don't strip out all your friendlies". We had made the mistake we repeated in Vietnam – offering everyone who wanted to leave, everyone with pro-Western sympathies, the chance to go. There was simply no one left in the North likely to help us.'[7]

It was a lesson that was learned at bitter cost in Korean lives: several hundred infiltrators and agents were landed in the North between 1951 and 1953, and pitifully few of them returned. It is difficult to regard the manner in which they were recruited and dispatched as any more than cynical exploitation of a supply of manpower whose depletion no one would bother to question. But for the CIA's future, the Korean operation paid off handsomely. In 1949 its covert activities branch possessed a staff of 302, seven foreign stations, and a budget of $4.7 million. By 1952, the staff had swollen to 2,812, with a further 3,142 'overseas contract personnel' on the payroll, forty-seven stations, and a budget of $82 million.

The simple truth was that, at this moment of history when the Cold War seemed so close to becoming a hot one, Washington's craving for information about the communists around the world was so great that it seemed necessary to seize upon any means by which to gain it. The crushing shocks of the North Korean invasion, the Chinese intervention, the sudden ruthless gambits of the Russians in Eastern Europe, created a desperate need to know more, much more, about the enemy. An organisation to achieve this had to be created from scratch. The wartime reputation of Bedell Smith, the Agency's director, did much to give the CIA credibility, and bankability, in Washington. Lower down the scale, among a number of distinguished and highly professional intelligence operatives, it is not surprising that the expansion of the CIA made room for a small army of adventurers, charlatans, and men more temperamentally suited to becoming rodeo riders. Let loose around the world with astonishing freedom of action, it was these men who conceived the plans to poison Patrice Lumumba's toothbrush, to parachute a long succession of doomed agents into Eastern Europe to foment hopeless revolutionary programmes, and to organise guerrilla operations in North Korea and China. To give the CIA its due, throughout the later war in Indochina, its intelligence assessments were consistently more realistic and better informed than those of the Pentagon. But in Korea, it is difficult to judge that its operations remotely justified the scale of resources it eventually deployed, or the lives that were squandered in its name.

14 » THE BATTLE IN THE AIR

Throughout the great conflicts of the twentieth century, professional airmen have asserted their claims to a unique status. They have argued that their ability to pass over the ground battlefield, to carry the campaign to targets miles behind the front lines, exempts them from the traditional precepts of warfare. In the First World War, until the last months, the technical limitations of aircraft restricted their role. Although they carried out some bombing operations, their principal importance was as scouts, reconnoitring and photographing the battlefield below. The see-saw struggle for air supremacy, waged between fighter aircraft, focused chiefly upon securing freedom for reconnaissance. The first generation of heavy bombers, the British Handley-Pages and German Gothas, inflicted some damage upon targets and civilian populations behind the lines in 1918. But it was the prophets of air power who were most excited by their achievements, who anticipated a future conflict in which great fleets of bombers could inflict fatal damage upon an enemy's industrial heartland, while the armies were still contesting irrelevant strips of earth hundreds of miles behind them.

The Second World War confirmed the decisive importance of aircraft in tactical support of ground and naval operations. But the conflict's message was far less certain about the effectiveness of bombing either as a means of destroying an enemy's industrial capacity to wage war; or in a long-range interdictory role, preventing an enemy from moving men and weapons to a battlefront. No one disputed that air attack had inflicted great damage upon lines of communications. Yet the fact remained that the Germans had been able to continue moving sufficient supplies to the front to fight with formidable effect for the last eleven months of the war, even in the face of absolute Allied command of the air. While vehicles moving in the open presented targets that could be attacked with devastating results, the impact of bombing upon footsoldiers in broken country – or well dug-in – remained far less impressive. Japan's surrender was precipitated by the effects of two air-dropped atomic bombs; but these demonstrated the intolerable consequences to humanity of the use of nuclear weapons, much more convincingly than they argued a new dimension for air power.

Viewed objectively, the experience of World War II suggested that air forces employing conventional weapons were subject to much the same constraints as ground and sea forces. The bomber possessed none of the mystic force with which it was endowed by the prophets of the thirties, who believed that air attack could terrorise a civilian population, or cripple vital industries, regardless of the scale upon which it was employed. The successful employment of aircraft, like that of any other instrument of military power, depended upon the weight of force available, the skill with which it was employed, and the suitability of the targets that it was offered. The more closely air forces worked in harness with ground or naval forces, the more effective they were. Their pursuit of a strategy independent of the other services produced more questionable results.[1]

Yet while these conclusions were readily accepted by generals and admirals, and even by military historians and defence intellectuals, in the years following World War II they were less enthusiastically adopted by professional airmen. Throughout their arm's brief history, the world's military airmen had striven for an independent role, divorced from the control of unsympathetic groundlings. Many senior airmen both in Britain and the United States simply declined to accept the unpalatable conclusion of the official post-war bombing surveys, which cast doubt on the achievements of the bomber offensive against Germany. They continued to assert that bombing had been a decisive – indeed, in the view of some, *the* decisive – force in the defeat of Germany and Japan. They were also enthused by the vital role they gained in post-war strategy, as a result of the invention of the atomic bomb. It was The Bomb, and the USAF's new stature as its carrier, that clinched the American air force argument for becoming a separate and equal service in 1947. In the post-war years of straitened service budgets, it was Strategic Air Command which absorbed the lion's share of funds for its big bombers. The air force sometimes gave the impression of wanting to forget all that it had learned with such pain during World War II about ground–air co-ordination and close support techniques. It carried its obsession for arranging matters differently from the ground forces to remarkable lengths: airmen wore their name badges on the opposite breast of their uniforms to the army, their officers even signed documents at the opposite corner of the paper. In 1948, a seminar was held at the Air University at Maxwell Field, Alabama, to discuss the question: 'Is there any further need for a ground force?'

The air war over Korea gave birth to a new concept – combat between jet aircraft – and revived all the traditional arguments about air support for ground operations. From the first days of the war, there was intense and often bad-tempered debate between the ground commanders and senior officers of Far East Air Force about the quality and quantity of close air support they received. This was heightened by army jealousy of navy and Marine organic air support, which the soldiers considered both more dedicated, and more professional, than that of the air force. 'Whenever we received close support from the Marine Air Wings,' said a sceptical army consumer, Colonel Paul Freeman of the 23rd Infantry, 'it was better than anything we got from the Air Force.'[2] It was not that the army disputed the vital importance of close support: indeed, soldiers freely declared that the army could not have stayed in Korea without it; the argument hinged upon the weight of air force effort that should be given directly to the ground forces, and at whose discretion this should be allotted. 'There was a lack of co-operation between the air force and army at all levels,' said Group-Captain 'Johnnie' Johnson, a British World War II fighter ace who flew some B-26 missions in Korea with the USAF. 'US Air Force morale was very high, and they thought they were doing a vital job. But there were not the army officers present at briefings that we had in Europe in World War II. In the first months, forward air control seemed very limited.'³ The ground forces were constantly frustrated by the difficulty of getting air support when it was needed, rather than when aircraft chanced to reach position over the forward area. Battalion commanders were irked by the arbitrary arrival of a flight of fighter-bombers, whose commander would radio laconically: 'I have twenty minutes on station. Use me or lose me.'

There is little doubt that in the first months of the war, thousands of the interdiction missions flown by the air force were valueless, because of inadequate targeting. 'The air force bombed and bombed all the main routes during the winter retreat of 1950,' said Major John Sloane, an officer on the ground with the Argyll & Sutherland Highlanders, 'but they achieved very little because they didn't understand Chinese techniques. The communists simply weren't on the main routes.'⁴ Attempts to identify and bomb communist troops on the move, especially during the first weeks of the war when target intelligence was almost non-existent, caused substantial casualties among friendly forces, and refugee columns fleeing desperately from the battlefield.

From the first day of the Korean War, the importance of fighter-bombers in a close support role was beyond doubt. The Yak piston-engined fighters of the North Korean air force were cleared from the skies within a matter of weeks, and the USAF's Mustangs, together with carrier-based American Corsairs and British Seafires and Sea Furies, played a critical tactical bombing role. In the last months of 1950, land-based UN aircraft were flying almost seven hundred fighter-bomber sorties a day, matched by a further three hundred from the offshore carriers. One of the most experienced and respected air commanders in the USAF, General O. P. Weyland, was dispatched to Tokyo to direct Far East Air Force. But serious problems quickly became apparent in determining the effective employment of medium and heavy bombers. There were pitifully few targets in North Korea large enough to justify attack by bombers in the big formations they were trained and accustomed to fly. How could fast modern aircraft fly effective interdiction missions against an enemy who moved most of his supplies by porter and bullock cart? This was a problem that would become familiar a generation later, in Indochina. In Korea, the United States Air Force encountered the difficulty for the first time, after a decade in which its commanders and its pilots had focused overwhelmingly upon the problems of fighting industrialised nations, which deployed vast mechanised power upon the battle-field. It would be absurd to dispute that the UN – or rather, overwhelmingly the US – air forces contributed greatly to the supply difficulties of the communist armies. But the central reality remained, that the North Koreans and Chinese continued to be able to move tolerable quantities of food, arms and ammunition to their front-line forces from beginning to end of the conflict. The air force commanders sought refuge for their disappointments and failures in incessant protest about the political limitations on their operations around and beyond the Yalu. But there remains no reason to suppose that, even had all political restrictions been lifted, strategic bombing could have decisively crippled the communist ability to sustain the war, any more than it was able to do so in the next decade, in Vietnam.

*

Lieutenant Oliver Lewis had spent the last months of World War II in the Pacific ferrying B-17s and B-29s, for he was too young to fly combat missions. On 26 June 1950, he was flying F-80s when he was abruptly ordered to the Far East. He had just time to take his wife home to Salt Lake City, before reporting to Travis Air Force Base. There, he was issued with a .45 pistol, a mosquito net, and a water canteen before boarding a C-54, still coated in coal dust from its role in the Berlin Airlift, for the long haul to Japan. He expected to be posted to fighters, but with his heavy aircraft experience, he was sent to the 3rd Bombardment Wing, flying B-26 bombers out of Iwakuni. 'The whole thing was pretty bad in Japan at that time,' he said. 'You can't believe the confusion. They were trying to get the dependents of the Australian Mustang squadron off the base and away home. They were trying to find some targets in Korea big enough for us to hit. They simply had not crystallised how to fight this type of war, when we had aircraft designed for large-scale formation operations.'[5]

Lewis spent forty-five minutes being 'checked out' on the B-26, flew two mail runs into Korea, and was then rostered for combat operations. At first they flew by day. Each pilot was allotted a stretch of road to patrol for a given period of time, with instructions to shoot up anything that moved upon it. Occasionally, they were directed to a specific target, perhaps a warehouse 'believed to contain war materials'. They had standing orders to attack all trains or suspicious concentrations. 'Trains were the best targets,' said Lewis. 'Hitting one made you feel like a king. But the Koreans got pretty good at blowing off steam from the engines to make themselves hard to see.' Within a few weeks of the outbreak of war, the communists had abandoned any attempt to make major movements by day. The bombers, too, were transferred to night operations. They carried a variety of ordnance: rockets, high explosive and fragmentation bombs. Some aircraft carried a devastating battery of fourteen fixed .5 calibre machine guns in the nose. Even in the darkness, at low speed and low level the pilots found that they could see reasonably well, with the instrument lights extinguished. Above all, they could detect motorised movement. In the first weeks of the Chinese intervention, crews sometimes found and attacked great convoys of trucks, moving with their headlights ablaze. The bombers would fly down the column, toggling a bomb every five hundred yards, then swing back to machine-gun the blazing ruins. But as the enemy became more practised at giving aircraft warning, as the extraordinary Chinese network of road sentries developed, halting every vehicle when a bomber was heard, it became far more difficult to spot targets. Novice crews preferred to fly in moonlight. The more proficient found that it was easier to identify enemy movement on clear dark nights, when the mountains were stripped of the haze that hung around them under the moon.

For the crews, a tour of operations consisted of fifty missions. Most wanted to get it over as speedily as possible, and go home. Thus, they would seek to fly every night, and some did. As winter came, the reflection from the snow made it possible to see more in darkness. But the lack of heating and de-icing gear in the aircraft began to cause serious problems. There were shortages of everything, in the air and on the ground. The weather became as dangerous a killer as the enemy. Every pilot had to make his own decision about the trade-off between layers of clothing to fight the cold, which caused some to climb into their cockpits looking like overstuffed teddy bears, and the clumsiness this created, hampering their ability to respond to the controls.

As the months went by and the problems of fighting a primitive enemy became more apparent, new equipment and new techniques were introduced: PQ-13 bombing radar, terrain radar to defeat the chronic bad weather. At the other extremity of the technological scale, some aircraft were fitted with troughs, into which the crews laboriously loaded the contents of keg upon keg of roofing nails. Over a North Korean road, the engineer shovelled these in a long stream out of a funnel at the rear of the aircraft, with the aid of a paddle. Later, the nails were replaced by purpose-designed tetraheydrons, designed to cripple the bare feet of men and beasts.

The more thoughtful pilots were far more conscious than some of their commanders in Tokyo of the uncertainty of assessing what they were achieving. 'We were very aware of how imprecise was our ability to judge what was being done,' said Lieutenant Lewis. 'But of course, the intelligence people are always eager to have you say that you've done well.'

The first MiG-15 jet fighters appeared in the skies over Korea in November 1950, sending a shockwave through the West comparable with that of the launch of the Sputnik satellite a few years later. Some fifty MiGs were initially deployed, flown by Chinese and Soviet pilots. The communists revealed their advance to the frontiers of technology. Within six months, there were 445 MiGs operating from the political sanctuary of air bases beyond the Yalu; by 1953 there were 830, mostly flown by Chinese pilots, though a Russian air corps also participated. The Soviets, like America's allies, used Korea as a proving ground where their pilots could be rotated in and out, to gain experience of the new shape of air warfare. The American B-29 bombers started to suffer a steady drain of losses to fighter attack, coupled with the impact of radar-controlled anti-aircraft guns. A struggle for air superiority began over North Korea, which continued until the end of the war. For the first few weeks after the MiGs' arrival, the available American fighters in the theatre, notably the F-80 Shooting Stars, were disturbingly outclassed. But then came the Sabre, the F-86 which became the principal weapon of the UN. The first wing was deployed in December 1950, reinforced by a second a year later. Sabres were in chronically short supply to maintain US air strength worldwide, and there were never more than 150 deployed in Korea, against the much greater number of MiGs. But the West, and the United States in particular, has always produced pilots of exceptional quality. From beginning to end, the UN proved able to maintain air superiority over North Korea, despite all that the communist air forces could throw against them. More than that, the Korean War and the shock of discovering the communists' possession of the MiG stimulated the United States to an extraordinary programme of technical innovation and aircraft development which continued long after the conflict had ended.

In Korea as in every war, the fighter pilots considered themselves the elite, despite the irony that their prospects of survival were significantly better than those of the ground attack pilots. Three squadrons of Sabres were based on the huge airfield at

Kimpo, a few miles west of Seoul, where they shared the strip with a squadron of Australian Meteors and another of B-26s. Each night, the squadrons' 'fragmentary orders' clattered down the teletypes from headquarters, decreeing the number of aircraft that would be required the following day. The pilots slept in quonset huts, little less cold or uncomfortable than those of army rear elements. Each morning, the rostered officers mustered for briefing, to be allotted their respective roles: high cover and close cover for daylight bomber missions, or routine combat patrols.

They took off one by one at three-second intervals, then climbed into formation, spreading out across the sky to cross the bomb line above the confronting armies. They patrolled at around 40,000 feet, or as low as 20,000 if they were escorting fighter-bombers. At those heights, the communist flak presented a negligible threat. They flew in fours – the famous 'finger four' created by Hitler's Luftwaffe, and the basis of all fighter tactics ever since. Larger formations were too difficult to control or manoeuvre. Number three commanded the flight, but the essential combat unit was the pair, each of the two leaders being protected by his wingman. They cruised steadily, for there was no purpose in exhausting their fuel at .9 mach if there was no enemy in sight. Pilots liked the Sabre – 'a very honest aeroplane', in the words of Lieutenant Jim Low, one of the Korean aces; 'it was a beautiful plane that sort of wrapped around you.'[6] Men who had trained or fought on the old propeller-driven fighters found the jets simpler to fly, without the problem of countering torque, and far less prone to technical failure – the lack of vibration placed less strain upon every mechanical element. At first, for a pilot reared to fly with the constant roar of a piston-engine in front of him, the muted vacuum-cleaner whine of the jet was almost unnerving. A careful pilot could extend his patrol endurance to as much as ninety minutes. A less skilled one – or a man feeling the strain of combat flying, eager for an excuse to return to the ground as fast as possible – might need to land after forty-five. In winter, their endurance was extended by the strong prevailing north-west jetstreams that pushed them home. It was also easier to spot the enemy in those months, when the cold, damp air created a prominent condensation trail behind an aircraft. In summer, they could only look for the glint of silver in the sun.

Throughout the war, the Sabres achieved almost undisputed dominance of the skies over Korea, North and South. Senior American airmen became exasperated by the manner in which the military took it for granted that they could conduct ground operations without the slightest threat of enemy interference in the air. 'It's a terrible thing to say,' remarked General William Momyer thirty years later,

> but I think we would be in a much stronger position today with regard to the importance of air superiority if the enemy had been able to penetrate and bomb some of our airfields and had been able to bomb the front lines periodically. It would have brought home to our ground forces and other people the importance of air superiority. The Army has never had to operate in an environment where it had to consider: 'Do we dare make this move at twelve o'clock noon because that road is under the surveillance of enemy aircraft, or can we move that division from here to here during this period of time?' Those considerations are absent in all of the planning by virtue of this experience: they have never had to fight without air superiority.[7]

Some American fighter pilots in Korea went weeks, even months, without glimpsing an enemy aircraft. Others, in inexplicable fashion, seemed to possess a magnetic force that drew the MiGs into the corner of the sky through which they flew. Jim Low, a twenty-six-year-old Californian, shot down an enemy aircraft on his first mission in Korea. Low was widely recognised as a natural hunter – indeed, a killer. It was a pilot in his squadron, James Horowitz, who later wrote the popular novel about the Korean air war, *The Hunters*. The picture that the book painted, of a group of men amongst whom a few were ruthlessly, competitively dedicated to 'making a score', was readily acknowledged by some of the survivors. Low himself suggested that there were three identifiable groups of fliers within his squadron, within most of the Korean squadrons. There were the average pilots, who merely did the job. There were the veterans of World War II, some of them highly skilled fliers, among whom were the foremost aces of the war – 68 per cent of pilots who destroyed MiGs in Korea were twenty-eight or over, and had flown an average of eighteen missions in World War II. But more than a few of the veterans had lost something of their cutting, killing edge with the passage of time. They wanted to stay alive. There were reservists among them, 'the retreads', men recalled from civilian life to fight again, who resented their presence in Korea. And finally, there were the young gladiators, the men like Low who had joined the air force not merely to fly, but to fight. 'I think wars are designed for twenty-three-year-olds,' said Flight-Lieutenant Roy Watson, a British pilot flying F-84 Thunderjets. 'I enjoyed it very much – it was the time of my life.'[8] Their enthusiasm, their hard-living, hard-dying, high poker-playing life style repelled some of their comrades. But in the air, few could dispute that they were good. When the priceless radar stations out on the islands off North Korea reported a 'bandit train' – perhaps eight successive elements of two MiGs – making for their sky, the hunger of their response could not be gainsaid. A flight leader once ran his entire flight out of fuel to reach a MiG and get a kill.

They cast off their wingtip tanks and swung towards an estimated rendezvous with the enemy, clawing height out of the sky, for the MiG's greatest advantage was its superior ceiling; that, and its tighter turning circle. The tactics of fighter combat in Korea were identical to those of World War II, save only that at higher speeds, the aircraft manoeuvred across greater spaces. The flight leader might radio to his second pair: 'You take the bounce!' indicating that he himself would watch the higher sky, cover the rear, while the other men dived, at a speed of perhaps five hundred knots. Sometimes, they would push their aircraft to its limits, frighten themselves considerably, shattering the sound barrier in their dive. If the MiGs saw them as they came, the enemy pilots would break sideways. Then, for the most part, there was merely a chase as the communist aircraft fled for home. On the rare occasions when the MiGs stayed to dogfight, the Americans knew that their opponents were uncommonly determined, and were likely to prove unusually skilled. Optimum killing range was around two hundred yards, and to gain an accurate shot a man might be flying as slow as two hundred knots.

The MiGs' cannon could be deadlier killers than the six .5 machine guns in the nose of the Sabres – if they could be brought to bear. But the Sabre was a more stable fighting machine at high speeds than the MiG, and the American pilots were of higher quality than the Chinese, or even the Russians when the Soviets sent a 'volunteer' air corps to fly some aircraft over North Korea. Each encounter came and went so fast: after weeks of boredom, one June morning on patrol Low's flight spotted two MiGs crossing the Yalu at low level. The Sabres rolled over, diving from 30,000 feet to 2,000 to intercept. Then Low channelled – made a fast climbing turn to the right – and fired a burst into a MiG's belly, momentarily glimpsing its pilot in a red silk scarf. The communist fighter exploded, its debris smashing the Sabre's windscreen. The Americans went home.

*

Flight-Lieutenant John Nicholls was an unusual member of the 4th Fighter Wing for which Low also flew, for he was an Englishman. While the Royal Air Force provided only a Sunderland flying boat squadron in Korea, its leaders were anxious to share the rewards of experience in the new art of jet warfare. A select group of British pilots was distributed among the American squadrons. Nicholls was twenty-four, one of the generation of fliers very conscious of having just missed World War II. He found his eight-week Sabre conversion course outside Las Vegas a revelation of the scale of American military power – 'there were more aircraft on the flight line at Nellis Air Force Base than in the whole of Fighter Command.' The instructors' motto was: 'Every man a tiger.' Nicholls was much impressed by the emphasis upon gunnery and air-to-air combat. His generation of British fighter pilots had been schooled overwhelmingly for the task of intercepting enemy bombers. He exulted in airborne visibility so much better than he had ever known in England. He also learned to have a cautious respect for the impact of G-forces at high speed.

Nicholls was fascinated by the Americans he joined at Kimpo: 'There were such a variety of types and backgrounds.' He discovered the existence of 'the warlovers', men like Jim Low and Pete Fernandez. Around half the pilots, he reckoned, were men determined to do their best, but also to stay alive.

> Another 25 per cent didn't give a damn – and that went for the ground crew as well. The other 25 per cent saw this as a great professional opportunity. If they could make their names in Korea, their careers were made. There was a lot of jockeying for position in the USAF. Shooting down a lot of MiGs was a passport to fame, though oddly enough in retrospect, few of the big MiG-hitters prospered professionally. There was a general acceptance of the need to do what we were trying to do, but they were not particularly articulate about it. There was no doubt that anything to do with communism was bad, and had to be resisted. In my experience, the American view of war is different from the European view. They still fight their wars in a remote sense, far from home. They send their people away to war – not like the Europeans, who have seen so much war around their own countries and homes. At Kimpo, it was rather like our participation in the Boer War. There was a vaguely early twentieth-century feeling about the place.[9]

When Nicholls first saw a MiG, it was too distant to have a chance of catching it up. He touched his gun button and watched the tracer lance into it, a glimpse of flame appear, before it disappeared into cloud. He could submit only a 'damaged' claim. By his ninety-ninth mission, he was becoming a little desperate, having fired at a succession of enemy aircraft without bringing them down. Colonel Royal Baker, one of the group's most cele-brated 'MiG-getters', with a legendary talent for finding enemy aircraft, invited the Englishman to change his luck by flying with him. Sure enough, just south of the Yalu they jumped a flight of four, and Nicholls achieved the only kill of his tour. Despite the strict rules against crossing into Chinese air spaces, many Sabres in hot pursuit did so: some claimed to have shot down aircraft in the traffic pattern at Mukden. On this occasion, as Nicholls was following his stricken prey down, desperate for confirmation, he heard his wingman give his fuel warning call: 'Bingo one first.' A few seconds later, he radioed: 'Bingo minus two,' and finally the crisis code: 'Joker.' At that moment, to Nicholls' exultation, the MiG below him began to burn, flew into the ground, and exploded. 'Can you see him?' Nicholls asked his wingman urgently. Having got his witness, he turned exultant homewards, with a bare mini-mum of fuel for landing.

*

If an American aircraft was hit, in winter the pilot would try to bale out overland, for the sea was too cold to offer much prospect of survival. A pilot who ditched in the winter months could last three minutes in the water before reaching his dinghy, and seven minutes thereafter before his saturated flying suit froze. But in summer, he would always opt for the sea if he could, where the huge and efficient rescue organisation might reach him, even under the communist guns. On the ships and the offshore islands, helicopters waited in constant readiness – for this, too, was the first war in which the 'whirlybirds' played a significant role, and became life-savers for so many wounded soldiers and downed airmen. If a wingman could mark his companion's ditching position, a rotating procession of fighters would fly cover above him until he was rescued. Gillies, a Marine pilot in the 4th Fighter Wing, was retrieved from the very mouth of the Yalu, after the first helicopter sent to rescue him itself ditched. Sometimes the overhead fighters were called in to drive off Chinese patrol boats. On North Korean territory, F-80s often attacked communist ground troops again and again, to keep them away from a downed pilot waiting desperately for a chopper. Scores of pilots were rescued successfully from the coastal areas of North Korea in the course of the war, a great boost to the confidence of UN aircrew, and a tribute to the extraordinary UN command of air and sea, even close inshore.

*

Kimpo was a dreary place, surrounded by rice paddies. There was little to do out of hours save play poker and gin rummy, or pay an occasional call on the nearby nurses' compound. The pilots were relatively rich, with their $60 a month combat pay and two bottles a month ration of Old Methusalem whisky which many gave away, for few fliers cared to drink seriously. It was mostly the older men who drank, and cured their hangovers by flying on 100 per cent oxygen the next morning. The Australian Meteor squadron also based there had a fine reputation, but the Australian pilots were chronically jealous of the Sabre. The Meteor was known as an aircraft that could take punishment, but it also possessed a highly vulnerable hydraulic system, that could be crippled by a single small-arms round through a leading edge. Heavy on the ailerons, it was hard work to fly from its cramped cockpit. The pressure on the pilots was intense: one British officer flew 114 Meteor sorties in six months, on one occasion five in a day.

Four Sabres sat permanently at readiness on the runway, the Alert Patrol, in case of some sudden report of an enemy take-off by the radar controllers. The pilots recognised the key role of the controllers in making their scores possible – Low took them a few cases of beer whenever he made a kill. Each flier had pet preferences about his aircraft and his weapons. Some loaded extra tracer in the guns. Many carried solid tracer at the end of their belts, to give warning that their three hundred rounds were close to exhaustion. Most pilots wore silk scarves, and many affected the old soft

leather World War II helmets, until they were ordered to change
to modern moulded designs.

The enthusiasm of the enemy varied greatly from month to
month. Sometimes, weeks would go by without a UN squadron
seeing combat. Then, without warning, the MiGs would embark on
a flurry of activity. In a characteristic month – December 1951 –
the statistics tell the story: 3,997 MiGs were reported seen in the
air by UN pilots; attempts were made to engage 1,849; twenty-
seven were confirmed destroyed. Enormous effort was expended
to achieve modest results in direct damage to the enemy. But much
more important, air supremacy over Korea was constantly maintained. Men like Jim Low, with his flamboyant taste for enormous
Havana cigars, his growing reputation as a 'honcho' – a top pilot –
revelled in the struggle. 'I enjoyed all of it,' he said later, 'the
flying, shooting down aircraft. I was too young to think about the
politics. It was just a job we were over there to do.'[10] Each pilot
flew around a hundred missions, perhaps six months' combat duty,
before being rotated back to the United States. There was, perhaps,
less tension among the squadrons in Korea than in World War II,
because the dominance of the American pilots was so great, their
casualties less alarming. Some celebrated pilots were lost – Bud
Mahurin, a World War II group commander, was shot down by
ground fire; George Davis, one of the most famous aces, was
brought down by a MiG when his score stood at fourteen victories.
But the odds on survival were good. Even those who were lost
were scarcely missed, when men were coming and going constantly on routine rotations. And as John Nicholls put it, 'in
England after a flying accident, there was a funeral. But in Korea,
somebody just wasn't there any more.' Jim Low went home after
ninety-five missions with five MiGs to his credit, and not a scratch
on him. He went on to fly fighters over Vietnam, and survive five
years in a communist prison camp. The Sabre remained unchallenged as the outstanding aircraft of the Korean War: of 900 enemy
aircraft claimed destroyed during the war by USAF pilots, 792 were
MiG-15s destroyed by Sabres, for the loss of just seventy-eight of

their own aircraft. It was, inevitably, a Sabre pilot who became the war's top-scoring ace, Captain Joseph McConnell with sixteen confirmed 'victories'.

*

If at least a proportion of fighter pilots found their occupation glamorous, it is unlikely that any of the heavy bomber crews would have said the same about theirs, flying a dreary daily shuttle to industrial and military targets in North Korea. Joe Hilliard was a twenty-seven-year-old Texas farmboy, who just missed World War II, and spent his first flying years as a navigator in what was then the USAF's only designated nuclear bomber group. He was newly returned from a tour of duty in England when Korea came, and he was rushed to Okinawa with the 307th Bomb Wing. They met none of the traditional comforts of combat aircrew: the only permanent accommodation on the base was occupied by another wing. They found themselves living in tents, which were razed to the ground at regular intervals by hurricanes. Their B-50 aircraft were taken from them, and they were given instead old B-29s, just out of mothballs, which posed chronic problems with mechanical defects: 'We were really mad about that. We got the feeling that the USAF just didn't want to waste its first-line equipment on Korea.'[11] To their disgust, they found that even the flight rations with which they were provided were of World War II manufacture.

Almost every morning, the Wing – an element among five B-29 groups operating over Korea – dispatched a formation of nine aircraft on a daylight bombing mission, in accordance with orders from 5th Air Force Headquarters in Tokyo. Then, with the coming of darkness, a succession of single aircraft was sent off, at intervals of ninety minutes, which flew and bombed under ground control. The next day, it was the turn of another squadron to provide the force, and so on in rotation. It was a round-the-clock war. The lights burned in the Operations Room twenty-four hours a day, seven days a week.

Yet it was also war reduced to a cold-blooded, mechanical

discipline. Daily Orders laid down the grid co-ordinates of the target, the altitude – perhaps 28,000 feet – the bombload – probably 144 hundred-pound bombs, or forty five-hundred-pounders – and the fuse settings, usually variable delays up to seventy-two hours. An average mission lasted around eight hours, from take-off to touchdown, which hardly seemed a serious business to men who had been training under Lemay to fly seventeen- or eighteen-hour missions to Russia. They flew the first five hundred miles, from Okinawa to the southern tip of Korea, at 4,000 feet; then began climbing to reach designated altitude around the 38th Parallel, flying at around 240 knots. The navigator and bombardier clambered down the fuselage to the bomb bay, to remove the cotter pins from the nose and tail fins of the load, their flying suits wringing wet from the exertion. In winter, they found flying very cold. In summer, it was intolerably hot: 'For most men, it was boring going up, boring coming down,' said Hilliard. 'One night, our wireless operator slept all through the flight, after a heavy drunk.'

In daylight, they flew in a formation of three loose vics, which tightened only as they approached the target. They attacked on the orders of a 'lead crew'. For a big operation, a 'Maximum Effort', there might be as many as seventy-two aircraft in the stream. The flak seldom troubled them. Most days, they saw no sign of enemy fighters. But one morning, suddenly, they might reach 'MiG Alley', twenty minutes short of the target, and hear their own radar controllers report urgently: 'Twelve trains leaving the station.' Then they knew that within a few minutes, the communist fighters would be swinging in to intercept. If the enemy was in determined mood, the Sabre top cover was seldom completely successful in keeping him away. The eternal controversy about the most effective means of giving fighter protection to bombers continued vigorously in Korea. The bomber men wanted escorts close in, where they could see them. The fighter men insisted that they could do much more for the bombers by ranging wide and aggressively at their own discretion than they could achieve – with fuel for only twenty-five minutes' 'loiter' over MiG Alley – hanging on to the flanks of the bomber wings. Both methods were tried, and neither prevented some MiGs from breaking through. When they did so, for all the B-29s' formidable weight of defensive armament, the gunners placed little faith in their ability to do more than throw the aim of the MiG pilots. In the autumn of 1951, the bombers found themselves under growing pressure from MiGs, until in October, casualties began to mount alarmingly. Five B-29s were lost in the month to MiG attack. The figure was a fraction of relative World War II bomber losses, but the aircraft were vastly more expensive and the commitment less absolute. Daylight operations were cancelled abruptly. Thereafter, the big bombers attacked by night.

The crews' enthusiasm was not increased by the living conditions on the base: rats in the tents, cold showers, naked light bulbs. One night when a typhoon blew, all the crews had to man their aircraft and sit in them through the night, engines turning into the wind for fifteen hours. Offbase, there were a few whores and a few restaurants, and the chance of an occasional trip to Japan. Many men had wives at home in the United States, less than enthusiastic about their husbands' role in Korea. Hilliard's was sharing a house in New Mexico with his flight engineer's wife. In the Second World War, there had been a sense of hardships shared among fighting men, in whichever theatre they were. Every man fighting in Korea was conscious that most of his fellow-soldiers and aviators around the world were living lives of infinitely greater comfort.

A man flew thirty-five missions to complete a bomber tour – ten more than the European wartime standard, a recognition of the better prospects of survival. There were few of the problems of stress that afflicted World War II bomber squadrons. One officer in Joe Hilliard's squadron suddenly declined to fly any further missions, and was simply given a ground job. But in Hilliard's view, 'morale wasn't good. We didn't think we had enough support':

When Vandenburg came down to inspect us, we really let him have it about that. A lot of us thought that if we were taking this thing seriously, we should have been able to bomb across the Yalu. We felt we should have had some better targets, or else some people felt that we shouldn't have been there at all. It was very discouraging when we found that they were repairing so many of the targets that we were hitting. There was a lot of criticism of Truman. Later, one looked back and felt that the whole thing had been a rehearsal for Vietnam – we just weren't getting the support from our government. Maybe if we had really hit North Korea with everything we had, it would have saved lives – there wouldn't have been any Vietnam.[12]

It was a source of constant irritation to the aircrew that they could only approach targets close to the Chinese border on an east–west course, to avoid the risk of infringing Chinese air space. Again and again, they were compelled to watch the enemy's fighters scrambling from the invulnerable sanctuary of their base at Antung. The American fliers' great fear was of capture, not death. Joe Hilliard was haunted by a vision of years of confinement on a diet of cold, soggy rice: 'I resolved I would starve rather than eat it.' His fantasy was not entirely fanciful – not a few American prisoners in communist hands indeed starved rather than eat what they were offered. The bomber crews received lectures on escape and evasion from comrades who had bailed out and survived. Most of those who had not suffered such a trauma found it chilling to think too much about the prospect. It was easier to get through a tour if you treated it as a job, a routine, and brooded as little as possible about the brutality of the enemy beneath. Yet it was the strange irony of the bomber men's business that, in six months of raining death and destruction upon the communist enemy in Korea, they never, even once, set eyes upon the face of a Korean.

*

Throughout the Korean conflict, one of the most important assets of the UN Command was its ability to deploy aircraft carriers relatively close inshore, almost parallel to the front lines, wherever these might be. The Americans and British – the dominant naval forces with some support from the Canadians and Australians – divided their areas of responsibility from the beginning of the war. The British Far East Fleet operated west of Korea, in the Yellow Sea, and normally deployed two aircraft carriers and their escorts on a rotating basis. The American Seventh Fleet cruised on station in the Sea of Japan, east of Korea, with up to three carriers at any one time providing strike aircraft. From the outset, the US Navy vigorously defended the claims of its carrier-based aircraft to operate independently of the land-based air forces. 'Command and control became a major problem in Korea,' as a senior air force officer wrote.[13] Only relatively late in the war did the navy concede the logic of joint target planning with Far East Air Force. The case for the independence of seaborne air operations normally rests upon the independence of the naval operations they are support- ing. Yet in Korea, the Allied fleets were merely providing mobile platforms for aerial sorties in support of the ground war. Without absolute command of the sea, the UN campaign could scarcely have been fought, since almost every soldier who fought, and every ton of supplies he consumed, was brought into Korea by ship. But since the communists never significantly challenged the UN's naval forces, their principal role became that of providing floating air bases.

For most of the ships' crews, it was a curiously unreal war. While the smaller vessels, destroyers and minesweepers, often worked close inshore and sometimes found themselves under fire from enemy shore batteries, the big bombarding cruisers and carriers steamed their racetrack courses, round and round a few square miles of sea, living out a daily routine that involved much hard work, much boredom, and only the smallest risk of enemy action. Yet aboard each of the carriers lived a few score men who were seeing the war at the closest and harshest proximity. The men of the air groups flew each day to the battle, then returned to the strange, cosy cocoon of their parent ship, where two thousand men laboured, most of whom never heard a shot fired in anger. As a British Fleet Air Arm pilot put it: 'You could fly four sorties in a day; then come below, change into mess undress, and sit down for an evening of sherry, bridge and brandy.' The US Navy and Marine pilots, of course, on their 'dry' ships, were denied the Royal Navy's alcoholic refinements. But the see-saw contrast in their lives between days of war and nights of naval comfort imposed almost a greater strain than the monotone discomfort of life on the line.

The Royal Navy's carriers worked a nine-day cycle of operations: four days' flying, one day's replenishment at sea, another four days' flying, then a brief trip to Japan. They aimed to fly 544 sorties in nine days, sixty-eight a day. Each aircraft might be called upon to fly up to 120 miles from the ship, and to remain in the air up to two hours. Aircraft took off in waves through the day, perhaps five or six in each, every two hours. The crews were briefed the previous night for the next day's operations. If it was summer, with dawn around 5 a.m., soon after four a Chinese steward might be shaking his officer awake: 'Must have blekfuss, Mr Jacob. Otherwise other officer have two blekfuss.'

Lieutenant William Jacob was posted to a Firefly squadron aboard the 23,000-ton light fleet carrier HMS *Ocean* in the spring of 1952. He was the son of one of Winston Churchill's best-known wartime staff officers, Sir Ian Jacob. As a boy, he was sent to Dartmouth, and felt deeply cheated that the Second World War ended when he was seventeen, just too young to take part. After a stint as a destroyer navigator, and with 350 hours' flying experience behind him, this gaily adventurous young man was thrilled to receive a posting to Korea: 'I simply loved the flying.'[14] The piston-engined Firefly was an old aircraft by 1952, slow and notoriously prone to bounce on making a carrier landing. If its pilots encountered MiGs over Korea, they were instructed to cut their speed to 125 knots, put their flaps down, and turn tightly; the jets should then have great difficulty in flying slowly enough to hit them. The merit of the Firefly as a ground support aircraft was that it could carry a heavy load – normally sixteen rockets and four

20mm cannon. But its pilots remained secretly somewhat jealous of the faster and smarter Sea Furies, of which *Ocean* also carried a squadron. Once, miraculously, a Sea Fury even shot down a MiG.

As always with carrier operations, take-offs provided some of the most frightening moments. The Fireflies ideally needed twenty-five or thirty knots of windspeed over the deck to get them into the air, fully laden. But *Ocean* could barely manage twenty-four knots, and on a still day the aircraft would sink alarmingly over the bows as it bolted from the catapult, then lumber uncertainly upwards towards 10,000 feet, collecting the other two or three aircraft in the flight as it climbed. Every hour of the day, one aircraft was detailed to fly a monotonous ASPRO anti-submarine patrol ahead of the carrier, while a flight of Furies mounted a Combat Air Patrol against the remote chance of enemy attack. But most days, most sorties were directed against enemy ground targets inland.

Operating in summer was the worst experience, with temperatures in the glasshouse cockpit soaring to 140 degrees, the crews flying in underpants and overalls, soaked in sweat from take-off to landing. Yet still they wore their chamois leather gloves and scarves, and covered every inch of exposed flesh against the dreaded risk of fire. Accidents accounted for a high proportion of carrier casualties – such daily mishaps as that of a man on *Ocean* who was blown overboard one morning and never recovered when a pilot ignited his Rocket Assisted Take-Off Gear without warning. Somebody had exchanged the positions of his RATOG and radio switches without telling him. Over the target, the tail fins of their 3-inch rockets were prone to break off after launching, and could hole the radiator, with fatal consequences. And always, of course, landing and take-off errors could prove fatal. On the ship, the intense physical demands of what the aircrew were doing magnified small irritants: the delayed arrival of mail, the absence of a new wardroom movie, an argument over who should lead a given sortie.

Yet still Jacob, and many of his colleagues, enjoyed immensely what they were doing: 'I adored it. We had a marvellous time. It was so good to be doing it all with friends.' For all the lectures they received about the political purpose of their mission, they cared little for the high politics: 'If we thought about it at all, we felt that we were really there to "show willing" to the Americans,' which indeed was a crudely accurate manner of expressing the view of the British government. Navigation was easy, and more often than not, they were shown a photograph of their target at briefing the previous night. The Fireflies possessed no sighting equipment for unloading their bombs and rockets. The pilots merely attacked by eye. The key factor was to judge the angle of dive correctly.

A few pilots became very 'wound up' by the strain of operations. But most treated it as a job: a dangerous job, sometimes a terrifying one, but most often exciting and satisfying. They flew, they attacked their targets, and sometimes they did not come back. They accepted it all without profound passion. Bill Jacob's logbook recorded a characteristic succession of strikes, near-misses, and brief tragedies: '. . . Dicky O shot down and killed . . . he was last seen going into a hill upside down . . .'; '. . . went on to strafe a number of villages and generally look around. I strafed an oxcart and I think hit it while I missed another. Each of the two runs I did and also Purnell's runs left the cart surrounded in dust and smoke from which emerged an oxcart going like a train. The man, however, was killed . . . My landing was good for a change . . .'

On 27 August, Jacob identified and photographed a communist radar station. The next day, he was sent back to attack it. Ground fire holed his radiator and coolant pipe. Knowing what would happen a few seconds later, he dragged back the stick and staggered hastily back up to 6,000 feet. There, the engine stopped. The Firefly began to drift downwards, belching smoke. Jacob dithered desperately. 'Prepare to bale out,' he told his navigator. 'No, we'll take her down and ditch.' 'No, let's bale out.' In the back seat was a chief petty officer with vast experience and two Distinguished Service Medals, named Hernshaw. The CPO was not impressed.

'Make your mind up,' he told Jacob crossly. 'I've been shot down seven times, and I don't mind what you do as long as you make your mind up.' Jacob ditched.

The Firefly cartwheeled as it hit the water, but to their overwhelming relief came to a stop the right way up. They tore open the canopy, conscious of the eight seconds in hand before the aircraft sank, and slipped into the brilliant warm water. Then they swam the few yards to the shore of the island of Chodo, where the UN Command maintained its superbly efficient Air-Sea Rescue Service. Within a few minutes, four F-86s from Kimpo, four US Marine Corsairs and four British Furies were circling Jacob's ditching position. Jacob was briskly interrogated by an American radar officer on the island, then swam back out to his aircraft in the shallow water, to dive for his radio set, gyro gunsight and other secret equipment, which they brought ashore in a dinghy. That night, Jacob and Hernshaw were back on *Ocean*. The following morning, they were sent to attack the radar station again. It was Jacob's 121st sortie: 'I thought my luck must be beginning to run out.' But it did not. A few weeks later, he completed his tour in one piece, and was posted home.

*

The vast majority of the 1,040,708 aerial sorties flown by UN aircraft in the course of the Korean War were like those of Lieutenant Jacob – to provide close support, or fighter cover. Their importance was undisputed. But America's leading airmen persistently urged a more ambitious role for their forces in Korea, and chafed at the frustrations of ground support. General Jacob Smart, Far East Air Force's Deputy Chief of Staff (Operations) for most of 1952, complained bitterly about 'the opinion so often expressed or implied, that the Eighth Army is responsible for winning the Korean War, and that the role of the other services is to support it in its effort'.[15] Here, yet again, was the airmen's search for a decisive independent role. Yet between June 1951 and the summer of 1952, the US Air Force attempted overwhelmingly its most ambitious independent contribution to the struggle, and suffered the most galling failure.

Operation STRANGLE was a systematic attempt to cut off the communist ground forces in the front line from their supplies, by the sustained exercise of air power. It began with a campaign of bombing the road network in North Korea, and in August 1951 was extended to the railways. Three-quarters of all land-based bomber effort, and the entire carrier capability were dedicated to this task. Day after day and night after night, the enemy's communications were pounded from the air. In a fashion disturbingly reminiscent of World War II, and prescient of Vietnam, air force intelligence officers produced extraordinary graphs and statistics to demonstrate the crushing impact of the campaign on communist movement. Yet, by the summer of 1952, none of this could mask the reality on the ground: the enemy's supplies were still getting through – between 1,000 and 2,000 tons a day continued to cross the Yalu at the height of STRANGLE, it was later discovered. Prodigious feats of repair by civilian labour gangs working around the clock kept just enough of the road and rail net open to move food and ammunition. Constantly improving communist anti-aircraft defences emphasised the eternal conundrum: to bomb low meant accepting unacceptable casualties; to bomb high meant a fatal loss of accuracy. STRANGLE cost the UN air forces 343 aircraft destroyed and 290 damaged, mostly fighter-bombers. It proved to objective observers, such as Ridgway, that there was 'simply no such thing as choking off supply lines in a country as wild as North Korea'.[16] In World War II, Allied intelligence estimates of German transport requirements proved to have been hopelessly distorted, because a German division required only a quarter of the daily supply of its Allied counterpart. In Korea, the ratio was even more dramatic: a Chinese division operated with a mere fifty tons of supply a day, against 610 for its American counterpart. The only means by which STRANGLE might have been made effective was to match the bombing of supply routes with intense pressure on the ground, to force up communist consumption of supplies. The will for this – or rather the will to accept the UN casualties involved – never existed.

STRANGLE was finally abandoned in the summer of 1952 in the face of severe aircraft losses for dubious strategic return. The airmen claimed that the campaign had at least prevented the communists from building up supplies to mount a major offensive, but most thoughtful observers doubted that this had anyway been the enemy's intention. The air forces turned instead to a succession of selective attacks upon power plants and dams in North Korea, about whose destruction the communists were expected to be especially sensitive. Operation PRESSURE PUMP was designed to impress upon the communist delegation at Panmunjom the urgency of signing an armistice. Bomber attack, wrote Bradley as Chief of the JCS in November 1952, 'constitutes the most potent means at present available to UNC, of maintaining the degree of military pressure which might impel the communists to agree, finally, to acceptable armistice terms'.[17] Yet American attacks upon the huge Suiho hydroelectric plant on the Yalu in June 1952 aroused intense controversy around the world, and especially in Britain where strategic bombing in Korea was a sensitive issue. Installations in Pyongyang were hit again by massed bomber raids in July and August, along with key mineral workings. By the end of 1952, every worthwhile industrial target in the North seemed to the planners in Tokyo, poring over their photo mosaics, to have been battered into ruin. Pyongyang and other major cities had been flattened, hundreds of thousands of North Korean civilians killed. Yet there remained no evidence of the predicted collapse in the communist will to win. In the summer of 1953, the airmen claimed that the communist signature on the armistice document represented a last victory for air power, following a new campaign of attacks on dams critical for the irrigation of North Korea. There remains no decisive evidence to support or deny their claims. It is probably fair to assume that once the communists had reached a political decision to accept the armistice, the prospect of further serious damage to North Korea's national infrastructure can scarcely have encouraged them to delay. The lessons of the Korean War for air power seemed self-evident to the ground force commanders, and to those politicians who took the trouble to inform themselves about such things. The experience of World War II showed that intensive strategic bombing could kill large numbers of civilians without decisive impact upon the battlefield, or even upon the war-making capacity of an industrial power. Bombing could inflict a catastrophe upon a nation without defeating it. North Korea was a relatively primitive society, which contained only a fraction of the identifiable and worthwhile targets of Germany or Japan. Nor could the airmen claim that this problem had never been foreseen. Alexander de Seversky was only one among many thoughtful students of air warfare. As early as 1942, he wrote: 'Total war from the air against an undeveloped country or region is well nigh futile; it is one of the curious features of the most modern weapon that it is especially effective against the most modern types of civilisation.'[18] In Korea, the USAF belief in 'victory thru air power' was put to the test, and found sorely wanting by many of those who were promised so much by it.

> The Eighth Army soldier [wrote an American officer in 1953] cannot but accept the destruction of that 'doctrine' [of air power] through demonstrations, costly to him, staged by his enemies the armies of Red North Korea and Communist China. For their troops and supplies moved, despite harassment from our air, consistently and in quantities sufficient to meet their needs ... Notwithstanding the all-out efforts of the Air Force in Korea, there was never a day when the trains did not run and the trucks did not roll behind the enemy lines in North Korea, from the forward enemy areas ... The Air Force in Korea did not fail to apply all the power of which it was capable. But it is plain that it could not, or at least did not, accomplish the mission Air Force theorists had repeatedly told the Army and the American people was sure to be accomplished, under conditions of such overwhelmingly one-sided aerial strength.[19]

No one could seriously dispute that to be bombed was a deeply distressing experience, and UN strategic bombing added greatly to the communists' difficulties in sustaining the war. But of all the governments upon earth, those in Peking and Pyongyang were among the least likely to be deterred from continuing a commitment to the conflict, merely because of the distress it caused to their peoples. Given time and labour to introduce counter-measures, above all putting key installations underground, the air-dropped conventional bomb proved as limited a weapon in the second half of the twentieth century as in the first. It is not surprising that the airmen's limitless faith in what they could achieve remained undiminished after Korea, as it had after World War II. If they admitted some of the bitter truths revealed by those wars, a critical part of the air force's rationale for its own independent operations would cease to exist. But it remains astonishing that ten years later, in Vietnam, they were allowed to mount a campaign under almost identical circumstances to those of Korea, with identical promises of potential and delusions of achievement, and with exactly repeated lack of success.

15 » THE PRISONERS

One day in the summer of 1951, a British lieutenant named Brian Hawkins found a tin in no-man's-land, containing a message from the Chinese. 'Officers and men of the 1st Division of the United Kingdom,' it proclaimed,

> in the April battle 701 officers and men of the British 29th Brigade were captured by one of our units. We had sent them to the safe rear for learning. They receive the best treatment from us. They play ball and amuse themselves after studying every day. So, don't worry about them please. We write the name of the officers here, expecting you to tell their parents and wives that they are safe and will go home in the future. Life is invaluable. You should keep your safety for a good turn. You may hide yourselves while you are ordered to fight. When you see China volunteers or Korean People's Army men, lay down your weapons and come over to us. We absolutely guarantee no harm, no abuse, and plenty of food for you. Otherwise, 'Death' is the only way before you,

> The Chinese People's Volunteer Forces[1]

In a curious sense, the Chinese in the forward areas of Korea were sincere in the pursuit of their 'lenient policy' towards prisoners. There were repeated examples, throughout the war, of Chinese – although never North Koreans – not killing UN soldiers even when they had the opportunity to do so, even releasing them and sending them back to the UN lines for propaganda purposes. Yet the clumsy efforts to display humanity that sometimes took place at the front masked a terrible reality in the rear. 'We do not

know about Geneva Convention,' a contemptuous communist officer told Padre Sam Davies when he was captured on the Imjin, and
then pointed to his interrogator: 'You must obey his orders.'[2] No
aspect of the Korean conflict caused greater bitterness – bordering
upon hysteria in the United States – than the post-war revelation
of the treatment of United Nations prisoners by their communist
captors. The bald figures speak more eloquently than any narrative.
Of 7,140 American prisoners to fall into enemy hands, 2,701 died
in captivity. Some fifty of the 1,188 Commonwealth officers and
other ranks posted as missing or prisoners died in enemy hands.
The West was appalled to hear of the discovery in a railway tunnel,
during the 1950 advance into North Korea, of the bodies of a
hundred American prisoners massacred by the retreating communists. From the outbreak of war, Kim Il Sung's army made it plain
that it killed American prisoners whenever it suited its convenience to do so.

'Would the Right Honourable Gentleman bear in mind,' Major
Harry Legge-Bourke MP told a British minister in the House of
Commons in January 1951, 'that those of our men who were
prisoners in Japanese hands during the last war all say that, of all
the guards they most feared, none were worse than the Koreans?
Therefore, will he make quite clear to the North Koreans that they
must abide by the [Geneva] Convention?'[3]

The minister replied that 'the Foreign Secretary is doing his
utmost through his representative, the British Chargé d'Affaires
at Peking'. But all concerned were aware of the futility of such
gestures. The North Koreans were a law unto themselves. The
only mitigating factor in judging their behaviour towards their
prisoners is the parallel attitude of many UN soldiers towards communist captives. Many American officers and men interviewed for
this book admitted knowledge of, or participation in, the shooting
of communist prisoners when it was inconvenient to keep them
alive. It is fair to suggest that many UN soldiers did not regard
North Korean soldiers as fellow-combatants, entitled to humane
treatment, but as near-animals, to be treated as such. As usual in

most wars, when the atmosphere at the front was relaxed, communist prisoners were perfectly properly used, and sent to the camps in the rear. But at periods of special stress or fear, especially in the first six months of the war, many UN soldiers shot down enemy prisoners – or even Korean civilians – with barely a moment's scruple. 'I couldn't get over how cruel we were to the prisoners we captured,' said Private Mario Scarselleta of the 35th Infantry. 'We'd strip them and tie them on the hood of a jeep and drive them around. A group would be taken back for interrogation and shot. My outfit didn't take too many prisoners.'⁴ Scarselleta's outfit was not untypical. Private Warren Avery of the 29th Infantry said flatly: 'We took no prisoners. Our interpreter, Lieutenant Moon, was always asking for a prisoner, but we never gave him one. Geneva Convention, my ass. I shot an old woman carrying an A-frame. We killed an awful lot of civilians over there. You just couldn't trust them. After you'd seen them kill a tank crew, you didn't take chances again. Anybody you saw wearing mustard-coloured sneakers, you shot.'⁵ It remains important and valid to make some distinction between the random acts of individual UN troops, and the systematic brutality of the North Koreans. But in Korea as later in Vietnam, it seems essential, more than thirty years later, to set the behaviour of the West's forces in context, when judging that of the communists.

Beyond anything that took place on the battlefield, Korea became notorious as the first major modern conflict in which a combatant made a systematic attempt to convert prisoners to his own ideology. The Chinese success in this may be partly measured by the statistics: twenty-one Americans and one Briton refused repatriation at the end of hostilities. By 1959, the Americans claimed to have identified seventy-five former prisoners in Korea as communist agents. The most serious case was that of George Blake, former British vice-consul in Seoul, who was seized and interned in June 1950, and remained in communist hands until 1953. A decade later, Blake was unmasked as a key Soviet agent inside the British Foreign Office. The deep fear that similar traitors still lurked undiscovered within the bureaucracies and bodies politic of the West persisted for a generation, and spawned such books and films as *Time Limit*, *The Rack* and *The Manchurian Candidate*. As the experiences of UN prisoners were revealed after the Panmunjom armistice, Americans were even more dismayed by the number of their own men who were found to have collaborated with the enemy, in greater or lesser measure, while behind the wire. Had the communists indeed, by their 'brainwashing' techniques in the cluster of camps along the Yalu, discovered a psychological formula for changing the loyalties of soldiers fighting for freedom? If this was indeed so, the implications for the future struggle against communism were disturbing indeed.

*

In any war against any enemy, the first minutes of captivity are most frightening, because it is then that the risk is greatest of being shot out of hand, in the hot blood of battle. When Captain James Majury was among a cluster of Ulster Riflemen overrun by the Chinese in January 1951, they were made to kneel in the courtyard of a Korean house. A Chinese officer told them: 'You have come here to murder the peace-loving people of Korea. But we shall treat you as students of the truth.' Corporal Massey of the machine-gun platoon, the battalion welterweight boxer, responded in the inimitable accent of the Belfast shipyards: 'Listen, mister: will you go f— yourself.'[6] From the beginning to the end of captivity, it was remarkable how many men there were, from all the United Nations contingents, with such foolhardy courage.

Most UN captives received some sort of introductory harangue in their first hours in communist hands. Padre Sam Davies recorded the speech of a senior Chinese officer to the captured Gloucesters after the Imjin battle, a characteristic performance:

Officers and soldiers of the British Army, you are now prisoners of the Chinese People's Volunteer Forces in Korea. You have been duped by the American imperialists. You are tools

of the reactionary warmongers, fighting against the righteous cause of the Korean people, supported by their brothers
the Chinese people. You are hirelings of the barbarous Rhee
puppet-government, but you will be given the chance to learn
the truth through study, and correct your mistakes. Do not
be afraid – we shall not harm you. At home, your loved ones
await you. Obey our rules and regulations, and then you will
not be shot.[7]

When Marine Andrew Condron was captured in Hellfire Valley
on 30 November 1950 along with some fifty Americans, during the
Chosin reservoir campaign, a Chinese officer harangued the group
in English, considerably to their bewilderment, about their bond
with their captors, as fellow-members of the proletariat. 'Proletar-
ians like us?' demanded a bewildered GI. 'I thought they were
f***ing communists.' The Chinese shook hands with them all, and
handed over some captured cigarettes and canned food before
shutting them up in a nearby hut. Their first conflict with their
captors came, wholly unexpectedly, when a guard brought in a
steaming gourd of hot water. Somebody had some soap. To the
delight of the prisoners, they were able to wash off the filth of
days. Then the guard returned, and gazed on the scene with sheer
horror. He fixed his bayonet, and for a tense moment the prisoners
were convinced that he intended to use it. They were herded
against the wall while the guard screamed and shouted at them.
Then he vanished.

When his officer returned, they were rebuked in English. The
guard had taken the risk and trouble of lighting a fire to heat
water for them. By using it to wash in, rather than to drink, the
prisoners had insulted him. 'It really was East meets West,' said
Condron. 'We simply didn't know.'[8] Belatedly, they were searched.
Knives, watches, lighters were taken away. So too were the
wounded. To the best of Condron's knowledge, none survived. In
justice to the Chinese, with their primitive medical facilities, few
of their own casualties were likely to fare better. One night, all the

unwounded prisoners were ordered to start marching. They continued to do so for almost a month.

Hundreds of men, above all the wounded, died on these marches from the battlefield, before they ever reached a camp. 'The signal for death was the oxcart following the column,' said James Majury. 'If you had to be placed upon that, you would freeze to death.' Pneumonia and dysentery took an early toll. Throughout the march towards the camps, every prisoner retained a keen sense of imminent death. One morning when a call came 'All British outside! All British outside!' the two dozen or so Royal Marines in Andrew Condron's party were convinced that they were about to be executed. The Chinese looked excited and nervous. For two hours, a Chinese officer delivered a political harangue. He seemed convinced there was an officer among their group, which there was not: 'I no believe you! Which one is officer?' In a long single rank, the British prisoners were marched along a railway line. Condron became maudlin, as he thought of breakfast at home in West Lothian – black pudding, sausage and eggs. Why had he not joined the air force, like most of his friends? His sense of self-pity was deepened by the sight of a cluster of Korean children, laughing and giggling at them from a ridge above. Around a corner, they reached a huge hole, a bomb crater. Condron was convinced it was to be their grave. Then the guards motioned them onwards, into a house. They sagged with compulsive relief. Another Marine, Dick Richards, muttered to Condron: 'Red, were you thinking what I was thinking?' After that moment, they began to feel a flicker of confidence that they might live.

In the three or four months that followed, they had no chance to wash or take off their clothes: they could only rub their hands with snow. Yet the Scottish socialist in Condron was impressed that on the march, their captors never asked them to carry their heavy equipment, and that as a matter of course the guards and their officers joined the daily queue for sorgum along with the prisoners. Condron admitted that it was only later that he understood the conscious political purpose behind this.

Among their party were two US Marines who had been prisoners of the Japanese, and could communicate with the Chinese. The Marines seemed to respond to the situation with less difficulty than the US Army prisoners. 'The American soldiers seemed to see the way out of the experience as individuals,' said Condron. 'If one stole a bit of food, he would scuffle into a corner and eat it alone. The British and American Marines took it in groups. We stuck together. When the marching was looking rough, we'd say to each other, "Come off it – the f—ing commando school was tougher than this."'

Their group's morale soared when they heard, through their American Japanese-speakers, that 'all prisoners go home'. To their utter astonishment, they were suddenly marched to a train. It began to head south. For four or five nights they travelled, halting throughout the daylight hours in tunnels. Near Pyongyang, they were shuttled into marshalling yards where they remained for a week. Then a handful of men were picked out, for no evidently logical reason, and taken away. These men were indeed returned to the UN lines, apparently as a propaganda move to convince the West that rumours that all prisoners were being shot were unfounded. The remainder began to receive more food – a little rice, chicken, soup. Some of the Americans were now euphoric, composing cables and letters to their families, ready for dispatch at the moment of their release. Some men spent hours discussing the menu for their first meal on their release. The British imposed a self-denying ordinance on themselves, not to discuss food. Suddenly, the Chinese brought news: 'You go north – prisoner-of-war camp.' The shock to those who had convinced themselves that they were going home was appalling. A few weeks later, Condron helped to bury one American, whom he had watched on the train working out the hour-by-hour programme for his first week of freedom.

Now, for the first time, they were interrogated. They were apprehensive at the prospect, and bewildered by the reality. They had spent some time discussing with an American captain how they should respond to military questions. Yet there were none.

Instead, an amiable Chinese officer sat on the floor, offered each man a glass of hot water, and asked: 'What sort of work does your father do? What sort of work does your mother do?'

'My mother does not work,' answered Andrew Condron.

'Why your mother no work?'

'She is a housewife.'

'What is housewife?'

'She just stays home.'

'How much your land your family own?'

'There's the back garden.'

'What you grow?'

'Potatoes, rhubarb.'

'How many cows have your family got?'

'We get milk from the dairy.'

'What is dairy? How many pigs you have? How many cows?'

At last, with a self-satisfied grin, the Chinese concluded, 'Ah, your family very small land. You are poor peasant.' The British laughed for weeks about the cockney Marine who was asked about his family's land, and vividly described his windowbox.

Yet if it is easy to find comedy in the naïveté of all this, among the prisoners a powerful undercurrent of fear was never far distant. Condron's group were relatively well treated by their Chinese guardians. Many men who fell into the hands of the North Koreans suffered dreadfully. Aircrew and those with special technical knowledge were singled out for far more sophisticated and brutal questioning. In the first months of captivity, many officers were treated with savage cruelty, and subjected to months of solitary confinement. The worst brutalities were suffered by those confined in the hands of the North Koreans in the transit or penal compounds around Pyongyang – 'Pak's Palace', 'The Caves', Camp 9 at Kangdong.

*

When Private Henry O'Kane of the Ulster Rifles was captured on the Imjin in April 1951, like Marine Condron, he and his group expected to be shot. A mate named Tommy Spears of B Company had seventeen cigarettes left in his pocket, and sat down to smoke the lot in the first half-hour, because he was certain he would never smoke again. O'Kane and his companions were reasonably well treated, given the usual 'safe-conduct passes' declaring that they had been 'liberated', then ordered to start marching. Their interrogations, like Condron's, focused upon personal histories rather than military information. O'Kane was told that he would be well treated. He pointed out that nothing had been done for his wounds. He was taken across the courtyard to a primitive aid post where the shrapnel fragments were extracted from his head and leg without benefit of anaesthetic, some black ointment 'such as we use for horses back home' was smeared on the wounds, then his original bandages were replaced. Their wounds, their filth, their exhaustion depressed O'Kane's group deeply. There were no officers among them. Each day an NCO would count out their ration of peanuts – sixteen to a man, the sort of statistic a prisoner remembers for the rest of his life. They were told that they were to be marched to catch a train to a place of safety. This raised their spirits, and for the first night or two they moved in good heart. Then, as night followed night and they realised that there was no train, morale fell again. There was no temptation to straggle from the column, for North Korean soldiers hung around constantly, begging to be given prisoners: 'We were very glad of Chinese protection.'

They spent some weeks at a village on the delta of the Taedong river, being given daily political lectures, before being set marching again, this time to their permanent home, Chayson, Camp 1, where they arrived in June 1951. Here, they joined some hundreds of Americans. The British were shocked. 'The atmosphere was pathetic. I have never seen men like it in my life,' said O'Kane. 'They were like the walking dead. They could not lift their heads, they seemed unable to speak. The appearance of fresh British troops seemed the end to them – it meant that the whole thing would go on for ever. I saw thirty men buried in one day, that first week.'⁹

*

Jerry Morgan was a twenty-five-year-old technical sergeant in the 24th Infantry, a black regiment, when his company heard the cry 'Every man for himself!' on the night of 27 November 1950. Most of them were rapidly rounded up by the Chinese, and marched north. They spent a month in the houses of a village at a place they called 'Death Valley', for many Americans died there. Then they were moved some twenty miles to their permanent home on the Yalu: Camp 5, 'Pyongdong University'. Here, in the hands of the North Koreans, they suffered through the rest of that first, terrible winter.

When Andrew Condron and his group were taken north again in March 1951 to Camp 5, they were appalled by what they found. They joined some seven hundred men at the limits of misery and hunger, among whom prisoners were dying every day. The camp was sited in a valley, on a peninsula overlooked by two hills. It was a place of great natural beauty, had the circumstances been such as to make them appreciate it. Here, confined chiefly by the geography and certainty of the impossibility of escape, with a single strand of wire marking the permissible limits of movement, many men stayed for up to three years. Only when the Chinese assumed control of Camp 5 in the spring of 1951 did conditions improve marginally, and the worst excesses perpetrated by the North Koreans cease.

The more thoughtful prisoners perceived from the outset that their wounded died for lack of medical attention and not, on the whole, as a matter of enemy policy. The communists themselves were entirely bereft of drugs and equipment, even for their own men. But it was also evident that in the first winter of 1950–51, the North Koreans were indifferent as to whether their captives lived, or died of starvation. Men who had been receiving a US

Army daily combat ration of 3,500 calories now found themselves provided with only 1,200 calories of corn and millet. It was a diet devoid of vegetables, almost barren of proteins, minerals, or vitamins. Leadership among the prisoners collapsed. A dreadful struggle for survival took over, the strongest ruthlessly stripping the weak of food. Up to thirty men a day were dying.

By far the most deadly killer, above all in those first months of 1951, was the dreaded 'give-upitis', which afflicted thousands of prisoners. In an extraordinary fashion, they lost the will to live, above all the will to eat. Many Americans simply declined to eat the mess of sorgum and rice with which they were provided. They chose instead to starve. The British would say laconically: 'If you don't eat, you don't shit. If you don't shit, you die.' Some men were fortunate enough to have friends and comrades who cosseted and cajoled them into eating. PFC Graham Cockfield of the 34th Infantry noticed that it was the younger prisoners who seemed most vulnerable:

> You'd hear mem sitting all day, planning the meal they were going to have when they got out. Then somebody came around with the millet, and they wouldn't touch it. We simply did our best to force food down any individual we knew wasn't eating. Natural physique had nothing to do with who survived and who didn't. It was all in the mind.[10]

Henry O'Kane was near the margin of survival when he reached Camp 1: his mouth was sore from lack of vitamins; like every other man, he was suffering from dysentery and beri-beri. All around him lay cases of malaria, jaundice, bone fever. O'Kane was placed in a hut with some forty Filipinos and Puerto Ricans: 'They saved my life. They were peasant characters, rice eaters, who simply understood that kind of life, could make medicine from herbs to keep themselves alive. That is what they did for me.'

But other prisoners refused help, resisted every blandishment. The 'no hopers' merely lay down, staring emptily into space, until one morning, they were dead. 'It was easier to die than it was to live,' in the words of Lieutenant Walt Mayo of the 8th Cavalry. 'We tried to do as much amateur psychology as we could, but the problem was sheer despair.'[11] It was an extraordinary phenomenon. A few men in the communist camps in Korea died as a result of deliberate brutality. Many suffered terrible beatings, punishments involving exposure to cold or heat that amounted to torture. Almost all were terribly weakened by hunger and disease. Yet there was never any equivalent of the systematic, wholesale brutality that the Japanese practised upon their prisoners in World War II.

The atmosphere in the camps, above all in the first months of most bitter starvation, was savage. As men's boots wore out, they saved the steels from the soles, and sharpened them into shivs, as tools for self-defence. There were endless petty power struggles, most about food. Terrible acts were perpetrated by prisoners upon each other. In one of the most notorious cases, US Army Sergeant James Gallagher was later convicted by court-martial of killing two seriously ill prisoners by throwing them out into the snow. 'I learned more about the way society operates in that camp than I could have learned in any university,' said Andrew Condron. With a kind of insanity, some prisoners sold scraps of food to others for money or scrip that was utterly worthless to them. In those first months of 1951, every man was entirely preoccupied with the struggle for survival. Racked with dysentery, a man's intestine would hang down inches below his anus, to be stuffed back with a surge of agony when the next call to defecate came. It was not uncommon to stagger thirty, forty times a day to the latrine, men finding themselves unable even to cross the compound without dropping their trousers. Prisoners drowned by falling in the latrine pits. Lice and bedbugs thrived. They held competitions to kill them – 123, 124, 125; their thumbs were black with ingrained blood. Condron became obsessed with this. 'If I live,' he thought, 'I shall never get rid of that blood.' They itched ceaselessly as they sat and talked; exchanged the plots of old films; signalled extracts from old newspapers to each other in morse or semaphore – anything to pass the dreadful, savagely cold days, until the time came to huddle desperately together for warmth through the icier nights.

For the weakened men, the greatest hardship was the regular wood detail. Their lives depended upon collecting sufficient fuel to keep their fires and cookers alive. Yet with each trip, they were compelled to forage further afield into the mountains. The supply began to falter. Crossly, the Chinese summoned a meeting, and harangued the prisoners upon their negative attitude to labour, pointing out that it was not for the captors' benefit, but that of the captives. Then, as spring came, there was a surge of volunteers for the wood detail. The Chinese were delighted to discover that 'your attitude towards labour has improved'. Yet it was not wood that called the men, but the discovery of marijuana. First identified by some of the Mexican prisoners, it grew wild on the hills. Through the next two years it became, for some men, the only means of making captivity endurable. It caused some excesses which puzzled the Chinese – sudden exuberant sing-songs from groups of black prisoners; one morning a helplessly stoned figure racing around the compound screaming: 'The Indians are coming! The Indians are coming!' But the Chinese were told that he was shell-shocked. Curiously enough, in two years they never appeared to grasp the truth.

*

In the spring of 1951, officers and men were held in the same camp areas. Each morning, they were herded together in their hundreds for political lectures, huddled shivering for four hours at a stretch: two hours in Chinese, two hours of translation, and any man found sitting back on his hands received a kick. 'Study hard, Comrades, with open minds, and you will get home soon,' the Chinese commandant told them. 'But if you don't, we'll dig a ditch for you so deep that even your bourgeois bodies won't stink.'

In the summer of 1951, there was a dramatic change in Chinese policy towards the prisoners-of-war. It was determined that if possible, they should be permitted to live. Conditions in all the camps improved markedly. Thereafter, the number of deaths among prisoners declined to a trickle. 99 per cent of all American prisoner deaths took place in the first year of the war. As Captain James Majury of the Ulsters put it laconically: 'The Chinese realised that they needed some survivors if their propaganda about "the lenient treatment" was to have any meaning.' At last, they were given the means to delouse themselves – and lice had been one of the most corrosive destroyers of morale. By the winter of 1951, to their astonishment the prisoners found themselves receiving sufficient food to sustain life. The Chinese killed an occasional pig, and its fat was distributed among the prisoners by self-administered roster. They began to receive a rice ration instead of millet. Captain Majury got his first letter home out of the officers' camp in August, and received his first from his family in October.

Then, as the Chinese arrangements became more organised, the prisoners were broken down into 'companies', for daily political study sessions, at which they were required to write long, allegedly self-analytical political tracts. As part of the deliberate communist policy of destroying their existing leadership, in October the British and American officers were gathered together, and marched some hundred miles into the mountains to the new Camp 2, which remained the officers' camp for the remainder of the war. Their uniforms were replaced by Chinese quilted suits and caps, a further blow to their identity as soldiers. The Chinese appointed company and platoon leaders from among the prisoners.

From beginning to end, the Chinese purpose was to reindoctrinate their prisoners politically, to convert them from their traditional political values to those of communism. Beyond obvious political instruction, the communists sought to destroy all existing structures of rank and command. No officer's rank was recognised. Any internal attempt by the prisoners to organise their own leadership without approval from the Chinese was interpreted as a 'hostile attitude'. When Sergeant Jim Taylor of the 8th Hussars, the senior British ranker in Camp 5, refused to salute a Chinese one morning, he was sent to 'The Hole' for three days, literally to roast in the summer heat in a hole covered with a sheet of corrugated iron. Some men were kept in it for weeks at a time.

The problem of 'hostile attitudes' occurred most often among the officers in Camp 2, and resulted in the frequent removal of officers to 'the cages', where they were held in solitary confinement, sometimes for months. Major Denis Harding, a Gloucesters company commander, was held in solitary confinement, mostly in a hillside cowshed, from January 1952 until his release in the summer of 1953. Major Guy Ward, RA, had already endured four years of captivity in World War II. Throughout that experience, he was sustained by a feeling 'that we were all together, like a family, that in the end things would be all right. In Korea, we asked ourselves: "How many years might this go on? Will it ever end?"' That first winter in the officers' camp, like his fellow-prisoners, Ward would find himself suddenly hauled from his bed at 3 a.m., when human resistance was lowest, and taken to an underground bunker for interrogation. Once again, this was overwhelmingly social, and wearily repetitive:

'What car does your father have?'

'Are you a large family?'

'How much capital have you?'

Ward said later: 'The only Chinese who understood us were the younger ones who had been educated in the United States. We were conscious that the way they treated us was the way they treated their own people. You might see fifteen or twenty Chinese by the roadside, being kicked about in just the same way that they kicked us.'

The sheer dreary monotony of the political lectures aroused their contempt: 'The Democratic Reformation and Democratic Structure in North Korea and the Peaceful Unification Policy of the North Korean Government'; 'The Chinese People's Right to Formosa'; 'Corruption of the UN by the American Warmongers'. They were permitted only communist newspapers – the *Daily Worker* and *Chinese Pictorial*. The loudspeakers blared forth news each day which announced fresh American defeats, never conceded a glimmer of United Nations success. Yet often, they would glimpse the white con-trails of high-flying aircraft, and occasionally they would see a dogfight, even see a communist MiG brought down. Thus they were reminded that the war was not yet over, that the communist armies had not yet triumphed.

There were a few tattered, dog-eared books which passed from hand to hand. Andrew Condron read Daphne du Maurier's *Rebecca*, and was driven mad by the absence of the very last page, torn out by his captors. Years later, Condron discovered that it contained a casually hostile reference to communists. Generally, they were allowed to keep books the Chinese considered ideologically sound: *Uncle Tom's Cabin*, *War and Peace*, Lenin's *One Step Forward, Two Steps Back*, some Steinbecks, those works of Dickens which were thought to present a sufficiently bleak portrait of the plight of the proletariat.

Men's reaction to imprisonment varied enormously. It was difficult to generalise about the kind of man who held together best. A US Marine pilot, who was little regarded at first by his fellow-prisoners because of his taciturn manner, his apparent inability ever to say more than 'Uh-Huh?' or 'Shit', proved one of the most rugged and respected 'reactionaries' in the officers' camp. A British officer who had been a prisoner of the Germans in World War II was one of the most visible resisters for months. Then, imperceptibly, he began to deteriorate. Like so many others, his will was weakened by illness and hunger. By the end, he seemed one of the most broken-spirited. To many British prisoners, it seemed a criminal blunder by the War Office to have recalled for service in Korea so many ex-World War II PoWs. It was an unspeakable experience for men who had already endured two, three, four years of their youth in captivity now to be exposed to the same misery once more. It was worst of all for those who had been held by the Japanese. At least five of the British prisoners had been captives in Korea in World War II. They, from the outset, remembered the Korean guards as their most atrocious and brutal tormentors. Colonel Fred Carne of the Gloucesters seemed, to most of his companions, astoundingly untroubled by captivity. The Chinese singled out Carne for special treatment, as the senior officer fellow-prisoners treated as their commander. He spent much of his time in their hands in solitary confinement. Yet Carne behaved throughout with his customary taciturn serenity. His example impressed his comrades for the rest of their lives.

By common consent, most of the doctors and chaplains – those with a very obvious and visible role to play in the camps – behaved well, some outstandingly so. Despite the pitiful absence of drugs and equipment, the doctors spent hours attempting to persuade men stricken with 'give-upitis' to eat. Among the padres, Sam Davies of the Gloucesters was remembered by his fellow-prisoners with immense affection and respect. But perhaps the most beloved of all was Father Emil Kapaun, Catholic chaplain of the US 1st Cavalry. Kapaun's cheerful selflessness, his genius for scrounging and devotion to the suffering, his nightly sick rounds, became a legend. He died in Camp 5 in May 1951, worn out by dysentery and a blood clot in his leg. In Camp 2, the prisoners hoarded rice paper on which to compile a copy of the Book of Common Prayer. When Padre Davies was dispatched to solitary confinement, James Majury took over the conduct of his services. Davies secretly baptised six Americans, and prepared nineteen British and American officers for confirmation, in the camp. He was bitterly chagrined that, because of his officer status, the Chinese would never allow him to go among the other ranks.

Lieutenant Bill Cooper found it helpful to demand of himself at the beginning of each day: 'What worthwhile thing are you going to do today?' He would often accept the job of washing the ghastly rags of men crippled by dysentery: 'It was horrible, but you felt that it was a job worth doing.'[12] For most men, the nights were the worst. It was then that they lay silent, but awake, brooding in the loneliness about their families and their societies, going indifferently about their business so many thousands of miles away. Desperately as they hungered for letters, life became almost more intolerable on the rare occasions when these came. In two years, Bill Cooper received three letters from home, and five of those he wrote reached his family. Jerry Morgan received his first letter from home in April 1952, enclosing a photograph of the son born in the United States whom he had never seen. Many men did not even achieve this level of contact. There was so much a man yearned to know, that was not in the simple scraps of paper they received.

'Dear Robert,' Lance-Corporal Bob Erricker's father wrote from his little house in Surrey to his son in Camp 5 on the Yalu,

> I have just received the news via the War Office that you are a Prisoner of War in North Korea, it's wonderful and we are so thankful to know you are safe and well, shall be watching every day for the post . . . Look after No. 1. I had a nice letter from Lt. Alexander's father. His death was in The Times. PC O'Halloran has been made Sergeant and is going to live at Milford. Daisy has got another Girl two month old. Mrs Terry has left Alford and Eileen Brunet is living in their bungalow. We celebrated the good news of your safety by going to the Daily Mail Ideal Home Exhibition at Olympia. Mum was 'Frisking about' like a 2-year-old, bought a Hoover Washing Machine for £31, and she aint got 4d.

It was a kind of agony, to hear this simple domestic small change amid the sorgum and dysentery of a hut on the Yalu. Camp 5 was for 'progressives', the men whom the Chinese considered to be adopting the most positive attitude to their own political education. If its inmates were marginally better treated than those in 'reactionary' camps, there is little evidence that most of them treated the Chinese any more seriously. Many British and American rankers simply decided that there was no harm in playing the Chinese game, if by doing so they could gain better food, and marginally improve their own chances of survival. Even when attendance at political lectures was made voluntary, in the later stages of imprisonment, some men continued to attend, merely to pass the day.[13]

The biggest enemy in a prisoner's life is boredom [said Henry O'Kane]. All the average British soldier ever read was the sports page. He didn't know much about Lenin's 'One Step Forward' or the crimes of John Foster Dulles. A lot of people appeared to take in the Chinese lectures, then you found afterwards it hadn't made the slightest real impression on them. They were simply playing it the safe way. You knew the answers the Chinese wanted, and a lot of the time you'd give them. You'd write any old propaganda nonsense they wanted to get a letter passed to be sent home. Then, every now and again, you'd get bored and kick against the traces, tell them what you really thought. Then the Chinese might forget the 'lenient policy' for a bit, and hand somebody over to the Koreans for a while. There were some people who always did it the hard way, who told the Chinese exactly what they thought of them – Kinney of the Northumberlands, Brierley, Richards, Andrew McNab of the RUR.

O'Kane shook his head: 'Two years, and the Chinese couldn't do a thing with McNab.' He laughed. 'But then, nor could the Royal Ulster Rifles.'[14]

The first serious shock to Western consciousness about the PoWs in Korea was the transmission by Radio Peking of broadcasts by American and British captives. Some made recordings at the behest of the Chinese because they could sincerely see no harm in them. Some represented communist successes in political indoctrination. Some were merely willing to pay any moral price for a greater prospect of survival. But the revelation in the West that some captives were co-operating, if not collaborating, with the communists was a profound shock. What was happening to men in the hands of the enemy, that they could be persuaded to speak to their own people across the airwaves in such terms?

Hello. This is Marine Andrew Condron speaking. Hello, Mum, Dad and all at home. By courtesy of the Chinese People's Volunteers I am broadcasting to you now, to tell you how we are getting on here, and about our preparations for Christmas . . .

A further confusing element in the lives and loyalties of the prisoners was the visits of Western communists to the camps. In World War II, the handful of British renegades who chose to put themselves at the disposal of the Germans were unhesitatingly branded as traitors, and several – including the son of a British Cabinet Minister – were hanged in 1945. Yet during the Korean War, as during Vietnam, the communists extracted a major propaganda advantage from invitations to Western left-wingers to visit their martyred country. In April 1951, Monica Felton, the communist chairman of Stevenage New Town, went East, and wrote a gushing little book about her uplifting experience. She eulogised the 'lively, critical, indoctrinated' schoolchildren she met in Prague, as against the 'docile blankness of English girls I knew whose minds were being kept antiseptically free from the infection of any contemporary ideas'.[15] She found that 'arriving in Moscow seemed suddenly like coming home'.[16] But she saved her highest flights of rhetoric for the heroic spectacle of North Korea under air attack, the tales of American atrocities and United Nations perfidy. She said nothing in her book about her proselytising visit to the Turkish UN PoW compound, where she spent several days. She was rewarded only with a contemptuous document drawn up by the Turks, suggesting that she peddled her ideological wares elsewhere. She anticipated by a generation the antics of Miss Jane Fonda in Hanoi. Representatives of the 'World Peace Council', together with such communist journalists as Alan Winnington of the *Daily Worker* and Wilfred Burchett of *Ce Soir* visited UN prisoners in their camps. Some prisoners such as Andrew Condron – not, perhaps, the most reliable witness on this issue – suggest that the Western visitors did what they could to get conditions for the prisoners improved. Others, however, recorded contemptible behaviour by the 'journalists', including taunting of the 'reactionaries' behind the wire. It is difficult to regard the behaviour of the visitors, to a nation with which their countries were at war, with much enthusiasm. It contributed something, at least, to the communist purpose of confusing the minds of the UN prisoners, as well as the world, about the unity of national purpose behind the UN war effort in Korea.

*

So much of the prisoners' experience teetered uneasily between tragedy and farce. 'You see that now?' said Comrade Lim to a Camp 5 group one morning, stabbing his blackboard as he denoted some refinement of proletarian organisation. A bee on the blackboard stung him, to the delight of his audience. 'You see that now?' demanded Lim furiously. 'That is a capitalist bee.' Chinese prurience was persistently affronted by the prisoners' language: 'Why all the time you effing, effing, effing?' The Chinese regarded the obscenities as a deliberate insult to themselves. The prisoners, in their turn, laughed at the Chinese habit of walking into the compound holding hands with each other: 'We thought they were a load of blooming fairies,' said Bob Erricker. The Chinese discovery of this belief led to yet another lecture, to 'correct their attitude'.

A fanatical young Marxist named Comrade Sun was Chief Political Commissar at Camp 2. His classes were conducted with weary, unrelenting zeal. The more senior an officer, the more likely to be singled out for correction:

> 'Davies, stand up' [he commanded the Gloucesters' padre one morning].
>
> I rose.
>
> 'What is your opinion of the chapter we have just read?' (It was from William Z. Foster's *Outline History of the Americas*.)
>
> Long pause, then:
>
> 'I'm afraid I was not listening.'
>
> 'Why not?'
>
> 'Well, I'm a British PoW and I have other interests than American history.'

Silence –

'You will pay attention. You must correct your attitude.'

Ponderously –

'I confess my crime.'

'Sit down.'[17]

Chinese behaviour was often unpredictable. Once, through the usual channel of the 'All China Committee for World Peace', Erricker received a letter from his mother, enclosing a photograph of the new Queen. He pinned it on the wall of his hut, and to his surprise, the Chinese made no attempt to remove it. Yet the Chinese at Camp 2 were furious when the British celebrated the Queen's coronation with a parade and stockpiled home-brewed rice wine. Rations were cut in punishment.

The Chinese made determined efforts to destroy prisoners' faith in religion. 'If you believe in God, why doesn't he help you now?' the commandant taunted NCO prisoners in Camp 4. Lieutenant John Thornton, USN, noticed that the black prisoners – whom the Chinese worked steadily to distance from their white compatriots, held on to their religious faith better than many whites. One of the prisoners best-loved by his companions was Captain John Stanley, who delighted them with his guitar-playing and exasperated the Chinese by his dogged insistence: 'I am an American, not a negro.'

Men became intensely moody, their spirits vacillating dramatically from one day to the next. Personal relations could become obsessive. Close friendships would form and persist for weeks, until broken by some fit of temper. But there was virtually no homosexuality: most men found, very early in their imprisonment, that they lost all interest in sex. It was only in the last weeks before their release, when the end was obviously near, that prisoners allowed themselves to think again about women. Most men believed that they learned from their time in captivity to count the blessings of daily life in freedom. Padre Sam Davies used to say: 'When I get out of here, I shall never again moan about waiting for a bus in the rain.'[18]

The attitudes of the 'reactionaries' – those who continued openly to defy the Chinese throughout their captivity – varied greatly. The most systematic defiance, not surprisingly, came from some of the inhabitants of the officers' camp. Some officers, for instance, refused to speak to a Chinese at all, if this could be avoided. Others, like Anthony Farrar-Hockley, talked and argued with them at every opportunity. It was a matter of personal inclination. The behaviour of all prisoners tends inevitably towards the juvenile, because they themselves are unwillingly placed in the position of captive children, unable to make their own decisions. Thus too, some of their acts of defiance were childish. One morning, a dozen men would work furiously for hours, digging in a deep hole in the midst of the compound. Then, with great ceremony, they would place a piece of paper in it, and fill it in again. Inevitably, the curious Chinese would re-excavate it, to discover the simple message 'Mind Your Own Business'. Some days, prisoners would reduce 'Loll Call' to chaos, only to parade with perfect discipline the next time. One morning, a group of men would run out into the compound, and spend an hour 'flying' around, pretending to be helicopters, amid the bewildered gaze of their guards. Another day, a crowd of spectators might stand watching two prisoners play ping-pong, their heads moving to and fro with the ball – except that there was no ball, no bats, no table – merely a mime show to needle the Chinese. Taking invisible dogs for a walk was always popular. One morning at Camp 3, 'all of us decided to go crazy,' according to Private David Fortune, 'we rode round on invisible motorbikes, sat playing invisible cards. Some men really were that crazy . . .'[19]

Perhaps the most imaginative pinprick 'tease' of their captors was perpetrated from the officers' camp, at the height of the Chinese propaganda campaign alleging that the Americans were employing bacteriological warfare in Korea. Some prisoners attached a dead mouse to a small parachute, and one morning when unobserved, they hurled it some yards beyond the wire of the compound. They were rewarded by the spectacle of an earnest cluster of Chinese, surrounding a doctor in a face mask who arrived to examine and at last, with infinite caution and ceremony, remove the specimen. It was another contribution to the prisoners' tiny, sometimes pathetic efforts to demonstrate to themselves, as well as to their captors, that they had not yet surrendered all control of their own affairs.

Although there were many friendships among prisoners that transcended nationality, in general each group hung closely together. The Turks were greatly admired for their indomitable toughness and resistance to the Chinese. Their only collaborator was quietly killed by his compatriots. When one of their men was sick, two of his comrades undertook responsibility for his survival. The British seemed to suffer fewer difficulties than the Americans with 'give-upitis'. Resignation and adjustment to the inevitable are British national characteristics. Most British prisoners took it for granted that it was preferable to eat the unspeakable food they were offered, rather than to die. There were sub-divisions within the national groups: the American aircrew, for instance, tended to distance themselves from their army counterparts. Each nationality tended to keep its own secrets, above all in Camp 2, the officers' camp. There was deep suspicion of a handful of American officers, one senior, who were believed to be collaborating with the Chinese, even to the extent of betraying escape plans.

The nationalities often argued about what approach to adopt to specific enemy demands. In the officers' camp, there was a protracted debate when the Chinese demanded that prisoners' group commanders should assemble and count them each morning. The Americans were uncertain whether or not this was a reasonable demand. The British flatly refused. They said: 'If the Chinese want to count us, okay. But we will not do it for them.' Two British officers were dispatched to solitary confinement in the course of that dispute. It would be foolish to deny that there were considerable tensions between the British and American officers in Camp 2. While the British greatly admired individuals, such as the Marine Major John McLoughlin, and Tom Harrison of the USAF, limping on his wooden leg, there was considerable mistrust at group level. The Americans considered some British behaviour and acts of passive resistance absurd and counter-productive. The British simply did not confide in some Americans about their plans or intentions, because they did not trust them. The British, historically conditioned to despise the open display of emotion, were bemused by the American readiness to weep. Lieutenant Bill Cooper was bewildered to see a US Army captain cry one afternoon, when one of his team dropped a catch during a softball game. Another officer burst into tears when he found his bedding had been switched, when he wanted to sleep next door to a friend. It was a difference of cultures. Lieutenant John Thornton, an American helicopter pilot universally known as 'Rotorhead', who behaved with great courage throughout his captivity, said afterwards: 'We were very poor PoWs – we envied the British regimental tradition. The attitude among most of our men was "hooray for me. Screw you." The communists were largely successful in isolating us from each other.'[20] Private David Fortune said: 'Among many Americans, one saw every principle of the code of conduct for PoWs break down. The whole idea of having faith in one's fellow-man collapsed.'

In the course of the entire war, there was not a single successful escape back to the UN lines by a prisoner in the Yalu camps. But there were many attempts. Some prisoners such as Captain Farrar-Hockley tried again and again, and remained at liberty for some days. PFC Fortune, a 35th Infantryman captured on 2 January 1951, got out of Camp 3 with a comrade, and remained at liberty for three days and nights in the winter of 1952. On the third night, the two men were peering curiously at a Chinese anti-aircraft battery when they were spotted and seized by North Korean militiamen. The Koreans behaved with predictable savagery. The Americans were stripped naked, paraded through the nearby village, and beaten up. Then they were tied up, to be mocked and spat upon by the local children for a few hours before being returned to the Chinese. Back at the camp, they were rewarded with two weeks' solitary confinement. The Chinese liked to say to the prisoners: 'The guards are not here to keep you in, but to save you from the Korean people.' There was a disagreeable strand of truth in this.

One of the most notable Chinese failures was the establishment, in August 1952, of a 'penal camp' for 'reactionary' non-commissioned prisoners. This was a fenced compound, where men were compelled to do hard labour, often as meaningless as digging holes and filling them in again. Yet the very qualities in a prisoner that qualified him for the penal camp were those that bound him to his fellow-'reactionaries' with a coherence that was achieved in no other compound. 'Everybody in that camp was a good man,' said Dave Fortune. 'Morale was much higher.' There were no informers, no collaborators, no burden of mutual mistrust. After a few months the Chinese realised their mistake, and redistributed the 130-odd inmates among the other camps.

The notion that the Chinese 'brainwashed' the bulk of their prisoners in Korea is simply unfounded. They appear to have employed the sophisticated techniques generally associated with this term only in one case: that of the American aircrew from whom they extracted confessions of participation in bacteriological warfare, their most notable propaganda achievement. In the Korean prison camps, the Chinese attempted large-scale thought reform, with a very modest degree of success. What was astonishing about their attempts to convert their prisoners to the cause of communism was the crudity, the clumsiness, the stupidity with which these were conducted. There is no difficulty in understanding their approach – the 'lenient treatment', the efforts to build a sense of community between captors and captives. It was precisely that by which the communists achieved such success during their civil war with the Kuomintang, by the end of which millions of Chiang Kai Shek's soldiers were successfully absorbed into the armies of Mao Tse Tung. It was founded upon the willingness of the defeated, throughout China's historical experience, to throw in their lot with the victors, to recognise a new leadership, a new source of power and patronage. Yet for the overwhelming bulk of the UN prisoners in Chinese hands, the notion that they had anything to learn from Mao Tse Tung's society was risible. Themselves the products of a highly technical, relatively educated society, they saw the absolute poverty, the pathetic ignorance of their guards and indoctrinators – and despised them. 'One or two of the Chinese were laughably pleasant,' said Major Guy Ward. 'But not one of them showed the intelligence really to make us like and respect them.'

> The Chinese were trying to persuade us: 'Our world is better than your world' [said Captain James Majury]. In my own mind, I would say, 'Okay, anything you've done with your own society has got to be better for you than Warlordism.' But there was no way that a Chinese could ever convince me that his world would be better for *me*. Very few people were truly brainwashed. I said to the Chinese towards the end: 'Surely you must realise that you will never change us?' And yes, I think they had given up. If they had really been smart, if they had really wanted to make an impact, they would have pampered us from the beginning.[21]

Yet two years of grinding repetition of political dogma, two years of isolation from their own society, two years of Chinese scorn – 'You know that your country is not interested in you' – made a decisive impact upon some men. 'Do not think that, because you get home, we cannot reach you – we can always get you if we want you,' they were told. In their impotence, some prisoners found this perfectly believable. The most effective means of breaking a man's will was the appeal to his physical weakness – offering secret access to the commodity whose absence dominated their lives, food. A prisoner who accepted an egg, a fistful of tobacco from a Chinese in return for some tiny act of betrayal was half-doomed already. His own self-respect was cracked. It remained only for his captors to make the treason absolute, to extract some hint about an escape plan, secret religious services, 'hostile attitudes'.

Why did such a man as Andrew Condron, the twenty-three-year-old barrack-room socialist from West Lothian, become, in the eyes of his countrymen, a traitor by refusing repatriation at the end of the war, along with twenty-one Americans? The simple answer, perhaps, is that he was ripe for it. Condron always refused to see himself as a traitor. He declared his lifelong pride in his country, in his service in the Royal Marines. But he had always been a member of 'the awkward squad' – 'Red' Condron, the man forever asking questions, who instinctively resisted authority in any form. In Camp 5, he became fascinated by Marxism:

> I had seen the suffering and hardship among people in the Mediterranean, and I related to it. Why were there the very rich and very poor? Surely life could be better organised than that. There was a large element of romanticism about China, a sense of adventure. At that time, I thought I'd go to China for a year or so, then come home. Had things not turned out the way they did, I might have become a missionary. I wanted to go and live in Russia afterwards. What I wanted to know was – Did it work? I wasn't a convinced communist, but a convinced Marxist. I have remained one all my life. I had lost my Catholic faith even before I went into the Marines. Perhaps I needed something to latch on to.[22]

Thirty-five years later, it seems much easier to accept the naive simplicity of Condron's reasoning than it was for his contemporaries. They perceived an enormity about his act, a sense of national disgrace which was shared by Americans towards their own prisoners who chose to remain in China. Condron 'the Bolshie', the instinctively bloody-minded, made a gesture which seems, with hindsight, to owe far less to the wiles of his communist captors than to his own wilfulness. It is striking that most of his British fellow-prisoners, even 'the reactionaries' who fiercely declined to co-operate with their captors, bear Condron little or no resentment today. At no time during their imprisonment was he suspected of the acts of personal betrayal of his comrades of which many other prisoners were guilty, who returned to their countries free of the stain of treason. It was men's personal betrayals that their peers found impossible to forgive. And these owed nothing to ideology, but everything to a pathetic collapse of will and self-discipline in the face of intolerable suffering and privation.

Guy Ward was cynically amused, on the eve of his release, to discover that the Chinese provided the same sort of demonstration of their generosity that he had received from the Germans. Just as in 1945 they had been given back lighters, pens, watches, so now the prisoners were given souvenir toiletries and fountain pens. Some of their captors sought to make amends for all that had happened in the previous two years: 'We are sorry, very sorry this has happened. We are friends. It is the American imperialists.' But even thirty-five years later, Ward would think of the Chinese and say simply: 'I loathe them.'

What was remarkable was not how many men were scarred for life by the experience of communist captivity, but how many shrugged it off with little long-term effect. General William Dean, the commander of the US 24th Division captured at Taejon in July 1950, was held for three years in solitary confinement near Pyongyang, subjected to intense Marxist-Leninist indoctrination. Yet Dean, on his release, merely remarked lightly: 'I'm an authority now on the history of the Communist Party and much of its doctrine.'

'I took the simple professional soldier's view,' said Captain James Majury. 'I certainly came out saying: "I shall never leave food on my plate again." But I felt that if one had been stupid enough to be taken prisoner, one must accept the consequences. It was an experience that I would not want to repeat, but it probably did not do me much permanent harm.' The most lasting mark of imprisonment upon Lieutenant Bill Cooper was the destruction of trust in his fellow-men: 'It made me look at people and say: "You are guilty until I have found you innocent." It also made me not care about things. If somebody said to me, "You mustn't do that," I would say: "Why? I'll make my own decision." ' Private Bill Shirk of the 15th Field Artillery found the whole experience 'a bad, bad, dream. All the time, I kept asking, "Why don't they come and get us out?" We were fighting these primitive people, for Chrissakes. I made up my mind: if I ever get out of this place, I won't ever put myself out for anybody. What the hell did we want with this country, anyway? I sure felt let down.'

The exact number of British prisoners who died in captivity is uncertain, but it was probably around fifty, against a total of 1,036 who were repatriated by the communists in 1953. 2,730 of the 7,190 American prisoners who fell into communist hands did not return. At least some hundreds of these were murdered in cold blood by the North Koreans. Many more died on the terrible journey to the camps, or in the first winter of the war. American students judge the casualties to represent the highest prisoner death rate in any conflict in the nation's history, including the Revolutionary war. Yet why was it that none of the 229 Turkish prisoners died, and only 13 per cent of US Marines, against 38 per cent of army prisoners? Part of the answer – a significant part – was that most of the non-American prisoners were captured after the winter of 1950, when the communists were making greater efforts to keep prisoners alive. But also, 'the army felt that its losses were due not so much to the Communists' disregard of the Geneva Convention – although this was unquestionably contributory,' wrote an American writer who investigated the issue in detail, 'as to the breakdown of discipline among the prisoners themselves. Many men after capture appeared to have lost all sense of allegiance, not only to their country but to their fellow-prisoners.'[23] One in seven of all US prisoners was considered by subsequent army investigations to have been guilty of 'serious collaboration'. The US Army's post-war reports upon the conduct of its own men in captivity inflicted a major trauma. It was felt necessary, in its aftermath, to draw up a Code of Conduct for US servicemen, reminding them of their obligations to their comrades, and to their country, if they fell into the hands of the enemy. It must be a measure of the success achieved by training in prisoner behaviour after Korea that US prisoners in Hanoi conducted themselves, as a group, incomparably better than those in the camps along the Yalu.

The revelation of what the communists had done to the UN prisoners in their hands had a profound influence upon the West's perception of the Korean War, and of the Chinese. For much of the conflict, the men on the line felt little hatred for their Chinese opponents, although the North Koreans enjoyed an unchallenged reputation for barbarism. But the shock of discovery of the plight of the prisoners placed Chinese conduct in a different, infinitely more sinister light. Mao Tse Tung's China acquired a far more frightening and disturbing aspect. From this, arguably, its image in the West never recovered. Long after the Korean War receded into memory, the fear of 'the Manchurian candidate' remained.

16 » ATTRITION: THE WAR ON THE HILLS

Through the last two years of the war, for all the periodic surges of tactical activity, the ferocious struggles which cost thousands of men on both sides their lives in pursuit of hill numbers or map references, the strategic situation in Korea remained unchanged. From time to time, the planners in Washington and Tokyo conceived grand initiatives for airborne drops or amphibious landings behind the enemy flank, designed dramatically to concentrate in Peking minds upon the negotiating table. Among many parallels between Korea and the later experience of Vietnam, as Dr Rosemary Foot has written, was 'the maintenance of the assumption expressed in the 1950s that using increased force can generate concessions at the negotiating table'. The confidence of many American commanders in their ability to smash the Chinese line and reach the Yalu once more, if the leashes were slipped and the UN armies plunged all-out for victory, remained a source of deep frustration. But the political realities ensured that their hopes were stillborn. The American public was weary of Korea. It was narrowly possible to sustain America's national will for the defence of a line across the peninsula until a compromise was reached, for avoiding the concession of defeat to the communists. But the political consequences of any action involving many thousands of casualties – as an all-out offensive must – were intolerable. There was no possibility that America's allies would countenance any dramatic expedient. It was proving difficult enough, diplomatically, to sustain the United Nations' support for a tough bargaining stance at Panmunjom. The possibility of a decisive outcome had vanished in the spring of 1951, when the recall of MacArthur decisively demonstrated Washington's rejection of all-out war with China as the price of victory in Korea. The Western powers were unhappily reconciled to the concept of Korea as a limited war, in which their highest aspiration was to demonstrate that their own will to defend the *status quo ante* would remain unbroken.

For many Americans at home, coming to terms with the limits of their own nation's power was a bitter process. Yet it was much more so for the hundreds of thousands of men in the bunkers and foxholes from sea to sea across the Korean peninsula. Each day, they faced the prospect of death or disablement with pathetically slender prospects of compensating glory, or even respect at home. A British officer spoke of the unhappiness among some of his subordinates in 29 Brigade, when they received letters from their wives at home describing the public indifference towards and ignorance about Korea. In the Second World War, men was sustained by the knowledge that their entire nation, on the home front, was committed to the struggle, and understood what those on the battlefield were seeking to do. The wives of the men in Korea found, instead, that some neighbours inquired clumsily where their husbands were, and showed surprise to be reminded that a war was still being waged in Asia. For the professionals, of course, this was less disturbing. If a British regular soldier was not in Korea, he would be in Malaya, or on the Rhine, or in the deserts of the Middle East. A Frenchman might be in central Africa or Indochina. An American might merely be stagnating at Fort Bragg. Korea offered career soldiers opportunities for combat experience, and for distinction. But for those who were conscripted, the equation was different. British National Servicemen in Korea were irked by the meagre pay they received, alongside that of Regulars sharing the same risks. Death along the 38th Parallel signified the termination of an adult life before it had usefully begun. The Western nations in Korea had borrowed the lives of some thousands of their young men for a cause few of them appreciated. Yet for more than a few, the loan was transformed into permanent confiscation.

In many ways, it was remarkable that the morale of the UN forces held up as well as it did, until the summer of 1953. Private James Stuhler of the US 3rd Division, who later served in Vietnam, remarked that his generation of soldiers had been reared in the 'Yours Not To Reason Why' tradition: 'The army in Korea was much less well informed than the army in Vietnam. In Korea, guys on line read comic books. In Vietnam, you'd see men reading the *Wall Street Journal*. That later generation was better educated, much more questioning. We just got on and did it without thinking much about why we were being asked to do it.'[1] Some officer veterans of both wars suggested another important contrast with Vietnam: 'In Korea, there was nothing to do but fight.' For some miles behind the front, a zone had been systematically cleared of all civilians, so that the defenders could be certain that any unidentified figure was hostile. With dogged cunning, a litter of prostitutes periodically defied the expulsion orders to ply their trade in primitive 'rabbit hutches' a few hundred yards behind the line. A sprinkling of refugees and infiltrators continued to test the vigilance of the outposts, despite the brutal risk that if they fell into South Korean hands and their *bona fides* was suspect, they would be shot out of hand. But for the most part, the forward area remained resolutely military territory, under military discipline. There were no officers' clubs or bars, no drugs or movies or diversions. There were only the mountain ridges, surmounted by the defences which both sides now dug with extraordinary care and caution.

Along most of the line, the United Nations and the Chinese faced each other a mile or so apart, from foxholes and observation posts sited on the forward slopes. But these were no longer the casual scrapes of troops in constant motion across a battlefield: they were fortresses, honeycombs of bunkers and tunnels bored into earth and rock by engineers with bulldozers and pneumatic drills, roofed with steel supports and timber, surmounted by many feet of earth or sandbags. They resembled the diggings of an army of monstrous moles, the setts of a great legion of badgers. Some

were surmounted by carefully emplaced tanks, providing not only
direct fire support, but night illumination from big searchlights
mounted upon their hulls. By day, the only sign of human occupation of the ridge line was an occasional fluttering national flag, or
a defiant gesture by a man recklessly exposing himself on the
skyline. Most men were asleep below ground on bunks woven
from planks and telephone wire, or standing watch at a BC scope
whose lenses filled the narrow firing slit in front of a bunker. 'You
could always tell how dangerous a position was by the size of its
front apertures,' said Sergeant Tom Pentony of the 5th Marines.
'A big aperture meant no one was doing much shooting. A small
aperture meant you were in trouble.'[2] When the World War I
veteran Field-Marshal Lord Alexander visited Korea, he observed at
once that the manner of warfare reminded him of Flanders.

It was only at night that intense muffled activity began, with
men shuffling forward in the darkness to work on improving
defences, or leading patrols through the wire into no-man's-land.
Down the slope from the bunkers, a host of ingenious and intricate
devices had been created and deployed to break the energy of an
assault: wire, minefields, trip flares, booby traps, and a few
uniquely Korean innovations, such as barrels of napalm or white
phosphorus, that could be unleashed and ignited by a wire pulled
from a foxhole. The slightest movement observed or imagined in
no-man's-land attracted the sudden pop and dazzling light of a
flare. For no apparent reason, a sector of the front would suddenly
erupt into an artillery duel that might last for weeks, with men
lying in their bunkers while shells pounded overhead for four, five,
six hours a day. Even the knowledge that the positions could
withstand bombardment on this scale was scant comfort for the
nerves of those within, or for the patience of the unit signallers
who knew that they must emerge, when it was all over, to replace
every telephone wire in the area for the hundredth time of their
tour.

On the reverse slopes behind the position, more open movement was usually possible. Here, company headquarters were sited,

with telephone wires running back to battalion, perhaps a ridge line further to the rear. By day, files of men seemed to be toiling up and down incessantly in the sisyphean labour of moving food, water and ammunition from the nearest point in the valley below that a truck could reach. American or Commonwealth fatigue parties were assisted by hundreds of the inevitable 'Chiggies', the Korean porters with their A-frames on their backs, whose dogged support even under fire became one of the most vivid of all foreign veterans' memories of Korea. Most units spent between two and three months at a time 'on line', before being withdrawn into reserve, or to a rest camp. Even when there was little fighting, it was extraordinary how great remained the strain and exhaustion of maintaining positions, standing watch, mounting patrols. There were aircraft recognition panels to be set out each day in different patterns, laundry to be gathered for the Korean 'dhobie-wallahs', PT sessions in most British units, and always digging, digging, and more digging. It was a modified animal existence. When there were scant facilities for washing, many men did not trouble to shave, and almost relished their shagginess. Some of the British cooked and heated their bunkers, at some personal risk, with tins of petrol. For the men of all the UN formations in winter, life centred upon the precious space heaters that were among the vital weapons of survival. They carried a spoon on a D-ring on their belts as a universal eating tool, occasionally supplemented with a bayonet. They wrote interminable letters home, detailing the tedium of their existences and the weary speculation about the end of the war. After a time, they scarcely noticed the tinny bellow of the propaganda loudspeakers from the Chinese lines: 'Come over, British soldier [or American, or Australian, or Turk, or who-ever he might be], you are on the wrong side!' Radio operators sometimes found a Chinese voice coming up on their frequencies: 'Hello, Tommy. You must be very cold. Missing your wife?' It was all very odd. But young Private Alan Maybury was frightened on his first day in the line, when he heard the communist tannoy proclaim: 'Welcome, 1st Battalion Durham Light Infantry!'[3] The enemy did his best to create a propaganda impression of omniscience.

Amidst it all, there remained the ceaseless danger of a sudden Chinese attack, a night when, without warning, a wave of screaming, bugle-blowing communist infantry would hurl themselves upon the wire, seeking to rush a position before its inhabitants could call down their devastating artillery fire support. Each platoon on each hill lived a self-contained existence, very conscious of its isolation. Few men took off their boots at night, and many slept on top of their sleeping bags rather than inside them, for fear of being surprised. The Commonwealth Division circulated repeated warnings to units about the need never to relax vigilance: '. . . Constant occupation of the same defensive positions tend to make infantry over-confident of their defensive works. Few positions will stand up to concentrated shelling, and many fire bays, weapons and stocks of ammunition are bound to be buried during the softening-up stages of an enemy attack'. '. . . counter-attack troops must be moved into assembly positions immediately there is the slightest real suspicion of an enemy attack, and must be launched BEFORE or AS the enemy penetrates the position. False alarms will be many, but this must be accepted.'[4]

Major John Sloane of the Argylls had formed his knowledge of the Chinese soldier in Burma, 'where they were always half an hour late for the attack'. But those men had been Kuomintang. Their successors of the PLA 'Volunteers' in Korea were vastly different. Western respect for the enemy had increased immeasurably: 'The Chinese infantryman is well-trained, well-equipped and efficient,' declared a Commonwealth Division report. 'He is an excellent night fighter, very brave, with good morale and good at finding his way in the confusion of battle. His limitations are due to lack of equipment and communications. The Chinese are prepared to take casualties and can therefore patrol in strength . . . There is little doubt that the war in Korea has been fought to suit the Chinese. His limitations in communications, his lack of air support and absence of heavy equipment and vehicles would make him a very vulnerable opponent in a war of movement.'⁵

On the night of Sunday 4 November 1951, the Commonwealth Division suffered a characteristic surprise Chinese attack. 1st King's Own Scottish Borderers were manning their positions on Hill 355, seized from the Chinese during Van Fleet's October limited offensive. For three hours, an intense bombardment rained down upon their bunkers. Then, with the usual horn and bugle accompaniment, the Chinese infantrymen stormed through what remained of their protective barbed wire. The KOSB's mortars ran red-hot as they fired their counter-bombardment, until the mortar platoon commander felt compelled to order his men to pour their precious beer ration down the tubes to cool them. Two platoons of B Company were driven from their positions. In the early hours of the morning, the company runner, a vast, slow Cheshireman named Bill Speakman, with a fearsome record of disciplinary offences, clambered to his feet in company headquarters, stuffed his pouches, shirt and pockets with grenades, and strode purposefully out into the darkness. 'And where the hell do you think you're going?' demanded the Company Sergeant-Major. 'Going to shift some of them bloody chinks,' replied Speakman. He charged alone on to the ridge, grenading as he went, then returned for more ammunition. This time, others went with him. After repeated counter-attacks through the night, at first light the KOSB's positions were once more in British hands, at a cost of seven killed, eighty-seven wounded, forty-four missing. Four DSOs were awarded for the night's work. Private Speakman, twice wounded, received the Victoria Cross. The story of his lonely action – and the legend of the alcoholic stimulus that played some part in it – passed into the history of the British Army. The battle? The battle was nothing, in the context of Korea: the kind of local action that units up and down the front found themselves compelled to fight at regular intervals through two years of positional war. If they won, they could pride themselves on a job well done. If they lost, the communists had gained another hill, and some other hapless unit would sooner or later have to pay the price for displacing them from it.

*

The UN troops were frequently impressed by the extraordinary dedication with which many Chinese soldiers would fight, and the lengths to which they would go to avoid being taken prisoner. Wounded communists sometimes struggled to resist the attentions of British or American medical orderlies. Nor did this always appear to be the product of mindless fanaticism, but of skilled indoctrination: 'On the average,' concluded a British intelligence report on deserters, 'the Chinese Communist soldier disposes of more information regarding commanders' plans and intentions than would normally be available to similar ranking soldiers in non-Communist armies. Once again this is believed to be the result of the frequent political meetings, when all ranks are encouraged to discuss future operations, even to the extent of criticising commanders' plans.'[6]

The familiar military routine of briefing took on a new meaning in Chinese hands. It was an article of faith among the leaders of the PLA's 'Volunteers' in Korea that hours each week were devoted to before and after action discussions on tactics, and political education. Such familiar slogans as 'Aid Korea to Fight America and Defend Our Motherland'; 'Love the Korean People, Love Everything in Korea', provided texts for regular harangues in a fashion not so very different from that in which verses from the Bible armed Christian padres for their sermons. It remains a measure of the success of political indoctrination that it proved so difficult for the UN forces to take prisoners, and that defectors remained few in number, despite the torrent of propaganda leaflets, promising good treatment, with which the UN deluged the Chinese lines.

For the communists, life on the line was troglodyte in an even more absolute fashion than for the UN. The UN's command of the air made it possible for its soldiers to move with relative freedom during daylight, as long as they were out of direct sight of the enemy. The Chinese had no artillery ammunition to waste upon random barrages. For Peng's men, however, every inch of territory in the forward areas was under constant threat from the air. Camouflage became an obsession, for they knew that if the Americans observed even a single moving figure in the open, a devastating barrage of bombs or artillery would follow. The Chinese lived, until darkness fell and often beyond, in the incredible honeycomb of tunnels that they created along their front, exceeding all that mechanical ingenuity achieved on the UN side. 'The tunnel became a great Chinese institution,' Hu Seng, one of Marshal Peng's staff, said wryly. Within its confines, the men of the 'Volunteers' passed their day in a mirror image of life on the UN side: listening to Peking Radio; reading; playing poker; singing and dancing to music made on Chinese violins, and instruments fashioned out of shell cases. Many men who went to Korea as illiterates used the opportunity lent to them by boredom, to learn to read and write in the flickering candlelight beneath the mountains. Disease, in those dripping caverns, was a chronic problem. Fever thrived in summer, and men welcomed the healthier chill of winter. If they were ill, or wounded, they depended upon traditional Chinese herbal remedies for a cure. Modern drugs were almost non-existent. Many men, much of the time, went hungry.

The Chinese suffered almost as acutely from the sense of distance from home as the men of the UN. 'Because we were fighting abroad, it was more difficult to sustain morale than during the Liberation War,' said Li Ben Wen, a regimental propaganda officer.[7] Few men even possessed a photograph of their families, for cameras were a rare luxury. Once a fortnight, they might receive mail from home – letters written, for the most part, by their village's professional letter-writer. Leave was almost unknown. Rarely, a man might be allowed to visit his village for compassionate reasons, if a close family member died. Wang Zhu Guang, a staff officer at 23rd Army Group, spent six years in Korea, and went home only twice. His wife, a factory worker, sent him such occasional remittances as she could spare from the upkeep of herself and their small daughter. Wang, like the rest of the 'Volunteers', received negligible pay, supplemented by cigarettes.

In assault, the Chinese specialised in infiltration and envelopment, at least one attacking group making immediately for the defenders' line of reinforcement. Thus, all-round defence was essential. As the war progressed, organisation and training improved markedly, with rehearsals for attacks being carried out behind the lines. Messages were passed in plain language over such radios as they possessed, or more often, by telephone. 'Encirclement and deep penetration are standard,' in the words of a British assessment of Chinese tactics.

The Chinese claimed to find *met juin* – the Americans – less formidable foes than the Japanese – 'they lacked the fighting will of the Japanese,' according to Li Hebei of the 587th Regiment. The communists developed night fighting to a fine art, because only in darkness could they overcome the overwhelming problem of UN air superiority. As the war progressed, their anti-aircraft capability increased dramatically: 35mm, 37mm, 100mm guns provided by the Soviets. 'We also became more and more experienced in dealing with "choke points",' said Wang Zhu Guang. 'We became accustomed to the way the Americans would bomb in fixed places at fixed times, and more skilled in moving trucks during the intervals.' Asked what shortages the Chinese felt most acutely, he replied unhesitatingly, 'aircraft'. The size of China's forces in Korea was restricted by the number of men for whom supplies could be moved south across the Yalu. Manpower as such was never a problem: thus the vast, ruthless sacrifice of lives in attack. 'We suffered very heavy casualties,' conceded Wang Zhu Guang, 'but it was worth it. We won the battle.'[8] More objective observers might reject his assessment. Even many Chinese officers today appear to look back on the crude, costly tactics of the Korean period with some embarrassment.

*

On the UN side of the line, opinion varied from unit to unit about the scale of risk that was acceptable in pursuit of the domination of no-man's-land by night. Among the Americans, Southerners often seemed the most enthusiastic soldiers. There was a West Virginian in PFC Mario Scarselleta's platoon of the 35th Infantry who was constantly volunteering for patrols: 'He'd say: "Oh Lord, please send over fifty gooks!" He loved it. I wish we'd had 50,000 like him, so the rest of us could have gone home.' Many men felt infinitely less inclined to take risks after the armistice negotiations began. 'It made it awfully hard to get people to do things, to go out on patrol,' said Corporal Bill Patterson of the 27th Infantry. 'A man would just say, "Aw, I'm on short time."'⁹ The British placed a high premium upon patrolling, in the interests of unit morale. The Commonwealth Division customarily occupied some nine miles of the line, each of its three brigades deploying one battalion back in reserve. Every unit organised frequent two- or three-day 'lie-up' patrols, and fifteen-man fighting patrols, supported by a 'flying squad' which remained on alert in the unit lines all night, ready to reinforce the men in the field if they got into trouble. But as a British report admitted: 'The enemy advantage of numbers means that in patrol battles, he almost always ends up dominating the ground, thus getting his own casualties out.'¹⁰

The British considered it essential to keep men occupied, to fight off boredom and monotony. Some official expedients were merely mildly comical, such as firing red, white, and blue smoke at the Chinese lines on Queen Elizabeth's coronation day. Others were more homicidal, such as maintaining an all-out artillery 'hate' on the enemy lines throughout May Day. Unit war diaries record a long procession of minor operations such as 'Operation POLECAT, 16–23 February 1953: sweep divisional area for enemy guerrillas; only a few civilians were apprehended.'¹¹ At night, men on line could see from miles away the barrage balloons floodlit by search-lights that marked the Panmunjom compound, where peace was being daily debated. These gave an added unreality to the little battles to the death in no-man's-land. In Korea, even professional soldiers encountered, for the first time in their lives, the pernicious difficulties of fighting in circumstances in which lives lost so often seemed wasted. Captain Peter Sibbald, a staff officer with the Commonwealth Division, reflected upon the sensation he and his colleagues encountered a decade later, fighting in the Radfan mountains in the last days of the British presence in Aden: 'We felt then: "Nothing we can do here is worth a single guardsman's life." The beginning of that insidious doctrine was in Korea.'[12]

Yet because it was plainly indefensible to expend men's lives except in pursuit of worthwhile objectives – whatever these might be – senior commanders in Korea also faced serious difficulty in checking the ambitions of professional soldiers who came to the country bent upon achieving a battlefield reputation. There were not a few American major-generals who arrived to take over divisions for a tour in the line, and had to be decisively checked in their determination to mount an attack in order to further their own careers. An officer came to assume command of a brigade of the Commonwealth Division, with an outstanding reputation for courage earned as a battalion commander in World War II: 'brave as a lion', as one of his colleagues said of him. Yet as a brigadier in Korea, his offensive instincts, his determination to carry the war to the enemy, appalled his subordinates. When he organised an attack on the Chinese positions which they believed would decimate their units, his battalion commanders protested strongly to the divisional commander. The brigadier was quietly relieved of his post. By the standards of conventional war, his enthusiasm was admirable. By those of Korea, it was merely foolish. Lieutenant Paul Sheehy of the US 7th Division reflected the feelings of many UN soldiers about over-zealous officers when he wrote to his parents in Maine in June 1952:

> We have a new battalion commander who is a 'son of a gun'. He came over to Korea in Sept 1950 when the division landed at Inchon, and he refuses to go home. He came over as a master sgt and is now a major. He is crazy for power and loves war. I

believe he is actually crazy and should be sent home to a hospital. He talks with a gleam in his eyes about the killing of Chinks in the coming operation. He hasn't any heart, and sent a brand-new 2nd lt., fresh from the States, out on a patrol the night he came to the battalion. And this crazy man is in charge. The high brass think he is No. 1 soldier. Boy will I be glad to get out of this outfit, I've sure had enough of Korea,

God bless you both, your loving son,

PAUL[13]

The British Commander-in-Chief in the Far East, General Sir Charles Keightley, visited Korea in April 1952 and reported to the War Office that 'the views of commanders there from top to bottom are really all in line: that the Chinese communist policy is directed from Moscow, and a forecast as to what will happen is as unpredictable as the rest of their actions throughout the world. The majority guess that it will be a stalemate. This sort of war, where the enemy is prepared to launch attacks apparently quite regardless of whether the losses are worth the objective, is a new one to us, and produces some quite new lines of thought. I was much impressed by the fact that the Chinese was showing himself a very skilful as well as tough fighter.'[14] Keightley described the main tactical problem as enemy infiltration at night, which was being met by 'wiring on the 1914–18 standards, thickened up with mines'. He was impressed with the men's morale, but dismayed by the extent of the chronic problem of venereal disease throughout the American and Commonwealth contingents. Keightley suggested making the cure more unpleasant, 'reintroducing some of the pre-war methods instead of penicillin'. The UN Command was constantly preoccupied with the problem of staleness among the men on the line: 'Ridgway says that if he had his way, he would change every man, divisional commanders included, every 90 days!' Senior officers were exasperated by the number of gunshot accidents in formal areas: an army doctor visiting a hospital found fifty-nine cases resulting from enemy action, and twenty-four accidental gunshot wounds, 'the great majority of which were self-inflicted'.[15] It was so in every war of this kind, that for every man who died facing the enemy, another was killed in some wretched truck accident, bar brawl behind the lines, mishap with munitions, or fatal step into an unmarked minefield. The static campaign in Korea was justly described as a platoon commander's war, because so much of the fighting followed small unit encounters in no-man's-land. Some units awarded seven days' leave to any man who could bring in a prisoner, and patrols went to extraordinary lengths to achieve this ambition, cutting Chinese telephone wires and then laying ambushes for the wiring parties that came to repair them, spending night after night with coshes clutched in their hands, awaiting an opportunity. One night, Lieutenant John Bowler of the Welch Regiment was lying out on a forward slope with a four-man reconnaissance patrol when by the light of flares they saw a long file of twenty-five Chinese padding silently past them. Half went by before one enemy soldier glanced and saw them. The darkness exploded in a hail of machine-gun fire. All four of the British soldiers' notoriously unreliable sten guns jammed. As they ran desperately for their own lines, three were hit and went down. The patrol lay mute, the wounded men struggling to keep silent in their pain, while the Chinese searched the surrounding area. They found one British soldier, and shot him. Bowler escaped, and was able to summon a stretcher party to recover the other two casualties.

Bowler was one of many young conscript officers who found the experience of National Service, even on the Korean battlefield, intensely challenging and rewarding. Like most British soldiers, he scarcely troubled himself about the great issues for which the war was being fought, but focused his thoughts overwhelmingly on his unit. The regiment and its totems meant much. When the Welch arrived in Hong Kong en route to Korea, halfway through an acclimatisation route march, the goat that was the unit mascot collapsed. For superstitious soldiers, the prospect of its death when the battalion was on its way to war was unbearable. The beast was carried home on a stretcher, and the goat-major nursed it night and day for four days until at last, to the vast relief of the whole unit, it staggered to its feet again.

The biggest action in which the nineteen-year-old Bowler participated during his service in Korea was a platoon-strength local attack. But amid so many weeks of tedium and inactivity, such miniature battles took on a significance far beyond their size, and attracted the attention of generals. The Commonwealth Division was constantly on its mettle, keen to demonstrate its professionalism. Bowler's thirty-man fighting patrol spent three days rehearsing their little operation behind the lines. On the afternoon of D-Day, the Chinese position they were to raid was softened up by an air strike, while the guns ranged in. At H-Hour, the platoon advanced across no-man's-land and up the enemy ridge in textbook extended arrowhead formation, two sections forward. They ran into the Chinese positions grenading as they went. A swarm of enemy soldiers scuttled out of the bunkers to meet them, and the British retired to their firm base, from whence they called down artillery fire. They went home having suffered one minor casualty, and had a radio operator blown off his feet by a grenade. The next morning, on the far side of the 400-yard-deep belt of wire fronting their own position, they saw a Chinese officer, demanding attention and indeed asylum. It emerged that he was the commander of the position the British had attacked, and his performance had attracted sufficient unfavourable attention from his superiors to make captivity an attractive alternative.

Yet even when a unit was not committed to offensive action, the strain of life on the line, and above all of patrolling, was considerable. John Bowler found one of his corporals, a married man with two children, sitting one day in a corner sobbing. The man said he would prefer to fight a battle and get it over, than sit each day under shellfire, wondering when an attack might come. The corporal, like most other such cases, was generously treated, and dispatched to become an instructor at a battle school in Japan. There was only one period, of intense cold and boredom, when the

whole platoon's morale seemed dangerously low. The young subaltern's platoon sergeant, a veteran of the Burma campaign, said
to him: 'Mr Bowler, sir. We've got a problem. The men have
stopped grousing. We've got to get them grousing again.' They
gradually restored the situation by summoning the men into their
biggest bunker for a daily 'bellyache'.[16]

Relations between the British and their American comrades
were generally cordial, encouraged by the characteristic, almost
embarrassing generosity of the US soldiers. 'Somebody said something one day to an American officer about liking their fruit juice
and behold, the next day a truckload of the stuff arrived,' said a
British sapper. The British liked to do things their own way,
preferring cap comforters or berets to helmets unless under direct
fire, unenthusiastic about American food. Some families in
rationed Britain were bemused to receive letters from their sons
amidst the privations of the Korean battlefield, complaining about
the surfeit of turkey at meals. As late as September 1951, in
England the butter ration was three ounces a week, bacon three
ounces, cheese one and a half ounces. Royal Marines of 41 Commando, gorging themselves on steaks aboard US assault ships on
their way to coastal raids on North Korea, astonished their American hosts by telling them that at every meal, they were eating a
British family's meat ration for a week. The British possessed the
belief in their own superiority which is a reasonable measure of
professional pride in any national army. But to this was added a
half-conscious, unhappy awareness of how far Britain had fallen in
the world by the early fifties. The generation of British soldiers
that fought in Korea had grown up amid their nation's possession
of the greatest empire the world had ever seen. Britain had borne
a far greater share of World War II's casualties than the United
States. Yet young British soldiers, now venturing overseas for the
first time in their lives, sadly perceived their shrunken greatness.
'You must remember that when we started soldiering, we assumed
the Empire would just go on and on,' said Brigadier William Pike
of the Commonwealth Division.[17] Yet now, men on leave in Japan

saw brand-new British cars that were unobtainable in rationed, austerity Britain being driven by their recent enemies. Major Gerald Rickord of the Royal Ulster Rifles was superintending the erection of tent lines one day, above which the British had hoisted a sign, 'BRITANNIA CAMP'. A GI lolling nearby poked his cigar towards it, and demanded of Rickord: 'Britannia? What's that?' 'Haven't you ever heard of "Britannia Rules the Waves"?' said the Ulsterman in astonishment. 'That's a bit out of date, isn't it?' said the American. Rickord was dismayed by the little encounter: 'I was saddened by how far we had come down in the world.'[18] Many of the British of his generation, serving as infinitely junior partners to the Americans in Korea, found the experience of decline too recent not to gaze somewhat sidelong at the new dominant force on the globe, and cherish unworthy thoughts about how much better the old team had done it. An American unit in the Commonwealth Division area posted a sign over its camp entrance, proclaiming itself 'SECOND TO NONE'. The Australian radio relay station a few hundred yards further down posted a sign proclaiming itself 'NONE'.

> *If there are any two things that I can't stand*

ran a characteristic little ditty in the Commonwealth Division news-sheet, *Crown News*,

> *It's a North Korean and a Chinaman.*
> *We're moving on, we're moving on.*
>
> *See the Chinks coming up 355,*
> *The Yanks pulling out in overdrive,*
> *They're moving on, they're moving on.*

The last verse, of course, referred to a hill crest the Americans had allegedly abandoned without reasonable cause. From General Cassels downwards, the Commonwealth Division argued that it was more economical to hold a position under attack than to adopt the American tactic of maintaining only a light screen in forward

positions, which gave ground under pressure and demanded a
set-piece counter-attack in strength to regain. A British company
commander who found himself posted alongside the Turkish
Brigade was exasperated to receive constant phone calls from its
liaison officer, accustomed to take a sceptical view of American
tactics, demanding: 'You still there, Tommy? You still there?' The
Englishman assented crossly, adding 'and let us be clear that we
have not the slightest intention of going.' Brigadier William Pike,
Cassels' CRA, said: 'It is a paradox that the British like Americans
very much, but do not have great respect for them as soldiers.'[19]
Pike and many of his British colleagues, with their reluctance to
accept casualties in pursuit of objectives which seemed to lack any
wider strategic value, much disliked the local attacks they were
periodically called upon to mount:

> If one had wanted to finish that campaign, it would have been
> perfectly possible to concentrate a corps and drive through.
> Instead, we would be asked merely to capture some hill. The
> Chinese would allow us to get on top, then retire into their
> bunkers while they called down mortar and artillery fire. These
> small attacks seemed to us singularly expensive. It would have
> been far more logical militarily to mount one good, big set-
> piece attack which could have taken us to the Yalu.[20]

But by 1952, the war in Korea was not an exercise of military logic,
but of national will.

*

Spring came with dramatic suddenness to Korea. The thaw followed by the monsoon rains played havoc with the fabric of
laboriously dug positions. Yet this was the most welcome, indeed
perhaps the only really enjoyable, season in Korea. The hillsides
burst forth in a riot of colours. Men were astonished by the speed
with which vegetation grew, and by the variety and profusion of
wild flowers. Then, with the coming of summer, the heat became
crippling. Western soldiers toiling up the mountainsides under

loads envied the infinitely greater endurance and carrying power of the little Korean porters. Infection and disease prospered in the damp warmth of the bunkers. The insects proved marginally more endurable than the stink of the repellent issued to suppress them, which was principally employed to soak rifle patches and make night lights. Rats scurried among the garbage behind the positions, and often in the tunnels beneath them. Some fortunate units possessed streams near enough to hand, and sufficiently screened from hostile observation, to wash. Those who did not were periodically ferried to the rear for showers. But most men were coated in sweat-soaked dirt most of their time on line. NCOs checked feet and socks to guard against chronic foot infections. Dust coated weapons, vehicles, food, clothing. Men in the forward positions counted off the days until they were rotated into reserve. But when their turn came, and they found themselves facing the same discomforts a few miles to the rear, constantly employed on fatigue parties, yet earning only half as many points towards their release date, they began to feel that it was better to be on line. Even the hardiest Chinese soldiers in the opposing positions declared that the Korean summer was unbearable.

Until winter came, that is. Then, as men plodded between positions with the studied clumsiness of spacemen, movements muffled by innumerable layers of clothing, they gazed in awed disbelief as the thermometers plunged to new depths. Starting a vehicle engine became a major undertaking. Laying or clearing mines was a nightmare in the frozen earth. The British cursed their ridiculous 1939-vintage 'Finnish pattern' snowboots, their inadequate camouflaged windproofs. The gunners found that the range of their weapons could vary by as much as 2,000 yards, according to the air temperature. An hour of carelessness in exposing a corner of flesh to the naked air was punished by frostbite. They experimented with hand warmers, foot warmers, belts stuffed with body warmers. They relieved the monotony of the rations by shooting the quail, pheasants and ducks which populated the countryside in such profusion. They devised crude practical jokes to make each other laugh – putting an electrical charge through a latrine seat by attaching it to a communication wire, lighting the ends of a screwed-up newspaper between a sleeping man's toes. But there were pitifully few trees to chop for firewood, pathetically few diversions beyond lying on one's back in a bunker listening to Hank Snow singing 'Moving On', Patti Page or Teresa Brewer, Connie Stevens or Eddie Fisher heart-throbbing across the air waves from a real world a planet away. All the UN forces observed a 'one winter' rule in Korea. No man, it was decreed, should be asked to endure more than one season of that terrible cold in the forward areas.

Perhaps once in a tour, most men were granted a week's 'R & R' – 'Rest & Recuperation' – which almost all of them spent in Japan. The memory of Japan in the early fifties is the most lyrical that most veterans brought back from Korea. 'At that time,' said Brigadier William Pike, 'it really did still have something of the romance of the Orient.' Men who sought a civilised release from the barbarities of the line found it in Japan, together with a real friendliness and kindness from the Japanese. For the British, it was a little painful to see recent enemies already in possession of consumer goods that were unobtainable in their own country, food beyond the dreams of rationed families in London or Glasgow.

But most men went to Japan seeking, above all, a woman and a drink. Many retained, until the end of their lives, memories of the bargirls they met there. A man stepped off the transport from Seoul, took the truck into town, and made a bargain with a girl for the three, four, five days he was at liberty: 'It was the land of the big PX,' said Private Warren Avery of the 29th Infantry. 'You drove to the Hotel Sun, got a girl, a room, and all the beer you could drink for five days for sixty dollars. I fell in love with Japan.'[21] So did hundreds of thousands of UN servicemen who fought in Korea. And for Japan itself, the war provided a staggering economic opportunity. The first, critical phase in the creation of Japan Inc. was made possible by the wealth the Korean War poured into the country, when it served as aircraft carrier, repair base, store depot,

commissariat, hospital, headquarters and recreation centre for the
United Nations force in the Far East.

*

In February 1953, Van Fleet handed over command of Eighth Army
in Korea to the veteran paratrooper Maxwell Taylor. The outgoing
general disappeared into retirement with bitter complaints that he
had been prevented from launching an all-out offensive to drive
the Chinese out of Korea once and for all. His frustration was
widely shared by other senior officers. It seemed profoundly unsol-
dierlike, to that generation which had come to maturity during
World War II in which defeat and victory were absolutes, to allow
an army to stagnate upon the mountains of Korea, restricted to
patrolling. Van Fleet was probably correct in believing that, with
the vast firepower at his disposal, the Chinese line could have been
breached and eventually rolled up. But such a campaign would
have cost many thousands of UN casualties. There was never the
remotest possibility that Washington or the Allied capitals would
entertain the plan. Yet the last months of the war saw some of the
fiercest fighting since the 1951 spring offensive. The Chinese made
a series of determined attempts to test the UN's will on the
battlefield, as negotiations at Panmunjom reached a critical stage.
On each occasion, they were thrown back; but only after bitter
struggles.

'Old Baldy', a hilltop in the midst of the peninsula that possessed no special strategic significance, nonetheless became the
focus of intense Chinese offensive effort in the summer and
autumn of 1952. In March 1953, at last they gained possession of
it after the collapse of a Colombian regiment rashly entrusted with
its defence. Taylor was reluctant to lavish lives upon its recapture.
But the communists quickly made it clear that they proposed to
make use of the advantage that they had gained, to advance
another bound: Old Baldy overlooked a feature named Pork Chop
Hill, garrisoned by two under-strength platoons of the 31st Infantry
of 7th Division. Soon after 10 p.m. on the night of 16 April 1953,

an American patrol moving into the valley between Pork Chop and the enemy positions opposite encountered two companies of Chinese sweeping forward to assault the hill. Within minutes, the ninety-six Americans on Pork Chop found themselves isolated under furious attack. The lieutenant in command lost radio and telephone contact with the rear, and summoned emergency artillery cover by flare. But when the barrage at last lifted, the Chinese stormed forward again. By 2 a.m., they held most of the hill. Two hours later, an American counter-attack managed to link with the surviving defenders on the high ground, but was not strong enough to recapture the lost positions.

All through the next day, some fifty-five Americans clung to their precarious foothold on Pork Chop, pinned down by the Chinese. At Eighth Army, the decision was made that at all costs, American dominance of the position must be re-established. It was essential that the communist delegation at Panmunjom should be denied the opportunity to claim a victory on the battlefield. At 9.30 p.m. on the night of 17 April, two companies of the 17th Infantry struck the western end of the feature from both sides. The battle continued all through the following day, with a stream of reinforcements being thrown in by both sides. By the night of 18 April, the Chinese had conceded tactical defeat. They withdrew their surviving elements from Pork Chop, while the Americans began an intensive struggle to rebuild the defences before the next assault came.

The battle for Pork Chop continued at bitter intensity deep into the summer of 1953. The US garrison on its blasted slopes grew to five battalions, under incessant communist mortar and artillery fire. On 10 July, a fortnight before the armistice was signed, Taylor and his commanders concluded that the cost of maintaining it, still under constant surveillance from Old Baldy, outweighed even the moral benefits. It was evacuated. The struggle for Pork Chop became part of the legend of the US Army in Korea, reflecting the courage of the defenders and the tactical futility of so many small unit actions of the kind that dominated the last two years of the war. It was said that there were eleven stars' worth of American generals at the regimental headquarters behind Pork Chop at the height of the battle. The divisional commander, Arthur Trudeau, won a Silver Star for personally leading a counter-attack battalion reconnaissance party on to Pork Chop under fire, after switching helmets with his driver. Some of the Allies were deeply sceptical about the price the Americans paid to regain the position. General Mike West, who succeeded Cassels in command of the Commonwealth Division, was asked what he would have done to recapture it, and answered: 'Nothing. It was only an outpost.' But this view reflected, yet again, the interminable conflict between military reason and political interest.

A succession of almost equally bitter battles was conducted for possession of a ridge within a few miles of the western coast of Korea, named 'The Hook'. On the night of 26 October 1952, the US 7th Marines fought a successful defensive action under the most unfavourable conditions. Thereafter, the Hook passed into the hands of the Commonwealth Division. The British lost more casualties on its steep flanks than on any other single battlefield in Korea. The 1st Black Watch fought the second Hook battle on 18 November 1952. The third battle, in late May 1953, was a much more protracted affair, of which the brunt fell on the 1st Duke of Wellington's Regiment. On each occasion, the Hook was the object of a set-piece Chinese night attack. 'It was a sore thumb, bang in the middle of Genghis Khan's old route into Korea,' said Major Lewis Kershaw of the Duke of Wellington's Regiment, one of the men who defended the position, 'it commanded an enormous amount of ground.'[22] Kershaw was a quiet-spoken forty-year-old Yorkshireman, who much regretted having spent World War II in inactivity, garrisoning Iceland and suchlike. He was commanding the Support Company of his battalion, which arrived in Korea in October 1952. Every platoon's establishment of weapons was dramatically increased when manning a sensitive sector like the Hook. Each man on the position knew that at any time, the Chinese could come.

On the night of 28 May 1953, Kershaw and his comrades were warned by the intense mortar and artillery bombardment that an attack was imminent. At 7.50 p.m., he himself had just come forward from the Battalion Command Post to D Company's positions, where it had been decided to send out a patrol, which he would control. Suddenly, the screams and bugles in the darkness told them the Chinese were coming. The defenders began to pour small-arms fire forward down the hill. Kershaw and the others in the forward platoon headquarters had to stumble out of the bunker into the trenches as it began to collapse under a succession of direct hits. Chinese soldiers were dropping in amongst them. There was a fierce short-range exchange of grenades. Alongside Kershaw, a conscientious, fresh-faced little National Service subaltern named Ernest Kirk was hit by a burst of burp-gun fire as he threw a grenade, and fell dead at Kershaw's feet. Kirk was twenty-one, a few weeks short of demob. He was planning to leave the army and become a school sports master. The defenders had been warned that if their position was overrun, British DF artillery fire would be called down upon it. When the shells began to land among the trenches, Kershaw swung himself down a ladder into an ammunition store as a Chinese stun grenade landed beside him. His legs and buttocks were peppered with fragments, his helmet blown off, his sten gun blasted out of his hands.

Kershaw staggered back into the trench above, grabbed his platoon sergeant's sten gun, and propped himself against the earth wall to remain upright. Fighting against spasms of blindness and unconsciousness, he tossed a few more grenades, then stumbled into a cave and fell down. When he came to, he found himself alongside four Korean 'Katcoms'. His leg was useless and bleeding. Clumsily, he tied a tourniquet with a bootlace. Then they lay in silence, Kershaw drifting in and out of consciousness, while the British artillery bombardment hammered the hill above their heads. Communications between D Company's forward positions and the rear had been shattered. Along the Dukes' front, most of the defenders were now trapped in tunnels and bunkers by earth-falls or shelling. After a time, Kershaw asked a Korean to look out and see if it was dawn. The man replied that he could see nothing, though Kershaw doubted that he had dared to put his head above ground level. A second man went, and returned to report that the Chinese were no longer on the position. An hour later, the company commander found them. Kershaw was dragged out on a ground-sheet, and transferred to a jeep at the foot of the Hook. His lower leg was amputated before he was put on a train to Seoul.

At first light on 29 May, the British surveyed the customary chaotic aftermath of battle on the Korean hills: positions painstakingly hacked out of the earth over months were flattened or caved in, the ground blackened and the scanty foliage stripped by bombardment. The forward area was littered with fragments of wire and shreds of sandbags, ammunition boxes and debris. The Dukes had suffered 149 casualties, including twenty-nine killed and sixteen taken prisoner. They estimated Chinese casualties at 250 dead and 800 wounded. It required hours of digging to extricate men buried by shelling. Soon after daybreak, communist artillery fire began again. Another battalion relieved the battered Dukes on the Hook, in expectation of another infantry attack. This never came. The Chinese had been too badly battered the previous night. The Dukes had mounted a fine defence for a battalion three-quarters composed of National Service conscripts, rewarded by a grateful country with the princely sum of £1.62 a week.

*

In the last months of the war, the names of the hills Carson, Vegas, and Reno became forever identified with the US Marine Corps, which fought so hard to retain them. Sergeant Tom Pentony was an artillery forward observer with the 5th Marines. He had found boot camp untroublesome after the rigours of a Catholic upbringing in New Jersey, 'where the nuns taught you that you would die as a martyr if you went fighting communism'. On 26 March 1953, Pentony was with the 3/5th behind Vegas, when the Chinese overran the American 'Combat Outposts', and the Marines went in to retake the position. Pentony watched, appalled, as the Americans fought their way up the hill under punishing Chinese fire: 'I used to think officers were smart. Now I felt: "This is stupid. Do they have any plan?" They just seemed to think: "The Marines will take that hill, frontal assault, that's it." '[23] On the afternoon of 27 March, Pentony's senior gunner officer, a major, was so appalled by the spectacle of infantry still struggling forward, having lost all their own officers, that he received special permission to go forward and lead them himself. His radio operator returned two days later with the dead major's pistol and watch. The March battles for Carson, Reno and Vegas cost the Marine Corps 116 men killed out of a total of over a thousand casualties, and inspired some of the most remarkable feats of American courage to come out of the Korean War.

Pentony found that his own mood, his attitude to the war, vacillated greatly from day to day: 'It was like indigestion: some days you felt very brave, nothing bothered you, sounds at night didn't worry you. Then on other days, for no special reason you were scary, jumpy – the smallest thing bothered you.' The atmosphere on the Marine positions was consciously 'macho' by comparison with that in the army lines. When the Chinese propaganda loudspeakers began to blare forth their raucous messages with their customary exhortation: 'American soldiers and officers!' the Marines at once interrupted to shout back: 'We're not soldiers! We're Marines!' Many men were reluctant to be switched out of the line into reserve, not only because they were earning fewer points towards their day of release, but because reserve units were nagged by training and inspections, and were still liable to be called forward to fill sandbags and dig trenches, often more dangerously exposed than the men on line.

The American points system was regarded as one of the most pernicious innovations of the campaign: a man needed thirty-six to go home; on line, he earned four a month; in the combat zone, three; in country but beyond reach of enemy action, two. Thus, most men serving with an American combat formation might expect to go home after about a year in Korea, while support personnel served eighteen months. It was a discipline which earned intense dislike among professional soldiers and commanders, because it caused men to become increasingly cautious and reluctant to accept risk as they grew 'short', and approached release date. It militated strongly against the unit cohesion the British achieved, by shipping men in and out of Korea by battalions, because each soldier focused upon the schedule of his own tour in country. Yet the system persisted in Vietnam throughout the sixties, with equally negative effects upon the US Army there.

*

Private James Stuhler was a New York high school drop-out who had run away to join the Marines at sixteen, been sent home again, and finally went to Korea for the last few months of the war with the 3rd Division, in the Kunwa Valley. An initial irony struck him on his way to the front, when the truck in which he and his draft of replacements were being carried forward was stopped and booked by the military police for speeding. Even at this late stage of the war, the routines and strains of life and death on the line were undiminished. They spent their first days in new positions digging incessantly, for the only contribution the unit they relieved had made to its own defence was to hang out a Chinese skull on a long pole. A squad leader in his platoon, obsessed with fear of being killed, deliberately put a bullet through his own hand. To pass the time, they fitted a telescopic sight on a .50 calibre machine gun, stabilised its tripod with sandbags, and sought to snipe at Chinese forward observers.

Then their company commander, an eager young first lieutenant, planned a raid to relieve the monotony. It went disastrously wrong. During their advance through the darkness, they walked into the American covering bombardment. Dankowski, their platoon leader, was killed almost immediately. 'O'B, what the f– are we going to do?' Stuhler cried desperately to O'Brien, their radio operator. The Chinese were now firing into them, hitting their squad leader as he ran along a ridge line. Stuhler's machine gun jammed. He pulled out a .45 pistol and fired in sheer fear and frustration. To his horror, he found that he had narrowly missed shooting an American lying in front of him. Then a rock splinter struck him on the finger, numbing his entire arm. A grenade exploded, horribly wounding his fellow machine-gunner in the face. Stuhler looked in horror at the man's eye, hanging loose from its socket. 'Pull back! Pull back!' shouted O'Brien among the chaos of explosion and pyrotechnics now breaking up the night sky. Discipline collapsed as they stumbled away into the valley towards their own lines. Stuhler hastily wrapped a field dressing on his companion's ragged face, and told the man to hold his collar while he guided him out. His helmet had fallen off, and a moment later he was stunned by a flying rock hitting him on the head. The New Yorker never knew how he got back. He and his companion waded chest-high through a creek, and were told later that they had walked through a minefield. Towards dawn, a sudden burst of machine-gun fire ripped over the exhausted men's heads. They threw themselves flat, the wounded man groaning: 'We're gonna get killed! We're gonna get killed!' Stuhler yelled to the Americans in front of him to hold their fire. They dragged the casualty in. 'Oh for Chrissake, will you look at this guy?' said the shocked medical orderly who examined his face. The victim was still conscious, and Stuhler said furiously, 'You're not supposed to say things like that.' Around half the platoon which had set out were dead or wounded. Stuhler received a Bronze Star for bringing back his buddy. To their fury, the company commander, who had never left the lines, was awarded a Silver Star. The battalion area was named Camp Dankowski, in memory of their squandered platoon commander. This pathetic little drama unfolded barely a month before the armistice was signed. Of such stuff was the armies' weary disillusion with the Korean War made, by the summer of 1953.

17 » THE PURSUIT OF PEACE

1. Koje-do

No aspect of the Korean War was more grotesque than the manner in which the struggle was allowed to continue for a further sixteen months after the last substantial territorial obstacle to an armistice had been removed by negotiation, in February 1952. From that date until the end in July 1953, on the line men endured the miseries of summer heat and winter cold; were maimed by mines and crippled by napalm, small arms and high explosive; while at Panmunjom the combatants wrangled around one bitterly contentious issue: the post-armistice exchange of prisoners.

Long after both sides had forsaken any hope of achieving decisive territorial gains on the battlefield, the impulse towards gaining a moral victory – or at least, avoiding a moral defeat – persisted. In the matter of the prisoners, there were two vital objectives for the UN Command: first, to gain the return to freedom of every man of their own held by the communists; and second, among Chinese and Korean prisoners held in the South, to ensure that only willing prisoners were returned to communist hands. The memory of Yalta, of hundreds of thousands of doomed, desperate Russians being herded by the Western Allies back into the bloody maw of Stalin in 1945, hung heavy over the governments of the West.

The first list of prisoners in communist hands given to the UN Command on 18 December 1951 contained just 11,559 names. Yet in March 1951, Peking and Pyongyang had claimed to be holding

65,000 captives. Even by communist standards, this was a huge discrepancy. Apart from South Korean captives, it left more than 8,000 missing Americans unaccounted for. The Chinese claimed that thousands of ROK army prisoners had been allowed to go home, and that the unlisted foreigners had died, escaped, been killed in air raids or released at the front. But Peking can never have supposed that this explanation would be acceptable in South Korea or the United States.

Even more contentious and complex, however, was the fate of the communist prisoners in UN hands. From the standpoint of Peking and Pyongyang, it was a matter of immense importance that all these should be seen to return to the bosom of the peoples' republics. The propaganda cost of many thousands being seen to 'choose freedom', to decline repatriation, appeared intolerable. On 2 April 1951, the communist delegation at Panmunjom demanded that the UN Command should prepare lists of prisoners willing to return north. To the astonishment of both delegations, only 70,000 of the total of 132,000 signified acceptance of repatriation. There was no possibility that such a situation could be accepted by the communist governments. A long, wretched struggle of wills began, in which the attention of the world became focused upon the vast UN prison compounds on the offshore islands of South Korea.

*

Until the war was well advanced, Koje-do remained one of the prettiest possessions of South Korea. A little fishing community, a few miles across the sea from the port of Pusan, went untroubled by the dramas and horrors that befell the mainland until a POW camp was established there in 1951. Communist prisoners were shipped in batches to Pusan by truck or train. At a compound on the edge of the city, the bewildered and demoralised men spent an average of two days while joint American and South Korean CIC teams interrogated them. They were given old American-style fatigues to replace their tattered uniforms, segregated by rank and ethnic group, and housed in big tents from which they were brought forth, one by one, to be questioned.

Millions of words have been written about the plight of UN prisoners in the hands of the communists in Korea. Much less has been said about the treatment of communist prisoners in the hands of the UN. Under the UN, nothing remotely resembling the indoctrination programme carried out in the Yalu camps took place. It may justly be claimed that the North Korean and Chinese prisoners in the southern camps were confined, for the most part, in conditions little worse, and with more and better food, than most would have enjoyed at home. Yet amid the profound humanitarian concern for the British, Americans, Turks being maltreated in the North, little has been said about the casual brutality to which thousands of communist prisoners were subjected. A host of UN veterans of Korea testify to the hostility and contempt in which most soldiers held 'the gooks', whether North or South Korean.

Western treatment of the Koreans and the Chinese was dictated by a deeply rooted conviction that these were not people like themselves, but near-animals who could be held at bay only by employing the kind of brutality they were wont to use upon each other. At the front prisoners were better treated, indeed greatly valued for intelligence purposes, from the spring of 1951 onwards. But in the camps of South Korea, many suffered as severely as their counterparts on the Yalu. 'The compounds at Pusan were run by military police who were very rough on the prisoners, often beat them up very badly,' said Private Alan Maggio, who served among the PoWs as a medical orderly for ten months from May 1951. 'Those MPs were just waiting for trouble. They wanted something to happen. The enlisted men ran the system. There were no officers who bothered to walk round or check what was going on.'[1]

From the Pusan compounds, the prisoners were herded into landing craft at the dockside, and ferried for three hours across the sea to Koje-do. Here beneath the shadow of the high hills that dominated the island, thirty-seven vast, adjoining, wired compounds had been constructed. Within these were confined, early in 1952, some 70,000 Chinese and North Korean prisoners. They were held at a density four times greater than that tolerated in US federal penitentiaries. A further 100,000, including 38,000 born in South Korea and conscripted into the North Korean army during the communist occupation, had already been screened and removed from the island.

They drifted upon an unbroken swell of boredom. There were a few daily fatigue parties – the details marching out of the compounds each morning carrying great drums of excrement slung between poles, the men working on the drainage ditches in endless, hopeless attempts to clear the mud which overlay the entire camp. But most prisoners sat in their tents all day playing a Korean version of mahjong, carving wooden figures, reading, playing cards, cooking over their little fires. Within each compound, the Americans left the prisoners entirely to themselves. But their lot was not enviable. From one of the little dispensaries outside the compound gates, Private Maggio found ample opportunities for exercising his medical skills:

> Koje-do wasn't managed properly – there were far too many men in one enclosure. There was a lot of bronchitis, pneumonia, malaria, dysentery, pinkeye. TB was widespread. There were men with open wounds that were still draining. All of them had lice. The problem was washing their clothes – it should have been compulsory, but it wasn't. The prisoners hated the delousing powder. Then there were always problems with the rats, which wasn't helped by the way they all hid food under their mats. The Chinese prisoners had the cleanest compound and highest morale. They were by far the most disciplined group on that island.[2]

The UN Command could claim that despite all the medical problems, only a very small number of communist prisoners died from disease on Koje-do, by comparison with the terrible toll on the Yalu. But the eyewitness evidence is also overwhelming that conditions among the prisoners would have been considered barbaric by, say, the inmates of a PoW camp in Germany in 1943. Their captors had simply installed the Chinese and North Koreans in the circumstances they considered appropriate to Asian peasants.

More serious than this was the rabble of the American and Korean armies who were entrusted with their custody. Maggio and other eyewitnesses describe the ferocious racial tensions between American groups among the guards – notably the blacks and Chicanos against the whites. For them, duty on Koje-do was almost as intolerable as for the prisoners. No serious attempt was made by officers to impose leadership or discipline. Gambling and local whores were the only diversions. Knife fights and brawls were commonplace. 'The disciplinary situation was unbelievable,' said Maggio. 'I found the whole place a living hell – I was in fear constantly. There were fights in the barracks, fights in the compounds. Anybody who couldn't make it on the line was sent down to do duty on Koje-do. We ended up with the scum of the army – the drunks, the drug addicts, the nutters, the deadbeats.' To his overwhelming relief, in February 1952 Maggio was able to gain a transfer to an ammunition trucking company.

Sergeant Robert Hoop was posted to the 595th Military Police company on Koje-do in October 1951, after being wounded in combat for the second time, serving with the 15th Infantry. In five months on the island, he only once set foot inside the wire of a compound, escorting a medical orderly – 'I was very scared every second I was in there. I just couldn't wait to get out.'[3] Hoop had constant disciplinary problems with his men – 'getting mixed up with whores and getting drunk on duty'. In his sector of the camp, there were just three MP companies, American and South Korean, to control and guard some 24,000 prisoners. By the spring of 1952, it was debatable whose predicament was more wretched – that of the prisoners within the wire, or the guards outside it.

The root of the huge difficulties that burst upon the UN prison camps in 1952 was that, once the prisoners had been sent to the rear areas and interrogated, their custody and welfare became very low priorities for the UN Command. The officers and men who were entrusted with running the camps were, for the most part, among the least impressive manpower in the US and Korean armies. Many of the guards treated the prisoners as animals. The chief objective of their officers was to distance themselves as far as possible from the prisoners, and leave them in their compounds to administer their own affairs. Thus it was that when in the spring of 1952 the communists began infiltrating men who deliberately allowed themselves to be taken prisoner, with orders to seize internal control of the PoW compounds, they were able to do so without the slightest difficulty. An extraordinary storm broke upon Koje-do Island, of a kind never witnessed before in any military prison camp in history.

The officers responsible for Koje-do had plenty of warning of the impending furore. In the first months of the year, there was growing evidence of ideological and military activity inside the compounds. Prisoners manufactured dummy rifles, uniform caps headed with bottle-top badges bearing the red star, flags, banners. Openly, by squads and companies, they began to drill inside the wire. Their commissars harangued them. The first evidence of ruthless internal discipline appeared: prisoners were badly beaten up, even murdered within the wire. Yet in the face of all this, their custodians did nothing. The inmates were left undisturbed. The prisoners' leaders began to make increasingly strident demands for improved conditions: writing paper, better food, changed routines. They were probing, testing the will of the Americans. It was found wanting. One morning, a crowd of prisoners began hurling cans of sardines and salmon back over the wire. The food was unsuitable, they proclaimed. They wanted fresh fish sent from Japan. The prisoners staged strikes in support of their demands. Their custodians, baffled, fearful of the wrath of this vast horde of apparent fanatics, desperate for tranquillity at any price, sought earnestly to appease them. An extraordinary psychological situation developed, in which it was the prisoners behind the wire who held the initiative. Their captors danced to their tune.

There were violent incidents as early as the summer of 1951. In June, after a prisoners' attack on a UN work detail, seven men were killed and four wounded by ROK fire. In August, there were demonstrations which ended with nine dead and twenty-five wounded on Koje-do, eight killed and twenty-two wounded at Pusan. Struggles in September caused twenty more deaths. In a more sinister development, on 23 December UN medical staff were unable to save the lives of ten prisoners fatally beaten by their fellow-inmates. No serious attempt was made to seek or punish the murderers. The same night, in a mass demonstration in another compound, fourteen prisoners were killed and twenty-four injured.

In the first months of 1952, the tempo of violence on Koje-do rose sharply. In February, the UN began its first attempts to screen the prisoners one by one, to determine who wished to be repatriated to North Korea and China. To the astonishment of the guards, the communist leaders of the first compound they entered launched a headlong assault with steel pickets, spiked clubs, barbed-wire flails and blackjacks. One American was killed – and seventy-five prisoners. On 10 April, when American medical orderlies entered Compound 95 on a routine visit to remove a wounded man, a wave of screaming prisoners charged them. Koje-do's commandant, Brigadier Francis T. Dodd, sent a hundred unarmed ROKs into the compound to retrieve the prisoners. One ROK soldier simply disappeared in the ensuing struggle. He was never seen again. Eventually, the guards on the perimeter tried to give their men inside covering fire. An American officer and several ROKs were wounded. In another incident, prisoners staged a massed rush on a compound gate. An American officer and two men fought them off with a jeep-mounted .30 calibre machine gun. Three prisoners were killed and sixty wounded, along with four ROK guards.

Koje-do was becoming, as the communists intended, a second front in the Korean War. Their purpose was to achieve a major propaganda victory – to project the United Nations as the brutal persecutors and murderers of their prisoners. To this end, the fanatics within the compound were able to inspire or intimidate thousands of their wretched fellow-prisoners to hurl themselves, often under suicidal circumstances, upon the guns of their captors. Those responsible for the camps now faced the worst of all possible worlds. In their fear, they made absurd concessions to the prisoners and allowed their leaders ludicrous liberty to create an ideological hell within the perimeter fence. But Koje-do was also becoming the focus of growing world controversy, as reports grew of the casualty lists in the island disturbances.

On 7 May 1952, a far more serious, indeed grotesque episode took place. In the midst of preparations for fresh political screening of the prisoners in Compound 76, which housed 6,400 of the most fanatical prisoners, the commandant Brigadier Dodd went in to reason with them. At 3.15 in the afternoon, as he prepared to leave, a whistle was blown. There was a rush of North Koreans around him. He was seized by the communists and held hostage. A sign painted on ponchos, obviously pre-prepared, was hoisted: 'WE CAPTURE DODD AS LONG AS OUR DEMAND WILL BE SOLVED HIS SAFETY IS SECURED, IF THERE HAPPEN BRUTAL ACT SUCH AS SHOOTING, HIS LIFE IS IN DANGER.' The following day, with the compound now under siege by tanks, guards, and offshore gunboats, and the island under the temporary command of Dodd's deputy, Colonel Craig, Dodd was allowed to communicate the PoWs' near-farcical demands: to be permitted to form an association, to be provided with office supplies and a telephone. From Tokyo, Ridgway instructed Van Fleet to take whatever measures were necessary to regain control. On 9 May, Van Fleet arrived personally to investigate the situation. There were now some 15,000 heavily armed UN troops on the island, facing the mass of unarmed communists behind the wire. On the night of the 10th, Dodd was released unharmed, after negotiations. But to the profound embarrassment of the Americans, it was found that he had signed a document which appeared to acknowledge a measure of justice in the prisoners' case.

The communists had scored a propaganda triumph, and focused the spotlight of foreign attention upon Koje-do. In the days that followed, a procession of official and unofficial visitors descended upon the island, and without exception castigated the authorities for the collapse of control. The British Air Vice-Marshal Bouchier reported on the lack of parades and rollcalls, the open display of communist flags and military drilling by prisoners: 'In short, the Communist PoWs in these compounds have held, and still hold, undisputed control within their own compounds.'[4] Van Itterson, the Dutch representative to the UN Korean Commission, who was a former PoW of the Japanese, declared: 'The Americans have no idea how to treat Asiatic PoWs. The fact that they still don't act strongly enough causes an ever increasing audaciousness of behaviour by the prisoners. It is clear that only drastic measures can help.'[5]

In the months that followed the Dodd seizure, far from improving, the situation appeared to deteriorate. 115 prisoners died in rioting between July 1951 and July 1952. American attempts to reassert authority generated only more unfavourable publicity. On 9 June 1952, *Pravda* reported gleefully that the Americans were employing gas chambers and torture, and forcibly preventing prisoners from expressing their wish to be repatriated. When General Mark Clark expressed his desire for token British and Canadian contingents to join the UN guard force on Koje-do, the British reluctantly complied, but the Canadian government agonised for days about whether it was willing to allow its troops to be associated with the unsavoury situation on the island. Renewed communist rioting was met with strong American repressive action, and scores more deaths. The communist 'journalist' Wilfred Burchett wrote in the *Daily Worker*: 'Two hitherto unreported massacres of Korean and Chinese prisoners in the American compounds on Koje-do have now come to light . . . The brutality used to make a prisoner agree not to return home is now clearly revealed.' Strained relations between London and Washington were worsened by the difficulty of gaining accurate reports about what was going on at Koje-do. The Washington Embassy minuted the Foreign Office: 'I think this is just one more instance of the difficulty of getting detailed information in Washington about operations in Korea.'

One of the most interesting outsiders' views of the Koje-do drama was presented in a report by Major D. R. Bancroft, the British commander of a company of the King's Own Shropshire Light Infantry sent to the island on 25 May 1952. Within hours of their own arrival, the KSLI had 'invaded' a compound and removed reserve food supplies, escape maps and contraband which it was plain had been sold to the prisoners by ROK guards. An hour later, two prisoners broke away from the compound and sought asylum with the British. They reported that the communist commissars were furious at having lost face, and had ordered that the prisoners must forcibly resist the next 'invasion'. Bancroft was appalled to discover that each compound possessed its own blacksmith's shop, in which prisoners could forge weapons, and that American supply vehicles were providing them with petrol, with which to start their fires. Accidental discharges from the weapons of guards, causing death or serious injury, appeared commonplace. On 10 June, some prisoners who sought to seek refuge from the commissars were speared to death by the inmates under the eyes of the guards. American troops entered the compound to restore order, and a battle followed. The Americans' 'bearing and control was of the highest order', reported Bancroft. 'The fanaticism displayed by the prisoners was alarming ... Even when half the compound had been cleared and there were over 100 dead and wounded lying around, the commissars harangued the masses to greater endeavours.' On 11 June, fifteen prisoners in one compound were murdered overnight by the commissars.

The British attempted a new approach in the compound under their control, to contest the commissars' supremacy. They ordered and supervised the election of prisoners' leaders by secret ballot. Thereafter, when the compound misbehaved, the prisoners' representatives were compelled to stand mute in the corner of the athletics field without food or water for up to twelve hours. The loss of face obviously caused them bitter pain. When the prisoners hoisted communist flags in their compounds, the British tossed in tear-gas grenades until they were taken down. Matters began to improve generally on Koje-do with the appointment of a new commandant, General Boatner. It was considered a damning comment upon the situation that prevailed before his appointment that, within a few days of his arrival, every single member of the former commandant's staff had been sacked and replaced. Efforts began to remove the 8,000 prostitutes who had taken up residence close by the compounds, for whose services so many sentries were accustomed to abandon their posts.

But the problem of the attitude of the guards to the prisoners persisted. '*All* US troops,' reported Major Bancroft,

> were apt to regard the PWs as cattle, and treated them as such. They were offensive in speech and manner towards the prisoners, and handled them, including cripples who had been badly wounded, extremely roughly. When witnessing this tendency, I asked both officers and men if they expected similar treatment to be meted out to their PWs in North Korea. Their reply was invariably: 'Well, these people are savages'; and on one occasion: 'Congress has never ratified the Geneva Convention anyway.'
>
> It was quite clear that the leaders [of the prisoners] could whip up mass hysteria among the PWs. It is therefore essential to segregate the ardent communist leaders as soon as they begin to make trouble. Their cruelty is beyond belief. Normal torture was to hang offenders to the ridge poles of tents by their testicles, place water hoses in offenders' mouths who were left to drown slowly, etc. As soon as it is known that atrocities are being committed, immediate action must be taken to release the victims. This was seldom done. The PWs

organised the running of their camps extremely well. Morale
was high under the most adverse conditions. Physical fitness
through organised PT was compulsory . . . I formed the opinion
that the North Korean was more honest, more militant, cleaner
and better-educated than the South Korean.[6]

Major Bancroft's extremely disturbing report was forwarded to
the Foreign Office in August 1952. An official attached a minute to
the text: 'The report confirms others accounts we have had of the
"Hate Asia" attitude so freely displayed by Americans in the Far
East. The harm which such behaviour does to our joint cause needs
no emphasising. It seems to us that if the United States' Joint
Chiefs of Staff were to take practical measures of indoctrination, a
good deal might be done towards improving the behaviour of the
US Armed Forces.'[7] If these remarks – intended only, of course, for
internal Whitehall consumption – sound somewhat complacent
and patronising, the seriousness of the problem of US attitudes to
the prisoners on Koje-do is confirmed by American reports to
Washington. A fatal combination of incompetence, lassitude, and
casual brutality by their captors had enabled the communists to
gain a bloody triumph in their propaganda struggle.

From the summer of 1952, the Americans sought to regain
control over their prisoners by dividing and relocating them
among a number of offshore island camps. Yet the savage revolts
continued. On 14 December, some 3,600 of the 9,000 prisoners on
Pongan-do fought a pitched battle with guards in which they
advanced, arms locked together, hurling a barrage of rocks and
missiles. Eighty-four prisoners died, and a further 120 were
wounded before peace was restored. Public controversy persisted
about the treatment of communist PoWs. 'The United Nations
refuse to return captives who would almost certainly be shot when
they got home,' commented the London *Daily Mail* on 18 December.
'But the effect of this humanitarian policy will be weakened by
continual shooting of prisoners, even in self-defence.' Yet how, in
the face of the fanatical and murderous behaviour of the commis-

sars behind the wire, was control of the prisoners to be maintained? An International Red Cross delegate, Colonel Fred Bieri, reported from Koje-do:

> Many prisoners' spokesmen have informed the delegate of their grave concern on the question of repatriation. According to their statements, it appears that there are North and South Koreans (both PoW and Civilian Internees) who wish to return to North Korea, and North and South Koreans who desire to remain in South Korea. Many Chinese PoWs desire to be sent to Formosa. Many men at present living in close contact with those of opposite political ideology are scared to express their real opinions; others have been forced by their comrades to make statements which are contrary to their wishes. Our delegate states that the effects of political pressure (from both sides) as applied to PoWs by PoWs themselves can be clearly observed. Most of the incidents which have occurred so far were actuated by purely political motives.[8]

Bieri and General Boatner discussed the seemingly intractable problem of communist terrorisation within the compounds: 'The Commandant regretted these incidents, but explained how difficult it is to keep each tent under observation in complete darkness. These beatings, which, unfortunately, often cause deaths, happen quickly and are carried out by well-organised groups. Even should culprits be recognised by tent inmates, fear prevents eye-witnesses from giving evidence.'[9]

In the last months of the war, control was tenuously maintained among the communist prisoners of the UN. But the Western powers had been dealt another bitter reminder that the conflict in Korea was being fought by new rules, far outside the historic experience of the democracies.

2. 'I shall go to Korea'

By the summer of 1952, the weariness of the United Nations, and above all the United States, with the war in Korea, was becoming intolerable. So too was the embarrassment of defending the excesses of President Syngman Rhee. In Tokyo, General Mark Clark, veteran of the World War II Italian campaign, had replaced Ridgway when the paratrooper departed for Europe to succeed General Dwight Eisenhower in command of the NATO armies. As the corrupt farce of a South Korean election loomed, Clark discussed with Van Fleet at Eighth Army by cable the possible implications of Rhee's defeat, in the unlikely event that the people of South Korea were allowed to achieve such a verdict:

'In the remote possibility that President Rhee accepts defeat gracefully,' said Clark sardonically, 'it is recommended that he should be urged to serve his country by making a worldwide lecture tour at UN expense to explain his country's problems and needs.'

But if Rhee forcibly resisted ejection, the UN would face serious problems: 'We do not have the troops to withstand a major communist offensive, to retain uncontested control of the prisoners of war on Koje-do, and to handle major civil disturbances in our rear areas at the same time. Therefore, we must swallow our pride to a certain extent until Rhee, through his illegal and diabolical action, has catapulted us into a situation where positive action must be taken.'

In other words, the US and the UN must somehow stomach almost any political excesses in Seoul. The military situation was causing equal dismay. '. . . it appears that, within current capabilities (in the true sense) and existing policies, there are no military courses of action that will ensure a satisfactory conclusion to the

Korean struggle,' the Assistant Chief of Staff (Plans) minuted on 15 September 1952.

> The problem of Korea is essentially part of a larger problem in Asia having its genesis in the aggressive posture and actions of communist China. The JCS recorded that the United States' objectives, policies, and courses of action in Asia should be reviewed, in order to determine the extent to which the United States military resources should be committed to deter or repel Chinese communist aggression.[10]

Here was a heartcry from the Pentagon to the Administration: What are we doing in Korea? How quickly can we get out? This private debate in the offices and corridors of Washington matched the great public one, fought out all that year, on the election platforms of the country.

In the early months of 1952, there was intense public debate on President Truman's prospects of gaining a third term. Towards the end of 1950, his 'favourable' ratings in the Gallup poll were running at 46 per cent, the highest he ever achieved. For the remainder of his term, popular approval of his performance never rose above 32 per cent, and sometimes fell as low as 23 per cent. On 29 March 1952, Truman chose the annual Jefferson-Jackson Day dinner at Washington National Guard Armoury to announce that he would not run for re-election. He always claimed thereafter that he made his decision because he believed two terms enough for any President, and that he could have retained the White House had he chosen to fight. This was unlikely, above all when it became apparent that his Republican opponent would be America's most celebrated living soldier, Dwight D. Eisenhower. Early in April, Eisenhower asked to be relieved of his military duties as NATO's first commander, because of his 'surprising development as a political figure'. For most of that year, Eisenhower sought to create the impression that he had somehow been drafted by popular acclaim, rather than made a conscious and ambitious decision to run. Likewise, he did his utmost to avoid explicit statements of political policy or intention. He was just Ike, and he believed that he could be elected for what he was, not for what he promised. He was almost right. Adlai Stevenson, the Illinois governor whom Truman had selected to succeed himself, could not unite even his own Democratic Party behind him, far less the nation. Eisenhower, with his great grin and good-natured professions of pious intention, his prudent equivocation about McCarthyism and invulnerable status as a national hero, was unstoppable. Pathetically, Douglas MacArthur still cherished hopes of the GOP nomination. At the convention, he received just ten votes. Ike won on the first ballot, by 595 votes to Taft's 500.

It would be wrong to suggest that the pursuit of an escape route from the war dominated the 1952 US Presidential election campaign. Indeed, by that year one of the foremost grievances of the men freezing or sweltering on the line was that so many of their own countrymen appeared to have forgotten that they were there. But weariness with Korea played its part not only in the political decline of Harry Truman, but in the election of Dwight Eisenhower. Korea was one of the 'four Cs', alongside Corruption, Crime, and Communism. The last glories of the New Deal had vanished in a welter of seedy Administration corruption scandals. Few Americans, few Westerners, any longer drew sustenance from a sense of high purpose in Korea. The cause was now tarnished by so many of the stains and blemishes that would assert themselves again in Indochina a generation later: the inglorious nature of a struggle that denied the promise of military success; the embarrassment of fighting for a regime whose corruption and incompetence were bywords; the difficulty of welding the South Korean army into a fighting force capable of meeting the Chinese on anything like equal terms; the reluctance of America's allies to shoulder a proportionate share of the burden. Before Vietnam was ever heard of, Americans discovered in Korea an unprecedented frustration of national will.

Despite the honourable character of both candidates, America's 1952 Presidential campaign was one of the most distasteful of modern times, dominated by the shadow of McCarthyism and the anti-communist crusade. MacArthur's objections to Eisenhower were partly founded upon the belief that Ike was insufficiently zealous in his hostility to communism, at home and abroad. Yet paradoxically, few American conservatives cried out for a more vigorous military policy in Korea, the one battlefield on which communism was being confronted at gunpoint. McCarthy and his acolytes declared that American blood was being wasted in a struggle that the Administration was conducting without conviction. Their isolationism militated against any display of enthusiasm for an increased American commitment to a campaign in Asia. Like most of their fellow-countrymen, they wanted to see America out of Korea. They sought only an escape without intolerable loss of face.

John Foster Dulles, the architect of Eisenhower's foreign policy for much of his election campaign and presidency, believed that Truman's decision to intervene in Korea had been 'courageous, righteous, and in the national interest'. But Dulles also considered that the broader Truman–Acheson strategy of containment of the Soviet Union by limited action and reaction had enabled the Russians to choose where, when, and how to confront the United States. Dulles wished to see America's military and foreign policy organised in a fashion that would enable the country to deploy its full might. He was the creator of the concept of 'massive retaliation' which somewhat troubled Eisenhower. Dulles proposed to keep the Soviet Union in a condition of permanent uncertainty and apprehension about where and when the United States would meet communist aggression with unbridled atomic reprisals. As a corollary of this policy, it was no longer in America's interest to become bogged down in limited local wars on distant battlefields against Soviet surrogates. Dulles favoured disengagement from Korea.

Eisenhower's early campaign statements on Korea were marked not merely by vagueness, but foolishness. In one speech in August, he claimed that the Administration had committed itself to the serious error of withdrawing US troops from Korea in 1949, 'despite menacing signs from the North'.[11] In reality, of course, Eisenhower himself had been a member of the Joint Chiefs of Staff who advised the Administration in September 1947 that the United States had 'little strategic interest' in maintaining a military presence in Korea. Truman was disgusted by Eisenhower's posture. He and the Democrats continued to demand insistently that Eisenhower should declare precisely what, if elected, he proposed to do about the war.

Truman's question was answered by Emmet John Hughes, a *Life* magazine editor who had become a speech-writer for Eisenhower, and Herbert Brownell, his campaign manager. In a long discussion over dinner in Brownell's New York apartment, the two men groped for a decisive declaration that their candidate could make, which would yet commit him to nothing. It was Hughes who seized upon the idea that Eisenhower should promise to go to Korea and make a personal assessment of the war. He and Brownell then distilled a single, simple, short phrase for Ike: 'I shall go to Korea.' The candidate himself proved uneasy about the idea, and the speech that was built for him around it. But on 24 October in Detroit, despite the doubts of some of his advisers, he took the plunge. In a speech at the Masonic Temple that was broadcast on nationwide television, he concluded with the declaration that his first priority upon taking office as President would be to bring an end to the war in Korea: 'That job requires a personal trip to Korea. I shall make that trip. Only in that way could I learn best how to serve the American people in the cause of peace. I shall go to Korea.'

The phrase passed into the textbooks of American politics, for it set the seal upon Eisenhower's victorious campaign. Two weeks later, he was elected President of the United States by 33,936,234 votes to 27,314,992. On 29 November 1952, he fulfilled his pledge. Under conditions of deep secrecy, his absence from New York concealed by an elaborate cover plan involving a procession of distinguished visitors to his empty apartment, Eisenhower flew to Korea.

The President-elect spent three days in the country. He visited a Mobile Army Surgical Hospital, and talked to wounded men. He travelled within earshot of artillery fire in the forward area, and inspected some troops. He passed an hour with a bitter and suspicious Syngman Rhee. He spent most of his time in the country with General Mark Clark. He saw General James Van Fleet, commanding the Eighth Army. He gave a press conference at which he conceded the unlikelihood of achieving 'a positive and definite victory without possibly running the grave risk of enlarging the war'. But he declared that America 'will see it through'. Then he flew home to New York.

The gesture had been made. That it was no more than a gesture was made evident by the subsequent testimony of Clark and Van Fleet, who had expected to take part in protracted debate about military options, only to discover that Eisenhower's mind was fixed upon the best means of achieving a truce. The exalted visitor had flown from Seoul to Wake Island, where he joined John Foster Dulles and other prominent advisers for a three-day cruise to Hawaii on the cruiser *Helena*. The world believed that the voyage was spent in intensive debate about Korea. In reality, however, it seems that little of substance was discussed. The new Administration's objective for Korea was already set: ceasefire. All that remained to be decided was how the communists could be persuaded to accede.

MacArthur was among the foremost to propose a solution. While Eisenhower was still at sea, he announced publicly that he had his own plan for ending the war, when the new President was willing to hear it. On 17 December, the two generals met at Dulles' home. MacArthur presented Eisenhower with a lengthy memorandum. He argued that the United States should demand from the Soviet Union the unification of Korea – and Germany. Their neutrality would be guaranteed by the two superpowers. Failing Moscow's agreement, 'it would be our intention to clear North Korea of enemy forces. This could be accomplished through the atomic bombing of enemy military concentrations and installations in North Korea and the sowing of fields of suitable radio-active materials, the by-product of atomic manufacture, to close major lines of enemy supply and communications leading south from the Yalu, with simultaneous landings on both coasts of Korea.'

It was a sad postscript to a great military career, this spectacle of an aged warrior casting his Jovian thunderbolts into oblivion. 'General,' said Eisenhower carefully, 'this is something of a new thing. I'll have to look at the understanding between ourselves and our allies, on the prosecution of this war, because if we're going to bomb bases on the other side of the Yalu, if we're going to extend the war we have to make sure we're not offending the whole . . . free world or breaking faith.' MacArthur went away home empty-handed. A fortnight later, Truman departed from office filled with distaste for both generals, Eisenhower perhaps most of all. Ike, Truman considered, knew better. Ike, who had sought to pretend that inglorious departure from Korea could be avoided, was in reality entirely committed to bringing this about.

The first plank of the new Administration's Korean policy was a dramatic expansion of the ROK army, to a strength of some 655,000 men, at an estimated cost of $1 billion a year. Thus, it was hoped, the principal military burden of the war could be transferred from the United States to the Korean people. 'Koreanisation' possessed precisely the same shortcomings as 'Vietnamisation' twenty years later. While the ROK army was a greatly improved fighting force since its lowest ebb in 1950–51, all the evidence on the battlefield continued to suggest that Korean formations were incapable of meeting their Chinese opponents on equal terms. But unlike Vietnamisation, Koreanisation would not be put to a decisive military test. The expansion programme began in the spring of 1953.

A development of much more direct impact upon the Korean peace negotiations was America's test detonation, in January, of the first nuclear device of a size capable of adaptation for artillery – a tactical atomic weapon. The Joint Chiefs of Staff recognised its relevance to the Korean stalemate in a study issued on 27 March:

> The efficacy of atomic weapons in achieving greater results at less cost of effort in furtherance of US objectives in connection with Korea points to the desirability of re-evaluating the policy which now restricts the use of atomic weapons in the Far East . . .
>
> In view of the extensive implications of developing an effective conventional capability in the Far East, the timely use of atomic weapons should be considered against military targets affecting operations in Korea, and operationally planned as an adjunct to any possible military course of action involving direct action against Communist China and Manchuria.

On 19 May, the Joint Chiefs recommended direct air and naval operations against China and Manchuria, including the use of nuclear weapons. There should be no gradual escalation of force, they argued, but a dramatic surprise attack. The next day, the National Security Council endorsed the JCS recommendation.

Dulles, the Secretary of State, was visiting India. He told her Prime Minister, Nehru, that a warning should be conveyed to Chou En Lai: if peace was not speedily attained at Panmunjom, the United States would begin to bomb north of the Yalu. The Pentagon had recently carried out successful tests of atomic artillery shells. The implication was plain. So too was the significance of Eisenhower's public announcement that the Seventh Fleet would no longer be committed to preventing military operations between Formosa and the mainland of China. Nationalist guerrillas, armed and trained by the CIA, embarked upon an intensified programme of raids against the mainland, more than two hundred in the first five months of 1953, according to Peking.

It will never be certain how close the United States came to employing nuclear weapons against China in the spring and summer of 1953, or how far the JCS study and the Dulles warning were intended as bluffs. If such they were, there is no doubt of their success. Through its agents in the United States and Europe, Moscow was undoubtedly informed of American progress on tactical nuclear weapons, and Washington's change of policy towards active consideration of their use. The Russians feared Dulles, and were disposed to believe that he meant business. There was a new confidence about American policy. In 1950, the uncertainty within the Administration was profoundly influenced by its perception of its own military vulnerability. By 1953, the rearmament programme was well advanced; aircraft production was at a post-war high; the United States felt less afraid of the Russians, more assured of its own ability to confront them. Eisenhower said after his return from Korea: 'We face an enemy whom we cannot hope to impress by words, however eloquent, but only by deeds – executed under circumstances of our own choosing.'[12] At a National Security Council meeting early in February, Dulles spoke of the need to make the idea of nuclear weapons more acceptable. He 'discussed the moral problem, and the inhibition on the use of the atomic bomb, and Soviet success to date in setting atomic weapons apart from all other weapons as being in a special category. It was his opinion that we should try to break down this distinction.' At the same meeting, Eisenhower suggested the Kaesong area of North Korea as an appropriate demonstration ground for a tactical nuclear bomb – it 'provided a good target for this type of weapon'.[13] By March, Eisenhower and Dulles were 'in complete agreement that somehow or other the tabu which surrounds the use of atomic weapons would have to be destroyed'.[14] At a special NSC meeting in March, Eisenhower said that although 'there were not many good tactical targets ... he felt it would be worth the cost' if a major victory could be gained in Korea.[15]

Here, then, is clear evidence that Eisenhower and his senior advisers talked with considerable open-mindedness about the possible use of nuclear weapons in Korea. Yet today, it remains difficult to believe that, had the military situation in Korea remained unchanged, Eisenhower would have authorised their employment.

It is entirely probable that he would have done so, had the Chinese offered some new and dangerous military provocation. But if America had detonated a nuclear weapon in cold blood, at a time of military stalemate on the battlefield, Eisenhower would have faced the certain, bitter, lasting anger and hostility of America's allies around the world. He was a cautious, humane man. It seems unlikely that he would have taken so drastic a step.

But in the spring of 1953, the Russians and Chinese almost certainly allowed themselves to be persuaded that the new Administration was willing to use nuclear weapons if the United States was denied an honourable escape from Korea. After so many months of deadlock, the talks at Panmunjom suddenly began to move with remarkable speed.

3. The Last Act

For almost two years, it had been apparent that the Korean War could not be settled on any terms that provided for the reunification of the country, nor that dispossessed either client regime in North or South. During the interminable struggle in which each side laboured for face, the fate of the prisoners held at the two extremities of the Korean peninsula remained the dominant issue. The prisoners. It always came back to the prisoners. They were no longer even prisoners-of-war, in any historic sense. Each side's captives had become hostages, whose treatment and disposal became the focal point of ruthless bargaining in those last, sterile months of the Korean War.

In December 1952, when the Red Cross in Geneva urged the exchange of sick and wounded prisoners in Korea as a 'gesture for peace', Mark Clark welcomed the proposal, but the Soviets and Chinese rejected it. Then on 28 March, without warning, Kim Il

Sung and Marshal Peng not only announced their acceptance of the swap, but also declared that this should pave the way to a settlement of the future of all PoWs, and a ceasefire 'for which people throughout the world are longing'. Chou En Lai endorsed this commitment in a Peking radio broadcast on 30 March. Although he restated Chinese rejection of an exchange which left any Chinese or North Korean prisoner in UN hands, he now proposed that any prisoner whose will was in doubt should be placed in the hands of a neutral state, for further investigation. For the Soviets, on 1 April Foreign Minister Molotov endorsed Chou's proposal and offered Moscow's support in seeing it carried out.

Washington at first regarded the Chinese declaration with deep suspicion. Again and again over the past two years, an apparently straightforward proposal from Peking proved, on closer inspection, to be capable of such different interpretation as to be worthless. Yet on 11 April at Panmunjom, the liaison officers at the conference table were astonished to reach rapid agreement with the communists for 'Operation Little Switch'. 700 Chinese and 5,100 Koreans were to be sent north. 450 Korean and 150 non-Korean soldiers were to come south. Between 20 April and 3 May, the exchange was completed at Panmunjom.

A new wave of revulsion about the communist conduct of war swept the West when its peoples beheld the condition of the UN prisoners who were released: in addition to wounds and disabilities that had effectively gone untreated for months, even years, many men were corroded by prolonged starvation, or psychologically crippled. Yet negotiations for the next exchange began at once, and the full UN and communist delegations met at Panmunjom on 26 April for the first time in six months. The main point at issue was the selection of a neutral 'quarantine nation' where prisoners refusing repatriation should be held. The UN opened by proposing Switzerland, with no man to be held in quarantine for more than two months. The Chinese rejected Switzerland, and demanded six months. Pressed for an alternative neutral site, they named Pakistan. Then the communist delegates appeared to undergo a sudden change of heart. They no longer insisted that the prisoners' political screening process should take place outside Korea, cut the proposed period from six months to four, and demanded the creation of a Neutral Nations Repatriation Commission made up of Poland, Switzerland, Czechoslovakia, Sweden and India.

The Americans were at last convinced that the communists genuinely sought peace. Stalin was dead, and in the dark shadows of the Kremlin new forces, albeit no less hostile to the West, were setting policy. Perversely, at this moment Dulles experienced a twinge of doubt about the wisdom of making a Korean peace based upon the *status quo* on the battlefield. Korea was the only shooting war that the United States was conducting with the communists anywhere around the globe. Was she now sacrificing a unique opportunity militarily to humble the enemy before the world? 'I don't think we can get much out of a Korean settlement until we have shown – before all Asia – our clear superiority by giving the Chinese one hell of a licking,' the Secretary of State told Emmet Hughes. But Eisenhower was by now wholly committed to a Korean settlement. Dulles buried his misgivings.

At last, the Americans perceived that they possessed the balance of strength at the negotiating table. It seemed that time was pressing the communists even more urgently than the UN. Mark Clark requested, and received from Washington, permission to drive home the advantage. The bombing campaign of Far East Air Force was intensified, with attacks on dams in North Korea deliberately intended to destroy crops and food supplies. The UN delegation at Panmunjom tabled a new, and declaredly final, proposal: a single neutral power would screen all reluctant PoW repatriates within ninety days, inside Korea. If this proposal was rejected, all unwilling North Korean repatriates would be unilaterally freed inside Korea within a month. The UN air attack on the North would also be intensified.

Yet even as the Western world waited impatient and expectant for a settlement at Panmunjom, for an end to the long stalemate of which the Allies had grown so weary, inside South Korea entirely different emotions reached boiling point. For President Syngman Rhee and his followers, the prospective armistice that offered peace to Seoul's foreign allies signalled the collapse of all their hopes. Always an obsessively stubborn man, Rhee was now also a bitter one. He saw plainly that Eisenhower proposed to accept a ceasefire based upon the permanent division of Korea, and the continuance of a serious communist threat to the Seoul government. The South Korean declared again and again that he would never countenance a settlement that did not remove the Chinese from North Korea, and effectively demilitarise the North. His warnings of imminent American betrayal made an impact upon even those of his countrymen who detested him. If the anti-American rallies in major cities were inspired by Rhee's agents, they were attended by many Koreans full of genuine fears for their society's future if the Americans withdrew, leaving South Korea at the mercy of the communists beyond the ceasefire line. Even opposition politicians in the National Assembly joined the desperate clamour. Rhee now directly threatened Eisenhower: if a deal was made at Panmunjom which permitted the Chinese to remain in North Korea, the ROK army would continue the fight unaided, if need be, until the communists were pushed north of the Yalu. However empty this threat in simple military terms, it caused the utmost alarm in diplomatic and political ones. Rhee's behaviour, it seemed, might now shatter the entire fabric of the peace talks.

Mark Clark did his utmost to assuage the Korean President's fears. The expansion of the ROK army would proceed whatever the outcome at Panmunjom, the American assured him. He believed that he had been successful in persuading Rhee of the futility of seeking to sabotage the peace negotiations. Clark cabled the JCS: 'He is bargaining now to get a security pact, to obtain more economic aid, and to make his people feel he is having a voice in the armistice negotiations.' The infinitely obstinate Korean was not finished yet.

Nor were the Chinese. On 26 April, their delegation at the peace talks entered a new proposal about the prisoners: three months after a ceasefire, those who refused repatriation should be moved for another six months to a neutral state, where representatives of their own government would have access to them. Those who still refused repatriation at the end of this process would remain in confinement while further negotiations were held to decide their fate. American counter-proposals were rejected. For four days, the communists harangued the UN delegation across the conference table, in a return to the exchanges of stultifying rhetoric that characterised the earlier stages of negotiations. Finally, the talks were adjourned. Clark consulted with Washington.

To the American's acute embarrassment, his government now determined to make the very concession that it had refused for so long, that was certain to provoke a new upheaval in relations with President Rhee: the UN delegation was to agree that Koreans, as well as Chinese, who refused repatriation should be handed over to the Indian neutral supervisory commission. Rhee's rage, when this news was broken to him, brought relations between Washington and Seoul to their lowest ebb since the war began. The Korean threatened to withdraw his army from the UN Command. The Americans, in their turn, undertook hasty secret preparations to implement Plan EVER-READY, a politico-military operation to seize control of South Korea from Rhee's regime. If it proved necessary to launch EVER-READY, the Korean President 'would be held in protective custody, incommunicado', unless he agreed to accept the terms reached at Panmunjom. Either his prime minister, Chang Taek Sang, would be installed as head of government, or failing his consent, a military regime would be established. On 29 May, Dulles and Wilson – the Defense Secretary – gave Clark authority to take whatever steps he considered necessary in Korea in the event of a 'grave emergency'. They did not explicitly approve the proposal for Rhee's detention. But they gave their Commander-in-Chief almost unlimited discretion to act as he saw fit in an internal crisis in Korea.

By 25 May, it was apparent that the communists were ready to accept the modified American proposals for the exchange of prisoners. Mark Clark drove to Rhee's home to present the bitterly unwelcome news. Rhee received him alone, forcefully denounced the armistice proposals, and the United States' foolish course of appeasement of the communists. Clark departed, still uncertain what the Korean intended to do. The negotiations at Panmunjom continued. On 8 June, agreement was at last reached on the terms for repatriation of prisoners. Those who wished to go home could be exchanged immediately. Those who did not would be left in the hands of the Repatriation Commission for ninety days, during which their governments would have free access to them. Their future would then be discussed for a further thirty days by a 'political conference'. After that period, those who remained would be considered civilians.

The details of this arrangement were still being concluded on the night of 18 June 1953, when to the astonishment and bewilderment of the handful of Americans at the huge Pusan PoW compound, they saw that the main gates were open, and a vast herd of North Koreans were streaming out into the countryside, watched with supine indifference by their South Korean guards. The same process was taking place at three other compounds around the country. Some 25,000 North Koreans who had expressed unwillingness to return to their homeland after the armistice disappeared into the darkness. President Rhee had acted. Seoul radio warned escapees to beware of American soldiers seeking to apprehend them. Seoul's soldiers and police gave the men clothing, and directed them towards shelter. Even as US troops were rushed to the compounds to take over guard duties, liberation operations continued. By 22 June, only 9,000 North Koreans remained in captivity, out of a total of 35,400. Only 1,000 of those who had gone were rounded up. The mass liberation was one of the most efficiently organised exercises in the history of the ramshackle Seoul regime.

In Washington, it caused genuine consternation. What now, if the communists regarded Rhee's action as sufficient cause to break off the negotiations? The Administration hastened publicly to deplore the Korean's action, and dissociate the United States from it. For days, Washington waited anxiously for a sign from Peking. When at last it came, deep sighs of relief were audible at the State Department. Broadcasts from the New China News Agency deplored the episode, but displayed a willingness to listen to American explanations. The delegation at Panmunjom provided them. They were accepted. The peace talks entered their final phase.

Yet now, the critical conversations were taking place not at Panmunjom, but in Syngman Rhee's office. It was a matter of paramount importance to secure the Korean President's public consent. To achieve this, the Americans were prepared to threaten to abandon absolutely the Seoul regime if it was not forthcoming. Yet it was essential that no word of the strength of American attitudes should leak out to the communists, for it would immeasurably reinforce their hand, and their determination. Through the last days of June and the early days of July, Rhee spent hours closeted in private talks with Mark Clark and President Eisenhower's special envoy, Walter Robertson. Into Robertson's ear, Rhee poured his interminable grievances against the United States. At each session, the elderly President appeared to change the ground of his demands.

Rhee's obduracy now remained the sole obstacle to the signing of an armistice. Even as he and his American guests talked in Seoul, on the battlefield United Nations troops were repelling the heaviest Chinese offensive for two years. After a long period of stagnation at the front, the communists plainly determined to drive home to the South Koreans their military vulnerability. Some 100,000 communist troops struck across the front of five ROK divisions. The South Koreans were thrown back in disarray up to five miles before a vast UN artillery concentration was laid in the path of the enemy offensive. 2.7 million rounds were fired on the UN front in June, a million more than in any month of the war thus far. While the communists sought to demonstrate their will to prevail on the battlefield, if they were denied an acceptable peace at the conference table, the UN proved its ability to deploy massed firepower to thwart them. Heavy fighting continued into July. The UN suffered 17,000 casualties, including 3,333 killed, in the twenty days between agreement in principle being reached between the delegations at Panmunjom, and Syngman Rhee acknowledging his readiness to accept it.

For accept Rhee finally did, on 9 July. He would not sign the armistice, he declared. But he would no longer obstruct it. On 12 July, the United States and the Republic of Korea announced their agreement on truce terms. Privately, the UN Command allowed the communists to know that they would give no support to independent offensive action by the ROK army.

Glimpses of sun broke through the heavy clouds overhanging Panmunjom on the early morning of 27 July. During the night, carpenters had worked in the rain to complete the building where the armistice was to be signed. Before the ceremony could take place, however, Mark Clark insisted upon the removal of two communist 'peace dove' propaganda symbols from the pagoda, and the creation of a new entrance, to avoid the necessity for his delegation to pass through the enemy area of the building. If such details seemed petty, their importance in negotiation with the communists had been grasped over two painful years of experience. A guard of honour, composed of representatives of each army that had fought for the UN cause, flanked the southern approach. Only the South Koreans were missing. Rhee would allow his soldiers no part in a process he detested.

At 10 a.m. precisely, the two delegations entered the building from opposite sides. It was two years and seventeen days since talks began. Some pedant or public relations man calculated that 18,000,000 words had been exchanged at 575 separate meetings. Now, Lieutenant-General William K. Harrison led in the UN contingent with studied casualness. His party strolled forward, and sat back easily in their chairs, while the communists, wooden-faced, took their places with an air of rigid formality. Harrison sat down at a table marked by a small UN flag, and began to sign the first of the nine blue-backed copies of the armistice agreement. General

Nam Il sat at the North Korean-flagged table. Without a word or a sign, the two men went through the formalities, while in the distance the crump of the guns went on. By 10.12 a.m., it was all over. Still without a word, the two men got up and departed through their allotted exits. It was done.

A few hours later, Mark Clark signed the documents at UN Advanced Headquarters at Mansan-ni. The former wartime commander of Fifth Army found the experience repugnant. 'I cannot find it in me to exult in this hour,' he said, in a short radio broadcast afterwards. 'Rather it is a time for prayer, that we may succeed in our difficult endeavour to turn this armistice to the advantage of mankind.' Later, in his memoirs, he declared that the moment 'capped my career, but it was a cap without a feather'. He bitterly regretted becoming 'the first US commander in history to sign an armistice without victory'. Clark was among those who always believed that the UN should have bombed beyond the Yalu, who shared many of Joseph McCarthy's fears of secret enemies at the heart of America's government. To the lanky, single-minded general, this inconclusive conclusion of the long and bloody experience of Korea was infinitely distasteful. To the end of their days, he and other senior American military men would continue to cherish the conviction that there was another, a better way to peace – through military victory. At the Korean Embassy in Washington, Han Pyo Wook sat in the office he had occupied through three long years of war, and where he had witnessed the first diplomatic acts of the drama: 'There was no celebration,' he said, 'only bleak looks. We had fought the armistice to the end. How could we survive, with a million Chinese in North Korea? There was a very great sense of disappointment.'[16] But many others, the men on the mountains from coast to coast of Korea, were merely content that there was peace.

*

In the last few hours before the ceasefire came into effect at 10 p.m., on some sectors of the front the artillery of both sides fired with redoubled, passionate futility. 'It was like the Fourth of July and New Year's Eve rolled into one,' said Lieutenant Bill Livsey of the 7th Infantry. He and many of the men around him could not believe that this vast, insensate din could be hushed according to a schedule. They were astonished, almost awed to discover that at 10 p.m., 2200 hours, a sudden deafening silence fell upon the line. 'There was no elation. We were just so damn happy that it was over,' said Livsey.[17] In the Duke of Wellington's Regiment sector, word came over the radio from battalion headquarters that other ranks might venture into no-man's-land, but no officers were to do so. Within a few hours, little clusters of Chinese appeared in front of the wire, bearing bottles of rice spirit and little glass rings inscribed with the word 'peace'.

At dawn on 28 July, Lieutenant Chris Snider of the Canadian Brigade watched fascinated with his men as the bare hillside opposite suddenly grew a forest of Chinese figures: 'They all came out. My God, there were thousands of them, more than I ever thought possible, on every hill, standing gazing at us. Some of our people thought they must have been brought forward specially, to impress us.'[18]

On the US 7th Division's sector of the front, the commanding general Arthur Trudeau ritually pulled the lanyard to fire his formation's last round of the war, picked up the shellcase as a souvenir, and drove back to his Command Post for a few celebratory drinks with his staff, to musical accompaniment from the CP band in which he played the banjo. 'I was happy it was over,' he said. 'It was apparent that all we were going to do was sit there and hold positions. There wasn't going to be any victory. All we could do was go on losing more lives. In those last few months, I lost men faster than Westmoreland at any stage of the Vietnam War except Tet.'[19] Private Alan Maybury of the Durham Light Infantry said: 'We didn't celebrate victory. We celebrated being able to go home.'[20]

Lieutenant Clyde Fore of the 27th Infantry was on his way home to America aboard a hospital ship when the truce was signed. 'There was no rejoicing – we were just sad and quiet. This was the first time Americans had ever accepted a no-win war. Everybody else was acclimatised to no-win wars, but we were not. To me, Korea had been an abomination. So many people had died, for what?'[21]

Many of the same mixed feelings pervaded the ranks of the opposing army. Were the men of the Chinese 23rd Army Group disappointed to go home without victory? Wang Zhu Guang, one of its staff officers, lingers before answering:

> We did our best. We felt that it was difficult to continue the war, to conquer the whole of Korea. We did our best. I was happy it was over. We talked to the men in the most down-to-earth manner, explained the situation. They were happy. We never expected to get the whole of Korea. We were told that we were going to support the Korean people in getting the Americans out of Korea, stopping the American invasion. But exactly how far – that was not made clear.[22]

When dawn came, men on the UN line peered out across the silent valleys between themselves and the Chinese. In many places, little clusters of bold spirits slipped forward through the wire and the minefields, searching with intense curiosity for their former enemies. What did they look like, these strange creatures who had been glimpsed only momentarily through binoculars, or as screaming shadows in the darkness of an attack? The same curiosity possessed their enemies. On the low ground between positions, there were stilted little encounters. The Chinese passed over beer and bottles of rice wine. UN troops offered chocolate and cigarettes. Some Chinese made it apparent that they were as delighted that the war was ended as the Westerners. But these meetings could scarcely be called fraternisation. They were impelled not by fellow-feeling for the enemy, but by the same impulses that would provoke any earthman to inspect visiting aliens.

*

Inevitably, the most intense emotional drama of the days after the armistice surrounded the release of the prisoners. The communists, truckload after truckload of them being driven north to the exchange point at Panmunjom, were in haste to dispel any suggestion that they had been well treated in the South. Some gashed their new fatigues into ribbons, to make clear that they had been clad in rags. Others cast out of the trucks the cigarettes, toothpaste, chocolate with which they had been provided. The most dramatic gestures of all were made in the last miles before the convoy reached the exchange point. Thousands of North Korean and Chinese prisoners stripped off their clothes and boots and hurled them away on to the road. They chose to return naked to their own people, uncontaminated by the contemptible handouts of capitalism. When the convoys had passed, one of the most unforgettable images of the post-armistice exchange was that of the empty road, strewn for miles with discarded fatigues and footwear.

Yet the other, still more memorable moment was that of the return of the United Nations prisoners from the North: some gaunt men; some broken men; some clutching the bitter shame and memory of collaboration: others physically devastated by paying the price of resistance. Some came weeping into 'Freedom Village', the encampment south of the exchange line, where beneath the 'Welcome Home' arch a small army of interrogators, doctors, and psychiatrists waited to receive them. Some strode boldly in, others shambled uncertainly into a life whose reality they had almost been taught to deny. '90 per cent of us would have much preferred to be liberated than released by the Chinese,' said PFC David Fortune. 'The shame, if it was shame, lay in being let go.'[23] But it was enough to be free. They gorged themselves on bowl after bowl of ice cream while the psychiatrists talked to them. Each man was processed and examined to check whether he was fit for press interviews, or immediate repatriation. The first bitter denunciations of collaboration spilled forth, from prisoners who had been containing their hatred and disgust for years, in anticipation of this moment. Others – those who nursed private guilts – began to mumble the excuses and explanations that would haunt the balance of their lives. 'The average PoW was not really a human being when he was released,' said Fortune. 'He was a wild animal.' Fortune, like many others, continued to lose weight for weeks after his release, and worked his way through many women and many bottles of whisky before he felt sufficiently sated to come to terms with life at a normal tenor.

Most of the British prisoners sought to maintain their national reputation for understatement at the moment of liberation. Colonel Fred Carne of the Gloucesters, three stone lighter in weight than he had entered captivity, worn down by nineteen months of solitary confinement, was chaired shoulder-high through Freedom Village by his cheering comrades. But imprisonment had done nothing to make him more communicative. He dismissed his experience laconically: 'The food was rotten, and I was damn bored.' The prisoners in Camp 5 had been forewarned that an announcement of an armistice would be made before they were paraded to hear it from the Chinese. The Americans exploded into spontaneous rejoicing. The British, by advance mutual agreement, dispersed in silence. On arrival at Freedom Village, the British shambled through their medical checks in an atmosphere of intense repressed emotion. One man, glimpsing a party of Chinese on their way north, said pityingly: 'There's nothing for them up there.' Some men were provoked to their first overt displays of emotion by such simple, unexpected gestures as being handed a shirt, or seeing a copy of the *Daily Mirror*. The first, urgent questions from interrogators about cases of collaboration, or brainwashing, were met with silence. It was only gradually, over the weeks that followed, that the truth spilled out. The most conspicuous symptom of the tensions between different groups of ex-prisoners emerged when they were put on a troopship to go home. It was found expedient to disembark certain controversial individuals at Hong Kong, for separate passage.

Within a month of the commencement of 'Operation Big Switch' on 5 August, 75,823 communist prisoners had been sent north, 5,640 of these Chinese. The communists, in their turn, handed over 12,773 men, 3,597 of them American, 7,862 South Korean. 22,604 prisoners in UN hands were surrendered to the Neutral Nations Repatriation Commission in the Demilitarised Zone. 137 eventually agreed to repatriation. The remainder elected for resettlement in South Korea or Formosa. 359 prisoners in communist hands initially declined to go home. Ten of these – two American and eight Korean – changed their minds while in the custody of the Repatriation Commission. But for the remainder – 325 Koreans, twenty-one Americans and one Briton – there was no emotional arrival at Freedom Village. To the astonishment and profound dismay of their fellow-countrymen, they chose to join the society of their former captors.

In the compound in the Demilitarised Zone where the British Marine Andrew Condron and the Americans refusing repatriation were held in Indian custody, the renegades appeared before a press conference to explain their conversion to the communist cause. Their decision sent shockwaves through their own societies. What diabolical techniques could the communists have employed upon them, to cause men to choose a life of rice and cotton suits in preference to a return to Glasgow or Jersey City? What sort of reflection was it upon American political motivation and military training, that while twenty-one Americans had been successfully communist-indoctrinated, not a single Turkish prisoner had succumbed? At a moment when American political self-confidence was under great strain from McCarthyism, the growing alarm about 'enemies within' their own society, here was hard evidence of the communist capability to make conversions even amid the brutality of a prison camp regime. Seeds of fear and doubt were sown in America which took years to root out. The British were disposed to take a less alarmist view of the impact of communist captivity upon their own men, proportionately fewer of whom proved to have been successfully indoctrinated than among the Americans. Yet a decade later, British complacency would be sorely shaken by the revelation that the diplomat George Blake, captured in June 1950 when he was serving as Vice-Consul in Seoul, had been successfully 'turned' during the three years that followed. He operated undetected for years as an important Soviet agent.

In August 1953, Andrew Condron was the only Briton to refuse repatriation, and to earn the disgust of his own nation. Condron, the chronic 'loner', the maverick, found himself the object of bitter press allegations, that he had been a 'King Rat' figure in his camp, and feared reprisals if he came home. In reality, most of his fellow-inmates rather liked and respected him as a man, and found his conversion pathetic or absurd, rather than evil. Condron himself sailed through his public appearances in the DMZ with the sublime assurance of the zealot: 'I was totally convinced that what I was doing was right. I felt no fear, no remorse. My only pang was about my mother. I knew that my family was very shocked. My brother, who had been a prisoner himself, was the only one who began to understand. He said that you shouldn't judge somebody unless you have shared that experience.'[24]

The Chinese, oddly enough, seemed profoundly embarrassed by their twenty-two foreign converts. They issued them with Western-style suits and fedora hats, and shipped them by train to Tsinan. From there, they were dispersed around China to spend as many years as they could endure studying or translating or working at such jobs as the Chinese could find them. They were actively discouraged from learning Chinese. Contact with civilians, above all women civilians, remained very difficult. Over the years that followed, most quietly trickled back to the United States as their patience with Chinese life – and Chinese patience with their Western habits – expired. Condron returned to Britain amid a brief blaze of publicity in 1962. He claimed to regret nothing, even if he had learned something: 'In those days, we felt that the Americans had started the Korean War. Today? I'm not so sure.' His son by a Chinese wife was educated at an English private school: 'If you can't beat 'em, join 'em.'

*

General S. L. A. Marshall, perhaps America's finest combat historian of the twentieth century, described Korea as 'the century's nastiest little war'. In those days before Vietnam, its claim to that title seemed unlikely to be eclipsed. 1,319,000 Americans served in the Korean theatre, and 33,629 did not return. A further 105,785 were wounded. 45 per cent of all US casualties were incurred after the first armistice negotiations with the communists took place. The South Korean army lost 415,000 killed and 429,000 wounded. The Commonwealth – Britain, Canada, Australia and New Zealand – lost 1,263 killed and 4,817 wounded. Belgium, Colombia, Ethiopia, France, Greece, Holland, the Philippines, Thailand and Turkey between them lost 1,800 killed and 7,000 wounded, of whom almost half were Turks. The Americans estimated that more than 1.5 million Chinese and North Koreans had died. If this estimate is exaggerated, it seems reasonable to assume that China cannot have lost less than half a million men given the manner in which she fought her war. Few people of any nationality, four years earlier, would have supposed that barren peninsula would ever be worth any fraction of those lives.

18 » HINDSIGHT

Many United Nations veterans came home from Korea to discover that their experience was of no interest whatsoever to their fellow-countrymen. The war seemed an unsatisfactory, inglorious, and thus unwelcome memory. It had begun as a crusade to save South Korea from communism, and enjoyed a brief public popularity in Europe as well as the United States. This died in the mud and blood of retreat in the winter of 1950. Thereafter, Korea was seen only as a running sore, belatedly cauterised in July 1953. A woman saw Private Warren Avery in the street of his home town in Connecticut when he was discharged from the service, and remarked severely: 'So you finally got out of jail?'[1] John 'Rotorhead' Thornton of the US Navy returned from captivity to hear his wife declare that he had been wasting his life. Once too often, friends had asked her: 'Gee, I haven't seen John for a while. Where is he?' The first day after his return, they argued into the night. Thornton said: 'I guess I just couldn't accept the fact that we hadn't won, that we couldn't beat the communists. The only people who welcomed me back were my neighbours in Philadelphia, who gave me a block party.' His Navy Cross had been posted to his home through the mail. 'I thought I would go round telling people what communism is – hanging Major Hume up by his thumbs until he froze, for instance. I ended up feeling like most returning PoWs I know – that I was shovelling shit against the tide. You talk about Mao and the millions he killed, and they just say you're a McCarthyite.' Many PoWs came home to discover that their wives had made 'other arrangements'. Most felt themselves returning to a new unfamiliar world that cared little for their experience.

'We went away to Glenn Miller. We came back to Elvis Presley,' said Thornton without enthusiasm.

In the Southern states, perhaps, traditional patriotism was a more active force than in the East. PFC David Fortune was embarrassed by the display that greeted him in his home town of Pickens, South Carolina, after more than two years on the Yalu. They gave him a brand-new 1953 Ford Fairlane, and treated him as a hero: 'In my part of the country, I don't know anybody who opposed the war.' He spent three years' pay in three months and declared proudly that at the end of it, he had nothing to show.

Stan Muir of 45 Field Regiment RA arrived back at Woolwich after a year in Korea to be apprehended by two Military Policemen at the station, who told him to take his hands out of his pockets. Lieutenant Bill Cooper of the Northumberland Fusiliers returned from two years in captivity to discover that most of his fellow-professional soldiers knew little about what had been happening in Korea, and cared less. He adjusted rapidly to saying nothing about his experience. His own mother forcefully chastised him for the damage he had done to his military career: 'How on earth did you allow yourself to be captured, boy? Three years wasted. You'd better get on and pull yourself together.' Which indeed Cooper did, and served for another twenty years in the British Army. Captain Tony Farrar-Hockley went on to a distinguished military career which culminated in the command of Allied Forces in Northern Europe. But some ex-prisoners suffered marriage break-ups, alcoholism, lasting physical and psychological damage. Private Henry O'Kane of the Ulsters endured months of difficulty with twilight blindness caused by vitamin deficiency, and years of chronic insomnia. For the rest of his life he could not trust himself to keep the peace in a Chinese restaurant after a couple of drinks.

For those who had merely served on the line in Korea, rather than faced the enemy at brutally close quarters in confinement, passions ran less deep. Captain Peter Sibbald of the Commonwealth Division expressed the archetypal view of the British professional soldier. 'In all my service career, I encountered hatred on the battlefield only in Northern Ireland. There was no hatred for the Chinese in Korea.' But if a career officer could adopt so relaxed a view, many rankers found their homecomings a sad anticlimax. 'There was absolutely no interest in Korea,' said Private James Cardinal of the US First Cavalry Division. 'I went into a depression – the sort the Vietnam veterans complain of today. People were bored with the war, as far as they were concerned we had been defeated in Korea. We weren't the glorious heroes of World War II. Civilians were quite unaware that this was the most difficult war the US had ever had to fight.'

It is a source of widespread bitterness among Korean veterans in the United States that their memories and sacrifices seem so much less worthy of attention than those of Vietnam veterans. It was their misfortune to endure a war that aroused less public emotion, because in those early days of television, it was infinitely less vividly projected, less impressed upon the consciousness of Americans. Even at the height of the Korean War, that Asian peninsula seemed a very remote place, far less real than Vietnam became, beamed nightly for years into the nation's sitting rooms. Rather than acknowledging that too little attention has been lavished upon the victims of Korea, it may be more just to suggest that too much has been heaped upon the veterans of Vietnam. It is an absurd conceit to suppose that, in Indochina, combatants suffered in a fashion unknown to others in other conflicts. Almost all men are marked in some way by the experience of taking part in any war. Those who fought in Korea are no more and no less deserving of respect – and of a memorial – than those who fought in Vietnam, World War II, World War I. Subsequent historical debate about the merits of a national cause should never be allowed to detract from the honour of those who risked their lives for it on the battlefield.

*

In the years that followed the Korean War, as the immediate sense of frustration and stagnation that attended the armistice faded, soldiers and politicians became disposed to think more favourably of its value as a demonstration of the West's commitment to the arrest of communism. If the United Nations failed to achieve the reunification of Korea, they had prevented the North from imposing its will by force upon the South.

Yet it was also self-evident that for the United Nations, the Korean commitment was an experience that would never be repeated. UN forces might be granted an international mandate to carry out policing and peace-keeping tasks around the world. But never again was it conceivable that such a mandate would be granted for a military commitment, in pursuit of ideological and political objectives. Even in the summer of 1950, it was only the accident of the Soviet boycott that made the UN vote possible, sending troops into Korea. The relatively small number of countries which then possessed UN membership, most of them sympathetic towards the United States, accepted American leadership in going to war for Korea. But only sixteen members provided any measure of military support, none of whom could properly be called non-aligned. The Korean War was fought by the United States, with token support from her allies in the capitalist world. Within months of the outbreak, these allies were displaying their dismay at the economic and military cost, and uncertainty about the merits of the regime they were committed to defend. The Allied contingents in Korea, the Commonwealth Division most notable among them, were maintained in the field by their respective governments until 1953 only because it was plain that their withdrawal would inflict deep damage upon Allied solidarity in confronting communism. It is a measure of the desperate economic plight of Britain, in contrast to booming post-World-War-II America, that the Korean War and the rearmament programme that it provoked drove the country to the brink of financial crisis.

Once the Korean War was ended, the old powers preoccupied with the abandonment of their overseas empires showed no stomach for fighting abroad alongside the Americans against communism. More than a decade after Korea, when President Johnson pleaded with British Prime Minister Harold Wilson for even a token British contingent in Vietnam, he received no comfort. The United States was compelled to look to its Pacific and Asian allies for such military support as it could muster. As for the United Nations, it was now a larger body than the nucleus of nations which made up its membership in 1950. Many newly-created nation members were chronically sceptical of American foreign policy.

Yet however great the misgivings of America's allies in 1950 about going to war for Korea, it remains a tribute to the respect the United States could call upon in 1950 that an international force was committed at all. For a brief historical moment, the combination of foreign gratitude for America's military role in World War II and economic assistance in its aftermath, together with real fear of imminent conflict with the Soviet Union, enabled Washington to mobilise Allied troops for an Asian war few Europeans believed in.

Only America's absolute dominance of the Korean campaign enabled it to be fought to a tolerable conclusion. Yet this very dominance also contributed greatly to Allied unhappiness about the course of the war. Beneath a thin veneer of respect for the authority of the United Nations, Americans conducted the war as they saw it. Many American soldiers and politicians were exasperated by the prevarication and scruples of allies who were making so small a material contribution to the conflict. 'It was a legacy of World War II that the United States was expected to accept the brunt of commitment and sacrifice,' acknowledged the British diplomat Roger Makins. Yet this created the conundrum of alliance, that the manner in which the war was commanded and conducted by one dominant nation made the presence of the United Nations flag seem to many foreigners a charade. 'Though we called ourselves the UN, there were so few of us,' said the British Group-Captain 'Johnnie' Johnson. 'I felt very much an observer of an American show.' The British, not excluding their Prime Minister, deluded themselves in supposing in 1950–53 that they could exert a decisive influence even upon American nuclear policy. Other nations were even less likely to rally to the UN banner again, because of the widespread view that this was employed in Korea in the foreign policy interest of the United States, whether or not this was also the cause of natural justice.

Much academic research has been devoted to exploring the shifting currents within the US military establishment, both in attitudes to embarking upon the Korean War, and professional debate about its conduct. 'Much of the analysis of military opinion,' wrote Dr Rosemary Foot, one of the most recent students of the period, 'has confirmed the conclusion of other students of American foreign policy, that once a decision is made to use force, the generals want to use it more quickly and decisively than do their civilian counterparts ... the navy and air force are likely to advocate more hawkish courses than the army.'[2] Field commanders in Korea, as later in Vietnam, were consistently more bellicose in the strategies they advocated than the politicians, or even the Joint Chiefs of Staff, in Washington. The doctrine of Limited War will always find more favour among those responsible for national policy than with those charged with implementing it upon the battlefield.

As to the military conduct of the war, a senior American veteran of both Korea and Vietnam remarked: 'We went into Korea with a very poor army, and came out with a pretty good one. We went into Vietnam with a pretty good army, and came out with a terrible one.' The performance of most elements of the US Army in the first year of fighting in Korea ranged between moderate and deplorable. Five years of fatal neglect between 1945 and 1950 produced a rundown of men, training, leadership and equipment that almost, but not quite, enabled the Chinese to inflict a wholesale disaster upon American arms in the winter campaign. But, having saved themselves narrowly from that disaster, in the two years that followed the Americans in Korea made themselves a far more effective, and above all self-confident fighting force. Matthew Ridgway deserves a great measure of credit for turning around a beaten army, and directing it in such a fashion that it inflicted a series of shattering defeats upon the communist invaders.

*

There are many important respects in which Korea was a rehearsal for Vietnam a generation later. It may be argued that the United States learned wrong lessons from the experience of the 1950–53 war, where a huge commitment of resources enabled her army to halt the communists at tolerable cost in casualties. The fact that Syngman Rhee was the unpopular leader of a thoroughly corrupt regime whose army was incapable of effective self-defence on the battlefield did not prove a fatal disadvantage to sustaining the South Korean cause. Nor was it only Americans who allowed themselves to be little concerned about the nature of the regime the UN presence was supposedly supporting. 'Of course we knew that Syngman Rhee was a pretty monstrous figure,' said Brigadier William Pike of the Commonwealth Division. 'But weren't they all out there?' Many Americans, inside and outside the Defense Department, concluded that with sufficient military and economic support, almost any anti-communist regime abroad could be kept afloat, regardless of its intrinsic viability. The government of President Thieu of Vietnam was certainly no worse, indeed almost certainly less oppressive, than that of President Rhee. But more sophisticated communist techniques of subversion and infinitely more sceptical world media attention undermined it. Thieu's regime was finally exposed to a military test of a severity which that of Rhee escaped. Had the ROK army ever been left alone to combat a full-scale communist offensive, its fate would most likely have resembled that of the ARVN more than twenty years later.

The American army emerged from Korea convinced that its vastly superior firepower and equipment could always defeat a poorly equipped Asian army, if it was provided with the opportunity to deploy them. Shrewd commanders were well aware of historic weaknesses in American infantry, dating back to World War II and before, in small unit leadership and tactics, fieldcraft and battle discipline. But most senior officers continued to believe that the historic American military virtues, centring upon the massive concentration of scientific and technical resources, could more than compensate for these deficiencies. They might have reflected, had they chosen, upon the unusual convenience of the Korean battlefield, where the mountains restricted movement by either side, and the narrow peninsula made it possible to fortify and defend a relatively short front. In Vietnam, there could be no such fixed line. The very tactics of lightly armed hit-and-run, in which the communists proved so formidable in the mobile winter campaign of 1950, could be employed daily in Indochina for years on end. 'It was amazing that so many of the mistakes we made in Korea, we repeated in Vietnam,' said Colonel Al Bowser of the US Marines. 'Why? I wish I could answer that. Something seemed to come over people who went over there. During Vietnam, I used to say to a colleague of mine, Lew Walt, "Lew, what in the name of God are you doing with all those tanks in a rice paddy?" I never got a good answer.' Colonel John Michaelis of the 27th Infantry argued that the US Army failed to learn the lessons of Korea because it became an unpopular war, and those who returned preferred to forget it, inside as well as outside the service: 'I don't think that, as an army or a nation, we ever learn from our mistakes, from history. We didn't learn from the Civil War, we didn't learn from World War I. The US Army has still not accepted the simple fact that its performance in Korea was lousy.'

It may be argued that the communists profited more than the United Nations from the painful military lessons they learned in Korea. Mao Tse Tung's conviction that any conflict could be conducted upon the principles, and with the organisation, of guerrilla war, was proved fallacious. Large-scale guerrilla tactics proved very effective in the first winter campaign of 1950, where rapid cross-country movement and surprise broke open MacArthur's army. But thereafter, even the infinite willingness of the communists to accept casualties went for naught when confronted with the air power and firepower of a Western army in prepared positions. To the end of the conflict, Mao Tse Tung retained a strong personal commitment to the massed 'human wave' assaults characteristic of his army since its inception. His generals had discovered their limitations by painful experience in Korea. In the positional war, the Chinese displayed remarkable skill and professionalism with their scanty resources. But they were unable to achieve a break-through, and paid a vast price for their attempts.

> The survivors [General Sir Anthony Farrar-Hockley has written] no longer believed that, armed with the philosophy of the Party, they could beat anybody however superior their tech-nology. They knew it was not true. So, too, did their senior commanders. Peng Te Huai eventually succeeded in convincing his Central Committee comrades that they must upgrade the basis of the army from that of a body armed with what it could capture to one enjoying standard equipment tables, not least a comprehensive communications system. For a time, he per-suaded enough of his colleagues that they must initiate a rational system of recruitment based on conscription; and that a properly selected and trained professional officer corps was essential to the future of the armed forces.[3]

Yet Mao alone remained unconvinced of these lessons, and above all disputed Peng's downgrading of the importance of polit-ical officers, who in the early stages of the Korean War constituted 10 per cent of every formation's leadership down to sub-unit level. If the PLA was to be armed and organised like any other army, then it must depend upon Soviet weapons and equipment to an extent Mao found intolerable. When he purged Peng Te Huai and other senior PLA officers, he reversed their policies and preserved the PLA in much the mould in which it was forged in the civil war. Yet in the words of Farrar-Hockley, the Korean War had 'raised doubts in the PLA concerning the wisdom and competence of the Party leadership'[4] which would not go away.

Senior Chinese soldiers – if not their leader – emerged from Korea having absorbed the central, critical lesson for future Asian conflicts: that they must never face a Western army on its own terms. They must seek to fight when Western resources and technology counted for least. They could exploit the West's greatest single weakness: the impatience of democracies. It proved difficult for the United States and her allies to maintain public tolerance and support for the Korean War for three years. Apathy and exasperation with a national effort which was yielding no evident result became apparent in the American electorate long before the armistice. The decisive reason why it was possible for Western statesmen to sustain their people's tolerance of the war was the memory of that devastating, indisputable act of communist aggression which began it all in June 1950. Even the least sophisticated, most xenophobic Iowa farmer or Bradford bank clerk could comprehend the nature of the North Korean invasion. Without that simple *casus belli*, it seems highly doubtful that the Korean War could have been fought to an acceptable finish. This message the communists surely absorbed: never again should they provide the West with so unclouded and comprehensible a reason to resist; and time must always be against the democracies in arms.

*

Thirty years later, Oliver Franks, the former British Ambassador in Washington, had no doubts about the merit of Truman's Korean commitment: 'The United States Administration acted in Korea – the United Nations involvement was merely a fig-leaf for executive action. It was a *bellum justum* – the use of force to put down a wrongful action, not a case of counter-aggression.'

'Worthwhile? It was more worthwhile than Vietnam,' said Major Ed Simmons of the US Marine Corps. 'In 1950, the individual GI couldn't see much to admire in the average Korean. But looking back on it, the war revitalised NATO. It caused us to drop the tradition of demobilising at the end of a war. It hastened the schism between China and the Soviets. It saved Formosa. It contributed greatly to Japanese recovery: they got rich out of Korea, and fabulously rich out of Vietnam. It probably saved the Philippines for a time. Yes, it was worthwhile.'

A less grammatical but almost more eloquently confused view, probably shared by thousands of American rankers who fought in Korea, came from Ecton Plaisance, a Louisianan, whom 1950 found as a private soldier in 7th Cavalry:

> A lot of us feel that Truman made a big mistake by not letting MacArthur bomb the bridges on the Yalu river, also not letting him bomb the Chinese that were massing in China. Another big mistake was in 1951, the Chinese made their last big offensive against us and we stopped them cold, right after that we could have gone north and set up a good line 20 miles north of Pyongyang . . . My family did not understand the war, except that they knew that the communists wanted South Korea. They supported our government in the war. The war set the Chinese back 10 to 20 years where in the United States the big companies got richer. Don't get me wrong, I am not sorry I went and fought, it was an honour to fight the communists because it had to be done, however I would not do it again for a million dollars.

PFC Bill Shirk, an Ohian who spent more than two years in captivity, thought of the war as 'a hell of a waste. I saw no reason for it when I went over, less when I went back. When Vietnam started, I just thought: "Here we go again, the same damn nonsense." Who gives a shit if they're North Korean or South Korean? You can't take a person living like an animal and expect him to act like a human being. They don't place the value on human life that we do. Lots of men felt the same as I did.'

Many American career officers were deeply dismayed by the precedent Korea established: the United States had failed to fight a war to a victorious conclusion. Lieutenant-General Arthur Trudeau, commanding the US 7th Division, spoke of 'that odious armistice . . . when we let the Russians and the Chinese off the hook in Korea, we opened the door for their victory over the French in

Vietnam. We should have let MacArthur go to the Yalu and bomb the piss out of them on the other side.' 'I still feel very badly about Korea,' said Colonel Paul Freeman.

> I thought there had been a lot of unnecessary bloodletting for a stalemate. To have had this thing drag on and on, fighting for every bloody little hill over there, was all wrong. We should have knocked the Chinese out of there, whatever it took. But some of the European nations were scared that we were going to start something . . . the absurdity of trying to destroy those Yalu bridges without bombing the other side, that isn't the way to fight a war.

Freeman's, of course, is the voice of a generation of post-World-War-II American professional soldiers, infinitely frustrated by the inability of their nation effectively to deploy its vast military power in limited conflict. MacArthur was the foremost protagonist of their argument. For a brief window of time in the early fifties, the United States possessed the unmatched atomic capability to take on and defeat the communist powers. Sooner or later, they believed, it was the destiny of the United States, as the greatest capitalist power on earth, to fight the communists. Better now, surely, when the nation possessed the means to achieve victory at minimal risk to the American continent, than a generation hence, at a time and place of the communists' choosing.

Much that has taken place in the world since 1950 reinforces the conviction of supporters of the MacArthur doctrine. Soviet nuclear power is now such that the United States could never hope to fight the Russians without suffering intolerable casualties. Asian communism has inflicted a crippling humiliation upon the United States in Vietnam, achieving victory in a war that was fought on communist terms. The political limitations imposed upon the deployment of American force in Korea were matched by the restrictions in Indochina, that caused the United States to fight 'with a hand tied behind its back', as so many Americans saw it.

Yet few uncommitted observers, looking back thirty-five years to Truman's dismissal of MacArthur, can doubt that the President was perfectly justified. If the old general's faculties remained undiminished, there is little question that his judgement had become fatally unstable. The shock of initial defeat in Korea, followed by the almost mystical triumph of Inchon against all odds, followed in turn by new humiliation at the hands of the Chinese, might have distorted the thinking of a much younger, more conventional mind than that of MacArthur. The general believed that he was facing the great historic issue of his time, from which Washington flinched. Yet his own preoccupation with the balance of world power, and the military means of changing this, blinded him to the huge, critical moral issue surrounding the use of the atomic bomb. Most of our post-Hiroshima generation are convinced that it is not acceptable to regard nuclear weapons, as did MacArthur and some of his contemporaries, as merely quantitative increments to the arsenal of war. A real political, military and moral chasm exists, most of us believe, between the employment of conventional and nuclear weapons. What would have been the moral standing of the United States in the world today, had she employed nuclear weapons in Asia in 1950–51, not in self-defence, but in pursuit of foreign policy objectives related to the defeat of communism? In the answer each of us makes to that question, must lie our own attitudes to MacArthur and the controversy surrounding his dismissal by Truman.

*

The Korean War occupies a unique place in history, as the first superpower essay of the nuclear age in the employment of limited force to achieve limited objectives. The United States might have come away from Panmunjom in a more satisfied frame of mind, had this perspective been clearly discernible at the time. Instead, however, many Americans were merely frustrated by discovering the post-World-War-II political limits of military power. A generation later, had America been able to do for South Vietnam what she had earlier done for South Korea, the achievement would have been a cause for national self-congratulation.

The war was a landmark in the post-1945 foreign policy of the United States. Before the North Korean invasion, though America mourned the 'loss' of China, she did not regard Asia as the principal battlefront against communism. This lay in Europe. But events in Korea focused the attention of Americans upon the Far East. As the political frontiers in Europe stabilised, and the prospects of further communist takeovers there by political or diplomatic means receded, Americans became increasingly preoccupied with Asia. They had always enjoyed a romantic fascination with the continent. Now, they saw within it a host of precariously governed small nations, highly vulnerable to communist intervention. The military and foreign policy energies of the United States became more and more dedicated to frustrating this turn of events.

Yet if this objective was not ignoble, it was founded upon one profound misjudgement: it greatly underestimated the influence of nationalist, as distinct from ideological, forces, among the nations it sought to protect. Among all the thousands of reports and assessments of Korea in the archives of the United States and her allies, depressingly few pay even lip-service to the needs or interests of the Korean people. Korea merely chanced to be the battlefield upon which the struggle against the international communist conspiracy was being waged. In Korea, Americans revealed all the arrogance, the paternalism, the insensitivity in handling of local people – and the local army – which later revealed themselves in Vietnam. South Korea did not gain the immense national pride it possesses today from its part in the war. Indeed most South Koreans emerged from the 1950–53 experience conditioned either to a cynical pursuit of personal survival, or burdened by self-disgust. South Korea gained its self-respect from what it achieved by its own astonishing industrial efforts in the generation that followed the war. If the UN army had abandoned the South Koreans before an armistice was signed, and left Rhee's regime to fend for itself, it would have collapsed as ignominiously as that of

Saigon twenty years later, with or without Chinese military support for Pyongyang. South Korea escaped the fate of South Vietnam chiefly because the accident of geography made it infinitely easier to defend; and because the West, in 1950–53, still possessed a sufficient reservoir of crusading zeal to sustain an overseas campaign against communism. This reservoir was all but drained by the 1970s.

In determining the justice of what was done in Korea in the name of the United Nations, it is necessary to pull away a great tangle of subsidiary issues that confused contemporary observers as much as they have complicated the judgements of history. American occupation policy in South Korea from 1945 to 1949 was clumsy and insensitive. A political structure was created whose chief merit was that it was professedly hostile to communism. Yet it is too easy for historians to argue that Americans misread the signals from North Korea, that the Soviets had no initial intention of creating a satellite state in the Korean peninsula. If American reaction to Soviet behaviour was at times alarmist, nothing alters the fundamental truth that in Eastern Europe from 1945 to 1950, the Russians were engaged upon the ruthless construction of an empire. They were determined to build a military buffer zone around their own frontiers, without the slightest regard for the liberty or interests of millions of people whose misfortune it was to live within it. Given the scanty intelligence available from North Korea, it was asking a great deal of the Washington Administration to divine and acknowledge the Soviets' non-imperialistic intentions in Korea – if such indeed they were. If the Americans behaved clumsily in South Korea, their conduct was understandable in the worldwide context of the period. It remains debatable whether, even if a broader-based government had been created in South Korea, this would have been immune from North Korean aggression.

By 1950, if the regime of Syngman Rhee in the South was dictatorial, it was no more oppressive than that of Kim Il Sung. And the Southerners had been deliberately denied by the Americans the means, even if they possessed the will, to carry out aggressive acts beyond their own frontier. By any reasonable measure, Kim Il Sung's invasion of June 1950 was an unprovoked act of raw aggression, which the South lacked the means to resist. If the Soviets did not directly encourage the invasion, it could not have been carried out without their consent. From Moscow's perspective, the invasion of South Korea can be regarded – as it was interpreted in Washington at the time – as an experiment. If the Americans merely abandoned their puppets, so much the better. Even if they did not, it is unlikely that the Russians anticipated an American reaction on the scale that in reality took place. The Soviet view was characteristically cynical, and there is no reason to doubt the sincerity of Russian expressions of alarm in the weeks that followed, as it became apparent that the United States was determined to repel the North Koreans with whatever resources were required.

The Soviets seemed persistently unhappy about the war thereafter. They supplied the North Koreans and Chinese, and provided the pilots of an air corps. But if the Chinese had not chosen to intervene in the winter of 1950, it seems doubtful whether the Russians would have done so, even with Americans camped on the Yalu. Moscow had miscalculated the strength of American reaction at the outset. In the winter of 1950, fear of provoking American nuclear retaliation would almost certainly have dissuaded Stalin from going to war with the United States on the borders of Korea. The strongest evidence of Moscow's lack of enthusiasm for the Korean War lies in the sluggishness with which Stalin supplied matériel to Mao. Only in the autumn of 1951 did Soviet military supplies begin to move in quantity to China, and to the bitter resentment of the Chinese, every ton had to be paid for. Korea precipitated the deep mutual mistrust between Soviet and Chinese communists, which has been evident ever since.

Yet the Chinese, who were the most passive partners in the original North Korean invasion of the South, could argue a legitimate determination not to tolerate an American presence on the

Yalu. It was MacArthur's commitment to sweep north from the 38th Parallel that introduced a new strand of confusion into the debate about the merits of the United Nations operation in Korea. Until that moment, few detached observers around the world could deny that the UN flag was flying in an honourable cause, the restitution of the *status quo* in Korea. But from the moment UN forces crossed the 38th Parallel, the highest ideals of the United Nations became submerged beneath the foreign policy purposes of the United States. MacArthur must not bear sole responsibility for the decision to drive north. Not only in Washington, but in London and other Western capitals, in the flush of victory at Inchon it seemed possible to achieve a cheap, absolute success over the communists. If some statesmen and diplomats possessed reservations, they did not express them very strongly. Their silence, or at least muted expressions of concern, could reasonably be interpreted as consent in Washington and at the Dai Ichi.

MacArthur's denunciation of the Chinese intervention as a treacherous act will not do. Peking gave repeated warnings of the limits of its patience. It could plead the interests of self-defence in crossing the Yalu with at least as much conviction as President Kennedy a decade later in threatening war if the Soviets placed missile bases in Cuba. The Peking government had only recently emerged victorious from a war against Nationalist armies supplied and supported by the United States. With American sponsorship, the Nationalists could still pose a formidable threat to Mao Tse Tung's fragile government. Some Americans today, as well as in 1950, would argue that since Mao Tse Tung's communist regime represented an evil force in the world, it was legitimate for the forces of justice to adopt any means to destabilise, and ultimately to undo it. But most of America's allies, today as in 1950, find this argument unacceptable. The British, in particular, have always sought accommodation with communist China, and acknowledged the legitimacy of the People's Republic. This much granted, it was unreasonable to expect the Chinese to stand idly by while the United States deployed an army along the Yalu.

Yet the Chinese, in their turn, displayed strategic naïveté. The testimony of Chinese officers makes clear that they greatly underestimated the power of a Western army. Because they had just defeated an American-sponsored and equipped Nationalist army, Mao Tse Tung and his commanders appear to have expected the same level of performance, and the same weaknesses, in the US Army itself. This view was reinforced by their early experience of fighting Americans in November and December 1950. The Chinese undoubtedly went into Korea with the limited objective of driving back the Americans to a respectable distance from the Yalu. But in December 1950, in the exultation of tactical success, they made a strategic error precisely mirroring that of the Americans a few weeks earlier: they saw an opportunity to expand a limited operation into a crushing and symbolic wider victory. Thus, they drove on southwards in hot pursuit of the fleeing Americans; and thus, with their supply lines over-extended and their resources of everything but manpower almost exhausted, they met the full might of a Western army, regrouped under Ridgway. Throughout the two years that followed, the combatant nations felt themselves engaged in an inescapable struggle for face. Each side having rashly overreached its limited war aims, peace only became attainable after a long process during which the combatants became once more reconciled to these. The war drove China into diplomatic and economic isolation, and made her an absolute dependent of the Soviet Union for a generation. 'Peking's action,' in America's view, assessed by Dr Rosemary Foot, 'displayed its revolutionary zeal, inexperience in world affairs, troublemaking capacity in the immediate vicinity of its borders, and exaggerated sense of its own power.'

But if China was denied its ideological triumph in Korea, the war made Mao Tse Tung's nation a great power in the eyes of the world. The impact of that first crushing Chinese victory in the winter of 1950 was never entirely lost. The spectacle of a heavily armed and armoured Western army fleeing before Marshal Peng's cotton-clad divisions was not forgotten. Most men who fought against the Chinese in Korea went home with a considerable regard for their fighting qualities, which made it all the more remarkable that, in Vietnam a decade later, a new generation of Americans proved once more reluctant to believe that Asian soldiers could match Westerners on the battlefield. In Korea, China convinced the world that she was a force to be reckoned with, after centuries in which she had been dismissed as an ineffectual society of mandarins and warlords. The chief negative cost of the war to Peking was that it prevented the communists – perhaps for ever – from gaining control of Formosa, today's Taiwan. In June 1950, Washington was weary of Chiang Kai Shek and his defeated Nationalists. Had it not been for the North Korean invasion, they would have almost certainly been left mouldering on Formosa until the communists overwhelmed them. Instead, they became a central element in America's policy for resisting communist expansion in the Far East, the beneficiaries of vast military and economic aid, which made possible the powerful modern industrial state they created over the next thirty years.

Thousands of men who fought for the United Nations in Korea are deeply moved today by the gratitude that South Koreans still display for the salvation of their country from the communists more than thirty years ago. Perhaps this has been enhanced by watching South Vietnam submerged into a communist state. 'I see Koreans today, and the respect they show for us,' said Private Bill Norris of the 27th Infantry, 'and I contrast this with the animosity I saw for us in Europe, after World War II ended. They didn't want us over there. In Korea, I see gratitude. I never felt exploited by a Korean, in the way we all were as GIs by the French and the Belgians in 1945. In the market place in Seoul, I could buy stuff for the same price a Korean paid for it. I felt safe there.' Sergeant John Richardson of 2nd Princess Patricia's Canadian Light Infantry believed passionately that the war was worthwhile: 'In October 1983, I had the great privilege of going back to Korea. It was the thrill of a lifetime. On my return, I simply told the Calgary Branch of the PPCLI Association that I was convinced that our fallen comrades rest in a country where their sacrifice is fully appreciated.'

'We stopped communism, didn't we?' said Bob Campbell of the 1st Marines. They did indeed. At the 38th Parallel, a border persists today between one of the most advanced, and one of the most backward societies in Asia. The people of North Korea have paid the bitterest price of all for Kim Il Sung's adventure in June 1950. To this day, they remain the prisoners of the ageing, obsessive, perhaps demented old dictator in his wretched self-created prison camp. Fifteen years after the Chinese set about opening up a new relationship with the West, the North Koreans reject any attempt to do so, and their relations even with Peking are strained. North Korea exists in pitiful isolation, a society dominated by poverty and the cult of Kim Il Sung.

South Korea, meanwhile, has become one of the greatest economic and industrial powers in Asia. The harshest price it has paid for the war is that, even today, it remains a society under siege. The threat from the North has never receded. Pyongyang maintains a constant propaganda war, and a military capability that cannot be ignored. North Korea's constant efforts to undermine the South by subversive activity, and periodically by guerrilla and terrorist operations across the border, provide the justification for the military machine that still dominates South Korea. Syngman Rhee was deposed in 1960, when the United States publicly withdrew its support from the old dictator after he had rigged one election too many. A generation after his fall, a procession of more or less repressive military, or military-influenced, governments rule from Seoul. Political dissent is ruthlessly suppressed. The United States maintains a strong military presence. Washington has always tacitly accepted the tough domestic policies of South Korea's governments, maintaining the bastion against communism. Seoul won the warm approval of the US during the Vietnam War, repaying the aid given in 1950 by sending a South Korean division to Indochina which proved one of the most formidable fighting formations in the struggle against the communists. It also earned a reputation as one of the most savage and ruthless in its dealings with the Vietnamese. Ironically, it was the Vietnam War which gave the Korean economy its decisive boost to take off. South Korea today displays all the traditional qualities of its people: energy, organisation, fiercely nationalistic competitiveness, ruthlessness. Much of the country the UN armies knew has vanished under unlovely steel and concrete.

Such critics as the British left-wing journalist James Cameron regarded all this, as they later regarded the shortcomings of the American-sponsored regime in Vietnam, as sufficient reason to deny the Seoul government a claim to legitimacy. In 1950, Cameron became a popular martyr-figure in the British media, when the proprietor of the weekly magazine *Picture Post* stopped the presses when he found an issue containing a denunciation of the Seoul regime by Cameron. Headed 'An Appeal to the United Nations', the article catalogued the brutalities and injustices of the Rhee regime, and argued that it was wrong that this should be defended under the flag of the UN. Cameron later called his piece 'an implicit criticism of the Americans for their endorsement of an arrogant tyranny'.[5] His eloquent reporting foreshadowed the veritable torrent of such prose which would flow from Indochina in the sixties and seventies. It stemmed from the conviction that civilised democracies should withhold their support – above all their military support – from flawed political structures, in which such wickedness flourished. Yet others – the author among them as a correspondent in Vietnam – acknowledged the failings of the Saigon or Seoul regimes, while denying that these provided sufficient reason to concede victory to the communists. The evidence of equal, indeed greater evils wrought by the communist forces could not be gainsaid. Rarely in the world is a choice offered between a cause of absolute virtue, and one of absolute evil: even the Allied cause in the Second World War was confused, for many participants, by discovering the bloody hand of Joseph Stalin on the side of the democracies. In Korea, as in Vietnam, the democracies supported the cause of a flawed society. Yet they were fighting against opponents representing an even harsher tyranny. Who can doubt that, if Hanoi had been defeated, South Vietnam would today enjoy the same affluence as South Korea, and its people at least a greater measure of freedom than they can look for under communism?

Today, the people of South Korea have achieved a prosperity and fulfilment that gives them immense satisfaction. In 1950, Won Jung Kil was twenty-one, an unemployed welder eking out an existence in Inchon, strongly hostile to the Rhee regime. He was conscripted in 1951 and spent six years of wretched near-starvation as an ROK army driver: 'I hated the officers. They had too much of everything. Pay? We had no pay, there was just a little food. No Korean enjoyed the war.' Yet today, Won can say: 'It was worthwhile. We are fine, we have enough to eat. I like our life now very much.' The simple, material satisfaction is very deep, for people who have come such a long way in thirty-five years. They look back upon the war as a nightmare for their nation. But they reveal a real gratitude for the campaign waged by the United Nations, that enabled their society to retain its independence, that made possible everything they have today. Few Westerners, looking upon the respective circumstances of North and South Korea today, can doubt that the West's intervention in 1950 saved the Southerners from a tragic fate, and indeed opened the way to a future for them infinitely better than anything attainable under Kim Il Sung. If the Korean War was a frustrating, profoundly unsatisfactory experience, more than thirty years later it still seems a struggle that the West was right to fight.

Appendix A: Chronology

1950

25 June	North Korean forces attack South Korean positions south of the 38th Parallel.
	The United Nations Security Council, in the absence of the USSR, adopts a resolution calling for the withdrawal of North Korean forces to the Parallel.
27 June	President Truman orders US air and sea services to give support to South Korean forces. UN Security Council calls on member nations to give aid in repelling aggression in Korea.
29 June	North Korean army seizes Seoul. Britain orders Far Eastern fleet to give aid.
30 June	Truman orders US ground troops to Korea and naval blockade of Korean coast. Authorises US Air Force to bomb North Korea.
1 July	First US combat troops arrive in Korea. Major-General William F. Dean placed in command of US forces in Korea.
4 July	US troops first meet enemy just north of Osan; forced to retreat.
7 July	General Douglas MacArthur named Supreme UN Commander.
13 July	Lieutenant General Walton H. Walker, commander of Eighth Army, assumes command of ground forces in Korea.
15 July	North Koreans cross Kum river.

18	July	US First Cavalry and 25th Infantry Divisions reach Korea.
21	July	24th Division troops fight out of burning Taejon. General Dean missing in action.
1	August	Second US Infantry Division reach Korea. Yakov Malik, the Soviet delegate to the UN, ends Moscow's boycott of the organisation and takes over the presidency of the Security Council.
2	August	First US Marine Brigade reach Korea.
8	August	North Koreans breach Naktong river perimeter line.
15	August	UN troops repel two attacks along Naktong.
29	August	British 27 Brigade arrive from Hong Kong.
3	September	Communist offensive threatens Taeju.
7	September	General Walker declares 'our lines will hold'.
15	September	US X Corps makes successful amphibious assault on Inchon, enabling UN forces to break out of Pusan and push towards the 38th Parallel.
19	September	X Corps starts to encircle Seoul; Eighth Army sweeps north and west with communists in flight. Filipino troops reach Korea.
26	September	Seoul falls.
29	September	General MacArthur enters Seoul with President Syngman Rhee.
1	October	South Korean troops cross 38th Parallel.
7	October	UN adopts resolution that 'all appropriate steps be taken to ensure conditions of stability throughout Korea'. US troops cross the Parallel.
8	October	Mao Tse Tung secretly orders Chinese 'Volunteers' to 'resist the attacks of US imperialism'.
15	October	Truman and MacArthur meet on Wake Island.
18	October	ROK troops occupy Hamhung and Hungnam.
19	October	Eighth Army take Pyongyang, capital of North Korea.

25	October	Chinese forces fight with ROK troops less than forty miles south of the Yalu river.
27	October	Eighth Army halted by Chinese.
29	October	X Corps halted by Chinese in north-east.
30	October	Eighth Army's 6th ROK Division overwhelmed by Chinese at Yongdu.
1	November	First Chinese MiGs appear along the Yalu.
3	November	US 25th Division driven back from Yalu area.
6	November	MacArthur charges Chinese with unlawful aggression. Chongchon river line held.
8	November	Air battle over Sinuiji.
11	November	Eighth Army again attacked.
12	November	US Army Third Division arrives in Korea.
16	November	Truman reassures China and other nations that he has never had any intention of carrying the hostilities into China. Lull in fighting.
24	November	Chinese special delegation arrives at UN Security Council. MacArthur launches offensive and troops approach Chinese border.
25	November	Chinese release fifty-seven US prisoners in propaganda move.
26	November	Chinese counter-attack.
27	November	Eighth Army halted by huge Chinese forces.
28	November	General Walker announces offensive at an end.
1	December	Eighth Army and X Corps begin withdrawing in face of Chinese offensive.
5	December	US/UN troops withdraw from Pyongyang. Chinese occupy the capital of North Korea.
9	December	X Corps forced to withdraw from Wonsan by sea.
11	December	X Corps evacuates Hungnam.
19	December	Truman declares state of National Emergency.
22	December	Chinese reject ceasefire: it makes no reference to

China's demands for removal of foreign troops from Korea and for a seat in the UN.

23	December	General Walker killed in jeep accident.
25	December	Chinese cross 38th Parallel.
27	December	Lieutenant-General Matthew Ridgway takes over command of ground forces in Korea.

1951

1	January	Communist offensive begins.
4	January	US/UN forces evacuate Seoul.
7	January	Communists enter Wonju.
8–15	January	US 2nd Division, with others, stops Chinese south of Wonju.
13	January	US delegation votes for UN ceasefire resolution.
17	January	China rejects ceasefire proposal.
		Eighth Army re-enters Suwon.
1	February	UN resolution declares China to be engaged in aggression.
10	February	Eighth Army retakes Inchon and Kimpo Airfield.
13	February	Major Chinese offensive against X Corps in Central Korea.
15	February	Communists defeated at Chipyong-ni.
21	February	Eighth Army launch Operation Killer.
7	March	Operation Ripper launched. Eighth Army cross Han river east of Seoul.
13	March	Communists start to withdraw across all fronts.
15	March	Eighth Army retake Seoul.
21	March	Eighth Army retake Chunchon.
22	March	Eighth Army reach 38th Parallel.
3	April	Eighth Army Divisions cross Parallel.
5	April	MacArthur's letter criticising Truman's strategy and the concept of limited war made public.

11 April	Truman relieves MacArthur as UN commander and appoints Ridgway to succeed him.
15 April	Lieutenant-General James Van Fleet takes command of Eighth Army.
19 April	MacArthur denounces the Truman Administration before Congress for refusing to lift restrictions on the scope of the war.
22 April	Chinese begin their spring offensive.
25 April	Start of Battle of Imjin river.
	Eighth Army pushed back 18–20 miles.
1 May	First phase of Chinese offensive halted north of Seoul.
16 May	Chinese launch second phase of spring offensive.
17 May	2nd Division again stop communists.
23 May	Eighth Army begin offensive.
28 May	Eighth Army take Hwachon and Inje.
3 June	Eighth Army move towards 'Iron Triangle' in Central Korea.
12 June	Eighth Army control 'Iron Triangle'.
Early June	At the MacArthur Congressional hearing, Secretary Acheson expresses willingness to negotiate a ceasefire near the 38th Parallel.
23 June	Yakov Malik, the Soviet Ambassador to the UN, calls for a ceasefire.
25 June	Chinese radio voices desire for ceasefire.
29 June	Ridgway offers to meet the communist commanders to discuss ceasefire and armistice.
1 July	Kim Il Sung, commander of the North Korean forces, and Peng Te Huai, commander of the Chinese 'Volunteers', agree to begin armistice discussions.
10 July	Armistice negotiations begin at Kaesong.
26 July	Agreement on the agenda for the armistice talks reached.

23 August	Communists suspend negotiations after alleged UN violation of the neutral zone at Kaesong.
25 October	Ceasefire discussions resume at Panmunjom.
13 November	US Administration proposes acceptance of current line of contact, provided other issues outstanding at the truce talks are settled within thirty days. US/UN ground action permitted to continue.
27 December	Thirty-day limit reached after establishing demarcation line on 27 November. No progress on other issues made, so line invalidated.

1952

January–April	Disorder in prison camps as screening of prisoners begins.
19 April	UN delegation informs the communists that only 70,000 of 132,000 prisoners-of-war willing to return home.
2 May	Communists reject UN proposals over question of voluntary repatriation.
7 May	Prisoners at Koje-do hold General Dodd hostage until 11 May.
	Both sides announce stalemate over prisoner-of-war issue.
12 May	General Mark Clark succeeds Ridgway.
23 June	US Air Force bomb Yalu river power installations to induce a more co-operative attitude at the truce talks.
29 August	Heaviest air raid of the war launched against Pyongyang.
8 October	The final offer on the prisoner-of-war question is rejected by the communists and an indefinite recess is announced.
24 October	Eisenhower announces that if he is elected President, he will go to Korea.
4 November	Eisenhower elected President with 55 per cent of the

vote. He visits units in Korea for three days on 5 December.

10 November
Van Fleet announces the mobilisation of two new South Korean divisions and six regiments.

1953

February
General Van Fleet retires, General Maxwell D. Taylor assumes command of Eighth Army.

22 February
Clark proposes an exchange of sick and wounded prisoners.

30 March
The Chinese agree and propose that prisoners unwilling to be repatriated be transferred to a neutral state.

20 April
Exchange of sick and wounded prisoners begins at Panmunjom.

26 April
Armistice negotiations resume.

13 May
Clark authorised to mobilise four more South Korean divisions.

20 May
The National Security Council decides that if 'conditions arise', air and naval operations will be extended to China and ground operations in Korea will be intensified.

28 May
The US/UN negotiating team presents its final terms and threatens to break off the talks if these are rejected.

Chinese attack outposts of US 25th Division.

8 June
Prisoner-of-war question resolved and principle of voluntary repatriation accepted.

10 June
Chinese open assault on ROK II Corps near Kumsong. By 16 June, ROK II Corps pushed back to new Main Line of Resistance.

15–30 June
Chinese attack US I Corps.

17 June
Revised demarcation line settled.

President Rhee orders South Korean guards to release

North Korean prisoners who do not wish to be repatriated.

20 July   New Main Line of Resistance established on south bank of Kumsong river.

27 July   Armistice signed at Panmunjom.

Appendix B

Offers of Military Assistance for Korea by UN Members

Summaries of Offers of Military Assistance for Korea by UN members as of 15 January 1952. Many of those marked 'Acceptance deferred' were never taken up: most conspicuously, Nationalist China's offer of three infantry divisions.

GROUND FORCES

Country	Date	Details of offer	Status
Australia	3 Aug. 1950	Ground forces from Australian Infantry Force in Japan	In action
		Additional battalion of Australian troops	In action
Belgium	13 Sept. 1950	Infantry battalion	In action
	3 May 1951	Reinforcements	In action
Bolivia	15 July 1950	30 officers	Acceptance deferred
Canada	14 Aug. 1950	Brigade group, including three infantry battalions, one field regiment of artillery, one squadron of self-propelled anti-tank guns, together with engineer, signal, medical, ordnance and other services with appropriate reinforcements.	In action
China	3 July 1950	Three infantry divisions	Acceptance deferred
Colombia	14 Nov. 1950	One infantry battalion	In action

Country	Date	Details of offer	Status
Costa Rica	27 July 1950	Volunteers	Acceptance deferred
Cuba	30 Nov. 1950	One infantry company	Accepted
El Salvador	15 Aug. 1950	Volunteers	Acceptance deferred
Ethiopia	2 Nov. 1950	1,069 officers and men	In action
France	20 Aug. 1950	Infantry battalion	In action
Greece	1 Sept. 1950	Unit of land forces	In action
	2 July 1951	Additional unit of land forces	Transmitted to Unified Command
Luxembourg	15 Mar. 1951	Infantry company integrated into the Belgian forces	In action
Netherlands	8 Sept. 1950	One infantry battalion	In action
New Zealand	26 July 1950	One combat unit	In action
Panama	3 Aug. 1950	Contingent of volunteers / Bases for training	Acceptance deferred
Philippines	10 Aug. 1950	Regimental combat team consisting of approximately 5,000 officers and men	In action
Thailand	23 July 1950	Infantry combat team of about 4,000 officers and men	In action
Turkey	25 July 1950	Infantry combat force of 4,500 men, later increased to 6,086 men	In action
United Kingdom	21 Aug. 1950	Ground forces	In action
	Official information communicated on 12 June 1951	Two brigades composed of brigade headquarters	In action
		Five infantry battalions	In action
		One field regiment	In action
		One armoured regiment	In action
United States of America	Official information communicated on 8 June 1951	Three Army Corps / One Marine Division } With supporting elements	In action

NAVAL FORCES

Country	Date	Details of offer	Status
Australia	28 July 1950	Two destroyers	In action
	29 July 1950	One aircraft carrier	In action
		One frigate	In action
Canada	12 July 1950	Three destroyers	In action
Colombia	16 Oct. 1950	One frigate – *Almirante Padilla*	In action
France	19 July 1950	Patrol gun boat	Withdrawn
Netherlands	5 July 1950	One destroyer – *Evertsen*	In action
New Zealand	1 July 1950	Two frigates – HMNZ *Tutira* and HMNZ *Pukaki*	In action
Thailand	3 Oct. 1950	Two corvettes – *Prasae* and *Bangpakong**	In action
United Kingdom	28 June 1950	Naval forces in Japanese waters diverted to Korea	In action
	Official information communicated on 12 June 1951	One aircraft carrier	In action
		Two cruisers	In action
		Eight destroyers	In action
		One survey ship	In action
United States of America	Official information communicated on 8 June 1951	A fast carrier task group with a blockade and escort force, an amphibious force, reconnaissance and anti-submarine warfare units	In action

AIR FORCES

Australia	30 June 1950	One RAAF fighter squadron	In action
		One air communication unit	In action
		Base and maintenance personnel	In action
Canada	21 July 1950	One RCAF squadron	In action
Union of South Africa	4 Aug. 1950	One fighter squadron, including ground personnel	In action

Country	Date	Details of offer	Status
United Kingdom	Official information communicated on 12 June 1951	Elements of the Air Force	In action
United States of America	Official information communicated on 8 June 1951	One Tactical Air Force, one Bombardment Command, and one Combat Cargo Command, all with supporting elements	In action

MATERIEL

Philippines	3 Aug. 1950	17 Sherman tanks and one tank destroyer	In action

TRANSPORT

Belgium	28 Sept. 1950	Air transport	In action
Canada	11 Aug. 1950	Facilities of Canadian Pacific Airlines between Vancouver and Tokyo	In action
		Dry Cargo Vessels (10,000 tons)	In action
China	3 July 1950	Twenty C-47s	Acceptance deferred
Denmark	22 July 1950	Motor ship *Bella Dan*	Withdrawn
Greece	20 July 1950 / 13 Oct. 1950	Eight Dakota transport planes	In action
Norway	18 July 1950	Merchant ship tonnage	In action
Panama	3 Aug. 1950	Use of merchant marine for transportation of troops and supplies	In action
Thailand	3 Oct. 1950	Transport *Sichang* to be attached to Thai troops	In action
		Air transport	
United Kingdom	Official information communicated on 12 June 1951	Seven supply vessels	In action

Country	Date	Details of offer	Status
United States of America		Air transport supply vessels	In action

MEDICAL

Country	Date	Details of offer	Status
Denmark	18 Aug. 1950	Hospital Ship *Jutlandia*	In action
India	29 July 1950	Field Ambulance Unit	In action
Italy	27 Sept. 1950	Field Hospital Unit	In action
Norway	6 Mar. 1951	Surgical Hospital Unit	In action
Sweden	20 July 1950	Field Hospital Unit	In action
United Kingdom	Official information communicated on 12 June 1951	Hospital Ship	In action
United States of America		Large-scale hospital facilities	In action

MISCELLANEOUS

Country	Date	Details of offer	Status
Costa Rica	27 July 1950	Sea and air bases	Accepted
Panama	3 Aug. 1950	Bases for training	Acceptance deferred
		Free use of highways	Acceptance deferred
		Farm lands to supply troops	Pending
Thailand	2 Feb. 1951	Treatment for frostbite	Pending

*Destroyed on grounding

Appendix C

United Kingdom Forces in the Korean Theatre of War

Period of Service	Armour
November 1950 to December 1951	8 King's Royal Irish Hussars
November 1950 to October 1951	'C' Squadron, 7th Royal Tank Regiment
December 1951 to December 1952	5 Royal Inniskilling Dragoon Guards
December 1952 to December 1953	1 Royal Tank Regiment

Period of Service	Royal Artillery
November 1950 to November 1951	45 Field Regiment
November 1950 to November 1951	11 (Sphinx) Independent Light A.A. Battery (converted to 4.2 Mortars in June 1951)
November 1950 to October 1951	170 Independent Mortar Battery
November 1951 to December 1952	14 Field Regiment
October 1951. Joined 61st Light Regiment in December 1952	120 Light A.A. Battery
November 1951. Joined 61st Light Regiment in February 1952	42 Light A.A. Battery (Redesignated 42nd Light Battery in January 1952)
	15 Location Battery
January 1952 to January 1954	61 Light Regiment
December 1952 to December 1953	20 Field Regiment
February 1953 to November 1953	74 Medium Battery

Period of Service	*Infantry*
August 1950 to May 1951	1 Bn. The Middlesex Regiment
August 1950 to April 1951	1 Bn. The Argyll and Sutherland Highlanders
August 1950 to March 1951	41 Commando, Royal Marines
November 1950 to October 1951	1 Bn. The Royal Northumberland Fusiliers
November 1950 to November 1951	1 Bn. The Gloucestershire Regiment
November 1950 to October 1951	1 Bn. The Royal Ulster Rifles
April 1951 to August 1952	1 Bn. King's Own Scottish Borderers
May 1951 to September 1952	1 Bn. The King's Shropshire Light Infantry
October 1951 to September 1952	1 Bn. The Royal Norfolk Regiment
October 1951 to June 1952	1 Bn. The Royal Leicestershire Regiment
November 1951 to November 1952	1 Bn. The Welch Regiment
June 1952 to July 1953	1 Bn. The Black Watch
August 1952 to August 1953	1 Bn. The Royal Fusiliers (City of London Regiment)
September 1952 to September 1953	1 Bn. The Durham Light Infantry
September 1952 to October 1953	1 Bn. The King's Regiment
October 1952 to November 1953	1 Bn. The Duke of Wellington's Regiment
July 1953 to May 1954	1 Bn. The Royal Scots

Period of Service	*Royal Engineers*
November 1950. Joined 28th Field Engineer Regiment July 1951	55 Field Squadron
1951 to	12 Field Squadron
July 1951 to 1955	28 Field Engineer Regiment (Commonwealth integrated unit)
July 1951 to 1955	64 Field Park Squadron (Commonwealth integrated unit)
	206 Army Postal Unit
July 1951 to 1955	28 Field Engineer Regiment (Commonwealth integrated unit
July 1951 to 1955	64 Field Park Squadron (Commonwealth integrated unit)

Period of Service   *Royal Signals*

                                             27 Brigade Signals Troop
                                             29 Brigade Signals Troop
July 1951 to 1955   Commonwealth Division Signals Regiment
                                                 (Commonwealth integrated unit)

Period of Service   *Royal Army Medical Corps*

December 1950 to 1954   26 Field Ambulance
                                             Commonwealth General Hospital, Kure, Japan
                                                 (Commonwealth integrated unit)
September 1952 to December 1954   Communications Zone Medical Unit
                                                 (Commonwealth integrated unit)

Royal Army Dental Corps

Queen Alexandra's Royal Army Nursing Corps

Royal Army Service Corps

57 Company
78 Company
76 Supply Company
37 Field Bakery Platoon
39 Field Bakery Platoon

Royal Electrical and Mechanical Engineers

10 Infantry Workshops
11 Infantry Workshops
16 Infantry Workshops

Royal Army Ordnance Corps

Intelligence Corps

904 Field Security Section
104 Army Photographic Interpretation Section

Royal Military Police

27 Brigade Provost Section
28 Brigade Provost Section
Commonwealth Division Provost Company
(Commonwealth integrated unit)

Royal Army Pay Corps

73 Forward Base Pay Office
204 Field Cash Office

Navy/Army/Air-Force Institutes/Expeditionary Forces Institute

2 Public Relations Service

ROYAL AIR FORCE

Far East Air Force Flying Boat Wing
Far East Air Force Transport Wing
1903 Army Observation Post Flight
1913 Light Liaison Flight

ROYAL NAVY

Period of Service	*Headquarters ships*
September 1950 to April 1953	*Ladybird*
April to July 1953	*Tyne*

Period of Service	*Light Fleet Carriers*
July 1950 to July 1953	*Unicorn*
July 1950 to September 1950	*Triumph* (800, 827 Squadron)
October 1950 to April 1951	*Theseus* (807, 810 Squadron)
April to September 1951	*Glory* (804, 812 Squadron, 801, 821 Squadron)
January to September 1952	
November 1952 to May 1953	
May to October 1952	
May to July 1953	*Ocean* (802, 825 Squadron; 807, 810 Squadron)

Period of Service	*Cruisers*
June to August 1950	*Belfast*
January 1951 to September 1952	
June to October 1950	*Jamaica*
July 1950 to August 1952	*Kenya*
August 1950 to July 1952	*Ceylon*
July 1952 to July 1953	*Newcastle*
September 1952 to July 1953	*Birmingham*

Period of Service	*Destroyers*
July 1950 to January 1951	*Charity*
July to September 1951	
December 1951 to March 1952	
August to November 1952	
February to April 1953	
June to July 1953	
July to November 1950	*Cockade*
March to August 1951	
October to December 1951	
January to March 1952	
December 1952 to February 1953	
April to July 1953	
July to November 1950	*Comus*
March to August 1951	
October to December 1951	
May to September 1952	
November 1952 to February 1953	
September 1950 to January 1951	*Concord*
April to May 1951	
August to November 1951	
January to April 1952	
July to August 1952	
May to July 1953	
June 1950 to April 1951	*Consort*
June to September 1951	
May to August 1952	
November 1952 to February 1953	
March to May 1953	
October 1950 to March 1951	*Constance*
June to July 1951	
November 1951 to February 1952	
June to December 1952	
June 1950 to October 1951	*Cossack*
February to May 1952	
July 1952	
September 1952 to January 1953	
May to July 1953	

Period of Service	*Frigates*
June to August 1950 February to June 1951 December 1951 to February 1952	*Alacrity*
August to October 1950 October 1951	*Alert*
February to June 1951 September 1951 to January 1952 April to July 1952	*Amethyst*
June to August 1950 February to June 1951 September to November 1951	*Black Swan*
November 1950 to January 1951 June to September 1951 January to April 1952 June to September 1952 January to July 1953	*Cardigan Bay*
March to June 1952 August to September 1952 November 1952 to March 1953 July 1953	*Crane*
June to August 1950 February to March 1951	*Hart*
April to June 1953	*Modeste*
October 1950 to January 1951 June to September 1951 March to May 1952 August to November 1952 May to July 1953	*Morecambe Bay*

Period of Service	*Frigates*
August to November 1952	*Mounts Bay*
December 1950 to January 1951	
June to September 1951	
December 1951 to April 1952	
June to November 1952	
March to June 1953	
November 1952 to April 1953	*Opossum*
December 1950 to January 1951	*St Bride's Bay*
August to December 1951	
July to October 1952	
April to June 1953	
December 1952 to February 1953	*Sparrow*
April to June 1953	
August to December 1950	*Whitesand Bay*
June to July 1951	
October 1951 to February 1952	
April to July 1953	

Period of Service	*Fleet Train. Royal Fleet Auxiliary*
June 1950 to February 1952	*Maine* (Hospital Ship Company
May 1952 to 1953	included Queen Alexandra's Royal
	Naval Nursing Service)
	Fort Charlotte (Naval and Victualling Stores
	Issuing Ship)
	Fort Rosalie (Armament Store Issuing Ship)
	Fort Langley
	Fort Sandusky
	Choysang (Merchant Fleet Auxiliary
	Armament Store Issuing Ship)
	Echodale (Oiler)
	Green Ranger (Oiler)
	Brown Ranger (Oiler)
	Wave Chief (Oiler)
	Wave Conqueror (Oiler)
	Wave Knight (Oiler)
	Wave Laird (Oiler)
	Wave Premier (Oiler)
	Wave Prince (Oiler)
	Wave Regent (Oiler)
	Wave Sovereign (Oiler)

Bibliography and a note on sources

The principal sources for this book have been oral interviews with participants in the Korean War, or those with pertinent diplomatic and political experience, together with the relevant files in the Public Record Office, London, and the National Archive, Washington DC. I have also consulted records and reports at the Staff College, Camberley, and personal correspondence preserved privately. The National Military Museum in Peking contains a large Korean section, and much visual material, but no important documentation is available to a foreign researcher. There are major oral history transcript collections at the US Marine Corps Museum, Washington DC, and at the US Army's Military History Institute at Carlisle Barracks, Pennsylvania. The list of secondary sources below does not include unit and formation histories, which exist for almost every fighting element on the UN side in Korea. I have drawn upon the contemporary files of major British and US newspapers, together with some locally published wartime English-language newspapers in Korea.

Acheson, Dean – *Present at the Creation* (Hamish Hamilton, 1969)
Ambrose, Stephen E. – *Eisenhower the President* (Allen & Unwin, 1984)
Anderson, William Ellery – *Banner Over Pusan* (Evans, 1960)
Barclay, C. N. – *The First Commonwealth Division* (Gale & Polden, 1954)
Barker, A. J. – *Fortune Favours the Brave* (Leo Cooper, 1974)
Bartlett, Norman – (ed.) *With the Australians in Korea* (Australian War Memorial, 1954)
Biderman, Albert D. – *March to Calumny* (Macmillan, 1963)
Blumenson, Martin – *Mark Clark* (Jonathan Cape, 1985)
Bohlen, Charles E. – *Witness to History, 1929–1969* (Norton, 1973)

Bradbury, William C., Meyers, Samuel M. & Biderman, Albert D. – *Mass Behavior in Battle and Captivity: The Communist Soldier in the Korean War* (University of Chicago Press, 1968)

Bradley, Omar N. and Blair, Clay – *A General's Life* (Simon & Schuster, 1983)

Bullock, Alan – *Ernest Bevin* (vol. II) (Heinemann, 1983)

Cameron, James – *Point of Departure* (Arthur Barker, 1967)

Carew, Tim – *The Commonwealth at War* (Cassell, 1967)

Caridi, Ronald J. – *The Korean War and American Politics: The Republican Party as a Case Study* (University of Pennsylvania Press, 1968)

Chae, Kyung Oh – *Handbook of Korea* (Pageant Press, 1958)

Chafe, William H. – *The Unfinished Journey* (Oxford University Press, 1985)

Collins, Lawton J. – *War in Peace* (Houghton Mifflin, 1969)

Cumings, Bruce – *Origins of the Korean War* (Princeton University Press, 1981)

Cutforth, René – *Korean Reporter* (Heinemann, 1951)

Davies, S. J. – *In Spite of Dungeons* (Hodder & Stoughton, 1955)

Dean, William F. – *General Dean's Story* (Viking, 1954)

Deane, Philip – *Captive in Korea* (Hamish Hamilton, 1953)

Donovan, Robert J. – *Tumultuous Years* (Norton, 1981)

Dulles, John Foster – *War or Peace* (Macmillan, New York, 1950)

Eisenhower, Dwight D. – *The White House Years: Mandate for Change, 1953–56* (Doubleday, 1963)

Farrar-Hockley, Anthony – *The Edge of the Sword* (Frederick Muller, 1954)

Felton, Monica – *That's Why I Went* (Lawrence & Wishart, 1953)

Field, James A. – *History of US Naval Operations Korea* (Naval History Division, Washington, 1962)

Foot, Rosemary – *The Wrong War* (Cornell University Press, 1985)

Foreign Affairs, Her Majesty's Secretary For, – *Survey of Events Relating to Korea* (HMSO London, 1950)

Futrell, George F. – *The United States Air Force in the Korean War* (Office of Air Force History, Washington, 1983)

George, Alexander L. – *The Chinese Communist Army in Action* (Columbia University Press, 1967)

Giesler, Patricia – *Valour Remembered: Canadians in Korea* (Department of Veterans' Affairs, Ottawa, 1982)

Gittings, John – *The Role of the Chinese Army* (Oxford University Press, 1967)

Goulden, Joseph C. – *Korea: The Untold Story* (McGraw Hill, 1982)

Griffith, Samuel B. – *The Chinese People's Liberation Army* (Weidenfeld & Nicolson, 1968)

Grist, Digby – *Remembered with Advantage* (Barton Press, 1976)

Gugeler, Russell A. – *Combat Actions in Korea* (Office of the Army Chief of Military History, Washington, 1970)

Gurtov, Hwang B. – *China under Threat* (University of California Press, 1956)

Harriman, W. Averell – *America and Russia in a Changing World* (Doubleday, 1971)

Heinl, Robert Debs – *Victory at High Tide* (Leo Cooper, 1972)

Hermes, Walter G. – *Truce Tent and Fighting Front* (Washington GPO, 1966)

Higgins, Marguerite – *The War in Korea* (Doubleday, 1951)

Higgins, Rosalyn – *United Nations Peacekeeping 1946–67* (Vol. II) (Oxford University Press, 1970)

Higgins, Trumbull – *Korea and the Fall of MacArthur* (Oxford University Press, 1960)

Holles, Robert – *Now Thrive the Armourers* (Harrap, 1952)

Howarth, T. E. B. – *Prospect and Reality* (Collins, 1985)

Hoyt, Edwin P. – *The Pusan Perimeter: On to the Yalu* and *The Bloody Road to Panmunjom* (Stein & Day, 1984 and 1985)

Isaacson, Walter & Thomas, Evan – *The Wise Men* (Simon & Schuster, 1986)

Johnson, Air Vice-Marshal J. E. – *The Story of Air Fighting* (Hutchinson, 1985)

Joy, C. Turner – *How Communists Negotiate* (Macmillan New York, 1955)

Karig, Walter, Cagle, Malcolm W. & Manson, Frank A. – *Battle Report: The War in Korea* (Holt Rinehart, 1952)

Kavanagh, P. J. – *The Perfect Stranger* (Chatto & Windus, 1966)

Kennan, George F. – *Memoirs, 1925–1950* (Little, Brown, 1967) *Memoirs, 1950–1963* (Little, Brown, 1972)

Kennedy, Edgar – *Mission to Korea* (Derek Verschoyle, 1951)

Kie-Chiang Oh, John – *Korea: Democracy on Trial* (Cornell University Press, 1968)

Kim, Chong Ik & Han-Kyo – *Korea and the Politics of Imperialism* (University of California Press, 1967)

Kinkead, Eugene – *Why They Collaborated* (Longman, 1960)

Knox, Donald – *The Korean War, an Oral History: Pusan to Chosin* (Harcourt Brace Jovanovich, 1985)

Kohn, Richard H. & Harahan, Joseph P. – (ed.) *Air Superiority in World War II and Korea* (USAF Warrior Studies, 1983)

Khrushchev, Nikita – *Khrushchev Remembers* (Little, Brown, 1971)

Langley, Michael – *Inchon: MacArthur's Last Triumph* (Batsford, 1979)

Linklater, Eric – *Our Men in Korea* (HMSO, 1954)

Lowe, Peter – *The Origins of the Korean War* (Longman, 1986)

MacArthur, Douglas A. – *Reminiscences* (Heinemann, 1965)

McGuire, F. R. – *Canada's Army in Korea* (Historical Section, General Staff, Army Headquarters, Ottawa, 1956)

McLellan, David S. – *Dean Acheson: The State Department Years* (Dodd Mead, 1976)

Manchester, William – *MacArthur: American Caesar* (Hutchinson, 1978)

Marshall, S. L. A. – *The River and the Gauntlet* (Morrow, 1953) *Pork Chop Hill* (Morrow, 1952)

Melady, John – *Korea: Canada's Forgotten War* (Macmillan Canada, 1983)

Mitchell, Colin – *Having Been a Soldier* (Hamish Hamilton, 1969)

Momyer, General William W. – *Air Power in Three Wars* (Ayre, 1979)

Montross, Lynn & Canzona, Nicholas A. – *US Marine Operations In Korea, 1950–53* (Vols. I–V) (Historical Branch US Marine Corps, Washington, 1957)

Morgan, Kenneth – *Labour in Power* (Oxford University Press, 1984)

Panikkar, Kavalam M. – *In Two Chinas: Memoirs of a Diplomat* (Allen & Unwin, 1955)

Pogue, Forrest – *George C. Marshall* (3 vols.) (Viking, 1963–73)

Porter, Brian – *Britain and the Rise of Communist China, 1945–54* (Oxford University Press, 1967)

Rees, David – *Korea: The Limited War* (Hamish Hamilton, 1964) (ed.) *The Korean War: History and Tactics* (Orbis, 1984)

Reeves, Thomas C. – *The Life and Times of Joe McCarthy* (Stein & Day, 1982)

Ridgway, Matthew B. – *The Korean War* (Doubleday, 1967)

Rovere, Richard H. & Schlesinger, Arthur M. Jnr. – *The MacArthur Controversy and American Foreign Policy* (Noonday Press, 1965)

Russ, Martin – *The Last Parallel* (Signet, 1957)

Scalpino, Robert A. – *North Korea Today* (Praeger New York, 1963)

Schaller, Michael – *The American Occupation of Japan* (Oxford University Press, 1985)

Schnabel, James F. & Watson, Robert J. – *History of the Joint Chiefs of Staff* (Vol. Ill, pt. II) (Historical Division, Joint Secretariat, 1979) *The US Army in the Korean War* (Vols. I & II), (Office of the Chief of Military History, Washington, 1972, 1984)

Stone, Isidor F. – *The Hidden History of the Korean War* (Monthly Review Press, 1952)

Stueck, William – *The Road to Confrontation: US Policy Towards China and Korea* (University of North Carolina Press, 1981)

Suk, Lee Hyung – (ed.) *History of UN Forces in the Korean War* (5 vols.) (Korean Ministry of National Defence, 1973)

Taylor, Maxwell D. – *Swords and Plowshares* (Norton, 1972)

Thompson, Reginald – *Cry Korea* (Macdonald, 1951)

Thorne, Christopher – *Allies of a Kind* (Hamish Hamilton, 1978) *The Issue of War* (Oxford University Press, 1985)

Thornton, Captain John – *Believed to be Alive* (Ericksson, 1981)

Truman, Harry S. – *Years of Trial and Hope* (Doubleday, 1956)

Vatcher, William H. – *Panmunjom* (Atlantic Books, 1958)

Vorhees, Melvin B. – *Korean Tales* (Secker & Warburg, 1953)

Watt, D. C. – *Succeeding John Bull: America in Britain's Place* (Cambridge University Press, 1984)

Whiting, Allen – *China Crosses the Yalu: The Decision to Enter the Korean War* (University of California Press, 1970)

Whitney, Courtney – *MacArthur: His Rendezvous with History* (Knopf, 1956)

Whitson, William W. – *The Chinese High Command* (Macmillan, 1973)

Willoughby Charles. A. & Chamberlain, John – *MacArthur, 1941–1951* (McGraw-Hill, 1968)

Young, Kenneth – *Negotiating with the Chinese Communists: The United States Experience, 1953–1967* (McGraw-Hill, 1968)

Notes and references

Prologue: Task Force Smith

1 Unless otherwise attributed, all direct quotations in the story of Task Force Smith are taken from the author's interviews with survivors: Lt.-Col. George Masters; Major Floyd Martain; Corporal Ezra Burke; Corporal Robert Fountain; Lt. Carl Bernard.

2 Donald Knox, *The Korean War, An Oral History*, p. 21 (Publication details of all titles cited in the notes are given in the bibliography)

3 *Ibid.*, p. 23

1. Origins of a Tragedy

1 The narrative of the arrival of the American advance party is based on an author interview with one of the participants, Lt. Ferris Miller USN, 12.10.85

2 Dennett quoted Bruce Cumings, *Origins of the Korean War*, p. 103

3 3.10.43, quoted Cumings, *op. cit.*, p. 114

4 *Ibid.*

5 Miller, *loc. cit.*

6 Cumings *op. cit.*, pp. 138–9

7 US National Archive, Foreign Relations of the United States, 1945 6: 1049–53

8 Miller *loc. cit.*

9 Edgar Kennedy, *Mission to Korea*, p. 14

10 FRUS *op. cit.*, 6: 1049–53

11 FRUS 1945 6: 1070–71

12   FRUS 1945 6: 1061–1065, Benninghoff to Secretary of State

13   FRUS 1945 6: 1023

14   Author interview Roger Makins (Lord Sherfield) 10.1.86

15   FRUS 1945 6: 1122–24

16   *History of the United States Armed Forces in Korea*, vol. II, chap. I, p. 11

17   FRUS 1945 6: 1133–34

18   FRUS 1945 5: 1144–48

19   HUSAFIK *op. cit.* vol. III, ch. IV, pt. 1, p. 1

20   Author interview General Paek Sun Yup, October 1985

21   Author interview Minh Pyong Kyu, October 1985

22   Author interview Kap Chong Chi, October 1985

23   Miller *loc. cit.*

2. Invasion

1   Public Record Office FO371/84076

2   US National Archive Defense Records OPS 091, RG319 G-3, Box 121

3   Nikita Khrushchev, *Khrushchev Remembers*, p. 367

4   Allan Whiting, *China Crosses the Yalu*, p. 77

5   William Manchester, *MacArthur: American Caesar*, p. 543

3. The West's Riposte

1   Narrative based upon an author interview with Han Pyo Wook, October 1985

2   Christopher Mayhew, conversation with the author, May 1985

3   Dean Acheson, *Present at the Creation*, p. 248

4   US National Archive, Record of JCS Action Relative to Korea, pp. 12–13

5   Truman Papers PSF, quoted Rosemary Foot, *The Wrong War*, p. 59

6   Douglas MacArthur, *Reminiscences*, p. 331

7   *New York Times*, 9.7.50

8   Author interview with Lord Franks, August 1985

9   *Ibid.*

10 Manchester *op. cit.*, p. 548

11 *Ibid.*, p. 4

12 Author interview with Colonel Fred Ladd, October 1985

13 *Ibid.*

14 *Ibid.*

15 Author interview Lt.-Col. George Masters, April 1985

16 Ladd *loc. cit.*

17 Cabinet Records CAB128, 27.7.50, Public Record Office

18 Kenneth Morgan, *Labour in Power*, p. 280

19 PRO: CAB128/17

20 Franks *loc. cit.*

21 PRO: CAB128/17

22 Some British State papers consulted by the author are not yet in the Public Record Office, and have thus not been given catalogue numbers. References are thus necessarily omitted from the text in certain cases, notably in this chapter.

23 *Reynolds News*, 9.7.50

24 Paek *loc. cit.*

25 Miller *loc. cit.*

26 Author interview Lee Chien Ho, October 1985

27 Author interview Suk Bun Yoon, October 1985

28 Author interview Won Jung Kil, October 1985

4. Walker's War

1 Knox *op. cit.*, pp. 38–9

2 William F. Dean, *General Dean's Story*, p. 25

3 Martain *loc. cit.*

4 Rosalyn Higgins, *United Nations Peacekeeping 1946–67*, vol. II, p. 179

5 Author interview General John Michaelis, April 1985

6 Masters *loc. cit.*

7 Author interview Patterson, April 1985

8 Author interview Avery, April 1985

9 Author interview Handler, October 1985

10 Author interview Sorensen, October 1985

11 Author interview Alton, April 1985
12 Author interview Cooper, December 1985
13 Author interview Muir, September 1985
14 Author interview Tisdall, July 1985
15 Author interview Rickord, June 1985
16 Author interview Varley, February 1985
17 Author interview Fore, October 1985
18 Author interview Taplett, November 1985
19 Author interview Waters, November 1985
20 Author interview Pearson, July 1985
21 Author interview Major-General Sir John Willoughby, June 1985
22 *Ibid.*
23 Minh *loc. cit.*
24 Kap *loc. cit.*
25 James Cameron, *Point of Departure*, pp. 106–7
26 Author interview Mayo, October 1985
27 Author interview General Paul Freeman, May 1985
28 *Saturday Evening Post*, 23 October 1950
29 *Ibid.*
30 Cameron *op. cit.*, p. 109

5. Inchon

1 Shepherd oral history transcript, US Marine Corps Museum
2 Author interview General Alpha Bowser, May 1985
3 Author interview General Ellis Williamson, May 1985
4 Ladd *loc. cit.*
5 Taplett *loc. cit.*
6 Smith oral history transcript, US Marine Corps Museum
7 *Ibid.*
8 Shepherd transcript *op. cit.*
9 Author interview Sheldon, May 1985
10 Williamson *loc. cit.*
11 Cameron *op. cit.*, p. 137
12 Author interview Brigadier-General Ed Simmonds, October 1985

13 Cameron *op. cit.*, p. 140

14 Smith transcript *op. cit.*

15 Michaelis *loc. cit.*

16 Williamson *loc. cit.*

17 Shepherd transcript *op. cit.*

18 *Daily Telegraph*, 26.9.50

19 David Rees, *Korea: The Limited War*, p. 90

20 Simmonds *loc. cit.*

6. To the Brink: MacArthur Crosses the Parallel

1 Shepherd transcript *op. cit.*

2 PRO CAB128/18

3 MacArthur *op. cit.*, p. 214

4 Paek *loc. cit.*

5 Colin Mitchell, *Having Been a Soldier*, p. 77

6 US National Archive FR7: 1108–9

7 Quoted Rosemary Foot, *The Wrong War*, p. 94

7. The Coming of the Chinese

1 Author interview Simon, May 1985

2 Mitchell *op. cit.*, p. 80

3 US National Archive, NSC Minutes 10.11.50

4 US National Archive, FR7: 1205–6

5 John Gittings, *The Role of the Chinese Army*, p. 43

6 *People's Daily*, 23 August 1950

7 Kavalam M. Panikkar, *In Two Chinas: Memoirs of a Diplomat*, p. 163

8 This version of the circumstances in which Marshal Peng assumed command of the 'Volunteers' is that given to the author by Chinese veterans in Peking in 1985. It must be treated with caution, and viewed against the background of Lin Piao's disgrace. But some sinologists consider it plausible.

9 Quoted Samuel B. Griffith, *The Chinese People's Liberation Army*, p. 135

10 Author interview Li Hebei, January 1985
11 Author interview Yu Xiu, January 1985
12 Author interview Li Hua, January 1985
13 To the author, May 1985
14 Author interview Mario Scarselleta, April 1985
15 Author interview Bill Shirk, April 1985
16 Quoted Griffith *op. cit.*, p. 145
17 Fortune *loc. cit.*
18 Author interview James Waters, May 1985
19 Mitchell *op. cit.*, p. 80

8. Chosin: The Road from the Reservoir

1 Smith transcript *op. cit.*
2 *Ibid.*
3 Author interview Andrew Condron, August 1985
4 Letter to the author, August 1985
5 McAlister letter to the author, August 1985
6 To the author, September 1985
7 Bowser *loc. cit.*
8 *Ibid.*
9 Taplett *loc. cit.*
10 Simmonds *loc. cit.*
11 Ladd *loc. cit.*
12 Shepherd transcript *op. cit.*
13 Williamson *loc. cit.*
14 Author interview Robert Tyack, October 1985

9. The Winter of Crisis

1 Freeman *loc. cit.*
2 Schultz letter to the author, March 1985
3 Bernard *loc. cit.*
4 Author interview Karl Morton, April 1985
5 Ladd *loc. cit.*

6 *Crossbelts*, regimental magazine of the Royal Irish Hussars, Spring 1951

7 Paek Sun Yup *loc. cit.*

8 Digby Grist, *Remembered with Advantage*, p. 86

9 PRO London, WO216/3821

10 *Ibid.*

11 Author interview Moon Yun Seung, October 1985

12 Cooper *loc. cit.*

13 Author interview Robert Erricker, June 1985

14 Martain *loc. cit.*

15 Quoted Walter Karig, *Battle Report*, p. 353

16 Author interview Hu Seng, February 1985

17 Li Xiu, *loc. cit.*

18 Li Hebei *loc. cit.*

19 PRO London WO216/836

20 *Ibid.*

21 *Ibid.*

22 Uncatalogued British records

23 *Ibid.*

24 James Cardinal, private correspondence loaned to the author

25 Fountain *loc. cit.*

26 Harry S. Truman, *Years of Trial and Hope*, p. 385

27 Acheson Papers, quoted Foot *op. cit.*, p. 103

28 US National Archive FR7: 1330

29 MacArthur interview with *US News and World Report*, quoted Joseph C. Goulden, *Korea: The Untold Story*, p. 393

30 Truman *op. cit.*, p. 381

31 PRO London WO216/836

32 *US News and World Report*, *op. cit.*

33 PRO London, CAB128/180

34 Labour Party Conference Report, 1950, pp. 146–50

35 Alan Bullock, *Ernest Bevin*, vol. II, p. 821

36 Franks *loc. cit.*

37 PRO London FO371/83018, 8.12.50

38 Schnabel & Watson, *History of the Joint Chiefs of Staff* vol. III, pt. 2, 6.12.50

39 *Ibid.*

40 Richard F. Haynes, *The Awesome Power: Harry S. Truman as Commander-in-Chief*, p. 95

41 US National Archive Records of Army Staff G3 091 Korea TS 5.7.51, Box 38a, RG319

42 US National Archive, FR7: 1326

43 Foot *op. cit.*, p. 132

44 US National Archive, Foreign Policy of the United States 7: 191–3

45 Matthew B. Ridgway, *The Korean War*, p. 86

46 *Ibid.*, p. 88

47 PRO London WO216/63 836

48 To the author, May 1985

49 Michaelis *loc. cit.*

10. Nemesis: The Dismissal of MacArthur

1 Manchester *op. cit.*, p. 617

2 Author interview General Charles Bolté, October 1985

3 Schultz *loc. cit.*

4 Uncatalogued British records

5 PRO London WO216/728

6 Ridgway *op. cit.*, p. 121

7 Courtney Whitney, *MacArthur: His Rendezvous with History*, p. 363

8 Minutes of British COS meetings, uncatalogued records

9 *Ibid.*

10 Author interview Air-Marshal Sir John Nicholls, April 1985

11 Williamson *loc. cit.*

12 Freeman *loc. cit.*

13 Ridgway *op. cit.*, pp. 147–9

14 Manchester *op. cit.*, p. 646

15 Kennedy *op. cit.*, p. 134

16 Sheldon *loc. cit.*

17 Ladd *loc. cit.*

18 Uncatalogued British records

19 *Ibid.*

20 Isaacson & Thomas, *The Wise Men*, p. 263

11. The Struggle on the Imjin

1 All quotations in this chapter, unless otherwise attributed, are based upon author interviews with participants.

2 P. J. Kavanagh, *A Perfect Stranger*, pp. 104–5

3 *Ibid.*

4 S. J. Davies, *In Spite of Dungeons*, pp. 18–19

5 *Crossbelts*, regimental magazine of the Royal Irish Hussars, Autumn 1951, p. 17

6 Anthony Farrar-Hockley, *The Edge of the Sword*, p. 89

7 *Ibid.*

8 Davies *op. cit.*, p. 13

9 Farrar-Hockley *op. cit.*, p. 93

12. The Stony Road

1 *The Second Indianhead Division in Korea*, p. 141

2 To the author, May 1985

3 Ridgway *op. cit.*, p. 157

4 Bullock *op. cit.*, p. 792

5 Author interview Tisdall, June 1985

6 US National Archive, Ridgway to JCS, 21.6.51

7 *Ibid.*, Ridgway to JCS, 14.7.51

8 *Ibid.*, FRUS 1951. Galleys 418–19

9 Uncatalogued British records

10 *Ibid.*

11 PRO London, FO371/92847

12 *Ibid.*

13 Author interview John Ellis, August 1985

14 Author interview Brigadier Chris Snider, November 1984

15 Author interview Stan Muir, August 1985

16 PRO London, FO371/92847

17 *Ibid.*

18 *Ibid.*, FO371/92848

19 Kauffroth letter to the author, July 1985

20 Author interview General Sir William Pike, April 1985

21 Snider *loc. cit.*

22 Suk Bun Yoon *loc. cit.*

23 Quoted Melvin B. Vorhees, *Korean Tales*, p. 150

24 Avery *loc. cit.*

25 Handler *loc. cit.*

26 Author interview Robert Sebilian, October 1985

27 Author interview Gordon Gayle, October 1985

28 Simmonds *loc. cit.*

29 Author interview William Norris, April 1985

30 US National Archive, Dept. Mil. Hist. ACMH 626

13. The Intelligence War

1 Lee Chien Ho, *loc. cit.*

2 William Ellery Anderson, *Banner Over Pusan*, p. 96

3 Author interview William Ellery Anderson, July 1985

4 Anderson *op. cit.*, p. 115

5 *Ibid.*, p. 182

6 Goulden *op. cit.*, p. 463

7 Author telephone interview General Jack Singlaub, October 1985

14. The Battle in the Air

1 For a more detailed discussion of these issues, see the author's *Bomber Command* (Michael Joseph, 1979)

2 Freeman *loc. cit.*

3 Author interview Air-Marshal J. E. Johnson, September 1985

4 Author interview General John Sloane, August 1984

5 Author interview General Oliver Lewis, October 1985

6 Author interview Jim Low, April 1985

7 General William Momyer, *Air Power in Three Wars*, p. 74

8 Author interview Roy Watson, June 1985

9 Nicholls *loc. cit.*

10 Low *loc. cit.*

11 Author interview Joe Hilliard, October 1985

12 *Ibid.*

13 Momyer *op. cit.*, p. 53

14 Author interview William Jacob, June 1985

15 Quoted George F. Futrell, *The United States Air Force in the Korean War*, p. 468

16 Ridgway *op. cit.*, p. 279

17 Quoted Momyer *op. cit.*, p. 170

18 Alexander Seversky, *Victory Thru Air Power* (Simon & Schuster, 1942), p. 102

19 Vorhees *op. cit.*, p. 170

15. The Prisoners

1 Pamphlet loaned to the author by a British veteran

2 Davies *op. cit.*, p. 29

3 *Hansard*, 23.1.51

4 Scarselleta *loc. cit.*

5 Avery *loc. cit.*

6 Author interview Major-General James Majury, June 1985

7 Davies *op. cit.*, p. 30

8 Condron *loc. cit.*

9 Author interview Henry O'Kane, July 1985

10 Author interview Graham Cockfield, April 1985

11 Author telephone interview Walt Mayo, October 1985

12 Cooper *loc. cit.*

13 Erricker, private correspondence loaned to the author

14 O'Kane *loc. cit.*

15   Monica Felton, *That's Why I Went*, p. 26

16   *Ibid*, p. 38

17   Davies *op. cit.*, p. 68

18   *Ibid*, p. 70

19   Fortune *loc. cit.*

20   Author interview Captain John Thornton USN, April 1985

21   Majury *loc. cit.*

22   Condron *loc. cit.*

23   James Kinkead, *Why They Collaborated*, pp. 153–4

16. Attrition: The War on the Hills

1   Author interview James Stuhler, August 1985

2   Author interview Tom Pentony, April 1985

3   Author interview Alan Maybury, June 1985

4   Commonwealth Division report, 26.10.52, Staff College Library

5   *Ibid.*

6   Commonwealth Division report to War Office Director of Intelligence, 21.9.52, Staff College Library

7   Author interview Li Ben Wen, January 1985

8   Author interview Wang Zhu Guang, January 1985

9   Patterson *loc. cit.*

10   Commonwealth Division report, 26.2.52, Staff College Library

11   *Ibid.*

12   Author interview General Peter Sibbald, July 1985

13   Paul Sheehy private correspondence loaned to the author

14   PRO London, WO216/720

15   *Ibid.*

16   Author interview John Bowler, May 1985

17   Pike *loc. cit.*

18   Author interview Col. Gerald Rickord, July 1985

19   Pike *loc. cit.*

20   *Ibid.*

21   Avery *loc. cit.*

22 Author interview Lewis Kershaw, June 1985

23 Pentony *loc. cit.*

17. The Pursuit of Peace

1 Author interview Alan Maggio, October 1985

2 *Ibid.*

3 Author telephone interview Robert Hoop, October 1985

4 Bouchier to War Office, 10.5.52. Uncatalogued British records

5 PRO London FO371/99640

6 *Ibid.*

7 *Ibid.*

8 PRO London FO371/99641

9 *Ibid.*

10 Schnabel & Watson, *History of the US Joint Chiefs of Staff*

11 12 August 1952

12 Ronald Caridi, *The Korean War and American Politics*, p. 253

13 US National Archive, minutes of the NSC meeting, 11.2.53

14 *Ibid.*, FR15: 827

15 Eisenhower Papers 31 March 1952, quoted Foot *op. cit.*, p. 215

16 Han Pyo Wook *loc. cit.*

17 Author interview General William Livsey, May 1985

18 Snider *loc. cit.*

19 Author interview General Arthur Trudeau, October 1985

20 Maybury *loc. cit.*

21 Fore *loc. cit.*

22 Wang Zhu Guang *loc. cit.*

23 Fortune *loc. cit.*

24 Condron *loc. cit.*

18. Hindsight

1 All quotations in this chapter are based upon author interviews with veterans, unless otherwise stated.

2 Foot *op. cit.*, pp. 239–40
3 'A Reminiscence of the Chinese People's Volunteers in the Korean War', *China Quarterly* No. 98, June 1984, pp. 303–4
4 *Ibid.*
5 Cameron *op. cit.*, p. 146

Acknowledgements

Thanks are due to a host of Korean veterans in Britain, the United States, Korea and China who not only contributed written or taped accounts of their experiences, but in many cases met and entertained me in the course of my researches. To all of them, I should like to express my gratitude, and my hope that they do not feel too exasperated or disappointed by the narrative that I have built around their stories and comments. The list below includes only field ranks and above, and omits decorations, which would otherwise overwhelm these pages.

Clyde Alton
Professor Eugene Alvarez
William Ellery Anderson
A. F. Antippas
Warren Avery
Tom Bagnall
A. D. Barnes
Moe Beaudin
Keith Bennett
Carl Bernard
D. O. Blackmon
Maj.-Gen. P. Bogert
Gen. Charles Bolté
Col. Donald W. Boose
Cdr. J. H. G. Bovey
John Bowler
Gen. Alpha Bowser
Maj.-Gen. Thomas Brodie
Ezra Burke
D. S. Caldwell
James Cardinal
John F. Carney
Deirdre Chappell
Graham Cockfield
Gen. Colter
Andrew Condron
Maj. William Cooper
James Coulos
C. W. Grassland
Harvey E. Dann

L. A. Davis
Kenneth G. Dibble
A. H. Donaldson
William Drummond
Matthew Dukes
Tony Eagles
Hamish Eaton
Capt. John Ellis
Jerry Emer
Robert Erricker
E. Esslinger
Col. M. G. Farmer
Peter Farrar
Gen. Sir Anthony Farrar-Hockley
Eric G. Fazan
Robert Flaherty
Richard A. Fleckenstein
Clyde Fore
Maj. J. A. Foulis
Capt. Robert Fountain
R. W. Fox
C. W. Franklin
Lord Franks
Gen. Paul Freeman
Jack Gage
T. J. Gallagan
Brig.-Gen. Gordon Gayle
Tom Glenn
Pip Wook Han
Selwyn Handler

Lawrence J. Hansen
Col. E. Denis Harding
Clyde A. Harriman
C. J. Harrold
Clifton W. Hastings
J. L. S. Haughton
Brian Hawkins
Cdr. R. Hennessy
Michael Hickey
Charles E. Higgins
Joe Hilliard
Charles F. Home
Robert Hoop
Seng Hu
Xiang Huan
J. Husher
William Jacob
Air Marshal J. E. Johnson
P. C. Jones
Brig. Amos Jordan
Bok Suh Kang
Chong Chi Kap
Arthur Karma
S. M. Kauffroth
P. J. Kavanagh
Bernard Loch
Col. George Masters
Christopher Mayhew
Walt Mayo
Don McAlister
John McQueen
John Merrick
Gen. John Michaelis
Ferris Miller
Patrick Min
Pyong Kyu Minh
Alan Moody
Yun Seung Moon
Karl R. Morton
John Mosse
Stan Muir
William Muncaster
Bill Myers
Fred Nelson
Air Marshal Sir John Nicholls
William Norris
Henry O'Kane
Capt. David Omer
Lt.-Col. Paul D. Orwoll
Nam Kyu Paek

Gen. Sun Yup Paek
Bill Patterson
Roy Pearl
John C. Pearson
Maj. Tom Pentony
Gen. Sir William Pike
E. J. Plaisance
Lt. Lloyd Pulton
Julio Ramon
Col. George Resula
Alistair Rattray
Barry Reed
J. Richardson
S. Richardson
Lt.-Col. G. P. Rickord
Bernard Rock
Mario Scarselleta
Ronald Schaffer
Peter F. Schultz
Robert Sebilian
Paul Sheehy
Bill Shirk
W. F. Showen
Gen. Peter Sibbald
Brig.-Gen. Ed Simmons
Gen. Jack Singlaub
Lord Sherfield
John Slackpark
Maj. Lester A. Sliter
Maj.-Gen. John Sloane
John J. Slonaker
George F. Smith
Brig. Chris Snider
Brig. Snow
Bill Sorensen
Robert W. Steffy
Capt. W. J. H. Stuart
James Stuhler
Bun Yoon Suk
Bill Swirk
Lt.-Col. Robert Taplett
Paul E. Tardiff
Raymond Tauszik
Bill Taylor
Brig. G. Taylor
Timothy P. Taylor
André Thiry
Cdr. I. P. Thorne
Capt. John Thornton US Navy
St Clair Tisdall

Thomas L. Tomlinson
Eric Townsend
Gen. Arthur Trudeau
Robert Tyack
J. W. L. Tyler
Albert Van Alstyne
Albert Varley
Mark Villanueva
Brian Wall
Melvin C. Walthall
Zhu Guang Wang
Maj. Guy Ward
James Waters
Roy Watson

Philip Welton
Lt.-Col. E. Williams
Gen. Ellis Williamson
Maj.-Gen. Sir John Willoughby
Brig. David Wilson
Blair Winer
Willis J. Wood
B. Woodhouse
Tom Worthington
Won Jung Kil
Professor Suk Bun Yoon
Maj.-Gen. Allan Younger
Xiu Yu

Index

extracts reading groups
competitions books new
discounts extracts extracts
competitions extracts discounts events
books new reading groups extracts reading groups
events books extracts events
extracts new titles reading groups
interviews reading groups events
events extracts extracts books
discounts events new books
new books events interviews n books new extracts
events new events

discounts extracts discounts
www.panmacmillan.com books
extracts events reading groups
competitions books extracts new